Lecture Notes in Artificial Intelligence 1010

Subseries of Lecture Notes in Computer Science
Edited by J. G. Carbonell and J. Siekmann

Lecture Notes in Computer Science

Edited by G. Goos, J. Hartmanis and J. van Leeuwen

T0180834

Springer
Berlin
Heidelberg
New York
Barcelona
Budapest
Hong Kong
London
Milan
Paris
Santa Clara
Singapore
Tokyo

Manuela Veloso   Agnar Aamodt (Eds.)

Case-Based Reasoning Research and Development

First International Conference, ICCBR-95
Sesimbra, Portugal, October 23-26, 1995
Proceedings

Springer

Series Editors

Jaime G. Carbonell, Carnegie Mellon University, USA

Jörg Siekmann, University of Saarland, DFKI, Germany

Volume Editors

Manuela Veloso
School of Computer Science, Carnegie Mellon University
Pittsburgh, PA 15213-3891, USA

Agnar Aamodt
Department of Informatics, University of Trondheim, UNIT-AVH
N-7055 Dragvoll, Norway

Cataloging-in-Publication Data applied for

Die Deutsche Bibliothek - CIP-Einheitsaufnahme

Case based reasoning research and development : first
international conference ; proceedings / ICCBR-95, Sesimbra,
Portugal, October 23 - 26, 1995. Manuela Voloso ; Agnar
Aamodt (ed.). - Berlin ; Heidelberg ; New York ; Barcelona ;
Budapest ; Hong Kong ; London ; Milan ; Paris ; Tokyo :
Springer, 1995
  (Lecture notes in computer science ; Vol. 1010 : Lecture notes in
  artificial intelligence)
  ISBN 3-540-60598-3
NE: Voloso, Manuela [Hrsg.]; ICCBR <1, 1995, Sesimbra>; GT

CR Subject Classification (1991): I.2, J.4

ISBN 3-540-60598-3 Springer-Verlag Berlin Heidelberg New York

Typesetting: Camera ready by author
SPIN 10487199   06/3142 – 5 4 3 2 1 0   Printed on acid-free paper

Preface

This book contains the papers presented at the First International Conference on Case-Based Reasoning - ICCBR-95 - held on October 23-26 1995 in Sesimbra, Portugal. ICCBR-95 marks the start of a joint CBR conference series that follows and extends the CBR workshops that have taken place in the United States since 1988 and Europe since 1993. The ICCBR conferences are planned to become biennial events, encouraging more specific workshops to be held in the immediate years.

The overall aim of ICCBR-95 was to advance the scientific and application-oriented state of the CBR field by bringing researchers and system builders together for presentation of results and discussions of problem issues. Case-based reasoning is now an established area of AI, with a continually growing world-wide research community and a number of fielded applications. ICCBR-95 was a broad-scoped conference, where recent research results were discussed in scientific papers and poster sessions, and where applications and system building tools were presented and demonstrated.

Out of a total of 89 received papers, 22 papers were selected for scientific talks, 10 papers were selected for application talks, and an additional 20 papers were selected for poster presentations. The papers were carefully reviewed by the Program Committee members and additional reviewers, and all papers accepted and presented at the conference are printed in this book. Based on the main issues addressed, the papers fell into the following categories (see the Main Topic Index on the last pages):

- case and knowledge representation
- case retrieval
- nearest neighbour methods
- case adaptation and learning
- cognitive modeling
- integrated reasoning methods
- application-oriented methods - planning, various
- applications - general decision making, diagnosis and interpretation, design

We would like to thank Roger Schank (Northwestern University) for giving his invited talk on "Non-conscious problem solving; why case based reasoning makes us rethink the consciousness bias in artificial intelligence", and Michael Richter (University of Kaiserslautern) for giving his invited talk on "The knowledge contained in similarity measures". Also thanks to David Leake for his tutorial on central CBR issues, methods, and technology. We further want to thank Pinar Ozturk and Marian D'Amico for all their help with organising the reviewing process, etc., and Stefan Wess for organising and chairing the application sessions. Particular thanks to Olga Costa and the other members of the local organising team lead by Carlos Bento at the University of Coimbra. The final thanks go to Springer-Verlag for their help and assistance in the publishing of this book.

Agnar Aamodt and Manuela Veloso

Program Conference Chairs

Agnar Aamodt
University of Trondheim, Norway

Manuela Veloso
Carnegie Mellon University, USA

Local Organization Chair

Carlos Bento, University of Coimbra, Portugal

Program Committee

David Aha	Naval Research Laboratory, Washington DC
Klaus Althoff	University of Kaiserslautern
Kevin Ashley	University of Pittsburgh
Ray Bareiss	Northwestern University
Brigitte Bartsch-Spoerl	BSR Consulting, Munich
Jeff Berger	University of Chicago
Karl Branting	University of Wyoming
Ernesto Costa	University of Coimbra
Paul Compton	University of New South Wales
Kris Hammond	University of Chicago
James Hendler	University of Maryland
Tom Hinrichs	Northwestern University
Carl Gustaf Jansson	Stockholm University
Jerzy Surma	University of Economics, Wroclaw
Eric Jones	Victoria University of Wellington, NZ
Mark Keane	University of Dublin
James King	AT&T GIS, USA
Janet Kolodner	Georgia Institute of Technology
David Leake	University of Indiana
Michel Manago	Acknosoft, Paris
Enric Plaza	IIIA, Spanish Scientific Research Council
Ashwin Ram	Georgia Institute of Technology
Michael Richter	University of Kaiserslautern
Chris Riesbeck	ILS, Northwestern University
Edwina Rissland	University of Massachusetts
Derek Sleeman	University of Aberdeen
Ian Smith	EPFL, Lausanne
Gerhard Strube	University of Freiburg
Katia Sycara	Carnegie Mellon University
Henry Tirri	University of Helsinki
Shusaku Tsumoto	Tokyo Medical and Dental University
Angi Voss	GMD, St. Augustin
Ian Watson	University of Salford

ICCBR-95 was supported by IJCAI Inc., MLnet, Acknosoft, Inference Corpoation, Banco Borges e Irmão, Câmara Municipal de Sesimbra, and Regiao de Turismo de Setubal, in cooperation with Associação Portuguesa para a Inteligência Artificial, and Departemento de Engenharia Informática da Universidade de Coimbra.

Table of Contents

Application Sessions

Integration of case based retrieval with a relational database system in aircraft technical support..1
Jonathan R. C. Allen, David W. R.Patterson, Maurice D. Mulvenna, John G. Hughes

Cost estimation of software projects through case base reasoning.........................11
Rossella Bisio, Fabio Malabocchia

Operator decision aiding by adaptation of supervision strategies...........................23
Béatrice Fuchs, Alain Mille, Benoît Chiron

PROFIL: A decision support tool for metallic sections design using a CBR approach..33
Frèderic Geffraye, Jean Luc Wybo, Aline Russeil

MacRad: Radiology image resource with a case-based retrieval system...................43
Robert T. Macura, Katarzyna J. Macura

Representing and indexing building refurbishment cases for multiple retrieval of adaptable pieces of cases...55
Farhi Marir, Ian Watson

Large-scale fault diagnosis for on-board train systems...67
B. D. Netten, R. A. Vingerhoeds

Case-based reasoning for expertise relocation in support of rural health workers in developing countries..77
Elisha T. O. Opiyo

Spatial composition using cases: IDIOM...88
Ian Smith, Claudio Lottaz, Boi Faltings

CBR and machine learning for combustion system design....................................98
Jutta Stehr

Scientific Sessions

KBS maintenance as learning two-tiered domain representation...........................109
Gennady Agre

A case-based approach for developing writing tools aimed at non-native English users...121
Sandra M. Aluísio, Osvaldo N. Oliveira Jr.

Reasoning with reasons in case-based comparisons..133
Kevin D. Ashley, Bruce M. McLaren

Towards the integration of case-based, schema-based and model-based reasoning
for supporting complex design tasks...145
Brigitte Bartsch-Spörl

Separating the cases from the data: Towards more flexible case-based reasoning.....157
Mike Brown, Ian Watson, Nick Filer

Route planning by analogy...169
Karen Zita Haigh, Manuela Veloso

Case adaptation using an incomplete causal model..181
John D. Hastings, L. Karl Branting, Jeffrey A. Lockwood

Evaluating the application of CBR in mesh design for simulation problems.........193
Neil Hurley

Case memory and retrieval based on the immune system....................................205
John E. Hunt, Denise E. Cooke, Horst Holstein

Using case data to improve on rule-based function approximation.......................217
Nitin Indurkhya, Sholom M. Weiss

Learning to improve case adaptation by introspective reasoning and CBR.............229
David B. Leake, Andrew Kinley, David Wilson

Retrieving cases in structured domains by using goal dependencies......................241
Héctor Muñoz-Avila, Jochem Huellen

An average-case analysis of k-nearest neighbor classifier...................................253
Seishi Okamoto, Ken Satoh

Cases as terms: A feature term approach to the structured representation of cases....265
Enric Plaza

ADAPtER: An integrated diagnostic system combining case-based and abductive
reasoning..277
Luigi Portinale, Pietro Torasso

Adaptation using constraint satisfaction techniques..289
Lisa Purvis, Pearl Pu

Learning a local similarity metric for case-based reasoning................................301
Francesco Ricci, Paolo Avesani

Experiments on adaptation-guided retrieval in case-based design.........................313
Barry Smyth, Mark T. Keane

Integrating rules and cases for the classification task..................................325
Jerzy Surma, Koen Vanhoof

Reuse of knowledge: Empirical studies.. 335
Willemien Visser

Weighting features..347
Dietrich Wettschereck, David W. Aha

An investigation of marker-passing algorithms for analogue retrieval....................359
Michael Wolverton

Poster Sessions

INRECA: A seamlessly integrated system based on inductive inference and
case-based reasoning..371
Eric Auriol, Stefan Wess, Michel Manago, Klaus-Dieter Althoff, Ralph Traphöner

DOM-ArC: An active decision support system for quality assessment of cases......381
Shirin Bakhtari, Wolfgang Oertel

A case-based reasoner adaptive to different cognitive tasks................................391
Isabelle Bichindaritz

On the use of CBR in optimisation problems such as the TSP..........................401
Pádraig Cunningham, Barry Smyth , Neil Hurley

Case-based diagnosis of multiple faults..411
Ralph Deters

On the automatic generation of case libraries by chunking chess games...............421
Stephen Flinter, Mark T. Keane

Learning to refine indexing by introspective reasoning....................................431
Susan Fox, David B. Leake

Problem solving with "The incredible machine": An experiment in case-based
reasoning..441
Mehmet H. Göker, Herbert Birkhofer

Integrating case-based reasoning and tabu search for solving optimisation
problems...451
Stephan Grolimund, Jean-Gabriel Ganascia

Systems, tasks and adaptation knowledge: Revealing some revealing
dependencies...461
Kathleen Hanney, Mark T. Keane, Barry Smyth, Pádraig Cunningham

Some limitations of feature-based recognition in case-based design.....................471
Thomas R. Hinrichs

A case based method for solving relatively stable dynamic constraint satisfaction
problems...481
Y. Huang, R. Miles

Learning strategies for explanation patterns: Basic game patterns with
applications to chess..491
Yaakov Kerner

A memory-based hierarchical planner...501
Deepak Khemani, P.V.S.R. Bhanu Prasad

Case-based reasoning for cash flow forecasting using fuzzy retrieval....................510
Rosina Weber Lee, Ricardo Miranda Barcia, Suresh K. Khator

A connectionist indexing approach for CBR systems......................................520
Maria Malek

Using a neural network to learn general knowledge in a case-based system............528
Eliseo Reategui, John A. Campbell, Shirley Borghetti

"Fish and sink": An anytime-algorithm to retrieve adequate cases........................538
Jörg Walter Schaaf

Knowledge engineering for CBR systems from a cognitive science perspective......548
G. Strube, A. Enzinger, D. Janetzko, M. Knauff

Towards using a single uniform metric in instance-based learning.......................559
Kai Ming Ting

Main Topic Index...569

Author Index...575

Integration of Case Based Retrieval with a Relational Database System in Aircraft Technical Support

Jonathan RC Allen[1], David WR Patterson, Maurice D Mulvenna and John G Hughes

Northern Ireland Knowledge Engineering Laboratory
Faculty of Informatics, University of Ulster at Jordanstown Newtownabbey
Northern Ireland, UK, BT37 0QB

Abstract. Case-Based Reasoning (CBR) is suited to problem solving in domains where there are recurring problems. This paper describes the development of a CBR system for use in such a domain, the Technical Support department of an aircraft manufacturing company. The system uses three types of indexing: knowledge-guided induction, inductive indexing and nearest neighbour matching. The resultant system integrates case based retrieval with a relational database system to provide a rich environment to help manage the life cycle of a technical support query. In early tests with the system, staff can discern if a new query is a recurring problem and has been solved before or if it is a completely new unsolved technical query.

1 Introduction

Quality, dependability, professionalism and cost effectiveness are all key features that assist a company in selling their product. In the situation where the product is a service, the same ethos applies. For this particular practical application the problem domain is the Aircraft Technical Support department of Short Brothers plc, an aerospace company based in Northern Ireland. The technical support is provided for a variety of short range commuter and military aircraft. The civilian aircraft range (designated SD3) consists of 118 SD3-30, 160 SD3-60, and in the military range 28 C23A and C23B. These aircraft are in service in over 40 countries with at least 40 different operators. Although the Company no longer manufacture this range of aircraft they are obliged to provide product and technical support to the operators of the aircraft. It is envisaged that the aircraft will be in operation for the next 10-20 years and will therefore require expert quality technical support during this period.

The Company have realised that the knowledge which the Headquarters Engineer (HQE) experts have developed in the solving of technical queries could be lost. Also, in conjunction with the need for fast response to all new queries, it is apparent that this is a domain where computer technology could be applied to assist the HQE. The

---

[1] Principal author's e-mail JRC.Allen@ulst.ac.uk

fact that there is an abundance of previously solved technical queries already in the office filing system means that potential cases for a CBR system are extant. This paper describes the development of a CBR system integrated with a Relational Database Management System (RDBMS) for 'SD3-Aircraft Product and Customer Support' using CBR software (ReMind), MS Access (RDBMS) and Visual Basic as the Graphical User Interface (GUI). The finished system utilises the *retrieval* component of the CBR software.

2 Technical Support

The main function of SD3 Aircraft Technical Support is to provide responses to technical queries from SD3 Aircraft operators. This often involves liaison between the operators and specialist departments within the Company. The vast majority of technical queries from operators arrive at technical support in the form of a fax. The queries are usually of an urgent nature with a status of AOG (Aircraft On the Ground) as grounded aircraft result in lost revenue for the operator. The scope of a technical query covers problems such as accident damage, corrosion, technical defects, or request for data.

Within technical support there is a wealth of information stored in maintenance manuals, flight manuals, and previously solved technical queries that are continuously being updated as new technical queries are solved. The HQE's use their expertise and knowledge of the domain to solve the new technical queries. Initially this may involve recalling a similar technical query that has been solved in the past. In this situation, they will go to the current filing system and try to locate such a similar case. The filing system works under the ATA 100[2] principle, where the aircraft structure is conceptually broken down into categories. An example of this is *'ATA 52 Doors', 'ATA 52-10 Passenger / Crew'* or *'ATA 52-20 Emergency Exit'*. The previously solved cases found in the current filing system can be used as a starting point to aid in the solving of new technical queries. If this is a new type of problem, the HQE will then use his own knowledge and experience to arrive at a possible solution. This may involve getting more information from the source of the query, using reference manuals , or contacting a specific department in the Company, such as Engineering Systems, Design & Structural, Airworthiness, Aerodynamics, or Weights & Stress. If the HQE is unable to recall solving a particular type of query before or if it was another HQE who had solved the query initially, this may lead to the situation where a time consuming search of the records produces no answer to the new technical query.

---

[2] Air Transport Association of America 100 is a set of standards which are used to identify particular systems within an aircraft.

3   The Case Base Retrieval Component

Case based retrieval compares a current situation (or case) with situations that have been encountered in the past to see if one or more of the earlier situations can provide a model for how to act in the current situation [1][2].

There are three basic steps in creating any case-based system, firstly data must be examined, and the significant features identified, secondly data must be acquired and represented, and thirdly data must be indexed for efficient retrieval [3].

3.1   Case Representation

The solved technical queries are all potential cases, containing information such as *operator name, subject of problem, detailed description of problem, staff member* who dealt with the query, *date received, reference number (In), detailed description of solution*, and *reference number (Out)*. Although all of these fields may provide good management information in the office environment for good house keeping purposes, it was decided from the offset that only those fields which would aid the retrieval process should be included in the case-base. Those fields that were not included in the case-base were placed in a relational database which directly interacts with the case-base through the GUI. The fields which best assist the retrieval process, i.e., fields on which indexing is performed, are *ATA Reference, Aircraft Type, Category of problem* and *Brief Description of Problem*.

There are two fields which do not affect the retrieval process but are necessary for the solving of new cases, namely, *Detailed Problem Description* and *Detailed Solution Description*.

Once the fields for inclusion in the CBR system were established the next step was to represent them as cases. ReMind provides a feature called *symbols* by which data being represented can be ranked and classified into a hierarchical structure. The symbol hierarchy is a branching graph structure of parents and children and is used to provide the system with knowledge about the domain data [3].

The symbol hierarchy was used to represent the *ATA Reference, Aircraft Type*, and *Problem Category*. The main purpose behind using the symbol hierarchy was to ensure that the users input would be well structured and be of a consistent nature as this input is used to generate several other fields using the CBR software's formula editor. The user is given a multiple-choice option to select the necessary information. *Aircraft Type* offers the complete range of aircraft for which technical support is provided. The *ATA Reference* symbol hierarchy consists of the complete range of ATA 100 Groups and the subsequent sub-sections used by technical support. The *Problem Category* symbol hierarchy includes the most common type of technical queries that arise: Request, Repair, Damage, Corrosion, Modification (see Fig. 1).

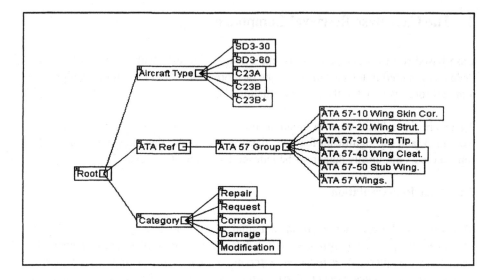

Fig. 1. Symbol hierarchy utilised for user selections.

The faxes that arrive at SD3 Aircraft generally have a short sentence highlighting the problem. The vocabulary used is of a very distinct nature, and generally refers to a particular section or part of the plane. Therefore when the HQE enters a natural language description of the problem there are only so many key words that appear, e.g., "Corrosion to port and starboard wing to lift strut", or "lugs part number SD3-23-1137XA on aircraft SH3063".

The free text that is inserted into the Brief Problem Description is parsed by a formula field to generate a list of symbol field called *Key Words*. The formula is derived from several symbols in the symbol hierarchy namely *Important Words, Unwanted Words* and *Morphology Rules*. The formula removes unwanted words such as *the*, *at* or *and* to leave possible key words that describe the problem. The remaining words have a set of morphology rules applied to them to strip the plural endings of the word, which leaves only the trunk of a word, e.g., ed -> e, ing->e. The resulting parsed sentence has only important domain or new words remaining.

Using several formulas the system is able to detect if the current domain word is important to the particular ATA reference section on which the new retrieval is being executed. The symbol hierarchy in the ReMind software enables a structure to be created that sets up each ATA 100 group and sub-section to be represented with its own dictionary of domain important words (see Fig. 2).

At this stage the remaining parsed words are compared with the relevant ATA 100 group's dictionary of domain important words, and if there is a match the word is added to the *Key Words* field for the case. Any words which the system does not recognise are placed into a *New Words* symbol hierarchy. The new words which have been detected by the system are not placed into one single list of new words but are represented in a symbol hierarchy under a particular ATA 100 group (Fig. 2.).

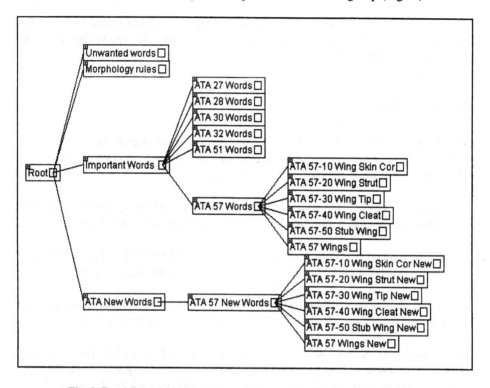

Fig. 2. Partial symbol hierarchy created to store the domain dictionary.

The symbol hierarchy of new words is a carbon copy of the ATA 100 groups and sub-sections and therefore allows a new word that is detected to be placed into the correct ATA 100 group for which it will possibly become a domain important word. Using this structure for representation of domain knowledge, the job of the Case Base Administrator (CBA) is made easier. One of the tasks that the CBA performs after a solved technical query has been made into a new case is to update the dictionary of domain words. Instead of just having a list of new words for which there is no way of tracing from which ATA 100 group they originated the CBA is able to know exactly what ATA 100 group the words should be placed in if they are to become important domain words. This task is fully automated and utilises visual programming techniques, where new words are dragged to important words on the interface and are thereby inserted into the correct ATA 100 group automatically. The same techniques are used for the unwanted words hierarchy.

There is also the added feature that the system is able to detect multiple occurrences of words. When a new word is added to the important words the system will check to see if that word already exists in another ATA 100 group for which it is 'domain important'. If this is true, then a link is created between that word and the ATA 100 group to which the new word is being added. This ensures that a word only ever appears once in the dictionary but can be domain important to many ATA 100 groups.

The general structure that has been adapted using the symbol hierarchy for case representation is ideal for any future additions of domain knowledge to *ATA Reference*, *Category* and *Aircraft Type*.

3.2 Case Indexing

The CBR software allows for four types of index strategies: pure induction, knowledge-guided induction, nearest neighbour matching and template matching [4]. The developed system uses three types of indexing:

1. Knowledge-guided induction, which takes into account specific domain knowledge about an application before inductive indexing is carried out.

2. Inductive indexing is done using clustering, where a decision tree is built based on features from past cases that discriminate between various outcome values [5].

3. Nearest neighbour matching, which enables retrieval of cases by comparison of a collection of weighted features in the input case to cases in the library [6].

In the developed system, the knowledge-guided approach is applied first. As the ATA Referencing is well structured it lends itself to knowledge-guided induction. A prototype was created for all groups of ATA 100 and for each of the sub-sections (Fig. 3). This allows the cases to be partitioned according to a set of pre-defined criteria.

The clustering process is then performed within the context of each of the knowledge -guided prototypes, i.e., each ATA sub-section. Inductive indexing is performed using the *Key Words* field. The cases are further split into a decision tree structure, which creates a smaller set of cases producing a more efficient and precise retrieval.

The final indexing method used is nearest neighbour matching. This retrieval method is applied to two fields; the aircraft type field where an exact match is requested, and the category field where an importance weight is applied.

The nearest neighbour matching process now singles out the type of aircraft that the user specifies by selecting either the SD3-30 , SD3-60 C23A, C23B or C23B+. The *Category* field is also used to narrow the set of cases retrieved. Initially, the system will try to retrieve those cases whose Category type the user stipulates, e.g., *Corrosion*. However if there are no similar matches in the case-base with *Category* type corrosion, then the system will still retrieve cases which have met all the other input selections but with a different *Category* type. The system will therefore retrieve a meaningful set of cases which may provide the complete solution to a new technical query or partial solution.

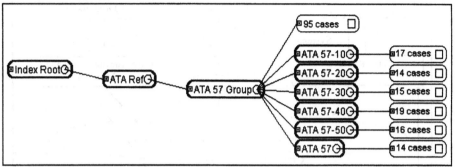

Fig. 3. Fragment of the knowledge-guided prototypes.

4 Integration of CBR System with Relational Database System

The CBR component of the system has been intimately inter-linked with a relational database in a seamless environment, providing full information flow through the resulting system. The use of CBR in aircraft product support is similar to work carried out by British Airways [7]. However, the preliminary work at Shorts highlighted the necessity for further work to integrate conventional RDBMS technology with CBR. The resulting hybrid system combines the full reporting functionality of a RDBMS with the heuristic retrieval capabilities of CBR.

The system has been designed to replace the current paper-based procedures in the Company's SD3-Aircraft support section. It provides instant access to the information needs of individual users through a customised form-based interface tailored to the specific needs of each user. As a result, each user has the specific information relevant to their needs displayed on their screen at any time. Figure 4 shows the system architecture.

The fields that are included in the case-base obtain their data from the database via the controlling GUI software. When a query has had all the necessary information added to it from each user, the next step is to find a useful solution. This is where the CBR aspect of the system is utilised. The relevant fields necessary for retrieval are taken from the database and used by the CBR system to find a similar case previously stored in the case-base. If such a case exists it will be retrieved and the user can view its solution. If the solution offered by the case-base is suitable, then it will be added automatically to the original database query.

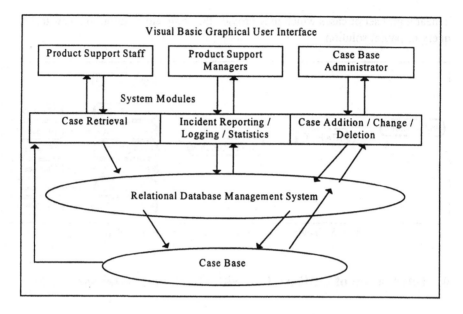

Fig. 4. Technical Support System Architecture

4.1 Using the Database to Acquire Knowledge

Each technical query may involve more than one correspondence between technical support and the operator. The initial technical query from the operator is classified as the 'parent' query and any subsequent related queries are classified as 'communication' queries. It was necessary to provide a solution to emulate electronically the processes involved in gathering information for a technical query as it passes through the office. Through the use of the relational facilities of the database, the physical method of compiling and 'stapling' all the individual related queries together to make one complete 'case' was incorporated into the system.

In this respect the database is being utilised as a knowledge acquisition tool as it facilitates two things. One, the building up of a query solution over time from its conception to its maturation when it is solved and made a case; and two, the ability to allow subsequent communication queries to be added and stored as related queries at a later date. In this latter use the database also overcomes the problem of the time lapse that often occurs between a parent technical query and its subsequent communication queries.

When a query has had all the necessary information added to it from each user, the next step is to find a useful solution. This is where the CBR aspect of the system is utilised. The relevant fields necessary for retrieval are taken from the database and used by the CBR system to find a similar case previously stored in the case-base. If such a case exists it will be retrieved and the user can view the solutions.

The retrieved cases can be used to give a complete solution or give partial information which can be used to guide the HQE. If the solution is not available from the case library, the CBA must add it to the case library for future retrievals once the query is solved. It is important that the CBA is someone who is a domain expert. The CBA has all the privileges for editing new and already stored cases within the case-base, as he/she makes the final decision on which newly solved technical queries in the database should be placed in the case library for future retrievals. *New words, important words* and *unwanted words* are also the sole responsibility of the CBA.

If a technical query arrives at technical support and is in some way connected to a previous query (i.e., a communication query) it is tagged electronically to the original query using the relational facilities of the database. This communication query is processed in the normal manner and a solution given back to the operator. Communication queries are an integral component of the problem and their solutions are an equally important part of the overall problem solving episode. Therefore it is imperative that all communication queries and solutions must be stored as one entity along with their parent queries in the case-base. If a communication query is solved and its parent query has been made into a case it is automatically '*appended*' to the original parent case in the case base and can therefore be retrieved in future as one single case.

The database stores all queries whereas the case-base stores unique problems (exemplar cases). The database stores both solved and unsolved problems while the case-base only stores those problems that have solutions. The database stores all information whether it is technical or non technical, while the case-base only stores unique problems.

As all faults are time-stamped at each stage of their journey through the system, the reporting component of the system can monitor their progress, and generate digital memoranda reminding support staff of outstanding work.

The statistical analysis component is used to determine the efficiency of technical support through database queries, and gives real time information on current technical queries, loads on the team's engineers and query solving time. It must be noted that such statistical information may not always give a true representation, as technical queries can have differing degrees of complexity which means a query can be answered within hours, days or weeks.

Another advantage of storing information in a database initially and then transferring it to the case base is that if the software is superseded by a more powerful case based reasoning shell the data is stored electronically and could be downloaded into the new software. The CBR software currently provides no facilities for the exporting of a case base to another format.

5 Conclusions

The system described in this paper is currently undergoing initial user testing, and it is expected that this integration of CBR with RDBMS technology will be employed by the Company throughout their organisation.

The GUI and harness for the system has been developed using Microsoft's Visual Basic. This harness controls all the interaction between the CBR software (ReMind) and the RDBMS (Microsoft Access). The users of the system view the software as one integrated package. Multi-user access across a network is facilitated by using the built-in networking capabilities of the RDBMS, and overcoming the single-user access restriction to the case base software programmatically. This work highlights the necessity to integrate conventional computing techniques with AI technology such as CBR to provide complete solutions.

The symbol hierarchy of the CBR software, ReMind, enables multiple-choice selection for the *Aircraft Type*, *ATA Reference* and *Category*. This ensures that the retrieval of cases by the HQE is rapid and accurate.

The current paper system in use at SD3-Aircraft has not been superseded but will run in tandem with the CBR system. The HQE, through the use of the CBR system will now know, in addition to the system retrieving nearest solutions, if a new query is a recurring problem and has been solved before or is a completely new unsolved technical query.

Further research is required on the key-words symbol hierarchy to aid the retrieval of stored cases.

References

1. Barletta R. An Introduction to Case-Based Reasoning, AI Expert 8, 1991.
2. Harmon, P. Case-Based Reasoning 2, Intelligent Software Strategies, 7(11), 1991.
3. Kriegsman, M., & Barletta, R. Building a Case-Based Help Application, IEEE Expert, 8(6), 1993.
4. Harmon, P. Case-Based Reasoning 3, Intelligent Software Strategies, 8(1), 1992.
5. Forsyth, R. Expert Systems: Principles and Case Studies, ed. Forsyth R, Chapman and Hall Ltd, (1989).
6. Michalski, R., Carbonnel, J., & Mitchell, T. Machine Learning: An Artificial Intelligence Approach, Tioga Publishing Corp, Palo alto, CA, 1983.
7. Magaldi, R.V., Maitaining Aeroplanes in Time-Constrained Operational Situations Using Case-Based Reasoning, EWCBR 1994 Chantilly, France.

Cost Estimation of Software Projects through Case Base Reasoning

Rossella Bisio and Fabio Malabocchia

Centro Studi E Laboratori Telecomunicazioni
Via Guglielmo Reiss Romoli, 274
10148 Torino, Italy
Fax: +39-11-2286862
Tel: +39-11-2286999 E-Mail : Rossella.Bisio@cselt.stet.it
Tel: +39-11-2286778 E-Mail : Fabio.Malabocchia@cselt.stet.it

Abstract. One of the most challenging goals for the software development community is the definition and assessment of techniques and tools
enabling the cost estimation of projects in the early phases of the software life cycle. Despite of the increasing needs and the available tools
and methods, a satisfactory solution is still to be found.
During the last two years, has gained some interest in this community
an approach based on analogy. Following this approach, an estimation
is made starting from analogies with other software projects met in the
past. The main reason for this trend is the increased flexibility with respect to other approaches. The main drawback of this method was the
inadequacy of the software technologies to provide an effective and efficient implementation.
The experience reported here, demonstrates that CBR techniques allow
a natural implementation of the estimation by analogy paradigm, and
the software estimation by analogy in particular.

1 Introduction

The extreme variability of software characteristics implies that it is getting
harder and harder to correctly estimate the software development costs. Despite of the methodological studies, and the ongoing efforts for the assessment
and standardization of the development processes, the evolution of the estimation methods hardly keeps pace with the increasing software complexity. While
standard products addressing a large market have prices not directly related to
costs, a great proportion of the software is developed for covering special requirements and is targeted for one or a few customers. In this case the price is
the result of a negotiation between the customer and the supplier. In telecommunications this is the most common case, and the strategical importance of
a laboratory devoted to cost estimation within the customer organization becomes concrete when the purchase department can base its offer on the result of
a reliable evaluation method.

By cost estimation of a software project we mean the identification of the
number of man months (i.e. the effort) required by the project development

until delivery. In the following, the attention will be on the effort, but the same approach applies to the duration as well.

Evaluation is generally carried out "a posteriori", when the project is already finished and the product is ready to be delivered or tested; at this stage the negotiation can only be about the price. Although this is a most important issue, early prediction is even more valuable as it allows to evaluate "a priori" the costs of a product. By early prediction is generally meant the evaluation during the first stages of the project life cycle, ranging from the specification stage up to the architectural design stage. At that time, the results are particularly useful for the definition of the feasibility study, for evaluating the suppliers' bids and managing the following negotiation.

While evaluation and early prediction are instances of the same problem, i.e. determining the effort, the latter problem is not supported by tools as it involves uncertainty characteristics that are rarely (if ever) taken into account by the classical estimation tools.

There are three main approaches for estimating software projects:

1. **Expert estimation:** experience is the basis, unfortunately, software typologies are so many and dissimilar that it is very hard to find a comprehensive experience like that. More usual is the availability of different experts for different software typologies.

2. **Algorithmic models:** some of them are very popular; generally they result from studies about the cost factors and take the form of an analytical function describing qualitatively the relations holding. Statistical regression is after used to tune the variables in this models. The most popular of this class is COCOMO. A second popular variety of these solution is the FUNCTION POINT method. This gives an estimation of the cost starting from the analysis of a number of parameters that can be representative of the software complexity, as the number of functionalities, the number and richness of the interfaces and so on. This works mainly for administrative software, whose costs are related to data management and transfer, but shows severe limitations for the evaluation of software whose algorithmic component is significant. In this case too, statistical regression has been employed for parameters' tuning.

   These methods perform reasonably well for the more common software typologies, on the contrary, their estimations can be unreliable when the project retains some unusual peculiarities. This is mainly due to the fact that the such peculiarities were not adequately covered in the training dataset.

   A second main problem is calibration. The relations holding between cost factors and cost vary depending on the context in which the parameters are tuned (e.g. the country, the project developers, the year, the industrial sector, and so on), so that all those tools should be tuned at the user site (like a barometer or a watch), otherwise their indications cannot be taken for granted. A further problem is that algorithmic models are almost useless in front of data incompleteness arising in the early prediction problem.

3. **Estimation by analogy:** this method is based on the retrieval of a number

of similar cases encountered in the past. Its main advantage is that this approach allows to appreciate the peculiarities of some regions of the project space that otherwise statistical regression would tend to neglect. In this field there is still little experience in the cost estimation community, but a lot of past successful applications of Case Based Reasoning [1, 2, 3, 4, 5] in different fields suggested that a CBR approach could overcome the limits inherent to the algorithmic models, and enable the development of a system suitable to the early estimation problem.

In the next section the problem is presented in more detail, in section 3 the AI solution is justified. The description of the system and its operational environment is given in section 4. As an introductory example, in section 5, is reported one of the benchmarks used for validation, it refers to COCOMO, the best known estimation model, that is well defined and simple.

2   Issues in the Effort Estimation of Software Projects

Building a cost model means providing an "object" that accepts a project description and evaluates the effort needed to deliver the software. Typical features are the software category, the programming language, the skill of the analysts, the programming environments and methodologies, and so on. The output, more than by a single value (deterministic function) is more adequately represented as an interval (probabilistic function) where the effort is defined with an average and a probability to fall into that interval. Perhaps the most important requirement in cost evaluation is flexibility. Algorithmic cost models are heavily affected by the dataset used for tuning the parameters. This phase is meant to reduce the error performed by the cost model; as the available methods (including neural networks, whose popularity is increasing in the software cost evaluation community) are based on the minimization of mean square error, they generally sacrifice precision over scarcely populated regions in the project space, in favour of precision over densely populated ones.

The reliability of the results of algorithmic models is therefore to be independently assessed by considering how similar the new project is to those used in the tuning phase. In scarcely populated regions the precision is poor, and algorithmic models can be complemented with other methods rating more the "locality" in the project space. Moreover, projects datasets convey information that cannot be kept by an average. If the user is provided with an estimation and the past cases considered by the evaluation process, the user can verify:

1. on his own, the similarity of the new project with those retrieved from the database;
2. if the effort associated to the various retrieved projects accounts for a low or a high variance;
3. how recent (i.e. up to date) are the projects upon which the estimation is based.

The requirements characterizing this domain are surveyed in the following. An important remark is that the cost evaluation process is too complex to even think of replacing the human expert with an automated system. At the same time, the economic relevance of the estimation implies that the user wants to understand any choices put forward by the system. An estimation computed starting from a number of past cases is a natural and generally well accepted explanation.

Data distributions

- **Few data** The stored projects are related to the software purchased in the past. Given the high variety of the projects, we have to deal with a project space with many dimensions (features) and scarcely populated. This makes the building of a single general cost model based on statistics unfeasible.
- **Non uniformity** The project space is not evenly covered at all, some regions show high density of cases, some others are totally uncovered. This sometimes happens due to correlations among the features that describe the projects (e.g. many programmers is related to many lines of code), other times because some types of projects are more uncommon (e.g. very large projects are more uncommon than small projects).
- **Outliers** They are the items that have costs far from the average. They are not uncommon and their importance cannot be underestimated. The regression base methods, represent pretty well the "average" case but can be unreliable for off standards projects.

Dynamical environment

- **Software evolution** As the software development process has not reached yet maturity, it is bound to smoothly change as it has done in the past. A good cost model should be able to follow this evolution that is witnessed by the content of the data base of projects. The natural learning capability of CBR systems fits very well into this requirement.
- **Change of the cost factors** As the development process change, some features like the CASE tool adopted gain higher importance, while the programmers' experience becomes less important.The considered features must be periodically updated and the similarity function correspondingly updated. CBR allows to keep these maintenance costs at an acceptable level.

Data Reliability

- **Subjective or estimated data** While some of the features can be unmistakably measured or obtained (for instance the programming language), some others depend on the human judgement and are bound to be subjective (e.g. the analysts' experience), other data are qualitatively estimated (i.e. the size in the early prediction problem). As this phenomenon is unavoidable, it must be explicitly controlled, and the cost model must show the capability to support it.
- **Level of detail** The level of detail of the available features is not ogeneous, some can be highly synthetical indicators, while others refer to technical

details. The cost model must be able to give more importance to the more informative features.

- **Description incompleteness** As data are acquired from the suppliers through questionnaires, some of the fields are left blank. Missing values are generally present both in the case under evaluation and in the stored projects. The cost model must be able to proceed even in front of partial descriptions. This is a main advantage featured by most CBR commercial systems.
- **Feature relevance** Each of the collected features contributes differently to the cost estimation.
- **Symbolic and numerical values** Some of the features take values from a predefined set, that can be partially or totally ordered. Numerical values can be integer, real and can take values from arbitrary ranges.

A further factor suggesting the application of AI methods is feature correlation. such dependencies can be located by the expert or by statistical analysis and are better captured by heuristics instead of expressions difficult to sinthesize and

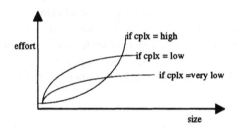

Fig. 1. Different effort-size relationships for different kind of projects.

represent.As an example. the relation between size and effort can vary depending on a third feature. that is complexity Fig. 2.

3 Why Case Based Reasoning

Classical algorithmic (sometimes referred to as parametric) methods are based on the statistical generalization principle. The cost model is represented by a mathematical function whose parameters are determined through statistical regression. Size and productivity are generally taken to be the principal features (main cost drivers) from which the basic cost is derived. Other less important cost drivers are generally devised and taken as modifiers for the basic cost.

A complementary approach. by analogy. is based on the following assumption:

similar projects have similar costs

and can be operationalized in this way:

1. Select one or more projects similar to the one to be evaluated.
2. Provide an estimation based on the retrieved projects.

A CBR solution can be set up to inherit the virtues of both approaches.
By maintaining a data base of projects, estimations and actual efforts, it is possible to find, on the bases of past similar cases, whether a predefined cost model can reliably estimate a new project or wheter analogy can be preferred.

4 Implementation and target environment

In the following, the operative environment of the system, and some implementation issues as the case representation, the retrieval and adaptation phases will be presented.

4.1 Operative environment

The system described here has been validated on a set of benchmarks and will be exploited in the cost estimation laboratory. This lab. avails of a number of tools (algorithmic) used by a number of professional evaluators. The choice of the tool follows a predefined schema. Currently, the software integrating FACE (Finding Analogies for Cost Estimation: the cost estimation system presented here) and the end user environment is under development. The start of the effective use of the system is planned for early October. A shared data base

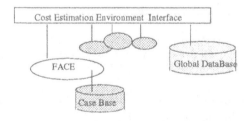

Fig. 2. Operative environment of FACE

collect all the projects estimated in the lab (see Fig. 3). This source is used for the case base of FACE, the cost estimation system presented here. The system implementation is based on the commercial tool CBR-Express. CBR-Express, being mainly oriented to help desk applications provides a good support to the phase of retrieval. The adaptation phase was developed using ART-IM [1], a hybrid shell available together with CBR-Express. The whole system runs on a PC 486 with Windows 3.1. The availability of tools like this allows to develop a prototype in a short time: problem analysis, learning the tool, functional and performance tests and documentation writing took about six man months. An

---

[1] CBR-Express and ART-IM are a trade mark of Inference Corporation.

additional period has been spent in a long and careful validation phase. expressly required by the customers.

4.2 Representation

Software projects are represented by means of a number of groups of homogeneous attributes dealing with all the relevant aspects. Six of them have been devised:

1. Class of the product: (e.g. network management system, administrative, ...)
2. Size: (e.g. code length and required documentation).
3. Program characteristics: (e.g. complexity, reliability, ...)
4. Developer group: (e.g. skill, experience, ...).
5. Development environment: (e.g. methodologies, tools, programming languages, ...)
6. User characteristics: (e.g. stability of the specifications, ...)

This information is collected by means of questionnaires designed by the software estimation group. When the supplier starts a negotiation, it has to provide this form compiled. The contents are checked for consistency, and a project description (amounting to about thirty features) is derived and inserted into the data base. Each project is then described by a set of features that are called cost factors (except for the size).

Within the system, features are distinguished by their usage, some of the attributes are used for retrieval, some others are instead used for adaptation, some at both stages. This solution follows from the need to concentrate in the retrieval phase on a space with a lower number of dimensions with respect to the number of cost drivers. From our experience the following heuristics can help in selecting the cost drivers:

- more abstract synthetic cost drivers are preferable. They generally have a limited number of values each representing a fairly different situation. If values to be acquired are less and more discriminant, they are easily understood by who fills in the questionnaire (data are more reliable) and the development of the similarity function is facilitated.
- it is not advisable to abstract over detailed continuous attributes (like size when expressed as the number of lines of code). Clustering these values for obtaining a restricted set can lead to meaningless clusters since there is no valid common criteria for all context.
- less relevant cost drivers can be dropped during an early feature selection phase.

Each symbolic feature is associated with two weights, representing the contribution to the similarity function. In the case of matching (i.e. when both features have the same value a) this weight is w+, otherwise the contribution is w-. For numerical attributes, the contribution to the similarity function decrease linearly with the distance of the retrieved value from the new project value, and evaluates 0 when this difference exceeds a given treshold. In order to exploit this approach, the weight definition and tuning is crucial. In the first release, we based on the expert indications, obtaining for each feature a weight in a range 1-10. Later we successfully experimented the use of a white box neural network model that allows to extract after the training phase a set of weights. This stage is most important even in the presence of the expert as the two weights could be compared and differences pinpointed. In our case the values were qualitatively compatible.

Each project description in the data base is stored together with its actual effort. Since locally (i.e. in some regions in the project space - see the discussion in section 3) some adaptation functions can be more suitable, further information can be recorded with each case. In particular when a cluster of similar projects is detected into the database a more specific adaptation function can be built. Each member of the cluster will host a reference to the cluster itself and the associated adaptation function will be applied in the future for the estimation of new similar cases. This means that the adaptation function and its parameters may vary from case to case.

4.3 Estimation of a new project

Given a new project, a set of most similar cases are extracted from the case repository. For each case a similarity score is computed. Scores are normalized in the interval [0 100], 100 means a perfect match. The obtained scores suggest how populated is the region around the new project. Similar cases are those having a score above a given threshold (θ) generally set to 70. All the cases found to be higher than the threshold are used to estimate the effort; we call them: θ-cases. If no cases can be found with this requirement no reliable estimation can be done.

Generally the size value is available for the new project; when missing, it is to be estimated and this is done on the basis of the size of the retrieved projects. After this step, from each θ-case an estimation is computed using the size/effort ratio, and the result modified on the basis of the cost factors specific for the adaptation stage. An integrated result is computed by balancing the different estimations generated by a subset of the θ-cases, the user has the capability of dropping some of the θ-cases from those to be considered. The general form used for an adaptation function for estimation by analogy is:

$$Effort(a) = Effort(b) \cdot \left(\frac{Size(a)}{Size(b)}\right)^{\alpha} \cdot \left(\frac{Context(a)}{Context(b)}\right)^{\beta} \qquad (1)$$

where a is the new project, b is one of the θ-cases, and context is a combination (e.g.: a sum) of a set of cost drivers expressing sinthetically the characteristics of the project.

5 Experimental Results

In the following we will give an example about how the system works. This experiment was considered very important by the cost estimation group because the model we were asked to emulate was very well known and allowed to make a good comparison.

Some of the goals of the validation activities were: verify that the features selected for the retrieval and adaptation phases were correct and good. For instance the features "Class of the product" were better exploited in the retrieval phase, and this agrees with the intuition that the typology of the product strongly correlates with the other features and consequently they will show a ratio size/development time comparable. The other cost drivers can act in the tuning of the effort especially when they diverge from the typical ranges of that class of products.

Perhaps the best known cost model is COCOMO [6]. It was built by a group of expert cost estimators; the parameters involved in the model were computed by regression over a set of 63 projects. These projects are described by the following attributes:

- **MODE:** information about the nature of the project. This attribute partitions the space into 3 groups of projects. Each group has a basically different behaviour regarding the ratio size/effort [7].
- **SIZE:** expressed in kilo lines of code.

And 15 cost drivers:

- **Products attributes:** (RELY, DATA, CPLX, TIME): take into account aspects like reliability, complexity, time constraint requirements.
- **Computer attributes:** (STOR, VIRT, TURN): describe the characteristics of the platform on which the project is developed
- **Human attributes:** (ACAP, AEXP, PCAP, VEXP, LEXP): represent the supplier's ability.
- **Project attributes:** (MODP, TOOL, SCED) capture the availability of tools, methodologies and development schedule.

A more detailed view of these attributes is beyond the scope of this paper. Furthermore at each project the real effort, expressed in man months, is associated.

5.1 Performance measures

The considered performance measures are:

$$MRE = \frac{1}{n} \sum_{i=1}^{n} \frac{|Actual_i - Estim_i|}{Estim_i} \qquad (2)$$

that is the average error computed over N cases. A slightly different measure, that takes into account the project size is:

$$WMRE = \frac{1}{\frac{1}{n} \sum_{j=1}^{n} Actual_j} \sum_{i=1}^{n} |Actual_i - Estim_i| \qquad (3)$$

WMRE, compared to MRE, weights heavier the relative errors for projects with actual effort over the average. An error of 30% is generally considered as acceptable in the early phases of the project.

5.2 Performed tests

The "Leaving-one-out" technique was used for the error estimation [8]. A set of test was performed to verify how different choices may affect the performance. Table 1 reports some test with results worth discussing. All the tests in Table 1 were performed with $\theta = 70$. For each test two rows are given: the first one reports the estimation performed over the best case retrieved, the second takes into account all the θ-cases retrieved.

In test 1, all cost drivers were taken into account during the retrieval phase, adaptation was performed using a simple function based only on size. The results were discouraging: few estimaded projects with an high error. Surprisingly (test 2), by simply narrowing the retrieval search space to the "class of product" kind of features (giving a higher w+ to these and lower w+ to the others); better result were obtained: more projects were estimated with a lower error. That means that the precision of the retrieval were increased not condsidering in this phase misleading features.

Following the hypothesis, that a more informed adaptation function will do the job equally well, two further tests were performed, both using an adaptation function taking into account the context given by the cost drivers other than the "class of product" features. One (test 3) with the all-features-retrieval, the other with partial-feature-retrieval (test 4), that is a sort of trade off between test 2 and test 3. The best result was obtained with the combined test, all the performance measure improved: lower MRE with lower standard deviation, lower WMRE, and more projects estimated with an MRE less that 25%. Adding all the details in the adaptation function does not improve meaningly the result (test 5). In fact even if the MRE is slightly lower, and error on big projects is decreased (lower WMRE) the percentage of prediction with an error less that 25% is reduced. The first two columns of Table 1 give names and numbers of the tests, the third one contains the number of cases whose estimation was possible. The fourth column indicates the predictive performance of the system, that is the ratio of cases whose estimation error is lower than 25%. The performance measures defined above are reported in the last columns. The standard deviation is added Another interesting issue is to evaluate the effectiveness of clusters with ad hoc adaptation functions. Three clusters were found, for a total of 32 projects with internal cross-similarity (still based only on product features) over score 75, the other projects remained isolated. For projects belonging to these clusters very interesting results were obtained, which are listed in Table 2. The third cluster is characterized by very similar projects. In the last row of Table 2 the performance measures are summarized for all projects to make them comparable to results in Table 1. A significant improvement was achieved. Some experiments for tuning the threshold showed that 70 is a good trade-off in order to allow the estimation of more cases (46) with still an acceptable error (40%). Table 3 reports the

No.	test name	Numb. of estimated	Pred (25)	WMRE	MRE avg.	std.dev
1	Simple	23	52%	0.62	54.58	70.42
		23	39%	0.62	59.78	71.24
2	Restricted no. of features retrieval	46	37%	0.55	52.26	56.72
		46	22%	0.59	65.52	69.44
3	all features retrieval	23	61%	0.58	45.49	70.75
		23	43%	0.58	52.90	67.65
4	trade off 2 - 3 retrieval	46	46%	0.48	40.41	37.46
		46	37%	0.51	50.74	52.35
5	Adaptation with complete inform.	46	39%	0.38	39.92	30.40
		46	33%	0.40	45.43	37.11

Tab. 1. Tests performed on COCOMO dataset

Test	No. proj. estimated	Pred (25)	WMRE	MRE avg.	std.dev
1 cluster	11	82%	0.18	21.52	10.15
2 cluster	16	50%	0.17	33.10	30.15
3 cluster	5	100%	0.13	13.05	4.33
review on clusters	32	69%	0.17	25.99	
Global result on					
partial inform & specific adaptat. function	46	61%	0.20	32.60	33.80

Tab. 2. Effectiveness of clusters

comparison varying θ in the context of test 4. Experimentations with the target data set are still on going, in that cases the performance results are much better. as the number of projects is much higher allowing a richer possibility for analogy. The main importance of COCOMO is of being a very popular benchmark, easy enough to understand but providing all the most important characteristics of its class. This is also the reason why although universally known, it is completely unused in practice. Another important point is that the experimentations carried out up to now are demonstrating that FACE shows a better performance and a higher stability with respect to the algorithmic cost models experimented.

6 Concluding remarks

We have shown how the CBR paradigm has been exploited for matching some uncovered requirements rising in the software cost estimation community. This

test performed	No.proj. estimated	Pred (25)	WMRE	MRE avg.	dev.
θ= 60	60	40%	0.43	48.81	46.1
θ= 65	55	45%	0.37	43.32	41.89
θ= 70	46	46%	0.48	40.41	37.46
θ= 75	30	50%	0.52	35.63	41.29

Tab. 3. Selection of the similarity threshold

domain lent itself to a solution like this as this is a natural way of representing how the expertise grows in an evaluation group. Software is in rapid evolution, to reuse past experiences, it is necessary to maintain the project descriptions in a data base, until they become no longer relevant and can be discarded (for instance because a dismissed CASE tool was used). Therefore the availability of a dynamical data base of projects is important (and was independently decided), CBR provides a conceptual and computationally efficient method that making an effective use of the similarity concept, overcoming the problem of the large and scarcely populated project space. The great importance is that it allows a natural achievement of the early prediction features still uncovered by commercial tools. In this moment is under development an integration of the system with a data base of projects related to Telecom Italia, and independently by another external lab. on a different base of projects.

Acknowledgements We warmly thank for their effective co-operation the colleagues of the Software Quality group. Among the others we particularly appreciated the contribution of Dr. Joannis Stamelos currently in STET HELLAS who made us available his deep experience.

References

1. Simoudis, E.: Using case-based retrieval for customer technical support. IEEE Expert **7** (Oct. 1992).
2. Hennessy, D., Hinkle, D.: Applying case-base reasoning to autoclave loading. IEEE Expert 7,5, (Oct. 1992).
3. Pearce, M., Goel, A.K., Kolodner, J. L., Zimring, C., Sentosa, L., Billington R.: Case-based design support IEEE Expert, October 7,5 1992.
4. Nguyen, T., Czerwinski, M., Dan Lee: Compaq Quicksource providing the consumer with the power of AI AI Magazine - Fall (1993)
5. Allen, B. P.: Case-based reasoning: business applications Communication of the ACM Vol 37 No 3, March (1994)
6. Boehm, B. W.: Software engineering economics Prentice-Hall, Englewood Cliffs, New Jersey (1981)
7. Subramanian, G. H.: An empirical examination of software development modes The Journal of Systems and Software 23:3-7, (1993)
8. Weiss, S. M., Kulikowski, C. A.: Computer systems that learn, Morgan Kauffman Publishers, 1990.

Operator Decision Aiding by Adaptation of Supervision Strategies

Béatrice Fuchs, Alain Mille, Benoît Chiron

CPE-Lyon, LISA , 31 place Bellecour, 69 002 Lyon, France
e-mail : {bf,am,chiron}@cpe.ipl.fr

Abstract. This paper presents a CBR application in the domain of industrial supervision. The domain knowledge is acquired at design stage through different models and some critical prototypical situations. At operating stage, new situations and their associated supervision strategy complete the supervision system and are reused by adaptation in later situations in similar contexts. The system can be viewed as an artificial operator who collects experiences from the operators in order to propose relevant variants in similar situations. First, we present current approaches in process supervision. Then, knowledge and cases representation that support case-based reasoning and the different stages of the reasoning process are presented. We focus on case adaptation, and show different degrees of case reuse, depending on available knowledge.

Industrial settings are complex, and their management needs powerful tools. The parts of the installation are interconnected but more and more autonomous and automatically driven, needing few manual intervention in normal operation.

In case of failure or troubleshoot, the system can't correct by itself, the operator must handle the situation and try to recover a normal operation. Human-machine interface and tools play a growing role, in that they give to the operator a perception of the current situation.

Usually, an industrial system is represented through synoptic and views that the operator can select by different ways. There are hundreds of different views for a complex system and all information cannot be represented and too much information produces an overloading of the operator's attention ([Millot, 1988]). In case of problem, it is the responsibility of the operator to look for the needed information to manage the situation.

1 Overview of Current Approaches

Some classical supervision systems (e.g. Imagin [SFERCA, 1993]) provide design tools specialized by function. Synoptics representing whole or part of the system are structured thanks to links and are built through a graphical editor. A synoptic consists of a *background* describing the fixed part of the installation, and a set of graphical configurable objects representing variables of the process (bar graphs, counters, animated symbols, telecommands ...). An example of such a system is presented in [Fuchs, 1995, Mille et al., 1995].

These systems provide various functionalities such as events and threshold management, recording of variable values, graphs displaying, process supervision and driving, process and data acquisition platform communication.

The use of these tools is left to the initiative of the operator, and no help nor suggestion is made to help managing a given situation. Moreover, the design of an application is tedious, subject to errors, because every element must be described and configured with different levels of detail.

More recently, supervision systems have been enhanced with hypermedia capabilities. The NeXTIM system illustrates such an approach ([Fuchs, 1995, Mille et al., 1995].

The basic interface object of a hypermedia system is a dashboard, which represents a point of view on the system to supervise. Dashboards are essentially windows onto the industrial system, and contain information about the system in the form of views. Views enable the displaying of multimedia information (variables, video, images, text, telecommands etc.). Dashboards are linked thanks to hyperbuttons which the user can use in order to navigate within the dashboard network.

The operator is helped in the supervision task by the automatic *display of dashboards* in response to an event occurrence, and the *record of dashboards* which starts on an event occurrence and continues while the corresponding state is true. The recorded data can be "replayed" as they evolved in the past ([Fuchs, 1995]).

Meanwhile, these systems, though easy and intuitive for the operator, don't provide guidelines for the designing of supervision applications. They provide no help for the choice of the appropriate strategy according to the context. The system to supervise is not modelled.

Padim's issues include first helping the design of a supervision system by providing generic tools adapted for the supervision domain, and second, facilitating its maintenance by acquisition of new supervision strategies and their reuse in later similar situations.

Padim acts as an artificial operator which interacts with the real operator to search for the appropriate strategy implementation according to the context, the supervision rules, and operator's experience of the supervision.

In this paper we will focus on the operating stage and the operator helping process. The design stage is part of other research works ([Chiron, 1995]).

2 CBR for Helping the Operator

At the operating stage, few dashboards are needed for routine situations. But in specific situations, other supervision strategies according to the current context must be implemented. A new supervision strategy implemented for a special purpose can be acquired to increase the supervision system and may be reused later in similar contexts by adaptation.

Case-based reasoning represents an interesting way in the acquisition of new experience ([Kolodner, 1993], [Riesbeck and Schank, 1989], [Slade, 1991]). There are several advantages of the CBR approach :

- It is an alternative to other methods when the domain knowledge is weak, or when we don't want to spend a lot of time for knowledge acquisition,
- It tries to reproduce the human reasoning mechanisms,
- A solution can be obtained without having to build it from scratch,
- It collects all experience to make it accessible by other people.

For Padim, the main aim is to avoid the need for big amount of knowledge. All available knowledge e.g. existing databases, must be exploited in order to facilitate knowledge acquisition. Furthermore, the CBR system must not be independent, but either integrated to other applications, and particularly the supervision system. The knowledge representation system must therefore meet these requirements.

The initial designed model represents a first domain knowledge of the system to supervise. This knowledge is linked to the description of known critical situations and stored as prototypical cases. The knowledge may be more or less well defined, so the CBR task must compensate the lack of knowledge. Less this knowledge is modelled, more important is the role of CBR.

The operator must be implied in this process. First, operator's profile must be taken into account for the supervision strategy construction, then, the results are validated and modified by him. Furthermore, the operator provides a feedback for controlling the quality of the adaptation which is done.

So, before discussing the CBR process, we'll describe what supervision knowledge and cases consist of, and then the knowledge framework which support cases and knowledge representation.

3 Knowledge Representation

The competence of a case-based reasoner is due to its ability to retrieve pertinent cases, and to adapt correctly a reminded case. Generally, domain knowledge is used to guide the process. So a minimal modelization of the domain is necessary. We'll first present a model to describe the supervision domain, and then we'll present our framework for knowledge representation.

3.1 The Supervision Knowledge

The aim of a human operator is to supervise the system according to different points of view in a given context. This point of view is named *supervision object*, i.e. the object on which the supervision must focus on, a goal for the supervision. The purpose of the modelization is to define classes and instances of supervision objects, with different points of view :

- *structures* : Objects are described with attributes, composition relations between other objects, and geographical information (A factory is composed of a pump unit, flood-gates, etc.)
- *topology* : Objects have a geographical disposition, and it is often useful to focus on a particular area.

– *functions* can be described with models such as IDEF0, associated with a
state transition graph ([Marca and Mc Gowan, 1988]). For example, starting
an oven, stopping a production factory.

In addition, *events* are defined through a dependency tree based on other
information, i.e. other events or variables. By following these dependencies, we
can reach objects that may be suspected in the occurrence of an event. This
model provides explanations.

concepts : Classes and instances of objects to supervise, abstraction / specialization relations are defined. For example, the object class PUMP defines all
common features of pumps and can be subclassed for several kinds of pumps.

The degree of modelization is variable, depending on the knowledge really
available, the effort spent for modelization and maintenance. So, the knowledge
may be weak and needs to be completed by cases constituting supervision experiences.

Supervision objects are described with attributes containing values, and relationships with other objects. They are represented through dashboards, their
attributes through views and their relationships through hyperbuttons (figure
1).

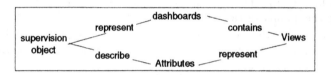

Fig. 1. supervision objects are linked to the supervision system

Generic dashboards are defined for a class of supervision objects. The instanciation of a generic dashboard with a real object allows the dynamic construction
of dashboards easily.

The description of some well-known typical supervision situations initializes
the case base.

3.2 The Supervision Cases

An atomic supervision case is a simple *supervision episode*. A supervision episode
is defined as a description of the starting *supervision situation* and the *supervision environment* to manage it. A starting supervision situation is described
by the sequence of events which lead to it and by the corresponding supervision
contexts. The sequence of events includes what occurred in the system and the
actions which have been done by the operator. Events are essential in the identification of a situation. They are filtered in order to eliminate redundant events,
and keep only higher level events (elaborated with lower level events).

1. *system events* come from the system and generally more or less precisely
   defined. They can be elaborated with other data, variable values, or by combinations of other events. Among events, there are state changing events

characterizing an evolution of the system, and dangerous events which must be avoided e.g. by analyzing the sequence of events that leads to.

2. *operator events* are actions performed on the system. Telecommand variable values, display or close dashboards, record dashboard are examples of such events.

A supervision environment describes the *system's state*, the *operator's state*, the *operating context* and is viewed thanks to some dashboards.

The system's state (relative to the supervision function) is described with a small number of states characterizing the operating state of the system and may be normal operation, degraded operation (with possible variants), breakdown stop, or maintenance stop.

The operator's state is useful to determine an user profile and operating conditions. The operator state is defined with an user profile (novice, experimented) and the operating conditions (night or day, team or not, ...).

The operating context is the set of supervision objects represented through the current dashboards. Each supervision object is characterized by its current state.

The solution is a new supervision environment, i.e. a set of dashboards to supervise and manage a new set of supervision objects.

Atomic supervision cases can be gathered in a strategy which is a consistent sequence of episodes.

The operator must take the initiative to change the supervision mode if he thinks the objectives have succeeded or failed. Furthermore, some conditions (urgency for example) may condition the strategy adopted by the operator.

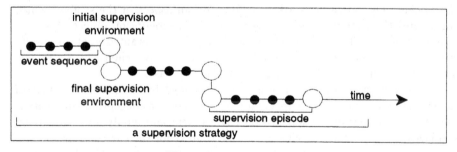

Fig. 2. A supervision case

3.3 The knowledge representation framework

Knowledge representation is frame-based. Objects are represented with a frame network linked by relations. A frame can represent classes or instances. The abstraction, specialization and instance links are particular relations. The set of frames is tightly coupled with cases. Cases are represented with particular frames. Every relation owns an inverse relation automatically updated by the system.

Attributes are characterized by a set of facets to ensure the consistency of the objects. The different kinds of facets are value facet, default value facet, type facet, constraint facets (cardinality, inclusion in a set, inclusion in an interval, ...) particular properties, and procedural facets (if-needed, if-added, if-removed, if-updated facets).

Procedural facets have multiple uses. First, they allow the definition of procedures to compute the value of a slot or to trigger a procedure when the slot's value changes. Second, they can be used to navigate within the information system, and then to augment the knowledge base with other information. They are the bridge between the system and the overall external information system, especially the supervision system.

Inheritance allows the definition of abstract objects and the inheritance of attribute definitions of superclasses. Inherited attributes can be modified according to the constraints defined in the superclasses. When an attribute is modified, modifications are propagated in all subclasses to check whether related constraints are satisfied after modification.

This is the framework that is used by the reasoner which we present now.

4 The CBR process

4.1 Case Retrieval

The first stage is the retrieval of cases relevant to the new problem to solve. This involves to find entry points in the case base in order to restrict potential cases.

Padim uses a discrimination network automatically built and maintained by the system. The operator is asked to focus on an aspect of the system, which constitutes the goal of the supervision : the focal supervision object. A supervision strategy will be very different according to the wanted goal, in similar situations, the goal of the supervision will condition the choice of a strategy. The supervision goal is the entry point in the case base.

The search space of the cases is strictly divided by the general context of the system and by the focal supervision object. Then, a conceptual similarity is used to find similar initial supervision environment and finally an event driven similarity allows to find the closest specific context for the current episode.

The conceptual similarity has to answer at the question "In which extent current supervision objects are the same *kind of* supervision objects than the reminded ones ?". Supervision objects are developed according to their relationships and a kind of subsumption process finds the level of matching between the current subgraph and the reminded one.

The event driven similarity measure takes into account the presence or not of the types of events, and their relative dispersion in the sequence. It is a kind of string matching. The current sequence is similar to the old one if all types of events in the current sequence are present in the old one and in the same order in both situations. The similarity measure is described in [Mille, 1994], an example is shown at figure 3.

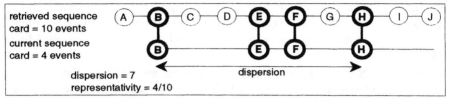

Fig. 3. An example of event sequences matching.

If the search process fails, constraints can be relaxed, e.g. by allowing minor differences between event sequences (elimination of less important events).

4.2 The Adaptation Process

There exist different adaptation methods depending on the type of problem to be resolved, the complexity of the problem, the availability of additional knowledge, the similarity degree of the input and retrieved case. In [Kolodner, 1993, Riesbeck and Schank, 1989, Smyth and Cunningham, 1993], several methods have been listed. A typology of these methods can be easily established :

- The methods that operate on the old solution directly to produce the new one : the techniques used depend on the nature of the components to adapt, and on the differences observed with the adapted case.
  - A copy of the solution of the old case is generally first done to serve as a basis for further modifications.
  - The substitution consists of replacing an element of the solution with another. The nature of substitution is done according to the type of the element concerned.
  - The transformation is a structural modification of the solution and consist of adding, removing or changing the order of the components.
- The reinstanciation of the inferences done in the old case to produce the old solution produces the solution of the new problem. The solution is then completely rebuilt. This suppose that the case include the inferences done to obtain the solution.

Padim's adaptation process uses different kinds of methods, depending on the correspondence of the features of the retrieved and new case, and the amount of domain knowledge available.

The matching process points out correspondences in the retrieved case and the new one (similar events and supervision objects). The different parts of the solution are linked with events of the sequence from which they depend on. The first stage is to project these links in the new solution, and copy the concerned solution elements. The copy is a reinstanciation process : first, the concerned parts of the old solution are abstracted and specialized for the need of the new case. Every detail of the solution is consequently adjusted to the current needs. The substitution method will be used e.g. for scale modifications of the variable views, (curves, bar graphs, ...), or time constants for the recordings. The kind of modification depends on the type of object. The different adaptation techniques presented above will be used depending on the nature of the elements. Some structural modifications will be done in order to preserve the consistency (e.g. the adaptation of a dashboard representing a group of pumps for another group with a different number of pumps will require to add or remove the corresponding views)

Then, the differences between old and new cases are analyzed. Solution elements of the old case linked to events which are not present in the new situation are left. The events in the new situation that are not present in the old one must be analyzed in order to determine what pieces of information depend on. The dependency is established by memory search using explaining links provided by event dependencies. The search process begins thanks to the connection between cases and objects of the model which are in turn linked to their representation. The exploration of the explanations dependencies is useful to retrieve related information. The exploration may be directed toward possible explanations of an event.

The memory search can be very expensive, may reach a lot (too many) information, or may fail. In case of memory search failure, the reasons of a failure can be due to a lack of domain knowledge (missing relations, for example), or a bad strategy. The origin of the failure cannot be diagnosed, but alternative can be considered. For example, an interesting investigation consists in searching in other cases for that event or supervision object, and reusing the search path used for navigation between an event and the related information. But we must not forget that the context of this event has an influence on the objects to supervise. The access to other cases may point out the need for additional index, which can be incrementally built as soon as their need appears.

Sometimes the memory search process may find too much information. Other cases, similar to the current situations (others than the one that has been chosen for adaptation) may be examined in order to determine which of them are relevant in the current context.

The memory search process points out the need to augment the solution of a case with additional information representing the memory search strategy used to produce a good adaptation.

The system checks the existence of a dashboard with these specifications and in case of failure, a new dashboard is built based on the retrieved information. Again, a retrieval process must allow the access to relevant dashboards. Here too, the index setting will facilitate this search.

Finally, when dashboards have to be created, some ergonomic constraints will guide the creation of dashboards, like :

- Avoid the overloading of information in dashboards, involving their structuration, using hyperbutton links,
- Prefer using dashboards already known by the operator,
- Take into account dashboards already viewed by the operator, the actions performed,
- Avoid creation of new dashboards if there exist a similar one differing only by few views.

Adapting a supervision episode is quite simple because the planification of the actions to be done has no particular importance. The major difficulty is to create and maintain indexes used by the adaptation process itself.

4.3   Test, Repair, Validate and Store the Solution

Once Padim has completed the adaptation of the supervision case, it proposes its solution to the operator. The operator has the ability to modify the proposed solution in a number of ways : add new interface elements, change the overall presentation of the dashboard, or change the way that some information is represented. These changes provide feedback to Padim about what makes a good dashboard, to recognize elements it may have failed to include, to enhance its memory search paths, or to adapt itself to the profile of its current operator.

The last stage allows to augment the case base with the new solved one. The expert of the domain analyses the case and a new feedback can be acquired. First, an analysis of the situation can be refined and a collection of incident tracing information enhances tracability. Second, it is the opportunity of the acquisition of new knowledge, or the refinement of existing ones.

The memorization stage must decide to store the case, to generalize if possible, depending on already existing cases in the case base. This stage must be controlled by an expert to avoid non relevant generalizations. The index setting stores the case at a good place in the discrimination network for later retrieval.

5   Conclusion

A prototype of this system is under development, implemented with the objective C language under NeXTStep. A this moment, the knowledge representation system is partially implemented.

The first perspective is to provide bigger supervision cases with supervision strategies, allowing to follow a sequence of supervision episodes and to detect any drift by analysis of the occurring events.

Other perspectives on this work are the enhancement of the adaptation process by introspection (see [Leake, 1993]) or by the analysis of the operator feedbacks, and the use of this framework for other domain knowledge.

References

[Chiron, 1995] Chiron, B. (1995). Aide à la conception dans le domaine de la supervision et le raisonnement à partir de cas. In Bichindaritz, I., editor, *4eme Seminaire raisonnement à partir de cas*, Université René Descartes, Paris V.

[Fuchs, 1995] Fuchs, B. (1995). Aide à la décision opérateur par adaptation de stratégies de supervision industrielle. In Bichindaritz, I., editor, *4eme Seminaire raisonnement à partir de cas*, Université René Descartes, Paris V.

[Kolodner, 1993] Kolodner, J. (1993). *Case-Based Reasoning.* Morgan Kaufmann.

[Leake, 1993] Leake, D. B. (1993). Learning adaptation strategies by introspective reasoning about memory search. In Press, A., editor, *Proceedings of the AAAI Workshop on Case based reasoning*, pages 57–63, MenloPark, CA.

[Marca and Mc Gowan, 1988] Marca, D. and Mc Gowan, C. (1988). *SADT: Structured Analysis and Design Technique*. Mac Graw Hill.

[Mille, 1994] Mille, A. (1994). Situations de supervision : similarite entre situations. Rapport interne.

[Mille et al., 1995] Mille, A., Chartres, J.-M., Niel, E., Fuchs, B., and Chiron, B. (1995). Intelligent workstation for immediate decision helping in process supervision. In Glavič, P. and Kravanja, Z., editors, *European Symposium on Computer Aided Process Engineering - 5*, Bled, Slovenia. Pergamon Press.

[Millot, 1988] Millot, P. (1988). *Supervision des procédés automatisés et ergonomie*. Hermès.

[Riesbeck and Schank, 1989] Riesbeck, C. K. and Schank, R. C. (1989). *Inside case-based reasoning*. Lawrence Erlbaum Associates.

[SFERCA, 1993] SFERCA (1993). Image, le manuel opérateur. Technical report, SFERCA S.A., 23, rue du Creuzat, 38 L'Isle d'Abeau.

[Slade, 1991] Slade, S. (1991). Case-based reasoning: A research paradigm. *AI magazine*, 12(1):42–55.

[Smyth and Cunningham, 1993] Smyth, B. and Cunningham, P. (1993). Complexity of adaptation in real-world case-based reasoning systems. In *Proceedings of the sixth Irish conference on Artificial Intelligence and cognitive systems*, pages 228–240.

PROFIL : a decision support tool for metallic sections design using a CBR approach

Jean Luc WYBO, Fréderic GEFFRAYE, Aline RUSSEIL

Ecole des Mines de Paris - CEMEF/IAM

B.P. 207 - 06904 Sophia Antipolis Cedex (France)

Abstract

This paper presents the PROFIL system, a Decision Support Tool for the Design of metallic sections production. The PROFIL system uses a Case-Based Reasoning approach for the selection of pertinent former designs.

Production of metallic sections is done by a succession of forming operations. The design task is composed of two parts : selection and scheduling of operations and assessment of forming tools geometry.

The PROFIL system also provides support to production technicians, to input process parameters and control measurements as part of cases, and to adjust settings during pre-production trials.

Selection of cases is made by following two orthogonal points of view, on similarity and quality of produced parts. Similarity is based on selection of relevant dimensions of the section, while quality is based on selection of potential defects. Each dimension or defect is associated to an evaluation function which uses a fuzzy logic approach. To improve ergonomy, relevant cases are displayed in a two-dimension space : similitude/quality.

Implementation of the system has been done on a computer workstation, using a commercial DBMS, in order to cope with industrial requirements.

The PROFIL system is operational in the industrial site and provides support to designers and process technicians.

1 Introduction

This study aims at providing an industrial company producing metallic sections with a decision support tool for design and production.

To solve this problem, we have chosen a global approach, starting from the studies on Interactive Decision Support Systems [Levine 89]. Such systems do not aim at reproducing the resolution process. The classes of problems that they manage are often multi-objectives and partially defined. This approach consists in providing tools and methods to evaluate a situation, the user adding his own experience, his own judgment in order to achieve the design task.

Starting from an analysis of the design process which demonstrated that it was not possible to model this task, we have decided to concentrate our efforts on providing design support by reusing similar parts already designed. Visser and Al. [Visser 93] show that support to reusing of past experiences constitutes the most important function of a design support tool. Actually, search of existing and potentially interesting solutions is one of the most difficult design tasks, even for an expert.

2 Origins of Case-Based Reasoning (CBR)

The origins of CBR are located at the intersection of two approaches : cognitive psychology (in the frame of the study of memory) and analogy reasoning. This technique emerged in US about ten years ago. Keypoints of the method may be found in [Darpa 89]. CBR consists in searching for a case similar to the problem to solve and reuse the solution or the reasoning which brought the solution for this case [Rougegrez 94]. Because the case extracted from the base is generally not identical to the problem, the complete reasoning includes a phase to adapt the case to the problem.

Concerning theories about memory, the works made by Schank [Schank 82] on organization of memory have been used in the first applications of CBR. Slade [Slade 91] presents this method as an alternative to rule-based reasoning. The author justifies his approach by the fact that CBR is founded on a more natural perception of reasoning : analogy.

Two application contexts of CBR can be identified [Cauzenille 85] :

- Heuristic analogy : when problem solving looks complex and difficult, using the solution of a problem formerly solved allows by-passing resolution process.

- last resort analogy : when there exists no theory or model to solve the problem, using the solution of a similar problem is the last resort.

CBR is based on reuse of knowledge. There are three main domains of application : problem solving, problem interpretation and training.

For problem solving, former similar experiences are used as design guidelines, they provide elements of the answer. This approach spread human experience gained on concrete examples and its training aspect is important : failures form an essential part of information and complete success cases.

Concerning CBR applied to design problems, Trousse and al. [Trousse 93] use experimental studies realized in cognitive psychology to show the importance of analogy reasoning in different types of design. Authors establish that reuse of former cases takes place at several levels, as designers tend to formalize new design problems in a reusable form.

3 Goals of the PROFIL System

The industrial plant is specialized in metallurgy and forming of copper alloys. We have studied the production of sections used by glasses industry to make hinges. These sections are obtained by a succession of forming processes and the design consists in assessing which operations are needed and what is the geometry of the forming tools. Two kinds of defects should be avoided : non respect of the precise dimensions required by the customer and surface defects, as scratches or differences in brightness.

Several studies have been made [Geffraye 94] to model or simulate the forming process and metal flow, in order to define relations between design parameters and results. Although some interesting results were obtained, these studies clearly demonstrated that knowledge is unsufficient to design tools and scheduling of forming operations from the required final shape.

Even with the lack of such general rules, designers succeed by using informal rules, experience and trial and error strategies which may result in high costs and long delays between the customer order and parts delivery.

From this analysis of the existing design process, two goals have been chosen : rationalize the design process and reduce production time and failures. To reach these goals, we have proposed to develop an Interactive Decision Support System, using a CBR approach, providing support to the designers and to the technicians in charge of production processes.

From the designer's point of view, the system is used to input and store new cases and to support design by identifying pertinent former cases. From the technician's point of view, the system is used to input process parameters, results of controls and to support evaluation of parts quality along production.

4 Methodology

4.1 Structure of Cases

A case is the representation of a problem and solution to this problem in the system memory. It is a set of data [Maurice-Demourioux 93] describing :
- the problem,
- process resulting in the solution,
- the solution,
- effects induced by the solution.

Some kinds of problems may depend from a context. It may be a set of constraints or informations out of which a solution is not valid. In our study, specific requests from customers or available machine tools form the context.

We call target-problem the problem to solve and source-problem a former problem which may be used to solve the new problem. Following Visser [Visser 93], the structure of a case is composed of 5 parts :
- situation, initial state and context,
- specification of the problem,
- processing steps to reach the result,
- description of result,
- non structured notes.

In this application, the context includes specification of requirements : surface aspect and nature of alloy. Problem specification is given by the required geometry of the section. Processing steps describe the forming stages applied to the material : machine tools and tool geometry. Description of result is a set of data representing the defects and values of control measurements (gloss, geometry). Finally, non structured notes are remarks from the designer about its choices and observations of technicians during forming operations.

Description of a case in three main parts (statement, solution, result) allows us to fit the requirements of CBR phases and specially selection of the best case. It corresponds also to the trial and error approach of design.

4.2 Selection of Cases

Selection of source-problems (former designs) is done by applying the criteria used by designers. In the catalogue of the company, sections are classified in "families", having some common characteristics. In a first step, we use this classification to extract from the base the cases descibing sections of the same family. This method raises two problems : it may be difficult to assign a family to a new section and by restricting the source-problems to the same section family, some experience is lost, as the one gained on sections belonging to a different family but having many characteristics in common with the target-problem.

In order to cope with the two main aspects of selection of interesting cases : similarity and overall quality of results, we propose to use an orthogonal approach based on points of view.

We define a point of view as the weighted combination of factors used by the designer to assess a value to similarity or quality. Each factor represents how the expert evaluates a parameter or the deviation from a reference. In order to provide degrees of freedom to the user, these factors are normalized in the [0, 1] range, in order to have the same influence and the sum of the weighting factors is equal to 1. In these conditions, all cases may be displayed in a [0..1] space. To define a point of view, the user selects a set of parameters and associates to each a weighting coefficient and a evaluation function.

4.3 Evaluation of Similarity

The target-problem is defined by a drawing of the final section and the associated dimensions. The point of view related with similarity is composed of a subset of the section dimensions and distance functions. Selection of relevant distances and weighting factors allows the user to define on which aspects he assesses the similarity, while defining the distance functions is a way to evaluate similarity for each distance. We use a fuzzy logic approach to define distance functions, as it may be seen on fig. 1.

Distance function : $POV_{Dis} = \Sigma a_i f(\Delta_i)$, with $i = (1, n)$: pertinent dimensions

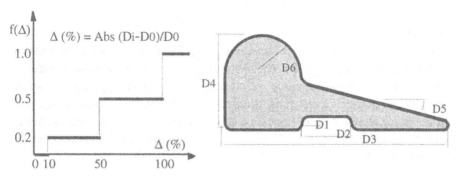

Fig. 1. Example of distance function

4.4 Evaluation of Quality

The overall quality of a design is evaluated by the expert from the associated production, as a distance between the results obtained in the source-problems with an ideal case (zero defect). This approach allows the user to process distance and quality in a comparable way : he selects a subset of potential defects, assigns to each a weighting factor and a defect fuction. We use also a fuzzy logic approach for these functions, extended to qualitative and symbolic values (cf. Figure 2), as defects may be described by quantitative, qualitative or symbolic values.

Defect function : $POV_{Def} = \Sigma a_i f(Q_i)$, with $i = (1, n)$: pertinent defects

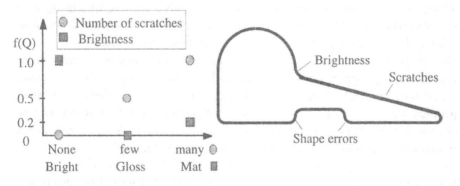

Fig. 2. Example of defect functions

Compared to geometry parameters, qualification of surface state quality is a real problem, as there is no objective method. Experts and customers appreciate it in a subjective way, by comparison to reference products. The method that we use has given to users the possibility to define points of view representing the different appreciations, for instance one customer requiring glossy parts (figure 2), another wishing bright ones. Quality may also involve cost aspects, as the company prefers the lowest cost possible at an equal level of quality.

4.5 Classification of Cases

As we have seen above, the interest of a source-problem for a new design depends on its similarity to the target-problem and on the quality of produced sections. In order to improve easiness of appreciation, we propose an orthogonal approach, in which similarity and quality are presented identically. To achieve this, we have designed a square display representing a 2-dimension space : horizontal axis represents similarity, vertical axis represents quality. Source problems are displayed as a set of points in this space (Fig. 5).

5 Presentation of the PROFIL System

In order to cope with the constraints of production in industrial companies, we have chosen a Unix workstation (Dec Alpha) and the INGRES® Database system.

All the structures needed by the application (description of cases, parameters of production, customers, alloys, ..) correspond to SQL tables.

INGRES® system includes a X-Window interface development tool : W4GL® which allows the design of interfaces and relations between graphical objects (buttons, lists, ..) with SQL commands. We have used this tool for the design of the user interface of PROFIL.

5.1 Main Functions

When a customer requests for a new section, he sends a drawing with his specific requirements : precise dimensions, surface state, alloy, .. The first function of PROFIL is to input and store this data, which forms the target-problem.

The second operation is to define the points of view. Depending on existence of the needed one, the designer may choose one in a list of existing points of view or create a new one. For each point of view (distance or quality), he chooses the set of pertinent parameters in a list and associates weighting factors. In a similar way, he chooses distance and quality functions or create new ones. Fig. 3 shows the window in which the user selects and adjusts his point of view on similitude.

Depending on the section family, the number and kinds of characteristics that form a point of view are different. Fig 3 shows an example of section family that the designers characterize with 5 distances. In this example, they focus on the section sole (l) by giving a weighting factor of 66% and on the diameter of the cylinder (Phi) with a weighting factor of 33%. The button in the upper-left corner gives access to the list of existing points of view. In this example, the designer is creating a new one.

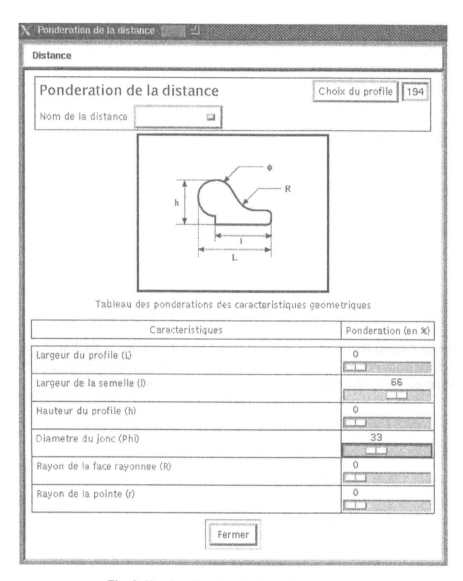

Fig. 3. User Interface for Similitude Point of view

In a similar way, the user creates and adjusts his point of view on quality by creating the list of defects that are to be included and weights them (Fig. 4). For this point of view, the number of characteristics (defect types) is not fixed and does not depend on the family. When the defect is associated to a qualitative or a symbolic value, the user chooses in the list of possible values, in order to avoid typing errors. As shown in Fig. 2, each of these values is associated with a number in the [0..1] range.

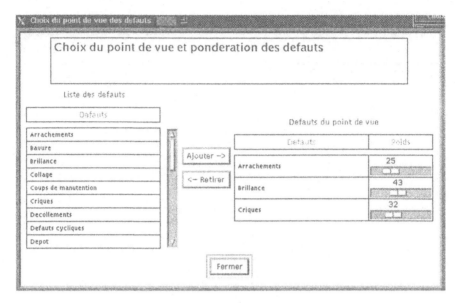

Fig. 4. User Interface for Quality Point of view

The third operation consists in analysing the set of cases selected by PROFIL. To do this, the designer uses the main display, in which all cases are displayed (Figure 5), the target-problem being located in the upper-left corner (identical, zero defect).

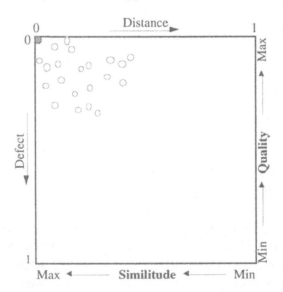

Fig. 5. The Similitude-Quality space of source-problems

To improve interactivity, we have used the reactivity provided by W4GL® to associate modifications in the points of view with refreshing of the displays, so any modification in a weighting factor or in a function has a visual effect on the position of cases in the similitude-quality space. Moreover, the designer may select any dot representing a source-problem and obtain full information on it.

To support his design, the user adjusts the points of view and compares cases, for example matching two cases having the same similarity but different quality levels often raises potential sources of defects. By focusing the quality point of view on a specific defect, the user may analyse the conditions in which it is present. If the target-problem is not similar enough to source-problems on a global point of view, he may focus first on one aspect of the section and extract design parameters, then focus on others.

5.2 Production Support

As we have seen, adaptation of cases is not yet implemented in PROFIL and it remains under the responsability of the designer to choose design parameters for producing the requested section. This task needs knowledge from the expert, that should be collected and formalized before integrating this function in PROFIL.

If the designer is the main user of PROFIL, a part of the study has been dedicated to define support tasks for the technicians in charge of producing sections.

The interface with this kind of users must be simpler, as their main task deals with production. On the other hand, they have an wide experience about processing and they are aware of all what happens during production and may be important for design.

The interface is used to input processing parameters, non-structured notes and results of quality testing. To facilitate the user task, control points are presented on a shematic drawing of the section and for each point, the input value is entered as a number (quantitative defects) or as a choice in a list (qualitative and symbolic). To provide in-line support, some of these answers are associated to warning messages to alert the user about gravity of defects and provide advices. This interface also uses interactivity, so it may be used for adjustments of forming operations. When correct settings are found, these data are stored in the database, as part of this new source-problem.

A first version of the PROFIL system has been launched on summer 94 and improvements are planned to extend functionnalities. The base is composed of more than 150 source-problems and is continually growing. The second workstation has been installed in the production hall during summer 95. It shares the database and communications with the designer workstation through an Ethernet network.

Conclusion

With the PROFIL system, we have demonstrated that CBR technique could be applied in the constrained environment of industrial design and provide support to designers.

A second result has been to formalize all the knowldge that is used during design and processing and to rationalize the tasks. A third result is to store in a common database all the designs made by several designers and allow by this way an efficient diffusion and sharing of knowledge.

Evolutions of the PROFIL system are currently studied. They deal with the adaptation phase, by formalizing the knowledge used by designers and with the integration of functions to support identification of optimal values of parameters to match given quality points of views.

References

[Cauzenille 85] Cauzenille-Marmeche E., Mathieu J., Weil-Barais A. "Raisonnement analogique et résolution de problèmes" l'année psychologique, (1985), 85, pp. 49-72

[Darpa 89] "Case-Based Reasoning" in Proceedings of the DARPA Workshop on Case-Based Reasoning, Machine Learning Program Plan, DARPA ed., Pensacola Beach Florida, 1989

[Geffraye 94] Geffraye F. "Aide à la conception d'outillage : apport de la simulation et du raisonnement par cas. Application à l'étirage de profilés métalliques" Thése de doctorat, Ecole des Mines de Paris, 1994

[Levine 89] Levine P., Pomerol J.C. "Systèmes Interactifs d'Aide à la Décision et Systèmes experts" Traité des nouvelles technologies, Hermés ed., Paris 1989

[Maurice-Demourioux 93] Maurice-Demourioux M., Lâasri B., Levallet C., Pinson S. "Le raisonnement à partir de cas : panorama et modélisation dynamique" in Séminaire Raisonnement à partir de cas, LAFORIA, Institut Blaise Pascal, Paris 1993

[Rougegrez 94] Rougegrez S. "Prédiction de processus à partir de comportements observés : le système REBECAS" Thése de doctorat, Université Paris VI, 1994

[Schank 82] Schank R. "Dynamic memory : a theory of reminding and learning in computers and people" Cambridge University Press, 1982

[Slade 91] Slade S. "Case-Based Reasoning : A Research Paradigm", AI Magazine, 1991, pp. 42-55

[Trousse 93] Trousse B., Visser W. "Use of Case-Based Reasoning techniques for intelligent computer-aided design systems" in 1993 IEEE International Conference on Systems, Man and Cybernetics, IEEE, pp. 513-518

[Visser 93] Visser W., Trousse B. "Reuse of designs : desesperately seeking an interdisciplinary cognitive approach" in Proccedings of IJCAI'93 Workshop on Reuse of designs, an Interdisciplinary approach, Chambéry, France, 1993

MacRad: Radiology Image Resource with a Case-Based Retrieval System

Robert T. Macura, M.D., Ph.D.
Katarzyna J. Macura, M.D., Ph.D.

Medical Informatics Section, Department of Radiology
Medical College of Georgia, Augusta GA 30912, U.S.A.

Abstract

We have compiled a case-based retrieval system for radiology, *MacRad*, that is structured around descriptors for radiology image findings. Our goal is to provide a feature-coded image resource that allows the user to formulate image content-based queries when searching for reference images. *MacRad* is implemented as a relational database with an image archive. Each image in the library is indexed according to its radiologic content. We structured an index for coding image content as a hierarchical image description index using the relational format. The hierarchical index of radiologic findings allows multilevel query formulation that depends upon the user's level of experience. The system uses rules to control the search direction within the case library and generate lists of diagnostic hypotheses for decision support. Rules are embedded within the database structure. At present, the case library consists of 300 cases and 3,000 images that present intracranial masses on skull X-rays, CTs, MRIs, and angiograms.

Keywords: image database, case-based retrieval, hierarchical index, neuroradiology

1 Introduction

References to accumulated knowledge and experience are an essential part of the diagnostic process in radiology. The visual analysis of an image relies on a comparison with meaningful image patterns that correspond to cases stored in the radiologist's memory [1-2]. Conceptually, the process a radiologist uses to solve new diagnostic problems conforms to the case-based reasoning. A complex problem is solved by making a reference to a similar problem rather than by reasoning from first principles. When making a diagnosis, radiologists frequently access image collections for reference, 1) to retrieve an image of a specific finding, a set of findings, or a diagnosis, 2) to identify the finding and/or diagnosis for an image, 3) to retrieve an image similar to a target image, and 4) to retrieve images that share findings but have different diagnoses (differential diagnosis). What radiologists need is the access to an image resource that will provide the experience stored in a significant number of solved case problems and offer searches based on combinations of radiologic findings.

Our goal is to capture the expertise of radiology specialists and codify it in the form of cases. The challenge is to determine a way to transform radiologic knowledge into usable case indices. Another major technical challenge is to design the case retrieval process, from formulation of a query, through the search, to the retrieval of the relevant images. The success that a particular retrieval process will have in meeting this challenge will depend upon the way that images are indexed and the way that the relevance of images is assigned on the basis of query.

To provide radiologists with a reference case resource, we have implemented a radiology feature-coded image database, *MacRad* (*Mac*-ura, authors name, and at present Mac-intosh; *Rad*-iology). *MacRad* encodes the image content using verbal descriptors for the domain-specific logic that underlies the image findings. In our project, we focus on the design of a structure for the classification of verbal descriptors for radiologic images that represent image content at different levels of granularity. Our overall goal is to provide radiologists at different levels of expertise with an image resource that would allow them to formulate image content-based queries when searching for reference images.

2 Methods

2.1 Case Representation
MacRad is implemented in 4th Dimension™ (ACI US Inc., Cupertino, CA), a relational database management system, on the Macintosh platform. The structure of the database is determined by the way we define a *radiologic case*. The case in our database is referred to as an example that presents a particular abnormality pertaining to a particular body location. The case is defined based on the diagnosis, anatomical lesion location, and the age group. Thus, the same patient in different life periods with different abnormalities in different anatomic locations may appear in as many cases as there are different age groups, anatomic locations, and diagnoses. The diagnosis for a case is represented as a list of features that lead to a particular outcome. There is a set of images related to each case. Images are grouped according to the modality. Each image is indexed based on its radiologic content. Radiologic findings (indices) are divided into three groups: lesion location, lesion characteristics, and associated findings. There are 11 main files within the *MacRad* [3]: 1) files storing information concerned with the images that belong to the case, files related to the [Image] file - [Lesion Location] file, [Lesion Characteristics] file, and [Associated Findings] file; 2) files related to the [Case] file - [Image] file, [Differential Diagnosis DDX] file, [Report] file; 3) files storing the information defining a case and the patient medical history (files related to the [Person] file - [Case] file, [Previous Pathology] file, [Clinical history] file); and 4) a [Person] file storing personal data that is related to the [Hospital] file.

2.2 Image Indexing with Hierarchies
MacRad is intended to provide multilevel, conforming to the user experience, access to data. The potential multilevel query formulation needs to be translated into a form that is recognizable by the database. This translation requires an organization of database indices that will be capable of conveying relationships between, and classification of, the image descriptors. The formation of a hierarchy is a useful way of achieving the desired organization. To be able to encode the image content through the radiologic findings, we have designed a hierarchical image description index that allows image indexing in neuroradiology (Figure 1). We use a semantic hierarchy composed of basic observations and interpretations that forms a continuum, in which higher level findings incorporate lower level findings. In this approach, the image details are coded by using both basic observations (such as the density of cerebral contents relative to normal brain tissue observed on the CT scans; e.g., hyperdense,

isodense, hypodense) and findings that express interpretation of basic observations (e.g., calcification, blood, cyst, fat) (Figure 1).

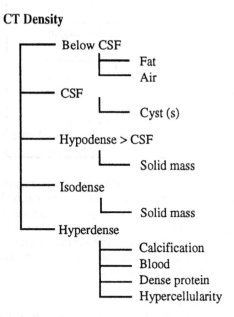

CT Density

Figure 1. A hierarchical structure of radiologic findings (CT density concepts) that are classified as basic observations and interpretations.

A hierarchy tree is implemented as a series of database records with the record keys representing nodes in the tree [3]. A record key is composed of slots that correspond to the levels in the hierarchy. A slot typically contains an alphanumeric code of one character (or more) enabling subsequent searching to be made with an alphanumeric key. The first slot of a record key corresponds to the highest level in a hierarchy (root level of a tree) and the last used slot corresponds to the lowest level in a hierarchy (leaf node of a tree). A record key contains as many slots as there are levels in the hierarchy. A particular record key inherits all of the slots of its immediate parent and uses the additional slot to uniquely identify itself. The hierarchy can easily be updated and expanded interactively with the user's assistance.

Each image in the library has a caption attached to it. The hierarchical image description index allows decomposition of the caption into searchable keywords for encoding the image content. The image caption "Coronal T1-weighted image after injection of gadolinium shows a ring-enhancing mass within the left parietal lobe with associated moderate vasogenic edema" will be indexed as shown in the Table 1. Moreover, each image in the library has an assigned age group that is based on the patient's date of birth and the exam date for a particular study. All index terms are searchable database fields that may be used for image retrieval.

In *MacRad* we use knowledge-based indexing that applies existing radiologic knowledge (such as expert opinion, textbooks, journal articles) to each case in the library to determine which features are important for retrieving each case.

Table 1. Indexing of a sample image caption.

Index Term	Value
Procedure	MR imaging
View	Coronal
Phase	T1 weighted
Contrast	Postcontrast
Lesion Location	Parietal lobe
Lesion characteristics	
Pattern of enhancement	Ring-like
Associated findings	Edema, moderate vasogenicity

Presently there are equal weights on all features considered important. The system would prefer a case matched on more features to a case that matched on less. Manual coding of radiologic features for a single image takes about 1-2 minutes. An additional 30 seconds per image are spent by a radiologist to verify the presence of features important for retrieving each image. The average time needed for a single image to be incorporated into *MacRad* (from image acquisition, through processing and indexing, to verification) is about 20 minutes.

2.2.1 Testing of Indexing System
One hundred nine (109) case studies that were "known" to the system (already encoded in the database) and had been used to test the indexing system incorporated into the earlier version of the case library [4], were presented to users who were not involved in the preceding testing (two residents in first and fourth year of training, and a radiology fellow). Radiologists were asked to retrieve cases from the case library based on observed findings for testing cases. We wanted to estimate the accessibility of cases incorporated into the database to users with different levels of experience and test the efficiency of the new indexing system. The accuracy of retrieval for "known" cases was 94.5% (for 109 cases tested, 103 were accessible to users, whereas the remaining 6 cases were not accessible and needed to be re-indexed).

2.3 Image Retrieval
The search criteria are transformed into the search keys in a way similar to the way the record keys are built, the difference being that they can be considered partial keys. A search in the database with a partial search key would return a selection of records that would belong to a hierarchically organized sub-tree (Figure 2).
The present retrieval method in *MacRad* is a template matching. Database records are retrieved only if they match precisely the constraints expressed in the query based on a sum of features in the input case that matches cases in the library. Important features are considered in the first order and determine the minimum range of match. Based on the age of the patient and the lesion location (mandatory inputs) as well as the clinical history and previous pathologies (optional), the differential diagnosis list (DDL) is formulated. The DDL is retrieved from the decision table implemented in the database structure. Decision table uses two diagnostic cues (age of the patient and location of the lesion) and the judgment of neuroradiology experts regarding the

probability of a given diagnosis (Table 2) [5]. The cases that match the search criteria are returned to the user. The order of case presentation is based on the DDL and the number of matched features.

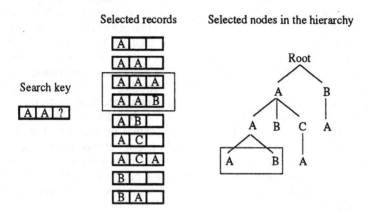

Figure 2. Diagram depicts the selection of records matching a search key. All records (cases) that belong to a hierarchically organized sub-tree are returned to the user.

When no matching case is available, *MacRad* uses two backtracking strategies to support the case retrieval. Since searches are done in two steps, temporary case sets are created and used during backtracking. The first step involves searching fields coding image findings and the second search uses the lesion location and the age fields. When there is no matching case for image findings input by the user, but there are cases that match the age of the patient and/or the lesion location, *MacRad* asks the user if he/she wants to browse cases representing pathologies from the DDL for a particular age and/or lesion location. These two diagnostic cues are used by experts during early hypothesis formation and dramatically narrow the set of possible outcomes. This way, the user may still retrieve images that represent highly probable pathologies. However, the findings might be somewhat different. When the system finds cases that match the image findings, but do not match the age of the patient and/or lesion location, *MacRad* asks the user if he/she wants to browse cases that present specified findings but in cases for different age group and/or location. This way, if the case library is missing an example for a certain pathology in a certain age group and/or location, the user may still be able to retrieve images matching the input image findings. The probability that the retrieved images will provide relevant cases is very high. However, the order of presented cases might not be relevant to the age and the lesion location specified by the user. The use of the DDL, that is retrieved independently from the decision table allows correction of the case order.

Table 2. Decision table for age & lesion location relationship.

Age	Child
Lesion Location	Cerebellum
Medulloblastoma	0.4
Astrocytoma	0.35
Ependymoma	0.15
else	0.1

2.4 Case Adaptation

Because the retrieved cases rarely match exactly the case in question, *MacRad* offers the user several features that allow the case adaptation. Each case in the library has a discussion text file attached to it that describes image findings, their importance to a particular diagnosis, and possible sources for misdiagnosis. Each case has its own list of differential diagnoses representing pathologies that are likely to be mistaken with the case. (Note, that this list is different from DDL, it pertains exclusively to a particular case). The diagnosis for a case is a keyword to the radiology information resource that allows retrieval of textbook-like documents describing particular pathology along with exemplary images illustrating the pathology. After the backtracking is used and only partially matching cases are returned to the user, the diagnoses for these cases represent pathologies that the user should seriously consider. Diagnosis field provides a link to textual descriptions for presented pathologies. The user may acquire information about various patterns of selected pathologies and use this information to derive at a conclusion for a case of interest. *MacRad* offers tools for making the case adaptation but the adaptation process is left to the user. For medical domain it is important that diagnostic judgment remains the user responsibility.

3 User Interface

3.1 Query Formulation

To initialize the search for reference images, the user may enter as many search criteria as desired at the level of granularity that makes the user most comfortable. A checklist type entry form allows the image reader to input a value for each radiologic finding that is listed on the entry. The data entry form suggests what findings are useful in diagnosis of intracranial masses. The user uses a pop-up menu for entering the structured information according to the hierarchical image description index (Figure 3-4). The lesion location is specified according to the ACR (American College of Radiology) index for radiology diagnoses. If a radiologist observes a hyperdense mass on the non-contrast CT and is not sure whether the lesion represents blood or calcified mass, and would like to retrieve from *MacRad* images that represent similar pattern, he/she may search for hyperdense lesions and the set of retrieved cases will contain both hematomas and calcified masses. If the user wants to search for different patterns presenting calcified lesions, the returned set of images will present hyperdense: calcified lesions only (Figure 1).

3.2 Image Browsing

The set of cases matching the search criteria is returned to the user in the Display Case screen (Figure 5). The Search Criteria field displays a summary of important features used for the case retrieval. The Cases Retrieved list displays all the cases found that match the search criteria. The images for a selected case are presented in thumbnail size. They may be expanded to a full size (512 x 512) upon clicking on them. Expanded image is presented with the caption describing image findings. If there is more than one study done for a case (e.g. MRI, CT, and angiography), the Procedure list activates and the user may change the modality (e.g. from MRI to CT). This function allows the user to compare the abnormality on different radiology modalities. The image correlation function provides very valuable diagnostic information. The Diagnosis field for a reference case provides a link to the textual documents describing selected pathology (Figure 6) and images illustrating this

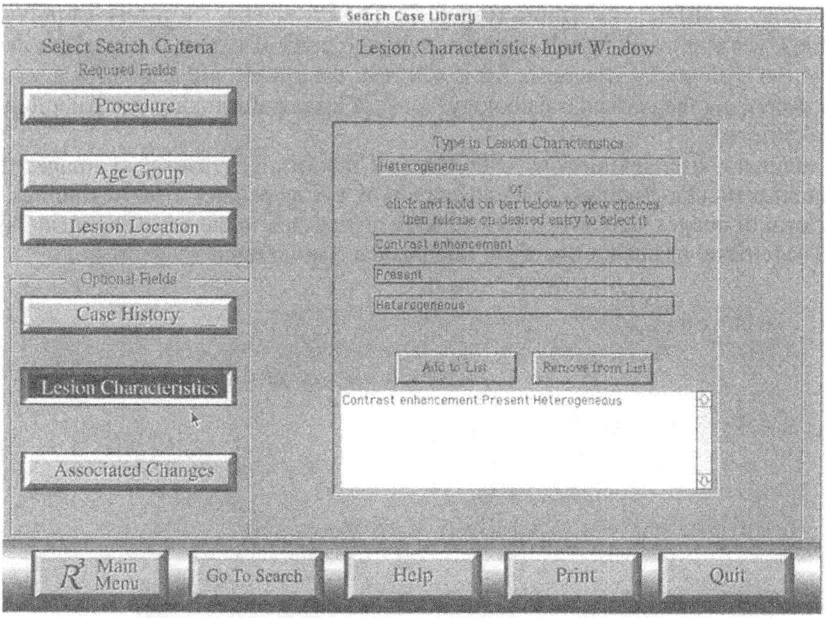

Figure 3. The Search Criteria selection screen. The user may specify radiologic findings of interest by typing in a request or using a pop-up menu.

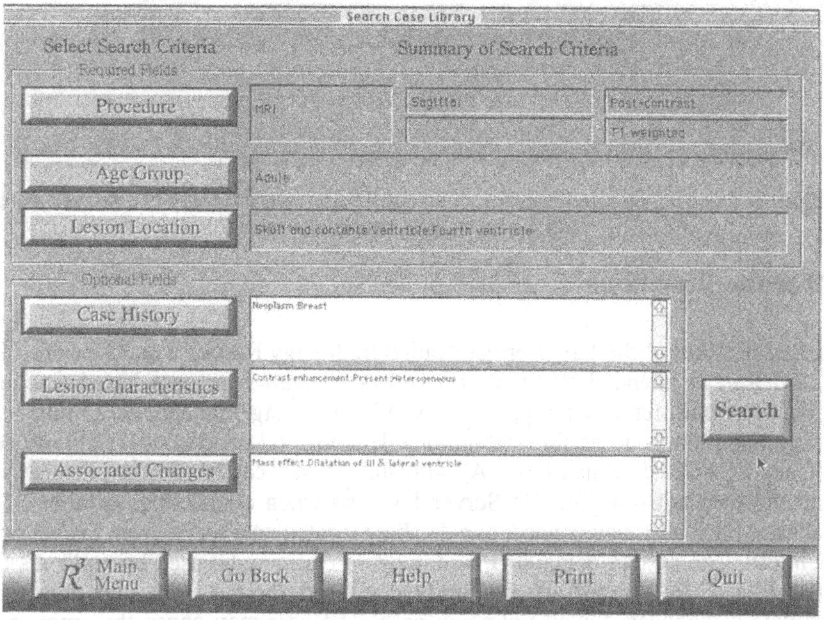

Figure 4. Summary of Search Criteria input screen.

pathology in different modalities (Figure 7). The Differential Diagnosis list provides pathologies that might be misdiagnosed with the particular case. If any of the items from the Differential Diagnosis list is selected, the system will search for a textual file describing the particular pathology. A set of images illustrating that pathology is also retrieved.

In summary, user interactions with *MacRad* involve: 1) retrieval of images that contain particular findings, 2) identification of a diagnosis for a set of findings, 3) retrieval of images similar to a target image represented in the set of input findings, and 4) retrieval of images that share findings but have different diagnoses.

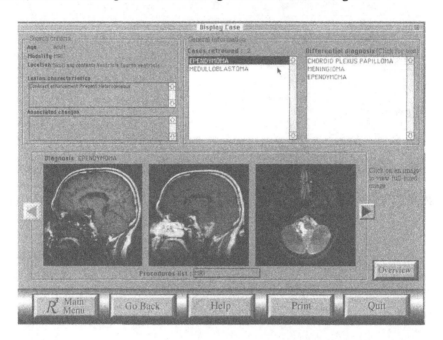

Figure 5. Based on the search criteria defined by the user relevant cases are retrieved along with the list of differential diagnosis.

4 *MacRad* Functions

MacRad is a part of the larger project called Radiology Resource and Review - R^3 [6]. *MacRad* is intended to be used as a case resource for case-based teaching applications and diagnosis support tools. We are using *MacRad* in a multi-user configuration that is accessible through the departmental network (4D Server® and 4D Client®, ACI US, Cupertino, CA). 4th Dimension™ can be used as client/server front end tool not only for 4D Server but also when connecting to other SQL databases. Each user may connect to a database located on a server from his/her own Macintosh. The system contains a Quiz module that may be used by residents for self-testing. Case images are randomly displayed for the user who may then formulate a diagnosis for an unknown case. The user may chose the amount of information needed to make a diagnosis (a caption for an image, a differential diagnosis) or may display a diagnosis as desired. Case-based teaching relies on the principle that learners will most naturally structure their own knowledge bases and gain correlative experience by visually memorizing radiological patterns and deliberation of cases. Our case library is accessible to applications that use cases for instruction [4]. As a diagnosis support tool, *MacRad* helps the user reach a diagnosis by providing images from proven cases that match the description of a specific case being evaluated along with the differential diagnosis list. Based on the search criteria defined by the user, relevant images including a textual description are produced for comparison to the case in question. The user may browse through retrieved cases, zoom images, make a correlation between different procedures, or access textual information if needed.

Figure 6. The Text screen presents description for a selected pathology.

5 Hardware Requirements

A Macintosh II model with 16 megabytes of RAM and a CD-ROM drive is the minimum recommendation for running the system as a stand-alone application. A 16" monitor is required. Any of the Macintosh II series computers with an 832 x 624 x 24 bit color display graphics card may be used.

6 Discussion

In our work we attempted to provide an effective way to capture radiology image content in terms of verbal expressions for image findings. There are several difficulties with encoding radiologic findings in the database. The currently available index for radiological diagnoses, ACR code, represents a significant amount of information concerned with anatomy and diagnostic categories but it does not allow coding the image-related data (verbal expressions for radiologic image content) [7].

Many researchers have experimented with application of different concepts to radiology image coding [8-12]. We structured radiologic findings as a hierarchical image description index for coding lesion characteristics and associated lesion findings. The form of indexing required in a database depends on the types of query that are anticipated. Indexing must anticipate the vocabulary a retriever might use. Indexing must incorporate concepts that are normally used to describe data being indexed. During report generation, radiologists use verbal expressions for description of the image content; we would like to capture those expressions to allow radiologists to retrieve the same images from the database later, when needed. Depending upon the expertise of the radiologist, image findings are communicated at different levels, ranging from the beginner's purely perceptual level (basic observations) to the expert's highly interpretative level. The potential multilevel query formulation needs to be translated into a form that is recognizable by the database. This translation requires an organization of the vocabulary that will be capable of classifying terms and conveying relationships between them. Thus, designing an image database that is accessible to users with different levels of experience requires multilevel indexing of image content. The hierarchical image description index offers a useful way of achieving the desired multilevel organization. During query formulation, less experienced users will use basic observations as an input, whereas more experienced users will use interpretations. The hierarchical index links basic observations with interpretations in a continuum, and the user may construct a query at the level that conforms to his/her level of experience and certainty. Cases are a repository of expertise so they are coded according to expert judgment. However, the end-users of case-based retrieval systems will not be experts. Experts do not need external case libraries for reference; they use their own memory. It is hard to predict all possible types of end-users. When the hierarchical index is used for case coding, the expert-level concepts incorporate lower-level concepts that are familiar to non-expert users. The accessibility of cases substantially increases and the system becomes more useful for different users. Preliminary testing of the new hierarchical indexing system showed the improvement of the retrieval accuracy, in comparison to the previous testing (from 80.7% to 94.5%) [4]. This course resulted from the correction of the index terms that were discovered to be inaccurate and/or missing in the previous version, and also from the implementation of the hierarchical indexing. We noted that users were very comfortable using hierarchical concepts, because this approach allowed them to formulate query at the level of specificity conforming to their needs. However, we need a large testing case set to estimate the real retrieval accuracy, especially against the "unknown" cases, which are cases not encoded in the system. Because the evaluation involved both a small number of radiology residents and cases tested, results from preliminary testing cannot be attributed entirely to the effects of the design of the system and its performance in clinical settings. We are preparing to test the case library outside the development laboratory; we will deliver *MacRad* on the CD-ROM.

There are two goals in defining the feature index for coding images: 1) to have a consistent way of coding and 2) to guide image retrieval. As users attempt to find information in an inconsistently indexed database, that inconsistency will be propagated into uncertainty as to how a particular information need concept can be expressed as a query. The development of a well-defined query language has the potential of improving information accessibility because the searcher utilizes a highly constrained vocabulary correctly. Improved performance is also obtained by simplifying the task of data entry. Our design provides the user with the possibility of searching for images using verbal expressions encoded into a hierarchical index of radiologic findings. The use of an image description index for coding image content permits the expression of image content-based queries. This is the most needed type of query when the radiologist searches for reference images.

The present retrieval method in *MacRad* is through the template matching with backtracking. The limitation of a deterministic retrieval is that images are retrieved only if they match precisely the constraints expressed in the query based on a sum of features in the input case that matches cases in the library. This method will preclude any match other than an exact match. This does not reflect the performance of the human perceptual system which retains the identity of images under certain transformation. To support the case adaptation, *MacRad* links cases with textual files that represent textbook-like descriptions of pathologies represented in cases. Thus, when the retrieved case does not perfectly fit the case in question, its diagnosis (solution to a case problem) provides a keyword for searching the textual files. The information provided in the textual description may be used to define a diagnosis for a case in question; the same way books are used for reference. The difference being that it is not a user but the system who suggests keywords to be used.

MacRad is intended to contain enough cases to clearly define most of the diagnostic categories (as many cases as many different patterns are possible for particular abnormality, not just one example per diagnosis). We have estimated that we would need about 100-150 more cases (about 500-700 images) to efficiently cover the domain of intracranial masses. Case collection is a laborious and time consuming process, but when the electronic patient records become a part of the hospital information systems in the near future, the possibilities for incorporating new cases will be unlimited.

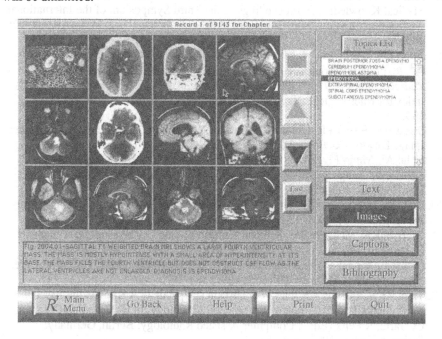

Figure 7. The Image screen presents pictorial information for a selected pathology.

We envision the use of *MacRad* as a part of the picture archiving and communication system (PACS) and teleradiology environment. The preliminary results have shown that *MacRad* is successful in supporting efficient access to reference cases, but further testing in clinical settings will show whether the system design has the potential of becoming a welcome addition to daily diagnostic practice in radiology.

Acknowledgments

The authors thank Drs. Eugene F. Binet and Jon H. Trueblood for their contribution to and support of the project. Many thanks go to Brandon D. Morstad for his programming work, Robert V. Finkbeiner for his work on the user interface, and Cliff W. Garzzillo for image digitization and processing.

References

1. Schmidt HG, Norman GR, Boshuizen HPA. A cognitive perspective on medical expertise: Theory and implications. Acad Med 1990; 65(10):611-621.
2. Pizer SM, ter Haar Romeny BM. Fundamental Properties of Medical Image Perception. J Digital Imaging 1991; 4(4): 213-225.
3. Macura KJ, Macura RT, Morstad BD. Digital Case Library: A Resourse for Teaching, Learning, and Decision Support in Radiology. RadioGraphics 1995; 15(1): 155-164.
4. Macura RT, Macura KJ, Toro VE, Binet EF, Trueblood JH, Ji K. Computerized Case-Based Instructional System for Computed Tomography and Magnetic Resonance Imaging of Brain Tumors. Invest Radiol 1994; 29: 497-506.
5. Macura RT, Macura KJ. The Usefulness of Decision Tables in Encoding of Medical Knowledge. In Proceedings of the Third Symposium of the International Association of Knowledge Engineers IAKE '92. Galthersburg, MD; IAKE, 1992: 263-269.
6. Binet EF, Trueblood JH, Macura KJ, Morstad BD, Macura RT, Finkbeiner RV. R^3, Radiology Resource and Reviev: From Floppy Disk to CD-ROM. *RadioGraphics* 1995; (July issue in print).
7. Index for Radiological Diagnoses, 4th Edition. American College of Radiology 1992.
8. Swett HA, Fisher PR, Cohn AI, Miller PL, Mutalik PG. Expert System controlled Image Display. Radiology 1989; 172: 487-493.
9. Cohn AI, Miller PL, Fisher PR, Mutalik PG, Swett HA. Knowledge-Based Radiologic Image Retrieval Using Axes of Clinical Relevance. Comput Biomed Res 1990; 23: 199-221.
10. Bramble JM, Insana MF, Dwyer III SJ. Information Retrieval for Teaching Files: A Preliminary Study. J Digital Imag 1990; 3(3): 164-169.
11. Greenes RA, McClure RC, Pattison-Gordon E, Sato L. The Findings-Diagnosis Continuum: Implications for Image Descriptions and Clinical Databases. In Proceedings of the 16th Symposium on Computer Applications in Medical Care. New York, NY; McGraw-Hill Inc., 1992: 383-387.
12. Taira RK, Cardenas AF, Chu WW, Breant CM, Hall T. A Knowledge-based Multi-media Database System for Skeletal Radiology. In HU Lemke, K Inamura, CC Jaffe, R Felix (Eds.). Computer Assisted Radiology. Berlin, Germany; Springer-Verlag: 1993, 649-654.

Representing and Indexing Building Refurbishment Cases for Multiple Retrieval of Adaptable Pieces of Cases

Farhi Marir and Ian Watson

Department of Surveying, University of Salford, M5 4WT. UK.

Abstract. CBRefurb is a case-based reasoning (CBR) system for the strategic cost estimation for building refurbishment. This domain is characterised by many uncertainties and variation. Its cost estimation involves large amount of interrelated factors whose impact is difficult to assess. This paper report on the problems faced by the building cost information Services (BCIS) databases and several rule-based expert systems to tackle this complex cost estimation problem and, the design and evaluation of CBRefurb system implemented using ReMind Shell. CBRefurb imitates the domain expert in its approach of breaking down the whole building work into smaller work (building items) by organising the refurbishment cases as a hierarchical structure composed of cases and subcases. The process of estimation imitate the expert by considering only these pieces of previous cases of similar situation (or context). For this purpose, CBRefurb defines some of the building and its component (or *items*) features as a *global context and local context* information used to classify cases and subcases into *context cases* and *subcases*, and to decompose the cost estimation *problem* into *adaptable subproblems*. This is followed by a two indexing schemes to suit the hierarchical structure of the case and the problem decomposition and to allow *classification* and *retrieval of contextual cases*. CBRefurb features consolidate the aim of the project that is allowing multiple retrieval of appropriate pieces of the refurbishment which are easier to adapt, reflecting the expert method of estimating cost for complex refurbishment work.

1. Introduction

Case-based reasoning (CBR) is a fresh reasoning paradigm for the design of expert systems in domains that may not be appropriate for other reasoning paradigms such as model-based reasoning [1]. As a result of this, and because of its resemblance to human reasoning, CBR has attracted increasing interest both from those experienced in developing expert systems and from novices [2, 3, 4]. This paper describes the design and the implementations of CBRefurb system for the strategic cost estimation of building refurbishment work using ReMind CBR shell.

Refurbishment is a work carried out on existing buildings in the attempt to improve and to update them to modern standards whilst retaining their current use. It represents a substantial part of the UK construction programme and is seen as an economic alternative to new build [5]. A recent investigation amongst the North West councils and contractors has shown the strategic importance of cost estimation for building refurbishment and the highly interrelated nature of the knowledge required to estimate efficiently this cost [6]. However, the design and development of several commercially available expert systems for the construction industry have shown the difficulties the knowledge engineer can meet during knowledge elicitation in such a complex domain [7]. Although the figures for each building repair can be produced using these expert systems or using Building Cost Information Service (BCIS) databases, we found that most of the experts use these sources to estimate costs of new build but never used them to estimate costs for building refurbishment work. Because the figures provided by these sources are calculated in the framework of new work rather than refurbishment work. Indeed, in new building work, the cost depends on quality, size and time. However, in refurbishment work, these factors are supplemented by many other features, or even outweighed, by major secondary (or broad-ranging) factors such as the safety of the structure and the effect of the repair of one building item on another. In the above systems, no considerations are given neither to the circumstance (or context) in which the work has taken places nor to the type and the size of the project in which the building or the item is repaired. Instead the repair cost is given on elemental cost basis as if each item or the element is repaired alone.

This paper presents CBRefurb as an alternative system using case-based reasoning (CBR). It estimates the strategic cost for refurbishing buildings by imitating the domain expert in its approach of breaking down the whole building work into smaller work (building items). This is by organising the refurbishment cases as a hierarchical structure composed of cases and subcases. Then it defines the contcept of context information to reflect the contextual reasoning of the expert who use only case of simailr context (or circumstances) to adapt previous solution. For this purpose, the building specification such as the state of the building, the type of work required and the size of the project as a *global contex.* Similarly the item state and the work required on that item as *local context.* CBRefurb use the concept of context to classify cases into *context cases* and *subacases*, and decompose the cost estimation *problem* into *adaptable subproblems*. In the same line, a convenient hierarchical indexing scheme to suit the hierarchical structure of the case and the decomposition of the problem is designed . In addition, this indexing scheme implements two interconnected schemes; *classification* and *retrieval* indexes. The classification indexes use *global* and *local context* features to classify cases and subcases into *context cases* and *subcases. This classification* reduces the retrieval search space within contextual cases instead of the whole case base. The retrieval indexes are used to select multiple cases and subcases among the context cases and subcases. These techniques implemented in CBRefurb allow multiple retrieval of pieces of case that can be adapted more easily.

To this end, section two presents the structural partitioning of building refurbishment cases and the classification of their features depending on their functionality's. Then the decomposition of the cost estimation problems presented. Section three is devoted to the two levels of indexing schemes. Section four describes the multiple case retrieval and the adaptation resulting from the decomposition of the cost estimation problem. The last section is devoted to the evaluation of the system and the contribution of CBRefurb to the CBR technology.

2. Representing and Reasoning with Cases

A building is a large complex artefact whose complete specification requires a high dimensional representational structure. Cost estimation involves finding and using the relevant information of a given job from a very large amount of information.. Moreover, some factors cannot be identified and their impact on the cost of refurbishment can neither be rigorously assessed nor predicted. It appears from this description that the building refurbishment case faces two major problems; the large number of factors involved in the estimation of the costs and the difficulty to quantify the effect of some of them on the costs.

2.1. Case Representation

Experience with monolithic case representation for real world large cases of a similar domain of construction has shown its limitations in accessing cases and in dealing with large number of cases [8]. To overcome these limitations and to allow efficient access and retrieval, several CBR systems have organised their cases into case-subcases hierarchies for different domains such as Clavier system for autoclave layout [9], Celia system for learning from expert problem solving [10] and PERSUADOR system for labour dispute [11]. We have been faced with a similar problem on how to represent this high dimensional real world case in ReMind environment. CBRefurb represents the refurbishment case as a flat structure combined with hierarchical subcases (Fig 1). Although this hierarchical organisation of cases is generally familiar, it goes beyond the normal ReMind framework. For practical reasons, each of the cases and subcases base is represented in a different case libraries. The link and the manipulation of these cases and their subcases is implemented using ReMind's *case field* and its C function library respectively.

Depending on the functionalities of the factors involved in the cost estimation, the main case contains, as shown in , essentially:

- The *Building Identification (bid)* identifies the characteristics of the building.
- the *Building Work Specification (bws)* describes the state and diagnosis of the building, a summary of the work required, and links to the item subcases involved in the refurbishment work.
- The *Building Subjective Parameters (bsp)* represents the factors whose impact on the cost is difficult to predict or quantify. This includes the state of the

building, type of refurbishment project, site access, occupancy and other environmental parameters,

- The *Building External Parameters (bep)* represents factors like the region and the state of the market, which can be used as parameters for indexing and updating the prices, and
- the *Building Costs and Advice (bca)* is composed of the cost estimation that states the derived solution and advice to prevent potential problems.

Similar parameters are also present in each subcase that represent the work for each item of the building . This partitioning can go further into decomposing the building items themselves into subcases for different purposes such as defining shared elemental work between different items or the need for elemental cost estimation..

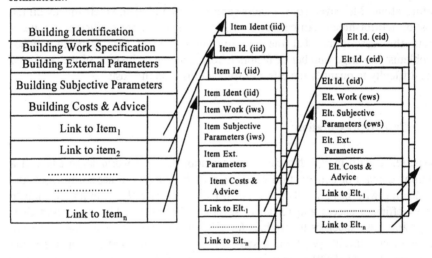

Fig. 1. The hierarchical Structure of the Case.

2.2. Context and Problem Decomposition

Even if the structural organisation resolves the problem of the high dimensionality of the cases, the impact of the interaction between the components of the building may prevent the decomposition of the cost estimation problem. In this situation, the hierarchical organisation of the case will have no benefit since the solution to the problem will require the retrieval and the process of *all* the items at the *same* time. . As a result the adaptation will be more complex and difficult to implement due the uncertainty that characterise the broad-ranging. (or secondary) factors whose impact on the costs is unpredictable. In practice the experts match the building items that need repair to previous items repairs which were in a similar situations (or context) and the overall cost can be estimated using the estimated cost of the items. This context information is given very high importance by the experts to the point that even very similar repairs are not considered if they took place in a different situation to the current one.

From the analysis of the refurbishment domain, the cost estimation problem is not a conflicting interaction of conjunctive goals that involve multi-agents who have different plans and goals as in PERSUADOR [11]. Instead, it is a single agent of high dimensional parameters some of which are difficult to assess given different circumstance (or context). The cost estimation problem does not require complex problem solving approach that use sequences of plans and subgoals [10,11,12] instead it is an equation whose solution will be the total amount that results from the addition of all items repair cost. The major problem however, is to define the context information in which the equation can be solved, since from one context to another the same equation may have different solutions. This is due to the impact on the costs of the wide-ranging parameters which tend to be stable for a given context but changes when this context changes.

We identified most of the wide-ranging factors whose impact on the costs is unpredictable and most importantly the factors that originate them and underline their importance. For instance, the impact of the safety factors on the costs depends in general on factors like the state and the type of the building, whether the occupants remain during refurbishing or not, the site access and the environment of the building. In CBRefurb these (subjective) parameters which are the source of the secondary or wide-ranging factors are used as context information. Context information is either *Global Context* if the subjective parameters concern the building or *Local Context* if they concern the building item. Global and internal or local context information are used in several work [9,10,13] for different purposes depending on the particularities of the domain and the type of the problem addressed which are different from one system to another. CBRefurb implements a practical solution to use the context information as a *similarity measure* to classify cases and subcases that share the same context information into *Context Cases* and *Subcases*. This is t allow the decomposition of the cost estimation problem into subproblems and to resolve the cost estimation equation. Using only context cases and subcases for any cost adaptation as the expert do, the impact in term of the cost of the secondary features on each item can be approximately defined in a boundary of figures. CBRefurb adaptation process implements a mechanism that uses these figures through its learning process to address more easily the problem of secondary factors and adapt them to new situations and save them in their appropriate case or subcase. To explain this the refurbishment cost estimation problem (BuildingCosts$_{bca}$) is represented in the following equation :

$$BuildCosts_{ica} \approx (Coeff_{bep} \oplus SubjFunc(bsp)) * \sum_{i=1}^{n} Item_i Costs_{ica} \oplus BuildCosts_{bid\&bws}$$

where :

- *Coef$_{bep}$* : a cost index used to update the costs of each item to meet the building external parameters requirements e.g. region and speed of work,
- *SubjFunc(bsp)* : function whose value depends on the subjective features,
- *Item$_i$Costs* : represents the estimated costs of each works, and
- *BuildCosts$_{bid\&bws}$* : represents added costs resulting from the new regulations, contingencies and other environmental aspects.

Both *Coef$_{bep}$* and *BuildCosts$_{bid\&bws}$* can be provided by BCIS databases or calculated using cost estimation techniques used in construction. However, the *SubjFunc(bsp)* function is in fact equation subjective parameters that is not taken into account in BCIS databases and previous expert systems approach when calculating repair cost In contrast, CBRefurb takes into account it when adapting the cost at both case and subcase levels. As explained previously, using the context information and the context cases and subcases the boundaries [Minimum of *SubjFun(bsp)* , Maximum of *SubjFun(bsp)*] of the *SubjFunc(bsp)* will be *approximately* defined and an estimated value *SubjValue$_{ctx}$* within this boundaries will be fixed and adapted to the new situation using previous similar experiences. Information on the boundaries and the importance of the subjective function for each secondary features will be saved in its appropriate case or subcase to reflect any changes as the domain evolve and to be used like any other parameter for future adaptation. The computation of the remaining *Item$_i$Costs* expression that represent the costs for each item will follow a similar approach as for the *BuildingCost$_{bca}$* equation. This means *Item$_i$Costs* will in turn be calculated using a similar equation that represent the subproblem. Once all the items equation are resolved and estimated cost for each item is adapted then their results will be used to resolve and adapt the *BuildingCost$_{bca}$* equation which represent the final cost estimation of the building refurbishment work. The resulting *BuildingCost$_{bca}$* will be represented as:

$$AdaptBuildCosts_{CTX} \approx (Coeff_{bep} \oplus SubjValue_{CTX}) * \sum_{i=1}^{n} Item_i Costs_{ica} \oplus BuildCosts_{bid\&bws}.$$

Providing global and local context information does not mean that the uncertainty that characterise the refurbishment domain is taken away and the subproblems are completely independent. However, by representing separately indexed, linked subcases, each associated with its costs will facilitate flexible iterative cost estimation while retaining the coherency by the entire cases.

A particular additional feature to CBRefurb is its use of global and local context information not only as a framework in which the decomposition of the cost estimation is possible but also as a *similarity measure* to differentiate and classify similar cases and subcases into *Context Cases* and *Subcases* at the learning phase of CBR i.e. the storage of the new solution, instead of its use at the retrieval phase. Such early classification of cases meets the expert requirements of using only context cases for adaptation and will reduce considerably the retrieval search space especially for large case base by directing it to context cases and subcases instead of the whole case base.

3. Case Indexing

In order for the mechanisms and data structure of case retrieval to be applicable to retrieving context cases and subcases, the indexing vocabulary for cases and subcases must be at an appropriate level of generality of the global and local context and to reflect the hierarchical structure of the cases. For this purpose, two main interconnected indexing schemes are provided in CBRefurb; the case indexing scheme and subcase indexing schemes(Fig.2). Each of the indexing scheme is composed of two type of indexes with different functionalities.

Classification indexes represents the global and local context features of cases and their subcases which represent the acquired knowledge in the domain. These indices are considered as difference-based indexing scheme by their main function of differentiating a case from another similar cases However, these indexes are mainly used to classify and direct the retrieval to *Context Cases* and *Subcases*. This reflects the importance given to the context information in which the expert domain retrieve and adapt cases and also adds an advantage to CBRefurb by reducing the scope of the retrieval search space to classes of similar cases rather than the whole case-base. In CBRefurb, these classification indexes compose the static part of the inductive tree (or *static subtree*) built using ReMind Cluster Editor.

Retrieval indexes is concerned by the details of the refurbishment work. They specify the defect diagnosis, the type and the quality of the repair for both the building and the items. These indexes are also used to further push down classification of context cases and subcases into groups that share further details. Their importance can be changed as the refurbishment domain evolves either by using the inductive learning process if they are represented as an inductive tree of or by assigning to them weights if they are represented as a vector. If the inductive process is used, they will represented as second part of the inductive tree (or *dynamic subtree*) whose leaves contain pointers to the cases and the ReMind inductive retrieval will be used to retrieve these cases. However, if they are represented as a vector, the nearest neighbour retrieval of ReMind will be used.

In CBRefurb, manual and automated have been mixed to identify the features to be used as indices for the refurbishment cases and subcases. The analysis of several specification documents for refurbishment work and discussion with expert has produced a list of most of the factors that have an impact on the cost. During this process we discovered which features of a case differentiate it from other similar cases, choosing as indices those features that differentiate cases best [6,14]. It is similar to the *checklist-based* indexing implemented in MEDIATOR to index on type and function of disputed objects and relationship of disputants, and CHEF [12] to indexes on texture and taste.

CBRefurb indexes on the circumstance of the project, the state of building, the extent of the damage and the type and quality of work required. Once the manual checklist is produced, further testing were performed on thirty real cases using ReMind's inductive learning methods [15] which has brought some adjustment to the predictions of the indexes of the checklist. This approach of combining manual and ReMind inductive learning methods for choosing the indices has shown interesting results in retrieving appropriate cases and subcases in

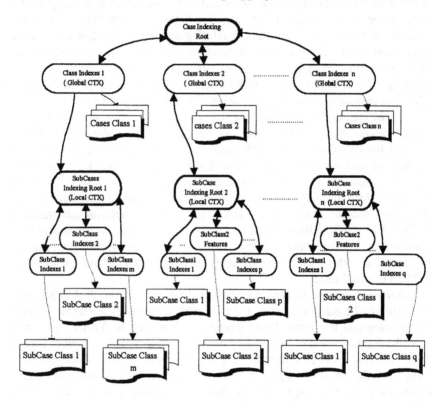

Fig. 2. CBRefurb Indexing Scheme

CBRefurb system.

This two-stage indexing schemes comes in line with the hierarchical case representation and the problem decomposition and consolidate the aim of the paper which is multiple retrieval of adaptable pieces of context cases and subcases. In addition, CBRefurb implements a mechanism that allows the user to make changes to the importance of the features to reflect his personal strategy of estimating cost.

4. Case Retrieval and Adaptation

Pieces from multiple previous cases have been used to come up with a proposed contract in PERSUADOR [11], a diagnosis [10] and proposed layouts in Clavier [9]. Estimating the cost of refurbishment involve collating information from several old cases thus a strategy of *multiple-case-retrieval* is also used (Fig. 2). Our approach of finding multiple relevant cases during building refurbishment cost estimation problem solving is based on the fact that the global and local context information can serve as basis for recognising cases and their subcases that can be used to adapt and estimate the costs.

Given the context information of a problem, a retrieval algorithm, using the indices in the case-memory, should retrieve the most similar cases to the current problem or situation. The retrieval algorithm relies on the indices and the organisation of the memory to direct the search to potentially useful cases. The issue of choosing the *best* matching case has been addressed in several works [16,17,18]. It is apparent that cases are selected on the basis of their closeness of their specification similarities rather than their solution similarities [19]. CBRefurb gives consideration to both solution and specification similarities. Its retrieval mechanism guarantees retrieval of cases that are easier to adapt by giving explicit consideration to how cases can be adapted during the design of the representation and the indexing of the cases. Moreover, CBRefurb implements the strategy of multiple features and multiple case retrieval instead of a single *'best'* or *'most similar'* case as the basis for a solution (Fig 4.). This approach is facilitated by the hierarchical structure of the case, the different level of indexing schemes for the main case and its subcases, and the decomposition of the problem into subproblems that can be adapted iteratively. In this context, CBRefurb follows a two stage process for the retrieval of the main cases. A *filtering stage* which uses the static subtree (or global context) to identifies candidates from the main cases that are deemed to be contextually relevant to the target. A *selection stage* that uses further information existing at the main case level concerning the items the building and the items to repair, the *selection stage* walks through some branch of the dynamic tree to select among the context cases more useful cases to the target case. At this level, identification of relevant information on the selected context cases and their nearest cases of nearest branches of the dynamic tree are saved in an external data structure which can be used for backtracking and walking again to the top of the hierarchy. At this level a *global ball-park solution* to the cost estimation problem is generated and used as a framework for all adaptation process and refinement of the different subcases. The same approach using the filtering stage with its static subtree (local context) and the selection stage with further information the item and elements for each subcases base. The result will be *local ball-park solution* to the cost estimation problem which will also be used for adaptation process and plans for the refinement of elements that can be shared by different building items.

The adaptation process is also performed in two stages: local adaptation for subcases and global adaptation for the whole case. Both implements parameter adjustment and derivational mechanisms during the adaptation of the cases. First, the local adaptation is triggered to adapt subcases in the framework of global ballpark and local ballpark using pieces from different subcases. If a piece is matched, its cost is adapted mixing the refurbishment regulation rules, parameters adjustment for updating prices, altering region, altering quantities, such as speed of construction and urban location. If no similar pieces of cases exist, CBRefurb provides a mechanism which use the external data structured and perform backtracking up to the hierarchy to return to context cases and search for other pieces of context cases that match the remaining unmatched features. The derivational mechanism is used to estimate additional cost resulting from the impact of each of secondary factors by using their boundary of figures and information on how it was estimated in a that similar situation. In the event of no similar pieces match, the derivational mechanism estimates the cost using elemental costs estimation techniques and the user altering procurement and adapt the resulting costs to the target context. Once the local adaptation i.e. solution of each equation of the subproblem, the global adaptation will add all the subcases costs and the result will be similarly adapted for the whole case i.e. solution to the cost estimation problem equation.

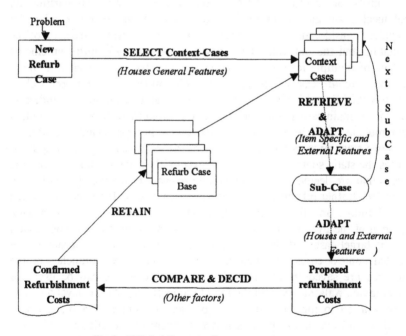

Fig. 3 : CBRefurb Reasoning Process.

5. Evaluation of CBRefurb

CBRefurb is being evaluated by experts in the domain of refurbishment, this feedback will serve to debug our approach of contextual retrieval and the adaptation. Several expert have been impressed by the systems which is in fact the automation of their approach of estimating refurbishment cost. CBRefurb can be seen as a real world intelligent database designed to give realistic refurbishment Costs. It can be used to respond to queries about the estimated cost of any size and type of repairs from large projects of building refurbishment to the building element repair. Moreover, CBRefurb can be used as a decision support tool for the managers while taking strategic decision to go for refurbishment or redevelopment of an important. In theory the technique should also be applicable to other estimating task that rely on prior experience.

The primary contribution to CBR field is the investigation of CBR for hard real-world domain and the application of ReMind to an interesting and challenging cost estimation for refurbishment. In addition CBRefurb contributes to CBR field by providing a "proof of concept" of a CBR architecture for reasoning with multiple cases and addresses the important issue of improving the adaptation process. The major contribution of CBRefurb are the method of hierarchical cases and subcases that goes outside the normal ReMind framework and the Context Information concept whose benefit cut across all the stages of CBR reasoning. Context information is used for many purposes. It provides means for the design of a hierarchical indexing that fits with the case representation. It is used as a similarity measure to classify cases into context cases that reduce considerably the search space of the retrieval process and more importantly used as a framework to decompose the complex problem into adaptable subproblems.

6. Acknowledgements

This work was partially funded by EPSRC project number GR/J42496.

7. References

1. Schank, R. (1982). Dynamic memory: a theory of reminding and learning in computers and people. Cambridge University Press, Cambridge, UK
2. Kolodner, J.L. (1993). Case-Based Reasoning. Morgan Kaufmann.
3. Aamodt, A. & Plaza, E. (1994). Case-Based Reasoning:
 Foundational Issues, Methodological Variations, and System Approaches. *AI Communications*, 7(i): pp 39-59.
4. Watson, I. & Marir, F. 1994. Case-Based Reasoning: A Review. The Knowledge Engineering Review, Vol. 9, No. 4: pp.327-354
5. Douglas J.F. and Peter S.B. (1991). Cost Planning of Buildings (6th Edition). BSP Professional Books
6 Marir, F., & Watson, I.D. ,(1995a). CBRefurb : Case-Based Cost Estimation. Colloquium on Case Based Reasoning: Prospects for applications. Organised by Professional Group C4 (Artificial Intelligence), 7, March, 1995.

7. Watson, I.D., & Brandon, P.S. (1992). Strategic Maintenance Prediction: An Expert System for Facilities Managers. In Facilities Management: Research Direction, Proc. 2nd. IFMA International Symposium. (Ed. Barett P.).

8. Pearce, M., Ashok K.G., Kolodner, J.L., Zimring, C. & Billignton, R. (1992) Case-Based Design Support- A case study in Architectural Design.*IEEE Expert* Oct. 1992

9. Hennessy, D. et al.[1992]. Applying Case-Based Reasoning to autoclave Loading., IEEE Expert,.Vol 17, pp14-20,pp21-25.

10. Redmond, M. A. 1992. Learning by observing and understanding expert problem solving. *Georgia Institute of Technology, College of Computing Technical Report no. GIT-CC-92/43.* Atlanta

11. Sycara , K. [1987] . *Resolving Adversial Conflicts: An approach Integrating cases-Based Reasoning and Analytic Methods.* PhD thesis , School of Information and Computer Science, Georgia Institute of Technology.

12 Hammond, K.J. (1986). CHEF: A Model of Case-Based Planning. *In Proc. American Association for Artificial Intelligence, AAAI-86, August 1986.* Philadelphia, PA, US.

13. Barletta, R. & Mark, W.,(1988). Explanation-Based Indexing of Cases.In DARPA'88 Proceeding , see Kolodner J.L.,(Ed.) 1988.

14 Marir, F., & Watson, I.D. (1995b). Can CBR imitate human intelligence and are such systems easy to design and *maintain? A critique.* Proceedings of the First UK CBR Workshop, 12th January at the University of Salford. (Ed. Watson I.D., F. Marir & Perera S.)

15. Lebowitz, M., (1987). Experimental with incremental concept formation: UNIMEM. *Machine Learning, 2(ii): pp 103-38.*

16 Navichandra, D. (1991). Exploration and innovation in design:towards a computational model. Springer Verlag, New York. NY, US.

17 Maher, M.L. & Zhang, D.M. (1991). CADSYN: using case and decomposition knowledge for design synthesis. In *Artificial Intelligence in Design*, Gero, J.S. (ed.), Butterworth-Heinmann. Oxford. UK

18 Domeshek, E., (1993). A case study of case indexing: Designing index feature sets to suit task demands and support parallelism. In, Advances in connectionnist and neural computation theory, Vol.2: Analogical connections, eds. J. Barenden and K. Holyoak, Norwood, NJ. US.

19 Smyth, B., & Keane M.T., [1993]. Retyrieving Adaptable Knowledge in Case Retriieval. EWCBR-93, 1st Worksop on CBR, Vol2 , 1-5Nov. 93, Germany

Large-Scale Fault Diagnosis

for On-Board Train Systems

B.D. Netten[1], R.A. Vingerhoeds[1,2]

1   *Delft University of Technology, Faculty of Technical Mathematics and Informatics,*
    Knowledge Based Systems Group, Julianalaan 132, 2628 BL Delft, The Netherlands.
    E-mail: bart@kgs.twi.tudelft.nl, rob@kgs.twi.tudelft.nl

2   *University of Wales Swansea, Department of Electrical and Electronic Engineering,*
    Singleton Park, Swansea SA2 8PP, United Kingdom.

Abstract

A new approach is developed for fault diagnosis during different stages of development and operation of large train systems, incorporating case-based reasoning, conditional probabilities and indexing networks. Due to the size and complexity, the explicit, complete and accurate modelling of the on-board train systems is regarded impossible. The knowledge is implicitly available in fault-cases with possible symptoms, test results and actions. Off-line, different diagnostic systems are automatically maintained and (re)generated. Knowledge and experience of manufacturers and railway companies are fed back into all systems, but only after validation by authorised personnel. On-line, the system responses are consistent and fast enough, despite the size and uncertainty in the fault-cases. Available case-based reasoning tools have serious limitations in permissible size of the problem, handling probability factors, meeting required response times and satisfying the real-time requirements. The novelty of the proposed approach is that fault-networks, rather than fault-trees, are built automatically as the indexing structure of the case-base for on-line use.

Keywords: case-based reasoning, fault diagnosis, network, probabilities, real-time.

1   Fault Diagnosis for On-Board Train Systems

A major problem in maintaining regular train services is diagnosing failures in on-board systems. These failures pose a technical problem to be solved, and an operational problem as well. A tight time-schedule must be maintained closely. Safe and efficient operation and maintenance of train systems involve several on- and off-board diagnosis tasks to determine which actions could be performed under the given circumstances and are most appropriate to the actual problem. Occurring failures may lead to simple on-board system recovery actions, quick repairs and delays, rescheduling traffic, moving scheduled maintenance to an earlier date, or even replacing a train unit.

In operational life, diagnosis tasks on the same technical train system are performed in alarm handling, trouble shooting, off-board analyses of on-board recorded data and reports, corrective and scheduled maintenance. These tasks have to be performed on-line by operators within a minimum of time, or even within strict time limits.

Modern trains have automatic failure detection systems on-board. These systems generate symptom-codes and alarm levels during operation, to signal for occurring failures and degradation of train functionality. The driver is obliged to take corrective actions to restore safety for continuous operation and to maintain the time-schedule.

Due to the complexity and the interaction of train systems, the fault or faults causing the failures may be very difficult to identify. The occurrence of failures depends on interactions with other faults, failures and external events. A fault may not always generate the same sequence of symptoms. Modern failure detection systems are extensive and complex, but are not accurate enough to precisely identify each fault under all circumstances. Additional tests are often required to identify the fault and the appropriate action. Diagnostic systems are necessary to determine the relevant additional tests and the consequences of the results.

Whenever proposed actions do not solve a problem during operation, the problem has to be solved during a train stop or maintenance. Tests and actions during operation and maintenance are largely complementary. The diagnosis objectives, time constraints and diagnosis strategy for each diagnosis task are, however, different.

The information obtained during operation provide valuable information for further diagnosis. This information consists of generated symptoms, results of tests and actions, and crew trouble reports. Vice versa, the knowledge gained during extensive diagnosis of unsolved problems provides valuable information for future on-board diagnosis, modification of the diagnostic systems and for the modification and future development of train systems. However, the newly gained information can only be implemented in diagnostic systems after validation and explicit approval of authorised personnel.

2   Analysis of the Fault Diagnosis Tasks

The fault diagnosis problem for this application is in many ways essentially different from diagnosis problems addressed in most case-based reasoning references, such as reported in Richter et al. 1993, Keane et al. 1994. Requirements for on- and off-line diagnosis are described by Vepa (1992) and are partially adapted for this application.

The typical size of the diagnosis problem, in terms of the number of occurring symptoms, faults, tests and actions, increases rapidly with the number of on-board systems. Johnson (1994) estimates the total number of different faults in a large civil aircraft at about 11.000. The diagnosis problem on aircraft is similar to trains, while the number of possible faults for the trains is estimated to be even larger.

The objective for the on-board diagnostic system is to find the *most appropriate action* in a *minimum of time*. This implies that only the most relevant tests should be determined, that require a minimum of time to perform. On-line diagnosis has to be performed in *real-time*. The diagnosis tasks have to be finished within a prescribed time-interval. To be able to achieve the real time requirements, the search-process for diagnosis has to be predictable and predefined.

The operational status of the train and the train systems, the activation of symptoms, tests and actions, changes the on-board situation *dynamically*. The situation cannot be "frozen", and on-board diagnostic systems should react immediately to any changes.

When a problem is not identified by the diagnostic system within the available time, its is stored as an *unsolved case*. The diagnostic system has to provide relevant information on possibly related faults and actions to allow the driver to make a decision.

The objective for off-board diagnostic systems is to identify the actual fault to be repaired for unsolved cases. The actions of previous diagnosis tasks appear as tests in following diagnostic systems. All information related to the unsolved case is recorded on-board. All diagnostic systems have to be fully *consistent* to use previously recorded information directly as input. Response time can be restricted for certain diagnosis tasks or by user-appreciation.

Fault diagnostic systems are initially developed from technical knowledge and lack the practical experiences of railway companies. Extensive testing and repair actions could result in suggestions for modifications of failure detection systems, additional tests during operation and modification of existing diagnostic systems. There is an essential difference between the technical knowledge of manufacturers and the operational experience of railway companies. The availability of additional knowledge is usually not enough appreciated, leading to duplication of diagnosis at high cost. Simplified and unambiguous *exchange of new information* between different operational and maintenance departments within railway companies and with train system manufacturers could well improve existing and future train systems and diagnostic systems.

The complexity and the size of train systems does not allow for development of models for the intended behaviour or malfunctioning of each system and for the interaction between systems. Many behavioural relations between symptoms and faults cannot be declared explicitly. Faults, symptoms, tests and actions are well defined facts, to which unique indices can be assigned. A *unique declaration* of diagnosis problems in terms of these indexed facts is required to facilitate incremental development and to maintain consistency of the diagnostic systems.

Faults can be declared in terms of possibly occurring symptoms and test results. The degree of *uncertainty* in the occurrence of facts is to be taken into account in the diagnosis process. These fault declarations could serve as a unique diagnosis problem declaration, provided that no additional relations between these facts are declared.

The objectives and requirements for each diagnosis task are essentially different. The technical diagnosis problem, however, is the same. Separate diagnostic systems are to be developed for trouble shooting, repair and maintenance, based on the unique problem declaration containing technical and experimental knowledge.

Additional explanation can be required for more *detailed descriptions* of faults, symptoms, and their relations. Detailed descriptions can also be required on procedures for tests and actions. The diagnosis tasks are to identify faults or actions.

Analysis and detailed explanations about the causes for behaviour or malfunction is not required.

Explanatory descriptions for each fact are to be in accordance with the terminology used by the operators of a diagnostic system. To improve user interaction, *symbolic* representations should be used rather than free textual descriptions. Standardised textual and graphical representations of the facts are retrieved from separate data-bases for each diagnostic system. The information in these data-bases can also be used for the production of operation, trouble-shooting and train system maintenance manuals as well.

During development and modification of train systems, a diagnosis environment can be used to identify where additional failure detections or tests are necessary. The results of detailed analysis of train systems can then be fed back for assessment in the diagnosis environment.

Special requirements are posed on the different diagnostic systems and to the approach for large-scale diagnosis, by the size of the problem, uncertainty in declarations, required response times, different objectives of diagnosis tasks, and exchange of new information. A generic approach for building diagnostic systems is presented in this paper and can be applied for many different diagnosing tasks in many different technical fields. An initial implementation of the work has been realised for trouble shooting on modern trains and was already reported by Netten en Vingerhoeds in 1994.

3 Diagnosis Problem Declaration

Only declarations of faults, symptoms, tests, results and actions are required for the declaration and explanation of the fault diagnosis problem. These declarations can be defined as unique and unambiguous indices for the definition of cases. A case is defined as a fault with features for the characteristic symptoms, test results and actions. The fault-case contains all features that may occur in any operational status and diagnostic system. The case-base, containing all fault-cases, provides the unique representational format for all diagnostic systems. The number of cases and features increases during train systems design, production, testing and operation.

3.1 Uncertainty in Fault Declarations

Not all failures in a fault-case will occur whenever the fault occurs, or may only occur after some delay in time. Test results may come out slightly differently. Several slightly different problems can be experienced in operational life for a single fault. Experienced problems could be categorised as individual cases for one fault. The differences in these problems indicate the degree of uncertainty in the effects of the fault.

The experience of train system designers and railway engineers is used to estimate the uncertainty in the fault-case declarations beforehand. A human expert expresses a belief in the probability that a feature of a case could occur, under the condition that the fault has occurred. A belief cannot be expressed in exact percentages for all features of all fault-cases. The size of the problem is too extensive to allow more accurate estimations. Belief is expressed in qualitative terms as likely, most likely or unlikely.

Reliable statistical data to determine all probability factors is usually not available. The prior probabilities do not provide enough information to determine the probabilities of possible faults for occurring symptoms (see Neapolitan 1990). However, the prior probabilities provide valuable information to determine a diagnosis strategy.

3.2 Diagnosis Strategy

Faults can be classified by their features into hierarchically ordered categories related to train systems, subsystems and components. During different stages of operation, different actions and tests can be performed for a fault. This implies that actions and tests can also be ordered hierarchically in different levels of detail, corresponding to the fault categories.

The objectives for each diagnosis task should determine the diagnosis strategy for each diagnostic system. According to the strategy, each diagnostic system is to be built from the case-base. The strategy prescribes what features to use in a particular diagnostic system. The operational status of the train and the available time for example, determine which tests and actions are relevant for a particular diagnostic system.

The strategy also prescribes how the case-base is to be searched to determine appropriate actions. The probability factors in the case-base are used to select the most appropriate test for a given problem situation. In the final stage of diagnosis, the probabilities are used as a similarity measure, not as an interpretation of the probability of a fault.

4   Fault Diagnosis using Case-Based Reasoning

Case-based reasoning techniques (e.g. see Aamodt and Plaza 1994), have been applied for many fault diagnosis applications (e.g. see Richter et al. 1993, Keane et al. 1994). Typically, these applications collect experienced faults in a case-base, whereas the current approach only uses a single case for each fault. New occurring symptoms are matched onto the symptoms of fault-cases. The similarity of fault-cases is a function of the number of occurring features and their prior probability factors (see Neapolitan 1990, Myllymäki and Tirri 1993).

Similar fault-cases have (almost) the same set of symptoms. If not all symptoms of a fault-case occur, similar fault-cases will match the current problem. Additional test results are required as new input features for further identification of the action or fault. In an incremental matching process, the most appropriate additional tests are to be determined and prompted to the operator for results. This process continues until the appropriate action is identified.

Due to the uncertainty in the occurrence of features, a variety of problems can be experienced for each fault-case. The total number of possible problems is a multiple of the possible faults. For the on-line diagnostic systems, only one case for each fault is used, for which prior probability factors are declared for the relevant features.

Occurring problems that can not be diagnosed and solved on-line, are recorded as a new problem case for further off-line diagnosis. Once the fault of the unsolved problem is determined, the fault-case can be modified or a new fault-case can be added. Modification of the on-line case-base is currently performed manually by authorised personnel.

Available case-based reasoning shells (e.g. see Woltering and Schult 1993) are not particularly suited for the current large-scale on-line fault diagnosis application. These available shells can handle only small case-bases, have no facilities for handling prior probabilities or response times are unacceptably long.

5   Indexing Structure for Diagnostic Systems

For on-line diagnosis, the use of the original case-base requires too much computer time and memory. In the on-line diagnostic systems only the indices of cases and features are used. In an off-line procedure, a structure is built from the indexed case-base. The structure should represent the implicit relations between features and fault-cases, direct the search process efficiently and has a minimal number of nodes and links. The efficiency of on-line diagnosis depends on the type of structure used. Three types of structures will be discussed in the following paragraphs.

5.1   Fault-Tree

Tree-structures are the most widely used to represent a logic structure for diagnosis and can be built from a case-base (e.g. see Auriol et al. 1994). A fault-tree consists of branches with nodes for symptoms and tests, and leaves (or end-nodes) with fault-cases. A large case-base is represented by a large number of (sub)trees. Searching trees has some serious disadvantages for the current fault diagnosis problem, resulting in complications of the search process and an unpredictable increase of response times.

The same features appear in many nodes of different subtrees. All related subtrees have to be searched, either sequentially or simultaneously. The diagnostic strategy is determined by the order of symptoms and tests in the branches. The initial choice of a starting node seriously affects the efficiency of the search and the response time. Changes in the status of symptoms and results of tests may diverge the search to other subtrees. Faults can be represented in different subtrees and are therefore difficult to diagnose when these faults occur simultaneously. Nodes, of which the feature value remains unknown, hinder the search process and more complex search strategies have to be adopted, or even the original case-base has to be consulted.

5.2   Connectionist Network

Most of the mentioned disadvantages of trees can be avoided by using a network structure. A 3-level connectionist network for case-based reasoning, incorporating prior probabilities, has been described by Myllymäki and Tirri (1993). The first level consists of input nodes for each feature. Individual networks of 2 layers for each fault-case are connected to the first layer. The conditional probability factors are assigned to the corresponding links.

This network structure still has some disadvantages for application for large fault-case-bases. Similarity is entirely based on the probabilities computed for faults. For every additional symptom or test result, the entire network has to be re-computed for accurate probabilities. The structure cannot identify the most appropriate test to be prompted to the operator. The diagnosis strategy cannot be incorporated in this structure, as it does not consider any hierarchical ordering in the intermediate layer. This structure does not take advantage of the common sets of features in similar fault-cases. A large reduction in the size of the network can be obtained by using common nodes for all related cases. This would, however, not allow the assignment or prior probabilities to links.

5.3   Fault-Network

In rule-based reasoning, the matching problem is efficiently solved using "Rete"-nets, see Forgy (1982). This structure can be applied to case-based reasoning as well, with the exception that the nodes are considered either as OR- or AND-ports. As in the connectionist network described above, each feature and fault-case are represented by an input node and an output node respectively, see Fig. 1. Every combination of features in the case-base is represented by 1 corresponding intermediate node.

The search through the network is data driven and the diagnosis strategy determines the ordering of the nodes in the network structure (see Netten and Vingerhoeds 1994). A different network is built for each diagnostic system. Building a network consists of 2 steps:

1. Determining the categories in the case-base as nodes in the network structure.

2. Linking the nodes in a network according to the diagnosis strategy.

Sets of characteristic features define categories in the case-base. The input nodes of the corresponding features are combined in a sequence of linked intermediate nodes. The automatic determination of categories is a straight forward process, because the features to match a category are well defined.

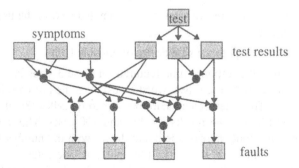

Fig. 1. Fault-network

Diagnosing a problem implies that the input nodes of the occurring features are activated, as well as all linked intermediate and output nodes. The links are used for multiple cases and have no conditional probability factors assigned. The similarities of fault-cases are determined in the corresponding output nodes only, partially based on the prior probabilities. Relevant additional tests can be identified from intermediate nodes with one input activated and one input unknown.

For case-bases with many similar cases, the number of nodes and links is considerably reduced with respect to fault-trees or connectionist networks.

6   Application

A prototype version has been developed to demonstrate the feasibility of the approach and achievable response times. To illustrate the practical advantages of the approach, a fault diagnostic system for a train system is currently being developed and tested. The simplified fault definition in the fault-base enables system engineers to concentrate on the most important aspects of the fault diagnosis problem: develop most appropriate actions to resolve failures. The representation of faults is very "natural" using probability factors for the occurrence of symptoms and test results for a given fault.

During development of a test application, the size of the case-base was increased both in the number of cases as well as in the number of features per case. The number of faults increased from 50 up to 800. Each fault consists of a number of symptoms and one or more additional tests. The total number of symptoms in the case-base rose to about 100, while the number of symptoms for each specific fault ranged from 1 to 10. The average number of features per fault was about 6.5. This implies that the number of layers in the fault-network remained about constant for all case-bases, while the total number of faults and symptoms increased.

In an off-line procedure, the network was built from the case-base. Before on-line diagnosis, the network is loaded into computer memory. On-line diagnosis is activated when a symptom status or test result is presented to the network. The following tasks are performed after every new input:

1. propagate the new input through the fault-network,
2. determine the most relevant test to be prompted next to the user according to the search strategy, and
3. if necessary, compute the similarities of possible faults.

An indication of the response time required for these 3 steps is given in Fig. 2. The highest measured response times (worst cases) from the test case-bases are presented as a solid line. The measurements are performed on a PC-486 at 33 MHz. A dotted line is drawn through the results for 200 and 400 cases. This dotted line indicates that the response time increases less than linear with the number of faults for larger case-bases of similar complexity. Extrapolation indicates a response time for diagnosis problems with similar complexity less than 1.6 seconds for 1000 faults.

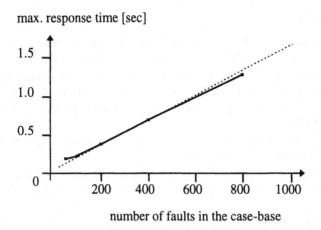

max. response time [sec]

number of faults in the case-base

Fig. 2. Maximum response times during development of the case-bases.

7 Conclusions

A new approach to case-based reasoning for fault diagnosis is presented for large scale technical applications. The feasibility is demonstrated by a prototype application for on-board train systems. Several major advantages of the approach are described:

1. Case-based reasoning is an adequate technique to develop large scale fault diagnostic systems. The problem description for the fault diagnosis problem is made much easier, and allows unambiguous exchange of knowledge between different users and experts. Available shells are not suited for large applications.

2. A network indexing structure for on-line diagnostic systems allows the use of larger case-bases, and results in fast response times. The search through a network is a more efficient and predictable than through a tree-structure. Incremental use can be made of data becoming available during on-line diagnosis, as symptoms and test results can be presented in any order to the system and are immediately evaluated.

3. Prior probability factors are used in the fault declarations to express experience and to guide the diagnosis strategy.

4. Development and maintenance of diagnostic systems are simplified. Dedicated and fully consistent diagnostic systems are generated automatically from the unique problem description.

8 References

Aamodt A., E. Plaza (1994). Case-Based Reasoning: Foundational Issues, Methodological Variations, and System Approaches. *AI Communications*, **7**, nr. 1, March, pp. 39-52.

Auriol E., M. Manago, K.D. Althoff, S. Wess, S. Dittrich (1994). Integrating Induction and Case-Based Reasoning: Methodolological Approach and First Evaluations. *2nd European Workshop on Case-Based Reasoning*, (eds.) M. Keane, J.P. Haton, M. Manago, Chantilly, 7-10 November, pp 145-156.

Forgy, C.L. (1982). Rete: A fast Algorithm for the Many pattern/Many Object Pattern Match Problem. *Artificial Intelligence*, **19**, pp. 17-37.

Johnson, K. (1994). Evolution of the Trouble Shooting Manual for the A319/A320/A321/A330/A340 Central Maintenance System. *FAST Airbus Technical Digest*, nr. 16, pp. 10-15.

Keane M., J.P. Haton, M. Manago, (Eds.) (1994). *Second European Workshop on Case-Based Reasoning*. AcknoSoft Press (Paris), Chantilly, 7-10 November.

Myllymäki P., H. Tirri (1993). Massively Parallel Case-Based Reasoning with Probabilistic Similarity Metrics. *First European Workshop on Case-Based Reasoning*, (eds.) M.M. Richter, S. Wess, K.-D. Althoff, F. Maurer, SEKI Report SR-93-12, University of Kaiserslautern, pp 48-53.

Neapolitan R.E. (1990). Probabilistic Reasoning in Expert Systems: Theory and Algorithms. John Wiley & Sons.

Netten B.D., R.A. Vingerhoeds (1994). Automatic Fault-Tree Generation, A Generic Approach for Fault Diagnosis Systems. *IFAC Workshop Safety, Reliability and Applications of Emerging Intelligent Control Techniques*, Hong Kong, 12-14 december, pp 182-187.

Richter M.M., S. Wess, K.-D. Althoff, F. Maurer (Eds.) (1993). *First European Workshop on Case-Based Reasoning*. SEKI Report SR-93-12, University of Kaiserslautern, 1-5 November.

Vepa R. (1992). Monitoring and Fault Diagnosis in Control Engineering. in: *Application of Artificial Intelligence in Process Control*, (eds.) L. Boullart, A. Krijgsman, R.A. Vingerhoeds. Pergamon Press, pp. 456-496.

Woltering A., Schult T.J. (1993). Management Strategy Consultation Using a Case-Based Reasoning Shell. *First European Workshop on Case-Based Reasoning*. (eds.) M.M. Richter, S. Wess, K.-D. Althoff, F. Maurer, SEKI Report SR-93-12, University of Kaiserslautern, pp 227-232.

Case-Based Reasoning for Expertise Relocation in Support of Rural Health Workers in Developing Countries

Elisha T. O. Opiyo

Faculty of Information Sciences, Moi University, P.O. Box 3900, Eldoret, Kenya.

Current address: Department of Computing Mathematics, University of Wales College of Cardiff, P.O. Box 916, Cardiff CF2 4YN, United Kingdom.
e-mail: elisha.t.o.opiyo@cm.cf.ac.uk

Abstract

Developing countries still suffer lack of adequate skilled medical health personnel and poor infrastructure. Expert systems have been identified as potential tools in addressing some aspects of these problems. In particular, most of the earlier researchers investigated the possibility of incorporating diagnostic-support applications in the medical work place. They did so by using expert systems that were built around representations such as production rules, frames, scripts and semantic networks. In this paper, a report on a different approach is given. A MEdical Reference SYstem(MERSY) is proposed. The basis of the design of MERSY is the case-based reasoning paradigm with some underlying domain model. This system therefore gets around the limitations of traditional expert systems that are related to knowledge representation and acquisition. The work also a emphasizes a high level of physical portability, hence the relocation of expertise. It is an on-going research.

1 Introduction

This paper discusses how Case-Based Reasoning is used in the design of an expert system that will support rural health workers by enabling the recall of relevant stored experiences. In particular it, announces an on-going research that targets developing countries and the improvement of the rural health services as the ultimate objective.

Most rural areas in developing countries are poorly served by infrastructure and health facilities [World Bank 93, 94]. Although most people live in the rural areas, it is the urban institutions that are relatively better equipped.

In this paper the extent to which other researchers have given attention to some aspects of the problems above will be highlighted. Some have looked at ways of improving health services by proposing rule based expert systems for use by paramedical staff [Forster 92, Kathleen & Howard 90]. A different approach, with emphasis on reference, rather than diagnosis, is proposed. To support, it a MEdical Reference System (MERSY) is presented. The system acts as a source of previous experiences which may be re-used in guiding problem solving when unfamiliar situations arise. MERSY will also be used as a general reference resource facility. Its design also emphasizes high portability of the target hardware. This is what is behind the relocation of expertise. This paper will also discuss some of the experiences as the work evolves. It will particularly point out the problems met, so far, and indicate the progress made.

2 Related work

2.1 Introduction

This section outlines the context of the general problem; reviews related work; points out possible causes of the difficulties with earlier systems, and gives grounds for choosing case-based reasoning.

2.2 The problem in context

The two quotations below indicate the general setting of the problem being addressed:-

"Population-based health services such as the EPI rely on personnel with limited training to provide drugs, vaccines, or specific health services directly to specific populations-in schools, at worksites, or in households." [World Bank 93 p.72].

"The poor also have considerably worse access to health care. A number of surveys show that low income households, especially in rural areas, have to travel considerably farther or longer to reach the first level of referral services, usually a primary health care centre or doctor's office." [World Bank 93 p.69].

The need to provide more information especially to those involved in health services but have only minimal training stands out. This is further motivated by the difficulties of access experienced by the rural poor.

2.3 How others have approached the problem

Expert Systems have been identified as potential tools in addressing some aspects of the problem of lack of trained medical specialists in developing countries. In particular, these expert systems would provide diagnostic support for use by paramedical workers [Forster 92].

These earlier expert systems used rules, frames, tables, semantic networks, scripts, decision trees and algorithms for knowledge representation. They were developed using a wide range of tools including BASIC, Pascal-USCSD, Turbo Prolog, GWBASIC, C, LISP, Hypercard, IQLISP and dBase III [Forster 92, Kathleen & Howard 90]. They were targeted for different hardware platforms ranging from mini, personal to hand-held computers. A number of them used the Essex Flowcharts and therefore were mainly concerned with the diagnosis of diseases. Most of these studies also focused on testing how well the programs would perform accurate diagnosis.

2.4 Problems with earlier work

Forster, pointed out that some of the expert systems for computer-assisted diagnosis could be expensive on some platforms [Forster 92]. Doukidis et al., evaluated ESTROPID(Expert System for TROPIcal Diseases) and questioned the need for computerized decision-aid technology by health personnel and suggested a paper-based one instead [Doukidis 94]. The relevant point is that they maintained the need for some decision aid.

Looking at most of these earlier systems, they could be regarded as based on earlier methods of building expert systems. The problems with these earlier techniques included inadequacy in the existing representation formalisms and the knowledge acquisition problems [Sloman 85, Waterman 86]. Furthermore the medical knowledge being inexact in nature makes the direct applicability of the usual representation formalisms difficult [Barr & Feigenbaum 82]. So these earlier systems had inherent limitations.

2.5 The relevance of Case-Based Reasoning

Kolodner, views Case-Based Reasoning (CBR) as a phenomenon that occurs when old solutions are: manipulated to meet new demands; used to explain new situations; used to critique new solutions; act as precedents to interpret new situations, or are used to create equitable solution to new problems [Kolodner 93 p.4]. She points out the extensive use of CBR in day-to-day commonsense reasoning and sees the regular recurrence of situations as the intuition behind it.

The main points brought out here are the re-use of old solutions and the natural way of problem solving using CBR. The range of possible uses of the old solution is wide and depends on the situation at hand. Kolodner also points out that those trained in making logical decisions use case-based inferences and this includes the doctors [Kolodner 93].

Slade, sees expertise as consisting of experience and views CBR as a general paradigm of reasoning from experience[Slade 91]. This raises the issue of expertise and experience. These two are richly documented in the medical records of the patient episodes. This documentation can be used by case-based reasoners to assist in handling new situations or as a basis of guidance in problem solving. The situation can be depicted as below:-

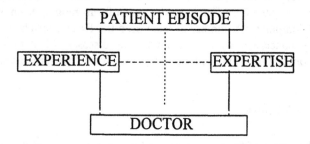

Fig.1. Basic doctor-patient episode with intervening experience and expertise.

Barr and Feigenbaum pointed out inexactness as a problem with medical knowledge [Barr & Feigenbaum 82] and therefore this called for other representations [Sloman 85]. Kolodner, however, pointed out the usefulness of CBR in the domains that are not completely understood [Kolodner 93]. CBR therefore is a technique that can be applied in the context of developing countries. It will minimize some of the problems inherent in traditional expert systems such as those related to knowledge acquisition. CBR will also lead to the advantages such as reduced development time, improved management of large volumes of information and easier maintenance [Watson 94].

CBR has been demonstrated successfully or shown to be potential in many areas including medical diagnosis, legal reasoning, explanation of anomalies, general diagnostics, arbitration, bridge design, general design, planning, software re-use and in some commercial tasks[Watson 94, Magaldi 94, Moore 94, Georgin 95, Price & Pegler 95, Maguire 95, Hammond 89].

It is, therefore, reasonable to expect CBR to yield useful results when used to address similar problems in the context of developing countries.

3 A different approach to the problem

3.1 Introduction

Earlier researchers approached the problem of lack of trained personnel in health services in developing countries by proposing the use of expert systems. Field trials have yielded mixed results and few of the projects, if any, have been adopted into the target health systems [Forster 92]. These earlier workers also investigated ways of supporting diagnostic processes at practice and, for some, at training levels. Few, however, aimed at decision support functions.   The MEdical Reference System

(MERSY) described below represents a different approach in that it is based on case-based reasoning and emphasizes the need to offer reference support.

3.2 Relocation of expertise

MERSY contains expert knoweledge, encapsulated in the stored past medical records. Expert knowledge is also held from other sources like literature and medical staff. Using it on portable hardware such as laptop, notebook or hand-held computers makes it possible to avail the expertise in different locations. This is relevant to health workers in remote locations who would use it with relative convenience. Given the wide range of the target hardware it is also desired that the costs be kept to a minimum. This would be consistent with the constraints identified by some earlier researchers [Kathleen & Howard 90, Forster 92].

3.3 The proposed System (MERSY)

The outline of the larger project and the structure of MERSY are described below.

3.3.1 Outline of the project layout

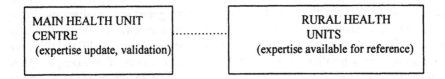

Fig.2. Overall project layout

A close association between the Main Health centres and the peripheral medical units is expected when MERSY is in use.

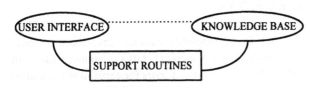

Fig.3. General structure of MERSY

The user interface will support both the system knowledge maintenance and its usage. The support routines are a group of modules that perform retrieval, matching and learning. The knowledge base holds data on both cases and the domain knowledge.

3.3.2 Contextual constraints

Since the intended user environment is developing countries, MERSY has to satisfy requirements similar to those pointed out by earlier researchers[Forster 92]. These include enabling user interface, low cost and ease of maintenance.

3.3.3 Progress so far

The modules that have been completed and have been extensively tested include data management functions, case extraction routine, case-feature association routines and retrieval routines. Some patient records have been entered into the system and further tests are being carried out.

3.3.4 Some technical aspects of MERSY

This section considers, briefly, knowledge representation, indexing, similarity measurement and the matching strategy in MERSY.

Knowledge representation. In MERSY a hierarchical conceptual view was adopted for representation. In this view, we have GROUPS, MEMBERS, and FEATURES (characteristics or properties). GROUPS are broad categories such as diseases, drugs, cases, terms, unknowns or habitats. MEMBERS are specific instances of group elements for example MALARIA is a member of the disease-group. FEATURES are the various characteristics of MEMBERS and their values. For example *'body temperature: 37.2 degrees centigrade'* may be a feature observed in a patient episode.

GROUP	MEMBER	FEATURE
case	patient-1	Patient-1 data (as much as available)
drug	quinine	quinine data (as much as available)

Fig.4. Knowledge representation in MERSY

Indexing. In MERSY, a case consists of case-identification, case-features, case-diagnoses, case-treatments and case-outcome. A medical staff confronted with an ill patient has to rely on observations which are used as a basis for explaining the causes of the illness. These observations (or features), therefore, hold the key to diagnoses.

(CASE IDENTIFICATION, FEATURES, DIAGNOSES, TREATMENTS, OUTCOME)

Fig.5. General case structure in MERSY; features are used to index the case

Similarity measurement. In MERSY similarity measurement is motivated by the question 'Given an observation how much does it tell?'. A feature is associated to a case by the amount of information content that it holds about the case. This is a sum of the information (in bits) that it holds about the case and in general.

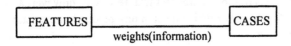

Fig. 6. Feature-Case association.

The association between a FEATURE and a CASE is a weight given as:-

weight = information about the case + general information;
Information about the case = $\log_2 (1/p\text{-}case)$;
general information = $\log_2 (1/p\text{-}feature\text{-}occurs)$.

where *p-case* is the probability that a feature occurs in a case, and *p-feature-occurs* is the probability that a feature occurs at all.

Matching strategy. When new set of features (problem set) is submitted, old feature-case associations are used to score various cases. The cases are ranked and those with information score above some threshold value are presented for consideration by the user. The matching strategy is outlined in the algorithm below:-

```
accept a problem set (new features);
while (more old feature-case associations){
      move to the first new feature
      do{
            if (old feature = = new feature){
                  add feature information score to the associated case;
                  note old feature for later explanation requests;
            } while (more new features)
        get another new feature;
      }
      get another old feature-case association;
}
sort cases;  present cases with scores above a cutoff value;  keep the solution set;
```

Fig.7. Matching algorithm in MERSY

3.3.5 Overview of system specifications

Functions. The system will offer some reference and diagnostic support based on stored experiences and relevant medical knowledge.

Software development tool. MERSY has been written using Turbo C.

Hardware. The target hardware platforms should be highly portable IBM PC machines or compatibles. These include Olivetti quaderno, Sharp PC3100, HP200LX, or any other suitable hand-held computers. So far an earlier model of Olivetti quaderno has been used.

Inputs. The bulk of the data consists of the features and feature values, however, a *feature* must belong to an existing *member* which must in turn belong to an existing *group*. An example is given below:

GROUP	MEMBER	FEATURES
Cases	patient-1	From Kisumu, hot body, elderly, etc.
Water sources	River Nyando	Some polution data on Nyando, etc.

Fig.8. Input data in MERSY

Outputs. These are mainly in the form of responses to information requests. For example suppose a health worker wants to check some allergies before administering a drug, data on the drug can be retrieved. Furthermore a health worker faced with a new situation can raise the question: *'Has such a situation been seen before?'*. When the current situation is described and submitted to the system as a set of features, the system will respond by retrieving earlier cases that could be similar to the situation. The user can then follow up with more information requests.

Users. The system is intended to be used by the rural health workers; medical staff at various levels and others who will tailor the information held to their reference needs. Since MERSY is a general information resource tool, it will be useful to people in other areas like agriculture and education.

3.3.6 Problems encountered

The first problem was related to the choice of software development tool. The C language. This led to a slow rate of development and drew attention away from the real issues in case-based reasoning for some time. The choice of C, however, was due to portability, cost and future maintenance considerations.

The second problem encountered was the search for a suitable representation combining domain model and case-based reasoning. It took time to settle for an acceptable representation. The initial version of MERSY was based on a relational model which turned out to be too rigid and could not cope with the information structures. The representation was then changed to only a two level hierarchical one of MEMBER-FEATURE which was also abandoned for being too general. The processing resources needed by MOPs or TOPs [Schank 82, Kolodner 93] are not available given the nature of functionality sought. We are looking for a low cost portable information resource tool. In the end, therefore, the current three level hierarchical representation of GROUP-MEMBER-FEATURES was adopted.

Thirdly, there are several problems related to case-based reasoning that are being addressed by various researchers. Some of these issues in case-based reasoning are enumerated in [DARPA 89] and have to do with matching, indexing, memory organization, case associations, sparse memory, forgetting, hybrid systems and training cases. In the previous sections it has been, very briefly, shown how some of the issues in CBR are handled in MERSY.

3.4 Promises, limitations and strengths of the study

In this research a minimized effect of the knowledge acquisition bottleneck is expected. Cases are easily obtained from the past medical records, and specific medical experts will not be the sole source of domain knowledge. Medical knowledge will be obtained from existing literature, medical records and other cooperative medical staff. It is also expected that the system will be more consistent with the professional practice and will have a wider scope.

MERSY inherits the limitations associated with the nearest neighbour search strategy and the use of surface features in indexing[Kolodner 93].

MERSY is, however, flexible and can be used even when the processing resources are low. It is functional as a reference resource, diagnostic guide and a classifier. It adds to the number of systems developed that re-use past experiences, particularly, in the medical domain.

3.5 The current constraints to the research

This research, especially for the field testing phase still calls for interested collaborators. Collaboration is still open at academic but is particularly needed at financial level.

4 Conclusion

This paper has described how the lack of trained health personnel in the developing countries can continue to be addressed. It has been argued that this can be done by restricting focus to the information requirements of the rural health workers. MERSY, a reference support system with diagnostic capabilities has been proposed and the progress of the on-going work indicated. It is also hoped that collaboration with other interested researchers will be initiated.

5 Acknowledgment

I am thankful to:- the Kenyan and the British governments for this limited scholarship; The British Council for the Quaderno; Dr K. W. Getao my country supervisor; Dr A. C. Jones for continuing supervision; Alec Gray for his contributions; Moi University for initial field work funds; Seth M. Dhidha for provision of some relevant literature before this research even started, and to the reviewers for criticisms that led to the inclusion of section 3.3.4.

6 References

[Barr & Feigenbaum 82] Avron Barr, Edward Feigenbaum (Editors), *The Handbook of Artificial Intelligence,* Volume II, Heuristech Press, 1982.

[DARPA 89] DARPA, Case-Based Reasoning from DARPA: Machine Learning Program Plan, in *Proceedings of a Workshop on Case-Based Reasoning,* Morgan Kaufmann Publishers, Inc., 1989.

[Doukidis 94] Doukidis G., I., Cornford T., Forster D., Medical Expert Systems for Developing Countries: Evaluation in Practice, in Jay Liebowitz (Editor), *Expert Systems With Applications*, Vol. 7, No. 2, pp. 221-233, 1994.

[Forster 92] Dayo Forster, *Expert Systems in Health for Developing countries: Practice, problems and potential*, International Development Research Centre, 1992.

[Georgin 95] E.Georgin, F.Bordin, J.R. McDonald, Using prototypes in case based diagnosis of steam turbines, in *IEE Case Based Reasoning:prospects for applications*, Digest No:1995/047,1995.

[Hammond 89] Kristian J. Hammond, *Case-Based Planning:Viewing Planning as a memory task,* Academic Press, Inc., 1989.

[Kathleen & Howard 90] Kathleen K., Howard B., Medical AI systems as appropriate technology for developing countries, in *The Knowledge Engineering Review*, No.5:4,1990,251-263.

[Kolodner 93] Janet Kolodner, *Case-Based Reasoning*, Morgan Kaufmann Publishers, 1993.

[Magaldi 94] R.V.Magaldi, CBR for troubleshooting aircraft on the flightline, *in IEE Case Based Reasoning:prospects for applications,* Digest No:1994/057, 1994.

[Maguire 95] P. Maguire, V. Shankaraman, R. Szegfue, L. Moriss, Application of Case-Based Reasoning (CBR) to Software Reuse, in I.Watson, F.Marir & S.Perera (Editors*)*, *Proceedings of the First United Kingdom Case-Based Reasoning Workshop*, The British Computer Society, 1995.

[Moore 94] C.J.Moore, M.S.Lehane, C.J.Price, Case Based Reasoning for decision support in engineering design, *in IEE Case Based Reasoning:prospects for applications*, Digest No:1994/057,1994.

[Price & Pegler 95] C.J.Price, I.S. Pegler, Wayland:Efficiency improvements in aluminium die casting, *in IEE Case Based Reasoning:prospects for applications*, Digest No:1995/047,1995.

[Schank 82] Roger C. Schank, *Dynamic memory: a theory of reminding and learning in computers and people*, Cambridge University Press, 1982.

[Slade 91] Stephen Slade, Case-Based Reasoning: A Research Paradigm, *in AI Magazine* 0738-4602/91.

[Sloman 85] Aaron Sloman, Why we need many knowledge representation formalisms, in M. A. Bramer (Editor), *Research and Development in Expert Systems*, Cambridge University Press, 1985.

[Waterman 86] Donald A., Waterman, *A guide to expert systems*, Addison-Wesley Publishing Company, 1986.

[Watson 94] Ian Watson, Case-Based Reasoning: A Review, in *Knowledge Engineering Review*, Vol. 9, No. 4, 1994.

[World Bank 93] World Bank, *World Development Report 1993:Investing in Health*, Oxford University Press, 1993.

World Bank 94] World Bank, *World Development Report 1994:Infrastructure for development*, Oxford University Press, 1994.

Spatial composition using cases : IDIOM

Ian Smith, Claudio Lottaz and Boi Faltings

AI Lab (LIA - DI)
Federal Institute of Technology (EPFL)
CH-1015 Lausanne

Abstract. This paper describes a system called IDIOM (Interactive Design using Intelligent Objects and Models) that was developed in order to study model-based case combination and adaptation in design. Intelligent objects are defined to be parts of cases that are interpreted at run-time by domain models and through user interaction. Incremental parameterization and dimensionality reduction ensures that design solutions are proposed quickly and reliably. An implementation in the domain of spatial composition for building designs demonstrates several aspects of the approach.

1 Introduction

Most design tasks require the determination of geometric parameters. To date, there are few case-based design (CBD) systems that are able to reason about geometry. For example, CBD systems such as CYCLOPS [18], KRITIK [8], CADET [21], ARCHIE [9], CADSYN [17], SEED [5] and the FABEL project [1] are proposed for mechanical engineering, civil engineering and architecture. Although all of these domains require the specification of geometry as part of the design solution, very little support for geometrical case adaptation is provided. Most systems are limited to treatment of symbolic information expressed in terms of discrete variables. Some systems, such as ARCHIE, are primarily intended for intelligent browsing. While this activity is an important stage in preliminary design, no computational support is provided for case adaptation. Where continuous variables are included in adaptation processes, such as in the case of CADSYN[24], only local constraint consistency is maintained during case adaptation. When local constraint consistency is maintained only, problems of looping, divergence and fictitious solutions are common, particularly when traditional algorithms are employed [4].

Support for case adaptation is important because creative use of design cases through adaptation may lead to innovative designs. This potential is especially attractive when two or more cases are combined. Adaptation issues for design are treated most extensively in papers which refer to Julia [10, 11], a system that interactively designs the presentation and menu of a meal. Through various design strategies, the system satisfies multiple, interacting constraints. This study introduced several new concepts related to case adaptation. Meal planning was chosen because this involved discrete variables; the researchers did not want to get "bogged down" [11] in issues related to geometric reasoning.

The CADRE system [12, 13] was the first to propose a solution for geometric adaptation. Methods were developed for adapting *exact* cases through a geometrical parameterization which occurs *at run time* according to the characteristics of the new context. Dimensional adaptation is supported in order to maintain the original topology of the case. Topological adaptation has been attempted for special cases of buildings using techniques such as shape grammars [13]. However, this has proven difficult to generalize for a range of buildings. In addition, run-time parameterization of topological adaptation knowledge for several abstractions has not been possible. This has lead to an investigation of combining two cases [3]. When these cases are complex, formulation of constraints necessary for successful combination have proved to be difficult.

This paper presents an approach where the *user* determines building topology through composition of intelligent objects, thereby avoiding the problems of topological adaptation. The next section includes a discussion of the evolution of case-based reasoning (CBR) adaptation research toward case combination and adaptation. In section 3, the IDIOM system is introduced. In section 4, we describe how objects are composed using incremental parameterization. Section 5 contains details of the current implementation of IDIOM and finally in section 6, limitations of the system are discussed.

2   Case combination and adaptation

Traditionally, CBR research has been divided into the following two themes: the study of case representation, indexing and retrieval and issues involving case adaptation [16]. Representation, indexing and retrieval topics are more extensively studied than case adaptation. This is partly because adaptation is seen to be difficult; indeed, few reliable adaptation systems are available. Case adaptation research is attractive because in order to properly index a case, one should know how to adapt it [14]. Some research has shown that people retrieve adaptable cases [15] and that adaptation-based retrieval increases reliability [20]. In design, users in professions such as architecture cannot ethically use geometrical cases developed by others; they are most likely to use their own cases and therefore, they do not need extensive support for retrieval. Finally, case adaptation requires methodologies such as problem-specific parameterization (not theory formation), thereby helping to distinguish case-based reasoning from other domains such as information retrieval and machine learning. The work described in this paper is a result of our research into case adaptation.

While much work on CBD adaptation has focused on modifying one case to suit design requirements, many designers use information from *several cases* in order to achieve design goals [23]. Treatment of several cases increases the capacity of CBD systems to handle complex designs. When combining cases only some information is needed from each case, each case must be interpreted for the problem in order to specify how the combination will be made and when combining, conflicts must be resolved between the various parts through adaptation. Therefore, case combination and adaptation research involves the following processes.

- **Analysis** - identification within each case the knowledge which is applicable to the current problem.
- **Interpretation** - requirements, established at run-time related to how the combination can be achieved for the current problem. Interpretation is carried out through : i) application of domain models and ii) user interaction.
- **Resolution** - constructing a feasible solution; satisfying, through adaptation, the requirements of users and two types of models, those related to each original case (that remain relevant) and those that become applicable to the new combination.

The following sections describe case combination and adaptation applied to building spaces. In this work we focus primarily upon the last two of the three processes described above, interpretation and resolution.

3   The IDIOM system

We have developed a system called Interactive Design using Intelligent Objects and Models (IDIOM) in an attempt to build upon successful aspects of CADRE while placing greater emphasis on interactivity and explicit domain modelling to guide adaptation, simlarly to Goel [8]. Figure 1 describes important aspects of IDIOM.

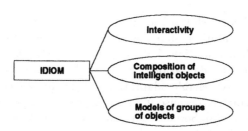

Fig. 1. *Important aspects of IDIOM*

The term, IDIOM, was chosen because its meaning reflects an important goal of this research. A dictionary definition for the word "Idiom" is

A phrase which means something different from the meaning of the separate words

This definition provides a useful analogy. We aim to provide support for incremental composition of design cases while allowing models of the design space to include holistic considerations of groups of objects. These models are applied to designs several ways; they are activated when certain groups of objects are present in the design, they are used to interpret designs in certain contexts and they are introduced by the designer incrementally as the design is composed.

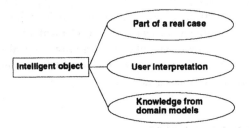

Fig. 2. *Information that contributes to the definition of an intelligent object. Note that an object becomes intelligent only at run-time, when it is interpreted by users and domain models for a specific design task.*

The information contained in an intelligent object is described in Figure 2. Our current research into case-based building design is motivated by two factors. The first factor arose through discussions with building designers. These discussions resulted in the observation that although they frequently reuse designs, they rarely wish to adapt whole building cases. Often, the cases which are most useful are spaces and collections of spaces [19].

The second factor is that most design domains cannot be modelled completely. Building designers know this intuitively since their designs are often influenced by complex considerations of social, political and economic factors. As a result, it is often the source of frustration when a design system performs automatic design, often providing just one design solution. A much better role for computer systems is to provide support for defining *allowable spaces of acceptable designs*. When exploring these spaces designers are able to introduce *their interpretation* of what is not modelled through adding constraints or through identifying design solutions for further development.

These two factors lead to the definition of an **intelligent object** that is used in this paper: an intelligent object is a *part of a real case* which can be interpreted for each new design task in the following two ways:

– through user interpretation in order to cover what cannot be modelled reliably. This avoids formulation of brittle heuristic rules.
– through reference to explicit models of their function, behavior and structure. Models provide explicit representations of physical principles, thereby again avoiding the brittleness associated with traditional rule based systems.

Therefore, an object becomes intelligent only at run-time after interpretation by users and domain models. An example of an intelligent object would be a living room taken from a case of a previously built apartment design. This living room becomes an intelligent object when i) the user interprets it in a new context by imposing conditions such as neighbourhood relationships and ii) when domain models add additional constraints, such as the size of the living room needed for the number of inhabitants in the apartment. More detail is provided in Section 5.

Rather than generate layouts automatically through techniques such as mathematical programming, space discretizations, graphs [6] and constraint satisfaction [22], IDIOM supports users with domain models while they build layouts incrementally using intelligent objects. A key element of this support is that IDIOM maintains design requirements at each stage and allows them to grow as objects are added. As such, layout designs benefit from incremental run-time parameterization; this is discussed next.

4 Incremental parameterization

When layout designs are composed using intelligent objects, dimensional constraints on geometric parameters are generated from an evaluation of the topology of the objects. These constraints are formulated in order to define conditions for maintenance of this topology, see Figure 3. The top drawing shows the constraints related to a primitive topology and the bottom one gives an example of the constraints for two spaces with a door between them. Additional con-

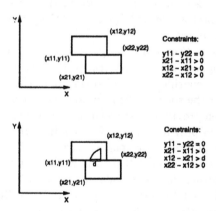

Fig. 3. Examples of parameterization with constraints on spaces. These constraints are used to maintain geometrical integrity.

straints originate from i) within the object; each object has constraints which determine acceptable positions of elements which make up the object, such as doors, windows and furniture, ii) from function-behavior-structure domain models that interpret the design; as objects are assembled, domain models introduce constraints related to issues such as circulation, building codes and thermal comfort and iii) from users through constraint posting: users introduce constraints in order to provide their interpretation of those aspects which are not covered in domain models.

Each time an object is added, the parameterization grows. Dimensionality reduction [12] is performed on the complete constraint set. Therefore, global constraint consistency is maintained since all constraints are considered simultaneously. This is valid for constraints expressed as equalities. Inequalities are checked once a solution has been generated. If an inequality is violated, it is transformed into an equality and the dimensionality reduction is recalculated. Once an acceptable solution is found, the user is free to add an additional object and consequently, more constraints are added to the parameterization.

An advantage of this approach is that, provided design criteria can be expressed as algebraic constraints, the process is independent of the discipline which generated the requirement. Thus, horizontal integration of disciplines such as structural engineering and architecture is possible through obtaining a parameterization which is simultaneously valid for both disciplines [14].

5 Implementation of IDIOM

We are testing the ideas presented in the previous sections within the domain of apartment floor layouts. Objects in IDIOM currently consist of spaces which are labeled according to their function. They are selected using a browser which is accessed through the main design window under *object* and then *add-object*. Once selected they are inserted into the main design window, see Figure 4. Objects may

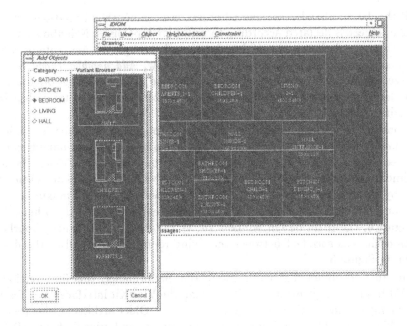

Fig. 4. The object browser and the main design window of IDIOM

be modified through rotation and mirroring using *modify-object*. Five functions for objects are currently available: bathroom, kitchen, bedroom, living room and hallway. Each object has been taken from a case and thus each has values for all dimensions.

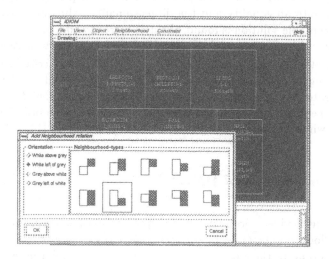

Fig. 5. Definition of neighbourhood relationships

If the design already contains an object, a neighbourhood relationship with another object is declared according to primitive topologies. Neighbourhood relationships are declared, changed and removed through the menu items *neighbourhood - add, modify* and *remove*. The window, *Add neighbourhood relation* in Figure 5 shows 10 primitive topologies for one of four possible orientations, *white left of grey*. A neighbourhood relationship can be specified for each pair of adjoining objects.

Constraints may be posted by the user through *object - modify* windows. The modify window in Figure 6 illustrates how object sizes and bounds can be changed. The desired values are values taken from the original case. The abs. minimum values are usually specified by codes while the minimum values are fixed by the user for a given design task. The user may also fix maximum sizes for rooms although this option is less frequently employed than the others. Also in Figure 6, the main design window shows the design after a neighbourhood relationship was specified between the living room and the hall in the design shown in Figure 5.

In order to obtain reasonable interactive performance, this first version of IDIOM has been implemented in C++ using the ViewKit interface tool. Testing with architects has resulted in divergent reactions. Older architects who are used to working hierarchically using well defined schemas and grids find that IDIOM does not reflect what they do and therefore, the system provides little support.

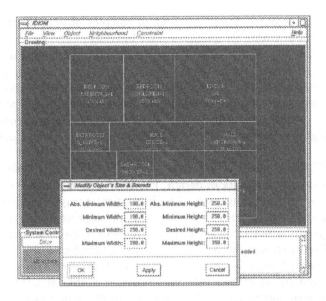

Fig. 6. Constraint posting with IDIOM

Younger architects, however have found that IDIOM provides an opportunity to get away from tradition methods, thereby allowing them to explore new approaches such as constructivism and space-based objects. IDIOM appeals more to architects who are inclined to participate in design competitions than those who do standard speculative construction projects.

6 Limitations and relation to other work

The dimensional parameterization described is limited to rectangular spaces and elements. Complex non-linear constraints slow the system down to the point where interactive design becomes difficult. For use in real time, constraints are formulated to be as close as possible to linear relationships. The current implementation of IDIOM allows for linear and simple non-linear constraints, such a those applied to floor areas.

Since this work is focused on run-time adaptation of values of continuous variables which represent spatial design attributes, there is very little relation to work of other groups in this area. Over the last few years, several German groups have been developing a system for building objects within the scope of a project called FABEL, run by GMD, St. Augustin [2]. Their concern has been storage and retrieval of cases and since in our project, we have concentrated on object combination and adaptation, we see this work as complementary. Other work includes the SEED project [5] where large numbers of cases are stored and indexed for retrieval using functional units. Although a case editor is a available for adaptation, no other computational support is reported. Our approach is different due to our capabilities to adapt complex objects through run-time parameterizations within an intelligent user interface.

An extension to CADSYN [24] employs constraint satisfaction techniques for verification and repair of adapted designs. CADSYN ensures only local consistency between constraints, thereby limiting its effectiveness to simple constraint networks where risks of divergence, looping and empty solution spaces are low. Our experience with geometric design has revealed that relevant constraint networks are highly interdependent and therefore, local consistency approaches are unreliable.

The ARCHIE system [9] was developed to help building designers during the initial exploratory stages of design. Previous designs are stored with annotations related to why things were done in particular ways. Architects perform this investigative work prior to addressing spatial aspects of designs. Since the ARCHIE system is not intended to generate geometrical information we view the IDIOM research and the ARCHIE system as complementary.

Closely related work is being performed by Giretti et al [7]. They report on a CBD system for architecture that supports graphical interaction. Their "theories" are similar to the models proposed in this paper and their "scenes" are analogous to groups of intelligent objects. However, there is no run-time parameterization and subsequent dimensionality reduction. Therefore, performance problems would be expected for designs of realistic size. In addition, it is not clear whether local or global consistency is achieved during constraint propagation.

7 Conclusions

Adaptation research has evolved from the study of modifying one case in a new context to combining and adapting information from several cases. The IDIOM system demonstrates that it is possible to perform spatial composition with cases by means of intelligent objects, domain models and user interaction. Incremental run-time parameterization of intelligent objects leads to consistent solutions nearly instantly for apartment layouts. We are currently extending the system to include soft constraints and more domain models.

Acknowledgments

This research is funded as part of the the National Priority Program in Computer Science (SPP-IF) and is a result of collaborative research with CAAD (Computer-Aided Architectural Design), ETH Zürich. Discussions and collaboration with Gerhard Schmitt (CAAD) have been most valuable. The authors would like to thank Christian Frei, Kefeng Hua, David Kurmann, Ruth Stalker for their ideas, collaboration and implementation of various versions of the IDIOM system. Finally, we are grateful for collaboration with two architectural firms, Philippe Guyot - Architects & Planners, Lausanne and Geninasca & Delfortrie Architects, Neuchâtel.

References

1. Bahktari S. and Bartsch-Spörl B. "Our perspective on using CBR in design problem solving" 1st European Workshop on CBR, Kaiserslauten, 1993
2. Bakhtari S. et al, "EWCBR93 : Contributions of FABEL" Fabel Report No. 17, GMD, Sankt Augustin, 1993
3. B. Dave, G. Schmitt, B. Faltings and I. Smith "Case-based design in architecture" *Artificial Intelligence in Design '94* 1994
4. Faltings, B. "Arc-consistency for continuous variables", Artificial Intelligence, **65**, 1994, pp 363-376.
5. Fleming U., "Case-based design in the SEED System", 1st Computing Congress, American Society of Civil Engineers, Washington, 1994
6. Flemming, U., R. Coyne, T. Glavin and M. Rychener, "A Generative Expert System for the Design of Building Layouts", AI in Engineering: Design, Elsevier 1988 pp 445-464.
7. Giretti, A., Spalazzi, L. and Lemma, M. "A.S.A. An interactive assistant to architectural design" Artificial Intelligence in Design '94, Kluwer, 1994, pp 93-108.
8. Goel, A.K. and Chandrasekaran, B. "Use of device models in adaptation of design cases" DARPA CBR Workshop, 1989, pp100-109.
9. Goel, A.K. and Kolodner, J.L. "Towards a case-based tool for aiding conceptual design problem solving" DARPA CBR Workshop, 1991, pp109-120.
10. Hinrichs, T. R. and Kolodner, J. L. "The Roles of Adaptation in Case-based Design" in: DARPA Case-based Reasoning Workshop, 1991, pp.121–132
11. Hinrichs, T. R. "Problem solving in open worlds" Lawrence Erlbaum, 1992
12. Hua, K. "Case-based design of geometric structures" Thesis No 1270, Swiss Federal Institute of Technology, Lausanne, 1994.
13. Hua K., Smith, I., Faltings, B., Shih, S., and Schmitt, G., "Adaptation of Spatial Design Cases" *Artificial Intelligence in Design '92*, Kluwer, Dordrecht, NL, 1992
14. Hua K., Smith, I. and Faltings, B. "Integrated case-based building design" Topics in case-based reasoning, Lecture Notes in AI, 837, Springer-Verlag, 1994, pp436-445.
15. Keane, M.T. "Analogical asides on case-based reasoning" Topics in case-based reasoning, Lecture Notes in AI, 837, Springer-Verlag, 1994, pp21-32.
16. Kolodner, J., Case-based reasoning, Morgan Kaufmann, San Mateo CA, 1993
17. Maher, M.L. and Zhang, D.M. "Case-based reasoning in design" Artificial Intelligence in Design, Butterworth-Heinemann, 1991, pp 137-150.
18. Navinchandra, D. "Case based reasoning in CYCLOPS" DARPA Case-Based Reasoning Workshop, 1988, pp286-291.
19. Schmitt, G., "Design reasoning with cases and intelligent objects" International Association of Bridge and Structural Engineering, Report 68, 1993 pp 77-87
20. Smyth, B and Keane, M.T. "Retrieving adaptable cases" Lecture Notes in AI, 837, Springer-Verlag, 1994, pp209-220.
21. Sycara, K.P. and Navinchandra, D. "Influences: A thematic abstraction for creative use of multiple cases" DARPA CBR Workshop, 1991, pp133-144.
22. Tommelein, I.D. "SightPlan - An expert system for designing construction site layouts", PhD Thesis, Stanford University, 1989.
23. Voss, A. "The need for knowledge acquisition in case-based reasoning - some experiences from an architectural domain", 11th ECAI, John Wiley, 1994, pp463-467.
24. Zhang, D.M. and Maher, M.L. "Using CBR for the synthesis of structural systems" Inter. Assoc. for Bridge and Structural Engineering, Report 68, 1993, pp143-152.

CBR and Machine Learning for Combustion System Design

Jutta Stehr

Daimler Benz AG

Dept. F3S/E

Postfach 2360

89013 Ulm, Germany

email: stehr@dbag.ulm.DaimlerBenz.com

Abstract

Nowadays the automotive industry has to face two major challenges. First products must meet continually increasing government requirements on fuel economy and low exhaust emission. Second the market demands product variety and short production cycles. The automobile's combustion system determines the exhaust emission rate, combustion system engineering is one of the crucial steps in the development process. Cylinder head design is a good example of showing how enhanced AI technologies like CBR and Machine Learning support high-level eingineering design tasks.

The work described was coordinated in a joint project between the Daimler-Benz research group on Thermo and Fluid Dynamics and our reasearch group on Machine Learning with the aim of improving of cylinder head engineering. This paper proposes how Machine Learning and specifically Case-based Reasoning (CBR) transform a traditional database containing both geometry and air-motion data into a so called *experience memory* for cylinder head design. We will present the initial steps of our database analysis in terms of different learning algorithms, then use the extracted knowledge to develop case-based design retrieval and quality prediction modules.

Keywords

Case-based Reasoning, Engineering Design Support, Knowledge Discovery in Databases

1. Introduction

Analogical reasoning and experience acquired in previous problem solutions have been found to be a powerful human problem solving technique [POL49], [DÖR76]. For a variety of tasks, people rely on experience when dealing with new problems. Companies only recently begun to realise that human expertise is a vital factor in market competition. Thus, corporate or organizational memories [WAL91] were developed with the idea of not only preserving existing knowledge but also making it accessible for laymen.

Traditional IT systems are not well-suited for implementing a corporate memory. Since conventional databases are designed for storing *data* and conventional programs are designed to manipulate it, searching a database for *information* on how to solve an actual problem is almost impossible.

Enhanced AI methods such as Case-based Reasoning (CBR) and other Machine Learning techniques can fill this gap. CBR has proved its potential of using experience knowledge for actual problem solving in a broad range of classification and diagnosis domains (for a good overview see [KOL93]. In fact, even industrial requirements in those domains are met as the variety of help desk-applications show [SIM89], [ACO92].

Applying CBR to other types of problem-solving tasks like planning and engineering design has been successful in more academic domains as well [HAM86], [KOL92]. Bridging the gap between academic research and industrial application is in progress [FAB92]. Some reasons for the small number of industrial systems (e.g. [BAR89]) may be:

1. Design engineers are highly respected for their knowledge and problem solving potential. These experts usually have psychological barriers against nearly all types of AI-based tools. Work on general problem solvers has led to their view that these systems are not meant to support but instead to replace the human expert.

2. In contrast to the newly implemented Help-Desk applications mentioned above, typical IT support for design tasks already exist, e.g. CAD tools, design databases. To be accepted, a CBR system has to fit seamlessly into both the designer's workflow and the existing IT environment.

3. Bridging the gap between academic research and practical application in industry usually takes 20 years. The idea of intelligent design support is a new one compared to classification and prediction support, with statistical research dating back to the 1950s. Only little experience is available on how to design a CBR system for complex and ill-structured design domains, not to mention a coherent methodology.

The work we report on in this paper mainly tackles the third point mentioned above. Integrating the developed CBR system into an existing IT environment and overcoming the prejudices towards AI-based tools are challenges we will be confronted with later.

The paper is organised as follows: In section 2 we give an in-depth introduction to the application domain of automotive cylinder head design. Section 3 presents the approach we took in developing solutions for the retrieval and prediction tasks required. Projected work is discussed in section 4.

2. Combustion System Engineering

Meeting the continually growing number of government requirements on fuel economy and low exhaust emission rates and the market demands for short production cycles and a variety in the range of product have led to the challenging situation that motor engineers have to develop an even greater number of automobile engines than ever before in less and less time.

2.1. The Automobile's Combustion System

The combustion system consisting of the combustion chamber inside the cylinder and the cylinder head with its parts is the heart of a motor (see Figure 1).

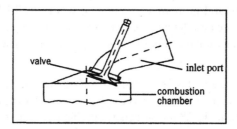

Figure 1: Cylinder Head

Optimum air-fuel mixture in the cylinder guarantees low smoke levels and low exhaust emissions. The mixture is determined by flow and in-cylinder air-motion values which are directly influenced by the geometry of the combustion chamber within the cylinder and the different cylinder head parts. The refinement of automobile engines is a research area of worldwide interest [TAK87], [BOE90].

Different types of inlet ports, their arrangement, the type of after casting-treatment of the port's inner surface, and components' characteristics produce different flow and air-motion values. Most of the relations between the cylinder head geometry and the flow/air-motion values are known: The flow value depends directly on the inlet port's cross section for example while the inlet port's curve determines the air-motion value.

The optimum values for these parameters vary from engine type to engine type. The rule of thumb is that the higher the flow and the air-motion value the better the air-fuel mixture generated by the cylinder head. Unfortunately increasing one parameter almost always reduces the other: e.g using 2 inlet ports instead of one results in a higher flow value but as a rule the air-motion value is worse because of air-fuel stream interference..

2.1.a. Cylinder Head Design

Deriving the flow and air-motion profiles from the requirements on the maximum exhaust emission rate is the first step in cylinder head design. When the original design is developed, a prototype of the cylinder head is built and evaluated in a port-blowing-box test. Ordinarily a first design has to be improved because it performs worse than it theoretically should. A good design engineer is guided by experience when deciding which parts of the design need to be refined and how. Nevertheless, in most cases various iterations in design, building and evaluation have to be performed until all requirements are met. Most problems arise because the domain is extremely complex due to knowledge on fluid dynamics within the cylinder is incomplete, often contradictory and vague.

One approach on improving this time-consuming process is by using simulation techniques to evaluate the cylinder head on the design level, thereby omitting the step of building a cylinder head prototype. Unfortunately the knowledge on how to develop a cylinder head's volume grid model for combustion simulation is sparsely spread. Moreover, model construction and simulation nowadays are almost as time-consuming and as expensive as the conventional design process.

Quality and speed of volume grid generation and fluid dynamics simulation are certain to increase over the years. However, it is doubtful whether the time required for the simulation can be reduced to a couple of CPU minutes at a designer's workstation. Chances are that only a limited number of the cylinder heads developed will be evaluated by simulation.

2.1.b. Improving Cylinder Head Design by Machine Learning

Improvement of the cylinder head development process is unavoidable. Machine Learning techniques seem to be a good mid- or even long-term solution since data on old designs is accessible. For design support our partners provide design engineers with a traditional IMS database, the Fluid Field Characteristics (FFC) database, which stores both design parameters and quality measurements on more than 10.000 cylinder heads.

The aims of the ML approach are twofold:

- Since the domain theory of cylinder head design is weak, experts are not sure whether the design information stored in the FFC database is complete and relevant for quality assessment. We hope to improve the domain model during the project by identifying the most influential design parameters.

- In discussion with cylinder head design engineers at Mercedes-Benz, we learned that any IT-based design support has to deal with typical questions questions:

  1. What ist the abstract concept of cylinder heads showing a certain flow/air-motion profile?
  2. What other cylinder head designs meet the specified requirements?
  3. What are the flow/air-motion values of a design consisting of two inlet ports of type X in a 115° arrangement and with a valve diameter of 31 mm?

We decided to develop a design support module consisting of a case-based design retrieval module, a quality prediction module, which might be also case-based, and a pattern-extraction module operating directly on the FFC database (see Figure 2):

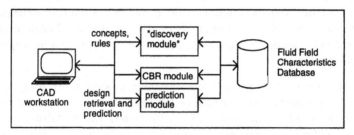

Figure 2: System architecture

A purely case-based solution is not suited for the support module since concept derivation is difficult to achieve using CBR. We chose a desision-tree generating ML algorithm for providing abstract knowledge (see point 1 above). The other two kinds of information mentioned can be obtained by a case-based approach:

- Case-based retrieval is a natural approach to implement search for similar objects.

- For a number of reasons we consider CBR as helpful for quality assessment:
  - Besides CBR all prediction techniques (e.g. regression analysis, symbolic ML algorithms, neural networks) are not suited well to deal with dynamic data. The FFC database is a dynamic database since every year it is augmented with data on new designs.
  - Since the domain is slightly chaotic there certainly are unstable regions in which prediction is almost impossible. These neighborhoods are hard to identify with generalization techniques. A solution can be to provide the design engineer with both the quality prediction and the cases used to let him decide on reliability.
  - It is known that most learning algorithms and particularly k-Nearest Neighbor Matching perform better when domain knowledge on attribute relevance is integrated. This knowledge can be easily integrated by adjusting attribute weights accordingly.

As automated adaptation of existing designs was considered an optional feature by domain experts, we will not focus on adaptation in the current project. Please note that our approach to predicting cylinder head quality will exclusively tackle routine design tasks [BRO89]. The domain of cylinder head design is too ill-structured (see Section 2.b) to allow analogical reasoning for quality prediction of dramatically new designs.

3. Knowledge Discovery and Quality Assessment in the FFC Database

As our activities are meant to improve expert knowledge too, we started with a knowledge discovery step. Knowledge discovery in databases (KDD), or data mining, is a new research topic with roots in data analysis, statistics, machine learning and expert systems [PIA91]. Activities are targeted of transforming the continually increasing amount of useless data stored everywhere in large databases into useful information. Depending on the task, e.g. classification, prediction, forecasting, planning, the database is searched for typical patterns. A KDD system integrates various Machine Learning and statistical algorithms to identify clusters, rules, dependencies, exceptions, etc., depending on the task to be supported.

The Esprit project Statlog [MIC94], an empirical comparisons of different ML methods, showed that no single classification or prediction method performs best in all possible domains. Therefore we conducted several classification experiments with symbolic and subsymbolic learning algorithms. Special emphasis was laid on k-Nearest Neighbor Matching. As it is known that the technique is sensitive to irrelevant attributes [AHA91] we used domain knowledge both from expert opinion and KDD results to experiment with the attribute weights used in the distance function.

3.1 Data Analysis

In analysing the FFC database we were inspired by colleages' recently proposed task model for KDD [WIR95]. The in-depth analysis of data is necessary because cylinder head design is an ill-structured domain since it lacks a general domain theory, knowledge is not complete, often contradictory and vague.

We decided on experimenting with decision-tree generating algorithms first. In our view decision trees can be interpreted as domain models containing hints on both the completeness of the design description and the relevance of the design parameters. Obtaining sufficiently accurate classification or prediction results proves the completeness of the design parameters. Stable trees regarding structure and selected attributes are the basis for distinguishing between the highly relevant root attribute, relevant lower layer attributes and irrelevant attributes never selected.

Data Preparation

We started evaluating the CBR approach with a database sample. It consisted of 282 cylinder head designs for one specific diesel engine type. In the first step of pattern extraction, we chose homogeneous data and not a statistical sample. The domain experts who are familiar with the engine type can evaluate the established patterns. Another advantage of this sample was the reduction in the number of geometry-related attributes from more than 60 to 8 by discarding all attributes with fixed parameters.

After the preparation step the examples had the following characteristics:

- 8 statistically independant attributes (4 numerical, 1 ordered, 3 discrete)
- the class of the example (good, bad) given by an expert according to the flow and air-motion values

We divided the examples into training sets consisting of 2/3 of the examples and a test set amounting to 1/3 of the data.

Knowledge Discovery

We analysed the data using

- Quinlan's C4.5 [QUI93] and
- commercially available simple feedforward Neural Networks [CHE94]

C4.5 is an ID3-like decision tree generating algorithm suited for classification tasks. From training examples a set of if-then-else-ules is derived on the basis of the information content of each attribute. The results were promising since we achieved simple classification trees with an average classification error rate of 8.5%. The trees consequently showed a similar structure and always took the same set of 5 attributes into account. The attributes C4.5 found relevant for the classification were only partly identical to expert opinion (see Figure 3).

In a second classification experiment we tried different neural networks - a 2-, 3-, and 4-layer feedforward network - on the same task. We derived a hypothesis of what attributes are relevant by interpreting the weights the input-layer neurons had after the training phase. The networks performed significantly worse. Here the average error rate was 14%. The attributes with the highest absolute weights match neither expert opinion nor C4.5 findings (see Figure 3).

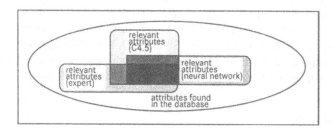

Figure 3: Non-Matching of classification-relevant attributes

3.2 Implementing Similarity-based Classification

For reference purposes we started a similarity-based classification on the normalised dataset without a refined domain model. We used unweighted k-Nearest Neighbor

Matching utilizing the Euclidian distance function to define the similarity of two instances X and Y:

- Similarity $(X, Y) = \sqrt{\sum_{i=1}^{d}\left(x_i - y_i\right)^2}$, d : number of attributes

We found that unweighted 1-NN-Matching performed best with average error rates of 8,5%. 3-, 5-, and 7-unweighted Nearest-Neighbor-Matching show average error rates of 16% (see Table 1).

In order to reduce error rates, we applied domain knowledge to implement weighted k-Nearest Neighbor Matching. The weights came from

- expert opinion on attributes' relevance
- C4.5 classification trees
- Neural Network weights
- a combination of expert knowledge and C4.5 results
- a random setting

It showed that weighted k-NN (k>1) Matching performed only slightly better than the unweighted one whereas error rates were lowest when using unweighted 1-NN Matching. Deriving weights from both expert knowledge and C4.5 findings was the best choice. Both expert knowledge and C4.5 rules alone performed slightly worse. Weighting the terms of the Euclidian distance function according to Neural network weights gave a classification error worse than a random weight setting.

		1-NN	3-NN	5-NN	7-NN
1	unweighted	8.5	16	16	16
2	experts' weights	9.5	13.8	14.9	13.8
3	C4.5 weights	9.5	14.9	14.9	13.8
4	Neural Net. weights	9.5	14.9	16	22
5	Combin. 2, 3	9.5	12.8	13.8	13.8
8	random weights	9.5	12.8	16	17

Table 1: Results of k-NN Experiments (Error Rates in %)

3.3. Discussion of Results

We presented two approaches to provide design engineers with different kinds of information needed during cylinder head design. A first step consisted of extracting knowledge from the design database provided, a second step was perfomed by evaluating several informed and uninformed quality assessment techniques.

The general concepts C4.5 derived from the data were quite good both in terms of decision tree stability and classification accuracy, i.e. they performed equal to the expert model. Problems arose because experts found the trees not intuitively understandable and the rules concluded therefrom do not match their domain model of which attributes are relevant. We hope to overcome the first problem by searching for ways how to visualize the results so design engineers are able to improve their domain knowledge. The second problem is tightly coupled to the overall acceptance of the support module and will require constant discussion with design engineers.

The empirical comparison of different machine learning algorithms in the domain of cylinder head design were ambiguous. The simplified version of classifying cylinder head designs led to error rates too high to accept. The best results were obtained when including domain knowledge into the similarity measure. Instead of eliminating irrelevant attributes [AHA94], learning weights [WES91] or applying genetic algorithms to adjust weights [KEL91], we kept it simple and derive weights from induced decision trees. The method of Cardie [CAR93] who reduced the attribute set by discarding all attributes which did not occur in the decision tree, was not promising. Classification accuracy improved when we weighted the attributes according to their layer in the tree, e.g. the root attribute and his immediate sons were weighted highest, lower layer attributes were weighted with medium weights and all other with small weights.

4. Conclusion and Future Work

In the next steps we will focus on improving classification accuracy by integrating more background knowledge into the similarity measure. As it is generally recognized that relationships between the geometrical attributes exist we will treat those dependencies. Another improvement is expected through integration of more construction-specific knowledge. From this point of view the database consists of positive examples only because impossible geometries have not been built at all. In addition next experiments will be conducted on a larger data sample to determine whether a global classification/prediction function is possible or a set of locally operating functions has to be developed.

The next project phase will not cover merely data analysis and the algorithmic part of case-based retrieval and prediction. Together with a domain expert, we intend to investigate visualisation aspects of both the KDD and the design retrieval steps. For system design purposes, we will research the need for information during cylinder head design process. Then intuitive visualisations for the communication of abstract knowledge on causal relationships, classification rules and exceptions will be developed.

5. References

[ACO92]   T.Acorn, S.Walden. SMART: Support Management cultivated reasoning technology for Compaq customer service. Proceedings of AAAI-92. MIT Press. 1992.

[AHA91]   D. Aha, D. Kibler, M. Albert. Instance-Based Learning Algorithms. Machine Learning 6 (1). 1991.

[AHA94]   D. Aha, R. Bankert. Feature Selection for Case-Based Classification of Cloud Types: An empirical comparison. Workshop Notes on Case-Based Reasoning. AAAI-94. 1994.

[BAR89]   R. Barletta, D. Hennessy. Case Adaptation in Autoclave Layout Design. DARPA Case-Based Reasoning Workshop. Morgan Kaufmann Publishers. 1989.

[BOE90]   C. D. de Boer, R. J. R. Johns, D. W. Grigg. B. M. Train. I. Denbratt. J.R. Linna. Refinement with perforamnce and economy for four-valve automotive engines. Society of Automotive Engineers. 1990.

[BRO89]   D. C. Brown, B. Chandrasekaran. Design Problem Solving: Knowledge Structures and Control Strategies. Pitman. 1989.

[CAR93]   C. Cardie. Using Decision Trees to Improve Case-Based Learning. Proc. of the 10th Int. Conference on Machine Learning. Morgan Kaufman. 1993.

[CHE94]   Cheshire Engineering Corporation. Neuralyst. User's Guide. 1994.

[COS93]   S. Cost, S. Salzberg. A weighted Nearest Neighbor Algorithm for Learning with Symbolic Features. Machine Learning 10 (1). 1993.

[DÖR76]   D. Dörner. Problemlösung als Informationsverarbeitung. Verlag W. Kohlhammer. 1976.

[FAB92]   FABEL-Consortium. Survey of FABEL, Fabel Report No. 2, GMD, 1992.

[HAM89]   K. Hammond. Chef: A Model of Case-Based Planning. Proceedings of the Nat. Conference on Artificial Intelligence (AAAI 86). MIT Press 1986.

[KEL91]   J. D. Kelly, L. Davis. A Hybrid Genetic Algorithm for Classification. Proc. of the 12zh Int. Joint Conference on Artificial Intellicence. 1991.

[KOL93]   J. Kolodner. Case-Based Reasoning. Morgan Kaufmann Publishers. 1993.

[LIN77]   P. H. Lindsay, D. A. Norman. Human Information Processing. Academic Press. 1977.

[MIC94]   D. Michie, D. J. Spiegelhalter, C. C. Taylor (eds.). Machine Learning, Neural and Statistical Classification. Ellis Horwood. 1994.

[PEA92]   M. Pearce, A. K. Goel, J. L. Kolodner, C. Zimring, L. Sentosa, R. Billington. Case-Based Design Support. IEEE Expert. October 1992.

[PIA91]   G. Piatetsky-Shapiro, W. J. Frawley (eds.). Knowledge Discovery in Databases. MIT Press. 1991.

[POL49]   G. Polya. Schule des Denkens. Francke Verlag. 1949.

[SIM92]   E. Simoudis. Using Case-Based Retrieval for Customer Technical Support. IEEE Expert. October 1992.

[QUI93]   J. R. Quinlan. C4.5 Programs For Machine Learning. Morgan Kaufmann Publishers. 1993.

[TAK87]   H. Takahashi, T. Ishida, K. Sato. Improvement of Diesel Emgine Performance by Variable Swirl System. Int. Off-Highway & Powerplant Congress. Society of Automotive Engineers. 1987.

[WAL91]   J. P. Walsh, G. R. Ungson. Organizational Memory. Academy of Management Review. 16 (1). 1991.

[WES91]   S. Weß. PATDEX/2 - ein System zum adaptiven, fallfokussierenden Lernen in technischen Diagnosesituasitionen. SEKI Working Paper SWP-91-01. Universität Kaiserslautern. 1991.

[WIR95]   T. Reinartz, R. Wirth. The need for a Task Model for KDD. Accepted by the MLnet Familiarisation Workshop on Machine Learning, Statistics and Knowledge Discovery in Databases. 1995.

KBS Maintenance as Learning Two-Tiered Domain Representation *

Gennady Agre

Institute of Information Technologies - Bulgarian Academy of Sciences
Acad. G. Bonchev St. Block 29A, 1113 Sofia, Bulgaria
Email: agre@iinf.bg

Abstract. The paper deals with the problem of improving problem-solving behavior of traditional KBS in the course of its real operation which is a part of the maintenance task. The solution of the problem is searched in integration of the KBS with a specially designed case-based reasoning module used for correcting solutions produced by the KBS. Special attention is paid to the methods of case matching and reconciling conflicts between CBR and RBR. The proposed solution for both problems is based on treating the maintenance task as a problem for learning two-tiered domain representation. From this view point rules form the first domain tier reflecting existing strong patterns in the representation of domain concepts, while the second tier is formed by the newly solved cases along with a special domain-dependent procedure for case matching. The main ideas of the approach are illustrated by the results of some experiments with the experimental system CoRCase.

1 Introduction

Recent experience in applying KBS in real domains has shown that for a KBS to be commercially viable it must be able to respond to the changes in the domain knowledge which it is based on i.e. it needs to be maintained. An important part of the maintenance task recognized as crucially important for KBSs [7] is the problem of developing methods for improving KBS problem solving behavior *in the course* of the system operation. Moreover, the ability of the system to avoid recurrent errors may be seen now as an implicit requirement for current KBSs. Promising results in this direction have been achieved by using case-based reasoning [11, 9, 1].

The problem addressed in the present paper is how to increase the correctness of the solutions produced by the "traditional" knowledge-based systems (i.e. the ones not originally designed as case-based) during their use in a real open environment. The detailed analysis of the process of real system operation [2] suggests the idea to search a solution of the problem in designing a CBR module able to correct solutions produced by the original KBS. Thus the system own

---

* This research was partially supported by National Science Foundation, Grant I-416/94

problem solving experience accumulated during its operation can be used as a source for corrections.

The architecture of such CBR module and the description of the principles of integration RBR and CBR are described in detail in [2, 3]. The present paper focuses on such crucial points affecting the effectiveness of approaches for integration CBR with other paradigms for problem solving as selection of an appropriate similarity measure (which is fundamental for organization of case matching) and determination of a method for reconciling paradigm conflicts.

The structure of the paper is as follows: the next section contains a brief description of the architecture for combining RBR and CBR which is necessary for better understanding of the approach to the problems addressed. In Section 3 transformation of the expert rules into two-tiered representation is considered. Sections 4 and 5 describe how the processes of case matching and conflict reconciling are organized. Section 6 presents the result of testing the proposed approach on two medical domains - prognosis of breast cancer recurrence and location of primary tumor and in Section 7 the approach is compared with related works.

2 Outline of the Approach to Integrating RBR and CBR

2.1 The Background Knowledge

The main idea of improving the performance of a KBS consists in constructing a special CBR module which is able to correct erroneous system solutions based on system own problem solving experience. The background knowledge for such module is the knowledge in and about the original KBS. The KBS is assumed to be an abstract nonprobabilistic rule-based system intended to solve a classification task. The task is considered as a hypothesis driven process. The RBR-system is able to perform both backward and forward chaining since forward chaining is normally used for generation of a list of differential diagnoses and backward chaining - for testing of hypotheses. A hypothesis (diagnosis) is considered to be confirmed if there is a satisfied rule having the diagnosis as its conclusion. A hypothesis is considered to be rejected if all rules leading to it have failed. The system stops its operation either if a confirmed hypothesis has been found or all generated hypotheses have been tested and rejected.

For simplicity in the rest part of the paper we will consider expert rules as flat structures which directly associate conjunctions of the problem features with problem solutions. This is not a real restriction since every rule base can be represented in such a way applying, for example, explanation-based generalization techniques [15] during KBS development phase.

2.2 The Case-Based Module Architecture

The architecture of the module is an example of a general architecture of a case-based planner [9] adapted for solution of the classification task. At the beginning, the current situation obtained *after* solving the initial problem by the RBR-system is analyzed by the **Analyzer** which produces a set of indexes used for determining cases similar to the problem at hand. The index information along with a predefined similarity metrics is used by the **Retriever** to find in the case memory the most similar case whose solution may be applied to the current problem. The decision about what solution should be preferred - the rule-based or the case-based one - is the responsibility of the **Modifier**. The final solution is given to the end user and the **Storer** forms and "remembers" the current case into the memory.

After receiving a "feedback" from the user who approves or rejects the final system solution, the **Repairer** starts its operation. In case of approval, the **Repairer** sends the confirmation to the **Storer** which then decides whether it is worthwhile to continue remembering this correctly solved case or it may be forgotten. Otherwise, the **Repairer** "explains" the failure using a failure vocabulary and the failed case. In such situations the **Repairer** creates failure predictors which play roles of indexes used by the **Analyzer** and allowing to avoid repetition of similar failures in the future.

2.3 The Memory Organization and Indexing

A case is represented as a single information structure containing the case name, a list of case features (attribute - value pairs) and the case solution - a category name obtained after the case classification. The use of CBR for improving the performance of the rules leads to employing an indexing schema in which a case is indexed by all possible roles it may play in the process of rule-based problem solving. Each solved case is indexed as *true negative (TN)* by each hypothesis rejected during problem solving and as *true positive (TP)* by the solution found along with the name of the rule inferred this solution.

TP- and TN-indexes are used for indexing cases which have been successfully solved by the RBR system, i.e. when the user has confirmed the solutions of these cases. A case is indexed as *false positive (FP)* by the rule if it satisfies the rule but the real case solution differs from the inferred one. A case is indexed as *false negative* with respect to a given category which is the real solution of the case if it has been tested and rejected as a hypothesis by the rules.

A special index is used to specify a failure which is caused by an inappropriate application of the domain knowledge rather then by its incorrectness. Such kind of failures may occur due to some deficiencies in, for example, the mechanism of formation of a list of differential diagnosis or because of erroneous termination of the process of hypotheses testing. A failed case is indexed as *untested* with respect to its real solution if the solution has not been tested by the rules during the problem solving session.

3 Converting Rules to Two-Tiered Representation

The proposed method for integration of rules and cases may be seen naturally as a method for learning *two-tiered representation* of the domain concepts [5, 14].

The rules may be considered as the first tier explicitly describing the base concept properties known by the expert *before* starting the real operation of the system. The procedure of *flexible matching* along with the memory of cases stored *after* starting the real system operation form the second tier which implicitly defines new boundaries of the domain concepts. The indexing scheme described above connects both tiers and coordinates their cooperation.

In contrast to other approaches for learning two-tiered representation we do not need to learn the first tier - it is known a priory and according to the specificity of the maintenance task can not be changed in spite of its incorrectness and incompleteness. So we should concentrate our efforts on learning only the second tier. Unfortunately, the approach proposed by Michalski and Bergadano [5, 14] is based on the rule significance calculated as the ratio of the number of training examples covered by a rule to the total number of training examples. Since we assume that the set of training examples used by the expert is not known the approach can not be applied.

To avoid the problem with the absence of training examples inducing the rules forming the first tier we consider these rules as generalized "typical" cases (or instances) of the domain concepts. Each rule is interpreted as a case represented by a list of features - attribute - value pairs extracted from the rule conditions. The rule conclusion defines the case classification. The typicality of a case is defined as its family resemblance and measured by the ratio of its intra-concept similarity to its inter-concept similarity. The intra-concept similarity of a case is its average similarity to other instances of the same concept and the inter-concept similarity - its average similarity to instances of all others concepts. The similarity $Sim(case^1(C_n), case^2(C_m))$ between two cases with known classifications is defined as the inverse of the distance between these two cases [19]:

$$Sim(case^1(C_n), case^2(C_m)) = 1 - Dist(case^1(C_n), case^2(C_m))$$

$Dist(case^1(C_n), case^2(C_m))$ is computed as the normalized Euclidean distance between the corresponding cases:

$$Dist(case^1(C_n), case^2(C_m)) = \sqrt{\frac{1}{k} * \sum_{j=1}^{k} w_j^2 * [case_j^1(C_n) - case_j^2(C_m)]^2}$$

where $case_j^i$ is the the value of the j-th attribute of case $case^i$, $k = |A^1 \cup A^2|$, A^i $(i = 1, 2)$ - the set of attributes of the corresponding case. Weight w_j denotes the importance of j-th attribute of the case and is calculated as the ratio of the number of all case containing this attribute to the whole number of all cases (rules) in the rule base. When the j-th attribute is symbolic-valued (in the paper we restrict only to this kind of attributes), $case_j^1(C_n) - case_j^2(C_m) = 1$ if they are different and $case_j^1(C_n) - case_j^2(C_m) = 0$ otherwise. For missing values $(case_j^1(C_n) - case_j^2(C_m))^2 = \frac{1}{L_j} * (1 - \frac{1}{L_j})$, where L_j is the number of possible values of the j-th attribute.

4 Case Matching

Similar to [19] each case is associated with a weight used for measuring the distance between a new instance (a case to be solved) and the stored case. The distance between a stored case X and a new instance Y is defined as:

$$DIST(X, Y) = W_X * Dist(X, Y)$$

where $Dist(X, Y)$ is the distance measure described in the previous section and W_X is the weight of X. The weight of a stored case is simply reciprocal of its typicality. As a result a more typical case will cover a larger area in the case space than a less typical one and an exceptional case will cover a very small area. So the proposed method for measuring distance in the case space provides a natural way for combining rules (generalized cases) and particular cases which are not covered or false covered by these rules.

The matching procedure is organized as a nearest neighbour algorithm in which a new instance is classified according to the class of the best matched case - the case with the minimum value of distance $DIST$. During the matching process the retrieved cases are used as templates for requesting the user about attributes of a new instance with still unknown values. When more than one best case belonging to different classes are found the most typical one (i.e. with the minimum value of weight W) is preferred. This allows us to effectively process cases with incomplete description i.e. cases in which values of some attributes are missing and can not be acquired from the user.

The distance is calculated according to the described above formula with one main difference - only a part of the attributes of the new instance is used in the calculation. Notice, that every new problem which should be solved by the CBR module has been formed as a result of a problem solving process determined by the initial problem description and the reasoning architecture of the original rule-based system. Thus the problem description may contain different features acquired during attempting to confirm different hypotheses. When measuring the similarity between an instance with unknown classification and a case belonging to a known category, it is naturally to consider only such features of this instance which are *relevant* to the category of the case. For each category the corresponding set of relevant attributes is defined as the union of all attributes which the rules corresponding to this category refer to. In such a way we avoid the influence of any redundant (for a particular category) features. Of course, this restricts the types of possible errors in the expert rules (i.e. a missing attribute) but since we assume that these rules are intensively refined during KBS development, the presence of such flagrant errors as not using some relevant attributes at all is unlikely to remain unnoticed.

5 Reconciling Conflicts between CBR and RBR

Conflicts between CBR and RBR occur in two situations: when the RBR system can not find any solution of the current problem (the so called "incomplete" situation) and when there is a failure predictor pointing that the problem solution found by the rules may be rejected by the user (as it had already happened in the similar situation in the system's past). In the previous version of the proposed approach for integrating CBR and RBR [3] such conflicts have been solved by applying a simple threshold scheme in which the threshold values used for evaluating similarity between matching cases have been determined ad hoc. This deficiency may be avoided by changing the set of cases to be retrieved. But before describing the method for constructing this set, we will discuss the question of when and how a case should be stored.

5.1 Storing New Cases

In our approach all cases erroneously solved by the system are stored. Such cases are indexed as false positive or true negative with respect to the faulty system solution and false negative, true positive or untested (depending on the results of the failure analysis made by the CBR module) with respect to the real solution of the problem. The solved case is also indexed as true negative with respect to all hypotheses tested and rejected by the system during problem solving session. So a stored case may be considered as a particular instance of some different generalized cases from the point of view of the semantics included in the corresponding index connecting the case and its "generalizations" (e.g. as a "positive" example confirming a rule or as a "negative" exception of the rule etc.).

A case successfully solved by the system is stored only if its solution has been found as a result of reconciling a conflict between the paradigms and an identical case has not been stored. Such cases confirm the correctness of applying the specific rule or using the specific case to obtain the problem solution.

For each newly stored case the value of weight W reflecting the case typicality is calculated. The calculation procedure is the same as for the rules but applied not only to all generalized cases but also to all solved cases which have not been covered by the generalized ones (i.e. indexed as false negative exceptions of the rules) [2].

5.2 Selection of Cases to be Retrieved

The set of cases to be retrieved is determined by comparing the main characteristics of the current situation (the rule which has inferred the problem solution and the set of rejected hypotheses) with indexes connecting the set to the cases stored in the memory. To avoid using a threshold scheme for evaluation of the degree of similarity of the best matched case, the set of cases to be retrieved is formed not only by the exceptional cases rejecting the particular rule but also by the cases confirming the rule. Since the set of such "positive" cases (i.e indexed as true positive with respect to the rule) may be empty the generalized case representing this rule is also retrieved and matched.

---

[2] As it is mentioned before, only relevant case features are used in this calculation.

When the CBR module tries to find a solution in an incomplete situation all generalized cases associated with the rejected hypotheses (suspected problem solutions) are retrieved along with all solved cases uncovered by the corresponding rules.

In both situations the final system solution is determined by the solution of the best matched case.

6 Empirical Evaluation

The presented approach for improving performance of traditional RBR systems by their integration with a specially designed CBR module has been implemented in the experimental system CoRCase (Correcting Rules by Cases), whose major components include a simple rule-based classification system, a method to convert rules to two-tiered representation, and a CBR module. The system performance will be illustrated in two medical domains - prognosis of breast cancer recurrence and location of primary tumor - well known in ML community data bases and used as test-beds for different ML algorithms. The data has been prepared by M. Zwitter and M. Soklic from the University Medical Center, Institute of Oncology, Ljubljana, Slovenia. The main characteristics of these databases are summarized in Table 1. (Both bases contain examples with missing values of some attributes).

Table 1: A characterization of two problem domains

Data base	Examples	Classes	Attrs	Vals/Attr
Breast cancer	286	2	9	5.8
Primary tumor	339	22	17	2.2

The first series of experiments was intended to evaluate the quality of the transformation of rules into two-tiered representation and the adequacy of the described above similarity measure. 40% of the examples in the breast cancer data base were randomly selected as a training sample and the rest of the database formed the database with testing examples. 5 sets of training examples and 5 set of testing ones have been constructed. This procedure was repeated for 50%, 60% and 70% of the examples. The training sets were used to induce corresponding sets of rules. Since we wanted to prove applicability of the transformation onto the expert rules with unknown principles of building, two algorithms of different types were used to simulate the rules. The first one was an ID3-like algorithm inducing discriminating rules and the second one was an AQ-type one producing covering rules [12]. Then the CoRCase system transformed each set of rules into two-tiered representation which was tested on the corresponding set of testing examples.

In order to evaluate the contribution of CBR and RBR to the final classification accuracy of the system four different algorithms for problem solving were tested. The first one was pure RBR implemented by the RBR system integrated in the CoRCase system. In the second algorithm the solution was searched by matching a problem at hand against the generalized ("typical") cases produced after rule transformation. In this algorithm (which we named TC-search) no testing cases had been stored. The third algorithm was incremental extension of the second one. In this algorithm each solved case had been stored and then used for searching solution of the next problem. This algorithms may be seen as a naive CBR method for problem solving with exhaustive search in the case space. And the last algorithm (named CoRCase) is an implementation of the method for integrating RBR and CBR described in the present paper. Since in CBR the final result is affected by the order in which cases are solved each next testing case was selected randomly. In order to obtain average evaluation of the algorithm accuracy each database was tested three times. The results describing the average of the 15 experiments per sample (from 40% to 70%) are presented in Fig. 1 and Fig. 2 as well as in Table 2 in which the results of experiments with training sets with 70% size are summarized.

The main result of these experiments is that they show a stable improvement in the classification accuracy obtained by the cooperative operation of RBR and CBR. This improvement is practically independent on the size of the training samples used to induce the rules and on the type of the algorithms generating these rules. This proves the adequacy of the chosen similarity measure and allows to expect the same behavior of the system in the case of rules build by the experts.

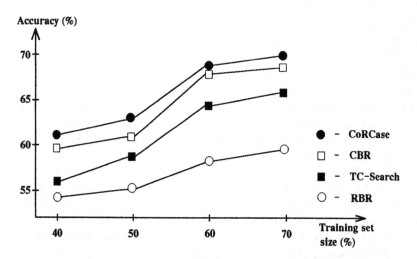

Fig. 1. The results of experiments with ID3-like rules

Another interesting result is the good behavior of the TC-search and the naive CBR algorithms. This may be explained by the fact [5] that the domain has a relatively strong patterns which are partially covered by "typical" cases. However searching a solution based only on the similarity with past cases (the naive CBR algorithm) gives worse results than combined use of both tiers (rules and cases). Explanation of this result may be searched in the fact that the generalized cases have been produced from the rules which are incomplete and incorrect and addition of new cases to the memory do not change the typicality of these generalized cases. On the other hand exhaustive search in the case space without any semantic restriction increases the possibility to select an inappropriate case with false similarity with the problem at hand.

The proposed algorithm for integration of rules and cases does not check rules that (up to the moment of solving the current problem) are proved to be correct and complete. An attempt to find a solution on the base of measuring similarity between cases is made only for rules which do not satisfy these conditions and carried out in the semantically restricted part of the case space. All this results in decreasing of the number of incorrect classifications.

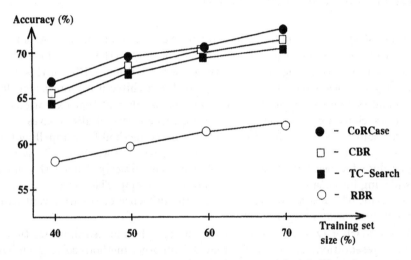

Fig. 2. The results of experiments with AQ-like rules

Table 2: The results of experiments with ID3-like and AQ-like rules

Rule base (for 70% sample)	RBR	TC-Search	CBR	CoRCase
ID3-like rules	59.23%	65.11%	67.18%	67.86%
AQ-like rules	61.98%	70.20%	70.64%	71.29%

The second set of experiments is related to the Primary tumor database. The domain is characterized with a large number of classes, absence of strong patterns and comparatively high level of noise [14]. For this domain 70% of examples were randomly selected for learning diagnostic rules, and the remaining 30% were used for testing. The rules which had been induced by the AQ-like algorithms were then converted to two-tired representation and tested by the CoRCase system. The experiment was performed five times using randomly chosen training and testing sets of examples. The results describing the average of these experiments are presented in Table 3.

Table 3: The results of experiments with Primary tumor database

Primary tumor	RBR	TC-Search	CBR	CoRCase
Accuracy (%)	34.65	33.46	33.07	37.03
# Rules/Cases	57.2	57.2	57.2 + 101	57.2 + 73.6

The results of the experiments indicate that the best accuracy is achieved by the proposed scheme for combination of rules and cases. It is particularly interesting that both the TC-search and the naive CBR methods used separately have worse performance than RBR. Once again it proves the effectiveness of the indexing scheme used in the proposed algorithm allowing to retrieve comparatively relevant cases for matching.

7   Discussion and Related Work

The proposed approach may be evaluated from various points of view. As an organization of the reasoning control the approach belongs to the group of methods concentrating on reconciling the conflicts between RBR and CBR. In this context it may be considered as an extension of the architecture proposed in [8] towards real system use, where the cases are used as different type exceptions of expert rules. Since we solve a classification task where several alternatives for a rule-based solution are possible, the similarity-based method for compelling the conflicts has been preferred. Moreover, by employing rules as "typical" cases in the procedure for case matching we avoid using heuristicaly defined threshold values playing important role in such kind of methods [4]. The interpretation of rules as "typical" cases allows also to avoid the influence of the irrelevant case features in measuring case similarity.

The approach may be seen as an incremental method for learning two-tiered domain representation. The main differences from other methods solving similar tasks (for example [14, 18, 19] etc.) are as follows:

First, we do not have to learn or refine as in [13] the first tier. It is formed by the set of flat rules associating different sets of problem features with the corresponding classification. These rules may be constructed from the original expert rules applying explanation-based generalization techniques. As a consequence of this the first tier may contain not only incomplete rules (as in the mentioned above methods) but incorrect rules as well.

Second, in contrast to other approaches to learning two-tiered domain representation our procedure for case matching which is the main part of the second tier does not need the set of training examples the rules were generated from. The proposed similarity measure uses only information about the domain encoded into the rules. This allows (and the experiment results have confirmed that) applying the method to improve performance of classification rules independently on the way of their construction.

And finally, the approach is incremental and allows refining the domain description by storing as a part of the second tier and further using cases uncovered or erroneously covered by the first tier. These cases along with the indexing information reflecting the roles they played in the problem solving, may be further used to real refinement of the first tier.

8 Conclusion and Future Work

The paper deals with the problem of improving problem-solving behavior of traditional KBS in the course of its real operation which is a part of the maintenance task. The solution of the problem has been searched in integration of the KBS with a specially designed case-based reasoning module which is used for correcting solutions produced by the KBS. Special attention has been paid to the methods of case matching and reconciling conflicts between CBR and RBR. The proposed solution for both problems is based on treating the maintenance task as a problem for learning two-tiered domain representation. From this point of view rules form the first domain tier reflecting existing strong patterns in the representation of domain concepts, and the second tier is formed by the newly solved cases along with a special domain-dependent procedure for case matching. This tier compensates some incompleteness and incorrectness in the first tier without its real refinement.

The main ideas of the approach have been illustrated by the results of experiments with the experimental system CoRCase. Using as examples the databases for prognosis of breast cancer recurrence and location of primary tumor it have been proved that the method is able to improve accuracy of classification rules independently on the type of algorithms used for their generation.

Currently we are preparing experiments with real medical data collected by the Laboratory of Electromyography of the Grenoble University Hospital Center in the framework of ESTEEM (A2010) European project. The experiment results will be compared with the results obtained during processing the same data by the hybrid expert system SHADE [10] using neural network to improve its behavior.

One of our goals includes improvement the CoRCase system behavior by using more sophisticated similarity measure based on the approaches described in [17, 16, 6].

Acknowledgment

The author thanks Zdravko Markov for providing ML algorithms used in the experiments and anonymous reviewers for their insightful comments that improved the final version of this paper.

References

1. Aamodt, A.: *Knowledge-intensive, integrated approach to problem solving and sustained learning.* Ph.D. Dissertation, University of Trondheim (1991).

2. Agre, G.: Improvement of KBS Behavior by Using Problem-Solving Experience. Ph. Jorrand and V. Sgurev (Eds.), *Proc. of the VIth Int. Conference AIMSA'94*, World Scientific Publ., Singapore (1994) 257–266.

3. Agre, G.: An Approach to Integration of Rule-Based and Case-Based Reasoning. *Problems of Engineering Cybernetics and Robotics*, **42**, Bulgarian Academy of Sciences, Sofia (1995) 40–49.

4. Barsalou, L., Hale, C.: Components of conceptual representation: from feature lists to recursive frames. I. Van Mechelen, J. Hampton, R.S. Michalsi and P. Theuns (Eds.) *Categories and Concepts - Theoretical Views and Inductive Data Analysis*, Academic Press (1993) 97–144.

5. Bergadano, F., Matwin, S., Michalski R.S., Zhang, J.: Learning two-tiered description of flexible concepts: the POSEIDON system. *Machine Learning* 8 (1992) 5–43.

6. Biberman, Y.: A Contex Similarity Measure. F. Bergadano and L. De Raedt (Eds.) *Machine Learning: ECML-94*. LNAI **784**, Springer-Verlag (1994) 48–63

7. Coenen, F., Bench-Capon, T.: *Maintenance of Knowledge-Based Systems: Theory, Techniques and Tools*, Academic Press (1993).

8. Golding A.R., Rosenbloom, P.S.: Improving rule-based systems through case-based reasoning. *Proceedings of the National Conference on Artificial Intelligence*, Anaheim, MIT Press (1991) 22–27.

9. Hammond, K.: *Case-Based Planning: Viewing Planning as a Memory Task*. Academic Press (1989).

10. Iordanova I., Giacometti, A., Vila, A., Amy, B., Reymond, F., Abaoub, L., Dahou M., Rialle, V.: Shade - A Hybrid System for Diagnosis in Electromyography. *Proc. of IXth Int. Congress on Electromyography*, Jerusalem (1992).

11. Kolodner, J.L.: Extending problem solver capabilities through case-based inference. *Proc. of 4th Workshop on Machine Learning*, UC-Irvine, June 22-25 (1987) 167–178.

12. Markov, Z.: *Private communication* (1995).

13. Matwin, S., Plante, B.: A Deductive-Inductive Method For Theory Revision. R.S. Michalski and Gh. Tecuci (Eds.) *Proc. of the First Int. Workshop on Multistrategy Learning* (1991) Harpers Ferry, 160–174.

14. Michalski R.S.: Learning flexible concepts: fundamental ideas and a method based on two-tiered representation. Y. Kodratoff and R.S. Michalski (Eds.) *Machine Learning: an Artificial Intelligence Approach* **3**, San Mateo, CA: Morgan Kaufmann (1990) 63–111.

15. Mitchell, T.M., R. Keller, Kedar-Cabelli, S.: Explanation-Based Generalization: A unifying view. *Machine Learning* 1 (1986) 47–80.

16. Cost, S., Salzberg, S.: A weighted nearest neighbor algorithm for learning with symbolic features. *Machine Learning* 10(1) (1991) 56–78.

17. Stanfill, C., Waltz, D.: Toward memory-based reasoning. *Communication of ACM* **29(12)** (1986) 1213–1229.

18. Zhang, J.: Integrating Symbolic and Subsymbolic Approaches in Learning Flexible Concepts. R.S. Michalski and Gh. Tecuci (Eds.) *Proc. of the First Int. Workshop on Multistrategy Learning*, Harpers Ferry (1991) 289–304.

19. Zhang, J.: Selecting Typical Instances in Instance-Based Learning. D. Sleeman and P. Edwards (Eds.) *Machine Learning - Proc. of the Ninth Int. Workshop (ML02)*, San Mateo, CA: Morgan Kaufmann (1992) 470–479

A Case-Based Approach for Developing Writing Tools Aimed at Non-native English Users

Sandra M. Aluísio[1] and Osvaldo N. Oliveira Jr.[2]

[1] Universidade de São Paulo
Departamento de Ciências de Computação e Estatística
CP 668, 13560-970, São Carlos, SP, BRAZIL
e-mail:sandra@icmsc.sc.usp.br
[2] Universidade de São Paulo
Instituto de Física de São Carlos
CP 369, 13560-970 São Carlos, SP, BRAZIL
e-mail:chu@ifqsc.sc.usp.br

Abstract

A writing tool has been developed for helping non-native English users to produce a first draft of Introductory Sections of scientific papers. A corpus analysis was carried out in 54 papers of Experimental Physics which allowed one to identify the schematic structure of Introductions and 30 rhetorical strategies generally employed. Each one of the Introductions analysed constituted a case. The user chooses from menus features related to the rhetorical strategies for each component and gives the intended order for his/her Introduction, thus forming the requisition. Using three types of metric, the tool recovers the best-match cases that can be later modified in a revision process. Preliminary experiments showed that high precision and recall will only be obtained if the number of cases in the case base is considerably increased. In the revision process, four operations are suggested which consist in modifying/adding/deleting the different rhetorical messages that constitute the strategies of the chosen case.

1 Introduction

Writing scientific papers in English is often a severe limitation for the career of many a non-native English user. In addition to difficulties in choosing appropriate rhetorical, grammatical and semantic itens, non-natives also face problems related to interference from their mother tongue (L1 interference). In order to overcome some of these difficulties, we proposed an empirical resource based on offering the writer a set of standard sentences and collocations which appear with high frequency in scientific texts [Oliveira-91]. A reference writing tool integrated in the AMADEUS (AMiable Article Development for User Support) environment was then developed [Caldeira-92] which provided excellent results when applied by some Brazilian graduate students [Fontana-93], for they were able to get started with their writing task and could produce good pieces of text. These particular users generally already had a good reception of the English language. However, the tool was not successful in helping less experienced writers, with poorer knowledge of English. This occurred mainly because such users had difficulties in localizing the collocations that were appropriate to their needs and, worst of all, they could not make sensible choices of cohesive links for building up a paragraph. It then became clear that these less experienced users require a writing tool which deals specifically with collocations in real contexts so that cohesive devices may be readily apparent. The utilization of reusable texts has already been exploited for producing standardized texts [Born-92], for reducing the duration of writing tasks [Buchanan-92] and in natural language generation or interpretation systems by way of phrasal lexicons [Kukich-83; Jacobs-85; Hovy-90; Smadja-91], but to our knowledge no tool has been devoted to non-native English users.

We take the view that a tool with the characteristics mentioned above could make use of the case-based approach, as a case would not only illustrate the rhetorical structure[1] of a given piece of text but would also instantiate the cohesive devices with real text. While the case-based approach applied to a writing tool for non-native English users is new, there are few existing case-based systems for natural language generation. One example is a case-based system that stores cases of actual utterances and uses them in order to generate sentences in the target language of a speech-to-speech dialog translation system [Kitano-90]. Another one is the LetterGen system for the generation of business letters in four languages [Pautler-94].

Our approach required a systematic corpus analysis of a number of papers, which is described in Section 2. The development of a writing tool for Introductory Sections of Experimental Physics papers is reported in Section 3. Upon selecting from menus various intended features for the Introduction, the user is returned real Introductions from the corpus which better map onto his/her requisition. It must be stressed that even if the recovered cases reflect the chosen features, this is still not sufficient. The user must be able to adapt/revise the case to input his/her own material. Suggestions are given to the user of the possible ways for revising the first draft. Section 4 discusses these issues, highlighting the strengths and limitations of the case-based approach for the development of this specific type of writing tool.

2 Schematic Structure of Introductory Sections

A corpus-based analysis was carried out for Introductions of experimental physics papers. Fifty-four (54) papers were selected at random from the years 1992-1994 from the journals Physical Review Letters (33 papers) and Thin Solid Films (21). The choice of these journals was based on their quality and also on the fact that their Introductions are reasonably short and standardized. In spite of its length, the Introduction in Physical Review Letters is more elaborate than in Thin Solid Films, for the intended audience is broader in the former journal. The analysis basically confirmed what has been proposed by Weissberg [Weissberg-90] and Swales [Swales-90] in that the most common schematic components of Introductions are *setting, review, gap, purpose, methodology, results, value and layout.* Some of these components are optional and may depend on the journal style and length of the article.

---

[1] The term rhetorical structure is used here for referring to the structuring of a particular text which may (or may not) obey strictly the canonical order of components of the schematic structure of a given genre of text.

The *layout* component, for instance, generally does not appear in Letters. In the corpus analysed the first four components above had very high frequency. The *gap* component is a strategic one since it points out the weaknesses and limitations of studies discussed in the *review* component, thus paving the way for a clear statement of the paper's intended contribution in the *purpose* component.

The corpus analysis also served to identify 30 rhetorical strategies (based on works by [Maybury-91; Huckin-91; Trimble-85, Weissberg-90; Swales-90]) for organizing 45 different types of information (called here as messages) that make up these strategies. Only papers written by native speakers were considered in order to avoid possible insertion of non-idiomatic linguistic structures into the corpus.

Some of the rhetorical strategies possess common characteristics and could be generalized. But they receive distinct names for helping the user in the gathering of features as they appear in different components. For example, both strategies *Historical review* from the Review component and *Listing the issues to be reported* from the Layout component are chronological strategies for narrative texts. They are temporally organized. The historical review pattern is used to recount a sequence of past events:

*Deposition of phthalocyanine derivatives as thin films by the Langmuir- Blodgett technique was **first** described by Roberts et al. who demonstrated that tetra-t-butyl substitution of the ring system facilitated deposition [1]. **Subsequently**, a number of groups worldwide have derivatised the ring system with a variety of substituents and substitution patterns in efforts to obtain improved LB films containing a high degree of molecular order [2]. **Recently** we described the film forming properties of the amphiphilic phthalocyanine (1) [3, 4].*

(Chesters,M.A et al. Structural evaluation of Langmuir-Blodgett films of amphiphilic phthalocyanines using infrared spectroscopy. Thin Solid Films, 210/211, (1992), pp. 538-541)

The layout pattern, on the other hand, describes step by step the parts of the article using a temporal series of adjuncts:

*The rest of this paper is organized as follows. We **next** describe our model of activation over fluctuating barrier and indicate the modes of analysis that are brought to bear its study. Exact and Monte Carlo results are **then** presented to both illustrate the resonant activation and provide an understanding of the mechanism responsible for this behavior. We **conclude** with a brief discussion of our results, pointing out some open questions.*

(Doering,C.R. et al. *Resonant Activation over a Fluctuating Barrier*. Physical Review Letters, October, 1992, pp. 2318-21)

In order to further illustrate how the strategies were identified and named, we describe the characteristics of the strategies from the Review Component. Similarly to *Historical review*, *Current Trends* uses a temporal organization but the main rhetorical pattern is one of contrast. The *General to particular ordering for citations* is a descriptive strategy and organizes topics/citations from distant (general area) to close (research topic). That is to say, it is topically organized. The *Citations grouped by approaches*, on the other hand, uses the listing pattern for organizing topics at the same level of closeness. It is similar to the *State of the Art* in grouping facts at the same level of closeness except that the facts reported in the latter are known facts and usually come without citations. Conversely, *Progress in the area* and *Requirements for the progress in the area* are argumentative strategies.

The resulting cases consist therefore of whole introductions, also encompassing information on the associated features and categorization of the strategies. Fig. 1 shows one of the 54 cases.

SETTING: FAMILIARIZING TERMS OR OBJECTS OR PROCESSES

1) Conductive LB films of charge transfer complexes based on TCNQ, TTF and related donors [1], are characterized by strong one-dimensional interactions and are therefore susceptible to stacking defects and the Peierls instability.

REVIEW: REQUIREMENTS FOR THE PROGRESS IN THE AREA

2) It should be possible to overcome such defects and thus produce films of higher conductivity if a complex of higher dimensionality is chosen.

3) Indeed, Nakamura et al. [2] have shown that monovalent salts of a range of long-chain alkylammonium salts of M(dmit)2, where M = Au, Ni, Pd, or Pt may be deposited as LB films and oxidised with bromine or iodine to yield molecular films with conductivities in the range 0.001-30S/cm.

GAP: RESTRICTIONS IN PREVIOUS APPROACHES

4) However, owing to their instability at the air-water interface, it was necessary in most cases to deposit the complexes as 1:1 mixtures with icosanoic acid.

PURPOSE: PRESENTING AN EXTENSION OF A PREVIOUS AUTHOR'S WORK + INTRODUCING MORE PURPOSES

5) § In a preliminary report [3], we have shown that it is possible to deposit LB films of the pure didodecyldimethylammonium salts of the divalent metal complexes [M(dmit)2]2- and [M(mnt)2]2-.

6) In this report we describe further investigations into the behavior of these compounds (complexes 1 and 2, respectively) at the air-water interface and extend our studies to the monovalent salt (complex 3) for comparison.

(Taylor,D.M.et alli. *Monolayer characterization and multilayer deposition of conducting Langmuir-Blodgett films*, Thin Solid Films, 210/211 (1992) pp.287-289)

Fig. 1. One of the Introductions of the case base

It can be seen that some fragments are underlined which correspond to the reutilizable parts of the text. The sentences are numbered because the basic unit of analysis is a sentence that is codified in a phrasal lexicon[2] . Information specific of the authors' work comes in normal text. The corresponding representation in Prolog is illustrated in Fig. 2.

---

[2] The phrasal lexicon indexes several sentences and clauses, as well.

```
case( tsf4,
      [c(setting,s(familiarizing_terms_or_objects_or_processes,
                    [m(semi_formal_definition, tsf4,1)])),
       c(review,s(requirements_for_the_progress_in_the_area,
                    [m(complexity_topic, tsf4,1),
                     m(requirements_progress,tsf4,2),
                     m(author_prominent,tsf4,3)])),
       c(gap,s(restrictions_in_previous_approaches, [m(restriction,tsf4,4)])),
       c(purpose,s(presenting_an_extension_of_a_previous_authors_work,
                    [m(author_prominent,tsf4,5), m(extension,tsf4,6)])),
       c(purpose,s(introducing_more_purposes, [m(addition,tsf4,6)]))], _ ).
```

Fig. 2. Rhetorical features represented in Prolog

A case is represented by the Prolog structure case(Case_Name, ListofComponents, ListofPragmaticFeatures). Each of the components in the ListofComponents is represented by c(Component_Name, Strategy). For each component only one strategy is chosen each time. The strategies have the Prolog structure s(Strategy_Name, ListofMessages) which should include a few messages (typically 3 or 4) taken from the 45 different types. Some of the messages are specific to the genre of scientific article, such as *extension, complexity_topic, requirements_progress* and *restriction*. Some are rhetorical relations which appear in other genres as well (such as *motivation, cause, addition, evidence*). Messages may also be recognized by the conventional order of their semantic components. In the latter class one may include *formal* or *semi_formal_definition*, and *author_prominent*. The Prolog structure of the messages is m(Message_Name, Case_Name, Sentence_Number). The messages have pointers to the phrasal lexicon entries. As already mentioned, our current implementation includes 45 message types, some of which are stand-alone messages. Other messages can be combined to form compound messages and there are also those that can be written in both stand-alone and compound fashions.

The last component of the structure of a given case, ListofPragmaticFeatures, is not being used in developing the present tool because the articles in the corpus possess several characteristics in common — such as the length of the Introduction, style of the journal, and to some extent, the intended audience. This component would be very important, however, when the approach is applied to other sub-genres or broader classes of scientific work. An Introduction of a review article or of a book chapter, for instance, is much longer, it has another purpose, being directed to another target reader, and therefore it possesses different components and/or arrangements.

3 The Writing Tool

The tool is being implemented in a Sun SparcStation using Sicstus Prolog with the interface being built with the XView toolkit and the Netscape browser. It is integrated into the AMADEUS environment which already offers a reference writing tool for more experienced writers [Fontana-93]. To use the tool in writing an Introduction the user follows a three-step procedure: i) gathering of features, in which the user selects from several menus the features intended for his/her introduction; ii) selection of the best-match case, following the case recovery by the system; iii) revision on the selected case. These stages are shown in the architecture of the writing tool (Fig. 3).

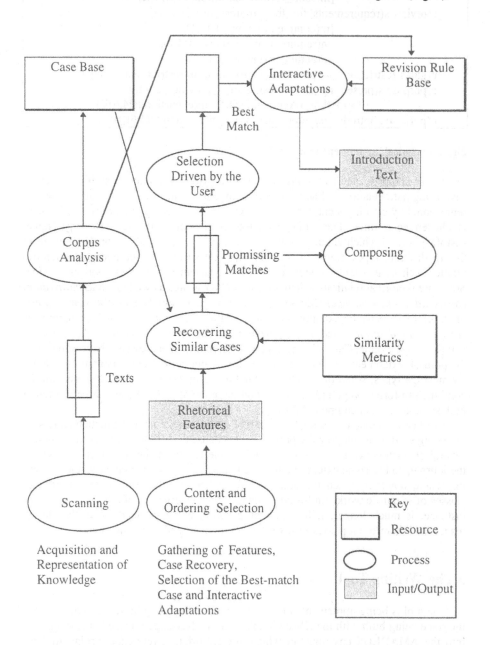

Fig. 3. The architecture of the case-based writing tool

3.1 Gathering of Features

In this stage the user selects in a menu system the components and strategies (and their order of appearance) for his/her introduction, forming the so-called requisition. The user also provides the system with information on the degree of certainty of the chosen order of components. There are 3 degrees of certainty which affect the choice of the metrics of similarity to be employed in recovering the cases: *sure about the chosen order, some doubts, many doubts.* Three distinct metrics were therefore implemented which only take into account the structural features of the Introduction: components, strategies, and their order of appearance. Messages are only considered at the Revision step (see below).

3.2 Cases Recovery

Three ways of pattern matching are used: perfect match (*equal lists*), proper undermatch (*sublist*) and non-proper undermatch (*intersection*). The tool selects cases to be returned to the user by employing these three metrics which are basically related to the degree of certainty on the part of the user about the order of the components and strategies (see Fig. 4). The number of returned cases (real introductions) is always 4. But the system may pick them up from more or less wide sources. The choice "Sure about the chosen order" activates *equal lists* and also recovers cases which contain the requisition (*sublist*). The choice "Some doubts about the chosen order" returns cases using the two previous types of search and other ones that are completely contained in the requisition (*sublist*). Finally, for the choice "Many doubts about the chosen order" the user is returned cases resulting from the previous searches and also from the intersections — requisition partially contained in the case, and vice-versa. Therefore, the search becomes more flexible when the degree of certainty is decreased.

3.3 Revisions: The Interactive Adaptations

Four revision operations were envisaged for this stage of the writing process: i) changes in the lexical and syntactic material of the messages; ii) changes applied to the selected strategies recovering similar ones; iii) addition of messages to a specific strategy; iv) deletion of messages, the opposite operation to iii). Operations i) and ii) are illustrated in Fig. 4. In operation i), there is simply the replacement of material within a given template. In operation ii), however, the changes may also affect the thematic structure of the sentence. In the example given, the type of claim in an argumentation strategy has been changed from *The research is part of a lively area* to *The research is part of a significant area.* As one may see, one goes from a temporally-driven to a topically-driven pattern.

Operation (i)
Initial sentence pattern: In recent years a considerable amount of effort has been devoted to the study of $<<\beta\beta$ decay of various nuclei$>>$. Lexical and/or grammatical changes: (a) (Recently/In previous years/Currently) a considerable amount of effort has been devoted to the study of ... (b) In recent years (a great deal of effort/ much attention/ a great deal of interest) has been devoted to the study of ...
Operation (ii)
Initial sentence pattern: In recent years a considerable amount of effort has been devoted to the study of $<<\beta\beta$ decay of various nuclei$>>$. Changes on the strategy: (a) $<<$topics$>>$ have been the subject of renewed interest ... (b) $<<$topics$>>$ have a wide-ranging importance in many areas of ...

Fig. 4. Examples of the revision process

The use of metrics of similarity employed for recovering cases (whole Introductions) can also be used for recovering strategies and ultimately messages from the phrasal lexicon, even if they belong to different cases.

3.4 A Sample Run

Fig. 5 and 6 show screendumps that illustrate how the tool is to be used. Fig. 5 shows the Gathering of Features stage in which the user chooses from a menu system the components and strategies for his/her Introduction. The user must also inform the degree of certainty for the order of components and strategies chosen. These pieces of information will guide the system with regards to the metrics to be employed. Because more than one case can be returned to the user, he/she has the choice of working on the cases returned by transferring linguistic material into his own working area (Composing process). But the user may also select the best returned case and activate the Revision process (in an another window not shown in Fig. 6) and then adapt it before taking material into the working area.

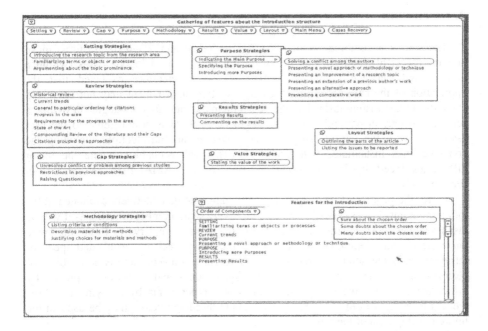

Fig. 5. Gathering of features

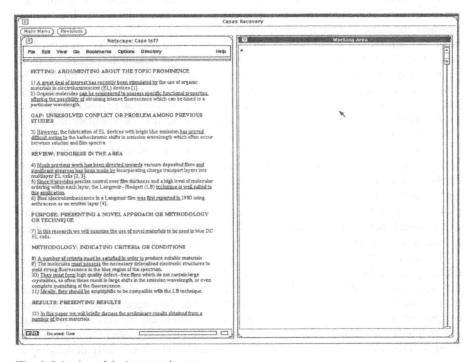

Fig. 6. Selection of the best match case

4. Discussion

The use of a combination of structural, semantic and pragmatic features make humans powerful agents in recovering information from analogous cases (within a domain and between domains) [Kettler-94]. It is therefore expected that the application of the case-based approach in a writing environment may not only help students in their writing tasks, but also teach them the most used strategies in writing a scientific paper. In particular because linguistic material is now offered to the user associated with the various strategies employed in an Introduction, including the cohesive links instantiated with real texts. This will probably obviate the major difficulties faced by less experienced users of the AMADEUS reference tool [Fontana-93].

As for the process of recovering cases, it cannot be quantitatively evaluated at the moment because the case base contains a relatively small number of cases, as it will be discussed later. An extension process for the base is underway. From the three parameters usually employed in such an evaluation - precision, recall and speed of retrieval - only the latter one may be considered now. Indeed, there is no problem of performance as the tool runs in a Sun Sparcstation and retrieval is practically instantaneous. We have nevertheless performed experiments by applying the three metrics to 5 cases in the case base. The results discussed below may be used in the future development of the tool.

The experiments showed in an unequivocal way that the current case base is too small for high recall and precision to be obtained. When the requisition consisted of a relatively long list, often only the identity case was recovered when the *sublist* and *equal list* were employed. The nearest-neighbor matching for these long lists, which provides the score of conceptual similarity, did not reach 50% in any of the cases when the *intersection* metric was employed. One feature that must be considered in recovering the cases is the length of the Introduction. Even though the papers are short (3 or 4 journal pages), their Introductions had lengths varying from 20 to 80 lines. In the longer Introductions some of the components may appear more than once; for instance, one may have a review about a general field and later on reviews on specific topics. Obviously these cases are represented by long lists of components which practically impair the use of the metrics *sublist* and *equal lists*.

The metric *intersection* must be used with caution, as it recovers a larger number of cases, some of which may not be appropriate. It is true that the user recognized that he/she did not know the best order for the components. But perhaps the most efficient way to deal with this problem would be to request the user to decide upon the best order, based on the several suggestions supplied by the system in initial runs. This metric would then only be used in a sort of screening process for the user to make up his/her mind with regards to the order of components.

In terms of implementation costs and portability of the present tool, the major difficulty lies in the need of corpus analysis. While the case-based approach including the metrics suggested here may be portable to other domains, the same is not true of the rhetorical structure of Introductions in other fields. Messages, strategies and even components are likely to depend to some extent on the idiosyncrasies of a particular research area [Crookes-86; Paice-90; Taylor-91]. In order to extend the approach to other Sections of a paper and for other research areas, we are currently developing a semi-automatic tool for compiling linguistic material and indexing it according to the messages and strategies already identified.

Finally, it must be stressed that the tool will only serve as a guide for the user to produce a first draft for his/her Introduction. No attempts to generate text automatically have been done. Nevertheless, even though the system cannot guarantee the final quality of the text, in particular because the user is to input his/her own material, the approach favours the writing of cohesive, coherent text. The user will also be helped in modifying the text through the revision operations offered by the tool. It is hoped that a case-based writing tool may also have pedagogical implications as the user may learn by analogy to work at all levels of the rhetorical structure of an Introduction: from the components to phrasal lexicon entries.

Acknowledgments

The authors are grateful to FAPESP and CNPq for financial support. They are also grateful to Prof. Stan Matwin for helpful discussions.

References

[Born-92] Born, G. *A Hipertext-Based Support Aid for Writing Software Documentation*. In Computers and Writing - State of the Art, P. O'Brian-Holt & N.Williams (eds), Kluwer Academic Publishers, Dordrecht, pp. 266-277, 1992.

[Buchanan-92] Buchanan, R.A. Textbase Technology: Writing with Reusable Text. In Computers and Writing - State of the Art, P. O'Brian-Holt & N.Williams (eds), Kluwer Academic Publishers, Dordrecht, pp. 254-265, 1992.

[Caldeira-92] (Caldeira), Aluísio S.M.; De Oliveira, M.C.F.; Fontana, N.; Nacamatsu, C.O. and Oliveira Jr., O.N. *Writing tools for non-native users of English*. Proceedings of the XVIII Latinamerican Informatics Conference, Spain, p. 224-231, 1992.

[Crookes-86] Crookes, G. *Towards a Validate Analysis of Scientific Text Structure*. Applied Linguistics, Vol. 7 No. 1, 1986, pp.57-70.

[Fontana-93] Fontana, N.; (Caldeira), Aluísio S.M.; De Oliveira, M.C.F. and Oliveira Jr., O.N. *Computer Assisted Writing--Aplications to English as a Foreign Language*. CALL, Volume 6 (2), p. 145-161, 1993.

[Hovy-90] Hovy, E. *Pragmatics and Natural Language Generation*. Artificial Intelligence 43, p. 153-197, 1990.

[Huckin-91] Huckin, T.N. and Olsen, L.A. *Technical Writing and Professional Communication for Nonnative Speakers of English*. McGraw-Hill, In. 1991.

[Jacobs-85] Jacobs, P.S. *PHRED: A Generator for Natural Language Interfaces*. Computational Linguistics 11(4):219-242.

[Kettler-94] Kettler, B.P.; Hendler, J.A. Andersen, W.A; and Evett M.P. Massively Parallel Support for Case-Based Planning. IEEE Expert, pp. 8-14, February 1994.

[Kitano-90] Kitano, H. *Parallel Incremental Sentence Production for a Model of Simultaneous Interpretation.* In Current Research in Natural Language Generation, Dale, R., Mellish, C. and Zock, M. (eds), Academic Press, Boston, 1990, pp. 321-351.

[Kukich-83] Kukich, K. *Knowledge-Based Report Generation: A Knowledge Engineering Approach to Natural Language Report Generation.* PhD Thesis, University of Pittsburg, 1983.

[Maybury-91] Maybury, M.T. *Planning Multisentential English Text Using Communicative Acts.* (PhD Thesis) Tech. R. 239, University of Cambridge, 1991.

[Oliveira-91] Oliveira, Jr. O.N.; (Caldeira), Aluísio S.M. and Fontana, N. *Chusaurus: A Writing Tool Resource for Non-Native Users of English,* In Proceedings of the XI International Conference of The Chilean Computer Science Society, pp. 59-70. Also In Computer Science: Research and Applications, R. Baeza-Yates and U. Manber (eds), Plenum Press, N.Y. pp. 63-72, 1992.

[Paice-90] Paice, C.D. *Constructing Literature Abstracts by Computer: Techniques and Prospects.* Information Processing & Management, Vol. 26, No. 1, pp. 171-186, 1990.

[Pautler-94] Pautler, D. *Planning and learning in domains providing little feedback.* AAAI Fall Symposium on Planning & Learning Notes'94.

[Smadja-91] Smadja, F. *Retrieving Collocational Knowledge from Textual Corpora. An application: Language Generation.* PhD Thesis, Computer Science Department, Columbia University, 1991.

[Swales-90] Swales, J. *Genre Analisys - English in academic and research settings.* Cambridge University Press, 1990.

[Taylor-91] Taylor, G. and Tingguang, C. *Linguistic, Cultural and Subcultural Issues in Contrastive Discourse Analysis: Anglo-amarican and Chinese Scientific Texts.* Applied Linguistics, Vol. 12, No. 3, 1991, pp. 319-336.

[Trimble-85] Trimble, L. *English for science and technology: a discourse approach.* Cambridge University Press, 1985.

[Weissberg-90] Weissberg R. and Buker, S. *Writing up Research - Experimental Research Report Writing for Students of English.* Prentice Hall Regents, 1990.

Reasoning with Reasons in
Case-Based Comparisons

Kevin D. Ashley and Bruce M. McLaren
University of Pittsburgh, Pittsburgh, Pennsylvania 15260

Abstract. In this work, we are interested in how rational decision makers reason with and about reasons in a domain, practical ethics, where they appear to reason about reasons symbolically in terms of both abstract moral principles and case comparisons. The challenge for reasoners, human and artificial, is to use abstract knowledge of reasons and principles to inform decisions about the salience of similarities and differences among cases while still accounting for a case's or problem's specific contextual circumstances. TRUTH-TELLER is a program we have developed and tested that compares pairs of cases presenting ethical dilemmas about whether to tell the truth. The program's methods for reasoning about reasons help it to make context sensitive assessments of the salience of similarities and differences.

1. Introduction

A rational approach to decision making involves, at a minimum, elaborating reasons for and against a proposed action. Since reasons both for and against an action usually exist, a decision maker also requires some method for deciding which reasons are more important and should be able to explain the decision in terms of the reasons for it and a justification for the preference.

In a wide variety of domains, such as law, practical ethics, business, and organizational policy, resolving conflicting reasons involves both reasoning with principles or policies and comparing cases. A principle is a fundamental rule, law, or code of conduct. A policy is a definite, but general, method of action for guiding future decisions. Both are more abstract reasons which may underlie and give symbolic weight to a reason for an action. When facing a problem presenting conflicting reasons in a field like practical ethics, a decision maker may assess the reasons in light of their underlying principles or policies *and* compare the problem to past cases, involving some or all of the same principles or policies, to buttress an argument that some reasons should override others in the problem context. The reasoner may select paradigmatic, hypothetical and past cases identifying the principles or policies which made a decision to act right or wrong in the case, compare the cases and problem to see whether those criteria apply more or less strongly to the problem, make arguments how to resolve conflicting reasons in terms of the criteria as they were applied in the similar cases, and evaluate the arguments to come to a decision (Jonsen & Toulmin, 1988, Strong, 1988).

In "Interpretive CBR" (Kolodner, 1993), computer programs that generate case-based arguments justifying decisions, researchers are just beginning to find ways to incorporate reasoning with principles or policies into their case-based comparative evaluation models. Integrating these different kinds of knowledge is a hard problem, even for humans, because they vary from very abstract principles through an intermediate range of reasons to very specific cases. Some people are better than others at resolving ethical dilemmas, cases presenting conflicting reasons for and against actions, backed by conflicting principles. Cognitive psychological evidence has shown, for instance, that gender and developmental differences affect a reasoner's ability to account for a dilemma's particular circumstances in applying general principles in moral decision making (Gilligan, 1982).

From an AI viewpoint, the challenge is to represent abstract principles and get programs to integrate reasoning with cases, reasons and underlying principles in a context sensitive manner. In general, context sensitivity in case comparison means knowing which similarities and differences are the most salient in different circumstances: which should a reasoner focus upon and which should it ignore. AI/CBR programs have explored different ways of representing the salience of similarities and differences and expanded the circumstances which a program can take into account in making a determination of salience. In HYPO (Ashley, 1990) and CATO (Aleven and Ashley, 1994), the circumstances included the side argued for, the set of cases being compared and the particular argument move involved (e.g., analogizing, distinguishing, citing counterexamples). In CABARET (Rissland and Skalak, 1991), the circumstances also included the arguer's viewpoint and various argument moves associated with broadening or restricting the meanings of decision rule predicates. GREBE (Branting, 1991) accounted for the presence or absence of criterial facts, facts an authoritative decision maker deemed important in a case. BankXX (Rissland, Skalak, and Friedman, 1993) added high level (legal) theories, standard stories and "family resemblance" into the mix. CASEY's justified match referred to a causal inference network and certain evidentiary principles to assess salience of differences (Koton, 1988). PROTOS employed weights reflecting explanatory significance and prototypicality (Bareiss, 1989). CHEF, PERSUADER, and PRODIGY-ANALOGY, in various ways, related the salience of similarities and differences to the existence or resolution of goal conflicts (Hammond, 1989, Sycara, 1987, Veloso, 1992). SWALE related them to expectation-violating anomalous outcomes (Kass et al., 1986), and CREANIMATE to functionality (Edelson, 1992).

We have made some progress in developing an AI/CBR program's ability to make context sensitive determinations of the salience of similarities and differences based on qualitative assessments of case similarity and general domain criteria for qualifying the absolute and relative importance of reasons. TRUTH-TELLER (TT) (Ashley and McLaren, 1994) compares pairs of cases presenting ethical dilemmas about whether to tell the truth and generates a comparison text contrasting the reasons in each case. The reasons may invoke ethical principles or selfish considerations. TT's comparisons point out ethically relevant similarities and differences (i.e., reasons for telling or not telling the truth which apply to both cases, and reasons which apply more strongly in one case than another or which apply only to one case). It is important to note that TRUTH-TELLER does not yet analyze problem situations by retrieving and selecting relevant paradigmatic cases. In this respect the work is quite different from the CBR programs referred to above, all of which retrieve and apply cases to problems. We hope to develop TRUTH-TELLER into such a program, computationally realizing, for instance, the case-based (i.e., "casuistic") model of moral decision-making proposed by the ethicist, Carson Strong (Strong, 1988) which integrates principles, reasons and cases into a five-step model (See discussion in Ashley and McLaren, 1994).

In a formative evaluation of an initial version of the program, as reported in (Ashley and McLaren, 1994), an ethicist criticized TRUTH-TELLER's inability to "marshal" its answers. The expert commented generally that TT's comparison texts lacked an "organizing roadmap" and a recommended final decision "which could guide thinking and in terms of which the similarities, differences, and ethical principles could be marshaled." Accordingly, we have reorganized the comparison texts around specific conclusions and developed techniques for marshaling the similarities and differences in a context sensitive way.

As a result of these changes, TRUTH-TELLER now selects similarities and differences for salience in light of an overall assessment of similarity of the two cases; the program marshals the comparisons differently depending on how close the cases are to one another in terms of categories that ethicists seem to regard as important. TT's other heuristics for reasoning about reasons identify additional criteria for regarding some similarities and differences as more important than others in terms of underlying principles, criticalness of consequences, participants' roles and untried alternatives. We have developed a mechanism for "tagging" reasons with qualifications based on a comparative analysis of the cases.

In this paper we describe TRUTH-TELLER's expanded comparison algorithm and illustrate it with an extended example focusing on the way it employs marshaling and other techniques for reasoning about reasons to assess the salience of reasons in the two cases in a context sensitive way. We also report the results of a new experiment in which five expert ethicists evaluated the quality of TT's comparisons.

2. TRUTH-TELLER's Algorithm and Knowledge Structures

TRUTH-TELLER has a set of methods for reasoning about reasons that enables it to integrate reasons, principles, and cases intelligently in its case comparisons. Broadly characterized, TT's methods comprise three phases of analysis for (1) aligning, (2) qualifying, and (3) marshaling reasons, followed by (4) an interpretation phase. Each of the phases is described in more detail below:

The Alignment Phase. Aligning reasons means building a mapping between the reasons in two cases. The initial phase of the program "aligns" the semantic representations of the two input cases by matching similar reasons, actor relations, and actions, by marking reasons that are distinct to one case, and by noting exceptional reasons in one or both of the cases.

The Qualification Phase. Qualifying a reason means identifying special relationships among actors, actions, and reasons that augment or diminish the importance of the reasons. The qualification phase adjusts the relative importance of competing reasons or principles in the problem. During the qualification phase, heuristic production rules qualify or "tag" objects and the alignments between objects in a variety of ways based on considerations like criticalness, altruism, participants' roles and alternative actions.

The Marshaling Phase. Marshaling reasons means selecting particular similar or differentiating reasons to emphasize in presenting an argument that (1) one case is as strong as or stronger than the other with respect to a conclusion, (2) the cases are only weakly comparable, or (3) the cases are not comparable at all. The marshaling phase analyzes the aligned and qualified comparison data, determines how the cases should be compared to one another based on five pre-defined comparison contexts reflecting a qualitative assessment of the overall similarity between the two cases, and then organizes information appropriate to that type of comparison.

The Interpretation Phase. A fourth phase of the program generates the comparison text by interpreting the activities of the first three phases.

The program employs various knowledge structures to support its algorithm, including semantic networks that represent the truth telling episodes, a relations hierarchy, and a reasons hierarchy. All structures are implemented using LOOM (MacGregor and Burstein, 1991).

The truth telling episodes were adapted from a game called Scruples (TM), from (Bok, 1989), and from a study that we conducted involving high school and ethics graduate students. Each episode includes representations for the actors (i.e., the truth teller, truth receiver, and others affected by the decision), relationships between the actors (e.g., familial, professional, seller-customer), the truth teller's possible actions (i.e., telling the truth, not telling the truth, or taking some alternative action) and reasons that support the possible actions.

The relations hierarchy is a taxonomy of approximately 80 possible relationships among the actors in a truth telling episode. Relationship types include familial, commercial, and acquaintance relations. The relations hierarchy is used to infer which relationships are "similar" for purposes of identifying levels of trust and duty that exist between the participants.

Finally, the reasons hierarchy represents possible rationales for taking action. Based on the formulation in (Bok, 1989), the hierarchy employs, at its top tier, four general reasons for telling the truth or not: fairness, veracity, producing of benefit, and avoiding harm. All other reasons are descendants of one of these abstract reason types. Each reason also has three other facets, criticalness, if altruistic, and if principled, each of which is important to ethical decision-making. The program accepts principled and unprincipled reasons as rationales for taking action.

3. An Extended Example

We now illustrate TT's algorithm and knowledge structures by providing an extended example of the program. A comparison of two cases by TT is depicted in Figure 1. We first describe the comparison text in its entirety, by describing in general terms what the program does, and then we focus on the underlined portion of the comparison text (the last paragraph of Figure 1), by guiding the reader through the four stages of the program.

The program starts by accepting semantic representations of each of the cases. The representation of a case is a manually constructed interpretation of the story. Figure 2 depicts the semantic representations of the Stephanie and Bruce cases. In Stephanie's case Stephanie is the truth teller, since it is she who is confronted with the decision to tell the truth or not. The experiment subjects will hear the truth, should Stephanie decide to divulge it, and thus are the truth receivers in this episode. Finally, the citizenry and the scientific community are affected others, since they would be affected by any truth telling disclosure (i.e., they stand to benefit in some way should the experiment result in an important scientific finding).

TRUTH-TELLER is comparing the following cases:
CASE 1: Should Stephanie, a psychology researcher, lie to human subjects about the intent of an experiment in order to study some aspect of the subject's behavior?
CASE 2: Bruce sells radios for a living. His favorite brother, Mark, picks out an expensive model with a history of maintenance problems. Selling this model would mean a big commission to Bruce but a big problem for Mark. Bruce has been doing very well lately, so the commission on this particular radio will not make much difference to his overall financial situation. Should Bruce warn his brother about the potential problems of this radio?
TRUTH-TELLER's analysis:
Stephanie and Bruce are faced with similar dilemmas. They abstractly share reasons to both tell the truth and not tell the truth. The cases also share similar relationship contexts. The relationship between Stephanie and the experiment subjects and between Bruce and Mark both involve a high level of duty.
Stephanie and Bruce abstractly share one reason to tell the truth. Both actors share the general reason to protect a right. More specifically, Stephanie has the reason to not

trick someone into a disclosure for the experiment subjects, while Bruce has the reason to provide sales information so that a consumer can make an informed decision for Mark.

The two cases also abstractly share a reason to not tell the truth. Stephanie and Bruce share the general reason to produce benefit. Stephanie has the reason to enhance professional status and opportunities for herself, while Bruce has the reason to realize a financial gain for himself.

However, these quandaries also have relevant differences. Arguments can be made for both Stephanie and Bruce having a stronger basis for telling the truth.

On the one hand, there is an argument that telling the truth is better supported in Stephanie's case. First, Stephanie has to decide whether to tell a blatant lie, while Bruce must simply decide whether to remain silent. This fact would tend to put more pressure on Stephanie to tell the truth. Second, Stephanie could possibly acquire information for her research by devising a different experimental procedure. However, according to the story, this action was not taken. Thus, there is a greater onus on Stephanie to be honest.

On the other hand, one could also argue that Bruce has a more compelling case to tell the truth. First, the shared reason for telling the truth 'to protect a right' is stronger in Bruce's case, since it involves a higher level of trust between Bruce and Mark. <u>Second, the shared reason for not telling the truth 'to produce benefit' is weaker in Bruce's case, since Bruce's potential profit will not make much difference to his overall financial situation. Third, Stephanie has the reason to not tell the truth to strive for a greater good for the citizenry. Finally, Bruce's motivations for not telling the truth, unlike Stephanie's, appear to be purely selfish. This increases the onus on Bruce to tell the truth.</u>

Figure 1: TT's Output Comparing Stephanie's and Bruce's Cases

The semantic representation also contains a set of possible actions that the truth teller could take and reasons supporting or justifying each of the actions. The actions and reasons are supplied manually. (In future work, we hope that TT will infer actions and reasons by comparing cases.) One of the possible actions is always to tell the truth and another is some version of not telling the truth, for instance, telling a lie or keeping silent (i.e., not disclosing information). In Stephanie's case, the choice is between telling the truth about the intent of the experiment or deceiving the subjects by telling a premeditated lie. The lie is premeditated since, supposedly, Stephanie would know the intent of her own experiment and would therefore have the opportunity to reflect on the decision to lie or not. Stephanie also has an alternative action she could take before deciding whether or not to lie to the experiment subjects: she could pursue an alternative experimental design that would not require deceit. (Notice that this alternative is not explicitly stated in the story. In interpreting the episodes for semantic representation, we sometimes extrapolated.)

In our knowledge representation, actions are supported by reasons; a reason is treated as a rationale for taking an action. For example, a rationale for Stephanie's telling the truth is to protect the right of the experiment subjects to not be tricked into the disclosure of information. A rationale for Stephanie telling the lie is to provide a "greater good" for the scientific community and the citizenry at large, i.e., the experiment may result in some general benefit for many people.

In this work, we focus on TRUTH-TELLER's techniques for reasoning about the reasons contained in a case in the course of comparing that case to another case. The underlined portion of the comparison text of Figure 1 is part of the argument for Bruce's having a more compelling case to tell the truth than Stephanie. A portion of the Stephanie and Bruce semantic networks and the comparison between these portions (Figure 3) is directly responsible for this text. The following paragraphs explain how this diagram and the four phases of the program led to the underlined comparison text.

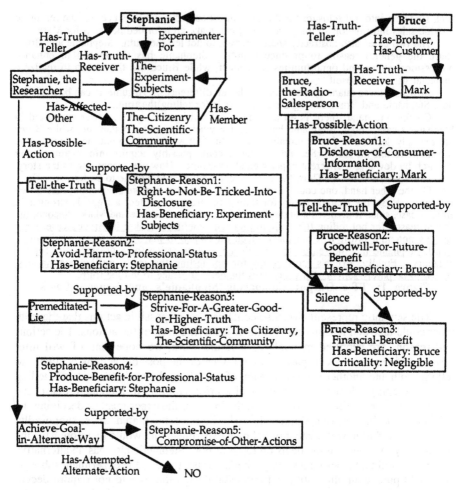

Figure 2: Representation: Stephanie's Case (l) & Bruce's Case (r)

Given the input representations, TT reasons about reasons by aligning, qualifying, and marshaling the semantic networks. First, the Alignment phase is initiated. The thin lines in Figure 3 depict alignments between the Stephanie and Bruce representations. First, Stephanie's reason involving a "greater good" is determined to have no counterpart in the Bruce representation (i.e., it is a clear distinction); thus it is "misaligned" and labeled as a reason distinction. Second, the premeditated lie for Stephanie and silence for Bruce -- possible actions for each case -- are aligned with one another because they abstractly match as a "do not tell the truth" action. Finally, Stephanie and Bruce have reasons that abstractly match and are thus aligned with one another (i.e., Stephanie may benefit professionally by lying to her subjects and conducting the experiment, while Bruce may benefit financially by withholding the truth from his brother). These reasons are not identical; however they match in the reason hierarchy at the level of "producing benefit."

The program next commences the Qualification phase. The italicized text in Figure 3 represents the qualifications that are applied to the comparison. During this phase individual objects and alignments between objects are qualified or "tagged" based on finer-grained knowledge. The first step is to qualify the individual objects. For instance, Stephanie's reason to produce benefit (i.e., to improve her professional status) is tagged (1) as having no duty or trust expectations, since it only involves herself, (2) as being unprincipled, since no ethical principle supports the reason, (3) as having average criticality, since no comment was made in the story about any critical consequences, and (4) as being self-motivated, since the reason is clearly selfish. Bruce's aligned reason (i.e., financial benefit) is tagged likewise, with the exception that its criticality is labeled as negligible, since the story states that the financial benefit to Bruce is not important.

The second step of Qualification is to qualify alignments. In Figure 3 there are three alignment qualifications. The first one is the reason distinction misalignment which is tagged as being a reason found only in case 1. Second, the alignment between Stephanie's premeditated lie and Bruce's silence is tagged as being fully selfish, and thus weaker, on Bruce's side, since Bruce has only a selfish reason for withholding the truth, while Stephanie has one rationale, the "greater good" reason, that is not selfish. Finally, the abstract reason match between Stephanie's possible professional gain and Bruce's financial benefit is tagged as stronger for Stephanie. This is the case because of the superiority of average criticality over negligible criticality. (A Reason A is said to be stronger than a Reason B iff Reason A has a higher criticality than Reason B OR Reason A has at least one qualifier (i.e., trust, duty, altruism, principled) that is stronger than Reason B's AND Reason A has no qualifier that is weaker than Reason B's.)

Next, the program begins the Marshaling phase. Its first marshaling task is to assign the case comparison to one of five possible comparison contexts. The five comparison contexts are defined as follows: (1) Comparable-Dilemmas/Reason-Similarity, if the cases present similar dilemmas. i.e., the reasons supporting both telling the truth and not telling the truth are similar either in an identical or abstract way, (2) Comparable-Dilemmas/Criticality-Similarity, if the cases are similar due to the critical nature of possible consequences, (3) Comparable-Reasons, if the cases share a similar reason or reasons for either telling the truth or not telling the truth but not for both possible actions, (4) Incomparable-Dilemmas/Reason-Difference, if the cases do not have any reasons supporting like actions that are similar, and (5) Incomparable-Dilemmas/Criticality-Difference, if the cases are incomparable due to a difference in the criticality of the possible consequences.

The Stephanie/Bruce comparison is classified as an instance of the Comparable-Dilemmas/Reason-Similarity comparison context, since it involves abstract reasons to tell the truth and abstract reasons not to tell the truth. After classifying the comparison, the program then marshals information that is appropriate to the classified context. There are two general categories of information that are marshaled, the *comparison focus* (i.e., information that is to be the initial focus of comparison and is typically the most important information to draw attention to) and the *distinguishing information* (i.e., information that contrasts with the comparison focus). For instance, for the Comparable-Dilemmas/Reason-Similarity comparison context, the program marshals the similar reasons and relations as the comparison focus and then, to distinguish the cases, marshals the information that supports arguing the relative merits of telling the truth in the two cases. As another example, if a comparison is assigned to the Incomparable-Dilemmas/Criticality-Difference, the program marshals the reasons that have greater criticality as the comparison focus, and then marshals, as distinguishing information, the contrasting, less critical reasons of the less critical case.

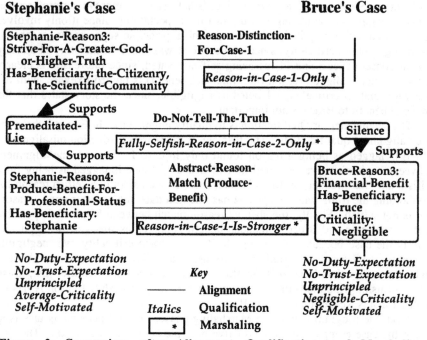

Stephanie's Case   Bruce's Case

Figure 3: Comparison after Alignment, Qualification, and Marshaling

Now let us return to Figure 3 to explain how the data in the figure is marshaled. Marshaled information is enclosed in a box with an asterisk. Only the marshaled distinguishing information is depicted in the diagram, corresponding to the underlined text in Figure 1. It is interesting to note, however, that the abstract reason match in Figure 3 is actually marshaled as part of both the comparison focus and the distinguishing information. This is so because the abstract reason match is a similarity, but qualification has also revealed that, at a more detailed level, it gives rise to a distinction. Note that the qualifier *Reason-In-Case-1-Is-Stronger* strengthens the case for Bruce's telling the truth relative to Stephanie, since Bruce's reason is less compelling for not telling the truth. This marshaled data corresponds to the sentence in the comparison text beginning "Second, ..." Stephanie's reason for not telling the truth to attain a "greater good" is also marshaled as a strength of Bruce's case relative to Stephanie's, because it is a misaligned reason distinction (i.e., it provides a justification for Stephanie to not tell the truth that is unshared by Bruce). This corresponds to the sentence "Third, ..." Finally, the program marshals the qualifier, *Fully-Selfish-Action-In-Case-2-Only*, from the matching actions in Figure 3. This also supports Bruce's case relative to Stephanie's, since it shows a weakness for not telling the truth that exists for Bruce but not Stephanie. This final marshaled data corresponds to the text in Figure 1 beginning "Finally, ..." The natural language text is generated in the final phase, Interpretation, using an augmented transition network.

To summarize, the extended example shows how TT uses its 4-phase algorithm to generate context sensitive and marshaled case comparisons. It "reasons about reasons" by aligning cases according to similarities and differences, and qualifying reasons in various ways including tagging reasons as altruistic, principled, critical, high trust, high duty, etc. and tagging alignments with relative strengths. The program marshals the reasons and qualifications by recognizing the context represented by a pair of cases. Figure 4 summarizes seven ways that TT reasons about reasons. The Alignment phase employs methods 1 through 4, the Qualification phase employs methods 5 and 6, and the Marshaling phase employs 7.

1. Elicit principles underlying reasons and classify reasons individually: Reason Hierarchy follows links from reason type to principles. Classify reasons as principled, self-motivated, or altruistic.
2. Classify reasons in the aggregate: Note if all reasons supporting an action are principled or unprincipled, altruistic or self-motivated.
3. Match reasons: Identify reasons for a particular action shared by cases and reasons not shared. Matches may be exact or abstract, based on a hierarchy of reasons and principles. Also, note exceptional reasons in one or both cases or reasons distinct to one case.
4. Map reason configurations: Mark shared configurations of reasons such as shared dilemmas (i.e., similar opposing reasons).
5. Qualify reasons by: (a) criticality (what happens if action is not taken?), (b) whether altruistic or not, (c) whether principled or not, (d) participants' roles and relationships (e.g. trust, duty), (e) existence of untried alternative actions, (f) how others are affected by action, (g) comparing actions (Lie vs. Silence, Premeditated vs. Unpremeditated)
6. Compare overall strength of reasons: Use the qualifiers to decide whether one reason is "stronger" than another.
7. Marshaling reasons: Select, collect reasons to emphasize based on the overall similarity of cases, nature of the reason mapping and qualifications on reasons.

Figure 4: TRUTH-TELLER's techniques for reasoning about reasons

4. The Evaluation

Our goal was to obtain some assurance that TRUTH-TELLER's techniques for reasoning about reasons generated case comparisons that expert ethicists would regard as appropriate. Our experimental design for this formative evaluation was to poll the opinions of five expert ethicists as to the reasonableness, completeness, and context sensitivity of a relatively large sampling of TT's case comparisons.

We divided the evaluation into two parts. The first experiment presented the experts with twenty comparison texts TT generated for pairs of cases randomly selected from three classes described below. The comparison texts were similar to and included the one in Figure 1. We also added two comparison texts generated by humans (a medical ethics graduate student and a law school professor). The experts were advised that the texts had been generated by humans or a computer program, but they were not told which texts or how many texts were generated by which. The second experiment presented the experts with five comparison texts in which TT compared the same case to five different cases. For each experiment, the evaluators were instructed: "In performing the grading, we would like you to evaluate the comparisons as you would evaluate short answers written by college undergraduates. ... Please focus on the substance of the comparisons and ignore grammatical mistakes, awkward constructions, or poor word choices (unless, of course, they have a substantial negative effect on substance.)" We also instructed the experts to critique each of the comparison texts.

In the first experiment, we instructed the experts to assign three grades to each of the twenty-two comparison texts, a separate grade for reasonableness, completeness, and context sensitivity. The scale for each grading dimension was 1 to 10, to be interpreted by the evaluators as follows: for reasonableness, 10 = very reasonable, sophisticated; 1 = totally unreasonable, wrong-headed; for completeness, 10 = comprehensive and deep; 1 = totally inadequate and shallow; for context sensitivity, 10 = very sensitive to context, perceptive; 1 = very insensitive to context. The twenty case pairs presented to TRUTH-TELLER were selected randomly as follows: (1) two cases selected at random from the training set (total of 5). (2) one case selected at random from the training set and one case selected at random from the test set (total of 5). (3) two cases selected at random from the test set (total of 10). The *training set* comprised twenty-three of the fifty-one cases in TRUTH-TELLER's case base; these cases were used to develop the program. The other twenty-eight cases served as the *test set* for the evaluation; these were used sparingly (or, in most cases, not at all) to develop the program.

The results of the first experiment were as follows. The mean scores across the five experts for the twenty TT comparisons were R=6.3, C=6.2, and CS=6.1. Figure 5 shows the maximum, minimum and mean scores per comparison for all three of the dimensions. By way of comparison, the mean scores of the two human-generated comparisons were R=8.2, C=7.7 and CS =7.8. The mean scores for the Stephanie/Bruce comparison, number 13, were R = 6.2; C = 7.2; CS = 5.8. Not surprisingly, one of the human comparisons, number 16, attained the highest mean on all three dimensions (R = 9; C = 8.8; CS = 8.8). Two of the program generated comparisons (numbers 2 and 14), however, were graded higher on all three dimensions than the remaining human comparison (number 22).

In the second part of the evaluation, we wanted to assess the program's sensitivity to context. To achieve this, we asked the experts to grade five additional TRUTH-TELLER comparisons. These comparisons all involved one case repeatedly compared to a different second case (i.e., a One-To-Many comparison). For this part of the evaluation, the experts were asked to grade the set of all comparisons with a single score along each of the three dimensions (i.e., reasonableness, completeness, and context sensitivity).

The results of the second part of the evaluation were as follows. The mean across all evaluators was R = 6.7; C = 6.9; CS = 7.0. Notice that the program fared better on the context sensitivity dimension than on the other two dimensions. This contrasts with the first experiment in which the mean CS score was the lowest of the three dimensions. Also, notice that the scores of all three dimensions were improved slightly over the first experiment.

5. Discussion and Conclusions

Our results should be viewed in light of our goals and the experimental design in this formative evaluation. We solicited expert opinions about the adequacy of TRUTH-TELLER's comparison texts in order to assess whether our knowledge representation and reasoning techniques were appropriate to the domain task and to obtain critiques identifying areas for improvement. Our primary intention was to determine if TT's comparisons were at least "within range" of that of humans and to determine the ways in which our model could be improved. We interpret the results as indicating that TRUTH-TELLER is somewhat successful at comparing truth telling dilemmas. Given the instruction to "evaluate the comparisons as you would evaluate short answers written by college undergraduates," we are encouraged by the grades assigned. We included the two human-generated texts as a calibration of the experts' scores; we are encouraged that some of the program's grades were higher than those assigned to texts written by post graduate humans.

On the other hand, our experiment does not involve an adequately sized sampling of human comparisons nor did we present the experts with outputs in which TRUTH-TELLER and humans generated comparison texts for the same pairs of cases. Quite simply, we felt it was premature to adopt this kind of experimental design for a formative evaluation. We recognize, however, that such an experimental design provides greater assurance of the quality of any results and will be employed for a future summative evaluation.

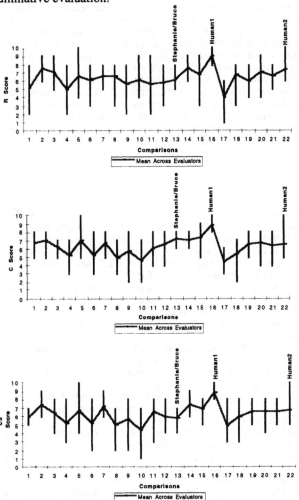

Figure 5: Max, Min, and Mean Values for R (top), C (middle), and CS (bottom) Scores in Experiment #1

The second part of the experiment attempts to address whether TRUTH-TELLER is competent at marshaling comparisons in a context sensitive manner. We believe that the slightly higher scores in the second part of the experiment are due in part to the fact that it would have been easier for the evaluators to recognize TT's sensitivity to context in the one-to-many part of the experiment than in the first part. Upon recognizing the difficulty of context sensitive comparisons and TT's ability to tackle them, the evaluators tended, we believe, to grade the program higher on all dimensions. In fact, as was noted, the context sensitivity dimension graded higher than the other two dimensions in this part of the experiment.

We also invited the evaluators to criticize the comparison texts. Several evaluators questioned TT's lack of hypothetical analysis; the program makes

144

immutable assumptions about reasons, actions, and actors. We will explore the possibility of hypothetically modifying problems in terms of factors as in HYPO (Ashley, 1990). Another repeated criticism involved the use of aggregate reasons to support an action. This was due, at least in part, to the fact that aggregate reasons are hard for the program to explain, since they require reference to other parts of the text. However, we have also considered that the calculus of support for actions and comparison of actions may be more complex than focusing simply on whether an action is fully supported by altruism or principled reasons. For instance, one could argue that an action that is mostly altruistic, but happens fortuitously to lead to a selfish side benefit, is as good as a fully altruistic action.

In conclusion, the evaluation encourages us that TRUTH-TELLER makes mostly reasonable comparisons of practical ethical cases with some ability to assess the salience of similarities and differences in a context sensitive manner. Its determinations of salience take into account a qualitative assessment of the cases' overall similarity and its other heuristics for reasoning about reasons identify additional criteria involving underlying principles, criticalness of consequences, participants' roles and untried alternatives.

References

Aleven, V. and Ashley, K.D. (1994). An Instructional Environment for Practicing Argumentation Skills; In the Proceedings of *AAAI-94*, pages 485-492.

Ashley, K.D. (1990). *Modeling Legal Argument: Reasoning with Cases and Hypotheticals*. MIT Press, Cambridge. Based on PhD. Dissertation.

Ashley, K.D. and McLaren, B.M. (1994). A CBR Knowledge Representation for Practical Ethics; In *Proceedings, 2d EWCBR*.

Bareiss, E. R. (1989). *Exemplar-Based Knowledge Acquisition - A Unified Approach to Concept Representation, Classification, and Learning*. Academic Press, San Diego, CA, 1989. Based on PhD dissertation, 1988.

Bok, S. (1989). *Lying: Moral Choice in Public and Private Life*. Random House, Inc. Vintage Books, New York.

Branting, K. L. (1991). Building Explanations From Rules and Structured Cases. In the *Journal of Man-Machine Studies*. 34, 797-837.

Edelson, D. C. (1992). When Should A Cheetah Remind You of a Bat? Reminding in Case-Based Teaching. In *Proceedings of AAAI-92*, 667-672. San Jose, CA.

Gilligan, C. (1982). *In a Different Voice*. Harvard University Press.

Hammond, K. (1989) *Case-Based Planning -- Viewing Planning as a Memory Task*. San Diego, CA: Academic Press.

Jonsen A. R. and Toulmin S. (1988). *The Abuse of Casuistry: A History of Moral Reasoning*. University of CA Press, Berkeley.

Kass, A. M., Leake, D., and Owens, C. C. (1986). Swale: A Program that Explains. In Schank, R. C. (ed.), *Explanation Patterns: Understanding Mechanically and Creatively*. Lawrence Erlbaum Associates, Hillsdale, NJ.

Kolodner, J. (1993) *Case-Based Reasoning* Morgan Kaufmann Publishers, Inc., San Mateo, CA.

Koton, P. (1988) *Using Experience in Learning and Problem Solving* . PhD thesis, MIT.

MacGregor R. and Burstein, M. H. (1991). Using a Description Classifier to Enhance Knowledge Representation. In *IEEE Expert* 6(3), pages 41-46.

Rissland, E. L. and Skalak, D. B. (1991). CABARET: Rule Interpretation in a Hybrid Architecture. In the *Journal of Man-Machine Studies*. 34, pages 839-887.

Rissland, E. L., Skalak, D. B., and Friedman, M. T. (1993). BankXX: A Program to Generate Argument through Case-Based Search. In *Fourth International Conference on AI and Law*, Vrie Universiteit, Amsterdam.

Strong, C. (1988). Justification in Ethics. In Baruch A. Brody, ed., *Moral Theory and Moral Judgments in Medical Ethics*, pp. 193-211. Kluwer, Dordrecht.

Sycara, E. P. (1987). *Resolving Adversarial Conflicts: An Approach Integrating Case-Based and Analytic Methods* Georgia Inst.Tech., Tech. Rep.GIT-ICS-87/26. Atlanta.

Veloso, M. V. (1992). *Learning by Analogical Reasoning in General Problem Solving*. PhD thesis, Carnegie Mellon University. Technical Report No. CMU-CS-92-174.

Towards the Integration of Case-Based, Schema-Based and Model-Based Reasoning for Supporting Complex Design Tasks*

Brigitte Bartsch-Spörl

BSR Consulting GmbH, Wirtstrasse 38, D-81539 München, Germany

Abstract. This paper presents an approach of how to build bridges between case-based and model-based reasoning. Unlike other approaches, these bridges do not intend to surmount the whole "abstraction distance" between concrete cases and generic models in one step. Instead they introduce and use a web of supporting columns which consist of useful intermediate representations called schemata, prototypes, patterns, templates or whatever is a suitable characterisation for their functional role in the design process.

The paper begins with a short summary of our knowledge acquisition experiences in a building design domain which led to the introduction of topological schemata. It continues with some concrete examples for the representation and integrated use of these different kinds of knowledge chunks introduced and gives a short overview of the state of our current implementation. In the end the paper summarises the main benefits of integrated case-/schema-/model-based approaches.

1 Introduction

There are application domains, especially in the customer support area, where pure case-based reasoning (CBR) has proven to be an adequate approach of problem solving and of providing software support systems which enhance the users' productivity in a very efficient way [3]. But there are also application domains, especially in the planning and design area, where the application of pure case-based reasoning approaches can cover only a part of the whole spectrum of the support functionality required and where CBR approaches have to be combined with other forms of reasoning and even with completely different kinds of non-AI tools e.g. for drawing or construction purposes [4].

This paper summarises an essential part of our experiences drawn from building a support system for a rather complex open world domain [8]. It mainly

---

* This research was supported by the Federal Ministry of Education, Science, Research and Technology (BMBF) within the joint project FABEL under contract no. 01IW104. Project partners in FABEL are German National Research Center for Computer Science (GMD), Sankt Augustin, BSR Consulting GmbH, München, Technical University of Dresden, HTWK Leipzig, University of Freiburg, and University of Karlsruhe.

concentrates on the problem of dealing with the heterogeneity of the design knowledge and of the reasoning processes and on the role(s) cases and abstractions from cases can play in such an environment.

2 Knowledge Acquisition Experiences

This chapter gives a brief summary of our knowledge acquisition experiences and in particular of the different viewpoints which evolved in the course of getting a deeper understanding of what is important for supporting design tasks.

For the FABEL project [10], we chose a rather complex building design domain because one of the methodological aims of the project is a seamless integration of case-based and model-based approaches and we wanted to build our application oriented demonstration prototypes in a domain which is heterogeneous enough to require and justify the combination of different reasoning approaches.

From the very beginning, it was clear that our architects and engineers use cases of different granularity for different purposes and during different stages of the design process. This starts with whole buildings which are used in the early phases for information gathering, for inspiration and for a first exploration of the design space. Then smaller pieces of buildings are looked at in order to identify interesting parts which are worth to be reused. At the end of this non-linear step-wise refinement process, concrete solutions for tricky tasks - in particular when there is very little space available - are searched for and reused in case they solve the actual problem at hand.

But using cases in the way described above is by no means enough for providing adequate design support. In the FABEL project, we use an installation methodology called ARMILLA [14] which was and is still being developed by the Institute for the Production of Industrial Buildings at the University of Karlsruhe. ARMILLA first provides a philosophy of how to make industrial buildings flexible, followed by organisational principles stating where to place the service spaces and how to distribute these spaces among the different subsystems etc. and last not least a collection of typical examples of how to find proper layouts e.g. for ducts of different capacity transporting different substances such as water, air or electricity.

When we went through the ARMILLA book [14] and other documentation material for the first time, we got the impression that this written material contains on the one side generic knowledge like e.g. parameterised models for the distribution of the service spaces, rules which decide whether certain combinations of parts and spatial arrangements are both possible and allowed, constraints for the capacity ranges or for the minimal/maximal distances between certain design elements etc. and on the other side cases showing concrete constellations of how to layout the return air system or the warm water ducts.

This impression became questioned as soon as we started to model the generic knowledge with the objective of building a domain ontology [15], [6]. We began with general concepts, relations, rules, constraints etc. and this worked fine for a while. But then we discovered more and more that many of the knowledge chunks we acquired are neither pure generic models nor representable as cases in an adequate way. Typical examples are e.g. knowledge chunks which represent good examples for how to solve certain layout problems that come together with a grid that makes them geometrically adjustable or with rules or constraints for guiding the implantation of the knowledge chunk in a variety of contexts. We realised that what we had in our hands were not merely cases but design templates equipped with knowledge about their proper use and adaptation hints, rules or constraints.

3 Design Expertise Embodied in Schemata and Patterns

Since we had explicitly noticed what was going to happen with our domain modelling efforts we began to look around and to get interested in similar experiences form other persons working on similar topics and we found astonishing parallels. A short summary of the most striking parallels is given in the following.

Akin writes about his experiments with novice and experienced architects [1]:

> Scenarios provide for the architect topological templates which are adaptable to different programmatic requirements. Scenarios are topological in the sense that they define physical relationships without fixed geometric attributes. These relationships link functions in desired ways and still allow malleability in geometric terms. Thus, they can be accommodated in sites with specific geometric dimensions and shapes and fixed window and door locations. Non-Architects and particularly students did not display any evidence that they were using scenarios and consequently, their solutions did not seem to benefit from known, topological patterns, as did the Architects.

Akin's observations are fully in accordance with our experiences in the FABEL project - with the only minor difference that we use the term topological schemata for what he has called scenarios.

A second source of parallels is Roy M. Turner's work on schema-based reasoning approaches in both a medical diagnosis and in an autonomous underwater vehicles domain [20]. Turner introduces and uses

- **procedural schemata** which contain task specific instructions an agent can perform in order to reach a goal
- **contextual schemata** which contain knowledge about a class of similar situations and about how an agent has behaved or should behave in new situations which are instances of this class
- **strategic schemata** which are more abstract than contextual schemata and summarise how to behave in similar classes of situations in terms of reactiveness to specified events and goals.

Turner's three kinds of schemata focus mostly on (re)action oriented and procedural aspects which seems to be natural for domains where the support system primarily aims at suggesting what to do next.

A third parallel is currently beginning to develop very actively in the domain of object-oriented software construction where Wolfgang Pree [17] and Erich Gamma et al. [11] recently published collections of so-called software design patterns and metapatterns. The term pattern they both use goes back to Christopher Alexander [2], an architect who suggested so-called pattern grammars for the definition of architectural building blocks and composition principles. Gamma et al. write in their recent book [11]:

> One thing expert designers know not to do is solve every problem from first principles. Rather, they reuse solutions that have worked for them in the past. When they find a good solution, they use it again and again. Such experience is part of what makes them experts. Consequently, you'll find recurring patterns of classes and communicating objects in many object-oriented systems. These patterns solve specific design problems and make object-oriented designs more flexible, elegant, and ultimately reusable. They help designers reuse successful designs by basing new designs on prior experience. A designer who is familiar with such patterns can apply them immediately to design problems without having to rediscover them.

Gamma et al. continue determining that a software design pattern consists of a pattern name, a problem description, a general solution and a set of consequences which result from applying the pattern. Both problem and solution description are abstracted from specific object-oriented programming languages in which they can be embedded without substantial structural changes. The patterns collected by Gamma et al. are classified as follows

- **creational patterns** which help to create object classes and instances
- **structural patterns** which help with the creation of larger object structures
- **behavioural patterns** which help to reuse algorithms and communication patterns.

All three kinds of patterns are natural ingredients for object-oriented software systems. With their collection of reusable patterns Gamma et al. do not aim at giving a complete alphabet of patterns in the sense of Alexander. They rather view the patterns collected as a starting point of a concerted action which is to produce a steadily increasing catalogue of reusable software building blocks.

After this excursion into several neighbouring fields we now return to the building design domain of the FABEL project. If we look at the different kinds of abstraction processes which are carried out there on the basis of concrete cases then we can determine that the major direction of abstraction in this domain is the abstraction from concrete geometrical information while preserving the essential topological structures and relations between the objects which constitute a case.

Therefore we introduce for our domain

- **topological schemata** which represent reusable design components equipped with knowledge how they can be embedded in an actual design context given by the concrete problem at hand.

As a short summary, we can state the following points about the emergence of topological schemata in building design:

- Schemata are very well suited to represent, communicate and apply design expertise.
- Schemata evolve in situations where a group of experienced designers work on recurring similar problems and where the people working together share at least to some extent ambitions to get more productive and produce better results through the reuse of former experiences.
- The documentation and distribution of design schemata requires additional work which is best done in small groups of experienced designers with strong abstraction capabilities and in a working environment where close cooperation and constant improvement of the design process are both encouraged and appreciated.

4 Case-Based Reasoning Approaches

In the first phase of the FABEL project, the main emphasis was laid on making case-based approaches [16] work. During this period, we particularly encountered that a major advantage of CBR approaches is their applicability even in ill-structured domains [4]. This is due to the fact that case-based reasoning does not require a complete and consistent domain model and does not rely on the closed world assumption as a necessary prerequisite.

So, the FABEL project started with the development of case-based retrieval functions in order to deal with the knowledge intensity of the design tasks. The first question to be answered was what do we regard as a case [21]. In principle, only buildings as a whole are real-world cases. But cases of this size are of rather limited usability and moreover very hard to manage. So we asked our experts what are meaningful parts of the building and began to regard all meaningful parts as potential cases. The size of the FABEL cases varies considerably from e.g. small parts of the return air system to parts of e.g. the fresh air system covering a whole storey or the whole building.

In order to grasp the notion of similarity in our domain we both developed classical feature based approaches as well as innovative graphically oriented approaches [22]. Till today the following case retrieval modules are implemented and can be used either stand-alone or in meaningful combinations [19]:

- a classical distance-based approach which determines the distances between cases from the numbers and types of the objects constituting the cases
- an indexing approach using also the objects constituting the cases which is implemented on the basis of an associative memory [13] and
- another approach based on the graphical appearance of the cases which compares abstracted bitmaps of design pictures.

These three modules can get enhanced by a fourth module using so-called gestalt indexes [18]. These gestalts represent characteristic patterns like a comb or a ring and can be used as additional case indexes. Further retrieval modules using tree- or graph-structured representations are still in the implementation and integration phase [22].

Within the current FABEL prototype no. 2 the user can select a part of the artefact already designed and activate the selection of similar cases according to either one or a combination of the retrieval methods mentioned above. The most suitable case found can then be taken over and adapted by hand.

It is important to note that we do not force the user in any way to use our case-based support functions. The functions are waiting in the background and only become active on explicit demand. Their activation requires that the user selects graphically the problem description part of his design and the kind of retrieval function he wants to use. Then he waits for the results and decides what to take over from the solutions suggested by the system.

One of the reasons for having implemented different retrieval methods is as follows:

Depending on the context and in particular on the user's intention, different retrieval methods are appropriate. E.g. if the user wants to have his design refined then the retrieval method should search for solutions which contain the user-selected design elements (that is the problem description) and at least some more refined design elements. Or if the user wants to see alternatives to his manually designed solution then the retrieval method should look for solutions which contain exactly the user-defined design elements - preferably in a different spatial arrangement.

Another requirement for different retrieval strategies comes into play when we think of combining the retrieval of cases with the retrieval of topological schemata: We need e.g. similarity functions that abstract from the concrete geometry when we want to retrieve for the same problem description both concrete cases and topological schemata which no longer carry concrete geometrical information with them. Or if we only stick to the function of cases and schemata and abstract from the layout at all then we need retrieval methods which focus exactly on the function and nothing else.

These considerations show that in complex design domains there is a need for different retrieval mechanisms which are dynamically adaptable to the actual context, the user's intention and to the problem solving methods available.

5 Model-Based Reasoning Approaches

The model-based reasoning (MBR) approaches in FABEL took a little longer because of the rather comprehensive knowledge needs of the model-based design support functions. Similar to the case-based retrieval field, there are again different approaches to knowledge-based assessment and adaptation functions under development [9].

One of these approaches is called DOM [5] which stands for domain onto-logy modelling. A short overview on DOM's main concepts, functions and roles follows.

The DOM ontology establishes the meaning and the permissible use of the design elements and the relations between these elements. Furthermore it in-cludes design maxims and rules relative to a given design methodology [14]. The domain ontology [15] plays a central role for

- supporting the group aspects because it lays ground for a common termino-logy and a shared understanding and use of the design elements
- defining what is the scope of the assessment functions and
- establishing a framework for the adaptation functions.

DOM provides the following design support functions:

- review a design layout in its current state in terms of the permissible use of the involved design elements
- assess the quality of a case in terms of coherence and conformance relative to the underlying ontology
- provide suggestions for improvement
- draw the user's attention to discrepancies and conflicts
- indicate alternatives and evaluate their merits.

The following figure 1 shows the assessment organisation with and around DOM. It indicates that drawn layouts are analysed with the goal of determining whether the design elements and relations contained adhere to the contents of the domain ontology. If this is not the case the system informs the designer about the detected discrepancies like e.g. missing elements or violations of maxims.

It is important to note that also this kind of design support functionality does neither require a complete or consistent domain model nor a closed world assumption. It is sufficient to have models for the criteria to be assessed and if unknown objects are detected the system will tell the user and ask what to do with them. At the moment the DOM assessment functions are implemented and further rectification and adaptation functions are the subject of ongoing work.

6 Schema-Based Reasoning Approaches

One of the essential insights of the FABEL project [10] is that cases play a useful role for the design of complex artefacts but a design theory is better expressed with more general terms and with adaptable templates [7]. This has to do with the fact that adaptability plays an important role and that schemata provide convenient ways to combine case knowledge with adaptation knowledge.

The general relations between generic models, episodic cases and schemata are shown in figure 2.

As already described in the chapters 2 and 3 of this paper, we have found that in domains like building or software design schemata evolve from a rational treatment with ways to improve the design process, in particular with the goal

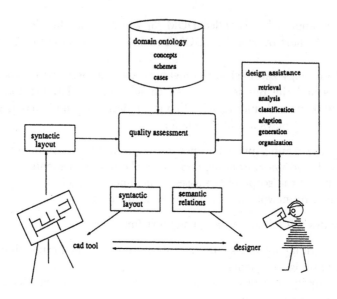

Fig. 1. Assessment organisation

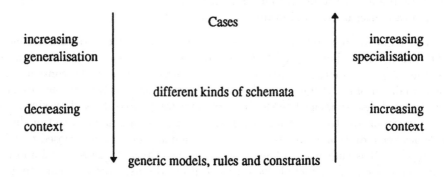

Fig. 2. Cases, schemata and generic knowledge

of gaining efficiency and ensured quality. As soon as schemata prove to be useful they have a chance to get documented in order to enforce their widespread use within the team or the organisation.

Most of the topological schemata we have collected till now are derived from the ARMILLA book [14] and consist of a semantically enriched representation of the layouts contained in the book. These layouts are combined with rules, constraints or procedures that guide the adaptation and embedding of a schema into a given context. We have found that in design domains like building or software design where the solution parts of a case do not stand alone but have to become a part of a much larger artefact, the adaptation is often easier to achieve than the embedding and the boundaries between these two tasks become blurred.

At the moment we have a collection of schemata which is going to be implemented as an extension of the DOM module's knowledge bases. For the retrieval of both cases and schemata we can use a subset of the case retrieval functions already implemented, in particular those which abstract from the concrete geometry and index with gestalt features [13], [18]. Some adaptation procedures are specified and others are the subject of ongoing work. An example for a topological schema follows in the next chapter.

7 Integrated Knowledge Representation and Knowledge Use

In the FABEL domain, we represent all knowledge and data about buildings, cases, generic models and schemata in an object-oriented way [6]. Cases are arrangements of complex design objects with fully instantiated slots. This means that all their attributes have concrete values like a type, a set of features, a location etc. or a reference to another existing design object.

Schemata are step-wise abstractions from cases where

- slots can be omitted or filled with "don't care"
- slots can be filled with variables taken from numerical intervals or from a set of defined values
- slots can contain a formula or an expression to be evaluated
- slots can be filled with references to virtual objects not yet placed etc.

Schemata can be instantiated and thus get specialised to cases. The constraints for the specialisation usually emerge from the concrete situation and from the surrounding context.

In the following we describe an example for the representation and integrated use of ARMILLA design knowledge in the form of cases, schemata and rules. A very small part of the ARMILLA design knowledge deals with using a grid for making the spatial organisation of the design objects easier, especially during the conceptual phases. The grid usage is determined as follows:

- During the conceptual phases a grid is used.
- The grid size has to be chosen before the design can start.
- All design objects that belong to the conceptual phases have to be placed with their center at a crossing point of the grid.
- The default ARMILLA grid has a side length of 12 units. (One unit usually stands for 0.1 metre.)
- If there are good reasons to deviate from this default, the following adaptations are possible:
    - It is possible to enlarge the grid in steps of exactly one unit.
    - It is recommended to enlarge the grid in steps of 3 units.

A layout pattern for how to solve a pipe arrangement problem, represented as a topological schema which incorporates the recommendations given above, is

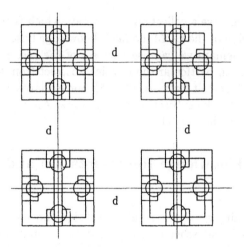

Fig. 3. Pipe layout pattern as a topological schema

shown in figure 3. The long lines annotated with d represent the grid, the other lines show where the pipes are to be placed.

The variable d has to be taken from the set of possible values 12, 15, 18, 21, 24. Analogously the rule about the one unit steps can be expressed.

In contrast to the rules and recommendations given above there exist buildings with a grid size of 10 units. According to the ARMILLA book [14] this is possible but not recommended because it leads to a series of modifications which are difficult to carry out. A building with a grid size of 10 units leads to a case which looks similar to the schema given in figure 3 with a distance of d=10.

Let's now imagine that there is a new building to be designed and there arises the need for a layout pattern for pipes. In this situation it is recommendable to search for layout patterns with a similarity function that considers the objects contained but abstracts from the exact geometry. With a similarity retrieval method like the one described in [13] the topological schema from figure 3 as well as the case with d=10 are found. The decision which result to reuse will be determined by grid size of the actual design. If this grid size is 15, the schema will be instantiated accordingly. If the grid size is 10, the case will be used without adaptation. If the grid size is 11, the architect can choose which result to take and try to adapt it by hand. If the grid size is 9, the adaptation by hand will fail because there is too little space available for placing all the objects in a way that is free from forbidden collisions between the conceptual design objects.

These examples show that generic knowledge and schema representations are more compact and convenient for assessment and adaptation purposes than a large number of concrete cases because they are able to represent the same amount of reusable design knowledge by a smaller number of objects enhanced with the necessary (mostly procedural) adaptation knowledge. In retrieval situations, it is usually not clear whether what is searched for will be found in the form of a concept, a schema or a case. Therefore the retrieval, assessment and adaptation procedures have to be able to deal with common (in our case object-oriented) knowledge structures on different levels of abstraction.

If we want to position our approach in the context of similar approaches, then it is clear that the idea of using cases and other forms of domain knowledge in an integrated way is by no means new [12]. But what we have developed in the FABEL project is a new mixture which seems especially suited for complex open world and at least partially innovative design domains where the goal of a software system is to provide support and not to solve the problem fully automatically in one step. These characteristic features also show the limitations of our approach for real world domains where the problems are not decomposable into subproblems which can be solved in a context-free manner.

8 Summary and Outlook

From our point of view, we have learned from the FABEL application domain that we need design support systems which play the role of a smoothly learning to get more competent and cooperative design assistant. Such an assistant should take over primarily the administrative, routine and some of the innovative tasks and leave the really creative tasks to the human designers. This last point is due both to acceptance and to feasibility reasons.

Besides this role determination we have shown that cases are a good and user-accepted vehicle to a better reuse of former designs. Case-based retrieval is the first step which can give inspiration and support for the reminding process. Case-based adaptation is the second step which is more knowledge-intensive and harder to build but can save a lot of manual effort.

Beyond the knowledge incorporated in cases it is very valuable to have a sharable domain ontology which can be used for a variety of purposes. We use the ontology e.g. for quality assessment of design fragments and for abstracting the knowledge incorporated in cases as well.

Last but not least we hope we have been able to demonstrate that schemata are very well suited for the representation of design knowledge and that schema-based reasoning is an important supplement to case-based and model-based approaches. Furthermore SBR is located at intermediate levels of abstraction and facilitates the seamless integration of CBR and MBR.

References

1. Akin, Ö.: Expertise of the Architect. In: Rychener, M. (ed.): Expert Systems for Engineering Design. Academic Press, London (1988) 173–196.
2. Alexander, C., Ishikawa, S., Silverstein, M., Jacobson, M., Fiksdahl-King, I., Angel, S.: A Pattern Language. Oxford University Press, New York (1977).

3. Althoff, K.-D., Barletta, R., Manago, M., Auriol, E.: A Review of Industrial Case-Based Reasoning Tools. AI Intelligence, Oxford (1995).

4. Bakhtari, S., Bartsch-Spörl, B.: Bridging the Gap between AI Technology and Design Requirements. In: Gero, J. S., Sudweeks, F. (eds): Artificial Intelligence in Design 94. Kluwer, Dordrecht (1994) 753–768.

5. Bakhtari, S., Oertel, W.: DOM-ArC: An Active Decision Support System for Quality Assessment of Cases. In: Aamodt, A., Veloso, M. (eds): Proceedings ICCBR-95. Springer, Heidelberg (1995), to appear.

6. Bakhtari, S., Bartsch-Spörl, B., Oertel, W., Eltz, U.: DOM: Domain Ontology Modelling for Architectural and Engineering Design. Fabel-Report Nr. 33, GMD, Sankt Augustin (1995).

7. Bartsch-Spörl, B.: KI-Methoden für innovative Design-Domänen. In: Richter, M., Maurer, F. (eds.): Expertensysteme 95. Infix, Sankt Augustin (1995) 137–151.

8. Bartsch-Spörl, B., Bakhtari, S.: A Support System for Building Design – Experiences and Convictions from the FABEL Project. In: Proceedings of the Lancaster International Workshop on Engineering Design. Springer, London (1995), to appear.

9. Börner, K. (ed.): Modules for Design Support. FABEL-Report No. 35, GMD, Sankt Augustin (1995).

10. Fabel-Consortium: A Survey of FABEL. Fabel-Report Nr. 2, GMD, Sankt Augustin (1993).

11. Gamma, E., Helm, R., Johnson, R., Vlissides, J.: Design Patterns – Elements of Reusable Object-Oriented Software. Addison-Wesley, Reading (1995).

12. Goel, A.K.: Integration of Case-Based Reasoning and Model-Based Reasoning for Adaptive Design Problem Solving. Ph. D. Dissertation, Ohio State University, Columbus (1989).

13. Gräther, W.: Computing Distances between Attribute-value Representations in an Associative Memory. In: Voss, A. (ed.): Similarity Concepts and Retrieval Methods. FABEL-Report No. 13, GMD, Sankt Augustin (1994) 12–25.

14. Haller, F.: ARMILLA - ein Installationsmodell. Institut für Baugestaltung, Baukonstruktion und Entwerfen, Universität Karlsruhe (1985).

15. Hedberg, S.R.: Design of a Lifetime, BYTE 10 (1994) 103–106.

16. Kolodner, J.: Case-Based Reasoning. Morgan Kaufmann, San Mateo (1993).

17. Pree, W.: Design Patterns for Object-Oriented Software Development. ACM Press, New York (1994).

18. Schaaf, J.W.: Gestalts in CAD-plans: Analysis of a Similarity Concept. In: Gero, J.S., Sudweeks, F. (eds.): Artificial Intelligence in Design'94. Kluwer, Dordrecht (1994) 437–446.

19. Schaaf, J.W.: "Fish and sink": An anytime-algorithm to retrieve adequate cases. In: Aamodt, A., Veloso, M. (eds): Proceedings ICCBR-95. Springer, Heidelberg (1995), to appear.

20. Turner, R.M.: Adaptive Reasoning for Real-World Problems: A Schema-Based Approach. Lawrence Erlbaum, Hillsdale (1994).

21. Voss, A.: The need for knowledge acquisition in case-based reasoning - some experiences from an architectural domain. In: Cohn, A. (ed.): Proceedings ECAI'94. Wiley & Sons, Chichester (1994) 463–467.

22. Voss, A. et al.: Retrieval of similar layouts - about a very hybrid approach in FABEL. In: Gero, J.S., Sudweeks, F. (eds.): Artificial Intelligence in Design'94. Kluwer, Dordrecht (1994) 625–640.

Separating the Cases from the Data: Towards More Flexible Case-Based Reasoning

Mike Brown[1], Ian Watson[2] and Nick Filer[1]

[1] Department of Computer Science, The University of Manchester, Manchester, UK
michaelb/nick@cs.man.ac.uk
[2] Department of Surveying, University of Salford, Salford, UK
i.d.watson@surveying.salford.ac.uk

Abstract. The number of successful, small-scale and purpose-built applications of CBR is growing rapidly. However, CBR has so far not been widely used as a methodology for reusing the large-scale data repositories typically maintained by a corporation. To facilitate this, cases must no longer be considered as concretely represented at the data level, but as virtual views of the underlying data. This paper argues that the basic requirement to support virtual cases are mapping functions between different data representations. It is argued that the use of mapping functions can increase flexibility in a number of ways. Multiple CBR applications can exploit a single database. Similarly, a single case representation can span multiple databases. Support for communication between different CBR applications as well as the evolution of case representation within a single application are also catered for by the same methodology. The paper provides reference to related work on database systems, with respect to the issues of mapping function implementation and management.

1 Introduction

Case-Based Reasoning (CBR) has rapidly reached a state of maturity as a practical solution to relatively small-scale problems. Many successful industrial applications have been developed and a growing number of commercial shells are available to aid in application development [4]. A typical application will use CBR for a single purpose and a standardised case template will be used to represent the data relevant to that application. CBR ought to be a technology that is also well-suited to the development of very large-scale Knowledge-Based Systems (KBS) as it has certain inherent advantages over other KBS techniques [22]. The storage of knowledge as modular cases, rather than as some coherent body of general-purpose rules, can greatly reduce the initial knowledge acquisition costs as well as improve maintainability [21]. In addition, CBR promotes cognitive economy [7], as it generally requires less effort to adapt the solution to a similar past problem than to derive a new solution from first principles.

Current attempts at applying CBR technology on a large-scale have involved a commitment to knowledge engineering, with the cases and the indexing structure that organises those cases being specifically created for the purposes of the CBR application [11]. However, a more commercially appealing approach is to use CBR as a technique for exploiting existing databases [20], so that the data held therein can be re-used. In this paper, it is argued that many CBR applications should be constructed on top of a single large-scale data repository, where each CBR application is tailored to a specific purpose to which that data can be put. It will be argued that, to support this type of reuse of data, the cases within each application must be virtual views of the underlying data.

2 Virtual Case Representation

In this section, a new approach to describing cases is introduced. Cases are not considered as being direct manifestations of the underlying data, but as virtual views of it. To support this, a mechanism for mapping between different data representations is required. As will be described, this leads to a number of ways in which the flexibility of CBR is enhanced, in comparison to existing technology.

2.1 Limitations of Current Case Representation

The prevailing approach in CBR tools is to treat cases as instances of some predetermined and static case template (e.g. CBR Express), even if cases are permitted to be hierarchically structured into standardised fragments (e.g. KATE, ReCall, ReMind). The use of standardised cases is popular because it greatly simplifies much of the CBR process, such as indexing, matching and retrieval. The representation of a case should directly reflect the purpose for which that case is to be used [6]. Even where multiple uses of a single case are considered, a single case representation is usually assumed and subsets of the case features are selected by each of a number of predetermined dimensions [3, 17]. It follows that adherence to a standardised case representation is well-suited if an application requires a single, problem-solving perspective. This is true in many small-scale applications, which, perhaps, explains why currently available commercial tools rely on standardised cases. However, tailoring a case representation to the requirements of a single application is not feasible in large-scale applications, where knowledge re-usage for a wide range of purposes will inevitably be required.

Another prevailing and limiting assumption is that the actual data that comprises a case base is stored in the same format as the cases themselves, i.e. the cases are inseparable from the data. In applications where the case data originates in pre-existing databases, this requires that either the cases conform to the format in which the data is stored, or a translation program is written to extract relevant data and store it within a new case base. This causes a problem of data redundancy as the case base is independent of the database from which it derives. Moreover, if multiple CBR applications are built on top of a single database, there is no scope for direct communication of data between the CBR systems, as each operates on its own localised case base.

This is the situation with the current generation of CBR tools. The more sophisticated tools have good data import facilities (e.g., ESTEEM, KATE, and ReMind). The exception to this approach is ART*Enterprise, which is able to

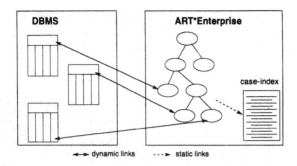

Fig. 1. ART*Enterprise Data Integration

map ART objects to data stored in relational tables (see Figure 1). The attributes of these objects will be updated if the data in the relational tables changes or vice versa. However, although ART*Enterprise has CBR functionality and can match and retrieve ART objects, it requires an index to be created. This index is static and will not be automatically changed if the underlying data changes.

What is proposed here is that the data required to populate a case base is derived by mappings attached to a standardised case format; hence, the cases are only indirectly linked to the raw data on which they are based. This indirection allows enhanced flexibility in a number of different ways, including:

- Multiple views of cases representing the same data
- Cases that span multiple databases
- Support for co-operative CBR
- Evolution in case representation

2.2 The Need for Mapping between Cases and Raw Data

To genuinely reflect different uses of the same episodic data, there is a need to support heterogeneous case bases, where several orthogonal cases may represent views of the data concerning a single episode [14]. As a hypothetical example, consider the situation of a large construction company. To a first approximation, it is assumed that the company routinely stores a detailed account of each building contract within a single unified database.

This hypothetical situation is typical for many companies in all areas of industry; the company has a massive amount of data which has the potential to be put to valuable usage. CBR is well-suited to this exploitation. For example, CBR may be a useful guide to a construction company in tendering for new contracts. Tendering requires cost estimation based on both inevitable expenditure (e.g. labour and materials) and more uncertain factors (e.g. the risk of legal cost from litigation resulting from carrying out the contract). CBR can allow cost estimation based on adaptation of the known costs of similar previous contracts. CBR can also be applied for risk factor analysis. For example, by recording the circumstances in which a company has been sued in the past, the recurrence of the same legal problems can be predicted in the future. This is just a variant of standard CBR approaches to failure avoidance (e.g. [15]).

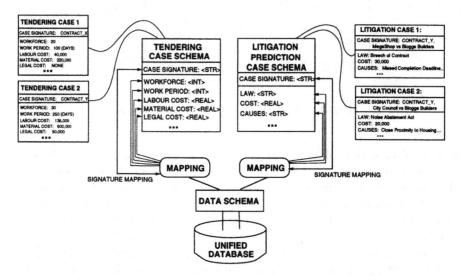

Fig. 2. Deriving Multiple Case Bases from a Single Database

The feature sets, relevant to the purposes of contract tendering and litigation prediction, will have little overlap, hence different case structures are ideally required for each application. However, the cases for each application should derive from the company's existing database. This is achieved by the establishment of a set of *mapping functions* between the data schema for the database and the specific data schema for each case base, as shown in Figure 2. Hence, cases are in fact virtual views of the underlying data. Nevertheless, to an external CBR application, these cases should behave as concrete data structures.

One use of mapping functions is to derive the values for the features of individual, virtual cases. These mapping functions will often be complex and must deal with the problem of semantic heterogeneity [1, 2, 9, 19]. For example, in a tendering case, a single feature value may represent the combined labour cost for a particular building contract. In practice, establishing this value may require a selective search through all records of the employees working on the project and a summation of their wages for the period of the contract.

As well as establishing feature values, a specific type of mapping function, referred to here as a *signature mapping*, is required to populate a virtual case base. A signature mapping is assumed to establish a set of data values (i.e. the *case signature*) that is necessary and sufficient to uniquely identify each virtual case instance. As an example (Figure 2), there may be exactly one tendering case for each building contract undergone by a construction company, hence a sufficient case signature may be the name of each contract. In contrast, there may be multiple litigation cases for each building contract requiring a more complex case signature (e.g. citing the plaintiff and defendant for the case). Issues concerning the implementation and management of the two types of mapping function are discussed in more detail in Section 3.

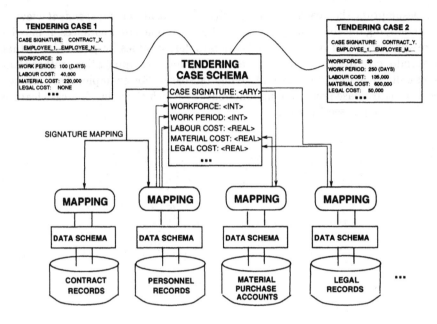

Fig. 3. Deriving a Single Case Base from Multiple Databases

In reality, the required mappings between data and virtual cases will be more complex because the assumption of a single unified database will not hold. A single virtual case may derive its feature values from multiple databases. This will allow a CBR application where the cases represent a purpose-specific, cross-sectional view of the activities of a company. For example (as shown in Figure 3), it is reasonable to assume that the variety of cost factors required to constitute a tendering case are in fact derived from multiple databases, covering varied aspects of a construction company's operation. Cross-sectional cases will generally be highly important for providing CBR support at an administration level, such as for project management.

The complexity, in terms of implementation, of building a virtual case base on top of multiple databases is manifest in the signature mapping function. The case signature must provide sufficient constraints to be able to identify all relevant data stored in *each* of the databases from which a single, virtual case is derived. For example, the name of a contract may not be explicitly stored in every database within a construction company. Identifying the data associated with each contract therefore requires additional information to be used as part of the case signature. For example, knowing which employees worked on a particular project might be used to indirectly infer data associated with that contract, where the name of the contract is an insufficient identifier (see Figure 3) .

2.3 The Need for Inter-Case-Base Mapping

The assumption that each virtual case base represents an *independent* view of the underlying databases may not always hold. In some circumstances, it may be more appropriate for one CBR application to derive values for part of its virtual cases indirectly from the virtual cases used by another application, rather than using a direct mapping to the underlying databases. For example, there are two general routes, based on mapping functions, by which the value of a case feature could be derived (see Figure 4):

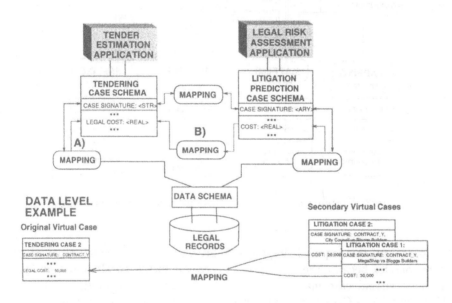

Fig. 4. An Example of Mapping Between Virtual Case Bases

- **A)** Directly, from the database; the signature of a virtual case is used to search the database records and the feature values of that case are derived from the selected records.
- **B)** Indirectly, via another virtual case base; the signature of an initial virtual case is used to match against the signatures of virtual cases in the other case base. The signatures of the secondary virtual cases are used to select records from the database. The feature values of the secondary cases can be derived by the mapping functions to the database. The feature values for the original case can then be derived by mapping functions to the secondary cases.

The indirect data access via route B) has two pragmatic advantages. Firstly, the inter-case-base mapping function may be easier to encode than ones that directly access a database. This is illustrated by the example in Figure 4. The matching between the case signatures of the tendering and litigation cases is straightforward (the first value being a subset of the latter). The legal costs of a tendering case can then be trivially derived by a summation of the costs of all selected litigation cases. Hence, assuming that the mappings from the litigation cases to the underlying database(s) are already in place, deriving mapping functions to compute the legal costs of a tendering case is a near-trivial task.

Secondly, despite introducing an extra level of indirection, in many cases the implementation of route B) may be more efficient than route A). This occurs when the matching of virtual case signatures causes additional information to be associated with the original virtual case. This is true for the example in Figure 4 where the tendering case signature (the name of a construction contract) gains additional information from the mapping to litigation cases (the names of specific legal cases). The inferred information can, in turn, be used to provide a more directed search of the underlying database(s).

The above discussion concerned the need for inter-case-base mapping for virtual case bases created for orthogonal purposes. The need may be greater if more than one virtual case base exists to serve a similar purpose. The support for *co-operation* between multiple reasoners is an appealing approach to problem solving in complex domains [5]. For example, multiple CBR applications could be used to assess the legal risk of a new contract, each application concentrating on a specific legal aspect (e.g. breach of contract, environmental pollution, etc.). For complex domains, it is likely that there will be some overlap in the content of different cases. For example, a single legal case will typically involve several legal aspects, hence, the data representing that case may be partially shared between multiple virtual case bases. Mappings are required to maintain equivalence relationships between the case bases (cf. [19]). This will allow the propagation of decisions between the co-operating CBR applications. So, for example, if one legal risk assessment application selects a particular virtual case as relevant, based on its own specialist criteria, the equivalent virtual cases of other CBR applications should receive greater importance. This information can, in principle, be communicated via the mapping functions.

2.4   The Need for Intra-Case-Base Mapping

A final source of flexibility is in the support of intra-case-base mappings. Intra-case-base mappings will be required where the representation of a case for a single application evolves over time. This will typically occur if multiple versions of the same CBR application need to be supported (see Figure 5), or if the underlying databases change. New case features will be added as new data types are made available and/or are required by the new application versions. Other case features will become obsolete (e.g. because the required data is no longer stored in the underlying databases). Finally, the format for the value for a particular case feature may change over time (e.g. from real number to integer).

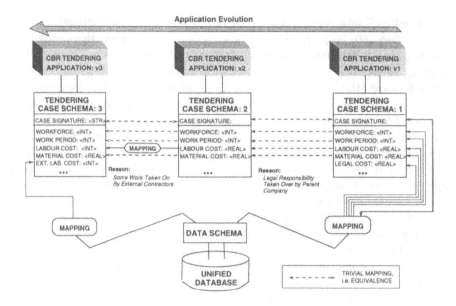

Fig. 5. An Example of Mapping Within a Single Virtual Case Base

Rather than generating a new set of mapping functions to the databases for each version of a virtual case schema, mappings between the schemas may be maintained, as shown in Figure 5. This is similar to the use of mappings advocated in section 2.3. The advantage of ease of implementation is still valid; a majority of the mappings between schema versions will typically be *trivial* (i.e. equivalences), hence, existing mapping functions to the underlying databases can be readily exploited. New mappings (either between case representations or to the underlying database) are only inserted where there is change in the representation. The indirection introduced will cause some degradation in access time for intra-schema mappings as, unlike for inter-schema mappings, no additional constraints concerning the case signature are likely to be inferred. However, where the intra-schema mappings are equivalence relationships, this loss in performance should be minimal. The biggest advantage for the intra-schema mapping approach is that it provides a neat way of maintaining the compatibility of a CBR application over time. For example, via the mapping functions, a current version of a CBR application will be able to access *legacy databases*, i.e. databases storing historical data, in an old version of the data schema.

3 Towards Virtual Case Bases

This paper has put forward a new approach to implementing CBR systems, where cases are represented separately from the underlying data. In this scheme, cases are virtual and act as application-specific views of the data. It has been argued that this methodology is essential for the future use of CBR technology to support large-scale, corporate-wide knowledge bases, where CBR must rely on the use of existing databases rather than specifically generated case data.

The key to virtual case bases has been seen as the implementation of inter-schema mapping functions. Two types of mapping function have been identified:

- **Signature mapping functions:** used to establish the set of case instances in a virtual case base.
- **Normal mapping functions:** used to generate the feature values for a virtual case instance.

Consideration of cases as virtual views of the underlying database is a promising new departure for CBR research. However, the issues involved have received considerable interest within the database community for over a decade [1, 2, 10, 19]. In particular, the problem of data integration in Heterogeneous Database Systems (HDBS) has a marked similarity to the problem discussed in this paper. However, a virtual case base requires only a *loose* coupling to the underlying databases, which simplifies the problem. In particular, unlike for HDBS, the maintenance of consistency is only one way. The virtual case base is derived from the databases, but modifications to the virtual case base should generally not be propagated as changes to the underlying databases.

To realise the ideas described in this paper, technology needs to be developed for two distinct aspects:

1. Interactive support for the encoding of each mapping (see section 3.1).
2. Automatic management of mappings during data access (see section 3.2).

3.1 Mapping Function Implementation

Significant advances in addressing the problems of data integration have recently been made at the University of Manchester as part of a project concerning the development of a CAD framework. CAD frameworks provide an environment into which separate software tools can be integrated [13], so that various management tasks, such as controlling the communication of data between tools, can be automated. Different tools can have different data representations, so a similar data integration problem to the one described here can arise.

It is practically impossible to provide an automated means of generating mapping functions as this task typically requires deep insights into the knowledge domains of the respective schemas, beyond the information stored within them [9]. However, it is useful to develop tools to support a knowledge engineer in the implementation of the mapping functions. A number of approaches to providing this support have been developed at the University of Manchester.

Firstly, a set of generic operators is provided which can enable a knowledge engineer to describe structural constraints upon the mapping [8]; such as the equivalence relationships that exist between features of different virtual cases. Some automated assistance for the task of establishing structural constraints is also possible. For example, finding similarities in the naming of constructs within two data representations is a powerful heuristic method for establishing where there is overlap in the semantics of the two representations [16]. In addition, consideration of the structural aspects of two data representations can be used to establish correspondences between them [18] (cf. approaches to analogical mapping, such as [12]). An area for current and future work is to amalgamate these various components into a single integrated environment to providing a methodology for mapping function development.

From the work on HDBS [1, 2, 19], a fundamental requirement for the integration of two heterogeneous data schemas is to provide a common data model to which the schemas can be translated, prior to generating the mappings between them. Hence, a central data access module is required. This module must provide a set of access routines that is generic enough to cover a wide range of data representations, yet simple enough to allow ease of porting to a wide range of database platforms. The existing GPIC system [13] for database access has been designed and implemented to fulfill these requirements. The proposed future development of GPIC is to provide facilities for storing mapping functions within the data access module. Meta-data concerning mapping (such as the declarative description based on mapping operators) will also be stored within GPIC to facilitate the management of the invocation of mapping functions. Hence, the future development of GPIC will provide the ideal basis for support for construction of virtual case bases and, by the arguments of this paper, an appropriate technology for the development of large-scale, multi-purpose CBR applications.

3.2 Mapping Function Management

A given mapping function is tied to a particular feature of a virtual case and is assumed to be triggered on request for the value of that feature. The examples in this paper have implied that cases should be purely virtual, in that there is no local case base into which the values generated by a mapping function can be stored. In practice, this is an extreme position. In reality, some local storage of data associated with a virtual case base will be required. It follows that several modes for the management of mapping functions can be identified, distinguished by the extent to which the resultant case base is virtual. The selection of which mode to apply is application-dependent. For example, purely virtual cases may only be required for real-time CBR applications or for CBR in highly volatile domains. The various modes are described below.

1) Single Call - Permanent Local Storage This is the mode currently supported by most commercial tools. In effect, the mapping functions provide a mechanism for translating from the database to the required data format of the CBR application.

2) Periodic Call On Request - Temporary Local Storage In this mode, the mapping function is called if a locally stored value for the case feature is not available. The value returned by the mapping function is stored locally and is used on subsequent accesses to the feature value. This has an advantage of efficiency, in that the same value is not repeatedly recalculated, but does not guarantee that the case base is a faithful representation of the underlying database.

By its precedent-based nature, CBR should be capable of tolerating some time-delay before a case base is returned to consistency with respect to the underlying databases. Hence, this mode may be the most practical for many CBR applications. Periodic use of the mapping functions to regenerate the values within the local data store of a virtual case base will be required to reinstate consistency. For example, all mapping functions may be called each time the CBR application is invoked (cf. [2, pp46-53]).

This mode is also most appropriate for signature mappings. Unlike other feature values, the case signature does *require* localised storage. This is in order to provide the case-based application with a handle by which to refer to each virtual case instance (hence, enabling virtual cases to appear concrete). Periodic use of the signature mapping to check the validity of the current set of virtual case instances is desirable, but the population should remain stable during a particular invocation of the virtual case base by the CBR application.

3) Always Call - No Local Storage This is the purely virtual mode. The mapping function is always called to regenerate a feature value, hence the virtual case base represents an *up-to-date* view of the underlying databases. The efficiency cost, in terms of having to repeatedly recalculate data values, may be high. This mode should, therefore, be reserved for critical or highly time-dependent case features.

4 Conclusions

Our experience of applying CBR to knowledge reuse within industrial sectors, such as the construction industry, has highlighted a severe limitation in the current generation of CBR tools. If the uptake of CBR is to become exponential over the next few years, as Alex Goodall states in his preface to a recent report on CBR tools [4], it is essential that CBR tools can use data in an organisation's existing databases. The creation of local data models, as in ART*Enterprise, is welcomed but is only a partial solution. This paper has set out a theoretical framework for deriving virtual cases from data, held in disparate heterogeneous databases, by using mapping functions. Although theoretical, it is based on sound research already carried out at the University of Manchester. The authors of this paper are now seeking research funding to develop a workbench that will combine conventional direct data retrieval with virtual cases and indirect retrieval using the methodology described here.

References

1. Special Issue on Heterogeneous Databases. *ACM Computing Surveys*, 22(3), September 1990.
2. Special Issue on Heterogeneous Distributed Database Systems. *Computer*, 24(12), December 1991.

3. R Alterman and M Wentworth. Determining the Important Features of a Case. In *DARPA CBR Workshop*, pages 197–202. Morgan Kaufmann, 1989.

4. K-D Althoff, E Auriol, R Barletta, and M Manago. A Review of Industrial Case-Based Reasoning Tools. AI Intelligence, PO Box 95, Oxford, OX2 7XL, 1995. ISBN 1 898804 01 X.

5. S Andreas, G Schlageter, and S Kirn. Problem Solving in Federative Environments: The FRESCO Concept of Cooperative Agents. In *The New Generation of Information Systems: From Data to Knowledge*. Springer-Verlag, 1992.

6. K D Ashley. Indexing and Analytical Models. In *DARPA CBR Workshop*, pages 197–202. Morgan Kaufmann, 1989.

7. M Brown. Case-Based Reasoning: Principles and Potential. AI Intelligence, PO Box 95, Oxford, OX2 7XL, 1992.

8. M Brown. Generic Operators for Schema-to-Schema Mappings. Technical Report JCF/MAN/111-05/31-Mar-95, The Uni. of Manchester, 1995.

9. M Brown, Z Moosa, N Filer, J Heaton, and J Pye. Close Integration of a CAD Vendor's Framework into the Jessi-Common-Frame Using a Flexible and Adaptable Procedural Interface. In *Proc. of The Int. Workshop on Concurrent/Simultaneous Engineering Frameworks and Applications*, Lisboa, Portugal, 1995.

10. C S dos Santos, S Abiteboul, and C Delobel. Virtual Schemas and Bases. *Lecture Notes in Computer Science: Proc. of EDBT 94*, (779):81–94, 1994.

11. D C Edelson. When Should a Cheetah Remind You of a Bat? Reminding in Case-based Teaching. In *Proc. of AAAI-92*, pages 667–672, 1992.

12. B Falkenhainer, K D Forbus, and D Gentner. The Structure Mapping Engine: Algorithms and Examples. *Artificial Intelligence*, 41(1):1–63, 1989.

13. N Filer, M Brown, and Z Moosa. Integrating CAD Tools into a Framework Environment Using a Flexible and Adaptable Procedural Interface. In *Proc. of EURO-DAC '94*, pages 200–205, Grenoble, 1994. IEEE-CS Press.

14. A K Goel, J L Kolodner, M Pearce, and R Billington. Towards a Case-Based Tool for Aiding Conceptual Design Problem Solving. In *DARPA CBR Workshop*, pages 109–120, Washington, D.C., 1991.

15. K J Hammond. Explaining and Repairing Plans That Fail. *Artificial Intelligence.*, 45:173–228, 1990.

16. S Mir. *Heuristic Reasoning for an Automatic Commonsense Understanding of Logic Electronic Design Specifications*. PhD thesis, The Uni. of Manchester, 1993.

17. M J Pazzani. Indexing Strategies for Goal Specific Retrieval of Cases. In *DARPA CBR Workshop*, pages 31–35. Morgan Kaufmann, 1989.

18. P K C Pun. *Knowledge-Based Applications = Knowledge Base + Mappings + Application*. PhD thesis, The Uni. of Manchester, 1991.

19. M P Reddy, B E Prasad, P G Reddy, and A Gupta. A Methodology for Integration of Heterogeneous Databases. *IEEE Transactions on Knowledge and Data Engineering*, 6(6):920–933, December 1994.

20. H Shimazu, H Kitano, and A Shibata. Retrieving Cases from Relational Data-Bases: Another Stride Towards Corporate-Wide Case-Based Systems. In *Proc. of IJCAI-93*, pages 909–914, Chambéry, 1993. Morgan Kaufmann.

21. J E Vargas and S Raj. Developing Maintainable Expert Systems Using Case-Based Reasoning. *Expert Systems*, 10(iv):219–225, 1993.

22. I Watson and F Marir. Case-Based Reasoning: A Review. *The Knowledge Engineering Review*, 9(4):327–54, 1994.

Route Planning by Analogy

Karen Zita Haigh and Manuela Veloso

School of Computer Science
Carnegie Mellon University
Pittsburgh PA 15213-3891
khaigh@cs.cmu.edu, mmv@cs.cmu.edu

Abstract. There have been several efforts to create and use real maps in computer applications that automatically find good map routes. In general, online map representations do not include information that may be relevant for the purpose of generating good realistic routes, including for example traffic patterns, construction, or number of lanes. Furthermore, the notion of a good route is dependent on a variety of factors, such as the time of the day, and may also be user dependent. This motivation leads to our work on the accumulation and reuse of previously traversed routes as cases. In this paper, we demonstrate our route planning method which retrieves and reuses multiple past routing cases that collectively form a good basis for generating a new routing plan. We briefly present our similarity metric for retrieving a set of similar routes. The metric effectively takes into account the geometric and continuous-valued characteristics of a city map. We then present the replay mechanism and how the planner produces the route plan by analogizing from the retrieved similar past routes. We discuss in particular the strategy used to merge a set of cases and generate the new route. We use illustrative examples and show some empirical results from a detailed online map of the city of Pittsburgh containing over 18,000 intersections and 25,000 street segments.

1 Introduction

Case-based reasoning is a powerful problem solving technique which enables flexible reuse of experience. It is an on-going research challenge to apply case-based reasoning techniques to real-world domains. We have been investigating the use of case-based reasoning methods to enable a planner to reuse solutions to previous similar problems in order to solve new problems. In this paper, we demonstrate how our retrieval and adaptation techniques are applied and extended to the problem of route planning.

We are interested in having a computer generate good routes from an online representation of a map. Online representations of maps however do not usually include information that may be relevant for route planning, including traffic patterns, construction, one versus multi-lane roads, residential areas, time of the day, or a particular user's driving preferences. The path finding task is therefore dynamic and complex, and learning from route planning and execution experience is necessary.

Case-based reasoning methods allow us to take advantage of prior routing and execution experience. Our general approach for incorporating case-based reasoning with planning, execution, and learning within this real-world task consists of:

- Accumulating route planning episodes in a case library so that we can reuse previously visited routes and avoid unguided search.
- Retrieving a set of similar routes that collectively form a good basis for generating a new routing plan by using the geometric features of the domain.
- Using execution experience to identify characteristics of particular routes that are not represented in the map and update the map and the *goodness* of the stored cases to reflect them.
- Using experience gained from altering plans during execution failures to acquire an understanding of when particular replanning techniques are applicable.

In previous papers, we presented several aspects of this project, including the similarity metric which effectively takes into account the natural geometric and continuous-valued characteristics of the map domain [4], and a discussion of the learning opportunities potentially offered by the real execution of the proposed planned routes [5].

The main focus of this paper is on presenting how the planning algorithm reuses the multiple similar retrieved cases. The paper is organized as follows. In Section 2 we show the representation of the real map, briefly introduce the planning domain itself, and discuss what information is represented and available to the planner. Section 3 reviews the storage and retrieval methods showing also how the goodness of a case is captured and used. Section 4 presents the analogical reuse of the multiple cases. Section 5 discusses empirical results and Section 6 describes related work. Finally, Section 7 draws conclusions on this work.

2 Representation of the Map Domain

Our current implementation uses the PRODIGY planner [1] and its analogical reasoning capabilities [11]. The route planning knowledge available to the planner consists of the map knowledge base, a set of operators (rules used to model changes in state), and the case library (described in the following section).

2.1 The Map

The map used in our work is a complete map of Pittsburgh containing over 18,000 intersections and 5,000 streets comprised of 25,000 segments. (An entire street is comprised of several segments corresponding to city blocks.)

The map is represented as a planar graph with the edges indicating street segments and the nodes indicating intersections. Associated with the intersections are the (x, y) coordinates of the intersection and a list of segments which meet at that intersection. Associated with each street segment is the name of the street containing it, and a range of numbers corresponding to building numbers on that block. In addition, there are several addresses of restaurants and shops in the city. Figure 1 shows a short excerpt from our files.

The representation, although it describes the map completely in terms of

```
(intersection-coordinates i0 631912 499709)
(intersection-coordinates i1 632883 485117)
(segment-length s0 921 )
(segment-street-numbers s0 4600 4999)
(segment-intersection-match s0 i0 )
(segment-intersection-match s1 i0 )
(segment-street-mapping 0 S_Craig_St)
(address Great_Scot 413 S_Craig_St)
```

Fig. 1. Excerpt from map database.

which streets exist, lacks in several areas important to an executing system. In particular, it does not indicate:

- existence of or direction of one-way streets,
- illegal turning directions,
- overpasses and other nonexistent intersections,
- traffic conditions,
- construction, and
- road quality, determined by factors such as number of lanes, surface (cobblestone, tarmac), and neighbourhood designation (residential, business).

This lack of information will lead to many situations in which the system needs to learn.

3 Storing and Retrieving Cases

A CBR planning system has to first identify cases that may be appropriate for reuse, and then modify them to solve the new problem. In order for the case identification phase to be efficient, the planning system must have a clear and easy method to store and subsequently retrieve past information. The following subsections describe our method for storing and retrieving routes. More detailed information regarding case retrieval (including run-time and efficiency results) can be found in a previous paper [4].

3.1 Case Representation and Indexing

When PRODIGY generates a plan, the detailed derivational trace of the successful planning episode is stored as a single case that can be multiply-indexed. Failed search decisions are annotated to be avoided at reuse time. For our route planning domain, the representation of each case will also include a detailed description of the situations encountered at execution time, including explanations of any errors that occurred and all replanning that was done to correct the problems.

Each case is also approximated by a set of straight line segments in a two-dimensional graph, and line segments are allowed to intersect only at their endpoints. The endpoints of these segments are generated at points where the new case intersects with existing cases as well as at points where the route changes direction and the segment would no longer approximate the route.

This graph acts as an index into the case library so that cases can be easily retrieved. The resulting graph, which we call the *case graph*, is illustrated in Figure 2b. Figure 2a is a map in which solid line segments represent previously

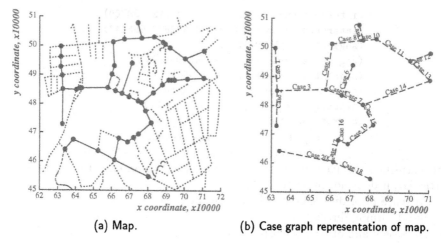

(a) Map.   (b) Case graph representation of map.

Fig. 2. Marked streets and intersections in the map (1% of the complete Pittsburgh map) are locations visited during previous planning.

visited streets, and dotted segments represent unvisited streets. Figure 2b shows the abstract manner in which these paths are stored in the CBR indexing file. Note that Case 20 oversimplifies the path, but the bend in the road would not change the final routing (since there are no intersections along the route), so this abstraction is acceptable.

Note that several segments may together describe one complete case route, and one segment may index several cases.

3.2 Similarity Metric and Retrieval

Identifying cases relevant to the new problem is done by the use of a *similarity metric*, which estimates the similarity of cases to the problem at hand. An ideal metric might:
 − take into account the relative desirability of different cases;
 − suggest how multiple cases may be ordered in a single new solution; and
 − identify which part(s) of a case are likely to be relevant.
Finding a similarity metric that is both effective and fast is a difficult task for the researcher. It is sufficiently difficult that many existing CBR systems identify neither multiple cases nor partial cases at all. The metric developed by Haigh and Shewchuk [4] effectively takes into account the geometric and continuous-valued characteristics of a city map, and can generate multiple and partial cases.

Suppose we undertake to plan a route on our map from some initial location i to some goal location g. Although we want to reuse cases, we want to avoid long meandering routes and are therefore willing to traverse unexplored territory. It is important to find a reasonable compromise between staying on old routes and finding new ones. Hence, we assign each case an *efficiency* value β, which is a rough measure of how much a known case should be preferred to unexplored areas β is an indicator of the "quality" of a case, and is independent of its length. After the case has been executed a few times, the β value associated with it will start reflecting the quality of the case as experienced in the real world. In particular, it will take into account traffic conditions, road quality and time of day. Each case-segment is annotated with information indicating what β should be as a function of the quality factors. For example, we might want to have a higher β value at rush hour:

$$\text{if } (15{:}00 \leq \text{current\_time} \leq 18{:}00)$$
$$\text{then } \beta = 1.5$$
$$\text{else } \beta = 0.6$$

Other possible comparisons might involve specific dates (e.g. construction), season or weather (e.g. impassability due to potholes, snow or mud), or direction (e.g. one-way streets). When invoked, the similarity metric uses the particular β associated with current conditions.

Since the only cases stored are those that the user executes, the metric will become biased towards routes that the user prefers.

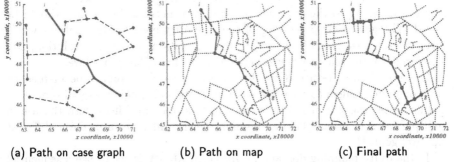

(a) Path on case graph   (b) Path on map   (c) Final path

Fig. 3. (a) The path found by the similarity metric in the case graph; dashed lines represent case edges, thick lines represent the path. (b) Path of cases superimposed on the real map; dashed lines represent where the planner needs to plan from scratch, solid lines represent cases. (c) Path modified by PRODIGY/ANALOGY to conform to real world constraints.

Figure 3 shows a path chosen by the similarity metric between the labelled initial (i) and goal (g) points and some β value assigned to each case in the case graph. Each segment in the path of Figure 3a corresponds to a case (or more than one) that the similarity metric believes will be helpful in solving the new problem. This path can also provide the planner with useful hints about how to link the cases together: where to change from case to case, as well as when to leave the cases entirely and start planning from scratch.

Note that a routing case is not used in reverse, since in general good routing situations are directional (e.g. one-way streets or traffic conditions). Note also that the path given to PRODIGY/ANALOGY would not be executable in the real world because it traverses several regions where there are no streets. It is the planner's job to knit this information together into a plan, taking into account details such as one-way streets and illegal turns that cannot be resolved by the geometric algorithm. This process is described further in the following section.

4 Route Planning by Analogy

We follow the analogical replay strategy developed by Veloso [11] in PRODIGY/ANALOGY. The replay technique involves a closely coupled interaction between planning using the domain theory (operators and other static knowledge of the world) and modification of a set of similar cases.

The cases are derivational traces of both successful and failed decisions in past planning episodes, as well as the justifications for each decision. The case replay mechanism of PRODIGY/ANALOGY involves a reinterpretation of the justifications for case decisions within the context of the new problem, reusing past decisions when the justifications hold true, avoiding failed decisions, and replanning using the domain theory when the transfer fails. The general PRODIGY/ANALOGY replay algorithm is domain-independent and is designed to replay multiple cases, and is capable of merging cases in several different manners. (Merge modes include sequential, interleaved, guided and random. [10].) The replay procedure provides guidance to the general choice points of the planner.

In this domain, the retrieval procedure returns a list of cases, $C_1, \ldots, C_n$, ordered according to the sequence in which the metric believes they should be reused. The geometric processing of the similarity metric also identifies which parts of each case should be used in the generation of the new solution, and therefore only the relevant steps are handed to the replay procedure.

The set of cases returned by the retrieval procedure should be merged by the replay mechanism to form the solution route to a single one-goal problem[1]. In this sense, the use of multiple cases in this domain differs from the use of multiple cases in other planning domains where different cases cover different top-level goals [11].

In the route planning domain, PRODIGY/ANALOGY is set to use a sequential merging strategy to combine the cases. Because of the partial match between the cases and the new situation, the replay algorithm is prepared to do any needed extra planning. In particular, any extra planning to *connect* a pair of cases is done by an iterative deepening search based on a estimated depth bound. Informally, at the end of each case, the replay algorithm proceeds by searching carefully for the next case. The illustrative example in the empirical section shows the effectiveness of this merging strategy.

An equivalent search process is performed if a case step becomes *invalidated*, for example, in a situation where the past case uses a segment (e.g. a bridge) that is not available in the current map. The map is updated by executions to reflect the change (see [5]) while the past cases still refer to the unavailable segment. We do not alter the cases since it could be computationally expensive in a large case library; instead we modify the β values of the case to reflect its poor quality. In addition, the case might become relevant at a later date.

Table 1 sketches the replay algorithm with this sequential merging procedure. We present the serial processing of the sequentially-ordered multiple cases.

---

[1] A single problem can consist of multiple goals, but the similarity metric is only called for a single source/goal pair. PRODIGY/ANALOGY is quite capable of handling multiple goals in this domain.

> - Input: The map description; the initial location; the goal location; and an ordered list of (chopped) cases $C_1, C_2, \ldots, C_n$ (each C_i consists of a sequence of relevant steps to the new situation).
> - Output: P, a route from the initial to the goal locations.
>
> **procedure** *sequential-analogical-replay*
> 1. $i \leftarrow 1; j \leftarrow 1$ (*i is the guiding case; j is the guiding step in the case*)
> 2. All case steps are marked usable.
> 3. Terminate if the goal location was reached.
> 4. Get the jth plan step from the case C_i, i.e. C_i^j.
> 5. Validate the case choice C_i^j.
> 6. If the case choice C_i^j is invalidated,
> 7.   then: Mark unusable the case steps strictly dependent of C_i^j.
> 8. $j \leftarrow$ next usable step in C_i
> 9.   Plan by searching on the map (heuristic or iterative deepening).
> 10.   If the new plan step matches some usable case step C_k^l,
> 11.   then: Mark unusable the steps in cases C_m, $i \leq m < k$, if $k > i$.
> 12.   Mark unusable the case steps C_k^m, $1 \leq m < l$, if $l > 1$.
> 13. $i \leftarrow k; j \leftarrow l$.
> 14.   Go to 4.
> 15.   else: Add the new step to plan P.
> 16.   Go to 3.
> 17.   else: Add the new step C_i^j to plan P.
> 18.   Link the new plan step to the case step.
> 19.   Advance case C_i to its next step: $j \leftarrow j + 1$.
> 20.   If the end of case C_i was reached,
> 21.   then: $i \leftarrow i + 1; j \leftarrow 1$.
> 22.   Go to step 2.
> 23. Return the plan P.

Table 1. Sketch of Serial Analogical Replay of a Sequence of Cases.

The adaptation in the replay procedure involves a validation of the steps proposed by the cases. When there is a need to diverge from the proposed case steps (step 9), note that the algorithm tries to return to the cases "as soon as possible" (see step 10, in which the algorithm tries to match a newly generated step with a case step, even when not the immediately obvious next one). This bias in the sequential merge combined with the β-biased similarity metric allows an interesting reuse of good quality previously visited routes.

5 Experiments

The experiments we describe in this section illustrate the use of our similarity metric combined with the sequential analogical replay of multiple cases. The ultimate goal of our work is to use real planning and execution cases to learn from and produce reliable routes. The experiments here are focused on the topic of this paper and do not address the complete goal of our work.

It has been claimed that complex adaptation strategies can be dangerous because it is difficult to guarantee a good final solution [6]. Our goal in these experiments, therefore, was to show that our method of selecting similar cases and subsequently merging them produces reasonable routes to new problems. The experiments we describe have been performed on a portion of the real map of Pittsburgh with approximately 18,000 intersections.

We randomly generated a set of 30 problems, and solved them using (a) A* to find the physically shortest path, (b) a heuristic based on a local desire to head in the direction of the goal (which corresponds to what someone might do while driving in unfamiliar territory), and (c) PRODIGY/ANALOGY using as a case library the combined set of A* and heuristic from the other 29 problems. In practice, we would prefer to accumulate cases from everyday planning and execution experience; something hard to capture in a heuristic function.

	Time (s)	Nodes	Route Length
A*	4881	1067	119567
Heuristic	686	167	153401
Analogy	604	155	129132

Table 2. Average time, number of nodes expanded and (Euclidean) length of solution for the three search algorithms.

Looking at the results from Table 2, it is clear that finding an optimal route is extremely expensive when compared to either the local direction-based heuristic or to analogy. Given that the improvement in solution length is only 22% and 8% respectively, it is hard to justify spending more than 600% of time and resources to find the optimal solution. Note that Analogy has less search to do than either of the other algorithms because the majority of the search was done in previous problem-solving episodes.

Figure 4 shows an example of one problem as it was solved by A*, PRODIGY/ANALOGY and the heuristic.

The A* route is the shortest route between the initial and goal points, however, it goes through a tightly congested residential area, rather than taking the larger street to the south[2]. In terms of convenience, the optimal route is in fact *worse* than either the heuristic- or analogy-generated routes. This situation occurs very often in real world cities because drivers select routes based on their convenience, familiarity and reliability rather than optimal length.

The heuristically generated path does very little search as it does no backtracking. Although reasonable in this situation, it can get sidetracked in non-grid-like cities, and even in this example meanders towards the goal. Several of the routes were distinctly unreasonable, more than doubling the length of the optimal route.

The similarity metric selected three relevant cases in the case library (Figure 4c). The metric examined all available routes (those generated by both A*

---

[2] For those readers familiar with Pittsburgh, the residential area is Shadyside, and Fifth Avenue is the larger street.

and the heuristic) and selected those which described the new problem most effectively. Note that case 0 eliminates the meandering of the heuristic path, while case 5 selects the better route near the initial point. The metric then returned the relevant parts of each case to the reuse algorithm, which faithfully followed the cases, adding the additional steps at the beginning and end of the cases and successfully switching between the cases along the route.

Based on these observations, we believe that an algorithm more reactive than A* is needed. Storing routes actually executed by the driver is a good way to

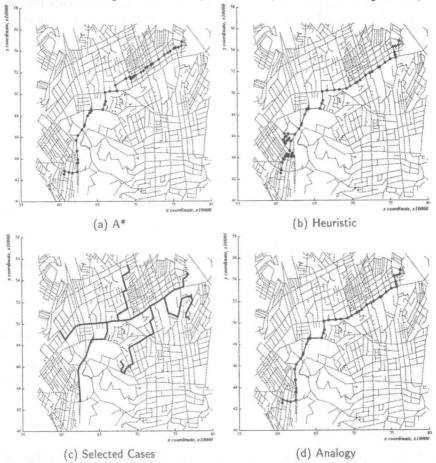

(a) A* (b) Heuristic

(c) Selected Cases (d) Analogy

Problem: initial location (762213,548347) to goal location (606469,425757)
Case 0 (A*): initial location (688451,553663) to goal location (625678,428191)
Case 4 (H): initial location (599257,493531) to goal location (769737,503789)
Case 5 (A*): initial location (678681,464750) to goal location (767392,546448)

Fig. 4. (a) The path as generated by A*. (b) The path as generated by a search heuristic. (c) The cases selected as being relevant to the current problem. (d) The path as generated by analogy.

bias the system towards routes that he prefers. The loss of physical optimality will be regained as the system increases its knowledge of the convenience and reliability of the route through experience. Solutions generated by analogy will therefore be better than generating solutions from scratch. We are currently implementing a model of the execution domain to test this theory[3]. To date, the β values output by the model have been accurate enough for the similarity metric to correctly identify two different routes for the problem described in Figure 4. Figure 5 shows the four relevant cases. During rush hour, when larger streets are more congested, the similarity metric selects the lower route through a park and residential areas. At other times, it selects the route along larger roads.

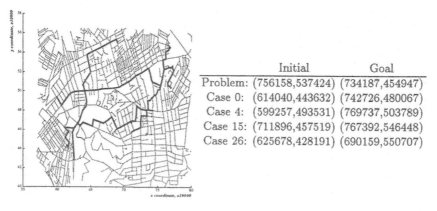

	Initial	Goal
Problem:	(756158,537424)	(734187,454947)
Case 0:	(614040,443632)	(742726,480067)
Case 4:	(599257,493531)	(769737,503789)
Case 15:	(711896,457519)	(767392,546448)
Case 26:	(625678,428191)	(690159,550707)

Fig. 5. The four relevant cases under different conditions for the problem described in figure 4.

Through our on-going experiments, which we briefly illustrated above, we have demonstrated that our method of retrieving and reusing multiple cases produces solutions that are reasonable and desirable, *i.e.* they correspond to familiar routes (the cases) and are not overly sinuous or long. With the learning methods described previously (see [5]), the map information and the knowledge about the quality of each case improves with experience.

6 Related Work

Most robotics path planners (e.g. Dyna [7], COLUMBUS [9], Xavier [3], NavLab [8]) don't remember paths or their quality, and typically use shortest path, dynamic programming or decision theoretic algorithms to determine routes. We do not believe these algorithms are sufficient in this domain for several reasons, including:

- they typically examine the entire map, doing a blind search ignoring the general direction of the goal, and in a large map will be very slow;

---

[3] Originally, we had planned to execute this on a real robot, but collecting sufficient data would have been too expensive.

1. Given a new problem, find a set of similar cases, using stored β values.
2. Modify case(s) into new plan.
3. Execute plan on real robot. (*Not implemented yet.*)
4. If execution of plan is successful:
   Then: Add new case to library.
         Assign appropriate β values.
   Otherwise: Identify reason for failure. (*Not implemented yet.*)
         Modify world knowledge as applicable.
         (β values, map)
         Add any successful parts of plan to case library

Fig. 6. Our integrated planning and learning route-planning algorithm. Current status of the various stages are marked in italics.

- they are unable to interleave planning with execution or deal with unexpected situations;
- they can not distinguish between multiple routes of equal length but different quality; and
- they are strictly shortest-path algorithms, not considering path reliability or convenience factors such as time-to-goal, road quality, or user preferences.

ROUTER (developed by Goel *et. al* [2]) and R-Finder (developed by Liu *et. al* [6]) are the only other case-based route-planning systems the authors are aware of. However they both have extremely simple retrieval and modification algorithms, considerably reducing the transfer rate of prior experience. In addition, they do not re-validate the plans in the up-to-date map, making it more likely that in a dynamic world they will return invalid solutions; nor do they remember the quality of cases in an attempt to improve retrieval and the quality of the plans they generate. Finally, the goal of their work is to speed up planning; we feel that fast planning can be achieved by a combination of Dijkstra's algorithm and goal-oriented heuristics, and therefore our focus is instead on the more difficult questions of plan quality and reliability.

7 Conclusion and Discussion

In this paper, we have described our approach to applying case-based reasoning methods to route planning. We motivated the need for an integrated system that incrementally acquires experience. We briefly presented a similarity metric that takes advantage of the geometric characteristics of the map and returns a set of similar previously traversed routes that are jointly relevant to the new situation. Our metric supports the need for more naturalized mechanisms for detecting similar cases. We discussed how the system creates a new route plan by merging guidance from the multiple retrieved cases and planning from the map description and the routing operators. We presented the analogical replay algorithm using a sequential technique to merge the multiple similar retrieved cases.

We believe that it is important to create good quality, reliable plans, and that using familiar well-indexed routes, shown to be successful in the past, is an effective way to do this. As our empirical results have shown, optimal algorithms seem far too costly for the benefits gained, while heuristically-based algorithms may get led astray.

The entire integrated planning and learning algorithm is summarized in Figure 6. Except where marked otherwise, it is fully implemented and running. The code is available on request. We are currently extensively evaluating our work and its impact in realistic route planning situations using the complete online map of the city of Pittsburgh.

We believe that any system that interacts with the real-world will have to deal with a changing environment. We hope that our system, with its robust integration of planning, case-based reasoning, and learning from real execution, will form a good basis for future exploration in this area.

References

1. Jaime G. Car bon ell, and the PRODIGY Research Group. PRODIGY4.0: The manual and tutorial. Technical Report CMU-CS-92-150, School of Computer Science, Carnegie Mellon University, June 1992.
2. Ashok Goel and et al. Multistrategy adaptive path planning. *IEEE Expert*, 6(6):57–65, December 1994.
3. Richard Goodwin and Reid Simmons. Rational handling of multiple goals for mobile robots. In J. Hendler, editor, *Artificial Intelligence Planning Systems: Proceedings of the First International Conference (AIPS92)*, June 1992.
4. Karen Zita Haigh and Jon athan Richard Shewchuk. Geometric similarity metrics for case-based reasoning. In *Case-Based Reasoning: Working Notes from the AAAI-94 Workshop*, pages 182–187, Seattle, WA, August 1994. AAAI Press.
5. Karen Zita Haigh, Jon athan Richard Shewchuk, and Manuela M. Veloso. Route planning and learning from execution. In *Working notes from the AAAI Fall Symposium "Planning and Learning: On to Real Applications"*, pages 58–64, New Orleans, LA, November 1994. AAAI Press.
6. Bing Liu and et al. Integrating case-based reasoning, knowledge-based approach and Dijkstra algorithm for route finding. In *Proceedings of the Tenth Conference on Artificial Intelligence for Applications*, pages 149–55, San Antonia, TX, March 1994.
7. Richard S. Sutton. Planning by incremental dynamic programming. In *Machine Learning: Proceedings of the 8th International Workshop*, pages 353–357. Morgan Kaufmann, 1991.
8. Charles E. Thorpe, editor. *The CMU Navlab*. Kluwer Academic Publishers, Boston, MA, 1990.
9. Sebastian B. Thrun. Exploration and model building in mobile robot domains. In *Proceedings of the IEEE International Conference on Neural Networks*, San Francisco, CA, March 1993.
10. Manuela M. Veloso. Automatic storage, retrieval, and replay of multiple cases. In *Preprints of the AAAI 1992 Spring Symposium Series, Workshop on Computational Considerations in Supporting Incremental Modification and Reuse*, Stanford University, CA, March 1992.
11. Manuela M. Veloso. *Planning and Learning by Analogical Reasoning*. Springer Verlag, December 1994.

Case Adaptation Using an Incomplete Causal Model*

John D. Hastings[1], L. Karl Branting[1], and Jeffrey A. Lockwood[2]

[1] Department of Computer Science
University of Wyoming
Laramie, Wyoming 82071-3682
{hastings, karl}@eolus.uwyo.edu
[2] Department of Plant, Soil, and Insect Sciences
University of Wyoming
Laramie, Wyoming 82071
lockwood@uwyo.edu

Abstract. This paper describes a technique for integrating case-based reasoning with model-based reasoning to predict the behavior of biological systems characterized both by incomplete models and insufficient empirical data for accurate induction. This technique is implemented in CARMA, a system for rangeland pest management advising. CARMA's ability to predict the forage consumption judgments of 15 expert entomologists was empirically compared to that of CARMA's case-based and model-based components in isolation. This evaluation confirmed the hypothesis that integrating model-based and case-based reasoning through model-based adaptation can lead to more accurate predictions than the use of either technique individually.

1 Introduction

Many types of diagnostic, monitoring, and planning tasks require prediction of the behavior of physical systems. Precise models exist for the behavior of many simple physical systems. However, models of biological, ecological, and other natural systems are often incomplete, either because a complete state description for such systems cannot be determined or because the number and type of interactions between system elements are poorly understood. Empirical methods, such as case-based reasoning, decision-tree induction, or statistical techniques, can be used for prediction if sufficient data are available. In practice, however, many biological systems are characterized both by incomplete models and insufficient empirical data for accurate induction. Accurate prediction of the behavior of such systems requires exploitation of multiple, individually incomplete, knowledge sources.

---

* This research was supported in part by grants from the University of Wyoming College of Agriculture and by a Faculty Grant-in-Aid from the University of Wyoming Office of Research.

This paper describes the use of model-based adaptation as a technique for integrating case-based reasoning with model-based reasoning in domains in which neither technique is individually sufficient for accurate prediction. The next section describes *rangeland pest management*, a task that requires predicting the behavior of a complex biological system, and sets forth a process description of expert problem solving in this domain. Section 3 briefly describes CARMA, a system that implements this process description, and describes how CARMA performs model-based case adaptation. Section 4 describes how CARMA learns match and adaptation weights. An experimental evaluation in which the predictive accuracy of CARMA's model-based adaptation component is compared to that of case-based and model-based reasoning in isolation is set forth in Section 5. This evaluation confirms that model-based case adaptation can lead to more accurate simulation of entomologists' predictions than empirical or model-based reasoning alone.

2   Rangeland Pest Management

Rangeland ecosystems typify biological systems having an extensive but incomplete causal theory and limited empirical data. Management tasks for rangelands include optimal stocking rates and grazing systems, water development, wildlife enhancement, noxious weed control, and insect pest management. Each of these management tasks requires evaluating alternative actions by predicting their potential consequences.

The particular rangeland management task of interest to us is pest management. On average, grasshoppers annually consume 21–23% of rangeland forage in the western United States, at an estimated loss of $400 million [HO83]. Rangeland grasshopper infestations can be treated with chemical or biological insecticides, but in many situations the costs of insecticide application exceed the value of the forage saved. Determining the most cost-efficient response to a grasshopper infestation requires predicting the forage savings that would ensue from each response and comparing the savings to the cost of the response itself.

While model-based reasoning can play a role in grasshopper management, there is a general recognition that the interactions affecting grasshopper population dynamics are too poorly understood and too complex to permit precise prediction through numerical simulation [LL91, Pim91, AH92]. However, entomologists and pest managers are able to provide useful recommendations to ranchers. This indicates that other sources of knowledge can compensate for the absence of a complete model of rangeland ecosystems.

Based in part on a protocol analysis of problem solving by experts in rangeland grasshopper management, we have developed the following process description of expert problem solving for this task:

1. Use rule-based reasoning to infer the relevant facts of the infestation case, such as grasshopper species, developmental phases[3], and density, from information provided by the user.

---

[3] During their lifetime, grasshoppers progress through three developmental stages: egg, nymph, and adult. The nymphal stage usually consists of five instars separated by molts. We define the **developmental phases** of a grasshopper's lifecycle to include egg, five nymphal instars, and adult.

2. Determine whether grasshopper consumption will lead to competition with livestock for available forage.

   (a) Estimate the proportion of available forage that will be consumed by grasshoppers using case-based and model-based reasoning.

   (b) Compare grasshopper consumption with the proportion of available forage needed by livestock.

3. If there will be competition, determine what possible treatment options should be excluded using rules such as "Wet conditions preclude the use of malathion"; "Environmental sensitivity precludes all chemical treatments."

4. If there are possible treatment options, for each one provide an economic analysis by estimating both the first-year and long-term savings using rule-based, model-based, and probabilistic reasoning.

We have implemented this problem-solving process in a system termed CARMA (CAse-based Range Management Adviser). This paper focuses on the components of CARMA that perform step 2(a), estimation of the proportion of available forage that will be consumed by grasshoppers. Making this estimation requires predicting the behavior of a rangeland ecosystem, a biological system with an incomplete causal model.

3   Model-Based Adaptation in CARMA

Our protocol analysis indicated that entomologists estimate forage consumption by comparing new cases to prototypical infestation scenarios. These prototypical cases differ from conventional cases in two important respects. First, the prototypical cases are not expressed in terms of observable features (e.g., "Whenever I take a step, I see 4 grasshoppers with brightly colored wings fly"), but rather in terms of abstract derived features (e.g., "Approximately 6 nymphal overwintering grasshoppers in the adult phase per square yard"). Second, the prototypical cases are extended in time, representing the history of a particular grasshopper population over its lifespan. Each prototypical case is therefore represented by a "snapshot" at a particular, representative point in time selected by the entomologist. In general, this representative point is one at which the grasshoppers are at a developmental phase in which treatment is feasible. An example prototypical case appears as Case8 in Table 1[4].

CARMA begins a consultation by eliciting information to infer the relevant features of a new case. When the relevant case features have been determined, CARMA can use a causal model to assist case-based reasoning in four different ways: case factoring; temporal projection; featural adaptation; and critical-period adjustment.

---

[4] This case is used merely to illustrate several of CARMA's features. In a typical consultation, a case occurring so late in the growing season would be classified as "too late" for purposes of insecticide application. A complete analysis of such a case would proceed only if requested by the user.

	Case8	New case		Case8
		SubcaseA	SubcaseB	after projection
Overwintering type	nymph	nymph	egg	nymph
Feeding types	grass 100%	grass 40% mixed 60%	grass 100%	grass 100%
Average phase	2.0	1.2	7.0	1.2
Density	12.0	13.0	7.0	13.3
Date	September 8	August 20		September 2
Precipitation	normal	dry		normal
Temperatures	normal	cool		normal
Infest. history	mod-low	mod		mod-low
Range value	mod	high-mod		mod
Forage loss	15% (mod-low)	?		15% (mod-low)

Table 1. Case examples.

Factoring Cases into Subcases. CARMA's consumption prediction module first splits the overall population into subcases of grasshoppers with distinct over-wintering types (*i.e.*, overwintering as nymphs or eggs), since forage consumption by those that overwinter as nymphs is much different from consumption by those that overwinter as eggs. CARMA uses a model of grasshopper developmental stages to estimate the hatch date and probable death date of each grasshopper population given the population's current developmental stage, growing season dates for the location, and current date.

Temporal Projection. To predict the forage loss of a subcase, CARMA first retrieves all prototypical cases whose overwintering types match that of the sub-case. Since prototypical cases are extended in time but are represented at a particular time, matching requires temporally projecting the prototypical cases forwards or backwards to align their average developmental phases with that of the new subcase. This requires using the model to simulate grasshopper attri-tion, which depends on developmental phase, precipitation, and developmental rate (which in turn depends on temperature) throughout the interval of the projection. An example appears in Figure 1.

The projected prototypical case whose weighted featural difference from the new subcase is least is selected as the best match. For example, the prototypical case that best matches SubcaseA after projection is Case8, shown in Table 1. Because the developmental phase of Case8 before projection is later than that of SubcaseA, Case8 must be projected backwards in time, causing grasshoppers that had been lost to attrition to be added back to the population.

Temporal projection aligns developmental phases but not necessarily dates. For example, the date of Case8 after projection is later than the date of Sub-caseA because the hatch date of Case8 was later than that of SubcaseA. As a result, the developmental phase of the grasshoppers in SubcaseA on August 20 are the same as those of Case8 two weeks later on September 2.

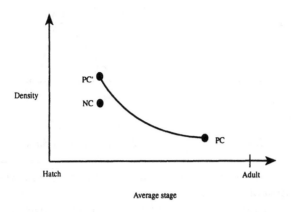

Fig. 1. Projection of a prototypical case from PC to PC′ to align its developmental phase with new case NC.

Featural Adaptation. The consumption predicted by the best matching prototypical case is modified to account for any featural differences between it and the subcase. This adaptation is based on the influence of each feature on consumption as represented by featural adaptation weights. For example, a lower temperature value means lower forage losses, because lower temperatures tend to slow developmental speed, increasing grasshopper attrition. Thus, the forage loss estimate predicted by Case8—15%—must be adapted downward somewhat to account for the fact that temperatures in SubcaseA (cool) are lower than in Case8 (normal).

Critical-Period Adjustment. Consumption is only damaging if it occurs during the critical forage growing period of a rangeland habitat. The forage loss predicted by a prototypical case must be modified if the proportion of the lifespan of the grasshoppers overlapping the critical period differs significantly in the new case from the proportion in the prototypical case. This process, termed *critical-period adjustment*, requires determining the developmental phases of the new and prototypical cases that fall within the critical period and the proportion of lifetime consumption occurring in these developmental phases. The critical period of a specific parcel of rangeland is determined from the parcel's latitude and altitude.

An example of critical-period adjustment appears in Figure 2. CARMA uses a model of grasshoppers' rate of consumption at each developmental phase to calculate the proportion of lifetime consumption occurring before the end of the critical period. For example, 47% of SubcaseA's consumption occurs during the critical period, whereas only 6% of Case8's consumption occurs within this period. CARMA therefore scales the initial consumption estimate by (47 / 6) = 7.8.

After adaptation, the consumption predictions for each subcase (*i.e.*, populations of grasshoppers with distinct feeding patterns) are summed to produce

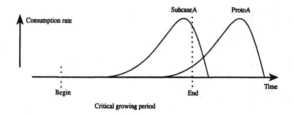

Fig. 2. Critical-period adjustment from Case8 to SubcaseA.

an overall quantitative consumption estimate. In the given case, the sum of predicted consumption of the two subcases is 57%.

In summary, CARMA can use a model of grasshopper developmental phases, consumption, and attrition, and a model of a rangeland's critical forage growth period to adapt the cases in its library. This adaptation is used both to determine the degree of relevant match between cases and to modify the consumption predictions associated with a prototypical case to apply to a new case.

4   Learning Match and Adaptation Weights

CARMA uses two sets of weights in case-based reasoning: match weights (used in the assessment of similarity between cases whose grasshopper populations have been aligned by temporal projection); and featural adaptation weights (used to adapt the consumption predicted by the best matching prototypical case in light of any featural differences between it and the subcase). General domain knowledge, such as the identifying characteristics and developmental phases of grasshoppers, can be provided by domain expert. By contrast, match and featural adaptation weights must be acquired by the system itself.

Match weights are set by determining the *mutual information gain* between case features and qualitative consumption categories in a given set of training cases, since recent research has indicated that this is often an accurate measure of featural importance for matching [WD95].

Featural adaptation weights are set by a hill-climbing algorithm, `AdaptWeights`, that incrementally varies adaptation weights A to minimize the *root-mean-squared error* (RMSE), *i.e.*,

$$\sqrt{1/n \sum_{i=1}^{n}[\text{PFL}(C_i, P, M, A) - \text{ExpertPred}(C_i)]^2}$$

for prototypical case library P and match weights M, where $\text{PFL}(C_i, P, M, A)$ is CARMA's predicted forage loss and $\text{ExpertPred}(C_i)$ is the expert's prediction of consumption for each training case C_i. CARMA can learn featural adaptation weights in either of two modes: *global*, in which a single set of weights are acquired for the entire entire case library; or *case-specific*, in which separate weights are acquired for each prototypical case.

5 Evaluation

The design of CARMA's forage consumption component was based on the hypothesis that an integration of model-based and case-based reasoning can lead to more accurate forage consumption predictions than the use of either technique individually. To test this hypothesis, we separated CARMA's empirical and model-based knowledge components, tested each in isolation, and compared the results to the performance of the full CARMA system under both global and case-specific adaptation weight modes.

The evaluation was complicated by the absence of empirical data against which to measure CARMA's predictions. We therefore turned to expert human judgments as an external standard. To obtain a representative sample of expert opinions, we sent questionnaires to 20 entomologists recognized for their work in the area of grasshopper ecology. Each expert received 10 hypothetical cases randomly selected from a complete set of 20 cases. The descriptions of the 20 cases contained at least as much information as is typically available to an entomologist from a rancher seeking advice. The questionnaire asked the expert to make several predictions about the case, including the predicted quantitative forage loss. A total of 15 recipients of the questionnaire responded. Much to our surprise, there was a very wide variation (from 25 to 90%) in consumption predictions among the experts over the set of 20 cases. The resulting experimental case sets consist of 15 sets of expert responses containing 10 cases each.

A complication introduced by the use of expert human judgments as an evaluation standard is the possibility that in making consumption predictions human experts fail to use of all aspects of the model of grassland ecology. To test this possibility, we performed an ablation study in which we tested the effect on prediction accuracy of removing each form of adaptation knowledge from CARMA. The configuration of CARMA with the highest predictive accuracy was then compared with purely model-based and purely empirical reasoning.

5.1 Experimental Design

Each predictive method was tested using a series of leave-one-out tests in which a set of cases (S) was split into one *test case* (C) and one *training set* (S - C). The methods were trained on the forage loss predictions of the training set and tested on the test case. This method was repeated for each case within the set (S). The forage loss predictions (0–100%) represent the proportion of available forage that would otherwise be available for livestock, but will instead be consumed by grasshoppers.

CARMA was tested using a protocol under which each set of training cases is used as CARMA's library of prototypical cases. This protocol is implemented in LeaveOneOutSpecificTest and LeaveOneOutGlobalTest, which perform the leave-one-out tests for the specific and global adaptation weights schemes, respectively. Both procedures call AdaptWeights, the hill-climbing algorithm described above. LeaveOneOutSpecificTest calls AdaptWeights with a prototypical case library containing only one case.

function LeaveOneOutSpecificTest(T)

1   **for** each case $C_i \epsilon T$ **do**
2        $P := T - C_i$;prototypical cases
3        $M :=$ global match weights for set P according to info. gain
4   **for** each prototypical case $P_j \epsilon P$ **do**
5            $T := P - P_j$;training set
6            $P_j(A) :=$ AdaptWeights(T, $\{P_j\}$, M)
7        $D_i := ($PredictForageLoss(C_i, P, M) - ExpertPred$(C_i))^2$
8   **return** ($\sqrt{\text{Avg}(D)}$)

function LeaveOneOutGlobalTest(T)

1   **for** each case $C_i \epsilon T$ **do**
2        $P := T - C_i$;prototypical cases
3        $M :=$ global match weights for set P according to info. gain
4        $G :=$ AdaptWeights(P, P, M)
5        $D_i := ($PredictForageLoss(C_i, P, M, G) - ExpertPred$(C_i))^2$
6   **return** ($\sqrt{\text{Avg}(D)}$)

Ablation Experiment. To determine the contribution of the various forms of model-based adaptation to CARMA's predictive accuracy, an ablation experiment was performed in which the performance of the full CARMA system was compared to CARMA's performance with various adaptation mechanisms disabled. The first column of Table 2 shows CARMA's average root-mean-squared error over the 15 expert sets using case specific weights (CARMA-specific). Columns two and three show CARMA-specific with, respectively, projection and critical period adjustment removed, and column four shows CARMA with featural adaptation removed. The performance of nearest-neighbor prediction (NN), *i.e.* CARMA with projection, featural adaptation, and critical period adjustment all removed,[5] is shown in column five.

These data show that full CARMA-specific actually performs worse than NN. Removing projection or featural adaptation makes performance still worse, but removing critical period adjustment makes CARMA's performance better than NN. From this, we conclude that critical period adjustment does not accurately reflect the problem-solving behavior of human experts in this predictive task.

Columns six and seven show CARMA using global weights (CARMA-global). As with CARMA-specific, CARMA-global is more accurate with critical period adjustment removed. However, CARMA-global with critical period adjustment removed, while more accurate than NN, is less accurate than CARMA-specific with critical period adjustment removed.

In summary, the ablation experiment showed that projection and featural adaptation each increased predictive accuracy but critical period adjustment decreased accuracy. Case-specific adaptation weights led to better performance

---

[5] Under this approach, cases are first factored into populations with distinct overwintering types, 1-NN prediction is performed for each population, and the resulting consumption predictions for all populations are summed.

than global adaptation weights. In the second experiment CARMA was therefore tested using case-specific adaptation weights and critical period adjustment disabled.

Comparison of CARMA with Empirical and Model-based Approachs.
CARMA's empirical component was evaluated by performing leave-one-out-tests for a nearest-neighbor approach and two other inductive approaches that used CARMA's empirical knowledge: decision tree induction using ID3[6]; and linear approximation, which consisted of using QR factorization [Hag88] to find a least-squares fit to the feature values and associated predictions of the training cases.

The predictive ability of CARMA's model-based component in isolation was evaluated by developing a numerical simulation based on CARMA's model of rangeland ecology. This simulation required two forms of knowledge implicit in CARMA's cases: the forage per acre based on the range value of the location, and the forage typically eaten per day per grasshopper for each distinct grasshopper overwintering type and developmental phase. The steps of the numerical simulation are as follows:[7]

1. Project each grasshopper population back to beginning of the growth season.
2. Simulate the density and developmental phases for each overwintering type through the end of the growth season based on the precipitation and temperature given in the case.
3. Calculate the forage eaten per day per acre based on the grasshopper density per acre and the forage eaten per day per grasshopper for each overwintering type and developmental phase as affected by temperature.
4. Convert the total forage consumed to the proportion of available forage consumed based on the forage per acre.

The effect of temperature on consumption (as a result of changing metabolism rates) was represented by multiplying a coefficient (determined from a lookup table indexed by temperature) by the forage eaten per day per grasshopper for each overwintering type. The numerical simulation was trained by hill-climbing on temperature-based coefficients to maximize the predictive accuracy on the training cases.

The accuracy of each approach was tested using leave-one-out testing for each of the 15 expert sets. The results, which appear in Table 3, include the root-mean-squared error for each of the methods.

---

[6] ID3 classified cases into 10 qualitative consumption categories representing the midpoints (5, 10, 15, ... , 95) of 10 equally sized qualitative ranges. ID3's error was measured by the difference between the midpoint of each predicted qualitative category and the expected quantitative consumption value.

[7] This model, which simulates each grasshopper population through the entire growth season, corresponds to the knowledge used by CARMA minus critical period adjustment. A simulation restricted to the critical period would correspond to the full CARMA system's knowledge.

Specific weights			No featural adaptation		Global weights	
Full	minus projection	minus CPA	minus featural adaptation	minus FA, P, CPA (NN)	Full	minus CPA
22.3	23.3	18.0	29.8	21.8	24.8	20.1

Table 2. CARMA's average percentage root-mean-squared error across 15 expert sets with various adaptation methods removed.

CARMA	Empirical Only			Model-Based Only
Specific weights minus CPA	CARMA minus FA, P, CPA (NN)	ID3	Linear appr.	Numerical simulation
18.0	21.8	29.6	31.1	28.3

Table 3. CARMA's average percentage root-mean-squared error across 15 expert sets compared with purely empirical and purely model-based approaches.

5.2   Discussion

The results of the second experiment provide initial confirmation for the hypothesis that integrating model-based and case-based reasoning through model-based adaptation leads to more accurate forage consumption predictions than the use of either technique individually. The root-mean-squared error for CARMA-specific minus critical period adjustment (18.0) is 17.4% lower than for the nearest-neighbor approach (21.8) and 36.4% lower than for the numerical simulation (28.3). The error rates for the other empirical approaches on this data set were higher than for nearest-neighbor and numerical simulation: ID3 (29.6) and linear approximation (31.1). This initial confirmation is tentative because the low level of agreement among experts and absence of any external standard gives rise to uncertainty about what constitutes a correct prediction. However, this validation problem appears to be an inherent property of the domain of rangeland pest management.

Consumption prediction can be viewed as approximating a function from derived case features to consumption predictions (a *consumption function*). Prototypical cases constitute representative points in feature space for which function values are known. The prototypical cases can be used to induce a representation of the function as a decision tree (*e.g.*, ID3) or a numerical function (*e.g.*, linear approximation). The poor performance of ID3 and linear approximation suggests that the biases of these inductive methods are poorly suited to the consumption prediction task.

Alternatively, simulation can be used to derive individual values for the function. However, the incompleteness of available models of rangeland ecology limits the accuracy of this approach.

A pure nearest-neighbor approach implicitly assumes that the consumption function is constant in the neighborhood of prototypical cases. CARMA's model-based adaptation approach uses a model of rangeland ecology to attempt to approximate the consumption function in the neighborhood of individual prototypical cases. For example, projection consists of simulation through the temporal interval necessary to align the developmental phases of two cases. Although the model may be insufficient in itself for accurate consumption prediction, it may greatly improve the accuracy of nearest-neighbor prediction.

We hypothesize that CARMA-specific outperforms CARMA-global because the latter depends on the assumption that the consumption function can be approximated by a single linear equation in the neighborhood of every prototypical case. However, the poor performance of linear approximation (31.1 as compared to 21.8 for the nearest-neighbor approach) indicates that no single linear function can accurately predict consumption. Thus, it is unlikely that a single linear function is sufficient to adapt the consumption prediction of every case. CARMA-specific does not depend on the assumption that the consumption function can be approximated by a single linear equation in the neighborhood of every prototypical case. However, CARMA-specific requires a large number of cases to accurately set the adaptation weights of every prototypical case.

6 Related Work

Several previous research projects have investigated the benefits of integrating case-based reasoning with model-based reasoning. However, these projects have generally assumed the existence of a correct and complete causal model. For example, CASEY [Kot88] performed diagnosis using model-based reasoning to assist both case matching and case adaptation. However, CASEY presupposed both the existence of a complete causal theory of heart disease and complete explanations of each case in terms of that theory. Goel's use of device models to adapt design cases also presupposes that the device models are complete and correct [Goe91]. Similarly, Rajamoney and Lee's *prototype-based reasoning* [RL91] presupposes a complete and correct (though not necessarily tractable) causal model.

Feret and Glascow [FG93] describe an alterative approach under which model-based reasoning is used for "structural isolation" (*i.e.*, identification of the structural components of a device that probably give rise to the symptoms of a fault). Cases are indexed by these tentative diagnoses, which are then refined using case-based reasoning. This approach, while appropriate for diagnosis, is ill-suited for behavioral prediction in the absence of faults.

CARMA's technique of model-based matching and adaptation represents an alternative approach to integrating CBR and MBR appropriate for domains characterized by an incomplete causal model.

7 Conclusion

This paper has described a technique for integrating case-based reasoning with model-based reasoning to predict the behavior of biological systems characterized both by incomplete models and insufficient empirical data for accurate induction. This technique is implemented in CARMA, a system for rangeland pest management advising. An empirical evaluation provided confirmation for the hypothesis that integrating model-based and case-based reasoning through model-based adaptation can lead to more accurate forage consumption predictions than the use of either technique individually.

We believe that the approach to model-based adaptation embodied in CARMA is appropriate for other domains in which empirical and model-based knowledge are each individually insufficient for accurate prediction. This approach may be particularly well suited for predictive tasks involving biological, ecological, and other natural systems.

References

[AH92]　T. F. H. Allen and T. W. Hoekstra. *Toward a Unified Ecology*. Columbia University Press, New York, NY, 1992.

[FG93]　M. P. Feret and J. I. Glascow. Hybrid case-based reasoning for the diagnosis of complex devices. In *Proceedings of Eleventh National Conference on Artificial Intelligence*, pages 168–175, Washington, D.C., July 11–15 1993. AAAI Press/MIT Press.

[Goe91]　A. Goel. A model-based approach to case adaptation. In *Thirteenth Annual Conference of the Cognitive Science Society*, pages 143–148, 1991.

[Hag88]　W. Hager. *Applied Numerical Linear Algebra*. Prentice Hall, 1988.

[HO83]　G. B. Hewitt and J. A. Onsager. Control of grasshoppers on rangeland in the united states: a perspective. *Journal of Range Management*, 36:202–207, 1983.

[Kot88]　P. Koton. *Using Experience in Learning and Problem Solving*. PhD thesis, Massachusetts Institute of Technology, 1988. Department of Electrical Engineering and Computer Science.

[LL91]　J. Lockwood and D. Lockwood. Rangeland grasshopper (orthoptera: Acrididae) population dynamics: Insights from catastrophe theory. *Environmental Entomology*, 20:970–980, 1991.

[Pim91]　S. L. Pimm. *The Balance of Nature: Ecological Issues in the Conservation of Species and Communities*. University of Chicago Press, Chicago, 1991.

[RL91]　S. Rajamoney and H. Lee. Prototype-based reasoning: An integrated approach to solving large novel problems. In *Proceedings of Ninth National Conference on Artificial Intelligence*, Anaheim, July 14–19 1991. AAAI Press/MIT Press.

[WD95]　D. Wettschereck and T. Dietterich. An experimental comparison of the nearest-neighbor and nearest-hyperrectangle algorithms. To appear in Machine Learning, 1995.

Evaluating the Application of CBR in Mesh Design for Simulation Problems

Neil Hurley

Hitachi Dublin Laboratory, Trinity College Dublin 2, IRELAND
{E-mail: nhurley@hdl.ie}

Abstract. One of the great difficulties facing a designer of a knowledge-based interface to a numerical simulation engine is acquiring sufficient domain knowledge to cover a significant range of problems to a depth that will make the system useful for real problem-solving. It is difficult to enumerate *a priori* all the different scenarios which may be encountered and to devise rules to cater for each. Indeed, it is true to say that often the tuneable parameters of a numerical algorithm (such as the error tolerance in a matrix inversion technique or the mesh density in a finite element analysis) are determined on a trial and error basis when the problem is first encountered. Setting up a knowledge-base therefore requires a lot of time-consuming experimentation over a range of different problems. There is no easy way to avoid this knowledge acquisition task if a robust system to tackle real-world problems is to be created. Furthermore, we must accept that the system at some stage is likely to encounter problems outside its coverage. It is therefore worthwhile examining alternative reasoning techniques which can be utilised when domain knowledge is lacking, as well as ways that new knowledge can be incorporated into the knowledge-base as problem-solving takes place. Towards this end, we have examined the application of case-based reasoning (CBR) to finite element simulation and in particular to the sub-task of finite element mesh design. In [5] a CBR approach to mesh design was outlined. In the current paper we evaluate that system, assess its performance at problem solving, discuss the lessons learned from its development and what implications these have for CBR in general.

1 Introduction

Partial Differential Equation (PDE) problems describe many engineering phenomena such as heat and fluid flow. The finite element method [5] is a technique for solving such problems on computer and involves discretising the problem, i.e. placing a grid or mesh over the geometrical domain and approximating the solution at the grid intersection points (nodes). The accuracy of a finite element model is highly dependent on the mesh. The greater the number of nodes, the greater the accuracy. Since the addition of nodes also increases the number of equations in the linear system of the discretised problem, the time required to complete the simulation is directly proportional to the number of nodes. There is therefore a trade-off between accuracy and efficiency. Most problems tend to be non-uniform in the sense that the solution varies more in one part of the domain than in another. To achieve sufficient accuracy in the area of high variation, a mesh of high node density may be required. Typically there is an upper limit to the total number of nodes which can be used due to time and memory restrictions on the machine and this precludes the placement of a uniformly fine mesh over the complete domain. Instead, a non-uniform mesh, whose density varies throughout the domain according to local requirements must be used.

Specifying appropriate densities for the mesh so that solution features are properly captured, is one of the most difficult tasks facing users of Finite Element Analysis. This issue is illustrated in Figure 1(b) in which the linear, steady-state, 2-dimensional heat conduction problem has a severe discontinuity in the boundary conditions in the lower right-hand corner (labelled by B in the diagram). The temperature profile shows a steep gradient due to this discontinuity between the points E and B. This will be correctly modelled only if a fine mesh is used close to the corner. A much coarser mesh will suffice further away from the corner. The difficulty is this : knowledge of the eventual solution (i.e. that a steep gradient will occur close to point B) is required, before a simulation to produce that solution can be properly set up. For many practical problems, it is not immediately obvious to the engineer or analyst what the solution will look like and hence where a fine mesh will be required.

In [5] a CBR approach to mesh design was outlined. The technique involved building a case-base of finite-element simulation problems solved using *adaptive* finite element analysis. Adaptive finite element analysis is an iterative simulation strategy which solves the simulation problem a number of times, refining the mesh on each successive iteration. Locations for mesh refinement are determined by applying an error estimator to the simulation results of the previous iteration. By the time the simulation is complete, an optimal mesh for the problem, in the sense that the mesh is fine only in areas of potentially high error, exists. Our CBR approach is to use a case-base of optimal meshes to design a mesh for new simulation problems. Thus knowledge gained through the solution of previous problems is stored and put to use in solving new similar problems.

In this paper the CBR system for mesh design is evaluated and lessons learned in its development are elicited. The paper is structured as follows : Section 2 gives a summary of the application domain, in Section 3 the CBR system is described, Section 4 evaluates the system and Section 5 discusses the results.

2 Preliminaries

2.1 The Problem Domain

We focus on heat analysis problems. Since the domain geometry for such problems is not as important as it is for structural analysis problems, for example, and our primary concern is how the mathematical model impacts on modelling decisions, our system design is concerned with encapsulating how the form of the PDEs, the type of boundary conditions and their relative positions influence the mesh granularity requirements throughout the domain. Our test system therefore fixes the shape of the domain and builds a case-base of heat conduction/convection problems over that domain.

The PDE which describes the temperature distribution is the standard form of the heat equation:

$$f(v,k,q) \equiv (v.\nabla)T - k\nabla^2 T = q$$

where T is the temperature distribution, v is the advective flow velocity, k is the conductivity of the material and q is a heat source or sink. A range of problems can be formed by varying the parameters v, k and q. The boundary conditions on each of the boundaries can be any of the following :

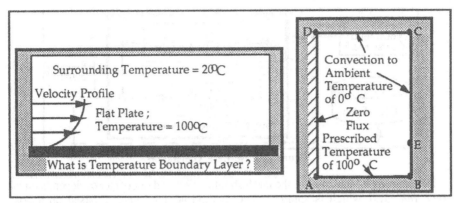

Figure 1: (a) Flow over a Heated plate; (b) Heat Conduction on a Flat Plate

Fixed Temperature   Fixed Flux   Convection

$B_1(T_o):T = T_o$ $B_2(f_o):(\mathbf{n}.\nabla)T = f_o$ $B_3(h,T_\infty):(\mathbf{n}.\nabla)T = h(T - T_\infty)$

Fixed Flux has sub-categories, OutFlux, InFlux and Insulated, depending on whether $f_0 < 0$, $f_0 > 0$ or $f_0 = 0$, respectively.

The domain is restricted to a simple rectangular domain, described by two parameters, its length and its breadth. This set of problems can nevertheless give rise to a wide range of behaviours, including as it does boundary-layer problems (Figure 1(a)) and problems such as that in Figure 1(b) which exhibits a quasi-singularity in the lower right-hand corner.

2.2 The Simulation Engine

The problem is modelled by applying a standard Finite Element Method to the PDE, incorporating streamline diffusion [6] to stabilise the solution when the advective term is dominant. Mesh generation is carried out by the *quadtree* method [3]. This method is based on recursively decomposing the domain into simple shapes. The decomposition proceeds by initially placing a square box (referred to as a root quadrant) over the entire domain. On the first recursive step, the root quadrant is quartered into four child quadrants. Each in turn may be quartered again and so on. The entire tree structure, called the *quadtree*, from root quadrant, through its child quadrants to the terminal leaf quadrants is stored in memory and used to facilitate geometric queries such as searches for points or line intersections. Each leaf quadrant contains sufficient information to carry out a local triangulation. Once each leaf quadrant has been triangulated, the complete triangulation is smoothed to produce the final mesh.

Since at each step the quadrants are quartered, the deeper a leaf quadrant is located in the tree, the smaller the mesh size will be in that quadrant. Non-uniform meshes can be generated by specifying control points through-out the domain and assigning a control level to each point. The control level is the depth to which the quadtree must be generated around that point. The mesh is updated after each adaptive step by refining or coarsening the quadtree data structure on which the mesh is based and regenerating the mesh on the modified quadtree.

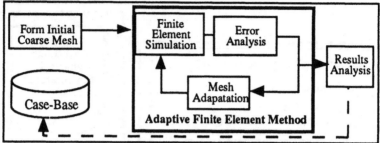

Figure 2: Case-Base Generation

Determining which areas of the mesh should be refined or coarsened depends on the *error indicator* which is applied. The method adopted here is based on a post-processing smoothing technique (see [4] for details).

3 A CBR Approach to Mesh Design

3.1 System Overview

The goal of the system is summarised in Figure 2. An adaptive finite element simulation engine is used to generate a case-base of finite-element problems with associated optimised meshes. This case-base organises the problems according to similarity and is used for initial mesh specification for new simulation problems.

3.2 Case Representation

The first step in designing a CBR system is to determine how cases and solutions should be represented. The description of the PDE problem above has already outlined a case representation. The PDE itself can be represented by specifying the parameters v, k and q. Each boundary of the domain is assigned a boundary type, from the five possible boundary condition types and depending on the type, the relevant parameters are also assigned.

Similarly the solution, that is, a particular mesh design for each case, can be represented as a set of parameters. This is achieved as follows :

A simple method of storing a mesh generated by the quadtree technique is to store the control points and control levels which are used to generate it. We use a grid of points spaced evenly throughout the domain and specify a control level at each of these points. This is demonstrated in Figure 3 for a 4x4 grid of control points. This set of points is sufficient for the quadtree mesh generator to generate a mesh. However, it should be noted that a fixed number of control points will not always be sufficient to represent any given mesh, if the variation in granularity occurs at a smaller scale than that used to separate the control points. In the case-base examples described later a 10x10 grid of control points is used and this has been found to give satisfactory resolution in practise.

The CBR problem is then formulated as : given a set of parameters describing a heat PDE on a rectangular domain (i.e. a target case) and a case base of previously solved heat PDE problems, together with their optimal mesh specification, retrieve

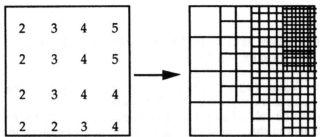

Figure 3: Representing Mesh Granularity using a Coarse Grid

one or more cases from the case-base which are similar to the given target case and adapt their mesh specifications to a new mesh appropriate for the solution of the target problem.

3.3 Case Retrieval

Forming a Qualitative Representation

In the description below we refer to qualitative values, but how should these be defined? Clearly the continuous real line must be discretised into a set of qualitative intervals, which distinguish clearly between positive, negative and zero values, since the sign of a number in this application generally has a clearly discernible physical meaning (e.g. the distinct qualitative difference between heat flowing into a domain across a boundary, heat flowing out of a domain or the boundary being insulated). In determining a proper characterisation of the interval size, the approach is to let the case-base itself decide. The purpose of using qualitative intervals is to partition the base cases into tractable sub-sets, so it makes sense to determine intervals by partitioning the base cases into reasonably sized sub-sets, through an ordering on the real-valued feature and to use this partitioning as a basis for the assignment of qualitative values to the feature.

Applying Retrieval Methods

The method of application of retrieval methods and the adaptation strategy employed are closely coupled. Rather than retrieving and adapting a single base case, multiple cases are retrieved and combined into a solution for the target problem. In order, the steps taken are :

(i)   *Retrieval* of relevant base cases
(ii) Formation of a *mapping* between the target problem and the retrieved cases.
(iii) *Adaptation* of retrieved base case solutions to form partial solutions of the target problem
(iv) *Aggregation* of the partial solution into the complete solution of the target problem.

(i) Retrieval

Retrieval is implemented as a series of filtering methods, which reduce the case base to a set of cases relevant to the target problem.

Characteristic Value Filter : Only those cases sharing the same qualitative characteristic value as the target pass through this filter.

The characteristic value filter plays the important role of determining cases which are broadly similar in character to the target case. It may be reduced to two separate filtering processes based on the following characteristic values :

-    The peclet number combines the flow-field, size of the conductivity and the length of the domain (in the flow direction) into a single qualitative parameter.

-    The approximate boundary fluxes are combined into a single holistic characteristic value for the domain, taken to be the maximum difference between boundary flux values.

Boundary Type Filter : This filters through only those cases whose boundary types intersect with the boundary types of the target problem. The filter can be tuned by setting the size of the intersection set required to allow cases to pass.

Boundary Value Filter : Each boundary is tagged with a qualitative boundary value, which combines boundary type with the values of the parameters associated with the boundary value. Thus if the temperature on a fixed temperature boundary is determined to be POS-LARGE, then the corresponding boundary is tagged with the qualitative value FIXED-TEMP-POS-LARGE. Qualitative boundary values are used in the same manner as boundary types, to allow only those cases which intersect to a specified degree with the boundary values of the target to pass through.

Source Value Filter : A qualitative size of the source term is calculated and only cases with similar sources pass through this filter.

(ii) Mapping

The retrieval mechanism has made no attempt to take into account the location of boundary conditions, searching only for the existence of similar boundaries in the base cases. A trivial mapping would map each of the four target boundaries (upper, lower, left and right) to the corresponding boundary in the base case. However, ideally the boundary types and boundary values of the corresponding boundaries should match. Since only the relative position of boundaries to each other is important rather than their absolute positions, each base case can be rotated or laterally inverted, to find the best correspondence between boundary types and values (see Figure 4). To determine which mapping is the best, the number of exact correspondences in boundary type and boundary value can simply be counted. However, we also add an additional weighting which prefers correspondences between connected boundaries over disconnected boundaries (for example, an exact match for B1 and B2 in Figure 4, would be preferred over an exact match for B2 and B4).

As well as determining the best mapping, the correspondence count can also be used as a measure of the quality of the mapping between base case and target problem

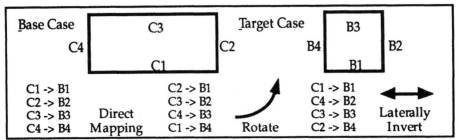

Figure 4: Mapping Target to Base Cases

(with large values implying closer matches). This measure will be used later during the aggregation process.

<u>(iii) Adaptation</u>

To apply the base case solution to the target problem, it is necessary to determine how to transform mesh control levels from one problem into control levels for another problem. This transformation would be trivial if the domains were exactly the same size, but the different dimensions of the target and base cases require more care to be taken.

Let the length and breadth of the base case domain be labelled L_b and M_b respectively. The root quadrant in the base case is a square of dimension $\overline{L}_b = \max(L_b, M_b)$. Each of the 100 control levels should determine the mesh density for the rectangular region of size $\dfrac{L_t}{10} \times \dfrac{M_t}{10}$ of which it is the centroid. A control level l corresponds to a mesh of approximate size $\dfrac{\overline{L}_b}{2^l}$. Thus there are approximately $\dfrac{L_b 2^l}{10\overline{L}_b} \times \dfrac{M_b 2^l}{10\overline{L}_b}$ mesh elements or $\left(\dfrac{L_b 2^l}{10\overline{L}_b} + 1\right) \times \left(\dfrac{M_b 2^l}{10\overline{L}_b} + 1\right)$ nodes contained within a control region of control level l. The mesh density therefore depends not only on the control level, but also on the dimensions of the domain. In order to map mesh densities from base case to target problem, it is necessary to transform the control level at each of the control points into an approximate mesh density using the above formula and to invert this formula to obtain a corresponding control level given the dimensions of the target problem. Although the above formulae are invertible to obtain a level l given a number of nodes in the control region, the approximations taken to arrive at this formula and more seriously the requirement that the control level be an integer, i.e. that the result be rounded, can in certain cases lead to meshes which are under- or over-refined, due not to an inaccuracy in the matching, but only to this error incurred in the adaptation phase.

<u>(iv) Aggregation</u>

Mapping information (i.e. whether the base case has been rotated or inverted to match the target) is used to determine a correspondence between the control points of the retrieved case and those of the target. The value at each control point in the target

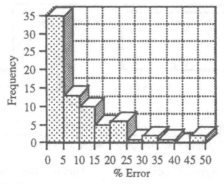

Figure 5: Percentage Error on Case-base designed Meshes

solution is calculated as a weighted average of the corresponding control values of the retrieved cases. The weighting is determined by the quality of the match, which was calculated at the mapping stage.

4. Evaluation

To evaluate the above method, a case-base of 250 randomly generated heat convection problems was created using the adaptive simulation engine to refine the mesh until an error of less than 5% was obtained. Since there are two qualitatively distinct situations, that of pure conduction, where the flow-field is zero everywhere and that of true heat convection, where the flow-field is non-zero, one third of the generated cases were chosen as pure conduction problems. The absolute values of the fixed temperatures and fluxes were restricted to lie in the range [0,100]. The norm of the flow-field was restricted to a range of [0,10000]. This range includes highly advective problems where the diffusion component is dominated by the advection component. These problems are the most difficult to simulate accurately. During random generation, only minor tests for consistency of the problem specification were carried out and thus some non-physical problems were generated which fail to reach the 5% tolerance during simulation. These are excluded from the case-base.

A test set of 75 target problems was generated using the same random method as for the case-base.

4.1 Quality of Case-base Solutions

To test the quality of the case-base, the CBR system was used to design a mesh for each of the 75 target problems, the simulation engine was used to solve the problem over that mesh and the error was calculated. Figure 5 is a histogram of the errors obtained. The y-axis shows the number of target problems which achieved the corresponding error shown on the x-axis. Thus, for example, 5 problems achieved an error of between 15 and 20% and 35 problems achieved an error of between 0 and 5%. The result demonstrates moderate performance by the system.

59 out of the 75 target problems, or 78.6% have achieved a reasonable error of less than 15%. However, only 35 out of the 75 target meshes have achieved the quality of

the base case meshes which were used to design it. Comparing these case-based generated meshes against the optimised meshes generated by the adaptive finite element system, it has been observed that in general the case-base succeeds in producing the correct mesh *pattern* i.e. for each generated mesh, the relative granularity of the mesh in different locations of the domain is similar to that of the optimised mesh; however the case-based method is let down because, overall, the mesh it generates contains insufficient nodes. This can be partly explained by the approximations which are necessary in the case-base mesh representation and in the solution adaptation process.

4.2 Performance of the Case-base Solution

One method to test the performance of the case-based solution is to use the mesh design generated by the case-base as an initial input to the adaptive finite element system. Since we expect the mesh to be close to optimal, the adaptive simulation engine should require fewer iterations to reach the 5% error tolerance. This is demonstrated by the histograms in Figure 6. Here the y-axis shows the number of target problems which required the corresponding number of iterations shown in the x-axis, e.g. 3 target problems required 4 iterations, starting from the CBR designed mesh, whereas 13 target problems required 4 iterations starting from a coarse initial mesh.

On the face of it, the case-based technique appears to yield good performance in terms of iterations taken. However, when a time analysis is carried out, we realise that the benefit gained in decreasing the number of iterations does not yield a net benefit in terms of reduction of simulation time. In fact, in general, when more than a single iteration is required, the total simulation time starting from the CBR designed mesh takes *longer* than when starting with an initial coarse mesh.

This negative result may be explained as follows :-

Firstly, simulations on coarse meshes are very cheap in comparison to simulations over fine meshes. Thus the standard adaptive Finite Element technique can perform its first few iterations very quickly. However, if iterations are required to fix the CBR designed mesh, then these will be expensive, since the initial mesh is already highly refined.

Secondly, the method used by the adaptive simulator is itself heuristic in nature. It determines how best to improve the global error by examining a local error indicator on each mesh element. Even if a mesh is close to optimum, there is a tendency for the simulator to over-refine it. The situation is illustrated in Figure 7, which shows a time profile for an example target problem Although an almost correct solution has been created by the case-based mesh designer, the two iterations required to reach the error tolerance can be more costly than the six iterations taken by the adaptive simulation engine, starting from a coarse mesh.

It should be noted that the time spent actually carrying out the mesh design, through retrieval and adaptation of cases, is insignificant in comparison to the time spend in the finite element simulation. The standard adaptive simulation engine employed here clearly does not integrate well with CBR mesh design. A more sensitive simulation engine which can make minor adjustments to an initial fine mesh may be one way of alleviating the situation. Also, in problems where the cost per iteration is greater, even for coarse meshes (e.g. time-dependent problems) a real time-saving might be observed.

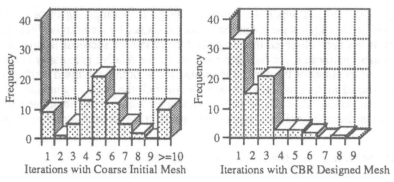

Figure 6: Comparison of Iterations during Adaptive Simulation

5. Discussion

A CBR approach to mesh design has been presented. As an approach, it is moderately successful. The meshes it produces are *qualitatively* correct - they exhibit the correct pattern of granularity. Quantitatively, they tend to fall short of being correct, failing in general to specify the correct number of nodes for a simulation to reach the specified error tolerance. Moreover this quantitative deficiency is significant enough to degrade the overall performance of the system, when combined with an adaptive finite element simulator. However, as a stand-alone system, its results appear to be comparable to those achieved in [1] using a rule-based approach. The development of this system has led to the following general observations about the application of CBR in domains such as ours :

Case Representation

The representation described in Section 3 is a very coarse representation of the problem domain. It is in stark contrast to the structured frame-based representations used in model-based approaches in this domain e.g. in [7]. In such systems, the structure is necessary to enforce modelling constraints. In CBR, such constraints are enforced in the retrieval and adaptation methods. The CBR approach we initially developed and described in [5] is based on a richer frame-based representation. However we found that the structured knowledge representation tends to be unwieldy and overly-detailed for retrieval. In practise, the lack of representation in depth in a simpler CBR system can be overcome by provision of a sufficiently large case-base. Moreover in more detailed representations, the necessary complexity of the retrieval mechanism tends to make it similar in nature to an inference engine used in a model-based approach. It can be argued that in this case, CBR is providing no more than a re-formulation of other reasoning techniques rather than a genuine alternative approach. It appears, from our experience, that CBR is more suited to shallow rather than deep representations.

Case Coverage

The success of CBR depends on case coverage - how many similar problems can be solved by application of the solution of a given problem. Case coverage depends on

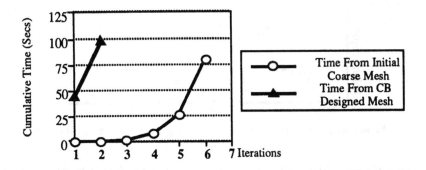

Figure 7: Graph of Cumulative Simulation Time against Iterations

the capabilities of the case adaptation module. In a domain where the problem space is continuous, a qualitative partitioning of the problem space is necessary and the case coverage depends on this qualitative partitioning. There are two conflicting considerations to be taken into account when deciding the partitioning. The partitioning should be fine enough so that only cases whose solutions are sufficiently similar that the adaptation module can transform one to the other should belong in the same partition. But also the partitioning needs to be coarse enough so that in a practically-sized case-base, there is a high probability of finding at least one case which matches the target problem.

These requirements cannot easily be satisfied and in our opinion can only be practically satisfied by relaxing the quality of solution one can expect to attain. In our system, this is manifest in our results which have produced broadly, but not exactly, correct mesh designs.

In general the mapping from problems to solutions might be described by some function,

$$f(P) = S.$$

In CBR, we attempt to approximate this function through retrieval and adaptation of cases. One way to describe the case-based reasoning method is that the function f is approximated by local adaptation functions in 'similarity intervals' around each of the base cases:

Given any base case P_o, there is some similarity interval I_{P_o} around it for which, if a target problem falls within that interval, the base case will be retrieved. Associated with P_o is an adaptation mapping a_{P_o} which maps problems in the interval into the solution space. The case-based reasoning approach will be completely successful if $a_{P_o}(P) \equiv f(P)$ for all problems $P \in I_{P_0}$, i.e. if the adaptation function applied to problems which are similar to P_o can exactly reproduce the correct solution. The stricter the similarity and hence the smaller the interval, then the less complicated the adaptation function needs to be.

However, the size of the interval impacts on the required case-base size. Indeed, in a continuous or very large problem space, as the similarity interval is reduced, the probability that a given target problem will fall within the interval approaches zero and hence more and more cases are required to cover the problem space.

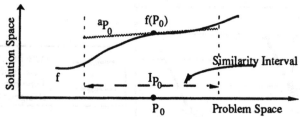

Figure 8: Local Approximation of Mapping from Problem to Solution Space

Our application domain can be described as one in which the situation of Figure 8 holds. When retrieval criteria are relaxed sufficiently so that problem solving can be accomplished on a practically-sized case-base, the variation in the solution space is still too great for the adaptation function to capture. The result is that, in general, only moderate quality solutions can be expected.

There is a danger of this situation occurring whenever the problem and solution spaces are large. Constraints on the size of the case-base dictate that large similarity intervals must be allowed, which shifts the burden of the solution formation task over to the adaptation module. Unless the mapping f is simple, or at least well-understood locally, the limited capabilities of the adaptation module can imply limited performance.

References

1. E. Kang & K. Haghighi: *A knowledge-based a-priori approach to Mesh Generation in Thermal Problems,* International Journal for Numerical Methods in Engineering 35, 915-937 (1992)
2. O.C. Zienkiewicz & K. Morgan: *Finite Elements and Approximations,* Wiley & Sons, (1983)
3. M. Shepherd: *Approaches to the automatic generation and control of finite element meshes* , Applied Mechanics Reviews vol. 41 no. 4 (1988)
4. O.C. Zienkiewiez & J.Z. Zhu: *A simple error estimator and adaptive procedure for practical engineering analysis,* International Journal for Numerical Methods in Engineering vol. 24, 337-357 (1987)
5. N. Hurley: *A priori Selection of Mesh Densities for Adaptive Finite Element Analysis Using a CBR Approach,* In : Topics in Case-Based Reasoning, Lecture Notes in Artificial Intelligence 837, 379-391, Springer Verlag (1994)
6. C. Johnson, J. Pitkaranta : *Finite Element Methods for Linear Hyperbolic Problems,* Comp. Meth. Appl. Mech. Eng. vol. 45 285-312 (1984)
7. D.P. Finn, N. Hurley, N. Sagawa: *AI-DEQSOL . A Knowledge-based Environment for Numerical Simulation of Engineering Problems Described by Partial Differential Equations,* AI-EDAM vol. 6 no. 3 199-212 (1992)

Case Memory and Retrieval Based on the Immune System

John E. Hunt, Denise E. Cooke and **Horst Holstein**

Centre for Intelligent Systems, Department of Computer Science,
University of Wales, Aberystwyth,
Penglais Campus, Aberystwyth, Dyfed,
SY23 3DB United Kingdom,
Email: {jjh,dzc,hoh}@uk.ac.aber
Tel: [+44] (0)1970 622537

June 27, 1995

Abstract

A variety of case memory organisations and case retrieval techniques have been proposed in the literature. Each of these has different features which can affect how useful they are for different applications. However, in applications which are likely to hold very large numbers of cases, which are highly volatile, and the structure of which is poorly understood, most of the current approaches are unsuitable.

In this paper we present a novel approach to case memory organisation and case retrieval based on metaphors taken from the human immune system. We illustrate how the immune system is inherently case based and how it relies on its content addressable memory, and a general pattern matcher, to help it identify new antigens (new situations) which are similar to old antigens (past cases). We construct a case memory based on the immune system theory and show how its pattern recognition, learning and memory operations can support CBR.

1. Introduction

Case Based Reasoning (CBR) has been applied to a wide variety of applications from device diagnosis and design, through interpretation and classification, to legal argumentation [9, 10, 12]. However, the most important element in any case based system is the case memory (case base) itself. This is a repository of past problem solutions and is the basis for the whole reasoning process. As such the way in which a case memory is organised is critically important. However, the design and maintenance of a case memory for a particular application can be problematic.

In this paper we present a novel CBR approach which relies on a theory used to explain the operation of the human immune system for its inspiration. We illustrate how the immune system is inherently case based and how it relies on its content addressable memory, and a general pattern matcher, to help it identify antigens (new situations) which are similar to existing antibodies (past situations). We construct a case memory based on the immune system theory and show how its pattern recognition, learning and memory can support CBR.

2. Case Based Reasoning

The basis of any CBR system is its case database. This means that the CBR system is only as good as the cases which it represents. It also means that the efficiency of the CBR system is mediated by the way in which the case database is organised as well as by the way in which the cases are retrieved. It is thus vitally important to adopt a suitable memory organisation and retrieval method for a particular application. However, in many situations it is difficult to identify the most appropriate organisation prior to actually constructing a system and experimenting with it (whether in software or on paper). This can significantly extend the development time of a CBR system as well as affect its overall success. In some application areas (e.g. data mining) it may prohibit or significantly reduce the potential of CBR systems.

A system which organises its own memory based on the information contained within the cases and utilises this organisation within its retrieval mechanism has a great deal of potential. Not only would it alleviate the time consuming and difficult task of case memory design, it could also allow CBR to be applied in situations where it has previously considered unsuitable.

Traditionally, case memories have followed human memory metaphors, however there is no reason why they should be limited in this way. Any system (biological or otherwise) which displays some form of memory could be considered as a metaphor for a case memory. In the next section we discuss just such a system: the human immune system. This system has a number of very important characteristics which are particularly significant for CBR. These include a content addressable memory, decentralised self organisation (see the immune network section), inherent pattern matching mechanisms, a learning mechanism and a retrieval mechanism. Its memory is constructed by experience from exposure to the same or similar diseases in the past. As such it can be viewed as an example of a naturally occurring CBR system.

3. The Immune System

The *immune system* protects our bodies from attack from foreign substances (called antigens) which enter the bloodstream. The immune system does this using antibodies which are proteins produced by the white blood cells called *B cells* (or B-lymphocytes) that originate in the bone marrow. When a B Cell encounters an antigen an *immune response* is elicited, which causes the antibody to bind the antigen (if they match) so that the antigen can be neutralised. The immune system possesses two types of response: primary and secondary. The primary response is the initial process by which the immune system destroys the antigen, this is referred to as immunisation. If the same antigen is encountered again a secondary immune response is normally activated. This is characterised by a quicker destruction of the antigen. This faster response is due to the immune systems ability to remember how it previously dealt with the antigen. The immune system thus possesses memory. This memory is *content addressable* memory since the secondary response can be elicited from an antigen which is similar, although not identical, to the original one which established the memory.

3.1 Antigen Recognition and Binding (Immune Response)

Antibodies identify the antigen they can bind by performing a pattern matching process. The strength of the bind depends on how closely the two match. The closer the match between antibody and antigen the stronger the molecular binding and the better the recognition. For an antibody to bind an antigen, the binding must be stable, that is the match must exceed a certain threshold before the binding can actually take place.

3.2 The Immune Network

There are a number of views on how memory works in the immune system. One for example, uses the concept of "virgin" memory cells. However, a controversial theory, which is still being debated in the immunological field, states that the B cells collectively form what is known as the *immune network* [11]. This network acts to ensure that when useful B cells are generated, they remain in the immune system until they are no longer required. The network maintains the B cells dynamically using feedback mechanisms. The feedback mechanisms allow the network to grow (and shrink) as required by its "environment", determining its size and the important features of the antibodies dynamically.

According to the immune network theory the level of B cell stimulation (the effect of the B cell's antibody binding an antigen) depends on how well it matches the antigen and also its affinity to (how well it matches) other B cells in the immune network [11]. The network is actually formed by B cells recognising other B cells in the system as being similar. The network is self-organising, since it determines the survival of newly created B cells as well as its own size (see [4]). The more neighbours a B cell has an affinity with, the more stimulation it will receive from the network. The fewer neighbours a B cell has an affinity with, the less stimulation it will receive. If the B cell's stimulation level falls below a certain level it will die. Thus, the immune network acts to reinforce the B cells which are useful and have proliferated and to kill off little used B cells.

3.3 Using the Immune Network for CBR

From the point of view of CBR, the concept of an immune network has a number of interesting (and potentially extremely useful) capabilities. For example, if something has been learnt by the immune network, it can be forgotten unless it is reinforced by other members of the network or by the environment. Thus antibodies which are no longer required can be forgotten. If this analogy is applied to a CBR system, it might be possible to "forget" cases which are no longer being used. Obviously care must be taken with such a process, as depending upon the application, the cases may become useful in the future.

The immune network is the approach we have chosen to explore. However, it should be noted, that the Immune Network theory is held by only a number of (the few) theoretical immunologists, and that it is supported by very few (of the many) experimental immunologists. The contentions are not of concern to us because we are using the theory as the inspiration for our CBR work, rather than trying to make an accurate model of the immune system. In addition, we only consider the aspects of the immune system which are of relevance to CBR. For example, we do not consider the issue of *somatic hypermutation* as CBR systems do not support the idea of mutation etc.

4. Immune Based CBR

This section applies the theories associated with the immune system to CBR.

4.1 The (Immune) Case Memory

The (immune) case memory actually forms a network which maintains the current set of cases and links between cases (which represent affinities between the cases). The network structure is based on the immune network theory, however for reasons of practicality it has deviated from the original theory. We do not believe that this is a problem as we are only relying on the immune system for inspiration.

In the immune-based case memory, a new case is inserted near to those cases which are "similar" to it. This measure of "similarity" is calculated using an immune system derived matching algorithm, described in the Case Matching subsection. The rules which govern case insertion automatically link similar cases together. This results in the emergence of regions within the network which can deal with similar problems. Between these regions, bridges exist which indicate common characteristics between different problem areas.

The novelty of this approach is that the case memory is self-organising. That is, it is not necessary to manually define or identify regions or indexes. This means that a CBR tool based on such a case memory can be easily applied to different problems (i.e., it does not require extensive development time to construct the hierarchy).

4.2 Case Matching

In terms of the analogy with the biological system, case matching mimics antibody/antigen binding. Case matching involves calculating how closely the case matches the current situation, and over how much of the case the match exists. This calculation results in a *match score*. If this match score is above a certain threshold the case may be able to *bind* to the current situation. Depending on the application, the binding threshold may be set as low as 1 or 0 or may be set such that only a very few, very similar cases are able to bind the current situation.

---

count = number of fields that match between
                the antibody and the antigen

For each region consisting of 2 or more matches record their length l_i

$$\text{match score} = \text{count} + \sum_i 2^{l_i}$$

If match score > binding threshold then return match score

Figure 1: The match algorithm

The actual match algorithm (illustrated in figure 1) counts each element in the new case (the antigen) which matches an existing case (an antibody). The match algorithm is also weighted in favour of continuous match regions. If a continuous region of 4 items of information matches, then such a region will have a value of 2 to the power of 4 (i.e. 2^4). For example, for a case to bind a new situation, the binding must be stable, that is the match score must exceed a certain threshold and exist over a certain number of elements of the case and the new situation. It should be possible to turn this feature on and off as it may have positive as well as negative effects depending on the application and the case structure.

Figure 2 illustrates the result of a case being matched with a new situation. The past case describes a holiday from the cabata case base (used later in this paper). As can be seen from the figure, the number of elements which match is 5. However, this number must be added to the value of each of the match regions (e.g. the 3 elements in the middle of the case). This means that the final match score for this example is 13. This approach is a variation on the matching algorithm used by [8].

New situation:	Adventure	2498	2	Egypt	Car	14	March	*
Past case:	Adventure	3066	3	Egypt	Car	14	April	*
Evaluation:	1	0	0	1	1	1	0	1	=> 5
Length:					3			
Match value:	$5 + 2^3$ => 13							

Figure 2: Calculating a match value

4.3 Case Insertion

```
For insertion factor do
    Randomly select n positions within the network
    Until there is no higher match score than current best set do
        From the n positions being considered find m cases with highest match score
        If one (or more) of the cases linked to these m cases have a higher
                match score than at least one of the current best set then
        Add them to the current best set, removing any poorer cases.
                Now consider the cases associated with the newly added case.
    End Until
End For
For each case x in best set do
    Link new case to x as a daughter of x.
    Link new case to any other daughter cases of x.
End For
```

Figure 3: Insertion algorithm

Case insertion mimics the way in which B cells are recruited into the immune network. This process links a new B cell to those B cells (already in the network) with which it has an affinity. This results in groups of B cells with associated features.

In the immune based case memory, a new case is inserted into the case memory near to those cases with which it has the highest affinity (where affinity equals similarity). The case insertion algorithm (illustrated in figure 3) ensures that the clustering nature of the network is automatically generated within the case memory.

The insertion algorithm performs the first loop insertion factor times. If the insertion factor is greater than one, then this increases the chances of selecting useful places in the network in which to insert the case. The first loop starts by randomly selecting n positions within the case network (where n is a number representing 10% of the size of the network). It then loops until no better matches are found than are currently present in the current best set. The current best set are the (10) best cases which have so far been considered. The inner Until loop considers each of the n insertion positions (which have been randomly generated). It checks to see whether any of the cases surrounding these points are better matches than any of the 10 cases currently in the *current best set*. If any are better matches then they replace the worst cases in the *current best set*. Next the cases associated with the ones which have just been added to the *current best set* are considered. This process results in a spreading of the influence of the new case amongst potentially similar cases. This continues until no cases can be added to the *current best set*.

The second loop then links the case to be inserted to each of the cases in the *current best set.*. This is done by linking the new case as a "daughter" case, which possesses an affinity to the parent case. It is also linked to any other cases which are currently daughters of the parent case[1]. This is illustrated in figure 4 where the new case has been linked to two existing daughter cases of x and to x as another daughter.

The network of cases which emerges from the application of the insertion algorithm captures the concept of "similarity" explicitly within it. Each case is linked with cases with which it shares certain features ("feature" does not equal an element of the case, rather it is some combination of elements). This means that one case may be linked to a case with which it shares one set of features and to another case with which it shares a different set of features. In the example, illustrated in the section 5.6, a new case could be linked to an existing case, which has a similar type of holiday at a similar price for a similar number of people, while also being linked to a case which represents a holiday in a similar part of the country, for a similar period at a similar time of year, etc.

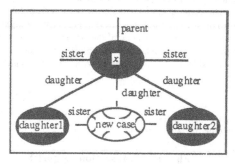

Figure 4: Inserting a new case

4.4 Case Retrieval (Immune Response)

The retrieval of a case mimics the secondary immune response. The aim of the case retrieval algorithm (illustrated in Figure 5) is to find a very close match in the case memory and retrieve it, without actually considering all the cases available.

The case retrieval algorithm effectively performs a beam search which is initialised to a random set of points within the case memory (network). In this situation, "expanding" a node means considering how similar the offspring of a case are to the new case. The value of a node relates to how similar the case is to the new situation. If the case is a close enough match to *bind* the new situation, then the stimulation level of the case is determined. If this is above a certain threshold then the

---

[1] The terms offspring, daughters, sisters and parents are taken from the terminology used to describe the operation of the immune system.

sisters and offspring of this case may be worthy of further examination. These associated cases are therefore added to the list of cases to be considered during the next iteration of the "do" loop. To keep this process tractable, at any one time the algorithm maintains at most n cases ready for expansion. This is necessary as the case database could grow very large and holding a large number of cases in memory would become prohibitive.

The search process continues until, one of the following condition sare met: 1) there are no cases left to consider, 2) a pre-specified elapsed time has been reached, or 3) the best case in the previous iteration is still the best case in the present iteration. Currently the best 10 cases are returned to the user (note this figure can be altered as required).

Randomly select n points in the case network
   Do until no further cases to consider
      Consider each of the cases at these points
         present the antigen to each case and determine whether this antigen
         can be bound by the case
      If the binding value is high enough, then mark the cases associated with
         this case as points for further consideration.
   End Do
Order these cases by binding value

Figure 5: The case retrieval algorithm

4.5 Case "Forgetting"

In order to provide an automatic method for case "forgetting" we have mimicked the B cell stimulation process. In the human immune system, if a B cell cannot bind the current antigen and it does not have a close affinity with other B cells in the immune network, it will die. In other words, if it is a poor solution to the current (or recent) problem(s), and it is not similar to other B cells, it will die. We have developed a case deletion approach based on this mechanism as part of the immune based case memory. In our model of the immune system we take into account both the strength of the match between the new situation and the existing case and the case's affinity to the other cases. The algorithm for calculating the stimulation level can be summarised by the following equation[2]:

$$stimulation = c\left[\sum_{j=1}^{N} m(x_i x_j) + k_1 \sum_{j=1}^{N} m(x_i y)\right] - k_2$$

in which there are N cases, and x_i represents the current case, x_j other cases in the case memory, y represents the current situation and m_{ji} relates to how closely the following two elements match. Then c is a constant that depends on the number of case comparisons per unit time, and k_2 models the tendency of cases to die in the absence of any interactions. Thus $\sum_{j=1}^{N} m(x_i x_j)$ represents the case's *affinity* to its

---

[2] This equation is based onthat presented in [5] for a mathematical model of the immune system.

neighbours, and $\sum_{j=1}^{N} m(x_i y)$ represents how well the case binds the new situation. The multilpier k_i is intended to ensure that a case which is an extremely good match for the current situation, but which is not supported by the network, does not die off. That is, the result of matching the current situation has a multiplication factor which ensures that it has a greater immediate influence than the network.

4.6 An Implementation of the Immune Based Case Memory

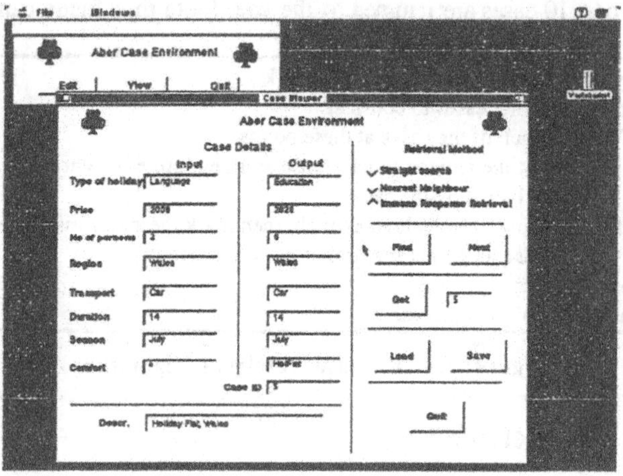

Figure 6: The Case Viewer window

The Aber Case Environment is an experimental environment which encompasses the immune system based approach described above. For comparison it also enables a nearest neighbour approach to be applied to the same case memory. Figure 6 illustrates the case viewer window of this environment. In the remainder of this section we consider the behaviour of this immune based system using the publicly available cabata case base. This case base represents 1470 different cases describing various features associated with holidays such as their type (e.g. adventure, diving, skiing, education etc.), cost, duration, location (e.g. Wales, Egypt etc.) and the type of location (e.g. holiday flats, one star hotel etc.).

In the example illustrated in figure 7, the user has input the requirements for a holiday and the system has retrieved an existing case using the case retrieval algorithm described previously. Note that this case has a continuous set of four elements which are the same (i.e. the region, the transport, the duration and the season) thus enabling a strong bond between this case and the input.

To retrieve this case the system had to consider only 365 cases, whereas the nearest neighbour algorithm had to consider 1470 cases. However, it should be noted that by its very nature the retrieval algorithm could potentially retrieve a different result if it is run again. This is because the retrieval algorithm picks n random points at which to start its search. If n is small compared to the size of the case memory, then it is possible that the points it picks may not allow it to find the best case. Similarly, the number of cases it must consider in order to find the best match will vary. Again this is due to the random choice of initial starting points. However, if it is important that a case be found in a relatively short time and that the result does not need to the best case available but a close match, then the immune based retrieval algorithm is potentially very useful.

Some interesting, and potentially very useful relationships amongst the cases can also be seen from an analysis of the case memory. For example, in the current case memory the experimental system has shown that holidays in Wales have a lot in common with holidays from England, Ireland, Scotland and Belgium. It has also shown that the majority of holidays involving diving are taken by 2 people, who travel by car for a period of 14 days (and are taken in countries as varied as Wales, Turkey and Rhodes). Explication of these relationships in itself may be a useful tool for further organisation of the case memory or as some form of "data mining". It is also the main strength of this approach, that is, the system has organised the case memory around common features which are exploited by the retrieval algorithm.

5. Comparison with Existing Approaches

5.1 Case Memories

Table 1: Comparison of Memory Organisations

	Structured memory	Incremental	Automatic creation	Inherent organisation	Case forgetting
Linear		■			
Hierarchical	■				
Nested	■				
Decision Tree	■		■		
Knowledge Guided Indexing	■				
Immune-based	■	■	■	■	■

Table 1 presents a comparison of a number of case memory organisations, the following discussion relates to this table.

Only the linear and immune based organisations inherently possess incrementally adaptable memories. In the case of the hierarchical, knowledge guided and nested approaches, they may require extensive maintenance if the original developer did not accurately predict the future contents of the case memory. It can also be necessary to rerun the induction process, in a decision tree oriented memory, when new cases are added to the case memory as they may change the structure of the decision tree used to organise the cases. However, it is worth noting that such systems might employ ID5 [14] an incremental an incremental decision tree induction method.

Only the decision tree approach and the immune based approach automatically create their memory structures / organisation. In each of the other systems a case memory designer must identify the appropriate structures / organisation. A decision tree oriented case memory is rarely produced "by hand". In general such an organisation will exploit some decision tree generating algorithm (such as ID3 or C4.5 [13]). The advantage of these techniques is that the relevance of case features to applications such as diagnosis is derived automatically [10]. A disadvantage is that a separate algorithm is required to generate this tree resulting in additional complexity. Another problem, common to all induction systems, is that the system might split on an apparently insignificant field. For example, the colour of houses, rather then the number of bedrooms in the houses. This can result in the system requiring apparently irrelevant information during the case retrieval process. It is also necessary to ensure that there is enough information (i.e. cases) available to clearly define the domain thus allowing the algorithm to partition the case memory appropriately. It is difficult to determine that enough information is available without actually running the induction process and examining the results produced.

The immune based memory is inherently self organising, requiring no external construction methods. It is also worth noting that the linear organisation is similarly self organising in that if new cases are always added to the front of the case base, then there is an implicit temporal ordering. However, only the immune based approach inherently incorporates a method for forgetting little used cases.

5.2 Case Retrieval

Table 2: Comparison of retrieval mechanisms

	Focus search	Handles noise and missing data	Deterministic
Nearest neighbour		■	■
Hierarchical	■		■
Decision tree	■		■
Knowledge guided retrieval	■		■
Immune based	■	■	

Table 2 compares a number of case retrieval approaches with the immune based approach. As before, a number of observations can be made form this table.

With the exception of the nearest neighbour approach, all the methods provide some way of focusing the search process. For example, in the decision tree approach most of the work associated with case selection has already been performed and pre-compiled into the decision tree. The advantage of this is that it is only necessary to follow the branch indicated by each decision point to find a small group of cases each of which may provide the required problem solution. The immune based approach inherently focuses the search process towards similar cases.

A new situation may possess noisey data or may be missing some information, however the only approaches which inherently handle these problems are nearest neighbour and immune based. In the decision tree approach, for example, these problems may result in limited performance as they may throw the decision tree of line. The same sort of problem can be found with hierarchical approaches. However, nearest neighbour and immune based both inherently handle both noise and incomplete information.

An important consideration, which the immune based approach fails to address, is determinism. That is, given the same inputs, will the system return the same result every time? Due to the way in which the immune based retrieval mechanism works, this cannot be guaranteed. This is in contrast to all the other approaches which should return the same result for the same inputs (assuming nothing else has changed).

Another potential problem with the immune based approach is that, although the matching algorithm is biologically feasible, it may not be applicable in a wide range of applications. This is because it places a large emphasis on the length of matched regions. While this algorithm has proved useful in the range of applications we have considered so far, there are many other applications in which such an emphasis is not appropriate (e.g., in diagnostic applications). Instead, it seems likely that in such an application that it would be desirable to eliminate the region weighting altogether. We could have introduced a concept of "nearness" into the algorithms (e.g. 2 persons is near to 3 persons or March is near to April). However, one of the aims of this research has been to minimise the level of specification and maintenance required by the case memory. By introducing additional domain knowledge in the matching process we would be undermining our own goals. However, in practice such an approach could be applied within the framework of the immune case memory.

6. Related Work

Although no work has previously attempted to apply theories relating to the immune system to CBR, some research has been done on using the immune system as the motivation for a number of other computer systems. Some models based on the immune system have been developed to aid the study of the operation of the immune system itself from a biological point of view [6]. Some of these researchers have identified the potential of immune-based computer systems for other applications. For example, Farmer and co-workers [5] recognised that their model had the potential to be used for artificial intelligence tasks, particularly pattern recognition.

Bersini and Varela [1, 2] have developed an approach which can be used for optimisation of functions or controllers. Gilbert and Routen [7] attempted to create a content-addressable auto-associative memory, based on the immune network theory, specifically for image recognition. Finally, Cooke and Hunt [3] have successfully applied an Artificial Immune System to the task of learning to recognise promoter sequences.

7. Further Work

There are a number of areas of further work which could be addressed. For example, one area of work would be to mimic the primary and secondary response operation of the immune system. At present we really only mimic the way in which B cells are recruited into the immune network and how the secondary response is elicited. The primary response could be based on an adaptation (and repair) step. This would allow the system to respond to new situations which cannot be directly addressed by the cases currently held in the case memory.

8. Conclusions

In this paper, we have presented a novel approach to case memory organisation and case retrieval based on metaphors taken from the human immune system. We believe that this approach has significant benefits in the applications with very large case memories, which are difficult to partition and maintain and which may be susceptible to constant change.

The primary advantage of the immune based approach is that the structure of the case memory is an "emergent" property of the system. That is, it does not require detailed domain analysis to define the case memory organisation, nor does it require extensive maintenance, nor does it rely on the application of a separate induction algorithm. This means that it could be applied in applications where little is known about the structure of the domain or about the cases involved (other than their specific content). This could make it very useful in applications where there are large amounts of data being processed into cases (e.g. gene sequence data or data mining).

The primary disadvantage of our immune based approach is that it does not guarantee to return the best match. Thus a system based on this approach would not be very useful in applications such as diagnostic help desk systems.

Acknowledgements

We would like to acknowledge Mario Lenz of the Institute for Computer Architecture and Software Technology of the German National Research Center for Computer Science, for making the cabata case base available.

References

[1] Bersini, H. 1991. Immune network and adaptive control, *Proc. 1st European Conference on Artificial Life*, ed. by F. J. Varela and P. Bourgine, Pub. MIT Press.

[2] H. Bersini, and F. Varela. 1994. The Immune Learning Mechanisms: Reinforcement, Recruitment and their Application, *Computing with Biological Metaphors*, ed. R. Paton, Pub. Chapman and Hall, London. 166-192.

[3] D.E. Cooke, and J.E. Hunt. 1995. Recognising Promoter Sequences using an Artificial Immune System, to appear in the *Proceedings of the Third International Conference on Intelligent Systems for Molecular Biology*. Pub. AAAI Press, California.

[4] De Boer, R. J. and Perelson, A. S. 1991. How diverse should the immune system be? *Proc. Royal Society of London B*, Vol. 252, 171-175.

[5] Farmer, J. D., Packard, N. H. and Perelson, A. S. 1986. The immune system, adaptation and machine learning. *Physica 22D*, 187-204.

[6] Forrest, S., Javornik, B., Smith, R. E. and Perelson, A. S. 1993. Using Genetic Algorithms to Explore Pattern Recognition in the Immune System, *Evolutionary Computation*, 1(3), 191-211.

[7] Gilbert, C. J. and Routen, T. W. 1994. Associative Memory in an Immune-Based System, *Proc. AAAI'94* , Vol. 2, 852-857.

[8] R. Hightower, S. Forrest and A.S. Perelson 1993. The Baldwin effect in the immune system: Learning by somatic hypermutation. Department of Computer Science, University of New Mexico, Albuquerque, USA.

[9] Kolodner, J. 1993. *Case-Based Reasoning*, Pub. Morgan Kaufmann CA.

[10] Kriegsman, M. and Barletta, R. 1993. Building a Case-Based Help Desk Application, *IEEE Expert*, Vol. 8, No. 6., 18-26.

[11] Perelson, A. S. 1989. Immune Network Theory, *Immunological Review*, 110, pp 5-36.

[12] Pu, P. 1993. (Guest Editor). 1993. Special Issue on Case-Based Reasoning in Design, *AI-EDAM* Vol 7 No 2.

[13] Quinlan, J. R. 1993. *C4.5 Programs for Machine Learning*, Pub. Morgan Kaufmann CA.

[14] Utgoff, P. E. 1989. Incremental induction of decision trees. *Machine Learning*, 4, 2, 161-186.

Using Case Data to Improve on Rule-based Function Approximation

Nitin Indurkhya[1] and Sholom M. Weiss[2]

[1] Department of Computer Science, University of Sydney
Sydney, NSW 2006, AUSTRALIA
[2] Department of Computer Science, Rutgers University
New Brunswick, New Jersey 08903, USA

Abstract. The regression problem is to approximate a function from sample values. Decision trees and decision rules achieve this task by finding regions with constant function values. While recursive partitioning methods are strong in dynamic feature selection and in explanatory capabilities, an essential weakness of these methods is the approximation of a region by a constant value. We propose a new method that relies on searching for similar cases to boost performance. The new method preserves the strengths of the partitioning schemes while compensating for the weaknesses that are introduced with constant-value regions. Our method relies on searching for the most relevant cases using a rule-based system, and then using these cases for determining the function value. Experimental results demonstrate that the new method can often yield superior regression performance.

1 Introduction

Given samples of output (response) variable y and input (predictor) variables $\mathbf{x} = \{x_1...x_n\}$, the regression task is to find a mapping $y = f(\mathbf{x})$. Relative to the space of possibilities, finite samples are far from complete, and a predefined model is needed to concisely map $\mathbf{x}$ to y. Accuracy of prediction, i.e. generalization to new cases, is of primary concern. Regression differs from classification in that the output variable y in regression problems is *continuous*, whereas in classification y is strictly categorical. From this perspective, classification can be thought of as a subcategory of regression. Some machine learning researchers have emphasized this connection by describing regression as "learning how to classify among continuous classes" [Quinlan, 1993]. However, the regression problem has been studied extensively in the statistical community and in this paper, the standard statistical terminology is employed.

Over time, many effective nonlinear regression methods [Efron, 1988] have emerged to expand the scope of classical linear least-squares regression [Scheffe, 1959], including projection pursuit [Friedman & Stuetzle, 1981], MARS [Friedman, 1991] and neural networks [McClelland & Rumelhart, 1988]. These methods produce results in terms of weighted models. In addition to these methods, disjunctive normal form (DNF) models, such as regression trees and regression rules can also be effective functional approximators [Breiman *et al.*, 1984, Quinlan, 1993, Weiss & Indurkhya, 1993].

DNF learning methods are noted to be strong when there are many higher order dependencies among the input variables [Friedman, 1991]. Two principal advantages of these methods can be cited: (a) dynamic feature selection in high dimensional applications and (b) explanatory capabilities for predicting a single numerical outcome. On the negative side, DNF methods cannot represent compactly many simple smooth functions because they represent a function as regions with single functional values. Regression rules are similar in character to regression trees, but the rules need not be mutually exclusive. They are potentially more compact and predictive than trees, but their learning methods are relatively more complex and time-consuming [Weiss & Indurkhya, 1993]. In this paper, we present a method that preserves the strengths of the partitioning schemes while compensating for their weaknesses. Our method relies on searching for the most relevant cases using a rule-based system, and then using these cases for determining the function value. Experimental results demonstrate that the the new method can often yield superior regression performance.

2 Model Combination

In practice, one learning model is not always superior to others, and a learning strategy that examines the results of different models may do better. Moreover, by combining different models, enhanced results may be achieved. A general approach to combining learning models was described in [Wolpert, 1992]. Based on this scheme, referred to as *stacking*, additional studies were performed in applying the scheme to regression problems [Breiman, 1993, LeBlanc & Tibshirani, 1993]. Using small training samples of simulated data, and linear combinations of regression methods, improved results were reported. Let M_i be the i-th model trained on the same sample, and w_i, the weight to be given to M_i.[3] If the new case vector is $\mathbf{x}$, the predictions of different models can be combined as in Equation 1 to produce an estimate of y. The models may use the same representation, such as k-nearest neighbors with variable-size k, or perhaps variable-size decision trees. The models could also be completely different, such as combining decision trees with linear regression models. Different models are applied independently to find solutions, and later a weighted vote is taken to reach a combined solution. This method of model combination is in contrast to the usual approach to evaluation of different models, where the single best performing model is selected.

$$y = \sum_{k=1}^{K} w_k M_k(\mathbf{x}) \tag{1}$$

While stacking has been shown to give improved results on simulated data, a major drawback is that properties of the combined models are not retained. Thus

---

[3] These weights are obtained so as to minimize the least squared error under some constraints [Breiman, 1993].

when interpretable models are combined, the result may not be interpretable at all. It is also not possible to compensate for weaknesses in one model by introducing another model in a controlled fashion.

In this paper, we hypothesize and empirically demonstrate that partitioning regression methods and k-nearest neighbor regression methods are complementary. Instead of inducing solutions independently and then (linearly) combining these two models, we examine the weaknesses and strengths of these two learning methods, and propose a new method that uses the decision rules to pick out the relevant cases, and then uses these cases for finding the function value. We also show how and why our method often yields strong results on real-world data.

In [Quinlan, 1993], model trees (i.e., regression trees with linear combinations at the leaf nodes) and nearest neighbor methods were also combined. The combination method is described in Equation 2, where the $N(\mathbf{x})^k$ is one of the K nearest neighbors of $\mathbf{x}$, $V(\mathbf{x})$ is the y-value of the stored instance $\mathbf{x}$, and $T(\mathbf{x})$ is the result of applying a model tree to $\mathbf{x}$.

$$y = \frac{1}{K} \sum_{k=1}^{K} V(N(\mathbf{x})^k) - (T(N(\mathbf{x})^k) - T(\mathbf{x})) \tag{2}$$

The k-nearest neighbors are found independently of the induced regression tree (results were reported with $K=3$). In that sense, the approach is similar to the combination method of Equation 1. The k-nearest neighbors are passed down the tree, and the results are used to refine the nearest neighbor answer. Thus, we have a combination model formed by independently computing a global solution, and later combining results. As we shall see, there are strong reasons for not determining the global nearest neighbor solution independently. Instead, the k-nearest neighbor result need only be considered for the cases covered by a particular partition. While this increases the interaction between the models and eliminates the independent computation of the two models, the model rationale and the empirical results are supportive of this approach.

3 Methods

3.1 Measuring Performance

The objective of regression is to minimize the distance between the sample output values, y_i and the predicted values y_i'. The mean absolute distance (deviation) of Equation 3 is used in our studies. This is a measure of the average error of prediction for each y_i over n cases.

$$MAD = \frac{1}{n} \sum_{i=1}^{n} |y_i - y_i'| \tag{3}$$

Because prediction is the primary concern, estimates based on training cases alone are inadequate. The principles of predicting performance on new cases are analogous to classification, but here the mean absolute distance is used as the error rate. The best estimate of true performance of a model is the error rate on a large set of independent test cases. When large samples of data are unavailable, the process of train and test is simulated by random resampling. In most of our experiments, we used (10-fold) cross-validation to estimate predictive performance.

3.2 Regression by Tree Induction

Like classification trees, regression trees are induced by recursive partitioning. The solution takes the form of Equation 4, where R_i are disjoint regions, k_i are constant values, and y_j^i refers to the y-values of the training cases that fall within the region R_i.

$$if \ \mathbf{x} \subseteq R_i \ then \ f(\mathbf{x}) = k_i = median\{y_j^i\} \qquad (4)$$

Regression trees have the same representation as classification trees except for the terminal nodes. The decision at a terminal node is to assign a case a constant y value. The single best constant value is the median of the training cases falling into that terminal node because for a partition, the median is the minimizer of mean absolute distance. Figure 1 is an example of a binary regression tree. All cases reaching shaded terminal node 1 (x1≤3) are assigned a constant value of y=10.

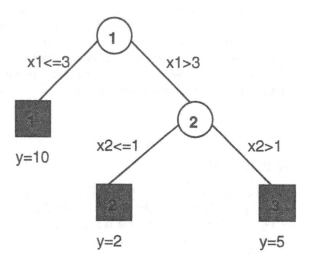

Fig. 1. Example of Regression Tree

More detailed descriptions of procedures for inducing regression trees can be found in [Breiman *et al.*, 1984, Quinlan, 1993, Weiss & Indurkhya, 1993].

3.3 Regression by Rule Induction

Both tree and rule induction models find solutions in disjunctive normal form, and the model of Equation 4 is applicable to both. Each rule in a rule-set represents a single partition or region R_i. However, unlike the tree regions, the regions for rules need not be disjoint. With non-disjoint regions, several rules may be satisfied for a single sample. Some mechanism is needed to resolve the conflicts in k_i, the constant values assigned, when multiple rules, R_i regions, are invoked. One standard model [Weiss & Indurkhya, 1991] is to order the rules. Such ordered rule-sets have also been referred to as *decision lists*. The first rule that is satisfied is selected, as in Equation 5.

$$if \ i < j \ and \ \mathbf{x} \subseteq both \ R_i \ and \ R_j \ then \ f(\mathbf{x}) = k_i \qquad (5)$$

Figure 2 is an example of an ordered rule-set corresponding to the tree of Figure 1. All cases satisfying rule 3, and not rules 1 and 2, are assigned a value of y=5.

$$\boxed{\begin{array}{l} x1 \leq 3 \ \rightarrow \ y=10 \\ x2 \leq 1 \ \rightarrow \ y=2 \\ \text{Otherwise } y=5 \end{array}}$$

Fig. 2. Example of Regression Rules

While rules are similar to trees, the rule representation is potentially more compact because the rules are not mutually exclusive. This potential of finding a more compact solution can be particularly important for problems where model interpretation is crucial. Note that the space of all rules includes the space of all trees. Thus, if a tree solution is the best, the rule induction procedure has the potential to find it. The expanded search space makes rule induction more complex than tree induction. Detailed descriptions of procedures for regression rule induction can be found in [Weiss & Indurkhya, 1993].

3.4 Regression by k-Nearest Neighbor

The k-nearest neighbor method is one of the simplest regression methods, relying on table lookup. To classify an unknown case $\mathbf{x}$, the k cases that are closest to the new case are found in a sample data base of stored cases. The predicted $y(\mathbf{x})$ of Equation 6 is the mean of the y values for the k-nearest neighbors. The nearest neighbors are found by a distance metric such as euclidean distance (usually with some feature normalization). The method is non-parametric and highly non-linear in nature

$$y_{knn}(\mathbf{x}) = \frac{1}{K} \sum_{k=1}^{K} y_k \ \ for \ K \ nearest \ neighbors \ of \ \mathbf{x} \tag{6}$$

A major problem with this approach is how to limit the effect of irrelevant features. While limited forms of feature selection are sometimes employed in a preprocessing stage, the method itself cannot determine which features should be weighted more than others. As a result, the procedure is very sensitive to the distance measure used. In a high-dimensional feature space, k-nearest neighbor methods may perform very poorly. These limitations are precisely those that the partitioning methods address. In theory, the two methods potentially complement one another.

3.5 Integrating Rules with Table-lookup

Regression trees and rules are induced by recursive partitioning methods that approximate a function with constant-value regions. They are relatively strong in dynamic feature selection in high-dimensional applications, sometimes using only a few highly predictive features. An essential weakness of these methods is the approximation of a partition or region by a constant value. For a continuous function and even a moderately sized sample, this approximation can lead to increased error.

To deal with this limitation, instead of constant-value functions, linear functions can be substituted in a partition, as was done in [Quinlan, 1993]. However, a linear function has the obvious weakness that the true function may be far from linear even in the restricted context of a single region. K-nearest neighbor methods are nonparametric and make no assumptions about linearity. At the limit, with large samples, they will correctly fit the function. In practice though, their weaknesses can be substantial. Finding an effective global distance measure may not be easy, particularly in the presence of many noisy features.

Hence, consider the following strategy: For determining the value of y-value of a case $\mathbf{x}$ that falls in region R_i, instead of assigning a single constant value k_i for region R_i, where k_i is determined by the median y value of training cases in the region, assign $y_{knn}^i(\mathbf{x})$, the mean of the k-nearest (training set) instances of $\mathbf{x}$ in region R_i. Thus for regression trees, we now have Equation 7. For regression rules, we also have Equation 8.

$$if \ \mathbf{x} \subseteq R_i \ then \ f(\mathbf{x}) = y_{knn}^i(\mathbf{x}) \tag{7}$$

$$if \ i < j \ and \ \mathbf{x} \subseteq both \ R_i \ and \ R_j \ then \ f(\mathbf{x}) = y_{knn}^i(\mathbf{x}) \tag{8}$$

We have a representation which potentially alleviates the weakness of partitions being assigned single constant values. Moreover, some of the global distance measure difficulties of the k-nn methods may also be relieved because the table lookup is reduced to partitioned and related groupings.

This is the rationale for a hybrid partition and k-nn scheme. Note that unlike stacking, our hybrid models are not independently determined, but interact very strongly with one another. However, it must be demonstrated that these methods are in fact complementary, preserving the strengths of the partitioning schemes while compensating for the weaknesses that would be introduced if constant values were used for each region. Two principal questions will now be addressed by empirical experimentation:

- Are results improved relative to using each model alone?
- Are these methods competitive with alternative regression methods?

4 Results

To evaluate the performance of the integrated partition and k-nn regression method, experiments were performed using seven datasets, six of which are described in [Quinlan, 1993]. In addition to these six datasets, new experiments were done on a very large telecommunications application, which is labeled pole. Experimental results are reported in terms of the MAD, as measured using 10-fold cross-validation. For pole, 5,000 cases were used for training and 10,000 for independent testing. The features from the different datasets were a mixture of continuous and categorical features. For pole, all 48 features were continuous. Descriptions of the other datasets can be found in [Quinlan, 1993].[4] Table 4 summarizes the key characteristics of the datasets used in this study.

Dataset	Cases	Vars
price	159	16
servo	167	19
cpu	209	6
mpg	392	13
peptide	431	128
housing	506	13
pole	15000	48

Table 1. Dataset Characteristics

Table 2 summarizes the original results reported in [Quinlan, 1993]. These include model-trees (MT), which are regression trees with linear fits at the terminal nodes; neural nets (NNET); 3-nearest neighbors (3-nn); and the combined

---

[4] The peptide dataset is a slightly modified version of the one Quinlan refers to as *lhrh-att* in his paper. In the version used in our experiments, cases with missing values were removed.

results of model-trees and 3-nearest neighbors (MT/3-nn).[5]

Table 3 summarizes the additional results that we obtained. These include the CART regression tree (RT); 5-nearest neighbors with euclidean distance (5-nn); rule regression using Swap1 [Weiss & Indurkhya, 1993]; rule regression with 5-nn applied to the rule region (Rule/5-nn); and MARS. 5-nn was used because the expectation is that the nearest neighbor method incrementally improves a constant-value region when the region has a moderately large sample of neighbors to average.

The MARS procedure has several adjustable parameters.[6] For the parameter mi, values tried were 1 (additive modeling), 2, 3, 4 and number of inputs. For df, the default value of 3.0 was tried as well the optimal value estimated by cross-validation. The parameter nk was varied from 20 to 100 in steps of 10. Lastly, both piece-wise linear as well as piece-wise cubic solutions were tried. For each of the above setting of the parameters, the cross-validated accuracy was monitored, and the value for the best MARS model is reported.

Dataset	MT	NNET	3-nn	MT/3-nn
price	1562	1833	1689	1386
servo	.45	.30	.52	.30
cpu	28.9	28.7	34.0	28.1
mpg	2.11	2.02	2.72	2.18
peptide	.95	-	-	-
housing	2.45	2.29	2.90	2.32

Table 2. Previous Results

For each method, besides the MAD, the relative error is also reported. The relative error is simply the estimated true mean absolute distance (measured by cross-validation) normalized by the initial mean absolute distance from the median. Analogous to classification, where predictions must have fewer errors than simply predicting the largest class, in regression too we must do better than the average distance from the median to have meaningful results.

In comparing the performance of two methods for a dataset, the standard error was estimated. If the difference in performance was greater than 2 standard errors, then the difference was considered statistically significant (This approximates to a confidence level of 95%). As with any significance test, one must also consider the overall pattern of performance and the relative advantages of competing solutions [Weiss & Indurkhya, 1994].

For each dataset, Figure 3 plots the relative best error found by the ratio of

---

[5] Because peptide was a slightly modified version of the *lhrh-att* dataset, the result listed is one that was provided by Quinlan in a personal communication.

[6] The particular program used was MARS 3.5.

Dataset	RT		5-nn		Rule		Rule/5-nn		MARS	
	MAD	Error	MAD	Error	MAD	Error	MAD	Error	MAD	Error
price	1660	.40	1643	.40	1335	.32	1306	.31	1559	.38
servo	.195	.21	.582	.63	.235	.25	.227	.24	.212	.23
cpu	30.5	.39	29.4	.38	27.62	.35	26.32	.34	27.29	.35
mpg	2.28	.35	2.14	.33	2.17	.33	2.04	.31	1.94	.30
peptide	.97	.46	.95	.45	.86	.40	.86	.40	.98	.46
housing	2.74	.42	2.77	.42	2.51	.38	2.35	.36	2.24	.34
pole	4.10	.14	5.91	.20	3.76	.13	3.70	.12	7.41	.25

Table 3. Performance of Additional Methods

the best reported result to each model's result. A relative best error of 1 indicates that the result is the best reported result for any regression model. The model results that are compared to the best results are for regression rules, 5-nn, and the mixed model. The graph indicates trends across datasets and helps assess the overall pattern of performance. In this respect, both Rule and Rule/5nn exhibit excellent performance across applications.

These empirical results allow us to consider the two questions posed at the end the last section:

1. *Are results improved relative to using each model alone?* A comparison of Rule/5nn with 5nn shows that for all datasets, Rule/5nn is significantly better. In comparing Rule/5nn with Rule, the results indicate that for three datasets (mpg, pole and housing), Rule/5nn was significantly better than Rule, and for the remaining three datasets both were about the same. The overall pattern of performance also appears to favor Rule/5nn over Rule. Thus the empirical results indicate that our method improved results relative to using each model alone. The general trend can be seen in Figure 3.

2. *Are these methods competitive with alternative regression methods?* Among the previous reported results, MT/3nn is the best performer. Other alternatives to consider are: Regression Trees (RT) and MARS. None of these three methods were significantly better than Rule/5nn on any of the datasets under consideration except for RT doing significantly better on servo. Furthermore, Rule/5nn was significantly better than MT/3nn on three of five datasets (servo, cpu and mpg) on which comparison is possible. The overall trend also is in favor of Rule/5nn. Comparing RT to Rule/5nn, we find that except for servo, Rule/5nn is significantly better than RT on all the remaining datasets. Comparing MARS to Rule/5nn, we find that for three of the datasets (price, peptide and pole), Rule/5nn is significantly better. Hence the empirical results overwhelmingly suggest that our new method is competitive with alternative regression methods, with hints of superiority over some methods.

Relative Best Erate

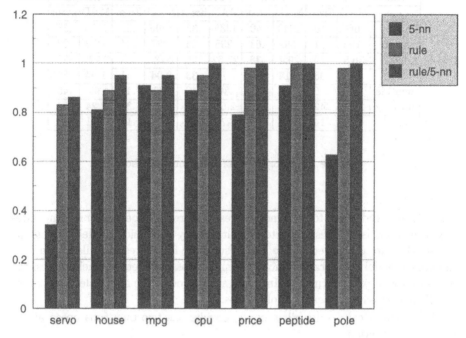

Fig. 3. Relative Best Erates of 5-nn, Rules, and Rule/5-nn

5   Discussion

Looking at Figure 3 and Tables 2 and 3, we see that the pure rule-based solutions are competitive with other models. Additional gains are made when rules are used not for obtaining the function values directly, but instead used to find the relevant cases which are then used to compute the function value. The results of these experiments support the view that this strategy of combining different methods can improve predictive performance. Strategies similar to ours have been applied before for classification problems [Ting, 1994, Widmer, 1993] and similar conclusions were drawn from those results. Our results indicate that the strategy is useful in the regression context too. Our empirical results also support the contention that for regression, partitioning methods and nearest neighbor methods are complementary. A solution can be found by partitioning alone, and then the incremental improvement can be observed when substituting the average y of the k-nearest neighbors for the median y of a partition. From the perspective of nearest neighbor regression methods, the sample cases are compartmentalized, simplifying the table lookup for a new case.

While not conclusive, there are hints that our strategy is most effective for small to moderate samples: it is likely that when the sample size grows large, increased numbers of partitions, in terms of rules or terminal nodes, can compensate for having single constant-valued regions. This conjecture is supported by the large-sample pole application, where the incremental gain for the addition of k-nn is small.[7]

In our experiments we used k-nn with k=5. Depending on the application, a different value of k might produce better results. The optimal value might be estimated by cross-validation in a strategy that systematically varies k and picks the value that gives the best results overall. However, it is unclear whether the increased computational effort will result in any significant performance gain.

Another practical issue with large samples is the storage requirement: all the cases must be stored. This can be a serious drawback in real-world applications with limited memory. However, we tried experiments in which the cases associated with a partition are replaced by a fewer number of "typical cases". This results in considerable savings in terms of storage requirements. Results are slightly weaker (though not significantly different).

A number of regression techniques have been presented by others to demonstrate the advantages of combined models. Most of these combine methods that are independently invoked. Instead of a typical election where there is one winner, the alternative models are combined and weighted. These combination techniques have the advantage that the outputs of different models can be treated as independent variables. They can be combined in a form of postprocessing, after all model outputs are available.

In no way do we contradict the value of these alternative combination techniques. Both approaches show improved results for various applications. We do conclude, however, that there are advantages for more complex regression procedures that dynamically mix the alternative models. These procedures may be particularly strong when there is a fundamental rationale for choice of methods such as partitioning methods, or when properties of the combined models must be preserved.

References

[Breiman et al., 1984] Breiman, L.; Friedman, J.; Olshen, R.; and Stone, C. 1984. Classification and Regression Tress. Monterrey, Ca.: Wadsworth.

[Breiman, 1993] Breiman, L. 1993. Stacked regression. Technical report, U. of CA. Berkeley.

[Efron, 1988] Efron, B. 1988. Computer-intensive methods in statistical regression. SIAM Review 30(3):421–449.

[Friedman & Stuetzle, 1981] Friedman, J., and Stuetzle, W. 1981. Projection pursuit regression. J. Amer. Stat. Assoc. 76:817–823.

[Friedman, 1991] Friedman, J. 1991. Multivariate adaptive regression splines. Annals of Statistics 19(1):1–141.

---

[7] Although small, this difference tests as significant because the sample is large.

[LeBlanc & Tibshirani, 1993] LeBlanc, M., and Tibshirani, R. 1993. Combining estimates in regression and classification. Technical report, Department of Statistics, U. of Toronto.

[McClelland & Rumelhart, 1988] McClelland, J., and Rumelhart, D. 1988. *Explorations in Parallel Distributed Processing.* Cambridge, Ma.: MIT Press.

[Quinlan, 1993] Quinlan, J. 1993. Combining instance-based and model-based learning. In *International Conference on Machine Learning*, 236–243.

[Scheffe, 1959] Scheffe, H. 1959. *The Analysis of Variance.* New York: Wiley.

[Ting, 1994] Ting, K. 1994. The problem of small disjuncts: Its remedy in decision trees. In *Proceedings of the 10th Canadian Conference on Artificial Intelligence*, 91–97.

[Weiss & Indurkhya, 1991] Weiss, S., and Indurkhya, N. 1991. Reduced complexity rule induction. In *Proceedings of IJCAI-91*, 678–684.

[Weiss & Indurkhya, 1993] Weiss, S., and Indurkhya, N. 1993. Rule-based regression. In *Proceedings of the 13th International Joint Conference on Artificial Intelligence*, 1072–1078.

[Weiss & Indurkhya, 1994] Weiss, S., and Indurkhya, N. 1994. Decision tree pruning: Biased or optimal? In *Proceedings of AAAI-94*, 626–632.

[Widmer, 1993] Widmer, G. 1993. Combining knowledge-based and instance-based learning to exploit qualitative knowledge. *Informatica* 17:371–385.

[Wolpert, 1992] Wolpert, D. 1992. On overfitting avoidance as bias. Technical Report SFI TR 92-03-5001, The Sante Fe Institute.

Learning to Improve Case Adaptation by Introspective Reasoning and CBR⋆

David B. Leake, Andrew Kinley, and David Wilson

Computer Science Department
Lindley Hall 215, Indiana University
Bloomington, IN 47405, U.S.A.

Abstract. In current CBR systems, case adaptation is usually performed by rule-based methods that use task-specific rules hand-coded by the system developer. The ability to define those rules depends on knowledge of the task and domain that may not be available *a priori*, presenting a serious impediment to endowing CBR systems with the needed adaptation knowledge. This paper describes ongoing research on a method to address this problem by acquiring adaptation knowledge from experience. The method uses reasoning from scratch, based on introspective reasoning about the requirements for successful adaptation, to build up a library of *adaptation cases* that are stored for future reuse. We describe the tenets of the approach and the types of knowledge it requires. We sketch initial computer implementation, lessons learned, and open questions for further study.

1   Introduction

Case-based reasoning (CBR) systems solve new problems by *retrieving* prior solutions of similar previous problems and performing *case adaptation* (also called *case modification*) to fit the retrieved cases to the new situation. Although much progress has been made in methods for case retrieval, both the American and European CBR communities have identified case adaptation as a particularly challenging open problem for the field (e.g., [1, 18]). The problem is so acute that the most effective current strategy for building CBR applications is to bypass adaptation entirely, building advisory systems that provide cases to human users who perform the adaptation themselves (e.g., [2, 14]). However, despite the practical benefits of retrieval-only advisory systems, successful use of advisory systems may require considerable user expertise. Consequently, automatic case adaptation is important from a practical perspective, not only to enable CBR systems to perform autonomously but to enable them to aid naive users. Likewise, as we discuss in [19], increased understanding of the case adaptation process and the knowledge required is also important from a cognitive modeling perspective, as a step towards understanding how humans adapt cases when they reason from prior episodes.

⋆ This work was supported by the National Science Foundation under Grant No. IRI-9409348.

This paper describes research based on characterizing case adaptation knowledge by decomposing it into two parts: (1) a small set of abstract structural transformations (e.g., [5, 9]), and (2) memory search strategies for finding the information needed to apply those transformations. This framework forms the basis of an approach to adaptation in which new adaptation problems are solved by first selecting a transformation indexed under the type of problem motivating adaptation, and then performing introspective reasoning about how to strategically search memory for the information needed to apply the transformation [17]. Not only does this approach provide increased flexibility in finding needed information, but it serves as a foundation for learning to improve adaptation performance from experience: A trace of this process can be stored as an *adaptation case* and used in future case-based reasoning about the adaptation process itself. Thus the approach is aimed at providing both the flexibility to deal with novel case adaptation problems and adaptation abilities that improve with experience.

We begin by discussing the significance of the case adaptation problem for CBR and the tenets of our approach. We then summarize an initial implementation that applies our approach to learning case adaptation for case-based planning (e.g., [8]) in the disaster response planning domain. We close by highlighting lessons learned and related research on case adaptation and memory search.

2 Acquiring Case Adaptation Knowledge

Coding effective adaptation rules can require extensive knowledge of the CBR system's task, its domain, and the contents of its memory. Unfortunately, this knowledge may not be available *a priori*. Thus in defining case adaptation rules, developers face the same problem of knowledge acquisition in imperfectly-understood domains that often impedes the development of rule-based systems in other contexts. In many of those contexts, the knowledge acquisition problem has been significantly ameliorated by the use of case-based reasoning. Consequently, it is natural to consider applying CBR to the case adaptation process itself, replacing pre-defined adaptation rules with adaptation cases that reflect prior adaptation experience [3, 17, 29].

An important question is the source of the needed library of adaptation cases. We propose a method that starts with a library of domain-independent adaptation rules, using them to solve novel adaptation problems. The results of applying those rules to specific adaptation problems are stored as adaptation cases to be re-used by case-based reasoning. The following sections first discuss the rule-based process and then the use of adaptation cases.

2.1 Adaptation = Transformations + Memory Search

Case adaptation knowledge is often characterized in either of two ways. The first is with abstract rules, such as the rule *add a step to remove harmful side-effect* for case-based planning [8]. Such rules are applicable to a broad class of plan adaptation problems, but give no guidance about *how* to find the specific knowledge needed to apply them (e.g., to find the right step to add in order to mitigate a given side-effect). For example, if the planning task is to generate X-ray treatment plans, and the retrieved plan administers the minimum X-ray dose required to destroy a tumor, but also has the bad side-effect of exposing the spinal cord to excessive radiation, deciding which step to add in order to remove the bad side-effect may require considerable domain knowledge.

The second way to characterize adaptations is by relying on adaptation rules that include the required specific knowledge. For example, in the radiation treatment planning domain, the general rule *add a step to remove harmful side-effect* can be replaced by specific rules such as *add the step "rotate radiation sources" to remove harmful side-effect "excess radiation"* [4].

Both these approaches exhibit the classic operationality/generality tradeoff from explanation-based learning (e.g., [28]). Abstract rules have generality: a small set of transformations appears sufficient to characterize a wide range of adaptations [5, 15]. However, abstract rules are difficult to apply. Specific rules, on the other hand, are easy to apply but have limited generality. In addition, defining such rules is difficult because of the specific knowledge that they require.

Kass [11] proposes one way to address the operationality/generality trade-off. His approach uses hand-coded *adaptation strategies* that combine general transformations with domain-independent memory search strategies for finding the domain-specific information needed to apply the strategies. Our approach to adaptation builds on this idea in treating adaptation knowledge as a combination of knowledge about general transformations and about memory search. However, instead of relying on hand-coded memory search strategies, our model builds memory search strategies as needed. When presented with a novel adaptation problem, it performs a planning process that reasons introspectively to determine the information required to solve the particular adaptation problem and to decide which memory search strategies to use to find that information. This process guides the search for information needed to perform the adaptation.

2.2 From Rule-Based Adaptation to CBR

After an adaptation problem has been solved by reasoning from scratch, a natural question is how to learn from that reasoning. Initially, it appears that explanation-based generalization (EBG) (e.g., [22]). would be the appropriate learning method, because it allows forming operational new generalizations: The memory search plan that found the needed information could be generalized and stored. However, one of the conclusions of our research is that using EBG to learn memory search rules is not practical [17]. For EBG to apply successfully to memory search rules, those memory search rules must provide a complete and correct theory of the contents and organization of memory. Unfortunately, the contents and organization of a specific memory are highly idiosyncratic [13, 27] and thus hard to characterize precisely. Consequently, a chain of memory search rules that finds desired information in one instance is not guaranteed to apply to other problems that appear to be within the scope of those same rules: explanation-based generalization may not yield reliable results.

In contrast, using case-based reasoning as the learning method for adaptation knowledge makes it possible for learned knowledge to reflect the idiosyncrasies of the memory's organization and its contents; unlike abstract adaptation rules, cases that package particular adaptation episodes encapsulate the system's experience on specific adaptation and memory search problems and reflect the system's specific task, domain, and memory organization. Consequently, we are applying CBR to learning adaptation cases. Thus our model acquires not only a library of problem-solving cases, but also a library of cases representing episodes of case adaptation. The following section discusses our computer model of the entire adaptation process, including both case adaptation from scratch in response to novel adaptation problems and case-based adaptation to re-use the results of previous adaptation episodes.

3 DIAL

The task domain for our research is *disaster response planning* for natural and man-made disasters. Examples of such disasters include earthquakes, chemical spills, and "sick building syndrome," in which occupants of a building fall victim to problems caused by low air quality inside a building. Studies of human disaster response planning support that case-based reasoning plays an important role in response planning by human disaster planners [26].

Our computer model, the case-based planner DIAL,[2] starts with a library of domain cases—disaster response plans from previous disasters—and general (domain-independent) rules about case adaptation and memory search. Like other case-base planners, it learns new plans by storing the results of its planning process. However, the central focus of our research is not on the case-based planning process *per se,* but on learning to improve case adaptation.

When DIAL successfully adapts a response plan to a new situation, it stores not only the problem solving episode, but also two types of adaptation knowledge for use in similar future adaptation problems: *memory search cases* encapsulating information about the steps in the memory search process, and *adaptation cases* encapsulating information about the adaptation problem as a whole, the memory search cases used to solve it, and the solution to the adaptation problem.

The entire DIAL system includes a schema-based story understander (that receives its input in a conceptual representation), a response plan retriever and instantiator, a simple evaluator for candidate response plans, and an adaptation component to adapt plans when problems are found. The case-based planning framework is based in a straightforward way on previous case-based planners (e.g., CHEF [8]). Consequently, this paper will only discuss the adaptation component.

DIAL's adaptation component receives two inputs: an instantiated disaster response plan and a description of a problem in the response plan requiring adaptation. To illustrate, one of the examples processed by DIAL involves the

---

[2] For Disaster response with Introspective Adaptation Learning.

following story: *At Beaver Meadow Elementary School in Concord, New Hampshire, students have been complaining of symptoms like unusual fatigue, eye irritation, respiratory problems, and allergic reactions from being inside the building.* When DIAL processes this story, a straightforward schema-based understanding process identifies the problem as an air quality problem. DIAL then attempts to retrieve and apply a response plan for a similar disaster. The response plan retrieved is the plan for the following factory air quality problem: *A & D Manufacturing in Bangor, Maine, has recently come under pressure from workers and union-representatives to correct perceived environmental problems in the building. Workers have been affected by severe respiratory problems, headaches, fatigue, and dizziness.* (These episodes are based on case studies from the *INvironment* newsletter for indoor air quality consultants.)

The response plan for A & D Manufacturing involves notifying the workers' union. DIAL's evaluator determines that the notification step does not apply to the current situation, because of a conflict with normative type restrictions on union members: elementary school students do not belong to unions. (The evaluation and problem characterization process is similar to that described in Leake [16]). Consequently, the response plan must be adapted to apply to the students. DIAL's adaptation component receives two inputs describing this situation: the response plan for the A & D Manufacturing problem, applied to the new situation, and a description of the problem to repair by adaptation: that trying to notify the students' union is not reasonable, because students do not belong to unions. After a description of the general processing done in response to adaptation problems, we will discuss how it applies to this example.

Given inputs describing a candidate response plan and a problem to be adapted, the process performed by DIAL's adaptation component is as follows:

1. **Case-based adaptation:** DIAL first attempts to retrieve an adaptation case that applied successfully to a similar previous problem. If retrieval is successful, that case is re-applied and processing continues with step 3.
2. **Rule-based adaptation:** When no relevant prior case is retrieved, DIAL selects a transformation associated with the type of problem that is being adapted (e.g., role/filler mismatches, such as the mismatch between unions and students, are associated with substitution transformations: a mismatch can be repaired by replacing the role being filled or how the given role is filled). Given the transformation, the program generates a *knowledge goal* [23] for the information needed to apply the transformation. E.g., for substitutions of role-fillers, the knowledge goal is to find an object that satisfies all the case's constraints on the object being replaced.

   The knowledge goal is then passed to a planning component that uses introspective reasoning about alternative memory search strategies [17, 20] to find the information needed. This search process generates a memory search plan whose operators include both an initial set of memory search strategies and *memory search cases* stored after solving previous adaptation problems.
3. **Plan evaluation:** The adapted response plan is evaluated by a simple evaluator that checks the compatibility of the current plan with explicit con-

straints from the response plan. A human user performs backup evaluation. If the new response plan is not acceptable, other adaptations are tried.

4. **Storage:** When adaptation is successful, the resulting response plan, adaptation case, and memory search plan are stored for future use.

The following subsections elaborate on the representation of knowledge goals, the memory search process, the adaptation case representation, and the examples currently processed.

Representing knowledge goals: In order to use our framework to guide rule-based case adaptation, a CBR system must be able to reason about how to find the information that it needs in order to apply a given transformation to a particular response plan. To do this reasoning, it must first have an explicit representation of the sought-after information. In DIAL, these needs are represented by explicit *knowledge goals* [23]. Previous study of knowledge goals has developed a two-part representation combining a *concept specification* [23] providing a template to match with candidate information and a description of how the information, once found, should be used.

To satisfy the requirements of memory search, however, we have found that the representation must include some additional components. First, as is reflected implicitly in the retrieval mechanisms of many CBR systems, the goals of memory search must often be described in terms of the available alternatives in memory (e.g., searching for the matching problem whose solution appears easiest to adapt, compared to other alternatives), rather than described by simply matching a template. Consequently, DIAL's knowledge goal representation also includes a *comparative specification* describing how to choose between multiple alternatives that satisfy the concept specification. Also, DIAL's knowledge goal representation includes information on the amount of search effort allowed for satisfying the knowledge goal (measured in terms of the number of primitive memory operations that may be applied during memory search).

The memory search process: During DIAL's initial rule-based adaptation process, it finds the information needed to apply adaptation transformations by an introspective reasoning process that implements memory search as a form of planning, using operators that describe actions within its internal, or "mental" world, rather than within the external world [10]. Using a planning process facilitates flexible re-combination of memory search knowledge. By decoupling memory search knowledge from specific adaptation rules, memory search knowledge can be applied to any problem for which it appears relevant.

Two types of memory search knowledge are provided to the system. First, the system is provided with *knowledge goal transformation rules*, similar to Kolodner's [13] query transformation rules, that reformulate the questions posed to memory. For example, one strategy for retrieving an instance of an event is to search for contexts in which it would have been likely to play a role. Second, the system is provided with a suite of domain-independent *memory search strategies* that depend on "weak methods" of memory search (e.g., ascending and descending abstraction hierarchies to find related nodes). DIAL currently includes six of these strategies. All strategies are defined in terms of a substrate of seven primitive memory access operations (e.g., to extract the "parent" of a node).

The results of the memory search process are filtered by constraints from the particular adaptation problem. The result is a relatively unguided initial search for information, but traces of this process are saved as *memory search cases* and made accessible for use during future memory search. These cases provide more precise guidance for memory search in similar future situations. In this model, cases are acquired solely by reasoning from scratch, which may require considerable processing effort. However, as will be discussed in a later section, we have also begun to investigate how this view of adaptation can be used to facilitate interactive acquisition of adaptation knowledge.

DIAL's memory search mechanism uses a reactive planning framework, inspired by the RAPS system [7], to interleave planning with execution and respond to problems during memory search (e.g., that needed intermediate information cannot be found). In this process, DIAL's rule-based adapter accepts a knowledge goal and chooses a strategy or stored memory search case indexed by the knowledge goal. In the course of processing, a strategy may transform the current knowledge goal or may generate sub-knowledge-goals, also to be satisfied by the planning process. Throughout the memory search process, the adapter maintains a reasoning trace of the operators it applies. That trace is packaged with the search result, as a memory search case, and stored for future use.

Representing and organizing cases learned from adaptation episodes: DIAL's *memory search cases* package the initial knowledge goal, a trace of knowledge-goal transformations and other memory search operations involved in the search process, a record of the search outcome (failure or success), the cost of the search in terms of primitive memory operations performed, and the information found. Memory search cases are indexed under the knowledge goals that they satisfy, and can suggest search operations to attempt in the future; they also have the potential to be used to warn of previous search failures. Memory search cases are accessible to the knowledge planning process for memory search, augmenting the initial library of built-in operators. For future searches, successful search cases that match the largest subset of the current knowledge goals are re-used. When the result of the stored search case does not satisfy current constraints, the search is continued by local search.

DIAL also packages *adaptation cases*, which include both the transformation used for the adaptation and pointers to memory search cases used to search for information to apply the transformation. These provide more specific guidance about how to adapt cases to repair particular types of problems.

Examples processed: DIAL's initial case library currently contains two disaster response plans, a response plan for the previously-described air quality disaster at A & D Manufacturing and a response plan for an industrial chemical spill. The system has been tested on four different stories exercising different parts of its adaptation mechanisms. The first concerns the indoor air quality problem at Beaver Meadow school, for which DIAL retrieves the A & D disaster response plan. (Like the stories processed, stored response plans are based on episodes from the *INvironment* newsletter.) The A & D disaster response plan includes many steps applicable to the new situation, providing the basis for a response to the school air quality problem. However, as previously described, one of the steps in the response plan for the air quality problem at A & D manufacturing does not apply: notifying the union of the victims. Because schoolchildren do not have unions, the notification step of the previous response plan must be adapted to apply to the schoolchildren. Many adaptations are possible, but a common suggestion from human readers is that the step involving notifying the union should be adapted into a step notifying the children's parents.

When DIAL is run on this example, no adaptations have yet been learned, so the program uses its rule-based adaptation process to perform the adaptation. It first selects a substitution transformation. (In DIAL, candidate transformations for repairing problems in retrieved cases are indexed directly under categories of problem types. For a description of possible problem types, see Leake, 1992.) In this case, the "role/filler mismatch" problem of the schoolchildren belonging to a union may be resolved by either of two substitutions: substituting a new filler (notifying someone else's union) or substituting a different concept in which the children play a similar role (notifying another group relevant to the children). To determine appropriate substitutions, the system must hypothesize the factors that were important in the relationship between workers and their union in the A & D manufacturing problem. Possible constraints can be obtained by examining alternative "views" of the relationship between the union and the workers in the original episode [31], based on the relationships represented in the system's memory. In DIAL's memory, one view of union membership involves the member *being represented*, suggesting searching for representatives of the children. This search yields "parents" as one possibility. (Other possibilities, like "student government" are also hypothesized but rejected during evaluation.) By storing the successful choices according to internal and external feedback, the system builds up information beyond the information in its initial world model about which adaptations to favor for particular adaptation problems.

A second example involves an air quality problem on a military base. The A & D manufacturing episode is the most similar in memory, but again the step of notifying the union fails to apply, this time because soldiers do not have unions. DIAL retrieves the previously-learned adaptation but finds that it too fails to apply: Notifying the soldier's parents is rejected by the user. Consequently, it applies a very simple adaptation to the adaptation case, discarding the final step in the memory search plan from the adaptation case and adding local search. In particular, it preserves that the *representation* relationship was important in the previous situation, and searches for representatives of soldiers. Using this guidance, it searches memory for representatives of soldiers and finds "commanding officers" as a possible group to notify.

Two additional examples involve another disaster at a school, to which the Beaver Meadow school response plan is reapplied in a straightforward way without adaptation, and the story of a chemical spill episode at a school. The chemical spill example illustrates the importance of learning new *adaptations* during CBR, instead of only learning new *cases* as traditionally done in CBR systems. For the chemical spill example, DIAL retrieves the previous chemical spill example as the most similar *case*, which is reasonable in light of the shared steps involved in cleaning up chemical spills—the response plan learned from the Beaver Meadow air quality problem is not the most similar response plan. However, the *adaptation* learned from processing the Beaver Meadow story is still useful: DIAL uses the adaptation learned from the Beaver Meadow school example to adapt the response to the previous chemical spill (which also involves notifying the workers' union) by substituting the students' parents. This demonstrates the value of decoupling case learning from adaptation learning: learning both new adaptation cases and new problem-solving cases increases the effectiveness of a CBR system in responding to new problems.

4 Lessons Learned and Open Issues

The conclusions drawn from the project to date include a number of points discussed in the previous sections: the usefulness of decomposing adaptation knowledge into two semi-independent parts, abstract transformations and memory search knowledge; the appropriateness of CBR; rather than explanation-based learning, as the mechanism for learning the needed memory search information; the need for a richer notion of knowledge goals than in previous research; and the usefulness of a reactive model of memory search planning in order to use incremental results of the search to guide further decisions.

Learning new strategies for adapting cases also has interesting ramifications for similarity assessment. In current CBR systems, similarity assessment is generally based on fixed criteria. However, as a CBR system learns how to adapt cases to deal with new types of problems, the similarity metric should be adjusted to reflect that (thanks to the adaptation learning), those problems are no longer as great an impediment to applying the case. Consequently, one area for further study is how best to make the similarity assessment process reflect the changing state of system adaptation knowledge.

We are now addressing a number of open questions. One of these is the level of granularity to be used for memory search cases. At present, memory search cases package entire memory search plans, but is possible that making subparts of the search plans available, as in Redmond's [24] *snippets,* would be beneficial.

Another question being studied is the effectiveness of the planful memory search process. To give an indication of the value of the knowledge planning framework for memory search, the current examples have been processed both using the planful process and using the simple *local search* strategy used by a number of CBR systems to find substitutions [15]. In this comparison, the knowledge planning method resulted in an order of magnitude savings in the number of primitive memory operations performed. This improvement is encouraging, although at this point it cannot be taken too seriously because of the limited set of examples used. Likewise, not enough examples are yet implemented to have reliable data on the tradeoffs between memory search by knowledge planning and CBR. We are now extending the system with the aim of performing additional tests. In particular, an important tradeoff to investigate is the *utility problem* [21] for learned adaptation knowledge: the danger that processing overhead due to the proliferation of adaptation cases and memory search cases will counterbalance the benefits of the additional guidance that they provide.

A final question involves the potential to apply this view of case adaptation to alternative methods for acquiring case adaptation knowledge. DIAL models the transition from adaptation by using unguided general rules to adaptation by using specific adaptation cases, by storing results of successful rule-based adaptation. With its method, the initial rule-based adaptation phase may be quite expensive. An alternative method for acquiring adaptation cases is to use its view of adaptation—as transformations plus memory search—as a basis for an interface to facilitate direct acquisition of adaptation cases from a human user. Such an interface could enable a user to suggest transformations and search strategies from a vocabulary of alternatives. We have begun to investigate this approach, both for its own potential and as a means of more rapidly acquiring a set of adaptation cases to test and refine DIAL's case-based adaptation process.

5 Relationship to Other Approaches

Memory search: Although many sophisticated memory search schemes have been developed in CBR research, they are normally driven by opaque procedures, rather than being accessible to explicit reasoning and learning. Our research follows an alternative course, developing explicit models of the memory search process to increase the flexibility and effectiveness of memory search, in the spirit of [13, 25], and to make it accessible to learning, as in [6, 12].

Case adaptation: Some previous systems are able to learn knowledge useful for guiding adaptation. For example, although CHEF [8] has a static library of domain-independent plan repair strategies, it augments that library with learned *ingredient critics* that suggest adaptations appropriate to particular ingredients. Likewise, PERSUADER [29] uses a combination of heuristics and case-based reasoning to guide adaptation, searching memory for similar prior adaptations to apply. In these systems, however, the adaptation information learned is quite domain and task specific, while memory search cases have more flexibility. The use of CBR for case adaptation has also been advocated by Berger [3], in the context of storing and re-using an expert's adaptations. An alternative approach to the case adaptation problem is to use derivational analogy, deriving a new solution by re-applying a prior solution process to new circumstances, rather than directly adapting the old solution itself [30].

6 Conclusions

Automatic case adaptation is necessary to enable CBR systems to function autonomously and to serve naive as well as expert users. However, knowledge acquisition problems for the rule-based adaptation methods used in many CBR systems have proven a serious impediment to developing CBR applications that perform their own adaptation.

We have described a framework for characterizing adaptation knowledge in terms of transformations and information search, have discussed how that framework is being used as the basis for a model of automatic learning of case adaptation knowledge, and have sketched an initial implementation of that model.

The model combines reasoning from scratch and case-based reasoning to build up expertise at case adaptation. The aim of this approach is to enable CBR systems to make the transition from adaptation guided by general rules (which may be unreliable and expensive to apply) to adaptation guided by adaptation cases that reflect specific case adaptation experience. Thus our method is a way for CBR systems to learn to become more effective at applying their existing cases to new situations.

References

1. Dean Allemang. Review of the first European workshop on case based reasoning EWCBR-93. *Case-Based Reasoning Newsletter*, 2(3), 1993. Electronic newsletter, special interest group AK-CBR, German Society for Computer Science.
2. R. Barletta. A hybrid indexing and retrieval strategy for advisory CBR systems built with ReMind. In *Proceedings of the Second European Workshop on Case-Based Reasoning*, pages 49–58, Chantilly, France, 1994.
3. J. Berger. Using past repair episodes. Unpublished manuscript, August 1995.
4. J. Berger and K. Hammond. ROENTGEN: a memory-based approach to radiation therapy treatment. In R. Bareiss, editor, *Proceedings of the Case-Based Reasoning Workshop*, pages 203–214, San Mateo, 1991. DARPA, Morgan Kaufmann, Inc.
5. J. Carbonell. Learning by analogy: Formulating and generalizing plans from past experience. In R. Michalski, J. Carbonell, and T. Mitchell, editors, *Machine Learning: An Artificial Intelligence Approach*. Morgan Kaufmann, San Mateo, CA, 1983.
6. M. Cox. Machines that forget: Learning from retrieval failure of mis-indexed explanations. In *Proceedings of the Sixteenth Annual Conference of the Cognitive Science Society*, pages 225–230, Atlanta, GA, 1994.
7. R.J. Firby. *Adaptive Execution in Complex Dynamic Worlds*. PhD thesis, Yale University, 1989. Computer Science Department TR 672.
8. K. Hammond. *Case-Based Planning: Viewing Planning as a Memory Task*. Academic Press, San Diego, 1989.
9. T. Hinrichs. *Problem Solving in Open Worlds: A Case Study in Design*. Lawrence Erlbaum Associates, Hillsdale, NJ, 1992.
10. L. Hunter. Planning to learn. In *Proceedings of the Twelfth Annual Conference of the Cognitive Science Society*, pages 261–268, Cambridge, MA, July 1990. Cognitive Science Society.
11. A. Kass. Tweaker: Adapting old explanations to new situations. In R.C. Schank, C. Riesbeck, and A. Kass, editors, *Inside Case-Based Explanation*, chapter 8, pages 263–295. Lawrence Erlbaum Associates, 1994.
12. A. Kennedy. Using a domain-independent introspection mechanism to improve memory search. In *Proceedings of the 1995 AAAI Spring Symposium on Representing Mental States and Mechanisms*, Stanford, CA, March 1995. AAAI.

13. J. Kolodner. *Retrieval and Organizational Strategies in Conceptual Memory.* Lawrence Erlbaum Associates, Hillsdale, NJ, 1984.

14. J. Kolodner. Improving human decision making through case-based decision aiding. *The AI Magazine*, 12(2):52–68, Summer 1991.

15. J. Kolodner. *Case-Based Reasoning.* Morgan Kaufmann, San Mateo, CA, 1993.

16. D. Leake. *Evaluating Explanations: A Content Theory.* Lawrence Erlbaum Associates, Hillsdale, NJ, 1992.

17. D. Leake. Towards a computer model of memory search strategy learning. In *Proceedings of the Sixteenth Annual Conference of the Cognitive Science Society*, pages 549–554, Atlanta, GA, 1994.

18. D. Leake. Workshop report: The AAAI-93 workshop on case-based reasoning. *The AI Magazine*, 15(1):63–64, 1994.

19. D. Leake. Combining rules and cases to learn case adaptation. In *Proceedings of the Seventeenth Annual Conference of the Cognitive Science Society*, Pittsburgh, PA, 1995. In press.

20. D. Leake. Representing self-knowledge for introspection about memory search. In *Proceedings of the 1995 AAAI Spring Symposium on Representing Mental States and Mechanisms*, pages 84–88, Stanford, CA, March 1995. AAAI.

21. S. Minton. *Learning Search Control Knowledge: An Explanation-Based Approach.* Kluwer Academic Publishers, Boston, 1988.

22. T. Mitchell, R. Keller, and S. Kedar-Cabelli. Explanation-based generalization: A unifying view. *Machine Learning*, 1(1):47–80, 1986.

23. Ashwin Ram. AQUA: Asking questions and understanding answers. In *Proceedings of the Sixth Annual National Conference on Artificial Intelligence*, pages 312–316, Seattle, WA, July 1987. Morgan Kaufmann Publishers, Inc.

24. M. Redmond. *Learning by Observing and Understanding Expert Problem Solving.* PhD thesis, College of Computing, Georgia Institute of Technology, 1992. Technical report GIT-CC-92/43.

25. E. Rissland, D. Skalak, and M.T. Friedman. Heuristic harvesting of information for case-based argument. In *Proceedings of the Twelfth National Conference on Artificial Intelligence*, pages 36–43, Seattle, WA, July 1994. AAAI.

26. Uriel Rosenthal, Michael Charles, and Paul Hart, editors. *Coping with crises: The management of disasters, riots, and terrorism.* C.C. Thomas, Springfield, IL, 1989.

27. R.C. Schank. *Dynamic Memory: A Theory of Learning in Computers and People.* Cambridge University Press, Cambridge, England, 1982.

28. A. Segre. On the operationality/generality tradeoff in explanation-based learning. In *Proceedings of the Tenth International Joint Conference on Artificial Intelligence*, Milan, Italy, August 1987. IJCAI.

29. K. Sycara. Using case-based reasoning for plan adaptation and repair. In J. Kolodner, editor, *Proceedings of the Case-Based Reasoning Workshop*, pages 425–434, Palo Alto, 1988. DARPA, Morgan Kaufmann, Inc.

30. M. Veloso. *Planning and Learning by Analogical Reasoning.* Springer Verlag, Berlin, 1994.

31. R. Wilensky. Knowledge representation—a critique and a proposal. In J. Kolodner and C. Riesbeck, editors, *Experience, Memory and Reasoning*, chapter 2, pages 15–28. Lawrence Erlbaum Associates, 1986.

Retrieving Cases in Structured Domains by Using Goal Dependencies*

Héctor Muñoz-Avila and Jochem Huellen

Centre for Learning Systems and Applications (LSA)
University of Kaiserslautern, Dept. of Computer Science
P.O. Box 3049, D-67653 Kaiserslautern, Germany
E-mail: {munioz|huellen}@informatik.uni-kl.de

Abstract. Structured domains are characterized by the fact that there is an intrinsic dependency between certain key elements in the domain. Considering these dependencies leads to better performance of the planning systems, and it is an important factor for determining the relevance of the cases stored in a case-base. However, testing for cases that meet these dependencies, decreases the performance of case-based planning, as other criterions need also to be consider for determining this relevance. We present a domain-independent architecture that explicitly represents these dependencies so that retrieving relevant cases is ensured without negatively affecting the performance of the case-based planning process.

1 Introduction

Reusing previous problem solving experience has proven to speed-up planning systems. Problem solving experience can be stored in generalized (Minton, 1988) or abstracted (Bergmann & Wilke, 1995) form, or it can be stored as cases (Veloso, 1994; Ihrig & Kambhampati, 1994; Yang & Lu, 1994). One of the methods better studied and used for adapting cases is derivational analogy (Carbonell, 1983; Veloso & Carbonell, 1993; Cunningham & Slattery, 1994) that basically consists of replaying the planning-decisions taken in selected cases, while solving a new problem. As other adaptation approaches (Smyth & Keane, 1994), the effectivity of derivational analogy depends on the adaptability of the cases selected. As a result, the derivational analogy replay method has been integrated with retrieval procedures in general problem solving systems (Veloso, 1994).

CAPLAN/CBC (Muñoz-Avila, Paulokat, & Wess, 1994) is a case-based planning system that is build on top of a partial-order nonlinear planner (Paulokat & Wess, 1994) and uses derivational analogy for replaying past solutions. To overcome the problem of retrieving adaptable cases, the first version of CAPLAN/CBC used classifications manually defined by domain experts as an index for the case-library. However, such classifications are not avaliable in every

---

* This research was partially sponsored by the Deutsche Forschungsgemeinschaft (DFG), Sonderforschungsbereich (SFB) 314: "Künstliche Intelligenz - Wissensbasierte Systeme", Project X9 (1991 - 1995).

domain. Further, domain-dependent classifications may be made, based on technological issues different than adaptability of the solutions. As a result, it was necessary to perform additional tests during the retrieval phase to ensure the relevancy of the cases retrieved, increasing thereby the average execution time.

There are domain where structural dependencies between certain key elements in the domain are defined. These dependencies are based on intrinsic processing restrictions and they form part of the problem descriptions. They also reduce the range of possible solutions for a problem as they establish relations between elements that must be meet by any solution. Thus, they must be taken into account when retrieving cases during a case-based solving process.

In this paper we define the notion of dependencies between elements of structured domains. Based on this notion a domain-independent architecture for the case-base is presented that extends the one developed in PRODIGY/ANALOGY (Veloso, 1994). By comparing it against the one in PRODIGY/ANALOGY, we show that this architecture ensures the retrieval of relevant cases for structured domains in better time ranges.

Subsequent sections present an example of a structured domain. Then, we state the requirements for a retrieval procedure and give a survey the architecture of the case-base in PRODIGY/ANALOGY. After that, section 4 defines the concept of dependencies. Then, we present the architecture of the case-base in CAPLAN/CBC (section 5) and introduce the retrieval procedure based on this architecture (section 6). In section 7, the results of an experiment comparing the retrieval times by using both architectures is discussed. Finally, a conclusion about our work is made.

2 Domain of process planning

An example of a domain with structural dependencies between goals is the domain of process planning for manufacturing mechanical workpieces (Paulokat & Wess, 1994; Yang & Lu, 1994). A planning problem in this domain is to find a sequence of processing operations in order to machine a workpiece, by considering the available resources (i.e. tools, machines) and technological constraints relative to the use of these resources. The process begins by clamping a piece of raw material on a lathe machine that rotates it at a very high speed. Then different tools are used to remove layers of raw material. Depending on the structure of the workpiece, several clamping operations may be needed to process the workpiece completely.

Fig. 1 shows an example of a workpiece. The grid area corresponds to the portion of raw material that need to be removed. Based on the geometry of the workpiece the grid area is decomposed in several processing areas, some of which are indicated explicitly in Fig. 1, such as *hor* (a horizontal outline) and *ucut1* (an undercut). The initial state of the planning problem is a collection of propositions regarding the resources available and propositions describing the relations between the processing areas. $rotary-cutting-tool(rct2)$ is an example of the first type of propositions, whereas $lies-below(ucut1, asc1)$ and

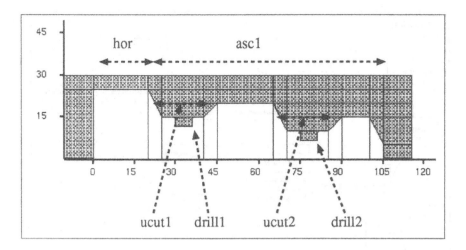

Fig. 1. Half display of a rotational symteric workpiece.

neighbour(hor, asc1) are examples of the second type. The goals of a planning problem are the processing areas encapsulated by the predicate *machined* (i.e. *machined(hor)*, *machined(ucut1)*). Fig. 2 shows a part of a plan[2] for machining the workpiece shown in Fig. 1. There are two possible reasons for a plan-step s_1 to be ordered before another plan-step s_2: first, if applying s_2 makes impossible to apply s_1. For example *Clamp(hor)* is ordered after *machine−outline(hor)*, because when the workpiece is clamped on *hor*, then it is impossible to machine *hor* as this area becomes unaccessible for the cutting tools. Second, when s_2 needs the effects of s_1 in order to be applied. For example, for machining the outline *hor*, the workpiece needs to be clamped on the outline *asc1*.

Notice that in Fig. 2 the processing areas are machined before the processing areas lain below them. For example, the undercut *ucut1* lies below the ascending area *asc1*. Then in order to achieve the goal *machined(ucut1)* it is necessary to achieve the goal *machined(asc1)* first. This kind of dependencies between certain goals can be determined independent from any consideration of the tools or clamping operations needed to achieve them. So they are established before the planning process begins. Thus they can be used as an order-constraint for achieving the goals during the planning process or as an additional constraint that must be meet by cases in order to be retrieved during a case-base planning process. This observation is one of the motivations for the architecture of the case-base presented in this paper.

---

[2] In this plan other processing areas and the steps for mounting cutting-tools are omitted.

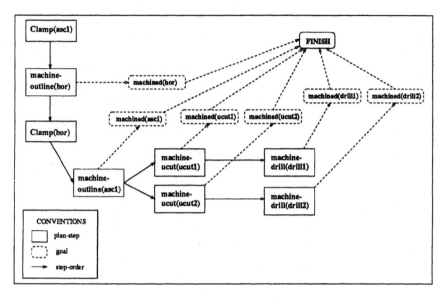

Fig. 2. Plan for machining a workpiece.

3 Domain Independent Case Retrieval

There are two basic restrictions that any retrieval procedure must meet: first, the cases retrieved must be relevant with respect to the planning problem (Veloso, 1994; Cunningham & Slattery, 1994). Second, the time to do this must be short enough, that the overall time for the case-based planner to solve a problem is shorter than the time that it takes to plan from scratch. We will refer to this restriction as the *time restriction*. In PRODIGY/ANALOGY an organization of the case-base has been proposed which enables the retrieval procedure to meet both restrictions. The basic idea is that after finding a solution plan that solves a problem, the problem description and the solution plan are stored together as a new case in the case-base. For indexing the case, an analysis of the problem description with respect to its solution plan is made. Based on this analysis a relation between goals is stated, which is defined as follows.

Definition 1 Interacting goals (Veloso, 1994). Given a solution plan that solves a problem and two goals g_1 and g_2 that appear in the problem. The goals $g1$ and $g2$ *interact* with respect to the solution plan, if $g1$ and $g2$ are achieved in the same connected component of the solution plan.

Consider the solution plan shown in Fig. 2. All the goals achieved in this plan interact with each other, as there is only one connected component in it with respect to the step-order. This is characteristic for the domain of process planning, although in other domains such as the logistic transportation domain and blocks world, plans may contain more than one connected component.

Giving a goal achieved in the plan, it is possible to perform goal regression (Veloso, 1994; Mitchell, Keller, & Kedar-Cabelli, 1986; Janetzko, Wess, & Melis, 1993) through the plan-steps in order to identify which propositions in the initial state had been used to achieved that goal, as stated by the following definition:

Definition 2 Foot-print of goals (Veloso, 1994). Given a solution plan that solves a problem. Then the foot-print of a goal g is constituted by the propositions in the initial state of the problem that contributed to achieve g. The foot-print of a set of goals is the union of the foot-prints for each individual goal in the set.

3.1 Organization of the Case-base

The case-base in PRODIGY/ANALOGY is organized as a three-level structure (Fig. 3). In the first level there are three access tables (not shown in Fig. 3). The second level is constituted by an initial-state discrimination network. Finally, the third level is constituted by the library of cases.

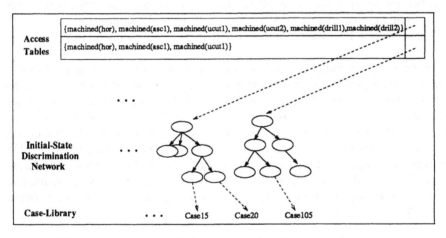

Fig. 3. Architecture of the case-base in PRODIGY/ANALOGY

The three access tables define entry points in the initial-state discrimination network, and their construction is based on the sets of interacting goals of each case stored in the case-base. Basically, these tables define a hash function that identifies for each set of goals, S, a tree in the initial-state discrimination network.

The initial-state discrimination network is constituted by a collection of trees. These trees serve to discriminate cases that have the same set of interacting goals.

The nodes of these trees contain sets of propositions and their leaves contain pointers to cases in the case-library. They are constructed in a way that by following any path from a leave to the root and collecting the set of propositions at each node, results in the foot-print for the set of interacting goals of the case pointed by the leave.[3]

3.2 Domain Independent Retrieval

The purpose of the retrieval phase is to find a collection of cases, so that their sets of interacting goals cover the new problem description. That is:

- For each goal in the new problem, there is one corresponding goal in one of the sets of interacting goals that matches it.
- The foot-print of each set of interacting goals matches the initial state of the new problem with a predefined accuracy. The accuracy indicates which percentage of the set of predicates need to be matched.

The strategy followed by PRODIGY/ANALOGY is to try to cover the new problem with as few cases as possible. So, at the first step, a case will be searched for that covers the whole problem description and more precisely that covers all the goals of the new problem. If this fails, PRODIGY/ANALOGY will try to find two cases: one that covers all the goals but one, and the other that covers the remaining goal. If this does not work, then the decomposition process will continue. At last PRODIGY/ANALOGY will try to cover each goal independ from the others.

Retrieving relevant cases and meeting the time restriction may be difficult. The matching process between sets of goals is one of the more expensive steps and it takes place each time the retrieval procedure is pursuing to cover a set of goals. The reason for this is the combinatorial factor involved when binding variables. However PRODIGY/ANALOGY has been tested massively in domains such as the logistical transportation domain, with good performances on the average. We argue that this performance may be threaten, when considering other classes of domains, where structural dependencies between goals need to be considered, and that by explicitly considering this dependencies between goals, the threat is reduced.

4 Dependencies between Interacting Goals

In some domains, it is necessary to consider the dependencies between goals that are included in the problem description. An example is the domain of process planning for mechanical workpieces, where the dependencies represent an order between steps for achieving certain processing areas. Thus, they establish

---

[3] Actually, they are not trees but graphs. The change was made for the sake of simplicity. There are other properties that characterize these trees (graphs), but they are not relevant for our discussion.

a partial order between the goals. So a problem description can be defined as follows:

Definition 3 Extended problem description. A problem description is constituted by an initial state, a set of goals to be achieved, and a partial order between the goals.

Comparing such a problem description against sets of interacting goals and their foot-prints will result in the selection of unadaptable cases, provided that a higher accuracy is not predefined. The reason for this is that these dependencies are hidden in the initial state of the problem and of the cases, so only high accurate matches between the initial states will ensure the consideration of all dependencies. But performing matches with high accuracy usually violates the time restriction of the retrieval procedure.

Before continuing, it is necesary to establish some conventions: a partial ordered plan $\mathcal{P}$ may be viewed as a pair $(\mathcal{S}, \rightarrow)$, where $\mathcal{S}$ represent the set of plan-steps of $\mathcal{P}$, and $\rightarrow$ the partial order of achievement between the plan-steps. For example, $Clamp(hor) \rightarrow machine-outline(asc1)$ is a plan-step order in the plan shown in Fig. 2. Given a goal g and a plan-step s_g, it is said that s_g achieves g if g is an effect of s_g. In the same way g is achieved by $\mathcal{P}$ if g is achieved by a plan-step in $\mathcal{P}$. So for example, the goal $machined(ucut2)$ is achieved by the plan-step $machine-ucut(ucut2)$. Given two plan-steps s_1 and s_2, the notation $s_1 \rightarrow^* s_2$, denotes: (1) $s_1 \rightarrow s_2$, or (2) there is a plan-step s, such that $s_1 \rightarrow s$ and $s \rightarrow^* s_2$ holds. For example $Clamp(hor) \rightarrow^* machine-ucut(ucut1)$. The notion of dependency between goals can be defined as follows.

Definition 4 Dependencies between goals. Let $\mathcal{P}$ be a plan and f and g two goals achieved by $\mathcal{P}$. Then f depends on g with respect to $\mathcal{P}$ if there are two plan-steps s_f, s_g in $\mathcal{P}$, such that s_f achieves f, s_g achieves g and $s_g \rightarrow^* s_f$.

For the plan presented in Fig. 1, the two machining-steps of the two undercuts $ucut1$ and $ucut2$ depend on the machining-step of the ascending outline $asc1$. It is easy to see that the dependency relation is strictly contained in the interaction relation: $machined(ucut1)$ and $machined(ucut2)$ interact, as they both are in the same connected component (Fig. 2). However, none of them depend on the other one. We used this refinement to construct an intermediate level between the access tables and the initial state network in order to represent explicitly dependencies between goals.

5 Indexing and retrieving cases in CAPLAN/CBC

Our approach consists of using the dependencies between goals in order to further structure the case-base. In this way irrelevant cases are rapidly discarded, enabling the retrieval procedure of CAPLAN/CBC to concentrate on a small portion of the case-base.

5.1   Architecture of the Case-Library

The case-base in CAPLAN/CBC is a four-level structure (fig. 4). There are three major differences with respect to the one presented in PRODIGY/ANALOGY (section 3.1): first, rather than explicitly representing the set of interacting goals in the access tables, chains of goals are used to conform a goal discrimination network. Usually an arc between two nodes in the chains of goals represents the dependency order, as for example the arc labeled with *A* in fig. 4. However, some arcs may represent an order that extends the dependency order, as for example the arc labeled *B* in fig. 4. The reason for this is that some information is lost due to the representation of the dependency order (which is a partial order) on chains of goals that are totally ordered. Even with this loss of information, the case-base is further structured, which results in better retrieval times as will be shown in section 6. Thus, the accuracy of the match can be improved, resulting in the retrieval of relevant cases.

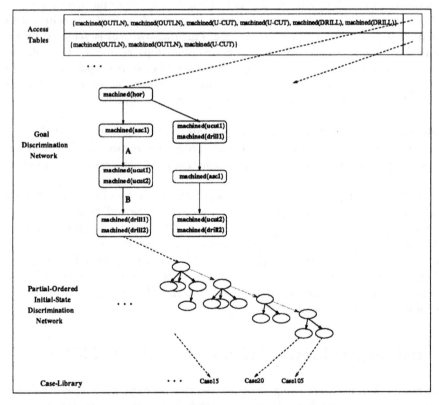

Fig. 4. Case-library in CAPLAN/CBC

The second difference is that the access tables contain only the class representation[4] of sets of interacting goals. The third difference is that the initial state discrimination network has been partially ordered through chains of threes. These chains serve to discriminate between cases that have the same representation in the chain of goals. Each node in the goal discrimination network points to a tree in the partially ordered discrimination network (not shown in figure 4). This initial-state tree contains the foot-print of the set of predicates included in the node. Only the leaves of the last initial-state tree in each chain point to cases in the case-library. Every link of each initial-state tree is labeled with one or more names of cases (not shown also in figure 4). These cases correspond to the ones pointed by the nodes in the last tree of the chain. Collecting the sets at each node that is pointed by a link labeled with the name of a case, results in the foot-print for the interacting goals of the case.

This organization is not well suited for domains without structural dependencies between their goals. For example, in the logistic transportation domain (Veloso, 1994), it is easy to state problems, so that for any combination of the goals, it is possible to obtain a plan that achieves the goals in the order stated through the combination. Thus the goal discrimination network tends to be very large for the same set of interacting goals. Further, no dependencies between goals can be predefined (we are not considering efficiency issues here), so there is no advantage of having the dependencies explicit in the case-base.

5.2   Retrieval of relevant cases in CAPLAN/CBC

CAPLAN/CBC follows the same strategy as PRODIGY/ANALOGY in order to retrieve relevant cases for the new problem: cover the goals with as few cases as possible and match the initial state with a given accuracy.

For finding a case that covers a partially ordered set of goals $(G_{prob}, \rightarrow_{prob})$, CAPLAN/CBC uses the access tables to identify a class representation of a set of interacting goals that is equal to G_{prob}. If none is found then there is no case that covers $(G_{prob}, \rightarrow_{prob})$ and the procedure terminates. Otherwise, a tree, $goal-tree$, in the goal discrimination network is accessed that corresponds to the class representation of G_{prob}. As we saw, $goal-tree$ is a tree representation of goal chains, where arcs between nodes represent the dependency order or an extension of it. So, a search on $goal-tree$ is made, looking for a chain that is consistent with the dependencies of the new problem, $\rightarrow_{prob}$. If no such chain is found, the procedure returns with a failure. Otherwise, a path from the root to a leave in $goal-tree$ has been identified that matches G_{prob} and that is consistent with $\rightarrow_{prob}$. Each node in the path contains a pointer to a tree in the partially-ordered initial state network. For the initial-state tree pointed by the root of $goal-tree$ the procedure identified the set of cases, $Cases$, that matches the

---

[4] The class representation (Veloso, 1994) of a set of predicates is obtained by replacing the arguments of each predicate with their types. For example, the class representation of $\{machined(ucut1)\}$ is $\{machined(U - CUT)\}$. Comparing class representations is not expensive, as the arguments of the predicates are constants.

initial state with the given accuracy. This is possible because all arcs in the initial-states trees are labeled with names of cases. This process is repeated recursively for all nodes of *goal−tree* in the path, excluding cases in *Cases* that do not meet the accuracy predefined. If at some point *Cases* is empty, then CAPLAN/CBC backtracks and continues the search in the goal tree. Otherwise, the leave of the path will be reached and one of the cases contained in *Cases* is returned.

6 Empirical Results

We implemented the architectures of the case-base presented in PRODIGY/ANALOGY (Veloso, 1994) and the one proposed here, integrating them in our case-based planning system CAPLAN/CBC, which is implemented in SMALLTALK-80. As a result, the basic operations such as matching between propositions, and the implementations of the basic data types such as set of propositions are the same for both architectures, so none of them takes advantage of the other based on implementation details. In both case-bases the same cases from the workpieces domain where added. In the experiment 60 new problem descriptions corresponding to complete descriptions of workpieces were given. We meassured the time that it took in each architecture to retrieve a case with an accuracy of 75%. The reason for retrieving just one case is that plans in this domain contain only one connected component, so no decomposition of the problem description based on interacting goals is possible. The results are shown in figure 5. The first 10 problems contained 7 goals, the next 10 problems contained 8 goals, and continuing with the same proportion, the last 10 problems contained 12 goals. Notice that for the last 20 problems, the increase in running time by using the architecture of PRODIGY/ANALOGY is higher than the one by using the architecture of CAPLAN/CBC. Thus, as the number of goals increases the architecture of CAPLAN/CBC leads to better retrieval times. There are two reasons for this: first, in PRODIGY/ANALOGY a matching between the sets of goals takes place, whereras in CAPLAN/CBC the match is between partially ordered collections of goals. Second, the initial state network in CAPLAN/CBC is constructed in a way, that the sets of predicates in the nodes tend to be smaller than in PRODIGY/ANALOGY. More precisely, the initial-state trees in CAPLAN/CBC store only foot-prints of small subsets of interacting goals, whereas in PRODIGY/ANALOGY these trees store foot-prints of all the interacting goals. As a result, matches in CAPLAN/CBC involve small sets of propositions only.

7 Conclusion

We have shown that the architecture of the case-library implemented in CA-PLAN/CBC ensures the adaptability of the cases retrieved for structured domains. In this class of domains it is necessary to consider structural dependencies

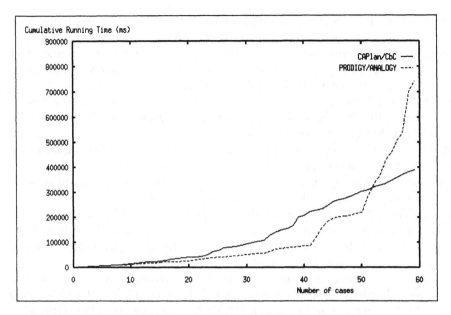

Fig. 5. Cumulative running times of the retrieval procedure by using the architectures of CAPLAN/CBC and of PRODIGY/ANALOGY

in the problem description in order to retrieve relevant cases during a case-base planning process. The architecture presented here is an extension of the one proposed in PRODIGY/ANALOGY, in that the concept of interacting goals has been refined to consider the dependencies between interacting goals. Based on this refinement the foot-print has also been partitionated. This partition is explicitely represented in the case-base and leads to an increased performance of the retrieval process.

Acknowledgements

The authors want to thank Michael M. Richter, Jürgen Paulokat and Frank Weberskirch for their contributions as well as Jürgen Paulokat, Ralph Bergmann and the reviewers for helpful comments on earlier versions of this paper.

References

Bergmann, R. (1995). Building and refining abstract planning cases by change of representation language. To appear in *Journal of AI Research*.

Carbonell, J. (1983). Derivational analogy in problem solving and knowledge acquisition. In *Proceedings of the 2nd International Workshop on Machine Learning*. University of Illinois, Monticello, Illinois.

Cunningham, P., & Slattery, S. (1994). Knowledge engineering requirements in derivational analogy. In *(Richter, Wess, Althoff, & Maurer, 1994)*.

Ihrig, L. H., & Kambhampati, S. (1994). Derivational replay for partial-order planning. In *Proceedings of the Twelfth National Conference on Artificial Intelligence, AAAI-94*. The AAAI Press/The MIT Press.

Janetzko, D., Wess, S., & Melis, E. (1993). Goal-Driven Simmilarity Assessment. In Ohlbach, H.-J. (Ed.), *GWAI-92: Advances in Artificial Intelligence*, Springer Verlag, pp. 283–298.

Minton, S. (1988). *Learning Search Control Knowledge: An Explanation-Based Approach*. Kluwer Academic Publishers, Boston.

Mitchell, T., Keller, R., & Kedar-Cabelli, S. (1986). Explanation-based generalization: A unifying view. *Machine Learning, 1*, 47–80.

Muñoz-Avila, H., Paulokat, J., & Wess, S. (1994). Controlling a nonlinear hierachical planner using case-based reasoning. In Keane, M., Halton, J. P., & Manago, M. (Eds.), *Proceedings Second European Workshop on Case-Based Reasoning, EWCBR-94*.

Paulokat, J., & Wess, S. (1994). Planning for machining workpieces with a partial-order nonlinear planner. In Gil, & Veloso (Eds.), *AAAI-Working Notes 'Planning and Learning: On To Real Applications'*. New Orleans.

Richter, M., Wess, S., Althoff, K., & Maurer, F. (Eds.). (1994). *First European Workshop on Case-Based Reasoning (EWCBR-93)*. No. 837 in Lecture Notes in Artificial Intelligence. Springer Verlag.

Smyth, B., & Keane, M. T. (1994). Retrieving adaptable cases: the role of adaptation knowledge in case retrieval. In *(Richter et al., 1994)*.

Veloso, M., & Carbonell, J. (1993). Derivational analogy in prodigy: Automating case acquisition, storage, and utilization. *Machine Learning, 10*.

Veloso, M. (1994). *Planning and learning by analogical reasoning*. Lecture Notes in Artificial Intelligence. Springer Verlag.

Yang, H., & Lu, W. F. (1994). Case adaptation in a case-based process planning system. In Hammond, K. (Ed.), *Proceedings of The Second International Conference on Artificial Intelligence Planning Systems, AIPS-94*. The AAAI Press.

An Average-Case Analysis of
k-Nearest Neighbor Classifier

Seishi Okamoto and Ken Satoh

Fujitsu Laboratories Limited
1015 Kamikodanaka, Nakahara-ku, Kawasaki 211, Japan
E-Mail: {seishi, ksatoh}@flab.fujitsu.co.jp

Abstract. In this paper, we perform an average-case analysis of k-nearest neighbor classifier (k-NNC) for a subclass of Boolean threshold functions. Our average-case analysis is based on the formal computation for the predictive accuracy of the classifier under the assumption of noise-free Boolean features and a uniform instance distribution. The predictive accuracy is represented as a function of the number of features, the threshold, the number of training instances, and the number of nearest neighbors. We also present the predictive behavior of the classifier by systematically varying the values of the parameters of the accuracy function. We plot the behavior of the classifier by varying the value of k, and then we observe that the performance of the classifier improves as k increases, then reaches a maximum before starting to deteriorate. We further investigate the relationship between the number of training instances and the optimal value of k. We then observe that optimum k increases gradually as the number of training instances increases.

1 Introduction

Recently, there has been growing interest in the learning frameworks using the knowledge from cases or instances such as case-based reasoning or instance-based learning. In these frameworks, similar case (instance) retrieval plays an important role and the k-nearest neighbor (k-NN) method or its variants are widely used as the retrieval mechanism. Certainly, the k-NN family can be easily implemented into a system, and the k-nearest neighbor classifier (k-NNC) exhibits high performance in many classification problem domains. However, in the actual use of k-NN methods, we are often confronted with some problems; how many training cases are required for the desired performance, or which value should be chosen as k for the highest accuracy. Indeed, the latter problem is crucial for k-NN application. These problems have been investigated by several experiments. These experiments, however, not only take a lot of time, but also do not guarantee system reliability in general. Therefore, we believe that the theoretical analysis of the k-NN family will greatly help us in solving these problems.

We can find the origin of k-NNC in the field of pattern recognition. As an early contribution to the theoretical analysis of k-NNC, it is well known that the upper bound of k-NNC error probability is twice the optimal Bayes risk [8]. Also, k-NNC is identical to the optimal Bayes classifier as k approaches infinity

[9]. These results, however, hold only for an infinite number of training samples. This assumption is not applicable for practical problems.

In recent years, there have been many empirical proposals for k-NNC, mainly to improve the classification performance [22, 1, 2, 12, 6, 7]. Stanfill and Waltz [22] proposed a weighted k-NNC using statistical information from the stored datum. Aha [1] proposed an incremental algorithm for learning weights in accordance with success or failure of classification of weighted NNC, and Aha and Kibler [2] extended this algorithm to detect and remove noisy instances. Kelly and Davis [12] learned the weights of features in k-NNC by using a genetic algorithm. Cardie [6] used a decision tree technique to extract relevant features which are subsequently used in k-NNC. Cost and Salzberg [7] proposed an instance-weighted NNC by modifying the method proposed by [22]. These proposals show high performance by empirical evaluation, but we need theoretical analyses for these proposals.

Some people have been investigating theoretical analyses for the k-NN family [19, 3, 4, 20]. Rachlin *et al.* [19] showed the remarkable result that the Bayesian classifier is not more accurate than the classifier given by [7] at the limit. This analysis, however, deals with a weighted NN algorithm, and we are interested in a k-NN method. Aha *et al.* [3] analyzed a NN algorithm on a model that is similar to PAC (Probably Approximately Correct) learning. Albert and Aha [4] generalized the result for the NN algorithm in [3] to a k-NN algorithm. In our paper [20], we gave a theoretical analysis of weight learning from qualitative distance information, which is related to the weighted NN algorithm. These theoretical analyses for the k-NN family are basically performed by using the PAC model. The PAC learning analysis allows us to know how many training samples are required for the desired performance. However, an appropriate choice of k seems to be hard to explore using the PAC model.

Average-case analysis is well known to be a useful framework to understand the behavior of the learning algorithm. Some researchers have made average-case analyses of several learning algorithms [11, 13, 17]. There are also two theoretical analyses of NNC by using this framework [14, 16]. Langley and Iba [14] made an average-case analysis of NNC for conjunctive classes. They showed that the accuracy of the classifier decreases gradually with an increase in the number of irrelevant features. In our previous paper [16], we analyzed the effect of the number of relevant features for two conjunctive classes on the predictive accuracy of NNC. However, these NNC studies are restricted to the case that $k = 1$.

In this paper, we perform an average-case analysis of k-nearest neighbor classifier for a subclass of Boolean threshold functions that are well known class in the field of concept learning. Our analysis assumes noise-free Boolean features and a uniform distribution over the instance space. We formally compute the predictive accuracy of k-NNC as a function of the number of features, the threshold, the number of training instances, and k. This accuracy function not only helps us to understand the predictive behavior of k-NNC, but also can give an optimal value of k, on our model. This is because we can plot the behavior of k-NNC by systematically varying the values of parameters of the accuracy function. We explore the predictive behavior of k-NNC by varying the value of k, and investigate the relationship between the number of training instances and the optimal value of k.

2 Problem Description

In this paper, we assume that every feature has a noise-free Boolean value and that the probability of occurrence for each feature is $1/2$. These assumptions generate a uniform distribution over the instance space. We then deal with the following class defined by the threshold.

$$C_p = \{ (a_1, a_2, \ldots, a_r) \mid a_1 + a_2 + \ldots + a_r \geq p \},$$

where $a_i (i = 1, 2, \ldots, r)$ is a feature value and p is a natural number threshold $(1 \leq p \leq r)$. This is a subclass of *Boolean threshold functions*, that are well known in the field of concept learning [18], because C_p has no irrelevant features. The class of Boolean threshold functions is also called as M-of-N class, where M and N represents the threshold and the number of features respectively [15]. Hence, we can also say that C_p is p-of-r class under the assumption that there are no irrelevant features.

Boolean threshold functions are shown to be not polynomially learnable unless **R**=**NP** [18], where **R** is the class of sets accepted in random polynomial time. On the other hand, C_p is polynomially learnable by using a standard enumerative algorithm. This class, however, is still attractive from a viewpoint of the practical use for the k-NN method. In most actual application cases, the k-NN method (unweighted) is used after performing the feature selection [6, 12, 21]. Hence, an analysis of k-NN is important for the class defined by the threshold.

In this paper, we deal with the following k-NNC for two classes (C_p and $\overline{C}_p$), assuming that k is an odd number to avoid a tie between classes.

> Each training instance is independently drawn from the instance space, then all training instances are stored into memory. When a test instance is given, the nearness of each training instance to the test instance is measured by its Hamming distance. Then, the test instance is classified into the major class of k nearest training instances. In the case that several training instances have the same distance from the test instance, the order of nearness among them to the test instance is decided randomly.

3 Predictive Accuracy

In this section, we formally compute the predictive accuracy of k-NNC for the class defined by the threshold. That is, we compute the probability that k-NNC correctly classifies the test instance after n training instances. The predictive accuracy will be represented as a function of the number of features (r), the threshold (p), the number of training instances (n), and the number of nearest neighbors (k).

If the threshold is p_1 ($1 \leq p_1 \leq \lceil r/2 \rceil$), then we have $\overline{C}_{p_1} = C_{p_2}$ and $C_{p_1} = \overline{C}_{p_2}$ by letting $p_2 = r - p_1 + 1$ ($\lfloor r/2 \rfloor \leq p_2 \leq r$). Clearly, the classifier has the same predictive accuracy for p_1 and p_2, and it is sufficient to compute the predictive accuracy only for the threshold p_1. Therefore, we assume $1 \leq p \leq \lceil r/2 \rceil$ throughout this paper.

Our mathematical computation for the predictive accuracy is performed by the extension of the method using the distance from the prototype for 1-NNC in [14, 16] to k-NNC. We use the instance for which all feature values are zero as the prototype for $\overline{C}_p$ to compute the accuracy. We designate this prototype instance with $\mathcal{P}$. We compute the probability that the test instance has distance d from $\mathcal{P}$ and the probability of correct classification for this test instance. We obtain the latter probability by using the distance from the test instance to the k-th nearest neighbor. Then, we can get the overall predictive accuracy by summing the products of these probabilities over all d.

We let t_d be an arbitrary test instance with distance d from the prototype $\mathcal{P}$. We denote the class of t_d with C_d, and the complement class of C_d with $\overline{C}_d$. From setting $\mathcal{P} = (0, 0, \ldots, 0)$, we have $C_d = \overline{C}_p$ for $0 \leq d < p$ and $C_d = C_p$ for $p \leq d \leq r$. We let $B_{n,k}(d)$ be the probability of correct classification for t_d after n training instances. For all test instances with the same distance from $\mathcal{P}$, the classifier has the same predictive accuracy. Hence, after n training instances, the overall predictive accuracy of k-NNC is given by

$$A_{n,k} = \sum_{d=0}^{r} \frac{\binom{r}{d}}{2^r} B_{n,k}(d) \, ,$$

where the first term in the sum denotes the probability of occurrence for t_d.

We compute $B_{n,k}(d)$ by using the distance from t_d to the k-th nearest neighbor (we denote this distance with e). We compute the probability that the k-th nearest neighbor has distance e ($0 \leq e \leq r$) from t_d and t_d is correctly classified into C_d (we designate this probability with $G_{n,k}(e, C_d)$), then we can obtain $B_{n,k}(d)$ by summing $G_{n,k}(e, C_d)$ over all e. We let $I_{i<e}$, $I_{i=e}$ and $I_{i>e}$ be a set of instances to which distance i from t_d is less than e, equal to e and greater than e, respectively. Regardless of the value of d, their cardinal numbers are written by

$$|I_{i<e}| = \sum_{i=0}^{e-1} \binom{r}{i} \, , \quad |I_{i=e}| = \binom{r}{e} \, , \quad |I_{i>e}| = \sum_{i=e+1}^{r} \binom{r}{i} \, .$$

Since we have $|I_{i<e}| = 0$ for $e = 0$ and $|I_{i>e}| = 0$ for $e = r$, we compute $B_{n,k}(d)$ by dividing $G_{n,k}(e, C_d)$ into three terms according to e, as shown below.

$$B_{n,k}(d) = F_{n,k} + \sum_{e=1}^{r-1} G_{n,k}(e, C_d) + H_{n,k}(C_d) \, ,$$

where $F_{n,k} = G_{n,k}(0, C_d)$ and $H_{n,k}(C_d) = G_{n,k}(r, C_d)$.

First, we compute $F_{n,k}$ by using the probability that exactly b of n training instances belong to $I_{i=0}$. We designate this probability with $M_0(b)$. Since we have $|I_{i=0}| = 1$ and $|I_{i>0}| = 2^r - 1$, $M_0(b)$ is written by

$$M_0(b) = \binom{n}{b} \frac{|I_{i=0}|^b |I_{i>0}|^{n-b}}{2^{nr}} = \binom{n}{b} \frac{(2^r - 1)^{n-b}}{2^{nr}} .$$

In the case that $e = 0$, all k nearest neighbors are identical to the test instance t_d, and k-NNC classifies t_d into the correct class regardless of the value of d. Hence, $F_{n,k}$ is equal to the probability that $e = 0$ holds, we have

$$F_{n,k} = \sum_{b=k}^{n} M_0(b) .$$

Second, we compute $G_{n,k}(e, C_d)$ $(1 \leq e \leq r - 1)$ by considering the case that exactly a of n training instances belong to $I_{i<e}$ and exactly b of n training instances belong to $I_{i=e}$. We let $M_e(a, b)$ be the probability that this case occurs, and $M_e(a, b)$ is written by

$$M_e(a, b) = \binom{n}{a} \binom{n-a}{b} \frac{|I_{i<e}|^a |I_{i=e}|^b |I_{i>e}|^{n-a-b}}{2^{nr}} .$$

We further consider the number of instances belonging to C_d, out of a training instances in $I_{i<e}$ and out of $(k - a)$ training instances in $I_{i=e}$. We let $I_i(\overline{C}_p)$ $(I_i(C_p),$ resp.$)$ be a set of instances belonging to $\overline{C}_p$ $(C_p,$ resp.$)$ with distance i from t_d. The cardinal number of a set of instances with distance i from t_d is written by

$$\binom{r}{i} = \sum_{j=0}^{i} \binom{r-d}{i-j} \binom{d}{j} .$$

Each instance with distance i from t_d such that $(d - j) + (i - j) < p$ belongs to $\overline{C}_p$, and each instance such that $(d - j) + (i - j) \geq p$ belongs to C_p. Hence, the cardinal numbers of $I_i(\overline{C}_p)$ and $I_i(C_p)$ are given by

$$|I_i(\overline{C}_p)| = \sum_{j=\lfloor \frac{i+d-p}{2} \rfloor + 1}^{i} \binom{r-d}{i-j} \binom{d}{j} , \quad |I_i(C_p)| = \sum_{j=0}^{\lfloor \frac{i+d-p}{2} \rfloor} \binom{r-d}{i-j} \binom{d}{j} .$$

We designate a set of instances belonging to $\overline{C}_p$ $(C_p,$ resp.$)$ in $I_{i<e}$ with $I_{i<e}(\overline{C}_p)$ $(I_{i<e}(C_p),$ resp.$)$. Their cardinal numbers are given by

$$|I_{i<e}(\overline{C}_p)| = \sum_{i=0}^{e-1} |I_i(\overline{C}_p)| , \quad |I_{i<e}(C_p)| = \sum_{i=0}^{e-1} |I_i(C_p)| .$$

We let $P_e(x, C_d)$ be the probability that exactly x of a training instances in $I_{i<e}$ belong to C_d. Since we have $|I_{i<e}(C_d)| \neq 0$ for $1 \leq e \leq r-1$, $P_e(x, C_d)$ is represented by

$$
P_e(x, C_d) = \begin{cases} 1 & \text{if } |I_{i<e}(\overline{C_d})| = 0 , \\ \binom{a}{x} \dfrac{|I_{i<e}(C_d)|^x |I_{i<e}(\overline{C_d})|^{a-x}}{|I_{i<e}|^a} & \text{otherwise.} \end{cases}
$$

We designate a set of instances belonging to $\overline{C_p}$ (C_p, resp.) in $I_{i=e}$ with $I_{i=e}(\overline{C_p})$ ($I_{i=e}(C_p)$, resp.). Put simply, we have $|I_{i=e}(\overline{C_p})| = |I_e(\overline{C_p})|$ and $|I_{i=e}(C_p)| = |I_e(C_p)|$. We let $Q_e(y, C_d)$ be the probability that exactly y of $(k-a)$ training instances in $I_{i=e}$ belong to C_d. Since $|I_{i=e}| \neq 0$, $Q_e(y, C_d)$ is written by

$$
Q_e(y, C_d) = \begin{cases} 0 & \text{if } |I_{i=e}(C_d)| = 0 , \\ 1 & \text{if } |I_{i=e}(\overline{C_d})| = 0 , \\ \binom{k-a}{y} \dfrac{|I_{i=e}(C_d)|^y |I_{i=e}(\overline{C_d})|^{k-a-y}}{|I_{i=e}|^{k-a}} & \text{otherwise.} \end{cases}
$$

We can compute $G_{n,k}(e, C_d)$ by using these probabilities. We get $G_{n,k}(e, C_d)$ for the following six cases according to $|I_{i<e}(\overline{C_d})|$, $|I_{i=e}(\overline{C_d})|$, and $|I_{i=e}(C_d)|$.

$Case\_1 : |I_{i<e}(\overline{C_d})| = 0 \wedge |I_{i=e}(\overline{C_d})| = 0.$
$Case\_2 : |I_{i<e}(\overline{C_d})| = 0 \wedge |I_{i=e}(C_d)| = 0.$
$Case\_3 : |I_{i<e}(\overline{C_d})| = 0 \wedge |I_{i=e}(\overline{C_d})| \neq 0 \wedge |I_{i=e}(C_d)| \neq 0.$
$Case\_4 : |I_{i<e}(\overline{C_d})| \neq 0 \wedge |I_{i=e}(\overline{C_d})| = 0.$
$Case\_5 : |I_{i<e}(\overline{C_d})| \neq 0 \wedge |I_{i=e}(C_d)| = 0.$
$Case\_6 : |I_{i<e}(\overline{C_d})| \neq 0 \wedge |I_{i=e}(\overline{C_d})| \neq 0 \wedge |I_{i=e}(C_d)| \neq 0.$

We designate $G_{n,k}(e, C_d)$ for each $Case\_m$ ($m = 1, \ldots, 6$) with $G^m_{n,k}(e, C_d)$. And we introduce the following notation in order to simplify the expression of $G^m_{n,k}(e, C_d)$.

$$
N_e(a) = \sum_{b=k-a}^{n-a} M_e(a, b) .
$$

The test instance t_d is correctly classified into C_d, if and only if $x + y \geq k/2$ holds. Moreover, we have $a + b \geq k$ and $a \leq k - 1$. Hence, each $G^m_{n,k}(e, C_d)$ ($m = 1, \ldots, 6$) is given by

$$
G^1_{n,k}(e, C_d) = \sum_{a=0}^{k-1} N_e(a) \qquad \text{for } Case\_1,
$$

$$
G^2_{n,k}(e, C_d) = \sum_{a=\frac{k+1}{2}}^{k-1} N_e(a) \qquad \text{for } Case\_2,
$$

$$
G^3_{n,k}(e, C_d) = \sum_{a=0}^{\frac{k-1}{2}} N_e(a) \sum_{y=\frac{k+1}{2}-a}^{k-a} Q_e(y, C_d) + \sum_{a=\frac{k+1}{2}}^{k-1} N_e(a) \qquad \text{for } Case\_3,
$$

$$G_{n,k}^4(e, C_d) = \sum_{a=0}^{\frac{k-1}{2}} N_e(a) + \sum_{a=\frac{k+1}{2}}^{k-1} N_e(a) \sum_{x=a-\frac{k-1}{2}}^{a} P_e(x, C_d) \qquad \text{for } Case\_4,$$

$$G_{n,k}^5(e, C_d) = \sum_{a=\frac{k+1}{2}}^{k-1} N_e(a) \sum_{x=\frac{k+1}{2}}^{a} P_e(x, C_d) \qquad \text{for } Case\_5,$$

$$G_{n,k}^6(e, C_d) = \sum_{a=0}^{k-1} N_e(a) \left(\sum_{x=\frac{k+1}{2}}^{a} P_e(x, C_d) \right.$$

$$\left. + \sum_{x=0}^{Min(\frac{k-1}{2}, a)} P_e(x, C_d) \sum_{y=\frac{k+1}{2}-x}^{k-a} Q_e(y, C_d) \right) \qquad \text{for } Case\_6.$$

Finally, we compute $H_{n,k}(C_d)$ by considering the case that exactly a of n training instances belong to $I_{i<r}$. We let $M_r(a)$ be the probability that this case occurs. Since we have $|I_{i<r}| = 2^r - 1$ and $|I_{i=r}| = 1$, $M_r(a)$ is written by

$$M_r(a) = \binom{n}{a} \frac{|I_{i<r}|^a |I_{i=r}|^{n-a}}{2^{nr}} = \binom{n}{a} \frac{(2^r - 1)^a}{2^{nr}} .$$

When we have $e = r$, $Case\_1$ dose not occur for each d because $C_p \neq \emptyset$ and $\overline{C}_p \neq \emptyset$. Moreover, $Case\_3$ and $Case\_6$ do not occur for each d in the case that $e = r$, since k-th nearest neighbor belongs to either $\overline{C}_p$ or C_p. It is therefore sufficient that we compute $H_{n,k}(C_d)$ only for three cases: $Case\_2$, $Case\_4$, and $Case\_5$. We designate $H_{n,k}(C_d)$ for each $Case\_m$ ($m = 2, 4, 5$) with $H_{n,k}^m(C_d)$. Each $H_{n,k}^m(C_d)$ can be obtained by replacing $N_e(a)$ in the corresponding $G_{n,k}^m(e, C_d)$ with $M_r(a)$, as shown below.

$$H_{n,k}^2(C_d) = \sum_{a=\frac{k+1}{2}}^{k-1} M_r(a) \qquad \text{for } Case\_2,$$

$$H_{n,k}^4(C_d) = \sum_{a=0}^{\frac{k-1}{2}} M_r(a) + \sum_{a=\frac{k+1}{2}}^{k-1} M_r(a) \sum_{x=a-\frac{k-1}{2}}^{a} P_e(x, C_d) \quad \text{for } Case\_4,$$

$$H_{n,k}^5(C_d) = \sum_{a=\frac{k+1}{2}}^{k-1} M_r(a) \sum_{x=\frac{k+1}{2}}^{a} P_e(x, C_d) \qquad \text{for } Case\_5.$$

At this point, we can get $B_{n,k}(d)$ ($0 \leq d \leq r$) by using $F_{n,k}$, $G_{n,k}^m(e, C_d)$ ($m = 1, \ldots, 6$), and $H_{n,k}^m(C_d)$ ($m = 2, 4, 5$).

First, we compute $B_{n,k}(d)$ for $0 \leq d < p$ (that is, $C_d = \overline{C}_p$). Fig.1 shows the regions according to the distance from the test instance t_d ($0 \leq d < p$). The meshed region and the striped region in Fig.1 represent $|I_i(C_p)| = 0$ and $|I_i(\overline{C}_p)| = 0$, respectively. That is, no instance belonging to C_p and $\overline{C}_p$ exists in the meshed region and in the striped region respectively. The black region in Fig.1(b) represents $|I_i(\overline{C}_p)| \neq 0$ and $|I_i(C_p)| \neq 0$, so that instances in the black region can belong to either class.

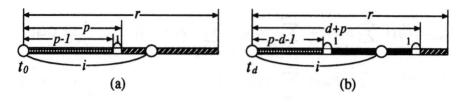

Fig. 1. The regions according to the distance from the test instance belonging to $\overline{C}_p$ in the case that (a) $d = 0$ and (b) $1 \leq d < p$. No instance belonging to C_p and $\overline{C}_p$ exists in the meshed region and the striped respectively. And the instances in the black region can belong to either class.

We divide the region according to d ($0 \leq d < p$) into $d = 0$ and $1 \leq d < p$, and we designate $B_{n,k}(d)$ for $d = 0$ and $1 \leq d < p$ with $B_{n,k}^0$ and $B_{n,k}^1(d)$ respectively. When $d = 0$, from Fig.1(a), *Case_1*, *Case_2*, and *Case_5* occur for $1 \leq e \leq p-1$, $e = p$, and $p+1 \leq e \leq r$, respectively. Hence, $B_{n,k}^0$ is written by

$$B_{n,k}^0 = F_{n,k} + \sum_{e=1}^{p-1} G_{n,k}^1(e, \overline{C}_p) + G_{n,k}^2(p, \overline{C}_p) + \sum_{e=p+1}^{r-1} G_{n,k}^5(e, \overline{C}_p) + H_{n,k}^5(\overline{C}_p) \,.$$

When we hold $1 \leq d < p$, from Fig.1(b), *Case_1*, *Case_3*, *Case_6*, and *Case_5* occur for $1 \leq e \leq p-d-1$, $e = p-d$, $p-d+1 \leq e \leq p+d-1$, and $p+d \leq e \leq r$, respectively. Hence, $B_{n,k}^1(d)$ is given by

$$B_{n,k}^1(d) = F_{n,k} + \sum_{e=1}^{p-d-1} G_{n,k}^1(e, \overline{C}_p) + G_{n,k}^3(p-d, \overline{C}_p) + \sum_{e=p-d+1}^{p+d-1} G_{n,k}^6(e, \overline{C}_p)$$

$$+ \sum_{e=p+d}^{r-1} G_{n,k}^5(e, \overline{C}_p) + H_{n,k}^5(\overline{C}_p) \,.$$

Next, we compute $B_{n,k}(d)$ for $p \leq d \leq r$ (that is, $C_d = C_p$). Fig.2 shows the regions according to the distance from t_d ($p \leq d \leq r$), and each of the three regions in Fig.2 have the same meaning as in Fig.1. We let $B_{n,k}^2(d)$ and $B_{n,k}^3(d)$ be the probability of correct classification for t_d in the case that $p \leq d \leq r - p$ and $r - p < d < r$, respectively. From Fig.2(a) and (b), these probabilities are written by

$$B_{n,k}^2(d) = F_{n,k} + \sum_{e=1}^{d-p} G_{n,k}^1(e, C_p) + G_{n,k}^3(d-p+1, C_p) + \sum_{e=d-p+2}^{d+p-1} G_{n,k}^6(e, C_p)$$

$$+ \sum_{e=d+p}^{r-1} G_{n,k}^4(E, C_p) + H_{n,k}^4(C_p) \,,$$

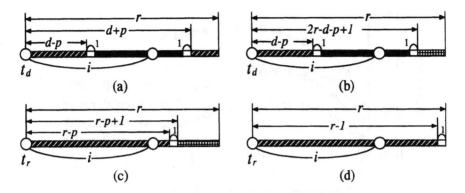

Fig. 2. The regions according to the distance from the test instance belonging to $\mathcal{C}_p$ in the case that (a) $p \leq d \leq r - p$, (b) $r - p < d < r$, (c) $d = r \wedge p \neq 1$, and (d) $d = r \wedge p = 1$. No instance belonging to $\mathcal{C}_p$ and $\overline{\mathcal{C}}_p$ exists in the meshed region and the striped respectively. And the instances in the black region can belong to either class.

$$B^3_{n,k}(d) = F_{n,k} + \sum_{e=1}^{d-p} G^1_{n,k}(e, \mathcal{C}_p) + G^3_{n,k}(d-p+1, \mathcal{C}_p) + \sum_{e=d-p+2}^{2r-d-p} G^6_{n,k}(e, \mathcal{C}_p)$$

$$+ \sum_{e=2r-d-p+1}^{r-1} G^5_{n,k}(e, \mathcal{C}_p) + H^5_{n,k}(\mathcal{C}_p) \ .$$

And, we let $B^r_{n,k}$ be the probability of correct classification for t_d in the case that $d = r$. From Fig.2(c) and (d), $B^r_{n,k}$ is given by

$$B^r_{n,k} = \begin{cases} F_{n,k} + \displaystyle\sum_{e=1}^{r-1} G^1_{n,k}(e, \mathcal{C}_p) + H^2_{n,k}(\mathcal{C}_p) & \text{if } p = 1, \\[4mm] F_{n,k} + \displaystyle\sum_{e=1}^{r-p} G^1_{n,k}(e, \mathcal{C}_p) + G^2_{n,k}(r-p+1, \mathcal{C}_p) & \text{if } p \neq 1. \\[4mm] \qquad + \displaystyle\sum_{e=r-p+2}^{r-1} G^5_{n,k}(e, \mathcal{C}_p) + H^5_{n,k}(\mathcal{C}_p) \end{cases}$$

From the above computations, we can compute the predictive accuracy of k-NNC on our model, as shown below.

$$A_{n,k} = \frac{B^0_{n,k}}{2^r} + \sum_{d=1}^{p-1} \frac{\binom{r}{d}}{2^r} B^1_{n,k}(d) + \sum_{d=p}^{r-p} \frac{\binom{r}{d}}{2^r} B^2_{n,k}(d) + \sum_{d=r-p+1}^{r-1} \frac{\binom{r}{d}}{2^r} B^3_{n,k}(d) + \frac{B^r_{n,k}}{2^r} \ .$$

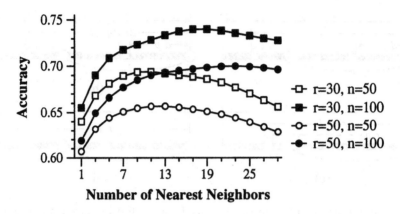

Fig. 3. The predictive behavior of k-NNC by varying the number of nearest neighbors. r and n represents the number of features and the number of training instances respectively.

4   Predictive Behavior

In the previous section, we could formally compute the predictive accuracy of k-NNC as a function of four parameters: the number of features, the threshold, the number of training instances, and the number of nearest neighbors. This accuracy function is very useful to understand the behavior of k-NNC on our model. This is because we can plot the predictive behavior of the classifier by systematically varying the values of the parameters of the accuracy function. In this section, we explore the predictive behavior of k-NNC on our model by using the accuracy function.

We present the predictive behavior of k-NNC by varying the value of k. Fig.3 shows the behavior where the number of features (r) is fixed at 30 or 50, the number of training instances (n) is fixed at 50 or 100, and the threshold is set at $p = r/2$. In all cases, we can observe that the classification performance of k-NNC improves as k increases, then reaches a maximum before starting to deteriorate. This is often referred to as the *peaking performance* of k-NNC by empirical analysis [5, 10]. Since the performance of the classifier is sensitive to the value of k, an appropriate choice of k is very important to achieve the high accuracy. We can also observe that the classifier has a similar behavior for the same number of training instances. This observation suggests that the effect of the number of training instances on the optimal value of k is greater than the effect of the number of features.

We further investigate the relationship between the number of training instances and the optimal value of k. Fig.4 shows this relationship where the number of features (r) is 30 or 50 and the threshold is set at $p = r/2$. In both cases, we can observe that the optimal value of k increases gradually as the number of training instances increases. From this observation, we can say that the optimal value of k is affected significantly by the number of training instances.

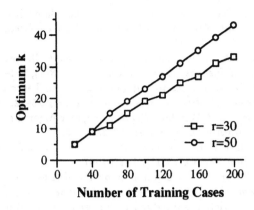

Fig. 4. The relationship between the number of training instances and the optimal value of k. r represents the number of features.

5 Conclusion

In this paper, we described an average-case analysis of k-nearest neighbor classifier for a subclass of Boolean threshold functions. We assumed that every feature has a noise-free Boolean value and that instances are uniformly distributed.

First, we computed the predictive accuracy for k-NNC as a function of the number of features, the threshold, the number of training instances, and the number of nearest neighbors.

Next, we plotted the predictive behavior of k-NNC by varying the value of parameters of the accuracy function. We presented the behavior of the classifier by changing the value of k, and showed the relationship between the number of training instances and the optimal value of k.

In the future, we must extend our average-case analysis of k-NNC to handle a broader class, noisy features, and also various distributions over the instance space. And we would like to perform an average-case analysis of a weighted k-NNC.

References

1. Aha, D. W. Incremental Instance-Based Learning of Independent and Graded Concept Descriptions. *Proceedings of the Sixth International Workshop on Machine Learning*, 387–391, 1989.
2. Aha, D. W. and Kibler, D. Noise-Tolerant Instance-Based Learning Algorithms. *Proceedings of the Eleventh International Joint Conference on Artificial Intelligence (IJCAI'89)*, 794–799, 1989.
3. Aha, D. W., Kibler, D. and Albert, M. K. Instance-Based Learning Algorithms. *Machine Learning, 6*, 37–66, 1991.

4. Albert, M. K. and Aha, D. W. Analyses of Instance-Based Learning Algorithms. *Proceedings of the Ninth National Conference on Artificial Intelligence (AAAI'91)*, 553–558, 1991.

5. Bailey, T. and Jain, A. A Note on Distance-weighted K-Nearest Neighbor Rules. *IEEE Transactions on Systems, Man, and Cybernetics, 8*(4), 311–313, 1978.

6. Cardie, C. Using Decision Trees to Improve Case-Based Learning. *Proceedings of the Tenth International Conference on Machine Learning*, 25–32, 1993.

7. Cost, S. and Salzberg, S. A Weighted Nearest Neighbor Algorithm for Learning with Symbolic Features. *Machine Learning, 10*, 57–78, 1993.

8. Cover, T. M. and Hart, P. E. Nearest Neighbor Pattern Classification. *IEEE Transactions on Information Theory, 13*(1), 21–27, 1967.

9. Cover, T. M. and Hart, P. E. Estimation by the Nearest Neighbor Rule. *IEEE Transactions on Information Theory, 14*(1), 50–55, 1968.

10. Dudani, S. A. The Distance-Weighted k-Nearest-Neighbor Rule. *IEEE Transactions on Systems, Man, and Cybernetics, 6*(4), 325–327, 1976.

11. Hirschberg, D. S. and Pazzani, M. J. Average-Case Analysis of learning k-CNF concept. *Proceedings of the Ninth International Conference on Machine Learning*, 206–211, 1992.

12. Kelly, Jr. J. D. and Davis, L. A Hybrid Genetic Algorithm for Classification. *Proceedings of the Twelfth International Joint Conference on Artificial Intelligence (IJCAI'91)*, 645–650, 1991.

13. Langley, P., Iba, W., and Thompson, K. An Analysis of Bayesian Classifiers. *Proceedings of the Tenth National Conference on Artificial Intelligence (AAAI'92)*, 223–228, 1992.

14. Langley, P. and Iba, W. Average-Case Analysis of a Nearest Neighbor Algorithm. *Proceedings of the Thirteenth International Joint Conference on Artificial Intelligence (IJCAI'93)*, 889–894, 1993.

15. Murphy, P. M. and Pazzani, M. J. ID2-of-3: Constructive Induction of M-of-N Concepts for Discriminators in Decision Trees. *Proceedings of the Eighth International Workshop on Machine Learning*, 183–187, 1991.

16. Okamoto, S. and Satoh, K. A Mathematical Predictive Accuracy for the Nearest Neighbor Classifier. *Proceedings of Second European Workshop on Case-Based Reasoning (EWCBR'94)*, 347–355, 1994.

17. Pazzani, M. J. and Sarrentt, W. A Framework for Average Case Analysis of Conjunctive Learning Algorithms. *Machine Learning, 9*, 349–372, 1992.

18. Pitt, L. and Valiant, L. G. Computational Limitations on Learning from Examples. *the Association for Computing Machinery, 35*(4), 965–984, 1988.

19. Rachlin, J., Kasif, S., Salzberg, S., and Aha, D. W. Toward a Better Understanding of Memory-Based Reasoning Systems. *Proceedings of the Eleventh International Conference on Machine Learning*, 242–250, 1994.

20. Satoh, K. and Okamoto, S. Toward PAC-Learning of Weights from Qualitative Distance Information. *Proceedings of AAAI'94 Workshop on CBR*, 128–132, 1994.

21. Skalak, D. B. Prototype and Feature Selection by Sampling and Random Mutation Hill Climbing Algorithms. *Proceedings of the Eleventh International Conference on Machine Learning*, 293–301, 1994.

22. Stanfill, C. and Waltz, D. L. Toward Memory-Based Reasoning. *Communication of the Association for Computing Machinery, 29*(12), 1213–1228, 1986.

Cases as terms:
A feature term approach to the structured representation of cases

Enric Plaza[*]

Institut d'Investigació en Intel·ligència Artificial, CSIC
Campus de la Universitat Autònoma de Barcelona
08193 Bellaterra, Catalunya, Spain

Email: enric@iiia.csic.es
URL: http://www.iiia.csic.es

1 Motivation

In our research work, we have come to represent cases as complex, structured data structures that we will formally described as *feature terms* (see [Arcos] for a description of the NOOS language for CBR and multistrategy learning). The advantage of using structured representations are twofold. Firstly, it offers a natural way to describe composite objects that if described by attribute-value representations cause some problems like dealing with irrelevant attributes, not-applicable values, etc (and this leads to problems when comparing similitude among cases in this descriptions). Secondly, structured-representation cases offer the capability of treating subparts of cases also as full-fledged *cases*: they can be stored, and retrieved and used to solve (sub)problems of new cases; also, a case may be solved using (subparts of) multiple cases retrieved from the system's memory. We will present here a formalization of structured (sometimes called *object-centered*) representations as feature terms and we will present how can we assess similarity between feature terms (cases) and determine the preferred (most similar) case from a set of cases.

1.1 Background

This approach is different from some usual notions of case-based reasoning (CBR). Usually, cases are (represented as) tuples of attribute value pairs for a known, finite vocabulary of attributes and values (except for numeric values that need not be finite). Then, similarity is estimated using some metrics (that may involve differential weighting of attributes, dynamic adjustment of the weights, etc). The usual thing is to have some attribute-wise distance measure, i. e. if attributes are $a_i (i = 1,...,n)$ and we use the notation $t.a$ to denote the value of attribute a in case t, then attribute-wise distance is some function $d(t_1.a_i, t_2.a_i)$ that may be defined according to the a_i attribute's type. Then some aggregation function D is defined as the weighted distance of two cases t_1, t_2, such as:

$$D(t_1, t_2) = \sum_{i=1}^{n} w_i \cdot d(t_1.a_i, t_2.a_i)$$

There are some problems that have to be solved, like missing values, irrelevant values, etc. Next, some similarity function is defined as $S(t_1, t_2) = N(1 - D(t_1, t_2))$ where N is a normalization function. Other CBR approaches do not use similarity but symbolic indices (sometimes learned by explanation-based generalization). However, this approach deal only with the what we call [Armengol] *retrieval task*, and not with the task of *selection task* of the retrieved cases [Plaza]; usually this CBR systems use some similarity-based or domain-specific strategy for ranking the retrieved cases. We will see how our approach deals with both retrieval and selection of structured cases.

---

[*] This work has been performed in the framework of Project ANALOG, CICYT grant TIC-122/93.

Indeed, the structured representation of cases we propose has the advantage of a wider expressive power than attribute-value representations. However, the classical approach of distance among tuples is not directly applicable. One option is that of extending distance metrics to structures representations as trees (see [Bunke]).

1.2 Towards similitude descriptions

Our approach is slightly different. Let's ask ourselves the reason of using distances: it is a way of estimating similarity between cases, and we want this because later the selection process in the CBR system will pick up as most relevant the most similar case. What we need then is a method for assessing similarity between cases (represented as structured terms) and obtaining a preference ranking among the cases based on that similarity. We do not need to use a distance (although it provides a complete ordering) if we have a way to obtain a preference ordering (albeit a partial ordering) based on a similarity estimate.

In the following we will formalize structured representation of cases as *feature terms* and we will show how this formalization allows us to define a natural characterization of similarity and how it can be used in the retrieval and selection of cases. This formalization is general and hopefully useful for other CBR systems, but we will explain specifically how NOOS, the language for CBR and multistrategy learning we have developed, is able to represent and implement all the concepts and methods we introduce. Feature terms can thus be considered as the foundation of CBR representation in NOOS-based applications [Arcos]. The structure of the paper is as follows: first feature terms are introduced and formalized, next the notions of subsumption and antiunification of feature terms are defined. Antiunification provides a *description* of the similitude among terms (cases). These notions are then used to realize a strategy for selection of retrieved cases using on a *preference ordering* based on a ranking of similitude descriptions.

2. Feature terms

Before defining formally feature terms, we will introduce intuitively some basic notions. A *structured representation* of cases is one where $t_1.a_i = t_2$, i.e. where the value of an a_i attribute of a tuple (case) t_1 is another tuple t_2. This fact allows to treat subparts of cases as full-fledged cases. The intuition behind feature terms is that the basic power of this representation is that of *path equality*. A *path* is a concatenation of attributes, e.g. if we have: $t_1.a_i = t_2$, $t_2.a_j = t_3$, $t_3.a_k = t_4$ then $p = t_1.a_i.a_j.a_k$ is a path. (with value t_4). Path equality ($p \doteq q$) is a restriction upon the values the term's attributes appearing in two paths may take. For instance a path equality such as: $t_p.a_i.a_j.a_k \doteq t_q.a_m.a_n$ constrains the term's attributes to have the same value. That is to say, they may have any value as far as among them the following relationship holds: following those paths they lead to the same term.

In fact, feature terms are just a generalization of first order terms that are useful to have a declarative representation of record-like structures without the loss of the convenient instantiation ordering unification operation [Aït-Kaci]. Using first order terms we can represent a person in this way:

person(John, Smith, 34, Jack-Smith, NYCity)

where we have to know the meaning of the arguments by its position, i.e. writing that predicate *person* is:

person(*firstname, lastname, age, father, city*)

Using feature terms each argument is denoted by a *symbol identifier* instead of position. This change allows to easily express incomplete information. We could not do that using the above first order term for *person*. Of course there is a way of representing incomplete information about persons by reification, i.e. saying *person*(p1) and then predicating about reification p1 such as: father(p1, p2) and having rules such as

$$father(x,y) \land lastname(y,z) \Rightarrow lastname(x,z).$$

For instance in a form of feature terms called unification grammars, the syntax for a person whose father is unknown can represented as follows:

$$
\begin{bmatrix}
person \\
name: \begin{bmatrix} name \\ first: John \\ \{1\}last: Smith \end{bmatrix} \\
lives-at: \begin{bmatrix} address \\ city: NYCity \end{bmatrix} \\
father: \begin{bmatrix} person \\ name: \begin{bmatrix} name \\ last: \{1\} \end{bmatrix} \end{bmatrix}
\end{bmatrix}
$$

The *tag* {1} is a syntactic way of expressing path equality, in this case if the feature term has name John-Smith, the equality

```
John-Smith.father.name.last ≐ John-Smith.name.last
```

The same term in NOOS syntax (and giving it the name John-Smith) is expressed:

```
(define (person John-Smith)
    (name (define (name)
            (first John)
            (last Smith)))
    (lives-at (define (address)
                (city NYCity)))
    (father (define (person)
                (name (define (name)
                        (last (>> name last)))))))
```

where path equality is expressed in position John-Smith.father.name.last by (>> name last) that determines a path starting at the root (i.e. John-Smith) and followed by name and last features.

2.1 Feature terms formalization

Regardless the concrete syntax used in feature terms, the abstract syntax of feature terms can be defined as follows (we will use [Carpenter] formalization, an alternative formalization may be found in [Aït-Kaci]). Let us have a finite set *Feat* of features (attributes) and a type hierarchy $\langle Type, \le \rangle$ that is a finite bounded complete partial order[1] over the type symbols of the set *Type*.

Definition 2.1 (Feature term)

A feature term[2] over *Type* and *Feat* is a tuple F=<Q, q_r, T, D> where

---

[1] A bounded complete partial order (BCPO) is a partial order just in case for every (possibly empty or infinite) set of elelements with an upper bound there is a least upper bound or join. A BCPO always has a least element ⊥ that is called *bottom* [Carpenter].

[2] There are different ways of describing feature terms, and the one used here is adapted from [Carpenter]. Another approaches is [Aït-Kaci]. There is no "canonical" definition of feature terms, because different authors define different semantics for them being an ongoing area of research and having different purposes. Not even the name "feature term" is standard, and they are also called "feature structures", ψ-terms, etc.

- Q : a finite set of *nodes* rooted at q_r,
- $q_r \in Q$: the *root* node
- $T : Q \rightarrow Type$: a total node *typing* function
- $D : Feat \times Q \rightarrow Q$: a partial *feature value* function

Let $\mathcal{F}$ denote the collection of feature terms. The intuitive way to picture a feature term is as directed labelled graphs such that Q is the set of nodes, T determines the labels of the nodes, and arcs are determined as follows: there is an arc from q to q' labelled by f, written $q \xrightarrow{f} q'$, if $D(f,q)=q'$. It is easy to make an analogy from feature terms to frame-based representations where frames correspond to nodes, features on arcs represent slot labels and the arcs points to their fillers.

References in feature terms are made of paths, defined as follows.

Definition 2.2 (Paths)

A *path* π is a sequence of features. Let *Path=Feat** and ε the empty path, we can now extend the feature value function D to paths as follows:

- $D(\varepsilon, q)=q$
- $D(f\pi, q)=D(\pi, D(f, q))$

That is to say, if $\pi = f_1...f_n$ then $D(\pi, q_0) = q_n$ if $q_0 \xrightarrow{f_1} q_1 \xrightarrow{f_2} q_2 ... \xrightarrow{f_n} q_n$. The set $\{D(\pi, q) \mid \pi \in Path\}$ is the set of nodes *reachable* from q by some path. The root of a feature term is the node q_r that satisfies $Q=\{D(\pi, q_r) \mid \pi \in Path\}$, i.e. the node from which all nodes in Q are reachable.

It is then apparent that defining a feature term is equivalent to assigning feature terms as the values of paths.

Definition 2.3 (Path Value)

If $F=<Q, q_r, T, D>$ and $D(\pi, q_r)$ is defined, then $F\backslash\pi = F=<Q', q_r', T', D'>$ where:

- $q_r' = D(\pi, q_r)$
- $Q' = \{D(\pi', q_r') \mid \pi' \in Path\} = \{D(\pi\pi', q_r) \mid \pi' \in Path\}$
  $D'(f, q) = D(f, q)$ if $q \in Q'$
- $T'(q) = T(q)$ if $q \in Q'$

There are two interesting properties of feature terms. The first one is that all subterms of a feature terms (that are also feature terms) are univocally determined by the path leading to it from the root. In the example above, the subterm that is the name of John-Smith is the term :

```
(define (name)
    (first John)
    (last Smith))
```

A second property of feature terms is that two terms may be equivalent up to the renaming of the their nodes if they represent the same information. This will be useful for defining the subsumption of feature terms.

We will later need the notion of *subsumption* for establishing a preference order, so we will introduce this notion presently. The intuitive idea is considering feature terms as *descriptions* of situations, then subsumption is the usual one: a description F subsumes another description F' if the F is more general than F'. Regarding feature terms, the essential idea is that a feature term F subsumes F', written F≤F', if and only if (1) the type of the root of F' is a subtype in $\langle Type, \leq \rangle$ of the root of F, (2) all features defined in F are also dfefined in features of F' (and the feature values of F subsuming the corresponding feature values of F'), and (3) all path equality constraints in F also hold in F'.

In the formal definition below, subsumption is given in terms of paths and we assume a fixed type structure $\langle Type, \leq \rangle$ and a finite set *Feat* of features. Notice that we treat subsumption ordering $\leq$ as an informational ordering, i.e. $a \leq b$ means that a has less or equal information content than b (a is more general and b more specific). This is standard practice in domain theory (and in feature terms literature) but goes against the common practice in AI where more general terms are directed towars the *top*. In feature terms the type hierarchy directs the more general concepts towards the *bottom* (because they have *less* informational content). In this approach the result of a *join* operation of two descriptions (intuitively: union of information content) is a description that has the union of the information (and thus is more specific than the two previous descriptions), while the result of a *meet* operation of two descriptions (intuitively: intersection of information content) is a description that has the information in common two both descriptions.

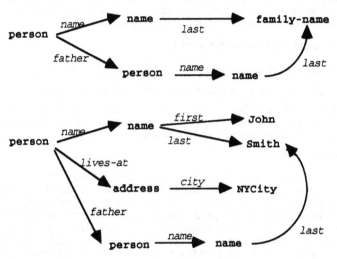

Figure 1. An example of subsumption between feature terms (where Smith is of type family-name).

Definition 2.4 (Subsumption)

$F = <Q, q_r, T, D>$ subsumes $F = <Q', q_r', T', D'>$, $F \leq F'$, if and only if there is a morphism $h: Q \rightarrow Q'$ such that:

- $h(q_r) = q_r'$
- $T(q) \leq T'(h(q))$ for every $q \in Q$
- $h(D(f, q)) = D'(f, h(q))$ for every $q \in Q$ and feature f such that $D(f, q)$ is defined.

The last condition, if expressed as a condition upon arcs, states that:

if $q \xrightarrow{f} q'$, then $h(q) \xrightarrow{f} h(q')$

This implies that a feature term subsumes another only if when there is a structure sharing in the more general one, then the same structure sharing appears in the more specific feature term. Deciding subsumption is quite efficient, in fact determining whether or not $F \leq F'$ is in time linear to the size of F [Carpenter]. Aït-Kaci [Aït-Kaci] shows that feature terms are formally equivalent to directed labelled graphs (i.e. every feature term F has a corresponding G$_F$ graph) and that determining the subsumption of feature terms F≤F' is equivalent to determining if graph G$_{F'}$ *approximates*[3] graph G$_F$. It is worthwhile to note that the notion of subsumption among feature terms (and graph approximation) is equivalent to the notion of *substitution* in first order terms.

The following example person-33 subsumes the feature term of John-Smith given above.

```
(define (person person-33)
    (name (define (name)
            (last (define (family-name)))))
    (father (define (person)
                (name (define (name)
                        (last (>> name last)))))))
```

And if we view these two terms as their corresponding graphs, we have the graphs in Fig. 1 where it is easy to see the subsumption relation (identifiers person-33 and John-Smith have been substituted by their root type person).

The subsumption relation over feature terms is transitive and reflexive (but not antisymmetric since two feature terms can subsume each other and still be distinct). This relation defines an ordering among feature structures, as follows.

Lemma 2.1 (Feature term pre-ordering)

The subsumption relation is a pre-ordering of the collection $\mathcal{F}$ of feature terms.

When two feature terms subsume each other (F≤F' and F'≤F) they are identical up to a renaming of nodes (F ~ F'). This relation F ~ F' in an equivalence relation over $\mathcal{F}$. Even if F and F' are distinct, we can treat them equivalently in that they convey the same information concerning the situation they are describing.

2.2 Antiunification

The notion we will use for assessing similarity of structured case representations, formalized as feature terms, is that of antiunification. Intuitively, the antiunification of two feature terms gives *that which is common to both* (yielding a generalization) and *all that is common to both* (the most specific generalization). In formal terms, the antiunification of two feature terms, F ⊓ F', yields the greatest lower bound with respect to subsumption ordering. The notion of intersection conveys the meaning of capturing the commonalty between sets: antiunification on feature terms, as before meet operation on types, conveys the meaning of yielding an element with the common information content (the greatest lower bound). Conversely, unification of two feature terms yields the least upper bound with respect to subsumption ordering (union of information).

The most intuitive way to present antiunification is to explain the procedure to compute the greatest lower bound of two feature terms and later give the formal definition. The procedure starts by taking the two root nodes of the feature terms and labelling the root node of the result with the antiunification of their types according to the type structure $\langle Type, \leq \rangle$, i.e. the *meet* operation[4] in this type structure, assuming there is a top element (meaning the *empty type* or *inconsistency*: ⊤) and a bottom element (meaning *anything*: ⊥) in it). Next we focus on the features that are common to both feature terms and identify the corresponding values. For those corresponding values we construct a new node labelled with the meet of their types before antiunification (given our type structure $\langle Type, \leq \rangle$ with

---

[3] A graph approximates another if it can be embedded in it with an homomorphism. Notice that this is *not* the process of deciding if an unlabelled graph is a subgraph of another that is NP-complete.

[4] The meet operation yields the greatest lower bound, while the join operation yields the least upper bound in a type lattice.

top and bottom, the meet of two types exists and is unique). Then we recursively proceed over this new nodes as roots (of the corresponding subterms). The procedure finishes when reaching closure, and if at any stage two feature (sub)terms have nothing in common their antiunification is simply ⊥ (the most general type) and the feature is discarded. A short description of the procedure is this:

<u>Procedure</u> AU(F, F')
    Let R and R' be the types of the root nodes of F and F'
    The root of the new term is of type *meet*(R, R')
    <u>For</u> all features *f* defined in both F and F'
        Let V and V' be the feature values of F and F' for feature *f*
        <u>If</u> V and V' are involved in a path equality constraints in both F and F'
        <u>and</u> they have already been antiunified in a feature *f*
            <u>Then</u> the value of feature *f* in the new term is the value of *f*
            <u>Otherwise</u> Let W=AU(V, V')
        <u>If</u> W=⊥
            <u>then</u> *f* is not a feature of the new term
            <u>otherwise</u> *f* is a feature of the new term with value W

We will now give a definition of antiunification. As the procedure, this definition is based on constructing a new node for every pair of nodes that are defined and have a type that is defined for both terms and whose antiunification is not *bottom*.

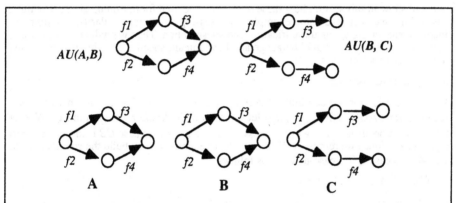

Figure 2. Antiunification gathers information common to two terms. Regarding equality constraints, they are kept in the generalization if it is common to both antiunifying terms (as in AU(A, B)) and new nodes are created otherwise (as in AU(B, C)).

Definition 2.5 (Antiunification)

Let F, F'∈ *F* be feature terms such that F~<Q, q_r, T, D> and F'~<Q', q'_r, , T', D'> are such that Q∩Q'=∅. We define an equivalence relation R on Q×Q' as a binary relation such that:

- $R \subset Q \times Q'$
- $R(q_r, q'_r)$
- $R(D(f, q), D'(f, q'))$ if and only if both are defined and $R(q, q')$.

The antiunification of F and F' is then defined to be:

$$F \sqcap F' = \left\langle \langle Q^R, \left\{ q_r, q'_r \right\}, T^R, D^R \right\rangle$$

where

$$Q^R = \left\{ \{q, q'\} \mid R(q, q') \right\}$$
$$T^R(\{q, q'\}) = T(q) \sqcap T(q')$$

$$D^R(f,\{q,q'\}) = \begin{cases} \{(D(f,q),D'(f,q'))\} & \text{if both } D(f,q) \text{ and } D'(f,q') \text{ are defined} \\ \text{undefined} & \text{otherwise} \end{cases}$$

In the longer version of this paper there is an Appendix A that shows that the result of this antiunification is indeed the greatest lower bound (report available at http://www.iiia.csic.es/Reports/1995/IIIA-RR-95.html).

Remark that this definition works recursively for all the meets in the definition of T^R that are not $\perp$ (the bottom element). The process starts by choosing a F and a F' in their equivalence classes so that they do not share nodes to avoid clashes. The binary relation R pick pairs of nodes when defined in both feature terms and constructs a new node in the new feature term. Function D^R defines the feature values that are common to both F and F'. The only subtle thing is the treatment of path equality. When there is a path equality $\pi \doteq \pi'$ in both F and F' the relation R detects this equality since it will build an identical pair for the value of paths π and π' in F and F' (see Fig. 2). However if only one feature term has a path equality constraint $\pi \doteq \pi'$ the result of the antiunification will not have this constraint (because R will create two different pair of nodes for the new term).

3 Retrieval and selection of cases

We will show in this section how these notions can be used for reasoning about structured cases. First we will give some examples of assessing structural similarity in a domain-independent setting using antiunification and subsumption. Then we will show how these notions are used in the NOOS language and how domain-specific knowledge can be used to retrieve and select cases.

3.1 Similitude terms

With antiunification we can build descriptions of the structural similitude between two feature terms: $AU(t_1, t_2) = t_{S(t_1,t_2)}$, and let us call it a *similitude term* of t_1 and t_2. What a CBR system needs now is a way to assess which case of a case base CB is more similar to a given case. Since we represent all cases by feature terms, we can build the *similitude term set* $\mathcal{S}$ of a case t_0 in a case-base CB as follows:

$$\mathcal{S}(t_0, CB) = \{t_{S(t_0,t_i)} \mid t_i \in CB\}$$

Since similitude terms in $\mathcal{S}$ are also feature terms, they are in $\mathcal{F}$ and we can use the pre-ordering of Lemma 2.1 to reason about them. In fact, we do not need to define a metric or a distance among them but only use the $\leq$-based ordering we have already defined. We can map the $\leq$-ordering over the similitude term set $\langle \mathcal{S}, \leq \rangle$ into a preference ordering upon the CB $\langle CB, \leq_{t_0} \rangle$ where $\leq_{t_0}$ is defined:

$$t_1, t_2 \in CB, \ t_1 \leq_{t_0} t_2 \ \textit{iff} \ t_{S(t_0,t_1)} \leq t_{S(t_0,t_2)}$$

Now, the most preferred cases in CB are the maximals with respect to $\leq_{t_0}$. This is what we expected since the maximals in $\langle CB, \leq_{t_0} \rangle$ correspond to the maximals in $\langle \mathcal{S}, \leq \rangle$ that are those similitude terms $t_{S(t_1,t_2)}$ that are more specific, i.e. those pairs (t_0, t_i) that are most similar (i.e. those that have more information in common).

Since we have a pre-order, we cannot assure that the maximal is unique. In the next section we discuss how we can use domain knowledge to improve this preference ordering so as to be able to better select a case from BC. However, in other applications it may be more useful to have an explicit explanation of why two cases are similar: the similitude term. In Figure 3 we show a term John-Smith and two terms in CB, namely person-1 and person-2. Although not shown in the picture, elements like John, Smith or NYCity, are

```
(define (person John-Smith)
  (name (define (name)
              (first John)
              (last Smith)))
  (lives-at (define (address)
                    (city NYCity)))
  (profession teacher)
  (father (define (person)
                  (name (define (name)
                              (last (>> name last)
))))))
(define (person person-1)
  (lives-at (define (address)
                    (city Amsterdam)))
  (name (define (name)
              (first Tom)
              (last Smith)))
  (nationality Dutch)
  (father (define (person)
                  (name (define (name)
                              (last Smith))))))
(define (person person-2)
  (father (define (person)
                  (name (define (name)
                              (last Johnson)))))
  (name (define (name)
              (last Johnson)))
  (lives-at (define (address)
                    (state California))))
```

Figure 3. Three cases as feature terms.

```
;;AU(John-Smith, person-1)

(define (person person-au-1)
  (name (define (name)
              (first first-name)
              (last Smith)))
  (lives-at (define (address)
                    (city city)))
  (father (define (person)
                  (name Smith))))
;;AU(John-Smith, person-2)
(define (personperson-au-2)
  (name (define (name)
              (first first-name)
              (last last-name)))
  (lives-at address)
  (father (define (person)
                  (name (define (name)
                              (last (>> last name)
))))))
```

Figure 4. Similitude terms for feature terms described in Fig. 1. person-au-1 is the antiunification of John-Smith and person-1 while person-au-2 is the antiunification of John-Smith and person-2.

of type first-name, last-name and city respectively. These types appear as feature values in the results of the antiunification in Figure 4. Figure 4 shows the similitude terms person-au-1 and person-au-2, the result of antiunifying John-Smith with the two other terms in *CB*. This symbolic description can be manipulated by a CBR system that has some domain knowledge about the importance of sharing some information (see §3.2). In our example here we can use the domain-independent criterion of subsumption ordering. If we observe the similitude terms person-au-1 and person-au-2, we can check that person-au-2 ≤ person-au-1, i.e. person-au-2 subsumes person-au-1. Since similitude term person-au-1 is more specific and it corresponds to the antiunification of person-1 with John-Smith, then person-1 is preferred to (is more similar that) person-2 with respect to John-Smith case.

3.2 Using feature terms in NOOS case-based applications

In this section we will show some examples of using *domain knowledge* for retrieval and selection of cases in developing a specific CBR application. For illustration, we will use CHROMA, a NOOS-based system uses a case-based method and an inductive method (based on antiunification) to recommend a plan for purifying proteins from a tissue or a bacterial culture [Armengol]. Currently we are using this approach in tasks such case-based planning, classification and configuration.

In NOOS we use feature terms (graphs) as queries for retrieval methods and for establishing preferences among retrieved cases. In fact, all methods (including retrieval methods) in NOOS are feature terms; this implies that reusing a method of a retrieved case in the current case ("derivational reply") is just taking the method's term and substitute its references for the references in the current case. Moreover, method applications are terms (and thus are cases) that can also be retrieved from memory. A method for retrieving cases is using determinations [Russell]. A determination states that the solution feature of a problem is determined by another feature (e.g. nationality *determines* language). Determinations are domain knowledge that allows us to justify the selection of a case as relevant. In the domain of CHROMA, where domain experts call their cases *experiments*, we know that the protein to be purified determines the purification plans that are relevant. A CBR-method in NOOS is just a method that has subtasks retrieve, select and reuse. Thus we use a retrieval method for CHROMA inside the retrieve task of the CBR-method based on this determination:

```
(define (retrieve-by-pattern Retrieve-by-Protein)
    (current-case my-experiment)
    (pattern (define (experiment)
        (protein (>> protein current-case)))))
```

Retrieve-by-pattern is a NOOS domain-independent method that retrieves the set of cases subsumed by the feature term given in the path retrieve-by-pattern.pattern. The new method Retrieve-by-Protein is a refinement of the last method that the retrieves all cases that have as protein the protein of our current case my-experiment. We can think of the retrieval methods as *queries* using graphs (feature terms) as patterns and returning the terms in memory that satisfy (are subsumed by) that particular graph specified in the query. NOOS implementation has a built-in indexing mechanism that will automatically retrieve the cases satisfying the query's graph.

Domain knowledge can thus prescribe that the comparisons and preferences are made only to a subset of relevant cases (here the feature terms retrieved by the method based on the protein determination). So, next we have to compare the relevant retrieved cases in order to determine which is more relevant to our current problem. We can use the domain independent schema presented in the last section, but we can also more focused domain-specific knowledge if we have it. In the protein purification domain, there is a *sample* (either an animal or vegetal tissue or a bacterial culture) from where the protein is purified. The domain experts can tell us that the most relevant experiments (cases) are those that have a sample with the same *species* or *source* (e.g. muscle). In fact, what we have now are a *domain-specific similitude terms*, i.e. similitude descriptions that are relevant according to the domain experts. The way to implement this knowledge in NOOS is to use a *preference method* that establishes a preference order such that the cases that satisfy this similitude descriptions (i.e. such that the similitude terms subsume them). For instance, a method for establishing a preference ordering based on having the same source of the sample is this:

```
(define (prefer-by-pattern prefer-by-experiment-by-sample-source)
    (cases cases-retrieved-by-protein)
    (current-case my-experiment)
    (pattern (define (experiment)
        (sample (define (sample)
            (source (>> source sample current-case)))))))
```

The method for preferring cases with the same species is analogous. Nothing else is needed for defining this CBR method, since NOOS automatically handles the preference ordering (including backtracking if needed when some preferred option turns out to be not so good) and the *reuse* task (implemented as "analogical replay" by reinstantiating the appropriate feature (sub)term of the selected case onto the current case). All kinds of retrieval and selection tasks can be specified in NOOS using these two kinds of methods: *preference* methods and *filter* methods (methods that select from a set of terms the subset that are subsumed by a graph: a *retrieve* method is a filter method that selects from the case-base).

4 Discussion

The notion of antiunification as generalization dates from 1970 [Plotkin]. There are some interesting articles on assessing similarity among structural representations. Bunke and Messmer [Bunke] define a distance between graphs d(g, g') as the (minimum) cost sequence of edit operations that transforms g into g'. Since feature terms are isomorphic with labelled directed graphs [Aït-Kaci], metric assessment of structural similarity is compatible with our approach of formalizing cases as feature terms and has the advantage that the work being done in this direction could be also applicable to the feature term approach. Although we have not taken this approach, we are currently investigating the possibility of defining an approximate subsumption operation (i.e. a form of partial pattern matching) based on fuzzy logic.

A precedent of the approach taken here is the study on structural similarity of first order terms performed in [Jantke]. In this article, an algorithm for antiunifying first order terms is proposed, but there is no proposal about what to do with the result of term antiunification like we do in section 3: how this antiunified terms are to be used? Part of the problem in doing so stems from the fact that seems difficult to describe a case as *one* first order term: usually one would thing of a *set* of first order terms as corresponding to a case[5]. We could think of applying our approach to *sets* of first order terms and establish a subsumption preorder (or even a lattice) over sets of first order terms that allows us to compare the similarity descriptions obtained by antiunification. However, defining a subsumption relation among collections of first order terms and using it for defining a preference order is not direct and in fact poses several fundamental problems that would need to be solved. Indeed, the fact that a case can be easily described as *one* feature term is a main reason to prefer the feature term approach when describing cases and case-based methods.

A related approach is that of "structural similarity" as used in [Börner]. First, a flat attribute-based representation is translated into a structured representation of a case. Next, "modification rules" are applied until a common structure of the current case and a retrieved case is found. Finally, the variable substitutions used in the modification rules are used as a guidance for the case adaptation phase. Although [Börner] uses first order terms, it seems in principle also amenable to a feature term formalization. However [Börner] do not use the subsumption relation among feature terms to build a preference order among them as we do, as she focuses on using these structural similarity for adaptation and do not use them during the retrieval phase ("superficial" features are used for retrieving and selecting cases). In our approach, the capability of *comparing* similarity terms, by means of the subsumption relationship, is the main advantage of using feature terms in the retrieval and selection phase of case-based reasoning.

The use of structured representations seems appropriate but some concerns about efficiency are still open. In NOOS we use feature terms (graphs) as queries for retrieval methods and for establishing preferences among retrieved cases. This gives the system developer a high level of abstraction in developing a CBR application, while the implementation of the language manages the indexing and retrieval. A way to improve efficiency is using parallelism, as done in the Parka language implemented in the Connection Machine, that uses a parallel algorithm for "structure matching" [Kettler]. This approach is compatible with our formalization, but in our experience a good indexing scheme offers enough efficiency in retrieval for several realistic domains.

The main goal of this paper has been to show that feature terms are a useful formalization that can be used to describe parts of the CBR process when using structured representations. We have introduced the formalization of feature terms and then we have seen how we can use some syntactic notions as notions useful for CBR: antiunification has been used for defining similitude terms and subsumption have been used to define preferential orderings in case retrieval. My goal has not been to formalize a specific CBR system (although I have shown an example of NOOS, because we came up with feature terms when we were trying to describe our language). Feature terms in NOOS are more complex: they include disjunction and values can be sets. Currently, we are studying the role of language bias in generalization: a series of more powerful languages $\{L_i\}$ can be defined inside NOOS starting from the language of terms presented here. Each language $\{L_i\}$ has a corresponding antiunification definition, and the system can decide to shift from a simple language to another more complex language when necessary. In this way, a declarative representation of language bias is obtained in a way similar to that proposed by [deRaedt].

---

[5] The example in [Jantke] uses mathematical formulas as "cases": this is probably one of the few domains in which cases can be easily described by unique first order terms.

Rather, my intention has been to show that certain aspects of CBR, hopefully in a variety of case-based systems, can be succinctly and clearly described with this formalization of declarative record-like structures called feature terms. Formalism developers focus on the unification operation on feature terms because they are interested in including record-like structures into logic-based languages, but I've tried to show here that for CBR systems (and in fact also for ML systems) feature terms, with operations of antiunification and subsumption, can be of help in the framework of structured representations.

An extended version of this paper is available at URL
http://www.iiia.csic.es/Reports/1995/IIIA-RR-95.html

Acknowledgements

This work has been performed in the framework of Project ANALOG, CICYT grant TIC-122/93. I am grateful to the discussions of the project members and to Josep-Lluís Arcos, Jaume Agustí, and Lluís Godo for enlightening debates on these and other topics.

References

[Aït-Kaci] H Aït-Kaci, A Podelski (1992), Towards a meaning of LIFE. PRL Research Report #11, Digital Research Laboratory (available at doc-server@prl.dec.com sending a message with subject line help).

[Arcos] Arcos, J. L., and Plaza, E. (1993), A Reflective Architecture for Integrated Memory-based Learning and Reasoning, In S. Wess, K.D. Althoff, M.M. Richter (Eds.), *Topics in Case-Based Reasoning. Lecture Notes in Artificial Intelligence*, 837, p. 289-300. Springer Verlag: Berlin.

[Armengol] Armengol, E. and Plaza, E. (1994b), Integrating Induction in a Case-based Reasoner. *Proceedings of the Second European Workshop on Case-based Reasoning.* Chantilly (France). pp. 243-251.

[Börner] Börner, K (1994), Structural similarity as a guidance in case-based design. In S Wess, K D Althoff, M M Richter (Eds.) *Topics in Case-Based Reasoning, Lecture Notes in Artificial Intelligence*, Vol. 837, p.197-208. Springer-Verlag 1994.

[Bunke] Bunke, H and Messmer, B T (1994), Similarity measures for structured representations. In S Wess, K D Althoff, M M Richter (Eds.) *Topics in Case-Based Reasoning*, p. 106-118. Lecture Notes in Artificial Intelligence 837, Springer Verlag.

[Carpenter] Carpenter, B (1992), *The Logic of Typed Feature Structures.* Cambridge Tracts in Theoretical Computer Science. Cambridge University Press, Cambridge, UK.

[deRaedt] deRaedt, L (1992), *Interactive Theory Revision.* Academic Press: London.

[Kettler] B P Kettler, J A Hendler, W A Anderson, M P Evett (1994), Massively parallel support for case-based planning. *IEEE Expert*, p. 8-14, Fed. 1994.

[Jantke] K P Jantke (1993), Nonstandard concepts of similarity in case-based reasoning. *Proceedings of the 17th Annual Conference of the "Gesellllschaft für Klassifikation e.V.".* Kaiserslautern, March 1993. Springer Verlag.

[López] B. López, E. Plaza (1991), Case-based Learning of Strategic Knowledge. *Lecture Notes in Artificial Intelligence 482.* Springer-Verlag.1991, pp. 398-411.

[Plaza] Plaza, E., Arcos, J.L. (1994), Integration of learning into a knowledge modelling framework. *Lecture Notes in Artificial Intelligence*, Vol. 867. Springer-Verlag 1994, pp. 355-373. Available online at URL "http://www.iiia.csic.es/People/enric/EKAW-94_ToC.html"

[Plotkin] Gordon D Plotkin, A note on inductive generalization. In B. Meltzer and D Michie (Eds.), *Machine Intelligence 5*, p. 153-163. Elsevier 1970.

[Russell] Russell, S. (1990), *The Use of Knowledge in Analogy and Induction.* Morgan Kaufmann.

ADAPtER: An Integrated Diagnostic System Combining Case-Based and Abductive Reasoning

Luigi Portinale, Pietro Torasso

Dipartimento di Informatica - Universita' di Torino (Italy)

Abstract. The aim of this paper is to describe the ADAPtER system, a diagnostic architecture combining case-based reasoning with abductive reasoning and exploiting the adaptation of the solution of old episodes, in order to focus the reasoning process. Domain knowledge is represented via a logical model and basic mechanisms, based on abductive reasoning with consistency constraints, have been defined for solving complex diagnostic problems involving multiple faults. The model-based component has been supplemented with a case memory and adaptation mechanisms have been developed, in order to make the diagnostic system able to exploit past experience in solving new cases. A heuristic function is proposed, able to rank the solutions associated to retrieved cases with respect to the adaptation effort needed to transform such solutions into possible solutions for the current case. We will discuss some preliminary experiments showing the validity of the above heuristic and the convenience of solving a new case by adapting a retrieved solution rather than solving the new problem from scratch.

1 Introduction

The idea of using different representations for diagnostic problem solving has attracted a significant amount of attention and a number of systems, exploiting some form of integration among different representations, have been developed (see [3]). These experiences pointed out two main problems: 1) how to guarantee consistency between different knowledge representations; 2) how to combine and integrate different reasoning mechanisms.

In the last years, the paradigm of Case-Based Reasoning (CBR) has shown to play a significant role in explanatory or abductive reasoning tasks like diagnosis, both as a "stand alone" mechanism [5, 8] and as integrated with Model-Based Reasoning (MBR) [7, 9, 4]. The use of cases seems to be very promising for addressing the two problems introduced above and for providing a model-based reasoner with some capability of learning by experience. In particular, problem 1 is greatly mitigated if both the case-based component and the model-based one share the same set and representation of data and the solutions stored in a case have the same form of those obtained by the model-based component alone. Approaches combining MBR with CBR can be roughly classified into two categories: approaches considering CBR as a speed-up and/or heuristic component for MBR [7, 9] and approaches viewing CBR as a way to recall past experience in order to account for potential errors in the device model [4]. Our proposal takes its place into the first category by means of the development of **ADAPtER** (**A**bductive **D**iagnosis through **A**daptation of **P**ast Episodes for **R**e-use), a diagnostic system integrating the model-based inference engine of AID (Abductive and Iterative Diagnosis [1] a pure model-based diagnostic system we have developed which solves diagnostic problems "from scratch"), with a case-based component intended to provide a guide to the abductive reasoning performed by AID.

The aim of this paper is to describe the architecture and the features of ADAPtER and to provide some preliminary experimental results. Differently from similar integrated diagnostic systems like CASEY [7], a basic feature of ADAPtER concerns the fact that model-based diagnostic problem solving relies on a formal logical theory of diagnosis and that the case-based component relies on such a characterization.

The paper is organized as follows: section 2 discusses the logical theory of diagnosis we rely on, section 3 is devoted to knowledge representation issues, in section 4 the architecture of ADAPtER is presented with a discussion concerning retrieval, ranking and adaptation of cases and finally, in section 5 we conclude by presenting some experimental results.

2 Characterizing Model-Based Diagnosis

In a formal characterization of diagnosis one has to define the type of model adopted for representing the system as well as a suitable notion of diagnostic problem and of diagnostic solution. A general theory of model-based diagnosis has been proposed in [2]. Here, we essentially adopt the same framework, where the model of the system to be diagnosed is represented by means of a logical theory T. In particular, we make use of different kinds of symbols for representing different kind of entities of the domain: STATE symbols represent non-observable internal states of the modeled system; CONTEXT symbols represent contextual conditions that may influence the behavior of the modeled system; MANIFESTATION symbols represent observable parameters in the modeled system which are the observable consequences of the behavior of the system; DIAG_HYP symbols represent the entities in terms of which diagnoses are expressed (i.e. diagnostic hypotheses)

Each one of these entities is characterized by a set of admissible values; for example, the manifestation *exhaust_smoke* (in a model covering car faults) can be characterized by the set of values $\{clear, grey, black\}$ and we use ground atoms to denote a particular assignment (e.g. *exhaust_smoke(black)*).

Formally, a *diagnostic problem* can be described as a 4-tuple $DP = \langle T, CXT, HYP, \langle \Psi^+, \Psi^- \rangle \rangle$, where: T is the logical theory modeling the system to be diagnosed, HYP is the set of ground atoms representing the possible instantiations of DIAG_HYP, CXT is the set of contextual data characterizing the case under examination, Ψ^+ is a set of ground atoms denoting the set of observable parameters that must be explicitly accounted for in the case under examination, Ψ^- is a set of ground atoms denoting the value of observable parameters that are known to be false in the case under examination. If OBS is the set of all the observed manifestations in the current case, $\Psi^+ \subseteq OBS$, while $\Psi^- = \{m(x)|$ for each admissible value x of manifestation m different than a, where $m(a) \in OBS\}$. This means that a conjunction of atoms representing different instances of the same entity yields an inconsistency. The choice of Ψ^+ is critical and cannot be done without taking into account the kind and the amount of knowledge captured in the logical theory T (see [2]).

Definition 1. Given a diagnostic problem $DP = \langle T, CXT, HYP, \langle \Psi^+, \Psi^- \rangle \rangle$, a set $H \subseteq HYP$ is a solution to DP (or , in other words, an explanation for the observations) if and only if:

$$\forall m \in \Psi^+ \ T \cup CXT \cup H \vdash m \quad \text{and} \quad \forall n \in \Psi^- \ T \cup CXT \cup H \not\vdash n$$

This means that H has to account for all observations in Ψ^+ (we say that manifestations in Ψ^+ have to be *covered*), while no atom in Ψ^- must be deduced from H. Given a diagnostic problem DP, there are potentially many (alternative) solutions to the problem and in most cases each solution involves more than one ground instantiation of DIAG_HYP. It should be clear that a solution H to a diagnostic problem identifies, together with contextual information CXT, a ground *trace* or *explanation* $EXPL(H, CXT)$ on the model T, containing the logical consequences of H and CXT.

3 Knowledge Representation Issues

3.1 Representing Domain Knowledge

For computational purposes, it is often convenient to restrict the logical theory T (representing the knowledge about the system to be diagnosed) to be a set of definite clauses. If we assume that the knowledge of the domain can be interpreted causally[1], it is quite useful to subdivide formulae of T into two sets in order to capture two different kinds of relations in the domain theory that are represented in a uniform way at the logical level.

- CAUSAL relationships represent cause-effect relations among states.
- HAM (Has As a Manifestation) relationships represent relations between states and their observable manifestations.

Each CAUSAL relation is modeled by a definite clause whose body involves ground instantiations of $\{s_1 \ldots s_n, c_1 \ldots c_k\}$ symbols ($s_i \in$ STATE and $c_j \in$ CONTEXT, $n \geq 1, k \geq 0$) and the head is an instantiation of a STATE symbol e. Such a formula is intended to represent the relationship "s_1 and ... and s_n cause e in the context formed by c_1 and ... and c_k". At the same way a HAM relation is modeled through a definite clause involving a STATE s in the body and a MANIFESTATION m in the head and is intended to represent the fact that m is an observable manifestation of state s.

Given this kind of characterization, we can assume that the set DIAG_HYP is composed by entities not appearing in the head of any clause (i.e. entities for which no explicit cause is provided in the model). Moreover, in order to model incompleteness in the specification of causal relations, new entities represented by ASSUMPTION

---

[1] Most of the work presented here can be adapted without much effort to the case where the domain knowledge is represented by a "structure and behavior" model [2].

DIAG_HYP: $\{prws, piws, roco, osga, \alpha_1\}$
CONTEXT: $\{casp, grcl, engi\}$

CAUSAL relations:

$prws(slightly\_worn) \rightarrow oico(increased)$ $prws(very\_worn) \rightarrow oico(very\_incr)$
$piws(slightly\_worn) \rightarrow oico(increased)$ $piws(very\_worn) \rightarrow oico(very\_incr)$
$casp(moderate) \wedge roco(very\_poor) \rightarrow jerk(strong)$ $casp(high) \wedge roco(poor) \rightarrow jerk(strong)$
$casp(high) \wedge roco(very\_poor) \rightarrow jerk(very\_strong)$ $roco(very\_poor) \wedge grcl(low) \wedge \alpha_1 \rightarrow oils(holed)$
$osga(very\_worn) \rightarrow oils(leaking)$ $oils(holed) \rightarrow laoi(severe)$
$oils(leaking) \wedge jerk(strong) \rightarrow laoi(moderate)$ $oils(leaking) \wedge jerk(very\_strong) \rightarrow laoi(severe)$
$oico(increased) \rightarrow laoi(moderate)$ $oico(very\_incr) \rightarrow laoi(severe)$
$laoi(moderate) \wedge engi(running) \rightarrow ente(increased)$ $laoi(severe) \wedge engi(running) \rightarrow ente(very\_incr)$

HAM relations:

$jerk(strong) \rightarrow vibr(strong)$ $jerk(very\_strong) \rightarrow vibr(very\_strong)$
$oico(increased) \rightarrow exsm(grey)$ $oico(very\_incr) \rightarrow exsm(black)$
$laoi(severe) \rightarrow owli(red)$ $oils(leaking) \rightarrow oibc(small\_amount)$
$oils(holed) \rightarrow oibc(huge\_amount)$ $ente(increased) \rightarrow htin(yellow)$
$ente(very\_incr) \rightarrow htin(red)$

Fig. 1. A fragment of a model for car engine faults

symbols are introduced; they are put in conjunction with the precondition of a
relation to model its incompleteness. Such symbols are also considered as being part
of DIAG_HYP. As an example, let us consider the simple model for the diagnosis
of car engine faults shown in figure 1 (table 1 shows the key of predicate symbols,
while α_1 is an ASSUMPTION symbol).

3.2 Representing Cases

Every case is represented by means of a 3-tuple $C = \langle CXT, OBS, SOL \rangle$ where
CXT and OBS represent the set of observed features characterizing the case (CXT
the contextual data and OBS the manifestations), while SOL is the set of solutions of the case. Each element of SOL is a pair $\langle H, EXPL(H, CXT) \rangle$ where H
is a set of DIAG_HYP instantiations satisfying definition 1 and $EXPL(H, CXT)$
is the explanation derived from H and CXT. For adaptation purposes, it is useful to characterized the whole set of manifestations related to a given solution
$S = \langle H, EXPL(H, CXT) \rangle$ of a case C: if $\epsilon(S, C) = \{m(a)/m$ is a manifestation
and $m(a) \in EXPL(H, CXT)\}$, the set $\pi(S, C) = \epsilon(S, C) - OBS$ represents the *predictions* of solution S on manifestations of case C that have not been observed; the
set of manifestations *related* to S is then defined to be $\mu(S, C) = OBS \cup \pi(S, C)^2$.
An example of a case in the domain described by the model of figure 1 is shown
in figure 2. In such an example the only solution is $S = \langle H, EXPL(H, CXT) \rangle$ and
$OBS \equiv \mu(S, C)$.
The methodology we adopted in ADAPtER for organizing cases in memory is based

---

[2] In general $\epsilon(S, C) \subseteq \mu(S, C)$ since there can be manifestations in OBS that are not
contained in $\epsilon(S, C)$.

ENTITY	ACRONYM	ENTITY	ACRONYM
car speed	casp	engine	engi
engine temperature	ente	exhaust smoke	exsm
ground clearance	grcl	high temp.indicator	htin
jerks	jerk	lack of oil	laoi
oil below car	oibc	oil consumption	oico
oil sump	oils	oil sump gasket	osga
oil warning light	owli	piston wear state	piws
piston ring wear state	prws	road conditions	roco
vibrations	vibr		

Table 1. Key for the predicates used in logical model

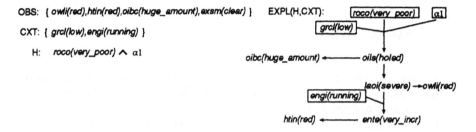

OBS: { owli(red),htin(red),oibc(huge_amount),exsm(clear) }

CXT: { grcl(low),engi(running) }

H: roco(very_poor) ∧ α1

Fig. 2. A Retrieved Case

on the notion of E-MOP [6]. An E-MOP is a generalization of a set of cases whose common characteristics are summarized into the E-MOP itself and are called *norms*, while discriminatory features are used as *indices* to retrieve the cases. In order to index cases, we use manifestations up to a given level of "cost": this exploits the facilities provided by AID to rank manifestations according to the degree of effort (cost) necessary to the user for providing them. In addition, also contexts can be used as indices; in particular, since a case is added to the case memory only after a solution for it has been obtained, if a contextual information is necessary to explain the observations (according to the criteria of definition 1), then it is used to index the case. Retrieval and matching mechanisms are described in section 4.1.

4 The ADAPtER Architecture

The architecture of the ADAPtER system aims at integrating aspects concerning case management and abductive reasoning in a uniform and flexible framework for diagnostic problem solving. The system involves the following basic components (see figure 3):

- a CASE MEMORY (or CONCEPTUAL MEMORY) where each case represents a diagnostic problem already solved as described in section 3.2;
- a DOMAIN KNOWLEDGE BASE identifying the behavior of the system to be diagnosed and described by means of a logical theory as described in section 3.1;
- a SUPERVISOR module controlling the activation of other modules;

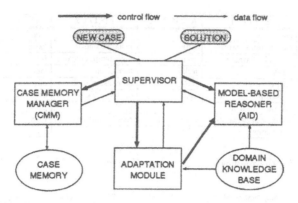

Fig. 3. ADAPtER Architecture

- a CASE MEMORY MANAGER (CMM) able to store and retrieve cases from the CASE MEMORY and to evaluate the degree of match between the current case to be solved and the retrieved ones;
- a MODEL-BASED REASONER (the AID inference engine) performing diagnostic reasoning by exploiting the logical theory representing the DOMAIN KNOWL-EDGE BASE;
- an ADAPTATION MODULE performing adaptation on retrieved solutions.

The system can work in two distinct phases: a *training phase* and a *consultation phase*. In the training phase, the system is provided with a set of (unsolved) cases in order to acquire some initial experience. In this phase, every case is solved by the AID inference engine and it is suitably stored in the case memory. The consultation phase is characterized by the following inference cycle: when presented with a new case, the SUPERVISOR first invokes the CMM in order to retrieve the most similar cases from memory, then it tries to use the solutions of retrieved cases in order to focus the model-based reasoner in the search for the actual solution. In particular, a ranking of cases is obtained by taking into account a heuristic estimate of the adaptation effort for each retrieved solution (see section 4.1); solutions with lowest cost are then passed to the adaptation module that makes use of suitable criteria which will be discussed in section 4.2. If adaptation fails, the control is switched to AID for solving the case from scratch[3].

4.1 Retrieval and Ranking of Cases

Case retrieval occurs by matching norms and following indices (see [10] for details). During retrieval the system can ask for additional data to the user; in particular, when there is no possibility of retrieving cases from a given E-MOP, the user is asked to provide values for some of the indices to be followed from the E-MOP (using a term borrowed from [6], this represents a kind of "discrimination strategy"). Moreover,

---

[3] More opportunistic strategies, choosing between turning control to AID or trying to adapt other solutions, are currently under study.

if a retrieved case has a solution involving contexts that are necessary to explain its observations, but are unspecified in the current case, the user is requested to provide a value for such contexts. In particular, it is possible to classify two different values of the same context as *slightly* or *totally incompatible*; if the value provided by the user is either exactly that present in the retrieved case C or it is slightly incompatible with that of C, then C is taken into account, by suitably weighting the possible incompatibility (see below); if the value provided by the user is totally incompatible, then C is not considered for adaptation.

Once a set of cases similar to the current one has been retrieved, the adaptation module should be provided with the most promising solutions. We have devised a heuristic function able to rank each solution of the retrieved cases according to the estimate cost of adaptation for solving the case under examination. This heuristic is associated with each solution S of a retrieved case C and it is based on a subdivision of manifestations into different classes. If the current case C' is characterized by $\langle CXT', OBS' \rangle$ and a case $C = \langle CXT, OBS, SOL \rangle$ is retrieved and $CXT = CXT'$ or CXT is slightly incompatible with CXT', we define the following partitioning of ground manifestations for each retrieved solution $S \in SOL$:

1. $O_{COMMON} = \{m(a) | m(a) \in OBS' \text{ and } m(a) \in \mu(S, C)\}$.
2. $O_{NEW} = \{m(a) | m(a) \in OBS' \text{ and } \not\exists m(b) \in \mu(S, C) \text{ for any value } b \text{ admissible for the manifestation } m \}$.
3. $O_{CONFLICT} = \{m(a) | m(a) \in OBS' \text{ and } \exists m(b) \in \mu(S, C) \text{ and } b \neq a\}$
4. $O_{RETRIEVED} = \{m(a) | m(a) \in \mu(S, C) \text{ and } \not\exists m(b) \in OBS' \text{ for any value } b \text{ admissible for the manifestation } m\}$.

The above partitioning reflects the different work needed in adapting a solution; in particular, manifestations contained in O_{NEW} should be explained (if required) since the retrieved solution does not account for them; manifestations in $O_{CONFLICT}$ require even more adaptation work since they represent points of conflict between the new case and the retrieved one (see section 4.2). We then introduce a heuristic function h_A (A stands for adaptation) intended to give a numerical score to retrieved solutions, trying to measure the adaptation effort they require. Such a function is defined as a linear combination of the cardinalities of O_{NEW} and $O_{CONFLICT}$, since the contribution of O_{COMMON} and $O_{RETRIEVED}$ to the estimate cost of adaptation can be defined to be 0. In particular, as we will see in section 4.2, there are two basic adaptation mechanisms: *inconsistency removal* and *explanation construction* (or *covering*). Let ρ be the (estimated) cost of inconsistency removal and γ be the (estimated) cost of the step of covering; for manifestation instances in $O_{CONFLICT}$ we consider 4 cases:

(i): $m(a) \in OBS'$ must be covered and $m(b) \in \mu(S, C)$ was covered;
(ii): $m(a) \in OBS'$ must be covered and $m(b) \in \mu(S, C)$ was not covered;
(iii): $m(a) \in OBS'$ must not be covered and $m(b) \in \mu(S, C)$ was covered;
(iv): $m(a) \in OBS'$ must not be covered and $m(b) \in \mu(S, C)$ was not covered.

The following coefficients are then computed:

$$\forall m(a) \in O_{CONFLICT}, \quad \alpha_{CONFLICT}(m(a)) = \begin{cases} \rho + \gamma & \text{if } (i) \\ \gamma & \text{if } (ii) \\ \rho & \text{if } (iii) \\ 0 & \text{if } (iv) \end{cases}$$

$$\forall m(a) \in O_{NEW}, \quad \alpha_{NEW}(m(a)) = \begin{cases} \gamma & \text{if } m(a) \text{ must be covered} \\ 0 & \text{otherwise} \end{cases}$$

We also choose to weight with a different factor δ the presence of a context slightly incompatible with the new case; let $SI(S)$ be the set of contextual information of solution S slightly incompatible with those of the new case C', then the heuristic function for S is defined as

$$h_A(S) = \sum_{m(a) \in O_{CONFLICT}} \alpha_{CONFLICT}(m(a)) + \sum_{m(a) \in O_{NEW}} \alpha_{NEW}(m(a)) + \sum_{c_i \in SI(S)} \delta$$

Function h_A is used for ranking the retrieved solutions and to select the one for which this heuristic function is minimum. The selected solutions are then considered for adaptation[4].

4.2 Adaptation Mechanisms

The ADAPTATION MODULE can be considered as a "focusing" module for the model-based reasoner, guiding the latter, by means of its adaptation strategies, in choosing the suitable inference control strategy (see also [11]). Rather that using such inference strategies in an uncontrolled way, the model-based reasoner is focused to work on the selected retrieved solutions. More precisely, the adaptation strategy is based on the activation in sequence of the following mechanisms: *consistency checking, inconsistency removal* and *explanation construction* (or *covering*). Given a retrieved solution S, the first step is performed by comparing the set Ψ^- with the manifestations under examination. If consistency is verified, S can be used as a potential solution for the current case and further work of adaptation is needed only if the user requires the covering of manifestations not accounted for by S. If an inconsistency is pointed out, then consistency must be re-established by the step of inconsistency removal; this mechanism disproves the explanation leading to the discovered inconsistency, by removing instances of states and/or manifestations (see the example at the end of this section). The covering mechanism builds abductive explanations for entities to be accounted for. It stops as soon as a state of the retrieved solution not disproved by the step of inconsistency removal is reached. In this way the amount of search for determining an abductive explanation is reduced.

Consider the model reported in section 3.1 and suppose that the case under examination is characterized by the following set of observed parameters:
$OBS_1 = \{vibr(very\_strong), owli(red), htin(red), exsm(clear)\}$
and by the contextual information $engi(running)$. Let us also suppose to retrieve from the case memory, the case of figure 2[5].
Notice that $O_{CONFLICT} = \emptyset$, $O_{COMMON} = \{owli(red), htin(red), exsm(clear)\}$,

---

[4] In case the heuristic function h_A is not able to discriminate, we take into account another heuristic function h_S (S stands for similarity) based on O_{COMMON} and $O_{RETRIEVED}$ and intended to prefer the retrieved solution with 1) highest cardinality of O_{COMMON}; 2) smallest cardinality of $O_{RETRIEVED}$.

[5] Notice that, since in the case to be solved no information about the context $grcl$ is given, the system asks the user to provide such information; in this example we are considering the case when the user's answer is $grcl(low)$.

$O_{RETRIEVED} = \{oibc(huge\_amount)\}$ and $O_{NEW} = \{vibr(very\_strong)\}$. Since manifestations in the retrieved case differ from those in OBS_1, a consistency check occurs by constructing the set Ψ^- as follows:

$\Psi^- = \{vibr(normal), vibr(strong), owli(off), htin(off), htin(yellow),$
$exsm(grey), exsm(black)\}$

The consistency check succeeds and therefore the retrieved solution can be considered a solution also for the current case unless the user requires a stronger form of explanation based on covering. In case he/she does not, the cost of adaptation is estimated as $h_A = 0$ for the retrieved solution, meaning that no real adaptation is needed. Let us suppose now that a test concerning the presence of oil below car produces the additional observation $oibc(small\_amount)$. We get $O_{RETRIEVED} = \emptyset$, $O_{CONFLICT} = \{oibc(small\_amount)\}$ and we can immediately point out that the retrieved solution is no longer consistent with $OBS_2 = OBS_1 \cup \{oibc(small\_amount)\}$. The cost of adaptation is then estimated as $h_A = \rho + \gamma$ if $oibc(small\_amount)$ has to be covered and $h_A = \rho + 2\gamma$ if we also require the covering of O_{NEW}. The adaptation strategy starts with a first step of inconsistency removal, trying to disprove the explanation leading to $oibc(huge\_amount)$. By removing the assumption α_1, the state $oils(holed)$ and the manifestation $oibc(huge\_amount)$ become unsupported and consistency is re-established; however, also the state $laoi(severe)$ is not supported and so it must be explained in an alternative way in order to account for its direct manifestation $owli(red)$ and its consequences. By considering the logical model, $laoi(severe)$ can be explained through the conjunction of states $jerk(very\_strong)$ and $oils(leaking)$ (the latter explaining also the manifestation $oibc(small\_amount)$). If then the user provides the value $high$ for context $casp$, then the system can reconnect the explanation process with the retrieved solution (i.e. $roco(very\_poor)$ can be re-used) and the adaptation process can be completed, by explaining $oils(leaking)$ with $osga(very\_worn)$. No additional work is needed to explain $htin(red)$ and, as a side effect of the adaptation, also the manifestation $vibr(very\_strong)$ is explained even if not explicitly required (i.e. $h_A = \rho + 2\gamma$ is a pessimistic estimate).

5 Experimental Results

In order to test the approach implemented in ADAPtER, we have conducted some experiments on two different knowledge bases concerning a mechanical (car troubleshooting) and a medical (hanseniasis diagnosis) domain respectively. In this section we report on some preliminary results obtained by using the medical domain (the most significative one). A first kind of test we have performed concerns the evaluation of the heuristic h_A. We randomly selected 30 cases out of 70 available and we determined the adaptation effort needed to solve such cases, when the conceptual memory was containing the remaining 40 cases. The results are summarized in table 2, where each row represents the retrieved solutions on testing a specific case (some of the input cases where tested by considering different values for contextual information and, in the table, situations corresponding to only one retrieved solution are not shown). The columns "Time" represent the adaptation time for the corresponding solutions (NA means that adaptation has failed). It is worth noting that only in one case the ranking obtained according to h_A does not correspond to the

RETRIEVED SOLUTIONS													
SOL. 1		SOL. 2		SOL. 3		SOL. 4		SOL. 5		SOL. 6		SOL. 7	
h_A	Time	h_A	Time	h_A	Time	h_A	Time	h_A	Time	h_A	Time	h_A	Time
1.2	0.517	3.6	2.067	3.6	2.717								
3.6	1.817	3.6	2.017										
2.6	0.967	3.6	NA										
0.6	0.433	1.2	0.467	1.6	0.583								
0.6	0.433	1.2	0.512	1.6	0.567	2	NA						
1	0.533	1.2	0.567										
0.6	0.417	1.6	NA	2	NA								
0.6	0.450	1	<u>0.567</u>	1.2	<u>0.500</u>								
1	0.617	1.2	0.750	1.2	1.433	2.2	NA	3.6	NA				
0.6	0.467	0.6	0.467	0.6	0.467	1	0.483	1.6	0.550	2	NA	2	NA
1	0.483	1.6	NA	2	NA	2.6	NA	2.6	NA	3	NA		
0	0.067	1	0.533	1	0.500	1	0.417	1.6	NA	2.6	NA		
0	0.050	1	0.500	1	0.500	1	0.383	1	0.483	2	NA		
0.6	0.417	0.6	0.417	0.6	0.300	0.6	0.400	0.6	0.283	1	NA	1.6	NA
0	0.050	0.6	0.400	1.6	0.567	1.6	0.517	1.6	0.567	1.6	0.517	1.6	0.500
0.6	0.417	0.6	0.400	1.6	0.517	1.6	0.633	1.6	NA	1.6	0.617	2.6	NA
0.6	0.400	1.6	0.533	1.6	0.650	2.6	NA	3.6	NA				
0	0.050	1	NA										
0	0.050	0.6	0.417	0.6	0.433								
0	0.050	2	NA	2	NA								
0.6	0.467	1.2	0.483										
1	0.550	1.6	NA	2	NA	2.6	NA	3	NA				
1	0.550	1.6	NA	2	NA	2.6	NA	3	NA	4.6	NA		
0	0.050	0.6	0.500	1	NA	2	NA	2	NA				
0	0.067	0.6	0.483	1	NA	2	NA	2	NA	4.6	NA		
0	0.033	0.6	0.417	1	0.500	1.4	NA						
0.4	0.400	0.4	0.433	1.4	NA								
0.6	0.483	0.6	0.417										
1.4	0.567	1.4	0.667	2.6	NA	2.6	NA						

Table 2. Results from testing heuristic for adaptation

one obtained by comparing the adaptation time (see underlined items), therefore, h_A seems adequate for safely restricting the solutions to be adapted to the ones with lowest h_A.

So far the heuristic function h_A has been used for selecting the most promising case(s) to be adapted. By inspecting the results reported in table 2 it is apparent to see some form of correlation between the fact that the adaptation mechanisms fail in providing a solution (NA in the table) with the value of the heuristic function. An opportunistic strategy could decide to avoid the invocation of the adaptation module when the value of the heuristic function is large since this could indicate the difficulty (or impossibility) of the adaptation module of adapting the retrieved solution to the new problem. More experimental work is needed to test this hypothesis and to learn how to determine a threshold on the value of the heuristic function.

A second type of experiments we have performed was concerning the comparison between the performance of ADAPtER and AID in solving a given case. This time, we randomly selected 40 cases out of 60 (in the hanseniasis domain), that have been subsequently solved by ADAPtER through adaptation (using the remaining 20 cases in memory) and by AID from scratch. In particular, we distinguished the set of input cases according to the different kind of adaptation they need. The results are summarized in figure 4 where the time spent by AID and ADAPtER are shown

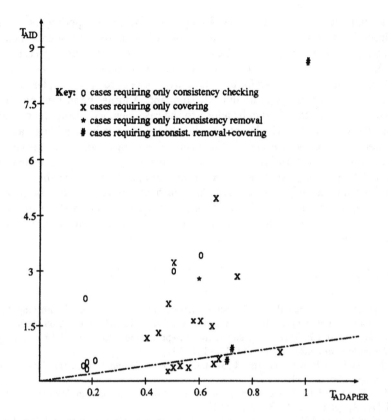

Fig. 4. Comparison between ADAPtER and AID

on the vertical and horizontal axis respectively (on a different scale)[6]. Points above the bisector represents cases for which ADAPtER has performed better than AID (and vice versa). For 11 cases ADAPtER was not able to retrieve any case from the memory (the number of stored cases was quite low), while for the remaining cases its performance can be considered in general satisfying; in particular, it was to be expected that ADAPtER performed better than AID in solving cases requiring only consistency checking and it should not be very surprising that, in some situations, the adaptation mechanisms could be computationally expensive, since they involve steps such as *explanation construction* (whose complexity could be exponential in the worst case) and/or *inconsistency removal* (that can disproves most, if not all, of the explanation associated with the retrieved solution).

A more general and comprehensive experimentation is in progress, with particular attention to the behavior of the integrated system with respect to the size of the case memory and to the comparison of the quality of the solutions it obtains with respect to those obtained by AID. Since the number of cases in the case memory

---

[6] All the timing measurements in the above experiments are given in seconds and are relative to the CPU time of a SUN Sparc station 10.

has an impact on the time needed for case retrieval, the experiments in progress are intended to test policies concerning cases to be stored in the case memory. In particular, during the training phase of the system we are storing cases not too complex (in terms of the interactions among DIAG-HYP) since they have better potential to be easily re-used for new cases with respect to very complex cases whose occurrence is very rare and are difficult to adapt. Another important parameter to be tested concerns the cases to be added to the case-memory during the consultation phase. We want to test the hypothesis that there is no gain in adding cases to the case-memory when a new case X has been solved via consistency checking of the solution associated to the retrieved case Y, since the new case X is essentially the same as Y. Similarly we expect that computational benefits can be obtained by adding to the case memory the cases for which no similar case has been retrieved or the adaptation mechanisms have failed to find a solution. In this case the MBR component solves the problem and the solution is saved in the case memory for a possible re-use.

References

1. L. Console, L. Portinale, D. Theseider Dupré, and P. Torasso. Combining heuristic and causal reasoning in diagnostic problem solving. In *[3]*, pages 46,68. 1993.
2. L. Console and P. Torasso. A spectrum of logical definitions of model-based diagnosis. *Computational Intelligence*, 7(3):133–141, 1991.
3. J.M. David, J.P. Krivine, and R. Simmons (eds.). *Second Generation Expert Systems*. Springer Verlag, 1993.
4. M.P. Feret and J.I. Glasgow. Experience-aided diagnosis for complex devices. In *Proc. AAAI 94*, pages 29–35, Seattle, 1994.
5. J. Kolodner and R. Kolodner. Using experience in clinical problem solving: Introduction and framework. *IEEE Trans. on Systems, Man and Cybernetics*, 17(3):420–431, 1987.
6. J.L. Kolodner. *Retrieval and Organization Strategies in Conceptual Memory: a Computer Model*. Lawrence Erlbaum, 1984.
7. P. Koton. Using experience in learning and problem solving. Technical report, MIT/LCS/TR-441, 1989.
8. D.B. Leake. Focusing construction and selection of abductive hypotheses. In *Proc. 13th IJCAI 93*, pages 24–29, Chambery, 1993.
9. D. Macchion and D.P. Vo. A hybrid KBS for technical diagnosis learning and assistance. In *Lecture Notes in Artificial Intelligence 837*, pages 301–312. Springer Verlag, 1993.
10. L. Portinale. Generalization handling in a dynamic case memory. In *Methodologies for Intelligent Systems*, pages 72–81. Lecture Notes in Artificial Intelligence 542, Springer Verlag, 1991.
11. L. Portinale, P. Torasso, C. Ortalda, and A. Giardino. Using case-based reasoning to focus model-based diagnostic problem solving. In *Lecture Notes in Artificial Intelligence 837*, pages 325–337. Springer Verlag, 1994.

Adaptation Using Constraint Satisfaction Techniques *

Lisa Purvis[1] and Pearl Pu[2]

[1] Dept. of Computer Science
University of Connecticut
U-155, Storrs, CT 06269
[2] Laboratoire d'Intelligence Artificielle & Robotique
Institut de Microtechnique / DMT
Swiss Federal Institute of Technology (EPFL)
MT-Ecublens, 1015 Lausanne, Switzerland

Abstract. Case adaptation, a central component of case-based reasoning, is often considered to be the most difficult part of a case-based reasoning system. The difficulties arise from the fact that adaptation often does not converge, especially if it is not done in a systematic way. This problem, sometimes termed the assimilation problem, is especially pronounced in the case-based design problem solving domain where a large set of constraints and features are processed. Furthermore, in the design domain, multiple cases must be considered in conjunction in order to solve the new problem, resulting in the difficulty of how to efficiently combine the cases into a global solution for the new problem.

In order to achieve case combination, we investigate a methodology which formalizes the process using constraint satisfaction techniques. We represent each case as a primitive constraint satisfaction problem (CSP) and apply an existing repair-based CSP algorithm to combine these primitive CSPs into a globally consistent solution for the new problem. The run time is satisfactory for providing a quick and explicable answer to whether existing cases can be adapted or if new cases would have to be created.

We have tested our methodology in the configuration design and assembly sequence generation domains.

1 Introduction

The domain of case-based reasoning (CBR) has received much attention as a viable and natural problem solving methodology for design, because the complexities of this domain often require past design experience in order to create effective new solutions. This past experience generally must be adapted to fit the new situation, since it is rare that an existing case exactly matches the demands of the new problem. Moreover, it is not enough to simply find one old case that is similar to a new situation and adapt from there. It is more likely that multiple cases contribute information that is necessary for solving the new problem.

* This research is sponsored by the National Science Foundation grant IRI - 9208429.

The solution to a new problem, then, results from merging the local solutions from previously solved problems to create a globally consistent solution for the new problem. However, the merging process is difficult since the local solutions typically exhibit conflicts when merged together. Furthermore, local solutions can be characterized by different representations, further intensifying the difficulty of synthesizing the global solution in an ad hoc way.

To overcome these problems, we investigate a methodology which formalizes the adaptation process using constraint satisfaction techniques. In our framework, each existing case is represented and stored in the case base as a solution to a primitive constraint satisfaction problem (CSP) with additional knowledge which facilitates retrieval and matching. The solutions to the primitive CSPs are combined into a globally consistent solution for the new problem using a repair-based CSP algorithm.

Our previous work [19] showed computational advantages over traditional methods when this case-based adaptation methodology is used to solve assembly sequence problems (ASP). The work described here further expands the applicability of the method to a larger class of problems by incorporating dynamic constraints into the CSP formulation and repair algorithm. This generalized formalism for case adaptation helps CBR systems achieve broader applicability and a better efficiency.

The rest of the paper is organized as follows: Section 2 reviews related work on case adaptation, Section 3 details the CSP formulation of cases, Section 4 describes the adaptation process itself, followed by current results in Section 5, and concludes with a summary and review of the key issues in Section 6.

2 Related Work

Adaptation can be described as the process of changing an old solution to meet the demands of a new situation [13]. Three important, well known adaptation methods are substitution, transformation, and derivational analogy methods. Substitution methods are used in the existing case-based design aids CHEF [9], JUDGE [1], and CLAVIER [10]. These methods choose and install a replacement for some part of an old solution that does not fit the current situation requirements. Transformation methods use heuristics to replace, delete, or add components to an old solution in order to make the old solution work in the new situation. Transformation methods can be found in the case-based system CASEY [14], in which transformation is guided by a causal model, and JULIA [11], which uses commonsense transformation heuristics to fix the old solution for the new problem context. Derivational analogy methods, found in ARIES [3] and PRODIGY/ANALOGY [4], use the *method* of deriving the old solution in order to derive a solution in the new situation [13].

Recently researchers have become interested in applying CBR techniques to the design domain [18]. Components of a design case often have strong relations among one another [13], and also tend to be large and therefore need to be decomposed to facilitate reusedoko93. Maher and Zhang [15] use an integration of case transformation and derivational analogies to tackle the adaptation problem in their system, CADSYN. Hua and Faltings combine multiple cases to achieve adaptation in their system, CADRE [12], where they observe that changing one feature during the adaptation process may result in non-convergent behavior for the adaptation algorithm.

3 CSP Formulation of Existing Cases

In our framework, existing cases are stored as primitive CSPs. A CSP consists of variables, values, and constraints. These CSP components are represented in a case as feature-value pairs. Along with the CSP variables, values, and constraints, a case also includes other characteristics in order to distinguish it during matching. Our cases allow not only static, but also dynamic constraints to be represented. Dynamic constraints are important in complex domains such as design, where the set of problem variables changes dynamically in response to decisions made during the course of problem solving.

Research on dynamic CSP can be found in the work of Bessiere [2], which describes an algorithm for computing arc-consistency for dynamic constraint satisfaction problems, Faltings [7], which explores dynamic constraint propagation in continuous domains, and Mittal and Falkenhainer [17], which identifies four types of dynamic constraints and implements them within an ATMS framework. Our research has implemented all four types of dynamic constraints identified in [17] within the minimum-conflicts CSP algorithm in order to extend the applicability of our adaptation methodology to all problems which can be described as either static *or dynamic* CSP's.

4 Adaptation

Adaptation is the process of changing an existing solution to fit the new context, thereby solving a new problem. The difficulties of doing adaptation in complex domains such as design prohibit its wide use in CBR systems. We attempt to formalize the adaptation process using CSP techniques. The general methodology for our approach is illustrated by Figure 1.

Cases which match portions of the new problem are retrieved from the case base, by first doing a structure mapping [8] using the spatial and geometrical features of each case to determine correspondences between variables of the old and new case, and then applying the nearest-neighbor similarity metric [13] to compute which of the structural matches are most similar. The matching cases contribute their constraints and solutions to form the new problem into a CSP, which is subsequently adapted using the minimum-conflicts adaptation algorithm to find a solution for the new problem.

The important pieces of information that are contributed by the existing cases are the *old solutions* and the *constraints*. Once a case has been identified as a match with the new problem, its variables and values can be used to initialize

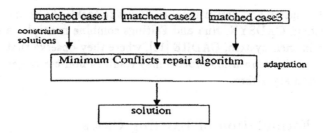

Fig. 1. Adaptation Methodology

the corresponding variables and values in the new case, thus providing guidance from past experience to help achieve a better CSP efficiency. In addition, the newly formed CSP obtains its constraints from the matched cases, thereby eliminating reliance on user input to determine the constraints, and reducing the significant computational burden necessary in other approaches in order to calculate the constraints from first principles. For dynamic design problems such as configuration design, the old cases also contribute the essential information about what variables compose the new problem; information that would not be available without the existing cases.

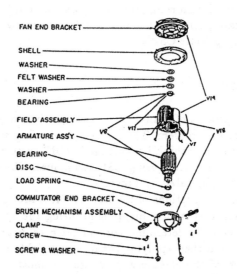

Fig. 2. Motor assembly

To illustrate in detail how the new problem is set up as a CSP, let us consider the assembly sequence problem of the motor shown in Figure 2 [6]. We will look at the correspondence between a subassembly of this new problem and the existing case for the receptacle shown in Figure 3.

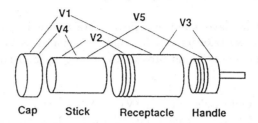

Fig. 3. receptacle

The constraints for the receptacle are such that the stick must be placed inside the receptacle either before the handle or before the cap is attached to the receptacle, otherwise there is no geometrically feasible way to insert the stick into the receptacle. This same principle can be found in a subassembly of the motor case, in that the armature must be placed inside the field assembly before either the fan end bracket or before the commutator end bracket is attached to the field assembly, otherwise there is no geometrically feasible way to insert the armature into the field assembly. This correspondence is found in our system by doing a structure mapping on the mating-relationship feature-values of the old and new case. From the structure mapping, we find the following correspondences between the old and new case:

HANDLE —⊱ COMMUTATOR-END-BRACKET
CAP —⊱ FAN-END-BRACKET
RECEPTACLE —⊱ FIELD-ASSEMBLY
STICK —⊱ ARMATURE
V3 —⊱ V18
V1 —⊱ V19
V2 —⊱ V7

Now, the nearest-neighbor similarity metric is applied using the correspondence information and the features' weights to determine whether the match is close enough to warrant using the old case as part of our new CSP. At this point, *all* of the case's features are considered, not just the mating-relationship features used during the structure mapping process. The more detailed case features allow a more accurate similarity score to be computed. In this example, additional case features of the receptacle case are:

(RECEPTACLE OPEN-CYLINDER 10)
(CAP BLIND-CYLINDER 10)
(HANDLE BLIND-CYLINDER 10)

Note that each of these detailed features has a weight of 10, out of a possible range from 1 to 10, indicating that each has significant importance to the case. In this example, the computed similarity measurement is large enough to warrant that the old case be used for the new CSP.

Now that we have found that the receptacle case is a match with part of our new problem, we take its solution and its constraints to set up the new CSP. The correspondences found provide the mapping information between old and new case.

> Old case's solution: (V1 1) (V2 2) (V3 3)
> Old case's constraint: (CONSTRAINT (OR (≺V2 V3) (≺ V2 V1)))

Since V3 from the old case corresponds to V18 from the new case, the initial value for V18 in the new problem is set to 3, which was V3's value in the old case. Similarly, the constraints for the new case are obtained by substituting the new variables for their corresponding variables in the old case's constraints.

> (CONSTRAINT (OR (≺ V7 V18) (≺ V7 V19)))
> (V19 1)
> (V7 2)
> (V18 3)

In this manner, each matching case contributes its constraints and solutions to the new CSP. The minimum conflicts algorithm is then applied to synthesize all of the primitive solutions into one globally consistent solution for the new problem. The minimum conflicts repair algorithm is illustrated by Figure 4.

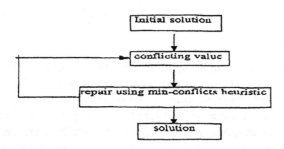

Fig. 4. Minimum Conflicts Repair Algorithm

The initial solution, made up of the primitive solutions found in the matching cases, is the starting point for the algorithm. A value that violates some of its constraints is chosen for repair from this initial solution, and repaired by finding a value for the variable which conflicts the least with the remaining values. Conflicting variable values continue to be repaired until there are no more conflicts, at which point we have found a solution to the new problem.

The empirical results for the algorithm reported in [16] showed that since the number of required repairs remains approximately constant as n grows, the algorithm's empirical time is approximately linear, as opposed to the exponential complexity of traditional constructive backtracking techniques. The effectiveness of the algorithm stems from using information about the current assignment to guide the search that is not available to standard backtracking algorithms. Our methodology capitalizes on the efficiency of the algorithm by providing it with a good initial solution based on the already solved cases in the case base.

Additional flexibility in our approach comes from the incorporation of *dynamic constraints* into the adaptation algorithm. We have modified the minimum conflicts algorithm in order to allow four types of dynamic activity constraints described in Mittal [17]. When a value is chosen for a variable, or a new variable becomes active in the problem, the activity constraints are tested using a forward-checking mechanism to identify any additionally required variables, and to eliminate any variables that are no longer required. This added flexibility has not only made the method more widely applicable, but also reduces the search space, and therefore provides a better efficiency from the minimum conflicts algorithm, as we will show in section 5 when detailing our results.

Let us now examine how a configuration design problem can be solved using our adaptation methodology. We will use the car configuration domain detailed in Mittal [17]. Consider two existing car configurations, represented in the case base as shown in Table 1.

Note that the cases include dynamic constraints: *RV* indicates a dynamic constraint meaning 'require variable', and *RN* indicates a dynamic constraint meaning 'require not' variable. Our new configuration problem is to configure a STANDARD, MODEL-80 car. We search the case base for cases with the requested characteristics, finding the two existing cases shown above. Case 1 matches the requested MODEL-80 feature, and Case 2 matches the STANDARD characteristic.

The variables and constraints related to the matched characteristics of the old case are used to set up the new CSP. Thus, from Case 1, all constraints having to do with MODEL-80 (C1, C2, C3, C4), and all variables encountered in those constraints (MODEL, FUEL-EFF, BODY, ENGINE, BATTERY) are added to the new CSP. Any constraints involving the added variables are also added (C7, since it involves FUEL-EFF). Any RV variables found in the added constraints are kept as reserve variables, in case any of the dynamic constraints later involve their activation. Thus, CONVERTER is kept as a reserve variable for the new CSP.

FEATURES	CASE #1	CASE #2
MODEL	model-80	model-70
STATUS	luxury	standard
FUEL-EFF	high	medium
BODY	convertible	hatchback
ENGINE	large	small
BATTERY	large	large
CONVERTER	cv1	
AIRCOND	ac2	
CD-PLAYER	sony	
DOORS		dr222
INSTRUMENT-PANEL		ip228
STEREO		st2
SEATS		s536
CONSTRAINT C1	(and (MODEL = model-80) (FUEL-EFF = high))	(and (BATTERY = small) (ENGINE = small)(RN CONVERTER))
CONSTRAINT C2	(and (MODEL = model-80) (RV BODY))	(and (STATUS = standard) (BODY ≠ convertible))
CONSTRAINT C3	(and (MODEL = model-80) (RV ENGINE))	(and (MODEL = model-70) (RV BODY))
CONSTRAINT C4	(and (MODEL = model-80) (RV BATTERY))	(and (MODEL = model-70) (RV ENGINE))
CONSTRAINT C5	(and (STATUS = luxury) (RV AIRCOND))	(and (MODEL = model-70) (RV BATTERY))
CONSTRAINT C6	(and (STATUS = luxury) (RV CD-PLAYER))	(and (MODEL = model-70) (RV DOORS))
CONSTRAINT C7	(and (FUEL-EFF = high) (RV converter))	(and (MODEL = model-70) (RV INSTRUMENT-PANEL))
CONSTRAINT C8		(and (MODEL = model-70) (RV SEATS))
CONSTRAINT C9		(and (STATUS = standard) (RV STEREO))

Table 1. Car configuration cases

Therefore, from Case 1, we have:

    (MODEL MODEL-80)
    (BODY CONVERTIBLE)
    (FUEL-EFF HIGH)
    (ENGINE LARGE)
    (BATTERY LARGE)
    (CONSTRAINT (C1 (AND (MODEL = MODEL-80) (FUEL-EFF = HIGH))))
    (CONSTRAINT (C2 (AND (MODEL = MODEL-80) (RV BODY))))
    (CONSTRAINT (C3 (AND (MODEL = MODEL-80) (RV ENGINE))))
    (CONSTRAINT (C4 (AND (MODEL = MODEL-80) (RV BATTERY))))

(CONSTRAINT (C7 (AND (FUEL-EFF = HIGH) (RV CONVERTER)))))
(Reserve Variable: (CONVERTER CV1))

The same process extracts the appropriate variables and constraints from Case 2:

(STATUS STANDARD)
(STEREO ST2)
(CONSTRAINT (C2 (AND (STATUS = STANDARD) (BODY ≠ CONVERT-IBLE))))
(CONSTRAINT (C9 (AND (STATUS = STANDARD) (RV STEREO))))

All of the extracted variables and constraints compose the initial solution to the new configuration design problem. The repair algorithm is now applied, finding that the dynamic constraint C7 from Case 1 is satisfied, and thus we add the reserve variable CONVERTER, along with its value CV1 to the problem. Furthermore, the repair algorithm finds that the value for BODY violates the constraint C2 obtained from Case 2. Thus, that value is repaired choosing a value for BODY that conflicts the least with the remaining values. A value of HATCHBACK is assigned to the variable BODY, resulting in a consistent final solution for the new configuration problem.

This example of a dynamic CSP illustrates how the existing cases not only provide the initial solution and constraints for the new problem, but also *formulate* the problem itself, by identifying the necessary problem variables.

5 Analysis and Results

Both configuration design using backtracking and assembly sequence generation have been characterized as NP-hard problems. Our intuition was that if a problem is hard to solve, then don't solve every one from scratch. In both domains, we found strong decompositional structures in the problems which allow application of old solutions to solve new problems. The computation time spent in adaptation is satisfactory compared to using conventional algorithms. Pu and Reschberger [20] and Pu and Purvis [19] discussed results of this framework applied in the domain of assembly sequence design. The work reported here showed that this framework can be further generalized to any discrete and static or dynamic configuration design problems. Response times for answering the question whether matched cases can be adapted to solve new problems are all within minutes.

To test the algorithm's performance against constructive backtracking, we tested using the well known n-queens problem as well as the assembly sequence design problem. These tests gave us positive confirmation that the minimum

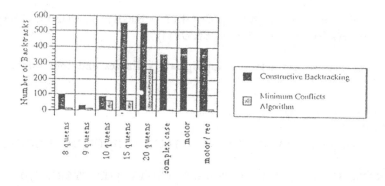

Fig. 5. Difference between constructive BT and min-conflicts algorithm

conflicts algorithm outperforms constructive backtracking, as can be seen in Figure 5.

To test the hypothesis that dynamic CSP outperforms static CSP, we formulated our assembly sequence design problems both in a dynamic representation as well as a static representation. We found that being able to remove variables from the problem dynamically improved performance significantly, as can be seen in Figure 6. This result corresponds to a similar result found by Mittal [17], in the configuration design domain.

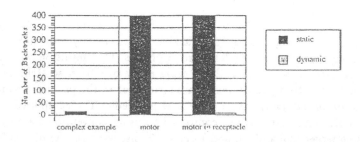

Fig. 6. Difference between static and dynamic min-conflicts algorithm

Finally, we tested whether the initial solutions taken from existing cases provide the minimum conflicts algorithm with more guidance than the minimum conflicts algorithm applied alone. As Figure 7 shows, the initial solutions do indeed provide more guidance and therefore less backtracks during the problem solving process.

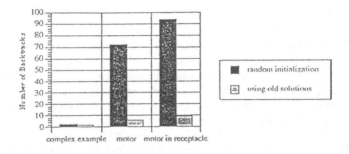

Fig. 7. Comparison of using old cases vs. random initialization

These experiments have confirmed the effectiveness of the minimum conflicts algorithm as a method by which to synthesize a global solution from several primitive solutions. Adding the possibility for dynamic constraints has improved its performance further, as well as extended its applicability, and the existing solutions from the case base provide the algorithm further guidance during the problem solving process.

6 Conclusion

CBR is becoming widely recognized as a viable problem solving methodology. It is being applied to a wide range of problem solving domains such as design, diagnosis, planning, customer technical support, legal reasoning, and education. Our methodology formalizes the case adaptation process in the sense of combining multiple cases in order to make the process applicable across varied application domains.

Our methodology uses the existing cases in order to cut down the necessary search space so that each new CSP does not need to be solved from the beginning. Incorporating constraint satisfaction techniques provides formalism to the approach which makes the methodology more widely applicable to any problem which can be represented as a discrete, dynamic or static CSP. In return, the case base provides important information about design variables, constraints, functionality, and characteristics which the CSP algorithm can capitalize on in order to provide efficient performance. Together, the CBR and CSP formalisms combine to provide a methodology for adaptation that will help CBR systems achieve a wider applicability and a better efficiency.

References

1. W. Bain. Judge. In R.C. Reisbeck, C.K.and Schank, editor, *Inside Case-Based Reasoning*. Erlbaum Publishers, 1989.
2. C. Bessiere. Arc consistency in dynamic constraint satisfaction problems. In *Proceedings of the 9th Nat. Conf. of AAAI, Anaheim*, 1991.
3. J.G. Carbonell. Derivational analogy: A theory of reconstructive problem solving and expertise acquisition. In *Machine Learning*, volume 1, 1986.
4. J.G. Carbonell and M.M. Veloso. Integrating derivational analogy into a general problem solving architecture. In *Proceedings: Workshop on Case Based Reasoning (DARPA) Clearwater, Florida*. Morgan Kaufmann Publishers, 1988.
5. Eric Domeshek and Janet Kolodner. Finding the points of large cases. *Artificial Intelligence in Engineering Design, Analysis and Manufacturing (AI EDAM)*, 1993.
6. W. Ewers. *Sincere's Vacuum Cleaner and Small Appliance Repair Service Manual*. Sincere Press, 1973.
7. B. Faltings, D. Haroud, and I. Smith. Dynamic constraint satisfaction with continuous variables. In *Proceedings of the European Conf. on AI, Wien*, 1992.
8. D. Gentner. Structure mapping: A theoretical framework for analogy. *Cognitive Science*, 7, 1983.
9. K. Hammond. Chef: A model of case-based planning. In *Proceedings of AAAI-86, Cambridge, MA*, 1986.
10. D.H. Hennessy and D. Hinkle. Applying case-based reasoning to autoclave loading. *IEEE Expert*, 7:21–26, 1992.
11. T.R. Hinrichs. *Problem solving in Open Worlds: A case study in Design*. Northvale Publishers, 1992.
12. Kefeng Hua and Boi Faltings. Exploring case-based building design - cadre. *Artificial Intelligence in Engineering Design, Analysis and Manufacturing (AI EDAM)*, 1993.
13. J. Kolodner. *Case Based Reasoning*. Morgan Kaufmann Publishers, 1993.
14. P. Koton. Reasoning about evidence in causal explanation. In *Proceedings of AAAI-88, Cambridge, MA*, 1988.
15. Mary Lou Maher and Dong Mei Zhang. Cadsyn: A case-based design process model. *Artificial Intelligence in Engineering Design, Analysis and Manufacturing (AI EDAM)*, 1993.
16. S. Minton, M. Johnston, A. Philips, and P. Laird. Minimizing conflicts: a heuristic repair method for constraint satisfaction and scheduling problems. *Artificial Intelligence*, 58:161–205, 1992.
17. S. Mittal and B. Falkenhainer. Dynamic constraint satisfaction. In *Proceedings of the 8th National Conference of AAAI*, 1990.
18. Pearl Pu. Issues in case-based design systems. *Artificial Intelligence in Engineering Design, Analysis and Manufacturing (AI EDAM)*, pages 79–85, 1993. As guest editor for a special issue on case-based design systems.
19. Pearl Pu and Lisa Purvis. Formalizing case adaptation in a case-based design system. In *Proceedings of the Third International Conference on Artificial Intelligence in Design (AID94)*, August 1994.
20. Pearl Pu and Markus Reschberger. Case-based assembly planning. In *Proceedings of DARPA's Case-based Reasoning Workshop*. Morgan Kaufmann, 1991.

Learning a Local Similarity Metric for Case-Based Reasoning

Francesco Ricci and Paolo Avesani

Istituto per la Ricerca Scientifica e Tecnologica
38050 Povo (TN)
Italy
email: {ricci,avesani}@irst.itc.it

Abstract. This paper presents a new class of local similarity metrics, called AASM, that are not symmetric and that can be adopted as the basic retrieval method in a CBR system. An anytime learning procedure is also introduced that, starting from an initial set of stored cases, improves the retrieval accuracy by modifying the local definition of the metric. The learning procedure is a reinforcement learning algorithm and can be run as a black box since no particular setting is required. With the aid of classical test sets it is shown that AASM can improve in many cases the accuracy of both nearest neighbour methods and Salzberg's NGE. Moreover, AASM can achieve significant data compression (10%) while maintainig the same accuracy as NN.

1 Introduction

Classification methods based on nearest neighbor (NN) have many advantages compared with other classification techniques. First of all, NN supports incremental learning from new cases without degradation in performance on previous training data. Moreover, NN methods work with an order of magnitude fewer parameters than back-propagation or radial basis function methods and are quite straightforward to implement.

Nevertheless classical NN methods have some negative points that limit their applicability. Classical NN methods exhibit poor generalization performance, suffer from the existence of noisy features, require big training sets and they suffer from the so called "curse of dimensionality". As the training set grows the run time performance of the system increases (see [9] for a large collection of papers on NN and his generalizations). These limitations have been addressed positively by a number of papers, which will be partially reviewed here, and are also the topic of our work.

NN methods are at the base of many implementations of case-based reasoning systems [25, 3, 24]. A training set in NN terminology is also called a case base, and an input to be classified is also called a probe case to be matched with the case base by the retrieval function. Both terminologies always will be adopted to stress the similarities between the two research areas. In a case-based reasoning framework our main goals may be stated as follows:

- Reduce the memory space required by the case base. The objective is to filter out cases in such a way that the accuracy of the system is not decreased (data compression).
- Speed-up on-line queries to the case base. This goal is related in some way to the previous one. NN algorithms usually have a linear time complexity with respect to the dimensionality of the case base. Therefore a reduction of the case base yields a proportional reduction in response time[1].

Researchers have recognized that many maladies of NN arise from the choice of the similarity metric, which is normally the classical Euclidean metric. First global modifications of the Euclidean metric have been considered and then a few researchers proposed local definition of the similarity metric [4, 5, 23]. A *global metric* is here defined as a simple generalization of the Euclidean metric, in this case a vector of weights is used to balance the contributions of different distances on the axes $(d(x,y) = (\sum_{i=1}^{N} w_i|x_i - y_i|^2)^{1/2})$. A *local metric* is a metric that depends on the point in the input space from which the distance is taken $(d(x,y) = (\sum_{i=1}^{N} w_i(x)|x_i - y_i|^2)^{1/2})$. Local metrics are context-sensitive [6], that is, similarity between cases depends also on the absolute value of feature values. Using a local metric one can express conditional expressions like "if feature A is greater that 70% then use only feature B and C to compute similarity". For instance, a local metric was used in a complex planning problem [7, 20] because an analysis of the domain knowledge raised the need of a context-sensitive similarity measure.

One of the basic tenets of our approach is that a local metric, which has been adapted to the problem domain, can lead to a significant reduction of the number of stored cases (data compression) and therefore to a substantial speed-up in run time performance. Moreover, adapting a local metric to an input space can also reduce the degradation of accuracy that is often associated with the introduction of irrelevant features.

This paper introduces a novel approach to compute nearest neighbor based on a local metric called AASM (asymmetric anisotropic similarity metric). This approach makes two basic assumptions. The first one (anisotropic) states that the metric is defined locally: the space around a case in memory is measured using the metric attached to that case. The second one (asymmetric) states that the distance between two points in a continuous feature space F_i is not symmetric, i.e., $d_i(x_i, y_i) \neq d_i(y_i, x_i)$. In fact two different weights for the "left" and the "right" directions are used per feature. In this way, as it is shown in a next section, one can more freely choose a representative in a set of cases that have to be commonly classified.

A reinforcement learning procedure [17, 14] also is provided for adapting the local weights to the input space. Our model basically implements an anytime algorithm that given an input case c decreases the distance between c and the nearest neighbor nn if nn correctly classifies c (reinforcement), and increases that distance if nn does not correctly classify c (punishment). A set of experiments

---

[1] Speed up can also be achieved compiling the case base in a k-d tree [25].

shows how a drastic reduction of the case base can be achieved, still maintaining the same accuracy of other methods.

Among the advantages of this new approach is the fact that AASM can be run as a black box without setting problem-specific parameters. Another advantage is that AASM can be assigned a fixed amount of memory and a fixed time to reply to a query. The system performs better and better as the amount of memory and the time to reply are increased. A drawback of our model is that for each case we need to store two additional vectors of the same dimension of the input space. We claim that this additional memory space is paid for by: a reduction of the cases needed to obtain the same accuracy of NN; an improvement in run time performance.

2 Previous Research

There are a number of generalizations of the basic nearest neighbor algorithm that address one of the points raised above: local metric, metric adaptation and case base reduction (data compression). A more extensive discussion of similar approaches and in particular of Learning Vector Quantization [13] can be found in [19].

Lowe [15] adopts a global metric and an optimization technique based on conjugate gradient method to optimize the similarity metric and the width of a Gaussian Kernel that is used to balance the contributions of k nearest neighbors. This method can cope with noisy features, but like others based on a global metric, it assumes that the noisy features are always the same in all the regions of the input space.

Cost and Salzberg [22, 8] use a global metric with an additional weight for each stored case, that measures how frequently the case was used to make a correct classification (prediction). Some cases are "generalized" by the learning process, i.e., they are replaced by the minimal hyperrectangle that contains that point. A hyperrectangle in $[0,1]^n$ is defined as: $H_{xy} = \{z \in [0,1]^N \mid z_i \in [min(x_i, y_i), max(x_i, y_i)] \ \forall \ i = 1, \ldots, N\}$. The distance between a point and a hyperrectangle is defined as the distance between a point and a set in Euclidean geometry, so for example if a point is inside a hyperrectangle the distance between them is zero. NGE uses a global definition of the metric weights but the metric is locally influenced by the dimension of hyperrectangles. Experimental results reported here, which were run on the same data sets used in [22], compare the accuracy achieved by EACH's learning procedure (Exemplar-Aided Constructor of hyperrectangles) with ours. A somewhat similar approach to generalization, which is exploited for rule induction, is also presented in [11].

Aha and Goldstone [4, 5] claim that an attribute's importance in human classification depends on its context and they provide a computational model that is able to generalize with results similar to those shown by experiments conducted with humans. One of the computational models proposed by the authors (GCM-ISW) uses an interpolation of local and global metrics. They show that GCM-ISW provides a better fit to the subject data than other methods with no local weights. Aha also introduced in [1, 2] an instance-based learning algorithm (IB4) that adopts a global metric and a non-parametric reinforcement learning strategy to incrementally change the weights. IB4's classification of an instance is decided by a vote among the k most similar instances and matches of instances in less frequent concepts yield larger adjustments of attribute weights.

3   Anisotropic and Asymmetric Metrics

Let C be a case space, $C = F_1 \times \ldots \times F_N$, where each F_i is the unit interval $[0, 1]$ or a set of symbols. Let us define a distance $d_i : F_i \times F_i \longrightarrow \mathbb{R}_{\geq 0}$ on each F_i with the following equation:

$$d_i(x_i, y_i) = \begin{cases} |x_i - y_i| & \text{if } F_i = [0, 1] \\ 0 & \text{if } F_i \text{ is a set of symbols and } x_i \neq y_i \\ 1 & \text{if } F_i \text{ is a set of symbols and } x_i = y_i \\ 0.5 & \text{if } x_i \text{ or } y_i \text{ is unknown} \end{cases}$$

These metrics on F_i spaces can be extended to a metric on C as usual: $d(x, y) = (\sum_{i=1}^{N} d_i(x_i, y_i)^n)^{1/n}$, where n is an integer greater than or equal to 1. This is the usual L^n metric on the product space C.

We shall now modify the Euclidean metric relaxing the symmetric condition $(d(x, y) = d(y, x))$ and enabling a different definition of the metric in different points of the case space. Let us first relax the symmetry of the metric d, we define a new metric $\delta_i : F_i \times F_i \longrightarrow \mathbb{R}_{\geq 0}$

$$\delta_i(x, y) = \begin{cases} p_i(x - y) & \text{if } x \geq y \\ q_i(y - x) & \text{if } x < y \end{cases}$$

where $p_i, q_i \in [0, 1]$ and $F_i = [0, 1]$. These two parameters are called the *left* and *right* weights of the i-th feature. A weighted metric can be defined also on a generic set of symbols but in this case an order relation could not always be defined, so we simply pose:

$$\delta_i(x, y) = w_i d_i(x, y)$$

where $w_i \in [0, 1]$. Let us suppose $\overline{C}$ be a subset of C. $\overline{C}$ represents the set of cases stored in memory. $\overline{C} = \{x_1, \ldots, x_M\}$ and for each $x_i = (x_{i1}, \ldots, x_{iN}) \in \overline{C}$ let $p_i = (p_{i1}, \ldots, p_{iN})$, and $q_i = (q_{i1}, \ldots, q_{iN})$ be two vectors in $[0, 1]^N$. Let us further suppose that $p_i = q_i$ if F_i is a set of symbols. The two matrices (p_{ij}) and (q_{ij}) are called a *System of Weights* for the case base $\overline{C}$. In other words a system of weights is a point in $[0, 1]^{2N|\overline{C}|} = W$.

We can now define an anisotropic and asymmetric metric on $\overline{C} \times C$, such that:

$$\delta : \overline{C} \times C \longrightarrow \mathbb{R}_{\geq 0}$$

$$\delta(x_i, y) = (\sum_{j=1}^{N} w_{ij} d_j(x_{ij}, y_j)^n)^{1/n}.$$

where

$$w_{ij} = \begin{cases} p_{ij} & \text{if } x_{ij} \geq y_j \text{ and } F_j = [0,1] \\ q_{ij} & \text{if } x_{ij} < y_j \text{ and } F_j = [0,1] \\ p_{ij} = q_{ij} & \text{if } F_j \text{ is a set of symbols} \end{cases}$$

So δ measures the distance between a point in the case base and a generic input. The following almost considers L^2 metrics, so we shall assume that $n = 2$ unless otherwise stated. The *retrieval function* (projection onto $\overline{C}$) on a case base C is defined as follows:

$$R_{\overline{C}} : C \longrightarrow \overline{C}$$

$$R_{\overline{C}}(y) = \overline{x} \text{ s.t. } \delta(\overline{x}, y) \text{ is minimum in } \overline{C}.$$

The retrieval function implements the basic nearest neighbor method: match a probe case with the most similar case in memory. Figure 1 shows a set of level

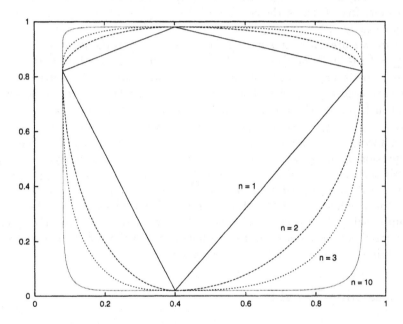

Fig. 1. Level curves for different values of p

curves for different values of n in a two dimensional space. Each curve is the set of points with distance 0.08 from point $(.4, .82)$ with different values for n. The weights chosen for the L^1 metric are $p_1 = .25$, $p_2 = 0.1$, $q_1 = 0.15$ and $q_2 = 0.5$. For $n = 2$ the weights are the square of the weights chosen for $n = 1$, for $n = 3$ they are the cube, and for $n = 10$ the weights are the tenth power of the weights chosen for $n = 1$. It is clear that for $n \to \infty$ the level curves tend to be rectangular[2].

---

[2] In fact L^∞ has the norm of the maximum: $d(x, y) = \max_i |x_i - y_i|$.

The retrieval function is generally used in a case-based system for approximation or classification purposes. Let D be a finite space[3], and let $G : C \longrightarrow D$ be a *goal function*. Let us suppose that G is known on $\overline{C}$, that is we know a correct solution for each case in $\overline{C}$. Here we want to approximate G on all the space C using its known definition on $\overline{C}$ and the retrieval function R. Let $\overline{G}$ be defined:

$$\overline{G} : C \longrightarrow D$$

$$\overline{G}(y) = G(R_{\overline{C}}(y))$$

In other words $\overline{G}$ maps a case y to the point (class/solution) that is mapped by the most similar case to y. Let us define the *accuracy* of a retrieval function $A = Prob[\overline{G}(y) = G(y)]$. If C is finite $A = |\{y \in C, \, | \, \overline{G}(y) = G(y)\}|/|C|$.

Allowing different weights for left and right directions in a local metric results in a more free choice of the cases in $\overline{C}$. Let us illustrate this point with a very simple example. Let us suppose $C = [0, 1]$, $D = \{0, 1, 2, 3\}$, $0 = a_0 < a_1 < a_2 < a_3 < a_4 = 1$ are five points in $[0, 1]$ and define $G(x)$ as the greatest k such that $a_k \leq x$ if $x \in [0, 1[$ and $G(1) = 3$. Suppose now that the case base $\overline{C}$ is composed of four points $\{x_1, \ldots, x_4\}$ with $a_{k-1} < x_k < a_k$. Using a symmetric metric we can have accuracy 1 provided that the four weights $\{w_1, \ldots, w_4\}$ (one for each point in $\{x_1, \ldots, x_4\}$) satisfy the three equations: $w_1(x_1 - a_1)^2 = w_2(x_2 - a_1)^2$, $w_2(x_2 - a_2)^2 = w_3(x_3 - a_2)^2$, $w_3(x_3 - a_3)^2 = w_4(x_4 - a_3)^2$. But, if for some reason w_1 changes, all the other weights have to change accordingly. Therefore, local adaptation of the weights is impossible. Conversely, using an asymmetric local metric the three equations on the weights become: $q_1(x_1 - a_1)^2 = p_2(x_2 - a_1)^2$, $q_2(x_2 - a_2)^2 = p_3(x_3 - a_2)^2$, $q_3(x_3 - a_3)^2 = p_4(x_4 - a_3)^2$. It is clear that in this case the weights are not linked as in a chain, and for example a change of q_1 requires only adaptation of p_2. Moreover in this case it is simpler to find out a "correct" set of weights because we have doubled the variables (weights) still maintaining the same number of constraints.

4 Learning Weights

We shall now present a procedure that, starting from a case base $\overline{C}$ and a system of weights w, iteratively changes the weights in w. The goal is to improve the accuracy of retrieval computed with respect to a given goal function G. A *learning step* is a map

$$T : W \times C \longrightarrow W$$

$$T : (p(n), q(n), y) \mapsto (T(p(n), y), T(q(n), y))$$

that maps a system of weights, defined at an instant n and a probe y in a new system of weights $(p(n + 1), q(n + 1))$ (see also [18] for more details on

---

[3] The extension to the approximation problem in infinite spaces will be considered in another forthcoming paper.

learning steps and learning procedures based on reinforcement). In the following, if $w = (p,q)$ is a system of weights we shall also indicate with $w' = (p',q')$ a system of weights obtained from w applying the transformation T. A *learning procedure* is an algorithm that iteratively chooses a case and calls the learning step on it until an exit condition is satisfied.

The following illustrates a particular learning step we have adopted and the results of our experiments. All our experiments adopt a very simple linear reinforcement scheme [17].

Let $w = (p,q)$ be a system of weights, $y \in C \setminus \overline{C}$ a probe case and $(p',q') = T(p,q,y)$. We shall now define the learning step. There may be two cases:

1. If $\overline{G}(y) = G(y)$ then we have:

$$p'_{ij} = T_{ij}(p_{ij}, y_j) = \begin{cases} p_{ij} - \alpha p_{ij}|x_{ij} - y_j| & \text{if } x_{ij} \geq y_j \\ p_{ij} & \text{if } x_{ij} < y_j \end{cases}$$

$$q'_{ij} = T_{ij}(q_{ij}, y_j) = \begin{cases} q_{ij} & \text{if } x_{ij} \geq y_j \\ q_{ij} - \alpha q_{ij}|x_{ij} - y_j| & \text{if } x_{ij} < y_j \end{cases}$$

if $F_i = [0,1]$.

$$w'_{ij} = T_{ij}(w_{ij}, y_j) = \begin{cases} w_{ij} - \alpha w_{ij} & \text{if } x_{ij} \neq y_j \\ w_{ij} & \text{if } x_{ij} = y_j \end{cases}$$

if F_i is a set of symbols.

2. If $\overline{G}(y) \neq G(y)$ then we have:

$$p'_{ij} = T_{ij}(p_{ij}, y_j) = \begin{cases} p_{ij} + \frac{\beta(1-p_{ij})}{1+|x_{ij}-y_j|} & \text{if } x_{ij} \geq y_j \\ p_{ij} & \text{if } x_{ij} < y_j \end{cases}$$

$$q'_{ij} = T_{ij}(q_{ij}, y_j) = \begin{cases} q_{ij} & \text{if } x_{ij} \geq y_j \\ q_{ij} + \frac{\beta(1-q_{ij})}{1+|x_{ij}-y_j|} & \text{if } x_{ij} < y_j \end{cases}$$

if $F_i = [0,1]$.

$$w'_{ij} = T_{ij}(w_{ij}, y_j) = \begin{cases} w_{ij} + \frac{\beta(1-w_{ij})}{2} & \text{if } x_{ij} \neq y_j \\ w_{ij} + \beta(1 - w_{ij}) & \text{if } x_{ij} = y_j \end{cases}$$

if F_i is a set of symbols.

$\alpha \in [0,1]$ and $\beta \in [0,1]$ are called the *reinforcement* and *punishment* rate respectively. We note that each learning step updates at most N parameters and maintains the weights in $[0,1]$. We can now define the learning procedure as a simple loop that after having initialized the system of weights[4], randomly chose a point in $(C \setminus \overline{C})$ (in fact we split $(C \setminus \overline{C})$ in two parts, one for training and another for test) and applies the T transformation on the system of weights using this point. The loop is terminated when an exit condition is satisfied. In all the experiments the process was stopped after a number of cycles proportional to the cardinality of $\overline{C}$ was completed.

---

[4] In all the experiments performed the weights were initially equal to .00001.

5 Experimental Results

We have conducted a set of experiments on four popular data sets[16]:

1. **Fisher's Iris Data Set.** This data set consists of four measurements made by E.Anderson on 150 samples of three species of iris [12]. Each example consists of four real-valued variables plus a known assignment of the example to a specie. This database doesn't have attributes with unknown values.

2. **Cleveland Data Set[5].** The Cleveland data set contains cardiological diagnoses [10]. The experiments with this data set aim to assess the occurrence of heart diseases. Each patient's record consists of 13 features (5 real-valued, 5 symbolic-valued, 2 boolean-valued). The goal is to distinguish the presence of heart diseases from the absence. The 303 instances are equally divided into the two classes.

3. **Breast Cancer Data Set[6].** This database contains 286 cases of patients who have been operated for tumor removal. Each example contains nine variables (6 symbolic-valued, 3 boolean-valued) that were measured plus a binary prediction: either the patient suffered a recurrence of cancer (30%) or not (70%).

4. **Echocardiogram Data Set.** Each example is a record for a patient who has had a heart attack. Some are still alive and some are not. The problem addressed by past researchers was to predict whether or not the patient will survive at least one year. The thirteen predictive attributes are all real-valued with meaningful occurrences of unknown values.

Fisher's Iris, Breast Cancer and Echocardiogram data sets were used, among others, by Salzberg to test NGE [22]. Wettschereck [26] compares a number of learning algorithms on different data sets, Fisher's and Cleveland data sets are two of those.

Table 1. Comparison of the accuracy, average memory size and average time to test obtained on different data sets by different algorithms

Data Set	Algorithm		
	AASM	EACH	NN
Breast Cancer	**66.0** 20 **1.73**	59.3 41.8 2.26	65.0 200 4.95
Iris	92.8 10 0.30	**93.8** 11.6 **0.26**	93.0 102 0.99
Echocardiogram	**70.0** 5 **0.11**	63.1 10.3 0.13	63.0 52 0.30
Cleveland	**76.5** 21 **3.21**	58.5 35.6 3.46	76.0 212 10.01

---

[5] The data have been provided by Robert Detrano from the V.A. Medical Center, Long Beach and Cleveland Clinic Foundation.

[6] The data have been provided by M. Zwitter and M. Soklic from the University Medical Centre, Institute of Oncology, Ljubljana, Yugoslavia.

For each data set 100 trials were executed subdividing the database into two parts: one for training, with 70% of the total database, and the other 30% for test. For each trial we have chosen a new random partition of the database and a different random set of seeds. The number of seeds both for NGE and AASM has always been taken as 10% of the training part and the seeds have been generated in such a way that each class has the same number of representatives in the set of seeds. The learning process in AASM was stopped after $10 * |TrainingSet|$ iterations of the learning step.

The results of these experiments[7] are shown in Table 1 and in Figure 2. Table 1 shows the accuracy obtained with different algorithms, the number of cases that were introduced into the memory ($|\overline{C}|$) and the average time for testing the classifier. The memory size does not change during learning for AASM, whereas it is equal to the final number of hyperrectangles generated by EACH algorithm. Our implementation of EACH is based on the generalization given in [26] and the parameters of the algorithm are set as Salzberg does in [22] ($\Delta_f = 0.2$). In particular the area of hyperrectangles is used to break ties when an input case has the same distance from two hyperrectangles[8]. Another important generalization concerns unknown values. In fact the original algorithm does not deal with both unknown features and symbolic features. The simbolic features are treated as in [26], but we decided to measure differently feature distance in the presence of unknow values. Our approach is similar to that used by Aha in [2], namely to assign feature distance equal to 0.5 when a feature value is unknown. While running our experiments we learned that EACH has to be tailored to the data set, and the configuration given by Salzberg is not always the best one. For example a little improvement in performance can be obtained in the Iris data set without updating the weights.

AASM has greater accuracy than NN in all data sets but Iris and uses 10% of the memory used by this last method. The comparison with NN is more clearly shown in Figure 2. Here the ratio of the accuracy obtained by AASM and that of NN is shown, with increasing values of the average number of times a training sample is presented to AASM. For Iris and Echocardiogram data sets AASM reaches (after 5 average sample presentations) more than 95% of the accuracy of NN, that stores in the memory all the training component. In the Breast Cancer and Cleveland data set AASM reaches a better accuracy than NN, only after each sample in the trial is showna couple of times on average.

AASM depends on two parameters, the reward and punishment factors α and β. A number of experiments were conducted with different pairs of values, but no significant differences were tested. All the data shown here were obtained with $\alpha = 0.2$ and $\beta = 0.1$. No particular procedure was used for reducinging the reward and punishment parameters as learning proceeds, but we expect to

---

[7] The experiments have been conducted using a public domain software written in LISP that is Copyright of Raymond J. Mooney (University of Texas at Austin). It includes automatic testing software for running learning curves that compare multiple systems and utilities for plotting and statistically evaluating the results.

[8] It is chosen that with minimal area.

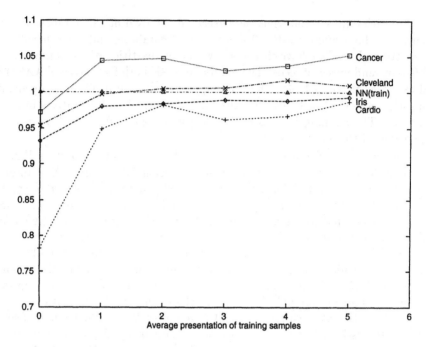

Fig. 2. Ratios of the accuracies of AASM and NN, with increasing average number of time each case is presented for training

improve the accuracy if the reward factor is gradually decreased after a first phase of learning, and the punishment is the only one to act in the second phase. Other experiments were also conducted, which cannot be shown here for lack of space, changing the cardinality of the initial set of seeds. The result is that accuracy increases with the cardinality of the set of initial seeds reaching an asyntotic value. So, applying these techniques one has to balance response times and accuracy choosing an appropriate number of initial seeds.

6   Conclusions and Future Directions

This paper presents a novel approach for learning a non symmetric local metric. The learning algorithm introduced here is based on a variation of the reinforcement/punishment paradigm. A set of experiments performed on standard datasets has shown that good data-compression can be achieved and therefore also good speed-up of run time (query retrieval) performance is obtained.

In the model presented in this paper the learning process starts with an initial set of stored instances (seeds). No method either for selecting a good initial set of seeds or for changing dynamically this initial set, as the training phase proceeds was discussed here. Moving the seeds in the input space would resemble other learning methods, for instance Learning Vector Quantization [13]. Significant improvements of our learning model may be attained as well by introducing a mechanism that dynamically changes the seeds, that is for deleting stored cases or adding new ones. That would provide a real incremental learning method with a capability to adapt to severe changes in the input space. Another improvement in the accuracy is expected when using a method for dynamically changing the punishment and reward parameters.

An application of the proposed techniques is ongoing on a real application domain whose main goal is to provide support for planning an initial attack to forest fires [21, 7, 20]. We are now acquiring a large case base that is being developed during simulated sessions with a domain expert. Among other advantages, the proposed technique for the automatic adaptation of the similarity metric will add great flexibility to the demonstrator and will simplify the porting of the demonstrator in a different context, for example for operating in a new operational region.

7   Acknowledgements

We would like to thank our anonymous reviewers for their insightful suggestions and remarks. Special thanks to David Aha for helpful discussions and ecouragement in pursuing this research. This paper benefited from the editing help provided by Susan Zorat. This work has been partially supported by the EspritIII project #6095 CHARADE (Combining Human Assessment and Reasoning Aids for Decision Making in environmental Emergencies). The partners of CHARADE are Alenia (prime contractor, Italy), Italsoft (Italy), Alcatel ISR (France), Inisel (Spain), ITC-IRST (Italy), Thomson-CSF/SDC and Thomson-CFS/LER (France).

References

1. D. W. Aha. Incremental, instance-based learning of independent and graded concept description. In *Proceedings of the Sixth International Workshop on Machine Learning*, Ithaca, NY, 1989. Morgan Kaufmann.

2. D. W. Aha. A study of instance-based algorithms for supervised learning tasks: Mathematical, empirical and psycological evaluations. Technical Report TR-90-42, University of California, Irvine, 1990.

3. D. W. Aha. Case-based learning algorithms. In *Proceedings of the 1991 DARPA Case-Based Reasoning WorkshopWorkshop 1991*, pages 147–158. Morgan Kaufmann, 1991.

4. D. W. Aha and R. L. Goldstone. Learning attribute relevance in context in instance-based learning algorithms. In *Proceedings of the Twelfth Annual Conference of the Cognitive Science Society*, pages 141–148, Cambridge, MA, 1990. Lawrence Earlbaum.

5. D. W. Aha and R. L. Goldstone. Concept learning and flexible weighting. In *Proceedings of the Fourteenth Annual Conference of the Cognitive Science Society*, pages 534–539, Bloomington, IN, 1992. Lawrence Earlbaum.

6. K. D. Ashley. Assessing similarities among cases: a position paper. In *Proceedings of a Workshop on Case-Based Reasoning*, pages 72–76, Pensacola Beach, FL, 1989. Morgan Kaufmann.

7. P. Avesani, A. Perini, and F. Ricci. Combining CBR and constraint reasoning in planning forest fire fighting. In *Proceedings of the first european workshop on Case-Based reasoning*, pages 235–239, Kaiserslautern, 1993.

8. S. Cost and S. Salzberg. A weighted nearest neighbor algorithm for learning with symbolic features. *Machine Learning*, 10:57–78, 1993.

9. B. V. Dasarathy, editor. *Nearest beighbour (NN) norms: NN pattern classification techniques*. IEEE Computer Society Press, Los Alamitos, CA, 1991.

10. R. Detrano, A.Janosi, W. Steinbrunn, M. Pfisterer, K. Schmid, S. Sandhu, K. Guppy, S. Lee, and V. Froelicher. Rapid searches for comples patterns in biological molecules. *American Journal of Cardiology*, 64:304–310, 1989.

11. P. Domingos. Rule induction and instance-based learning: a unified approach. In *Proceedings of the Fourteenth International Conference on Artificial Intelligence*, 1995.

12. R. A. Fisher. The use of multiple measurements in taxonomic problems. *Annals of Eugenics*, 7:179–188, 1936.

13. T. Kohonen. The self-organizing map. *Proceedings of the IEEE*, 78(9):1464–1480, Sept. 1990.

14. M. M. Kokar and S. A. Reveliotis. Reinforcement learning: Architectures and algorithms. *International Journal of Intelligent Systems*, 8:857–894, 1993.

15. D. G. Lowe. Similarity metric learning for a variable-kernel classifier. *Neural Computation*, 7:72–85, 1995.

16. P. M. Murphy and D. W. Aha. *UCI Repository of Machine Learning Databases*. University of California, Department of Information and Computer Science, Irvine, CA, 1994.

17. K. S. Narendra and M. A. Thathachar. *Learning Automata*. Prentice-Hall, 1989.

18. F. Ricci. Constraint reasoning with learning automata. *International Journal of Intelligent Systems*, 9(12):1059–1082, Dec. 1994.

19. F. Ricci and P. Avesani. Learning an asymmetric and anisotropic similarity metric for case-based reasoning. Technical report, IRST, Apr. 1995.

20. F. Ricci, S. Mam, P. Marti, V. Normand, and P. Olmo. CHARADE: a platform for emergencies management systems. Technical Report 9404-07, IRST, 1994.

21. F. Ricci, A. Perini, and P. Avesani. Planning in a complex real domain. In *proceedings of the italian planning workshop*, pages 55–60, Rome, 1993.

22. S. L. Salzberg. A nearest hyperrectangle learning method. *Machine Learning*, 6:251–276, 1991.

23. D. B. Skalak. Representing cases as knowledge sources that apply local similarity metrics. In *Proceedings of the Fourteenth Annual Conference of the Cognitive Science Society*, pages 325–330, Bloomington, IN, 1992. Lawrence Earlbaum.

24. C. Stanfill and D. Waltz. Toward memory-based reasoning. *Communication of ACM*, 29:1213–1229, 1986.

25. S. Wess, K.-D. Althoff, and G. Derwand. Using k-d trees to improve the retrieval step in case-based reasoning. In *Topics in Case-Based Reasoning, First European Workshop, EWCBR-93*, pages 167–181, Berlin, 1993. Spinger-Verlag.

26. D. Wettschereck. *A study of distance-based machine learning algorithms*. PhD thesis, Oregon State University, 1994.

Experiments On Adaptation-Guided Retrieval In Case-Based Design

Barry Smyth[1] and Mark T. Keane[2]

[1]Hitachi Dublin Laboratory, Trinity College, Dublin 2, IRELAND
{E-mail: barry.smyth@hdl.ie}

[2]Department of Computer Science, Trinity College, Dublin 2, IRELAND

Abstract. Case-based reasoning (CBR) has been applied with some success to complex planning and design tasks. In such systems, the best case is retrieved and adapted to solve a particular target problem. Often, the best case is that which can be most easily adapted to the target problem (as the overhead in adaptation is generally very high). Standard CBR systems use semantic-similarity to retrieve cases, on the assumption that the most similar case is the easiest case to adapt. However, this assumption can be shown to be flawed. In this paper, we report a novel retrieval method, called adaptation-guided retrieval, that is sensitive to the ease-of-adaptation of cases. In the context of a CBR system for software-design, called Déjà Vu, we show through a series of experiments that adaptation-guided retrieval is more accurate than standard retrieval techniques, that it scales well to large case-bases and that it results in more efficient overall problem-solving performance. The implications of this method and these results are discussed.

1 Introduction

Most case-based reasoning (CBR) systems replace a first-principles problem-solver with cases and knowledge-weak adaptation rules to modify these cases. The success of such systems depends on selecting the best possible case during retrieval. The majority of CBR systems retrieve cases using semantic-similarity metrics; the assumption being that the most semantically-similar case to the target problem will be the most useful and easiest to adapt. However, this assumption is often flawed; the most similar case may *not* be the easiest to adapt and may even be impossible to adapt.

This realisation has led some researchers to augment semantic similarity with other factors. Kolodner [1] proposed that some mappings between a target problem and a candidate case should be preferred over others if they were, for example, more *specific* or *goal-directed*. She also argued that "easily-adapted" matches should be preferred over "hard-to-adapt" matches. Goel's KRITIK system [2] also prefers candidate design-cases that satisfy the functional specifications of the target design and hence have easily-adaptable matches. Birnbaum, Collins, Brand, Freed, Krulwich & Pryor [3] proposed a system that learns to index cases on the basis of their adaptability, overriding semantic similarity where appropriate, a proposal that has been implemented by Fox & Leake [4]. Their system avoids cases with feature combinations that were difficult to adapt in previous problem-solving episodes. Leake's [5] method of constructive similarity also addresses the fundamental importance of adaptability in case retrieval. Cases matched is not viewed as from the viewpoint of known and fixed base and target feature sets, but is instead viewed as an elaborative process where initial target features are refined and elaborated in order to meaningfully link them to a base case.

We agree with the spirit of these proposals but favour a different solution. The above systems involve an across-the-board promotion (or demotion) of certain matches based on their *likely* rather than their *actual* ease-of-adaptation. They make an "educated guess" as to the adaptability of cases rather than a detailed assessment of their adaptation requirements. We advance a novel technique, called *adaptation-guided retrieval* (AGR), that assesses the adaptation requirements of cases during retrieval. AGR makes direct use of specially-formulated adaptation knowledge to determine simple surface-changes, structural transformations, and complex interactions [6]; our integration of adaptation knowledge into retrieval is influenced by techniques used to introduce other forms of domain knowledge into retrieval [7,8]. Furthermore, AGR works without incurring the full cost of adaptation during retrieval. Indeed, AGR can be more efficient than standard methods in CBR.

AGR is implemented in Déjà Vu, a case-based reasoning system for software design (see section 2). In section 3, we show how adaptation-guided retrieval works; how cases are selected based on their adaptation requirements and how subsequent adaptations are predicted during retrieval. In section 4, we present experimental evidence to demonstrate some of the performance and competence advantages offered by adaptation-guided retrieval.

2 Déjà Vu & The Plant-Control Domain

Déjà Vu is a case-based reasoning system for software design boasting two main novelties. Firstly, it uses adaptation-guided retrieval. Secondly, it integrates case-based and decompositional design methods by imposing a hierarchical structure on the case-base such that complex problems are represented as hierarchies of cases at varying levels of abstraction. The primary application domain of Déjà Vu is plant-control software design. Plant-control programs regulate the action of autonomous vehicles within real industrial environments.

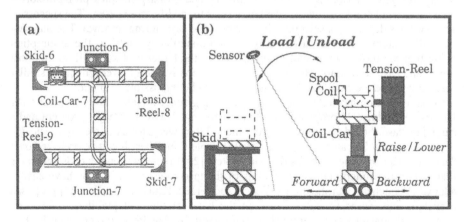

Fig. 1. (a) Track Layout; (b) Load/Unload Task Schematic

The examples in this paper are taken from a steel mill environment where a system of track-bound vehicles (called coil-cars) load and unload spools and coils of steel. Figure 1(a) illustrates a sample plant layout and 1(b) a schematic of a basic Load/Unload task with a coil-car, a mill (tension-reel), a loading-bay (skid), and a spool or coil of steel.

Déjà Vu's decompositional design component enables complex problems to be broken up into simpler tasks by the retrieval of abstract cases. Actual solution code is then produced by the retrieval and adaptation of the appropriate design cases with the resulting solution segments being integrated into the overall solution structure on the fly (unfortunately Déjà Vu's decomposition component is beyond the scope of this paper and the interested reader is referred to [9]). Problem solving activity is co-ordinated using a blackboard architecture with dedicated knowledge agents handling such tasks as indexing, retrieval, adaptation, decomposition, and integration.

3 Adaptation-Guided Retrieval

Déjà Vu retrieves the best case by determining the adaptation requirements of candidate cases during retrieval. In this section, we outline Déjà Vu's adaptation component, how AGR works and present some examples of its use.

3.1 Déjà Vu's Adaptation Component

Déjà Vu's adaptation component adapts candidate cases using two forms of knowledge: (i) *adaptation specialists* to perform specific, local modifications to cases, and (ii) *adaptation strategies* to solve problematic interactions within cases.

```
SPEED-SPECIALIST*1

Capability

  (:TASKS        Move)
  (:MAPPINGS     ((VEHICLE CONSTRAINT-SPEED Target-Speed?)
                  (VEHICLE CONSTRAINT-SPEED Base-Speed?)))
  (:TESTS        (eq Target-Speed? 2-SPEED)
                 (eq Base-Speed?   1-SPEED))

Action
  (INSERT-COMMAND
    (Def-Command Move <vehicle> Fast <direction>)
    :BEFORE
      (Def-Command Move <vehicle> Slow <direction>))
  (INSERT-COMMAND
    (Def-Command Distance-Check <vehicle>
                                <slowing-distance>
                                <orientation>
                                <destination-location>)
    :BEFORE
      (Def-Command Move <vehicle> Slow <direction>))
```

Fig. 2. A Speed Specialist

Adaptation specialists correspond to packages of design transformation knowledge concerned with a specific adaptation task. Each specialist can make specific, local modifications to a retrieved case. For instance, in the plant-control domain, retrieved "move" cases often differ from a target problem in the speed of the coil-car (one- or two-speed). So, Déjà Vu has a dedicated *speed specialist* to modify the coil-car speed in retrieved cases to meet the appropriate target specifications (see Figure 2). Specialists contain two parts: (i) *capability* - information describing the nature of the adaptation task (e.g., the specialist in Figure 2 is designed to alter the speed constraint of a movement task from 1-speed to 2-speed). (ii) *action* - the procedural know-how needed to perform a particular kind of adaptation (e.g., to upgrade the speed of a case a number of additional solution nodes must be added to the 1-speed solution chart). In short, the capability information describes *what* must be adapted and the action information describes *how* this adaptation can be carried out. As we shall see, it is the capability information that allows specialists to be used during retrieval. During adaptation many specialists may act on the retrieved case to transform it into the desired target design. Thus, through specialist activity, the differences between the retrieved case and the target are reduced in a piecemeal fashion.

Adaptation strategies deal with interactions that arise during the adaptation of a case by the specialists. Specialists are local and therefore ignorant of global interactions between case elements that may lead to problem-solving failures; interactions cause problems in many planning and automated design systems. Déjà Vu's adaptation strategies detect and repair different classes of interactions that arise. The strategies are organised in terms of the interactions they resolve and each is indexed by a description of the type of failure it can repair. Each strategy also has a set of repair methods for fixing a particular interaction.

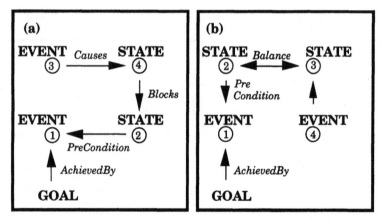

Fig. 3. (a) Blocked-Precondition; (b) Balance-Interaction

For example, one common interaction involves the effect of one event preventing the occurrence of a later event. Figure 3(a) depicts this situation; a goal event (1) is prevented by the disablement of one of its preconditions (2), the precondition having been blocked by some earlier event (3) causing a conflicting state (4). This *blocked-precondition interaction* could occur when the speed of a coil-car is increased (during adaptation), causing a power availability problem that results in the coil-car running out of power (power being a precondition of the movement goal). This interaction can be repaired by adding an event before the blocking event (3) that prevents its blocking effect; for example recharging the coil-car before initiating the move. The blocked pre-condition adaptation strategy contains a description of this situation along with appropriate repair methods.

Another type of interaction, a *balance-interaction*, can occur when the value of one state is proportionally dependent on another (see Figure 3(b)). Here, some necessary goal-achieving event (1) has a precondition state (2) that depends on another state (3) that has resulted from some other event (4). For example, before moving a coil-car across the factory floor the height of the carrying platform must be adjusted to accommodate the load being transported; there is a balance condition between the height of the lifting platform and the diameter of the coil of steel being carried. If this balance is not properly maintained then a failure may occur (the coil-car may collide with an overhead obstacle).

The system currently uses 10 strategies to deal with all the interaction problems that arise in the plant-control domain. Our investigations suggest that many of these strategies are applicable to other domains, although other new ones may also be required. Hammond's CHEF [10] uses similar types of knowledge to identify failures during recipe generation and as index features to signify failure conditions.

3.2 The Adaptation-Guided Retrieval Procedure

Table 1 shows the three-stage process used to determine the adaptation requirements of cases during retrieval. *Candidate Selection* is a base-filtering stage that quickly eliminates irrelevant cases from further consideration. Basically, it removes any cases that have no specialists in common with the target specification. This stage treats all adaptable features as equally relevant and simply locates cases that are potentially adaptable to the target situation.

Input: T,   a target specification; CB, a case-base
            AK,   adaptation knowledge
Output: C,   the most "adaptable" case
            AK',   its relevant adaptation knowledge

1. **Candidate Selection**
   1.1 Locate candidate cases (CB') with target adaptable features
   1.2 For each candidate, collect its specialists.

2. **Assessing Local Adaptability**
   2.1 **Compute Case Coverage** --
       Map target and case features that are adaptable and remove any case that
       leaves some portion of the target unmapped (uncovered).
   2.2 **Compute Local Adaptability** --
       Estimate the complexity of each case's local adaptation requirements in terms
       of the relevant specialists.

3. **Assessing Global Adaptability**
   3.1 **Find Applicable Strategies**-- For each case collect applicable strategies.
   3.2 **Compute Global Adaptability** --
       Estimate the complexity of each case's global adaptation requirements
       (interaction problems) in terms of the strategies.

Table 1. The Adaptation-Guided Retrieval Procedure

In the *Assessment of Local Adaptability* the target's features are aligned (or mapped) with those of candidate cases. A feature mapping is only constructed if it is deemed adaptable, that is if there is a specialist to support the mapping. Briefly, a case is said to *cover* the target if some feature of the case can map on to each relevant feature of the target and if all of these mappings are adaptable. A local adaptability metric is applied to the remaining cases to estimate their ease of adaptation in terms of their applicable adaptation specialists.

Finally, during the *Assessment of Global Adaptability* the strategies that are applicable to each of the remaining candidates are determined and a second metric is used to grade these cases according to the different repair methods that are suggested by each strategy. Exactly how strategies are determined is beyond the scope of this paper. In brief, it is similar to the determination of specialists in that each strategy has capability information (a set of features) that describes when a certain type of failure is likely to occur. In this way strategies are coded up to recognise certain special-purpose interactions -- more general techniques are likely to be prohibitively expensive and were judged to be unnecessary in this domain where only certain types of interaction problems tend to occur. Different strategies are differentially weighted according to the amount of change their repair strategies incur. Some repair methods will significantly reorder a proposed solution whereas others may just require a simple deletion of an existing goal structure. Overall, the candidates are ordered according to both their local and global adaptability and the case that minimises both measures is chosen.

The output of the retrieval stage is a ordered set of candidate cases, their feature mappings, and the adaptation specialists and strategies applicable to each candidate. So, AGR is unlike conventional retrieval methods which simply return the chosen case, the feature mappings, and a similarity measure, with no support for adaptation and repair.

3.3 An Example

The following example works through a sample retrieval session taken from the plant-model of Figure 1(a). The target problem is to move coil-car-7 from tension-reel-9 to skid-7 using 2-speed motion carrying coil-1, a coil of steel and the case memory contains just a single case for moving a coil-car from tension-reel-8 to skid-6 using 1-speed motion, and carrying no load. The adaptation knowledge consists of a number of specialists designed to cater for transformations involving speed, direction, start and end locations, and the contents of vehicles in movement tasks. Two strategies are relevant; the blocked-precondition strategy and the balance-interaction strategy, both mentioned above.

Figure 4 is a representation of the types of structures built during retrieval. Since the target and base differ in terms of speed, direction, locations, and vehicle content, a variety of relevant specialists are activated and shown. A number of points are worth noticing here. First, only *relevant features* (i.e., features that are adaptable) partake in the mapping process. This contrasts with many knowledge-weak retrieval methods that *have to* consider the mapping of all specified problem features[1]. As a result adaptation-

---

[1] One could of course build in some notion of relevance or context and many existing systems do use such techniques to greatly improve retrieval performance. However it is our contention that rather than building separate models of relevance, adaptation knowledge should be used, since after it is adaptability that we are trying to measure.

guided retrieval computes significantly fewer mappings than other methods. Secondly, at this early stage non-adaptable cases can be identified and eliminated. For example, if a speed specialist did not exist then Déjà Vu would have no alternative but to find a different case, namely one that matched exactly on speed.

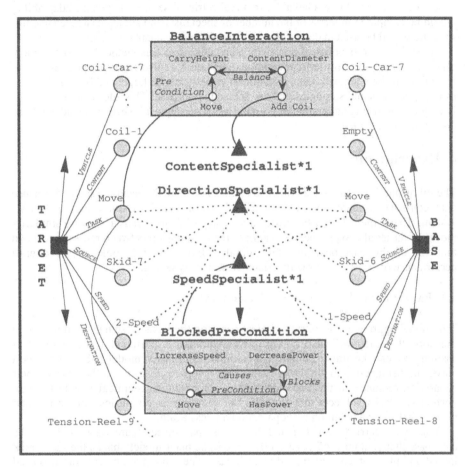

Fig. 4. Retrieval Snapshot

In this example, when the specialists are applied (during adaptation) further problems in the form of blocked-preconditions and balance-interactions arise (see Figure 4). For instance, the content-specialist is set to change the base solution so that the target coil-car is carrying the target coil. However, there is a balance condition between the coil diameter and the carrying-height of the coil-car. This is detected at retrieval time because the content-specialist is known to affect a balance-state feature. Consequently, the balance-interaction strategy is stored with the applicable specialists. The speed specialist also results in a problematic interaction. A pre-condition of movement is that power be available to the coil-car. An effect of the speed-specialist is that the power consumption of the coil-car will increase and possibly lead to the lack of power, thereby blocking the movement pre-condition. Again this is spotted during retrieval and the blocked-precondition is also marked as applicable. In conclusion, the base case is judged to be adaptable. In a real retrieval session its precise adaptability would be computed in terms of the number of specialists and strategies needed and this measure would be used to discriminate among alternative adaptable cases.

Apart from the benefits of retrieving adaptable cases this method also offers more that just a case and a similarity measure to adaptation. It also offers a representation of the nature of the similarities and dissimilarities between the target and base in the form of the specialists and strategies that are deemed applicable. This additional knowledge is very useful during adaptation in pointing out precisely *what* needs to be adapted and *how* it may be adapted.

4 Experiments

The following three sets of experimental data demonstrate the accuracy and performance characteristics of adaptation-guided retrieval. All of them were run using the Déjà Vu system. Experiment 1 tests the retrieval accuracy of AGR versus a standard similarity model of retrieval. Experiment 2 examines the relationship between retrieval cost and the size of the case-base in AGR. Finally, Experiment 3 looks at the overall performance of AGR compared to a standard similarity model.

4.1 Experiment 1: Accuracy of Retrieval

Traditional approaches to retrieval select cases on the basis of semantic similarity in the hope that they will also be the most adaptable. Experiment 1 shows that this assumption can be unwarranted. The standard similarity model (SS) used was a classical, distance-based similarity metric that compares features on the basis of their separation distance in the knowledge-base; for example, identical matches obtain perfect similarity, objects that shared a common parent obtain less similarity, and objects that share a common grandparent obtain less again.

Trials were carried out with two different case-bases (see Figure 5(a)). Trial 1 used a case-base that contained 45 cases all from the same plant-model; that is, the same track layout and plant objects were used in each case. The same plant model was also used for the 45 target problems of the first trial (see e.g., Figure 1). The most adaptable case in the case-base was computed for each target problem. The accuracy of the two retrieval methods was then measured for the 45 targets. The results showed that AGR selected the most adaptable case 100% of the time whereas the SS method was only accurate 70% of the time; this difference was statistically significant (see Trial 1 in Figure 5(a); $chi^2(1) = 14.295$, $p < .0001$).

In the second trial, we used a case-base containing 120 cases involving 8 different plant-models. Various plant models were also used in the 45 target problems employed. The SS method fares even worse on this more realistic case-base; AGR was still 100% accurate, but SS decreased to 12% (see Trial 2 in Figure 5(a); $chi^2(1) = 65.34$, $p = .0001$). The standard similarity method degrades because it selects cases from the same plant-model rather cross-model cases. It is mislead by exact entity matches between the target and cases involving the target's plant-model even though cases from different plant model are often easier to adapt.

Clearly, the standard similarity method could be improved with a more elaborate weighting scheme to closer approximate the concept of adaptability. However, such improvements would implicitly include the knowledge that is explicitly used in the AGR method. Furthermore, the tailoring of similarity metrics is a complex trial and error process that depends greatly on the current state of the system. Finally, as we shall see in the other experiments, it is not clear that such remedial adjustments actually result in any computational gain over AGR (see Experiment 3).

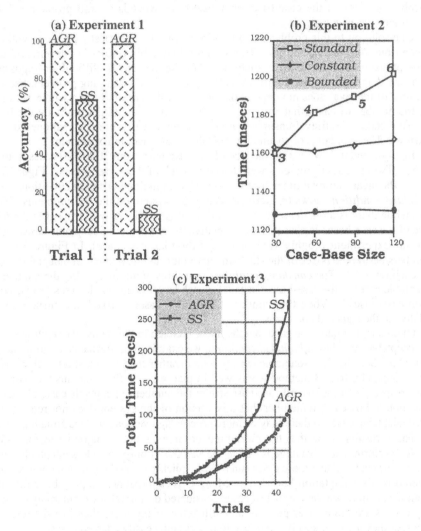

Fig. 5. Experimental Results:
(a) Retrieval Accuracy (b) Retrieval Performance (c) Overall System Performance

4.2 Experiment 2: Avoiding Swamping Problems

The AGR method is clearly more complicated than standard similarity methods. It is, therefore, important to ascertain whether it is particularly prone to a special case of the utility problem in CBR systems, known as the *swamping problem* [11]. Utility problems occur when the uncontrolled accumulation of knowledge results in a performance degradation because the cost of locating relevant knowledge is (on average) more than the saving obtained in using this knowledge. In many CBR systems the swamping problem arises because the cost of retrieval is directly proportional to the number of cases in the case-base; as a case-base expands overall problem solving performance may actually degrade.

One solution to this problem is to limit retrieval time; the best case found within a given time limit is selected [8]. This solution invariably results in the retrieval of a sub-optimal case and, of course, such sub-optimal cases may be difficult or impossible to adapt. Adaptation-guided retrieval is less prone to the swamping problem, because the cost of retrieval does not depend on the size of the case-base as a whole but more on the number of cases that are adaptable (relevant) to the target problem; the base-filtering stage of retrieval ensures that non-adaptable cases are not examined during retrieval. The avoidance of swamping in AGR is illustrated in Experiment 2.

In Experiment 2, we varied the size of the case-base from 30 to 120 cases in units of 30. Twenty target problems were tested on each of these case-bases. Figure 5(b) shows the mean retrieval times for the test problems in three different conditions. The *standard condition* shows the performance of the system on the test problems. Note that while there is an increase in retrieval time, it is not linear with respect to the total size of the case-base. Rather it is linear relative to the number of adaptable cases found (in this experiment roughly 10% or less of the total case-base). In Figure 5(b) the numbers beside the boxes of the standard curve indicate the number of adaptable cases on each retrieval. The *constant condition* proves this point, by holding the number of adaptable cases in the case-base constant for each target (3 adaptable cases were used in each case-base). When the number of adaptable cases is fixed, the curve flattens relative to the standard condition.

Of course, it could be argued that the linear increase in the standard condition is still unacceptable. So, in the *bounded condition*, we examined performance by terminating retrieval when the first adaptable case is found (rather than the most adaptable case). This bounded retrieval method works well in that retrieval time remains more or less flat irrespective of the overall case-base size or the number of adaptable cases available. We should, however, remember that this version of the system does not retrieve the most adaptable case, so there may be more processing overhead in the adaptation stage.

These results show that the swamping problem is not a major issue for AGR. AGR's performance advantage is due to the fact that it only considers adaptable cases during retrieval and that these cases can be very quickly located by the indexing scheme offered by the adaptation knowledge. Many CBR approaches employ base-filtering methods to cut down the number of cases considered during retrieval but many of these approaches are either over general, and still select many more than just the relevant cases, or they are over specific and tend to ignore some easily adapted cases.

4.3 Experiment 3: Overall System Performance

In Experiments 1 and 2 we just considered retrieval. However, AGR should also have benefits for overall system performance (i.e., combining retrieval and adaptation). We have seen that AGR's retrieval accuracy is very respectable relative to a standard similarity model. AGR should be more accurate and faster in the adaptation stage because the retrieval stage identifies what adaptation knowledge should be used. In Experiment 3, we examined the effect of adaptation-guided retrieval on the overall problem-solving time. Two versions of Déjà Vu were used; one that used AGR (the AGR-system) and another that used semantic similarity-based retrieval and an adaptation component (the standard similarity-based, adaptation system or SS-system). Each system had the same case-base of 100 cases, the same adaptation knowledge and was tested with the same 45 target problems.

Figure 5(c) shows the cumulative solution times for the two systems over the 45 problems (problems were roughly ordered in terms of their complexity). The AGR-system was considerably better than the SS-system taking only 120 seconds to solve the 45 problems compared to 280 seconds in the SS-system. The mean solution time for problems in the AGR-system ($M = 2.07$ secs; $SD = 2.07$) is about three times faster that in the SS-system ($M = 6.22$ secs; $SD = 5.66$); a difference that is statistically reliable ($t(44) = 5.65$, $p < .0001$).

The performance of the AGR-system is much better than the SS-system because it retrieves the most adaptable case and locates the relevant adaptation knowledge for this case during retrieval. Furthermore, the benefits of AGR emerge most strongly when problems become more complex, because the sketchy nature of standard, similarity-based retrieval has a greater tendency to be mislead.

5 Conclusions

Many researchers have been attracted the idea of adaptation-guided retrieval but have worried about its computational efficiency. In this paper, we have tried to show that these worries can be unfounded. First, the explicit use of adaptation knowledge ensures that adaptation-guided retrieval is more accurate than more conventional approaches (see Expt. 1). Second, adaptation-guided retrieval maintains the cost of retrieval at an acceptable level or can be bounded to achieve near-constant retrieval times (see Expt. 2). So, the technique should scale well on larger case-bases. Third, the overall adaptation costs are greatly reduced because the most adaptable case is always selected and preliminary adaptation work is performed during retrieval. So, there are considerable performance improvements in the overall cost of problem solving (see Expt. 3).

In addition, the closer integration of retrieval and adaptation provides a much more flexible CBR model. With conventional approaches, changes to the adaptation capabilities of a system are not immediately reflected in the retrieval preferences of the system. Instead changes must be made to the retrieval heuristics in order to capture the new adaptation possibilities. In contrast, because the retrieval and adaptation stages are directly coupled in Déjà Vu, any changes to its adaptation capabilities *will* be immediately available to the retrieval system; this is because the altered adaptation knowledge itself is used explicitly in retrieval.

We acknowledge that standard similarity models of retrieval and standard CBR architectures could be parametrically varied to improve the performances we have shown here. However, we doubt whether any such systems could better the results found for the AGR-system. Furthermore, the likelihood is that any such system would be merely trying to mimic AGR within the confines of standard approaches.

Finally, the representational requirements of the approach are domain independent and thus facilitate the adoption of the technique across a range of CBR application domains. Already Déjà Vu has been used to investigate a number of different software design domains. As well as plant-control software, a Motif graphical user interface design has also been investigated. Initial results suggest that AGR transfers well to this quite different software design domain.

6 References

1.   Kolodner, J. (1989). Judging Which is the "Best" Case for a Case-Based Reasoner. Proceedings of the Case-Based Reasoning Workshop, Florida, U.S.A.

2.   Goel, A. (1989) Integration of Case-Based Reasoning and Model-Based Reasoning for Adaptive Design Problem Solving. *Ph.D. Thesis*. Ohio State University, USA.

3.   Birnbaum, L., Collins, G., Brand, M., Freed, M., Krulwich, B., Pryor, L. (1989) A Model-Based Approach to the Construction of Adaptive Case-Based Planning Systems. *Proceedings of the Case-Based Reasoning Workshop*, Florida, USA.

4.   Fox, S. & Leake D. (1994) Using Introspective Reasoning to Guide Index Refinement. *Proceedings of the Sixteenth International Conference of the Cognitive Science Conference*, (pp. 324 - 329)

5.   Leake, D. (1992) Constructive Similarity Assessment: Using Stored Cases to Define New Situations. *Proceedings of the Fourteenth International Conference of the Cognitive Science Conference*, (pp. 313 - 318)

6.   Smyth, B., & Keane, M. (1994). Retrieving Adaptable Cases: The Role of Adaptation Knowledge in case Retrieval. *Topics in Case-Based Reasoning*, Springer Verlag (pp. 209-220).

7.   Cain, T., Pazzani, M. J., and Silverstein, G. (1991) Using Domain Knowledge to Influence Similarity Judgements. *Proceedings of the Case-Based Reasoning Workshop*, (pp. 191-198). Washington D.C., U.S.A.

8.   Veloso, M. (1992) Learning by Analogical Reasoning in General Problem Solving. *Ph.D. Thesis* (CMU-CS-92-174). Carnegie Mellon University, Pittsburgh, USA.

9.   Smyth, B., & Cunningham, P. (1992). Déjà Vu: A Hierarchical Case-Based Reasoning System for Software Design. *Proceedings of the 10th European Conference on Artificial Intelligence.* (pp. 587 - 589). Vienna, Austria

10. Hammond, K. J. (1989). *Planning from Memory*. New York: Academic Press.

11. Francis, A.G., & Ram, A. (1993) Computational Models of the Utility Problem and their Application to a Utility Analysis of Case-based Reasoning. *Proceedings of the Workshop on Knowledge Compilation and Speed-Up Learning.*

Integrating Rules and Cases for the Classification Task

Jerzy Surma
Department of Computer Science
University of Economics
Komandorska 118/120, Wroclaw, Poland
Email: surma@ksk-2.iie.ae.wroc.pl

Koen Vanhoof
Faculty of Applied Economics Science
Limburgs University Center
B-3590 Diepenbeek, Belgium
Email: vanhoof@rsftew.luc.ac.be

Abstract. The recent progress in Case- Based Reasoning has shown that one of the most important challenges in developing future AI methods will be to combine and synergistically utilize general and case-based knowledge. In this paper a very rudimentary kind of integration for the classification task, based on simple heuristics, is sketched: "To solve a problem, first try to use the conventional rule-based approach. If it does not work, try to remember a similar problem you have solved in the past and adapt the old solution to the new situation". This heuristic approach is based on the knowledge base that consists of rule base and exception case base. The method of generating this kind of knowledge base from a set of examples is described. The proposed approach is tested, and compared with alternative approaches. The experimental results show that the presented integration method can lead to an improvement in accuracy and comprehensibility.

1 Introduction

The recent progress in Case- Based Reasoning has shown that one of the most important challenges in developing future AI methods will be to combine and synergistically utilize general and case- based knowledge (Aamodt 1995). The presented approach has an origin in Riesbeck and Schank's psychological consideration (Riesbeck & Schank 1989, pp.11): " When an activity has been repeated often enough it becomes rule- like in nature. We do not reason from prior cases when well- establish rules are available. [...] When the rule fails, the only alternative for its user is to create a case that captures that failure". Let us assume that our task is classification, and the knowledge is represented in: *rules* - that represent a standard and/or a typical situation, and *cases* - that represent the particular experience, exceptions and/or non-typical situations. The problem solver can classify a new case by means of the following algorithm:

> **If** a new case is covered by some rule
> **Then** apply a solution from a rule with the highest priority
> **Else** adapt the solution from the most similar case

This algorithm is based on the following heuristics: "To solve a problem, first try to use the conventional rule- based approach. If it does not work, try to remember a similar problem you have solved in the past and adapt the old solution to the new situation". The rules are evaluated first because standard situations occur more often, so it is more probable that input case is a standard case.

In section 2., we present an overview of related work on integrating Case- Based and Rule- Based Reasoning. In section 3 the different approaches for splitting Case Base are introduced. In section 4 we show the results of comparisons between the integrating approach and alternative approaches. The paper concludes with a short presentation of an algorithm learning from failures, and a discussion about the advantages and disadvantages of the suggested approach.

2 Related Work

The mixed paradigm involving case- based and traditional rule- based reasoning was included in the original CBR systems. The CHEF contained a rule- based sub module to support Case- Based Reasoning (Hammond 1988), and the CASEY used cases to supplement rule- based mechanism (Koton 1988).

The advanced studies in this field were made in the 1990s. Rissland and Skalak described a system CABARET that integrates reasoning with rules and reasoning with previous cases (Rissland & Skalak 1991). This integration was performed via a collection of control heuristics. Golding and Rosenblum propose the architecture for combining Rule- Based and Case- Based Reasoning for the task of pronouncing surnames (Golding & Rosenblaum 1991). The central idea of their approach is to apply the rules to a target problem to get a first approximation to the answer, but if the problem is judged to be compellingly similar to a known exception of the rules, then the solution is based on the exception rather than the rules. A good example of combined reasoning in the framework for problem solving in knowledge rich environment is the CREEK system (Aamodt 1991). Here, the system first attempts to solve the problem by case- based reasoning, and if an acceptable match is not found, rule based reasoning is attempted.

The selected studies in inductive learning were based on an integration with the case- based approach. Utgoff showed how the updating costs of incremental decision tree algorithms can be significantly decreased by saving specific instances (Utgoff 1989). Cardie proposed a method for using decision trees to specify the features to be included in k- nearest neighbor retrieval (Cardie 1993). The classic application of the decision tree as an index for case- based retrieval is implemented in commercial CBR tool ReMind, described and evaluated by Barletta (Barletta 1994).

In Europe a numbers of systems has recently been constructed, exploring various approaches of case and rule integration, including Cabata (Lenz 1993), and BUBE/CcC+ (Bamberger & Goos 1993). Malek and Rialle developed a computer- aided medical diagnosis system for neuropathy diseases where the domain knowledge is represented in prototype cases, and non- typical cases. During a diagnosis phase prototypes matched to the presented case are extracted, if no prototype is matched then the group of non- typical cases is retrieved (Malek & Rialle 1994). Armengol and Plaza presented the general knowledge modelling framework for solving the purification task of proteins. This task can be solved in different ways, especially by combining case- based retrieval and by using domain knowledge in the form of prototypes that are generated by an inductive method (Armengol & Plaza 1994).

The four possible levels of integration between the Induction and Case- Based Reasoning method were established and tested in the INRECA project (Manago et al., 1993), (Auriol et al., 1994). In terms of stand- alone, co-operative, workbench and seamless levels of integration, the approach presented in this paper is co-operative. This means that both methods are kept separated but they co-operate.

Some of the studies in machine learning that are concerned with the instance prototypicality are very important in the context of this research. Especially Matwin's and Plante's prototypical and marginal examples (Matwin & Plante 1994), Zhang's measure of instance typicality (Zhang 1992), and more recently Biberman's prototypicality approaches (Biberman 1995).

3 Integrating Rules and Cases

3.1 The Main Idea

The main source of knowledge for the problem solving heuristic (introduced in section 1) is a set of rules (Rule_Base) and a set of exception cases (Exception_Case_Base). In the traditional approach the rule base is obtained after a difficult and time consuming knowledge acquisition process. The main idea of the integrated approach is shown in Fig.1.

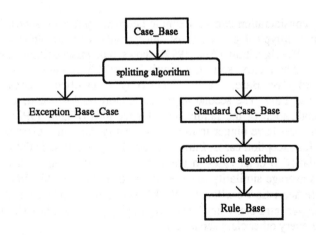

Fig.1. Generating Exception_Case_Base and Rule_Base

The given set of cases (Case_Base) is split into two disjoined subsets: Exception_Case_Base and Standard_Case_Base, and then the induction algorithm (e.g. C4.5) generates rules (Rule_Base) from standard cases (Standard_Case_Base).

Now we can describe the problem solving heuristics from section 1 more precisely. To classify a new case, the ordered list of rules from the Rule_Base is examined to find the first whose condition is satisfied by the case. If no rule's condition is satisfied, the case is classified by means of the Nearest- Neighbor algorithm on exception cases (Exception_Case_Base).

3.2 Splitting Approaches

One of the most important problems in the present approach is to find a suitable Case_Base splitting procedure. In general this can be done by:

• *an expert* - the split obtained from an expert is very valuable (see result of experiments in section 4), and gives an opportunity to obtain an additional explanation for an exceptions.

• *a statistical approach* (e.g. cluster analysis) - this is a quite interesting approach from a formal point of view. Unfortunately, conventional statistic methods are mainly useful when the case is described by continuous features.

• *a heuristic approach* - there are a lot of informal approaches based on geometrical interpretations. The split can be based on weighting schemes as well, where exceptional cases can be determined to their performance and/or frequency of use for problem solving. This kind of method for identifying exceptional cases was introduced in Salzberg and Cost MVDM metric (Cost & Salzberg 1993).

We take into consideration two very simple heuristic split approaches. The first one assumes that non-typical cases can be interpreted as near-boundary cases. Aha's study on the IB2 algorithm (Aha 1992) shows that misclassified cases are more likely to be near-boundary, so in this heuristic correctly classified cases are put into the Standard_Case_Base, and incorrectly classified cases into the Exception_Case_Base. The second approach is more sophisticated, and is based on Zhang's formalization of the family resemblance idea (Zhang 1992). We assumed that standard cases have bigger intra-class similarity than inter-class similarity, and the opposite for exception cases. Intra-class similarity of a case is defined as a case's average similarity to other cases in the same class, and the inter-class similarity is defined as its average similarity to cases of all other classes. This kind of intra/inter similarity split heuristic we will call "Weak". The "Strong" one is when the standard cases have bigger intra-class similarity than the biggest inter-class similarity, that is computed for every other class separately.

Formally those heuristics can be defined as follows. There is a given set of cases: $C_{set} = \{c_1, c_2, ..., c_N\}$. Each case c_j j=1..N is described by a list of attribute values $c_j = \langle f_j^1, f_j^2, ... f_j^m \rangle$. For each case $c_j \in C_{set}$ the classification: class(c_j) is given, that belong to the finite pre-numerated set. The task is to split C_{set} into two disjoint sets: C_{std} - set of standard cases (Standard_Case_Base), and C_{exc} - set of exception cases

(Exception_Case_Base), $C_{set} = C_{std} \cup C_{exc}$. The similarity measure between two cases c_x and c_y is:

$$\text{Sim}(c_x,c_y) = 1 - \sqrt{\frac{1}{m} \sum_{i=1}^{m} \text{dis}(f_x^i,f_y^i)^2} \quad \text{where: } \text{dis}(f_x^i,f_y^i) = \frac{\left|f_x^i - f_y^i\right|}{max_i - min_i}$$

for numeric- valued attributes, max_i, min_i respectively are the maximum and minimum value of the i-th attribute. For symbolic-valued attributes: if $f_x^i = f_y^i$ then $\text{dis}(f_x^i, f_y^i)=0$ (including both unknowns) else $\text{dis}(f_x^i, f_y^i))=1$. If one attribute value in unknown and the other is known, then they are of distance one. This similarity measure is reflexive, symmetrical, and normalized to the range from 0 to 1.

```
Begin
C_std ← C_exc ← ∅
For each c_x ∈ C_set
   Begin
      For each c_y ∈ {C_set - {c_x}}  sim(c_y) ← Sim(c_x,c_y)
      y_max ← max{sim(c_y)}
      If class(c_x)=class(y_max) Then C_std ← C_std ∪ {c_x} Else C_exc ← C_exc ∪{c_x}
   End
End
```

Fig.2. IB2 split heuristic

```
Begin
C_std ← C_exc ← ∅
For each c_x ∈ C_set
   Begin
   sim' ← sim" ← 0
      For each c_y ∈ {C_set - {c_x}}
         If class(c_x)=class(c_y) then sim' ← sim' + Sim(c_x,c_y) else sim" ← sim" + Sim(c_x,c_y)
      intra_sim ← sim' / (| class(c_x) | -1)
      inter_sim ← sim" / (N-| class(c_x) | )
      If intra_sim > inter_sim Then C_std ← C_std ∪ {c_x} Else C_exc ← C_exc ∪ {c_x}
   End
End

where: | class(c_i) | - number of cases from class: class(c_i)
```

Fig.3. Weak Inter/Intra similarity split heuristic

The first heuristic (based on IB2 algorithm) is presented in Fig.2, and the second one (Weak Intra/Inter similarity) is shown in Fig.3. The Strong Intra/Inter similarity heuristics can be easily obtained after slightly changing the code in Fig.3.

4 Experimental Results

The experiments were performed in order to compare the integrated approach based on the different split heuristic with rule based (rules from C4.5 algorithm), and the nearest- neighbor approach. The tests were based on three databases . The LED Display (with seven attributes) symbolic- valued artificial database with 10 % amount of noise. The U.S. Congressional Voting 1984, symbolic valued database with unknown values, and the Nurses (Surma 1994), a real database with numeric and symbolic attributes. Table 1 briefly characterises the domain and the experiments.

Table 1. Databases characteristics

Characteristic:	Database:		
	LED Display	**Voting (1984)**	**Nurses**
Train size	200	300	115
Test size	500	135	51
No of attributes	7	16	3
No of classes	10	2	5

All three databases were split into standard and exception subsets by means of IB2, Weak Intra/Inter similarity, and Strong Intra/Inter similarity heuristics. Additionally we obtain from the domain expert split for Nurses database. The characteristics of the knowledge base, respectively for Nearest- Neighbor (1-NN), C4.5 rules and Integrated approaches (Integration) are presented in Table 2. For example the knowledge base in the integration approach (with IB2 heuristics) for the database Voting consists of 26 exception cases and 4 rules. Those rules were generated from 274 standard cases (300 cases from Case_Base - 26 cases from Exception_Case_Base).

Table 2. Knowledge base sizes

Method:	Database:					
	LED display		**Voting (1984)**		**Nurses**	
1-NN (no. of cases)	200		300		115	
C4.5 rules (no. of rules)	15		7		9	
Integration (IB2)	85	11	26	4	52	12
Integration (Strong)	54	12	34	6	61	4
Integration (Weak)	5	14	34	6	11	6
Integration (Expert)	-		-		39	6

Legend for Integration rows:
a | b ≡ no. of exceptions cases | no. of rules generated from standard cases

The results of the accuracy comparison are shown in Table 3. The results for Nearest- Neighbor (1-NN) were obtained thanks to the Inducer utility from the

MLC++ Machine Learning Library in C++ (Kohavi et al. 1994). In all experiments the rules were generated and tested thanks to Quinlan's C4.5 Machine Learning programs (Quinlan 1993). For testing the integrated approach we created a special Case/Rule- Based System in the Kappa PC expert system shell.

Table 3. Average classification accuracies

Method:	Database:		
	LED display	**Voting (1984)**	**Nurses**
1-NN	69.3	94.1	56.9
C4.5 rules	69.9	95.6	60.8
Integration (IB2)	69.1	95.6	49.0
Integration (Strong)	69.7	97.0	58.8
Integration (Weak)	70.3	97.0	51.0
Integration (Expert)	-	-	66.7

To avoid overgeneralization, the rules for the integrated approach were induced based on standard and exception cases. But all exception cases had the same fictitious value of the decision variable. Next, the rules with fictitious variable were excluded from the obtained rule set. All the classifiers were tested on randomly drawn and separate training and test sets.

The accuracies for the integrated approaches on the LED with 10% noise are quite reasonable taking into account that LED consists of noisy or noisy free cases. The results for Voting are comparable with C4.5 rules, and much better than simple 1-NN. The Voting database has only 2 classes so the Weak Inter/Intra similarity split heuristic is equivalent to the "Strong" heuristic. If we compare split heuristics, it is easy to see that in all experiments results for the Inter/Intra similarity split are better than results for the IB2 split. The results on "Nurses" shows that the "Strong" split is much better than the "Weak" one. In this experiment all cases from the two classes were recognized by the "Strong" split as exceptions ! The outstanding result was obtained for "Nurses", where the expert was responsible for splitting. These experimental results show that in terms of the accuracy the integrated approach is not worse than conventional approaches, and can give quite impressive outcomes for a suitable splitting procedure.

The explanatory ability of the integrated approach seems to be much better than the C4.5 rules or 1-NN. If the user requests an explanation, the system is showing a rule (if an input problem was interpreted as a standard) or a case (if an input problem was interpreted as an exception). The rules based on the standard cases are much more closer to the expert ones, than rules induced from the whole training set. In order to verify this hypothesis a simple experiment was done. According to the expert the Nurses set consists of 39 exceptions and 76 standard cases. From all 115 examples: 8 rules (R1) + a default rule were generated. Next, from 76 standard cases: 6 rules (R2) were generated as well. The rules from sets R1 and R2 were mixed and given to the expert for examination. The expert task was to evaluate each rule in terms of a nonsense, wrong, tolerable, or good rule. The result of this subjective evaluation is presented in Table 4.

Table 4. Expert evaluation of the "Nurses" rules

Rule set:	Expert evaluation:			
	"nonsense" (no. of rules)	**"wrong"** (no. of rules)	**"tolerable"** (no. of rules)	**"good"** (no. of rules)
R1 (based on 115 cases)	3	1	2	2
R2 (based on 76 cases)	0	2	2	2

The rules from the R2 set are much closer to the expert opinion than the rules from R1. In fact no rule from R2 was judged as a nonsense rule. Of course it is easy to falsify only one experiment, but this result opens up promising avenues for further evaluations.

5 Overview of the Learning Procedure

Unfortunately, even in such a simple integrated approach as is presented in this paper, the case retainment (learning) is very complex. In Fig.4 overview of the procedure of learning from failures is shown.

```
Begin
If is(input_case, exception)
 Then
   Begin
     If solution_from_rules Then
                             Begin
                                 specialize(Rule_Base, input_case)
                                 add(input_case, Exception_Case_Base)
                             End
     If solution_from_exceptions And solution_is_false
                             Then add(input_case, Exception_Case_Base)
   End
 Else { is(input_case, standard) }
   Begin
     If solution_from_exceptions Then generalize(Rule_Base, input_case)
     If solution_from_rules And solution_is_false Then modify(Rule_Base, input_case)
   End
End
where:
specialize(Rule_Base, case) - modify Rule_Base in order to not cover a case by any rule,
generalize(Rule_Base, case) - modify Rule_Base in order to cover a case by at least one rule
                             and classify a case correctly,
modify(Rule_Base, case) - modify Rule_Base in order to classify a case correctly.
```

Fig.4. Overview of learning from failures procedure.

We assumed that the case revision is done by asking an expert. In this process three sub- procedures on a Rule_Base are involved (i.e. generalize, specialize, and modify). In the conventional approach everyone of those sub- procedures needs an access to the whole Standard_Case_Base. This problem can be partially overcome by some incremental techniques (Utgoff 1989).

6 Concluding Remarks

The solution of the classification task that is proposed in this paper seems to be valuable for the three reasons. First, the knowledge acquisition process for obtaining Exception_Case_Base and Rule_Base is relatively easy. Second, the outcomes of the initial accuracy comparisons are acceptable, and very promising when splitting is based on the domain knowledge. Finally, a good comprehensibility of this approach is given to the end user.

The approach presented in this paper is one of the possible ways of integration. There are a lot of possibilities of integrating Case- Based and Rule- Based Reasoning. For instance a framework for integrating different integration strategies based on the NOOS object oriented language is presented in the mentioned Armengol and Plaza paper. Unfortunately the presented approach can be applied only where the underlying heuristic is appropriate for the domain.

Acknowledgements

We are very grateful to Eva Armengol, Eric Auriol, Maria Malek, and Enric Plaza for providing comments on the initial stage of this research. We also want to thanks P.M. Murphy and D.W. Aha who are in charge of the UCI Repository of Machine Learning Databases at the University of California (Irvine). Special thanks to Jerzy Stefanowski for outstanding support during the composition of this paper.

This research was undertaken with support from the European Commission's Phare ACE Programme under contract 94-0028-F

References

Aamodt, A. (1991). A Knowledge- Intensive, Integrated Approach to Problem Solving and Sustained Learning. *A Doctoral Dissertation* - University of Trondheim.

Aamodt, A. (1995). Knowledge Acquisition and Learning by Experience - The Role of Case-Specific Knowledge. In Kodratoff, Y., Tecuci, G. (eds.) *On Integration of Knowledge Acquisition and Machine Learning*. Academic Press (in press).

Aha, D.W. (1992). Tolerating noisy, irrelevant and novel attributes in instance- based learning algorithms. International Journal of Man Machine Studies, vol.36, pp.267-287.

Armengol, E., Plaza, E; (1994). Integrating Induction in a Case- Based Reasoner. In *Proceed. of the Second European Conference on Case- Based Reasoning*. AcknoSoft Press, Paris, pp.243-252.

Auriol, E., Manago, M., Althoff,K.D., Wess, S., Dittrich,S. (1994). Integration Induction and Case- Based Reasoning: Methodological Approach and First Evaluation. In *Proceed. of the Second European Conference on Case- Based Reasoning*. AcknoSoft Press, Paris, pp.145-156.

Bamberger, S.K., Goos, K. (1993). Integration of Case- Based Reasoning and Inductive Learning Methods. *In Proceed. of the First European Conference on Case- Based Reasoning*. SEKI Report SR-93-12. University of Keiserslautern, pp. 296-300.

Biberman, Y. (1995). The Role of Prototypicality in Exemplar-Based Learning. In Machine Learning: ECML-95, (Eds.) Lavrac, N., Wrobel, S., Springer Verlag, pp.77-91.

Barletta, R. (1994). A Hybrid Indexing and Retrieval Strategy for Advisory Case- Based Reasoning Systems Built with ReMind. In *Proceed. of the Second European Conference on Case- Based Reasoning*. AcknoSoft Press, Paris, pp.49-58.

Cardie, C. (1993). Using Decision Trees to Improve Case- Based Learning. In *Proceed. of the Tenth International Conference on Machine Learning*. Morgan Kaufmann, pp.25-32.

Cost, S., Salzberg, S. (1993). A Weighted Nearest Neighbor Algorithm for Learning with Symbolic Features. *Machine Learning* vol.10, pp.57-78.

Golding, A.R., Rosenbloom, P.S. (1991). Improving Rule- Based System through Case- Based Reasoning. In *Proceed. of the 1991 National Conference on AI*. The MIT Press, pp.22-27.

Hammond, K.J. (1988). Explaining and Repairing Plans That Fails. *Artificial Intelligence* vol.45, pp.173-228.

Kohavi, R., John, G., Long, R., Manley, D., Pfleger, K. (1994). MLC++. A Machine Learning Library in C++. In *Tools with Artificial Intelligence* Conference.

Koton, P.A. (1988). Reasoning about Evidence in Causal Explanations. In *Proceed. AAAI-88*, Morgan Kaufmann, Los Altos, pp.256-261.

Lenz, M. (1993). Cabata - A hybrid Case- Based Reasoning system. In *Proceed. of the First European Conference on Case- Based Reasoning*. SEKI Report SR-93-12. University of Keiserslautern, pp. 204-209.

Malek, M., Rialle, V. (1994). A Case- Based Reasoning System Applied to Neuropathy Diagnosis. In *Proceed. of the Second European Conference on Case- Based Reasoning*. AcknoSoft Press, Paris, pp.329-336.

Manago, M., Althoff, K.D., Auriol, E., Traphoner, R., Wess, S., Conruyt, N., Maurer, F. (1993). Induction and Reasoning from Cases. In *Proceed. of the first European Conference on Case- Based Reasoning*. SEKI Report SR-93-12. University of Keiserslautern, pp. 204-209.

Matwin, S., Plante, B. (1994). Theory Revision by Analyzing Explanations and Prototypes. In Michalski, R., Tecuci,G. (eds.) Machine Learning vol.4, Morgan Kaufmann, San Mateo.

Quinlan, J.R. (1993). *C4.5: Programs for Machine Learning*. Morgan Kaufmann, San Mateo.

Riesbéck, C.K., Schank, R.C. (1989). *Inside Case- Based Reasoning*. Lawrence Erlbaum, Hillsdale.

Rissland, E.L., Skalak D.B. (1991). CABARET: rule integration in a hybrid architecture. *International Journal of Man- Machine Studies*, vol.34, pp.839-887.

Surma, J. (1994). Enhancing Similarity Measure with Domain Specific Knowledge". In *Proceed. of the Second European Conference on Case- Based Reasoning*. AcknoSoft Press, Paris, pp.365-371.

Utgoff, P.E. (1989). Incremental Decision Tress. *Machine Learning*, vol.4, pp.161-186.

Zhang, J. (1992). Selecting Typical Instances in Instance- Based Learning. *In Proc. of the 9th Int. Conf. on Machine Learning*. Morgan Kaufmann, pp.470-479.

Reuse of Knowledge: Empirical Studies

Willemien VISSER

Ergonomic Psychology Project - INRIA
Domaine de Voluceau - Rocquencourt - B.P. 105 - 78153 LE CHESNAY Cedex - France
email: Willemien.Visser@inria.fr

Abstract. This paper presents empirical studies, mainly from psychology, on reuse of knowledge, especially in design. The results are considered relevant to research and development in the domain of CBR because of the support function generally attributed to CBR systems. The data exposed concern both representational and processing aspects of reuse. The topics discussed are: reuse vs. design "from scratch"; different stages in reuse, especially retrieval; types of entity reused (with respect to their abstraction level, origin, and "product"-solution vs. "procedure"-solution character) and types of their exploitation; strategies of reuse; frequency of effective reuse; effects of reuse on designers' productivity; difficulties and risks of reuse. The paper closes with possible repercussions for CBR systems based on the results presented, and research topics in the domain of reuse of knowledge (conditions of reuse, retrieval from memory, and reuse and analogical reasoning).

1. Introduction

Case-based reasoning (CBR) systems are generally considered as support, not autonomous, systems (Kolodner, 1993; Pu, 1993). Although this means that data on human cognition should be taken into account, this is rarely the case (see Trousse & Visser, 1993; Visser & Trousse, 1993). This paper presents a state of the knowledge with respect to cognitive aspects of representations and processes implemented in reuse -considered in this paper as the human reasoning process corresponding to CBR. This introduction presents a definition of reuse, and delineates the focus of the paper, i.e. reuse in real design tasks. The second section, which constitutes the main body of the paper presents results from empirical studies on reuse. The discussion section introduces several questions which remain to be examined, and discusses repercussions of the results for CBR systems.

1.1 Reuse of Knowledge: a Definition

All use of knowledge could be called "reuse": knowledge is indeed based on the processing of previous experience and/or data encountered in the past. We reserve "reuse" (vs. other "use" of knowledge) for the exploitation of knowledge which is at the same level of abstraction as the "target" (the problem to be solved or utterance to be understood) for whose processing the knowledge in question is retrieved. Generally, this knowledge is specific, thus reuse of knowledge is opposed to the use of more general, abstract knowledge (i.e. knowledge structures such as schemas and rules). The knowledge reused seems therefore to correspond to the entities which are generally considered the "cases" in CBR. It is, however, different from the "components" advocated to be reused in the software-engineering community working on reuse[1].

Terminology. "Target" - "Source". Following on this point the analogical-reasoning tradition, the problem to be solved is called the "target (problem)"; and the knowledge elements reused the "sources" ("cases" in CBR).

1.2 Focus on Reuse in "Real" Design Tasks

This paper focuses on "design reuse", i.e. reuse in a particular form of problem solving. Several authors in the CBR community have argued that CBR is particularly well suited to design problem solving (e.g. Pu, 1993). On the basis of cognitive-psychology data, Visser and Trousse (1993) also stressed the important role of exploiting specific experiences from the past in this type of problem solving, especially in nonroutine design (cf. the workshop organised at IJCAI93 on "Reuse of designs: an interdisciplinary cognitive approach", Visser, 1993).

Indeed, a considerable proportion of the empirical research on reuse has been conducted on design tasks, mostly in the domain of software: object-oriented (OO) (Burkhardt & Détienne, 1995; Détienne, 1991; Lange & Moher, 1989; Lewis, Henry, Kafura & Schulman, 1991), LISP (Weber, 1991), industrial programmable controllers (Visser, 1987); but also in other domains: mechanical design (Visser, 1990, 1992a, 1995), aerospace structures (Falzon & Visser, 1989; Visser, 1991) and architecture (De Vries, 1993). Reuse has also been examined in other tasks: several types of decision-taking tasks (Klein & Calderwood, 1988) and diagnosis (process control, Baerentsen, 1991; telephone-traffic monitoring, Perron, 1995).

The explicit mention of the "real" character of the design tasks studied may sound strange to computer scientists -even if their research is also often based on data gathered in artificially restricted situations. Classically, psychological studies on problem solving have been conducted on very simple tasks, requiring no experience in any particular task domain. It is the cognitive-ergonomics approach -aiming the collection of data required for the specification of support systems, computerised or not- which has insisted on the importance of studying problem solving in "real", i.e. professional, real-work, situations. From this viewpoint, it is important to note that most studies on reuse were conducted on real, professional activities.

N.B. There is another -not very broad- tradition in cognitive psychology relevant to the reuse of specific knowledge. Generally it is not referred to as "reuse", and not examined in work situations. The research in question concerns "autobiographical" memory (Norman & Bobrow, 1979; Reiser, 1986; Williams & Hollan, 1981).

---

[1] We do not discuss neither a possibly justified distinction between reuse of "knowledge", "information", "data" and "solutions" (Visser, 1995); nor the one between "specific" and "episodic" knowledge (Tulving, 1983): all reuse is considered to be reuse of "knowledge". In spite of their relevance, data on analogical reasoning cannot be presented due to space constraints (for a good literature review, see Keane, 1988; see also Visser, 1992b).

2. Reuse of Knowledge: Results from Empirical Studies

This section presents data on reuse, both representational and processing, as identified in empirical studies on the way humans (try to) proceed to reuse (thus, not A.I. research referring to "human cognition", but not based on particular empirical investigations on this cognition). Such research has mainly been conducted by psychologists, but some authors come from computer-science or other disciplines.

2.1 Reuse or Design "from Scratch"

When do designers proceed to reuse to solve a design (sub)problem[2], rather than design "from scratch", i.e. base their problem solving on general knowledge? There are few data on this point -and, with one exception, they do not come from studies conducted on designers in a professional-work situation. Let us just remark before the presentation of the available data, that, as a problem-solving activity, a design project generally involves solving a great number of subproblems, and that these different problems probably are not all solved using the same form of reasoning. So, during a project, designers generally proceed to both reuse and design from scratch.
Woodfield, Embley and Scott (1987) examine professional programmers not accustomed to proceed to reuse. They ask them to judge when reuse of components (from abstract-data-type libraries) would be more interesting than to (re)create the code. The factors mentioned by the subjects are aspects of the components rather irrelevant for reuse (their size and the proportion of required additional operations, rather than, e.g., the proportion of operators to be modified).
When Burkhardt asks seven OO-software designers to name elements they might want to (re)use, half of them remark that there are reusable elements whose actual reuse they would not envision because of the "cost" of their reuse (Burkhardt & Détienne, 1995).
Data gathered by Visser (1987) using observation of a programmable-controller software designer provide one example of a factor contributing to this "cost of reuse" (once candidate sources have been retrieved!). This is the "cost of required adaptation", itself a function of "target-source similarity". Visser indeed notices that the designer examines candidate sources, asking himself if they are "sufficiently similar" to the target (for details on the way the designer considers "similarity", see Visser, 1987).

2.2 Reuse: Various Processing Stages, but Mainly Data on Retrieval

Reuse takes place in, at least, three "stages"[3] -preceded by one, and followed by another stage, not specific to reuse, but too important to be omitted in a general description: construction of a representation of the target problem; retrieval of one or

---

[2] As "problem" and "subproblem" are relative notions (like "solution" and "subsolution"), we will use the term "problem" (and "solution") except if there is a risk of confusion.

[3] Our use of this term does not mean that stages are purely consecutive, and that designers cannot come back to a stage, once they have gone through it.

more sources; adaptation of the source into a target-solution proposal; evaluation of the target-solution proposal; and integration into memory of the resulting modifications in problem and solution representations.

This section discusses only stages on which empirical data exist, i.e. mainly retrieval.

In CBR, one generally distinguishes two retrieval stages, the retrieval of possibly several candidate sources, and the selection of the "best" source to be adapted. No empirical data are available to give a "cognitive status" to this distinction.

Empirical research shows that the target-source relationship, or rather its mental representation, seems to play a major role in retrieval. In at least two studies (Visser, 1987, 1990), we have shown that different types of similarity (or "analogy", depending on the definition given to these terms) between target and source are exploited by designers: one is opposition, i.e. target and source differ on only one attribute, on which they have opposite values.

Scope of retrieval. When a designer retrieves a source, "what" is it that is retrieved (see Visser, 1991)? The distinction between product- and procedure-solution (see below) an orient the search for elements of response; and so can the analysis of a "solution path" into, at the one hand, alternatives, sideways, dead ends, etc., and at the other hand, other elements taken into consideration by the designer, such as criteria, constraints, justifications and other "underlying" elements. The observation of two designers reconstructing together a solution path corresponding to a problem solved in the past and whose product-solution they remembered, showed that reminding such a product-solution does not imply recall of the corresponding procedure and/or other "underlying" elements (data collected, but not presented, in the study discussed in Visser, 1991).

2.3 Types of Entity Reused

This is the aspect of reuse on which empirical studies provide most data.

2.3.1 Abstraction Level

Our definition of reuse as use of a source at the same abstraction level as the target may be interpreted as meaning that sources are generally concrete, i.e. low-level knowledge elements, but the definition does not imply so. Empirical studies mostly show reuse of concrete sources, but Visser (1987) e.g. observed that sources from at least three levels were reused to solve target problems at the corresponding levels:

- a "high" level: the software designer reused the structure of the software he had developed in the past for a similar problem;
- an "intermediate" level: in order to attribute software variables to domain entities, the designer used the variables on the listing of another, similar program;
- a "low" level: the designer also heavily reused code.

2.3.2 Origin

Sources may have an "external" or an "internal" origin -i.e. come from the designer's

memory. Sources from external origin may be of various types:
- The designer may be, or not, their author. The software designer observed by Visser (1987) mainly reused two different listings of programs, both written by himself.
- The sources may come from another design project, but also from the target, i.e. the solution under construction. Both Visser (1987) and Détienne (1991, OO software) observe "intra design-project reuse", i.e. a software solution developed on the current design project is used later on, during this project, as a source for the development of other target solutions. Visser (1990) observes this same intra-project exploitation in mechanical design (functional specifications). In both studies (1987, 1990), she also identifies "inter design-project reuse".
- Sources may come from human or non human information sources. Visser (1995, backpack-to-mountainbike attachment) discusses the pros and contras of both forms.
- They may have a descriptive (technical, commercial information), or more evaluative character (manufacturer tests, user evaluations, expert assessments) (Visser, 1995).

2.3.3 "Product"-Solution vs. "Procedure"-Solution
This distinction (cf. "derivational" vs. "transformational" analogy, Carbonell, 1986) has generally not been made in empirical studies on reuse. Generally, reuse implicitly refers to reuse of the product of a design problem-solving process (but see Visser, 1990, who also observed that the mechanical designer reused source-solution procedures as sources for the development of target-solution procedures).

2.4 Types of Exploitation of Reusable Entities

In the software-engineering community, a distinction is made between "design for reuse" and "reuse for design" (Thunem & Sindre, 1992): the construction of reusable entities ("components" organised into a "library") is often considered an independent design task, not necessarily executed by the same designer as the one who is going to reuse these entities. No empirical studies have been conducted in situations where these two tasks are presented to designers as separate tasks. Two series of results, however, may be relevant in this context. One of them will be discussed under the heading "Anticipation of reuse" (see below).
The other series of results comes from the study by Burkhardt (Burkhardt & Détienne, 1995), in which the OO-software designers explicitly distinguish, in their description of elements relevant in the context of reuse, elements they would like to be able to re-trieve (in order to develop their target program) and elements (developed in their target program) which might be reused (for the development of other target programs) -but which may be considered too "costly" (cf., above, "Reuse or design 'from scratch'").
Visser (1995) observes that reuse takes place in all three problem-solving "stages" classically distinguished in the psychological problem-solving literature: construction of a problem representation, solution development, and solution evaluation.
Reuse for the construction of a problem representation e.g. serves the anticipation of possible problems (and possible solutions).
Solution development through source-solution reuse is the common form of reuse

noted in empirical studies. Visser (1995) observed that both analysis and evaluation of a source may contribute to the proposal of a target-solution; and that source analysis is used to adapt the proposed solution (or to modify the problem representation).

She noted that, during solution evaluation, constraints on the source solution play an important role in determining the importance of constraints on the target solution. Another application of reuse in evaluation was use of a source solution to confirm the possibility and/or validity of a target-solution proposal.

An important role of sources in all these "stages" was "possible-problems signalling", leading to e.g. the adjustment to the "reality" accessed via the source, of a solution-attribute value developed on purely "theoretical" grounds.

Neal (1989, "example-based programming") also observed that the examples (i.e. the sources) were used for both development and evaluation of target solutions. During development, half of her subjects used the examples only for target coding, whereas the other half used them for both design and coding. All subjects used them rather for syntax than for construction of algorithms.

2.5 Strategies of Reuse

Détienne (1991) distinguishes two code-reuse situations: when reusing code "in a row", all exploitation of a source is done in one, continuous episode[4]; whereas, when designers proceed to "scattered" reuse, the reuse episode of a source is interrupted by other processing. This second strategy leads to errors in the target solutions, which the author attributes to problems of information management in working memory.

Anticipation of reuse. In her study, Détienne also identifies reuse anticipation. She observed that, when her subjects develop a schema instance which is going to be used as a source, they may anticipate the later exploitation of this source. They do so by constructing an operative representation of it, i.e. by distinguishing constant and variable parts, and sometimes by constructing source-modification procedures.

Visser (1987) observes that, through inter-solution homogenisation, the designer anticipates possible future reuse of certain subsolutions of the project currently under development. This homogenisation may take two forms: solutions are created right from the start according to certain homogeneity-assuring rules; or they are modified later on, when the creation of other solutions retroactively imposes such modification in order to homogenise the different solutions in question.

2.6 Frequency of Effective Reuse

Depending on the authors, the software-engineering literature asserts that 40 to 80 % of code is non specific, thus reusable. Many authors advancing 80 % refer to the same paper, i.e. Jones (1984), who himself summarises four studies conducted between 1977 and 1983. In 1989, Biggerstaff and Perlis assert, however: "over the broad span

---

[4] An "episode" is defined by the use of one and the same source.

of systems, reuse is exploited today but to a very limited extent".

Empirical studies providing quantitative data all concern OO software, which -due to its mechanisms of inheritance, abstraction and encapsulation, and polymorphism- is considered to particularly "favour reuse", so the conclusions may be specific to this form of design. Lange and Moher (1989, OO software) indeed observe "massive" reuse: over 85 % of the 99 new methods were developed using pre-existing methods; all nine new classes were defined using existing classes. In Neal's (1989) study, "only" some 33 % of the subjects proceed to reuse.

The conclusion of analogical-reasoning research, however, is that "spontaneous" source retrieval is rare ("spontaneous" meaning that subjects do not have been cued or suggested by the experimenter -contrary to the common practice in analogy research).

2.7 Effects of Reuse on Designers' Productivity

Among the rare empirical studies on reuse conducted by non-psychologists, is the experimentation by three members of a computer-science, and one of a statistics department, Lewis, Henry, Kafura and Schulman (1991, differences between OO and procedural languages concerning effects on productivity). In this study, reuse augments productivity, independently of the software paradigm adopted.

2.8 Difficulties and Risks of Reuse

Sutcliffe and Maiden (1990b, software specifications) observe a significant correlation between the time spent by experts attending to the source and the completeness of the target solution -but not its correctness. "Successful" experts spent 90 % of their time studying the source. In a comparison between experts and novices in the same type of task, Sutcliffe and Maiden (1990a) observe differences: whereas the two groups take the same time to study sources, novices take more time to use them.

The main risks of reuse, identified in several studies, are source-comprehension avoidance and/or failure. Lange and Moher (1989) conclude to such comprehension avoidance, in spite of their experienced professional software designer having a mature mental model -so that it was not in order to compensate for an incomplete model.

Sutcliffe and Maiden (1990b), in their study on reuse by experts, observe that "direct source copying" accounted for many errors; the failure to understand the source led to both mappings based on surface similarities between source and target, and an incapacity to construct mappings where no surface similarities existed.

In their experiment on experts and novices, Sutcliffe and Maiden (1990a) observed that 40 % of novices began reuse without reading the source-narrative; 80 % of novices retrospectively admitted to copying and word substitution during reuse -whereas 70 % of experts said to deliberately having avoided a copying strategy.

3. Discussion

This section discusses two points: repercussions of the results for CBR systems, and research topics in the domain of knowledge reuse.

3.1 Reuse of Knowledge: Repercussions for CBR Systems

3.1.1 Which Reuse Activity Should be Supported?

One often reads that it is the access to sources. We did not find in the literature any data on adaptation or evaluation of a source. If one considers that results on analogical reasoning are relevant to reuse, one might conclude that, amongst the main three stages, retrieval is indeed the "bottleneck" in reuse.

But how should source access be supported? According to analogical-reasoning research, retrieval is so difficult because people refer to inappropriate attributes. In addition, in design -particularly nonroutine design- categorisation of solutions is hard because of their diversity, their non-repetitive character. That is why Falzon and Visser (1989) propose a system supporting not only source access using guiding of its users in their description of the target problem (by proposing them with category attributes), but also abstraction of design-solution categories on the basis of the problems solved.

Green, Gilmore, Blumenthal, Davies and Winder (1992), on the basis of their empirical studies on OO software, propose to attach a "description level" to the program "in which arbitrary attributes and relationships can be recorded in a 'browsable' form" (p. 1). The studies by Perron (1995) on telephone-traffic monitoring also show that predefined categories will not do for characterising sources. Rather than to propose a completely "free" source characterisation, however, she examines if a finite set of attributes is sufficient for characterising sources so that those needed for a particular task can be retrieved.

3.1.2 "What's in a Case?"

Our answer to this question, often asked by CBR-system developers, follows two non exclusive lines based on a cognitive-ergonomics approach: examine how designers proceed, and what they need. Concerning the first line, we saw that, according to the subproblem a designer is solving, a source may take different forms: from a rather abstract structure to a concrete, low-level solution implementation (Visser, 1987). Perron (1995) showed that, according to their task, monitors focus on different source attributes. Thus: cases at different levels and represented from different viewpoints, according to the problem, the problem solver, and the task.

With respect to the other line, arguments concerning the "scope" of recall plead for inclusion in a case, in addition to a product-solution, of "underlying" information (procedure, justifications, history). This proposal is backed up by the result from the Visser (1991) study, presented above, showing that even the authors of a project themselves may not always remember this information: in the study, authors were observed to reconstruct the path leading to a solution whose product they remembered.

3.1.3 Source Construction and Source Exploitation

Rather than to focus on the possibility to consider these two aspects of source processing as two separate tasks, we think it important to examine their relatedness. The observations by Détienne (1991) on source-modification procedure construction, and by Visser (1987) on future-source homogenisation (in "Anticipation of reuse") may suggest that support could be useful (a detailed analysis of the data might suggest modalities).

3.1.4 Source Analysis

Preventing source-comprehension avoidance and/or failure -identified as the main risks of reuse- probably is rather a question of education than of tests -or other conditions on access- built into a system. Access and exploitation should be as easy as possible, but users should be convinced of the necessity to understand the source they plan to use.

3.2 Reuse of Knowledge: Research Topics

Many questions remain to be examined. A few only are alluded to here (see also Visser & Trousse, 1993).

3.2.1 Conditions of Reuse

When does a designer consider to proceed to reuse (rather than to proceed from scratch)? One may formulate the hypothesis that concrete, specific knowledge is used before abstract, general knowledge -an assertion which many authors in the domain of CBR advance without any empirical basis, or referring to not further specified "psychological data". Once again a conclusion from analogy research may be used as an argument, i.e. that surface attributes are more easily accessible than structural features -but data directly concerning this specific question are not available. This is not surprising, given the late start of studies on tasks in domains where the use of specific knowledge is needed; until recently, psychological studies concerned tasks requiring people to refer to only general knowledge (Hunt, 1991; Medin & Ross, 1989).

3.2.2 Retrieval from Memory

As noted already when discussing the question of the "scope" of retrieval, we know that possession of knowledge (in memory) does not imply retrieval of this knowledge when necessary. Possession of knowledge on a product-solution does not imply possession or retrieval of knowledge on the corresponding procedure-solution or underlying justifications. The reconstructive nature of recall -an outcome trivial for linguistic material- still needs to be stressed in the context of problem solving (Ross, 1990).

3.2.3 Reuse and Analogical Reasoning

We kept until the end the question about the possible differences between analogy-based problem solving and problem solving on the basis of reuse. At least four dimensions may play a role to this respect.

• *Domain(s) of target and source.* This is the difference between the two forms of reasoning generally advanced in the CBR community: analogies come from "remote" domains (relative to that of the target), whereas cases are supposed to be intra-domain entities. In human memory, however, separations between domains may be too unstable and/or vague to be operative, i.e. to allow distinctions between domains of knowledge (Visser, 1995, discusses this point in greater detail).

• *Abstraction level(s) of target and source.* We asserted that, in reuse, target and source are at the same abstraction level -as they are in analogical reasoning; but this definition may be questioned.

• *Retrieval: target-source relationship(s) (R).* In analogical reasoning, R(target-source) is analogy (and, for certain authors, other types of similarity). In reuse, in addition to similarity, other types of relationship may lead to target-source evocation.

• *Adaptation mechanism(s).* The transfer and/or mapping mechanisms used in analogical reasoning may be supposed to be used also for source adaptation in reuse; no other mechanisms have been proposed in the literature. Empirical data are needed on this point (also).

In conclusion: this paper has shown that, even if many questions are still asking for research, empirical studies on reuse have led to a number of results which may be interesting for research and development in the domain of CBR.

Acknowledgements

The author wishes to thank Andrea Enzinger and two anonymous reviewers for comments on the first version of this paper.

References

Baerentsen, K. B. (1991). Knowledge and shared experience. Proc. of the Third European Conference of Cognitive Science Approaches to Process Control, Cardiff, Univ. of Wales, 217-232.

Biggerstaff, T. J., & Perlis, A. J. (1989). Introduction. In T. J. Biggerstaff & A. J. Perlis (Eds.), Software reusability, Vol. I, Concepts and models. Reading, MA: Addison-Wesley.

Burkhardt, J.-M., & Détienne, F. (1995). An empirical study of software reuse by experts in object-oriented design. Proc. of Interact'95, Lillehammer (Norway), 27 - 29 June.

Carbonell, J. G. (1986). Derivational analogy: a theory of reconstructive problem solving and expertise acquisition. In R. S. Michalski, J. G. Carbonell & T. M. Mitchell (Eds.), Machine learning. An artificial intelligence approach (Vol. II). Los Altos, CA: Morgan.

Détienne, F. (1991). Reasoning from a schema and from an analog in software code reuse. Fourth Workshop on Empirical studies of programmers, New Brunswick, N.J., Dec. 6-8.

Falzon, P., & Visser, W. (1989). Variations in expertise: implications for the design of assistance systems. In G. Salvendy & M. Smith (Eds.), Designing and using human-computer interfaces and knowledge based systems. Amsterdam: Elsevier.

Green, T. R. G., Gilmore, D. J., Blumenthal, B. B., Davies, S., & Winder, R. (1992). Towards a cognitive browser for OOPS. International Journal of Human-Computer Interaction, 4, 1-34.

Hunt, E. (1991). Some comments on the study of complexity. In R. J. Sternberg & P. A. Frensch (Eds.) Complex problem solving: principles and mechanisms. Hillsdale, N.J.: Erlbaum.

Jones, T. C. (1984). Reusability in programming: a survey of the state of the art. IEEE Transactions on Software Engineering, Special issue on Software reusability, SE-10 (5), 488-493.

Keane, M. (1988). Analogical problem solving. Chichester: Horwood.

Klein, G. A., & Calderwood, R. (1988). How do people use analogues to make decisions? In J. Kolodner (Ed.), Case-based reasoning. Proc. DARPA Workshop. San Mateo, CA: Morgan.

Kolodner, J. L. (1993). Case-based reasoning. San Mateo, CA: Morgan.

Lange, B. M., & Moher, T. G. (1989). Some strategies of reuse in an object-oriented programming environment. In K. Bice & C. Lewis (Eds.), CHI'89 'Wings for the mind' Conference Proc.. Reading, MA: Addison Wesley.

Lewis, J. A., Henry, S. M., Kafura, D. G., & Schulman, R. (1991). An empirical study of the object-oriented paradigm and software reuse. In Proc. of OPSLA'91 Object-Oriented Programming, Systems and Applications'91. New York, NY: ACM Press, 184-196.

Medin, D. L., & Ross, B. H. (1989). The specific character of abstract thought: categorization, problem solving, and induction. In R. J. Sternberg (Ed.), Advances in the psychology of human intelligence, Vol. 5. Hillsdale, N.J.: Erlbaum.

Neal, L. R. (1989). A system for example-based programming. In K. Bice & C. Lewis (Eds.), CHI'89 'Wings for the mind' Conference Proc.. Reading, MA: Addison Wesley.

Norman, D., & Bobrow, D. (1979). Descriptions: An intermediate stage in memory retrieval. Cognitive Psychology, 11, 107-123.

Perron, L. (1995). La réutilisation de cas 'une problématique commune entre I.A. et ergonomie cognitive ... des points de vue différents'. Actes de JAVA-JAC'95, Grenoble 5 - 7 avril.

Pu, P. (1993). Introduction: Issues in case-based design systems. AI EDAM, 7 (2), 79-85, and the other papers in this special AI EDAM issue.

Reiser, B. J. (1986). Knowledge-directed retrieval of autobiographical memories. In J. L. Kolodner & C. K. Riesbeck (Eds.), Experience, memory, and reasoning. Hillsdale, N.J.: Erlbaum.

Ross, B. H. (1990). The access and use of relevant information: a specific case and general issues. In R. Freedle (Ed.), Artificial Intelligence and the future of testing. Hillsdale, N.J.: Erlbaum.

Sutcliffe, A., & Maiden, N. (1990a). Cognitive studies in software engineering. Proc. of ECCE-5, Fifth European Conference on Cognitive Ergonomics, Urbino, Italy, Sept. 3-6.

Sutcliffe, A., & Maiden, N. (1990b). Software reusability: delivering productivity gains or short cuts. In D. Diaper, G. Cockton, D. Gilmore & B. Shackel (Eds.), Human-computer interaction - INTERACT '90. Amsterdam: North-Holland.

Thunem, S., & Sindre, G. (1992). Development with and for reuse. Guidelines from the REBOOT-project. Proc. of the ERCIM Workshop "Methods and Tools for Software Reuse", Heraklion, Oct. 29-30 (pp. 2- 16).

Trousse, B., & Visser, W. (1993). Use of case-based reasoning techniques for intelligent computer-aided-design systems. Proc. of the IEEE/SME'93 International Conference on Systems, Man and Cybernetics-Systems Engineering in the Service of Humans, Le Touquet, France, Oct. 17-20.

Tulving, E. (1983). Elements of episodic memory. Oxford: Oxford University.

Visser, W. (1987). Strategies in programming programmable controllers: a field study on a professional programmer. In G. Olson, S. Sheppard & E. Soloway (Eds.), Empirical Studies of Programmers: Second Workshop. Norwood, N.J.: Ablex.

Visser, W. (1990). More or less following a plan during design: opportunistic deviations in specification. International Journal of Man-Machine Studies. Special issue: What programmers know, 33, 247-278.

Visser, W. (1991). Evocation and elaboration of solutions: Different types of problem-solving actions. An empirical study on the design of an aerospace artifact. In T. Kohonen & F. Fogelman-Soulié (Eds.), COGNITIVA 90. At the crossroads of Artificial Intelligence, Cognitive science, and Neuroscience. Proc. of the third COGNITIVA symposium. Amsterdam: Elsevier.

Visser, W. (1992a). Designers' activities examined at three levels: organization, strategies & problem-solving. Knowledge-Based Systems, 5 (1), 92-104.

Visser, W. (1992b). Use of analogical relationships between design problem-solution representations: Exploitation at the action-execution and action-management levels of the activity. Studia Psychologica, 34 (4-5), 351-357.

Visser , W. (Ed.). (1993). Proc. of the Workshop of the Thirteenth International Joint Conference on Artificial Intelligence "Reuse of designs: an interdisciplinary cognitive approach", Chambéry (France), August 29, 1993. Rocquencourt: INRIA.

Visser, W. (1995). Use of episodic knowledge and information in design problem solving. Design Studies, 16 (2), 171-187.

Visser, W., & Trousse, B. (1993). Reuse of designs: desperately seeking an interdisciplinary approach. In Visser (1993).

De Vries, E. (1993). The role of case-based reasoning in architectural design: stretching the design problem space. In Visser (1993).

Weber, G. (1991). Explanation-based retrieval in a case-based learning model. Proc. of the Thirteenth Annual Meeting of the Cognitive Science Society, Chicago, IL. Hillsdale, N.J.: Cognitive Science Society, 522-527.

Williams, M. D., & Hollan, J. D. (1981). The process of retrieval from very long-term memory. Cognitive Science, 5, 87-119.

Woodfield, S. N., Embley, D. W., & Scott, D. T. (1987). Can programmers reuse software? IEEE Software, Special Issue on Reusability, 4, 52-59.

Weighting Features

Dietrich Wettschereck[1] and David W. Aha[2]

[1] German National Research Center for Computer Science,
53754 Sankt Augustin, Germany (dietrich.wettschereck@gmd.de)
[2] Navy Center for Applied Research in AI, Naval Research Laboratory,
Washington, DC 20375 USA (aha@aic.nrl.navy.mil)

Abstract. Many case-based reasoning algorithms retrieve cases using a derivative of the k-nearest neighbor (k-NN) classifier, whose similarity function is sensitive to irrelevant, interacting, and noisy features. Many proposed methods for reducing this sensitivity parameterize k-NN's similarity function with feature weights. We focus on methods that automatically assign weight settings using little or no domain-specific knowledge. Our goal is to predict the relative capabilities of these methods for specific dataset characteristics. We introduce a five-dimensional framework that categorizes automated weight-setting methods, empirically compare methods along one of these dimensions, summarize our results with four hypotheses, and describe additional evidence that supports them. Our investigation revealed that most methods correctly assign low weights to completely irrelevant features, and methods that use performance feedback demonstrate three advantages over other methods (i.e., they require less pre-processing, better tolerate interacting features, and increase learning rate).

1 Case Retrieval Using k-Nearest Neighbor

Variants of the k-nearest neighbor (k-NN) classifier are frequently used for case retrieval in case-based reasoning (CBR) algorithms. k-NN assumes each case $x = \{x_1, x_2, \ldots, x_n, x_c\}$ is defined by a set of n (numeric or symbolic) features, where x_c is x's class value. Given a query q and a case library L, k-NN retrieves the set K of q's k most similar (i.e., least distant) cases in L and predicts their weighted-majority class as the class of q. Distance is defined as

$$\text{distance}(x, q) = \sqrt{\sum_{f=1}^{n} w_f \times \text{difference}(x_f, q_f)^2} \qquad (1)$$

where w_f is the parameterized weight value assigned to feature f, and

$$\text{difference}(x_f, q_f) = \begin{cases} |x_f - q_f| & \text{if feature } f \text{ is numeric} \\ 0 & \text{if feature } f \text{ is symbolic and } x_f = q_f \\ 1 & \text{Otherwise} \end{cases} \qquad (2)$$

The probability $p(q, c, K)$ that q is a member of class c is defined as

$$p(q, c, K) = \frac{\sum_{x \in K \wedge x_c = c} 1/\text{distance}(q, x)}{\sum_{x \in K} 1/\text{distance}(q, x)} \qquad (3)$$

Table 1. Dimensions For Distinguishing Feature Weighting Methods

Dimension	Possible Values
Feedback	{Available, Not Available}
Weight Space	{Continuous, Binary}
Representation	{Given, Transformed}
Generality	{Global, Local}
Knowledge	{Poor, Intensive}

where small addends (not shown) are used to prevent zero division. For classification tasks a class c with a largest $p(q, c, K)$ is output. k is set using leave-one-out cross-validation (LOOCV) on L. Numeric features are normalized (i.e., by subtracting their mean and dividing by their standard deviation) to ensure they have the same range (and expected impact) in Equation 2. k-NN does not address CBR issues other than case retrieval, and requires extension when applied to case representations not defined by a flat set of features.

In Equation 1, k-NN assigns equal weights to all features (i.e., $\forall_f \{w_f = 1\}$). This bias handicaps k-NN, allowing redundant, irrelevant, and other imperfect features to influence distance computations. Thus, k-NN can perform poorly when such features are present. Many variants of it have been proposed that instead assign higher weight settings to the (presumably) more relevant features for case retrieval. Although many feature-weighting variants of k-NN have been reported to improve its retrieval accuracy on some tasks (e.g., Aha, 1990; Kelly & Davis, 1991; Wettschereck, 1994), their relative merits are not known; previous comparisons focussed on specific algorithm pairings (e.g., Wettschereck & Dietterich, 1995; Kohavi et al., 1995) or present only case study results (Mohri & Tanaka, 1994).

We introduce a framework for feature-weighting methods in Section 2 and empirically compare a specific subset of them in Section 3. Case studies are not particularly informative. Therefore, in Section 4 we present hypotheses for explaining these results and investigate each empirically. Section 5 includes a summary discussion.

2 Framework and Examples

The feature weighting methods reviewed here modify the standard k-NN similarity function by allowing feature weights to have different values. We briefly introduce our framework in Section 2.1 and detail examples of its first dimension in Section 2.2. Wettschereck et al. (1995) discuss details on the other dimensions.

2.1 A Framework for Feature-Weighting

We distinguish feature weighting methods along five dimensions (Table 1).

Dimension 1: Feedback This dimension concerns whether the feature weighting method receives feedback from the k-NN variant being used. We discuss this dimension in detail in Section 2.2.

Dimension 2: Weight Space This concerns the size of the space of feature weights searched by the algorithm. Many feature weighting methods perform *feature selection*, which constrains the search space to binary values. Feature selection has a long history in pattern recognition (e.g., Devijver & Kittler, 1982). Several researchers have recently reported accuracy and/or speed improvements for k-NN variants in CBR systems (e.g., Cardie, 1993; Moore & Lee, 1994; Skalak, 1994; Aha & Bankert, 1994).

Feature selection methods can reduce the task's dimensionality when they eliminate irrelevant features. Kohavi et al. (1995) present evidence that continuous weighting increases accuracy when features vary in their relevance for classification, though it requires searching a much larger space.

Dimension 3: Representation This concerns whether the feature set is transformed (i.e., replaced with a different set) before weighting, which can sensitize CBR algorithms to interacting or correlated features. For example, Mohri and Tanaka (1994) used *Quantification Method II* (QMII) to transform the feature set. After *binarizing* the symbolic features (i.e., replacing each feature defined over v values with $v - 1$ binary features), QMII computes weights that maximize the ratio of the variance between each class' cases to the variance of all cases. Mohri and Tanaka introduced a k-NN variant of QMII named QMIIy and reported that it performed best among the algorithms they tested.

Dimension 4: Generality Most weighting methods learn settings for a single set of global weights, but their assumption that feature relevance is invariant over the domain is constraining and sometimes inappropriate. Other methods instead assume weights differ among *local* regions of the case space, either for different values of a feature (e.g., Stanfill & Waltz, 1986; Creecy et al., 1992; Ricci & Avesani, 1995) or on a case-specific basis (e.g., Domingos, in press). Case specific weighting provides great flexibility in assessing feature relevance, which is required to model subject data accurately (Aha & Goldstone, 1992).

Dimension 5: Knowledge This is the most important dimension for distinguishing feature weighting methods. Domain-specific knowledge can be used, for example, to constrain the case representation (Stanfill & Waltz, 1986), guide feature transformation (Aha, 1991), or assign case-specific weight settings (Cain et al., 1991). We focus on automated algorithms that do not receive much task-specific knowledge. A comparison of knowledge-intensive methods for weighting features in CBR algorithms would complement this paper's contribution.

2.2 Details on the Feedback Dimension

This first dimension refers to whether the feature-weighting method uses feedback from the k-NN variant to assign weights or not; we refer to these as *feedback* and *ignorant* methods in our paper. Kohavi et al. (1995) presented favorable comparative evidence for one feedback method. We review two sets of feedback methods and three sets of ignorant methods in this section.

2.2.1 Feedback methods.

Incremental hill-climbers: These methods modify feature weights to (a) increase the similarity between a query q and nearby cases in the same class and (b) decrease its similarity with nearby cases in other classes. They process each training case once and are thus sensitive to their presentation ordering.

Salzberg (1991) used this method in EACH. When a correct classification occurs, if feature f matches, then its weight w_f is incremented by Δ_f. Mismatching features have their weights decremented by this same amount. For incorrect classifications, the weights of *mismatching* features are incremented while the weights of matching features are decremented. Salzberg reported that different values of Δ_f worked better for different datasets.

Wettschereck and Dietterich (1995) argued that EACH's weighting method is insensitive to skewed concept distributions, a problem that IB4 (Aha, 1990) addresses. It computes weights using

$$w_f = \max \left(\frac{\text{CumulativeWeight}_f}{\text{WeightNormalizer}_f} - 0.5, 0 \right), \tag{4}$$

where CumulativeWeight$_f$ is expected to asymptote to $\dfrac{\text{WeightNormalizer}_f}{2}$ for seemingly irrelevant features. Let Λ be the higher observed frequency among the two concepts x_c and q_c. CumulativeWeight$_f$ is incremented by

$$\begin{cases} 1 - \text{difference}(x_f, q_f) \times (1 - \Lambda) & \text{if } x_c = q_c \\ \text{difference}(x_f, q_f) \times (1 - \Lambda) & \text{Otherwise} \end{cases} \tag{5}$$

and WeightNormalizer$_f$ is always incremented by $(1 - \Lambda)$. Aha (1990) reported good results for IB4 on tasks involving irrelevant features.

IB4 assumes a uniform distribution for irrelevant feature values. Kira and Rendell (1992) removed this constraint in RELIEF. It selects a random training case x, a similar positive case p, and a similar negative case n. It then updates the feature weights using

$$w_f = w_f - \text{difference}(x_f, p_f) + \text{difference}(x_f, n_f) \tag{6}$$

Kira and Rendell reported good results for RELIEF on parity tasks. We evaluate a hill-climbing variant of RELIEF-F, Kononenko's (1994) extension of RELIEF, in our experiments.

Continuous optimizers: These feedback methods iteratively update feature weights using randomly-selected training cases. For example, GA-WKNN (Kelly and Davis, 1991) uses a genetic algorithm to update feature weights, where search is guided by five genetic operators and fitness is based on both training accuracy and recency. GA-WKNN attained lower error rates than k-NN for three datasets. Skalak (1994) instead used only the mutation genetic operator to select features (i.e., binary weights) for 1-NN. His algorithm retains the best-performing bit sequence and terminates after a fixed number of iterations since finding a new best string. It attained higher accuracies than 1-NN on four datasets while halving the number of features used to compute distances.

Other continuous optimization algorithms use knowledge of the function's gradient to increase learning speed, which works well for reasonably smooth target functions. Lowe (1995) employed this approach in the *variable kernel similarity metric* (VSM), which optimizes feature weights using the conjugate gradient algorithm to minimize the summed LOOCV error on the training set. The derivative of this error with respect to each feature weight is used to guide the search. The VSM performed as well or better than several other algorithms on two datasets yet required far less training time than some other algorithms.

We experimented with k-NN$_{VSM}$ (Wettschereck et al., 1995), a variant of the VSM that isolates its feature-weighting method. k-NN$_{VSM}$ computes the distances between all pairs of training cases using Equation 1, assigns the same value to each weight (i.e., $\forall_f\{w_f = 1\}$), then optimizes the value of k, and finally uses conjugate gradient to optimize feature weights so as to minimize LOOCV training error. The error function is (i.e., for a set of classes C)

$$E = \sum_{x \in L} \sum_{c \in C} \begin{cases} (1 - p(x, c, K))^2 & \text{if } x_c = c \\ p(x, c, K)^2 & \text{Otherwise} \end{cases} \tag{7}$$

2.2.2 Ignorant methods.

Conditional probabilities: This group consists of two methods that assign feature weights using simple conditional probabilities, discretize numeric features, and binarize symbolic features (Creecy et al., 1992). The *per category feature importance* (PCF) method assigns high weight values to features that are highly correlated with the given class using

$$w_f(c) = P(c|f) \tag{8}$$

That is, the weight for feature f for a class c is the conditional probability that a case is a member of c given the value of f. This algorithm tends to classify too many cases according to the majority class (Mohri & Tanaka, 1994).

The *cross-category feature importance* (CCF) method averages across classes. It computes weight settings using

$$w_f = \sum_{c \in C} P(c|f)^2 \tag{9}$$

Since Mohri and Tanaka (1994) reported good results for CCF, we included it in our experiments.

Class projection: The more sophisticated *value-difference metric* (VDM) (Stanfill & Waltz, 1986) does not binarize symbolic features. It computes similarity between individual (symbolic) feature values, defining distance using

$$\text{distance}(x, q) = \sum_{f=1}^{n} w_f(f, x_f) \times \text{difference}(f, x_f, q_f) \tag{10}$$

$$w_f(f, v) = \sqrt{\sum_{c \in C} \left(\frac{\lambda(c, f, v)}{\lambda(f, v)} \right)^2} \tag{11}$$

$$\text{difference}(f, v_1, v_2) = \sum_{c \in C} \left(\frac{\lambda(c, f, v_1)}{\lambda(f, v_1)} - \frac{\lambda(c, f, v_2)}{\lambda(f, v_2)} \right)^2 \tag{12}$$

Equation 11 computes the weight of feature f with value v. $\lambda(c, f, v)$ is the number of times that cases of class c in the case library have value v for f, whereas $\lambda(f, v)$ is the same value summed over the set C of all classes. The VDM assigns higher weights to features whose distribution of values across classes are highly skewed. Equation 12 computes the difference of two values for f. It assigns greater differences to values whose corresponding sets of cases have highly disparate class distributions. Thus, two cases are similar if they have feature values whose respective projections on the training library have similar class distributions. We included the VDM in our experiments.

Mutual information: This third ignorant approach assigns feature weights using the *mutual information* (MI) (Shannon, 1948) between the values of a feature and the class of the training cases. The MI of two variables is the reduction in uncertainty of one variable's value given knowledge of the other's value, computed using

$$w_f = \sum_{v \in V_f} \sum_{c \in C} p(x_c = c \wedge x_f = v) \cdot log \frac{p(x_c = c \wedge x_f = v)}{p(x_c = c) \cdot p(x_f = v)} \tag{13}$$

where $p(x_c = c)$ is the probability that the class x_c of an arbitrary training case x is c and $p(x_f = v)$ is the probability that its value for feature f is v, where f's set of possible values is V_f. Daelemans and van den Bosch (1992) reported that MI significantly improved k-NN's accuracy for one task. Wettschereck and Dietterich (1995) reported that MI significantly increased EACH's (Salzberg, 1991) accuracy. In our experiments, we examined a variant of this approach that discretizes continuous features using Fayyad and Irani's (1993) algorithm.

Table 2. Algorithms Selected for Experimentation

| | Weighting Method | |
Name	Category	Subcategory
RELIEF-F	Feedback	Incremental hill climber
k-NN$_{VSM}$	Feedback	Continuous optimizer
CCF	Ignorant	Conditional probabilities
VDM	Ignorant	Class projection
MI	Ignorant	Mutual information

Table 3. Characteristics of the selected datasets. B = Boolean, C = Continuous, S = Symbolic. The relevant features in the datasets located above the horizontal divider are approximately equally relevant.

Domain	Set Size		Number and Type of Features	Number of Irrelevant Features	Classes
	Training	Test			
Banded	350	150	2 C	1	10
Sinusoidal	350	150	2 C	1	2
Gauss-band	350	150	4 C, 1 B	2	14
Parity	350	150	11 B	7	2
LED Display	200	1000	7 B	0	10
LED+17	200	1000	7 B, 17 C	17	10
Waveform	300	100	21 C	0	3
Waveform+19	300	100	40 C	19	3
Cleveland	212	91	5 C, 3 B, 5 S	0	2
NETtalk phonemes	5000	2500	7 S	0	54

3 Comparing Feedback with Ignorant Weighting Methods

This section reports an empirical comparison that motivates the selection of our summary hypotheses in Section 4. We focus on the first dimension of our framework.[3] Each selected algorithm (Table 2) represents a subcategory of the methods described in Section 2.2; they differ only in how they assign weights to features. Not shown is k-NN, the control algorithm.

For this paper, we selected ten datasets (Table 3) that test the algorithms' capabilities for tolerating irrelevant, interacting, and/or redundant features. Cases were selected randomly from a uniform distribution in the first four datasets. First, *banded* has one relevant and one irrelevant feature, and ten equal-sized classes. Second, *sinusoidal*'s two-dimensional concept boundary is a sine curve with eight peaks; its vertical dimension is nearly irrelevant for distinguishing cases in the two classes. Third, *gauss-band* has interacting features. It extends *sinusoidal* with three additional features; two of these define four Gaussian distributions, while the fifth determines whether the class is determined by the first or second pair of features. The fourth dataset is a parity problem on 11 binary

---

[3] See (Wettschereck et al., 1995) for a more extensive evaluation.

Table 4. Mean Accuracy of Feature Weighting Algorithms Relative to k-NN

| Dataset | k-NN | Feature Weight Learning Algorithm | | | | |
| | | Feedback Method | | Ignorant Method | | |
		Relief-F	k-NN$_{VSM}$	CCF	VDM	MI
Banded	83.0±0.4	**11.2**	**12.8**	**12.8**	**12.8**	10.8
Sinusoidal	74.2±0.8	**5.9**	**14.4**	**-9.1**	**-9.1**	**-4.6**
Gauss-band	78.3±0.5	**8.6**	**16.6**	**14.9**	**15.5**	12.1
Parity	67.3±0.1	**32.7**	**32.7**	1.3	1.7	2.2
LED Display	72.7±0.4	**-1.0**	0.0	**-1.5**	**-1.4**	-1.2
LED+17	68.8±0.6	**3.3**	**2.0**	**-5.6**	**2.0**	3.6
Waveform	82.1±0.4	0.3	-0.5	**-6.1**	**-3.7**	0.5
Waveform+19	81.3±0.9	**1.7**	1.2	**-3.4**	-0.7	1.0
Cleveland	82.4±0.8	-0.5	0.0	**-1.3**	0.2	-0.6
NETtalk	69.6±0.2	**9.2**	**6.6**	7.7	**10.0**	9.7

features, where positive cases have an odd number of the first four features set. Thus, it has both interacting and irrelevant features.

The remaining datasets are obtainable from the UCI Repository (Murphy, 1995). Whereas LED's relevant features are roughly equally relevant, Waveform's vary in their relevance. Waveform+19 (LED+17) is identical to Waveform (LED) with the addition of 19 (17) continuous irrelevant features. The Cleveland dataset contains some redundant features, while the NETtalk dataset has no irrelevant or redundant features (Wettschereck, 1994).

Each dataset was randomly partitioned 25 times into disjoint training and test sets. Table 4 lists the algorithms' average test set accuracy relative to k-NN, whose standard error is also listed. Significant differences are highlighted using **boldface** (i.e., two-tailed t-tests, confidence level 0.05). We used LOOCV to tune the algorithms' free parameters (i.e., except for the large NETtalk dataset, where we optimized parameter settings on a cross-validated subset of the training set). k's optimal value was estimated for all methods. k-NN$_{VSM}$'s number of epochs was limited to the number required for minimization along one conjugate direction. Fayyad and Irani's (1993) algorithm was used to discretize continuous features for RELIEF-F, CCF, VDM, and MI.

4   Evaluating Summary Hypotheses

These results motivated us to test the four hypotheses addressed in this section. Wettschereck et al. (1995) describe a more extensive analysis.

H1: Most feature weighting methods can tolerate irrelevant features unless there are many highly interacting features. The results generally support this hypothesis except for the *sinusoidal* task (see **H2**). However, the size of the case library must also be considered. For example, k-NN 's average performance decreased by only a small amount when adding the 19 irrelevant

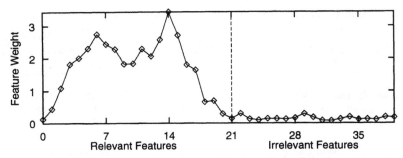

Fig. 1. Feature Weights Computed by MI in the Waveform+19 Task

Table 5. Average Accuracies on the Waveform Tasks Relative to k-NN

Dataset	Training Size	k-NN	Feature Weight Learning Algorithm		Ignorant Method
			Feedback Method		
			Relief-F	k-NN$_{VSM}$	MI
Waveform	100	77.0±1.0	79.1	77.2	78.0
	300	82.1±0.9	82.4	81.6	82.6
Waveform+19	100	73.4±1.0	**78.4**	**76.7**	**78.6**
	300	81.3±0.9	**83.0**	82.5	82.3

features to the Waveform task. Although the *relative* accuracies of the other methods all increased as expected and they computed low weights for the irrelevant features (e.g., see Figure 1), only RELIEF-F significantly improved accuracy. We surmised that smaller case libraries would prevent k-NN from performing as well as the other algorithms. Our results from a follow-up study (Table 5) support this hypothesis.

H2: Ignorant methods can suffer substantially when the data are not carefully pre-processed. We hypothesized that the ignorant methods performed comparative poorly on the *sinusoidal* task because their discretization procedure did not work well for this task, as revealed by subsequent inspections.[4] The accuracies of all ignorant methods improved significantly (Table 6) in followup experiments with user-provided discretizations. Discretization is not performed for k-NN or k-NN$_{VSM}$ and had no positive effect for RELIEF-F.

H3: Feedback methods attain higher accuracies than ignorant methods in tasks with a few interacting features. This is evidenced by the performance differences between MI and k-NN$_{VSM}$ in tasks with interacting features (e.g., *parity* and LED). We tested them on the parity concept, varying the number of relevant binary features in a ten-dimensional space. Although

---

[4] The vertical, more relevant, dimension was generally split into only three intervals, where one interval covered nearly the entire range. There exist 16 equally-sized intervals.

Table 6. Average Accuracies for the *sinusoidal* Task Relative to *k*-NN

Discretization Method	*k*-NN	Feature Weight Learning Algorithm			
		Feedback Method	Ignorant Method		
		k-NN$_{VSM}$	CCF	VDM	MI
none	74.2±0.7	88.6			
(Fayyad & Irani, 1993)			-65.1	-65.1	-69.6
Manually Set			81.6	82.8	88.5

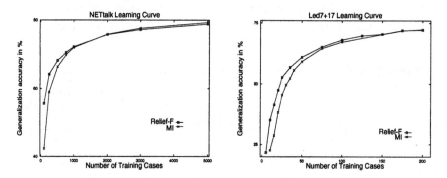

Fig. 2. Learning curves for MI and RELIEF-F for two tasks.

k-NN$_{VSM}$'s significantly outperformed MI for up to four parity features, they performed equally poorly for larger numbers of interacting features.

H4: Feedback methods have faster learning rates than ignorant methods. We selected the two most computationally efficient methods from each category (i.e., MI and RELIEF-F) to investigate this hypothesis. The learning curves from experiments with three tasks where these methods attained approximately equal accuracies (Table 4) indicate that RELIEF-F's learning rate is indeed faster than MI's. Two of these curves are shown in Figure 2.

In summary, these results provide confirming but incomplete evidence for hypotheses designed to help determine which methods should perform well for some given task characteristics. The reason *why* they perform differently is due to their only difference: their similarity function and, in particular, their feature weighting method.

5 Implications

This paper focussed on empirical evaluations of knowledge poor feature weighting methods for CBR algorithms. The dimensional framework can be used to relate methods for weighting features, motivate experiments to distinguish their comparative abilities, and suggest future work (e.g., selection followed by continuous weighting, locally estimating where weighting might be profitably explored, etc.). New weighting methods can be categorized according to this framework, which would simplify their comprehension. Further investigations could focus on the latter four dimensions.

The evidence for our hypotheses is limited to the algorithms and datasets tested. For example, H3 suggests feedback methods are preferred for tasks with interacting features, yet this could be contradicted by designing an ignorant method to account for such features. Also, we examined only a binary feedback/ignorant distinction rather than gradations of that dimension.

The scope of our investigation is also limited; it ignores k-NN methods that incorporate domain-specific knowledge (i.e., Dimension 5 of our framework in Section 2) and task-appropriate case representations. When designing practical CBR applications, a feature-weighting method should be selected in the context of these and other crucial design decisions.

Acknowledgements Thanks to our anonymous reviewers for their suggestions.

References

Aha, D. W. (1990). *A study of instance-based learning algorithms for supervised learning tasks: Mathematical, empirical, and psychological evaluations* (TR 90-42). Irvine, CA: University of California, Department of Information and Computer Science.

Aha, D. W. (1991). Incremental constructive induction: An instance-based approach. In *Proceedings of the Eighth International Workshop on Machine Learning* (pp. 117–121). Evanston, IL: Morgan Kaufmann.

Aha, D. W., & Bankert, R. L. (1994). Feature selection for case-based classification of cloud types: An empirical comparison. In D. W. Aha (Ed.) *Case-Based Reasoning: Papers from the 1994 Workshop* (TR WS-94-01). Menlo Park, CA: AAAI Press.

Aha, D. W., & Goldstone, R. L. (1992). Concept learning and flexible weighting. In *Proceedings of the Fourteenth Annual Conference of the Cognitive Science Society* (pp. 534–539). Bloomington, IN: Lawrence Erlbaum.

Cain, T., Pazzani, M. J., & Silverstein, G. (1991). Using domain knowledge to influence similarity judgement. In *Proceedings of the Case-Based Reasoning Workshop* (pp. 191–202). Washington, DC: Morgan Kaufmann.

Cardie, C. (1993). Using decision trees to improve case-based learning. In *Proceedings of the Tenth International Conference on Machine Learning* (pp. 25–32). Amherst, MA: Morgan Kaufmann.

Creecy, R. H., Masand, B. M., Smith, S. J., & Waltz, D. L. (1992). Trading MIPS and memory for knowledge engineering. *Communications of the ACM, 35*, 48–64.

Daelemans, W., van den Bosch, A. (1992). Generalization performance of backpropagation learning on a syllabification task. In *Proceedings of TWLT3: Connectionism and Natural Language Processing* (pp. 27–37). Enschede, The Netherlands: Unpublished.

Devijver, P. A., & Kittler, J. (1982). *Pattern recognition: A statistical approach.* Englewood Cliffs, NJ: Prentice-Hall.

Domingos, P. Context-sensitive feature selection for lazy learners. To appear in *Artificial Intelligence Review.*.

Fayyad, U. M., & Irani, K. B. (1993). Multi-interval discretization of continuous-valued attributes for classification learning. In *Proceedings of the Thirteenth International Joint Conference on Artificial Intelligence* (pp. 1022–1029). Chambery, France: Morgan Kaufmann.

Kelly, J. D., Jr., & Davis, L. (1991). A hybrid genetic algorithm for classification. In *Proceedings of the Twelfth International Joint Conference on Artificial Intelligence* (pp. 645–650). Sydney, Australia: Morgan Kaufmann.

Kira, K., & Rendell, L. A. (1992). A practical approach to feature selection. In *Proceedings of the Ninth International Conference on Machine Learning* (pp. 249–256). Aberdeen, Scotland: Morgan Kaufmann.

Kohavi, R., Langley, P., & Yun, Y. (1995). Heuristic search for feature weights in instance-based learning. Unpublished manuscript.

Kononenko, I. (1994). Estimating attributes: Analysis and extensions of RELIEF. In *Proceedings of the 1994 European Conference on Machine Learning* (pp. 171–182). Catania, Italy: Springer Verlag.

Lowe, D. (1995). Similarity metric learning for a variable-kernal classifier. *Neural Computation, 7,* 72–85.

Mohri, T., & Tanaka, H. (1994). An optimal weighting criterion of case indexing for both numeric and symbolic attributes. In D. W. Aha (Ed.), *Case-Based Reasoning: Papers from the 1994 Workshop* (TR WS-94-01). Menlo Park, CA: AAAI Press.

Moore, A. W., & Lee, M. S. (1994). Efficient algorithms for minimizing cross validation error. In *Proceedings of the Eleventh International Conference on Machine Learning* (pp. 190–198). New Brunswick, NJ: Morgan Kaufmann.

Murphy, P. (1995). *UCI Repository of machine learning databases* [Machine-readable data repository @ics.uci.edu]. Irvine, CA: University of California, Department of Information and Computer Science.

Ricci, F., & Avesani, P. (1995). Learning a local similarity metric for case-based reasoning. To appear in *Proceedings of the First International Conference on Case-Based Reasoning.* Sesimbra, Portugal: Springer-Verlag.

Salzberg, S. L. (1991). A nearest hyperrectangle learning method. *Machine Learning, 6,* 251–276.

Shannon, C. E. (1948). A mathematical theory of communication. *Bell Systems Technology Journal, 27,* 379–423.

Skalak, D. (1994). Prototype and feature selection by sampling and random mutation hill climbing algorithms. In *Proceedings of the Eleventh International Machine Learning Conference* (pp. 293–301). New Brunswick, NJ: Morgan Kaufmann.

Stanfill, C., & Waltz, D. (1986). Toward memory-based reasoning. *Communications of the ACM, 29,* 1213–1228.

Wettschereck, D. (1994). *A study of distance-based machine learning algorithms.* Doctoral dissertation, Department of Computer Science, Oregon State University, Corvallis, OR.

Wettschereck, D., Aha, D. W. & Mohri, T (1995). *A review and comparative evaluation of feature weighting methods for lazy learning algorithms* (TR AIC-95-012). Washington, DC: Naval Research Laboratory, Navy Center for Applied Research in Artificial Intelligence.

Wettschereck, D., & Dietterich, T. G. (1995). An experimental comparison of the nearest neighbor and nearest hyperrectangle algorithms. *Machine Learning, 19,* 5–28.

An Investigation of Marker-Passing Algorithms for Analogue Retrieval

Michael Wolverton

Knowledge Engineering and Image Processing Group, SINTEF DELAB,
N-7034 Trondheim, Norway,
e-mail: Michael.Wolverton@delab.sintef.no

Abstract. If analogy and case-based reasoning systems are to scale up to very large case bases, it is important to analyze the various methods used for retrieving analogues to identify the features of the problem for which they are appropriate. This paper reports on one such analysis, a comparison of retrieval by marker passing or spreading activation in a semantic network with *Knowledge-Directed Spreading Activation*, a method developed to be well-suited for retrieving semantically distant analogues from a large knowledge base. The analysis has two complementary components: (1) a theoretical model of the retrieval time based on a number of problem characteristics, and (2) experiments showing how the retrieval time of the approaches varies with the knowledge base size. These two components, taken together, suggest that KDSA is more likely than SA to be able to scale up to retrieval in large knowledge bases.

1 Introduction

Most research in retrieval in case-based reasoning and analogy has focused on retrieving same-domain analogies, often from relatively small case and knowledge bases. Relatively little attention has been given to retrieving cross-domain analogies, specifically those where the two analogues are *semantically distant* from one another – i.e., the analogues mismatch on all but a few key aspects, and those aspects that do match do so only at a high level of abstraction. These semantically distant analogies have been identified as one possible source of support for creative reasoning in intelligent systems [5], which is quickly becoming an important goal for artificial intelligence. Semantically distant analogies pose difficult computational problems for analogy retrieval algorithms, since such analogies are only feasible in very large multi-domain knowledge bases, and since the high degree of mismatch between the analogues make the connection between them difficult to find in a tractable amount of time. It is important, then, to study how well analogy retrieval algorithms meet these computational demands – i.e., how the cost of retrieving analogies changes with the size of the knowledge base and the semantic distance of the analogues.

This paper reports of the results of one such examination. We have looked at the behavior of a commonly-used class of retrieval algorithms – the marker passing or spreading activation approach [1, 2, 3, 8, 10] – and compared it to a technique called Knowledge-Directed Spreading Activation (KDSA) [12], a method developed to be appropriate for retrieving semantically distant analogies. Our analysis is specifically designed to examine how the two approaches are affected by the required semantic distance of the analogy and by the size of the knowledge base from which the analogues are drawn. The analysis has two components: (1) a theoretical model of the retrieval time for each approach based on a number of problem characteristics, and (2) an experiment with an implementation of the two approaches showing how the retrieval time of the approaches varied with the knowledge base size. These two components, taken together, suggest that KDSA is more likely to be useful for retrieving semantically distant analogues from large knowledge bases.

2 Knowledge-Directed Spreading Activation

Before describing how the two approaches to analogue retrieval were modeled in this theoretical analysis, we will briefly describe the two approaches themselves. We will use the term "Spreading Activation" (SA) in this paper to cover the various retrieval approaches that pass values along links in a semantic network. While the data type being passed and the exact method of passing varies from project to project, the salient steps in the operation of these methods for the purpose of this investigation are: (1) mark the nodes in the network representing the target concept with some value; then (2) continually pass values from each marked node to all of its neighbor (linked) nodes, until (3) the nodes representing some other concept in the network meet a retrieval condition (often when the percentage of the concept's nodes exceeds some threshold, or when the cumulative activation of those nodes exceeds some threshold). Whenever a concept is retrieved in this way, it is further evaluated as an analogue to the target; if it does not meet the criterion of being an analogue, we will assume here that the spreading activation process continues from the state at which it left off until a suitable analogue is retrieved. This general description covers both numeric spreading activation models, e.g. [2], and passing non-numeric markers, e.g. [8]. This method and close variants of it have been used in analogy and case-retrieval mechanisms (e.g., [1, 3, 10]), in information retrieval and question-answering systems (e.g., [8]), and as general models of human associative memory (e.g., [2]).

As described here, SA essentially performs blind search in a semantic network. When the network is large and the search is deep, therefore, SA is subject to the same combinatorial explosion problem that applies to all blind search mechanisms. KDSA is an attempt to overcome this problem while still maintaining an important benefit of SA: domain- and problem-independent indexing of the knowledge base (a general-purpose semantic network). We will give a very brief description of KDSA here; a more detailed description, and an example of its use, is presented in [12]. KDSA works by introducing a feedback cycle into the spreading activation process, as shown in Fig. 1. KDSA starts the same way as SA, by marking the nodes in the target concept and beginning the spread of activation starting from the target along the network's links. Each time this spreading activation process retrieves a concept, it is evaluated as an analogue

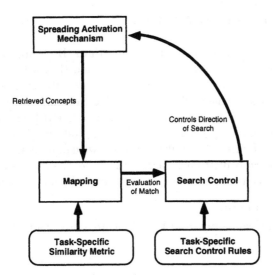

Fig. 1. Knowledge-Directed Spreading Activation

by a heuristic Mapping component. This Mapping component returns a measure of how close the retrieved concept is to being a useful analogue for solving the system's current task. Based on this evaluation, KDSA's Search Control module modifies the direction of subsequent spreads of activation into more promising areas of the knowledge base. For example, if the retrieved concept was evaluated as very close to being a useful analogy, the Search Control module can clear all activation in the network and start a new SA search from that retrieved concept. Or, if the retrieved concept was evaluated as very far from being a useful analogy, the Search Control module can clear its activation to keep subsequent spreads of activation from exploring that area of the semantic network. Once the Search Control module has made these changes, spreading activation begins again and the entire process iterates until a final analogue is found.

We have identified several ways in which the Mapping and Search Control modules can interact to efficiently guide the search to an analogue, and we have implemented a specific set of heuristics for the task of creative design [13]. In the analysis that follows in this paper, however, we will consider only the first example search control heuristic mentioned above: whenever the Mapping module identifies that a retrieved concept is closer to being a final analogue than the previous one evaluated, the search control module clears the activation in the network and restarts the search from this new concept. In this way, KDSA can operate as a series of smaller spreading activation searches between *beacon concepts*, where each beacon concept (hopefully) takes the search closer and closer to the final analogue.

3 Analysis of Retrieval Cost

Now let us turn to the analysis of these algorithms. Both approaches perform a search in a semantic network knowledge base, and that will be modeled as a directed graph. Let $S = (V, E)$ be the knowledge base with nodes V and links E. The size of the knowledge base will be measured as the number of nodes $K = |V|$. The branching factor of the knowledge base is $b = |E|/|V|$, and is assumed to be constant throughout the entire KB, i.e., each node in V is assumed to be adjacent to exactly b links. The links in the knowledge base are assumed to be randomly and uniformly distributed across the nodes. I.e., the semantic network can be thought of as having been constructed with the following algorithm:

> **for** each $v \in V$ **begin**
>> pick b nodes randomly from V and create a link from v to each of them; add the new links to E;
>
> **end**.

All concepts or types will be defined in the semantic network as subgraphs $(V' \subset V, E' \subset E)$ of S.

3.1 Time cost of SA

Standard spreading activation will be modeled as marker passing through S starting at a target graph G_T, and finishing when some designated base graph G_B, which meets the desired similarity metric, is retrieved. The marker passing in this theoretical model will be strictly breadth-first. That is, each marked node will pass a mark to all of its neighbors in a cycle. The *spreading activation path distance* between two graphs G_1 and G_2, $d(G_1, G_2)$ will be defined as the number of spreading activation cycles needed to retrieve G_2 after making G_1 (and only G_1) a source. This is the operational definition of semantic distance we will use in this paper.

The computational cost of a spreading activation search will be assumed to be the number of nodes marked during that search. Modeling this breadth-first search algorithm in a graph differs from modeling breadth-first search in a tree because, unlike nodes in a tree, nodes in a graph that have already been marked will be re-encountered by the search. As the search progresses, a higher and higher percentage of the total knowledge base will have already been marked. We do not want to double-count these previously-marked nodes, because they represent a portion of the search that has already been performed and does not need to be performed again.

The total number of nodes marked by a spreading activation search up to and including cycle i, N_i, is given by the recurrence relation:

$$N_i = \begin{cases} 0, & i = 0 \\ |G_T|, & i = 1 \\ N_{i-1} + K \left(1 - \left(\frac{K-1}{K}\right)^{b(N_{i-1}-N_{i-2})}\right)\left(1 - \frac{N_{i-1}}{K}\right), & i > 1 \end{cases} \quad (1)$$

(Here $|G_T|$ represents the number of nodes contained in G_T.)

We will not give the derivation of this formula here, and will instead refer the interested reader to [11] for the full derivation. However, we will provide some intuitive evidence that this formula is the right one by pointing out that this function's graph gives the exact qualitative behavior we would expect from the SA algorithm. Fig. 2 shows a graph (labeled "SA") of N_i as i increases. For small values of i, where relatively few of the KB's nodes have been marked, the value of N_i starts out with exponential behavior. However, as i grows and a higher and higher percentage of the KB's nodes are marked, the growth of N_i slows, and it eventually converges asymptotically on a value near the KB size.

This recurrence equation represents the total computational effort in a spreading activation search of depth i. The computational cost of searching from G_T to G_B by standard spreading activation will then be $N_{d(G_T,G_B)}$. This recurrence equation does not have a known closed form, but even in its present form it allows us to inspect and analyze the behavior of SA and KDSA under a variety of general problem types.

3.2 Time cost of KDSA

KDSA between G_T and G_B will be modeled as a sequence of standard SA searches along a sequence of beacon concepts, $G_T, G_1, G_2, \ldots, G_{n-1}, G_B$. That is, KDSA will consist of first an SA search from G_T to G_1, followed by an SA search from G_1 to G_2, and so on until G_B is retrieved. The benefit of an individual beacon search, $\Delta d(G_i, G_{i+1}, G_B)$, will be defined as how much closer to the base G_{i+1} is than G_i:

$$\Delta d(G_i, G_{i+1}, G_B) = d(G_i, G_B) - d(G_{i+1}, G_B)$$

The total cost of KDSA between G_T and G_B will depend on the cost of each beacon subsearch, $N_{d(G_i,G_{i+1})}$, and the benefit gained from each beacon subsearch, $\Delta d(G_i, G_{i+1}, G_B)$. In particular, the cost of a KDSA search from G_T to G_B is given by the rather complex formula:

$$KDSA(G_T, G_B) = \sum_{i=0}^{\sum_{j=0}^{i} \Delta d(G_j, G_{j+1}, G_B) \geq d(G_T, G_B)} N_{d(G_i, G_{i+1})} \tag{2}$$

In other words, the cost of KDSA is determined by summing the costs of individual beacon searches between G_i and G_{i+1}, until the sum benefit of the beacon searches so far (in terms of path distance) equals or exceeds the path distance between G_T and G_B.

This formula can be simplified significantly by making the assumption that each beacon search is of a constant depth d_p, and has a constant benefit Δd_p. In this case, the number of searches will be simply $d(G_T, G_B)/\Delta d_p$, and the cost of each search will be N_{d_p}:

$$KDSA(G_T, G_B) = \frac{d(G_T, G_B)}{\Delta d_p} N_{d_p} \tag{3}$$

4 Theoretical Results

The analysis above allows us to examine the predicted performance of KDSA under a wide variety of circumstances, and compare its performance to standard spreading activation. Each section below describes the behavior of KDSA and SA as a specific parameter of the model – semantic distance of the analogy, size of the KB, etc. – changes. For each section, a graph will demonstrate the behavior of KDSA compared to standard SA. The time cost of standard SA in these graphs is calculated as $N_{d(G_T, G_B)}$ by formula 1, and the time cost of KDSA is calculated as $KDSA(G_T, G_B)$ from formula 3. In each case, the values of other parameters were chosen to reflect a "typical" case of interest to our study of KDSA – i.e., finding a semantically distant analogy in a large knowledge base – and to reflect conservative values for the cost and benefit of each KDSA beacon search – i.e., the cost/benefit ratio of each beacon search was high. In particular, for each graph the variable values except the independent variable for the graph are set as follows: the spreading activation distance between target and base is 13 cycles, the knowledge base size is 1,000,000 nodes, the branching factor is 4, each KDSA beacon search was assumed to be of path length 7, and each beacon search was assumed to lead to a graph that was path distance 2 closer to the base graph.

4.1 Time cost as semantic distance grows

Fig. 2 graphs the costs of SA and KDSA as they vary with $d(G_T, G_B)$, the path distance between the target and the base graphs. KDSA's computational cost

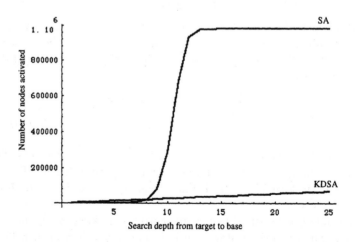

Fig. 2. Cost of search as search depth from target to base ($d(G_T, G_B)$) grows. $K = 1,000,000$, $b = 4$, $d_p = 7$, $\Delta d_p = 2$, $|G_T| = 1$.

is linear in the path distance between G_T and G_B (Equation 3). The cost of

SA, on the other hand, increases roughly exponentially with path distance until the algorithm starts encountering a significant number of nodes it has marked before, at which time the graph asymptotically approaches some number less than the total KB size, K. The conclusion we can draw here is that, when a very high degree of semantic distance between analogies is required, KDSA is likely to be much less computationally expensive than standard SA.

As Fig. 2 shows (for search depths between 0 and 8), it is possible for KDSA to be more expensive than SA. There are two reasons for this. First, the model assumes (realistically) that KDSA's beacon searches are not along the ideal path to the base graph. Second, in graph search, there is an overhead involved in doing multiple graph searches – each new beacon search visits and marks nodes that were already marked in previous beacon searches. Fig. 2 shows that, even when the search:benefit ratio of the beacon searches is high (it is 3.5:1 in the graph shown), and therefore the amount of overhead involved in KDSA is also high, KDSA is still able to avoid searching a large portion of the knowledge base that is searched by standard SA as the analogy desired becomes more and more semantically distant.

4.2 Time cost as KB size grows

Fig. 3 graphs the cost of SA and KDSA as K, the number of nodes in the knowledge base, varies. In the range of KB sizes considered by the figure (0 to

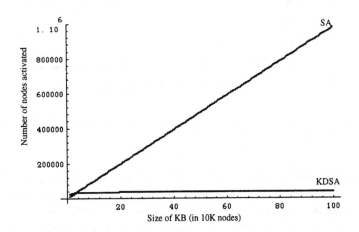

Fig. 3. Cost of search as knowledge base size (K) grows. $d(G_T, G_B) = 13$, $b = 4$, $d_p = 7$, $\Delta d_p = 2$, $|G_T| = 1$

$1,000,000$ nodes), the graph shows the cost of SA as increasing roughly linearly with the KB size. In this range of KB sizes, SA will examine most of the nodes in the KB before retrieving the analogy, and therefore it is natural that the cost of SA is roughly directly proportional to KB size. KDSA, on the other hand, reaches an asymptote as the size of the KB grows. This is because, as the size of the KB gets large, a shallow search marks a progressively smaller proportion of the KB, and therefore the probability of encountering nodes that have been marked before gets smaller. In this situation, the behavior of each (relatively shallow) KDSA beacon search approaches that of a breadth-first tree search, costing approximately b^{d_p}. Therefore, for a given b, a given Δd_p, a given $d(G_T, G_B)$, and a given d_p, the cost of KDSA (equation 3) will approach (and be bounded by) a constant – namely, the cost of doing $d(G_T, G_B)/\Delta d_p$ tree searches. Standard SA will also exhibit this behavior for extremely large KBs; however, it will asymptotically approach a much higher cost.

4.3 Time cost as cost/benefit of beacon searches changes

Fig. 4 graphs the cost of SA and KDSA as Δd_p, the benefit (in terms of semantic distance) gained by each beacon search, varies. The cost of standard spreading

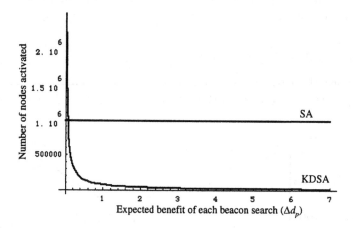

Fig. 4. Time cost as benefit of beacon search (Δd_p) grows. $K = 1,000,000$, $d(G_T, G_B) = 13$, $b = 4$, $d_p = 7$, $|G_T| = 1$

activation of course does not change as Δd_p is varied, since it is not using beacons to control its search. This graph shows that KDSA can be much more efficient than standard SA even when the cost of each beacon search is very high relative to the benefit gained from it. Fig. 4 shows for these parameters that when a search of depth 7 shrinks the expected distance to the base by only 1 or even 0.5, KDSA is still many times more efficient than standard SA.

There is no guarantee that every beacon KDSA encounters during its search will actually be closer to the eventual base than the previous beacon, and this portion of the analysis quantifies that issue. Fig. 4 shows that KDSA can be robust in the face of "bad beacons", provided the overall effect of those bad beacons is not enough to bring the total expected benefit of all beacons below 0.

5 Experiments

The results of the previous section show that KDSA is more likely than SA to be a tractable mechanism for retrieving semantically distant analogues from a large KB, under some theoretical assumptions. A complementary method of evaluating the approaches is to examine their behavior on real problems using a computer implementation. We used an implementation of KDSA, called IDA, to perform such an experimental evaluation. IDA is a program that uses KDSA to search for an analogue that is useful for an innovative redesign of a given target device [13]. We observed KDSA's behavior by running the full IDA implementation, and we observed SA's behavior by running IDA without its mapping evaluation[1] and search control modules.

We ran experiments with IDA retrieving analogues for innovative design in a diverse knowledge base of devices. The full knowledge base used for these experiments consists of 29 fully represented models of devices. Each device is represented by a high-level description of its structure, behavior, and function. The devices chosen for representation reflect a diverse collection of domains and diverse sources of expertise. The representations of these devices, along with the type hierarchy of concepts used in those representations, comprises about 1100 total objects. While this is not a very large knowledge base of the type for which KDSA was designed, we can extrapolate from the trends shown in experiments with this KB to predict KDSA's behavior in a very large KB.

The experiments were designed to answer the same question as the theoretical graph of Sect. 4.2: How are the approaches' retrieval times affected by growth of the KB? To answer this question, we ran a single retrieval example under randomly chosen knowledge bases of different sizes. In the particular example we ran, IDA is given the goal of redesigning the blinkered railroad crossing technology – the mechanism by which drivers are informed to stop their cars at a railroad crossing by a light that flashes when a train is approaching. IDA retrieves an on-off (fluid) valve as an analogue, and proposes a high-level redesign based on this analogy. For each run, a random collection of n devices were loaded to form the system's knowledge base, with n varying from 0 to 24 [2]. We did a total of 37 runs with varying KB sizes, and for each run we retrieved the analogue with both KDSA and SA. We measured the CPU time taken for IDA to retrieve the on-off valve as a useful analogy for innovative design.

The graph of total CPU time vs. KB size for this example is shown in Fig. 5. These results mirror the theoretical results shown in Fig. 3. They show the retrieval time for SA rising roughly linearly with the KB size, while the retrieval time for KDSA changes very little as the KB grows. The same experiment run with a different retrieval example produced a similar graph, although there the slope of KDSA's retrieval time was not quite as flat. These experiments con-

---

[1] The only part of the mapping evaluation module loaded in the SA runs was the similarity metric, which determines whether or not a retrieved concept meets the condition for being an analogue.

[2] The target, base, and beacon concepts for this example were always loaded.

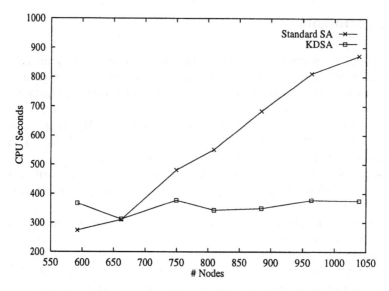

Fig. 5. CPU time taken to retrieve analogy as KB size grows, railroad crossing example

firmed the results of the theoretical analysis, and provide more evidence that KDSA will be a tractable retrieval mechanism in very large knowledge bases.

6 Related Work and Discussion

There are a number of other approaches to case and analogy retrieval that were not included in the analysis reported here, but each of them has limitations as a retrieval mechanism for semantically distant analogies in large KBs. Many case-based reasoning systems use a retrieval mechanism based on traversing discrimination networks (see [7] for an overview). This class of approaches requires that the set of features useful for retrieving a concept as an analogy is known at concept storage time, so that these features can be used to index the concept. However, this requirement is unreasonable for a general analogy retrieval mechanism in a large multi-use knowledge base, where the KB can be used in the service of a very large number of goals, each of which can have a different feature set for retrieving useful analogues. A possible solution to this problem is to add redundancy to the discrimination network, in effect indexing each concept on all (or most) possible combinations of its feature values and their supertypes. For a large multi-domain KB, though, a redundant discrimination network would be prohibitively large, and searching it would be prohibitively complex [5]. Similar limitations apply to the related method of indexing concepts as graphs with hierarchies of subgraphs [4]. Another analogy retrieval approach is Thagard *et. al.*'s ARCS [9], which constructs a constraint network between the target and plausible bases and uses a connectionist relaxation algorithm on that network to calculate the relative quality of the plausible bases as analogues. This approach takes time proportional to the square of the KB size in the worst case, and experiments show roughly this K^2 behavior in actual retrieval episodes, so this approach does not seem well-suited for retrieving analogues from very large KBs.

So far, the amount of work on combined theoretical and experimental analyses of analogy or case retrieval algorithms has been limited. One project that involved this sort of analysis is reported in [14]. This work is similar to ours in that Zito-Wolf and Alterman evaluated their approach to knowledge retrieval against other existing approaches both by developing a theoretical model of retrieval and by experimentally validating the theoretical results by measuring the execution of an implemented system. However, Zito-Wolf and Alterman's analysis makes specific assumptions about the cases being retrieved – retrieval of plans and plan steps – and the type of retrieval method used – searching a decision tree based on feature matches – that are incompatible with the assumptions made in our analysis.

From a mathematical standpoint, a class of analyses that match more closely with ours are analyses of hierarchical planning such as the one reported in [6]. Like our analysis, Knoblock's investigates the degree to which search time can be lowered by breaking a deep search down into a sequence of smaller searches toward intermediate subgoal states. In KDSA, the beacon concepts serve as these subgoal states; in hierarchical planning, the goal states are selected by a search at a higher level of abstraction. The work presented in this paper analyzes analogue retrieval rather than planning, and for this reason differs in two important ways from Knoblock's analysis: (1) it analyzes search in a semantic network (i.e., a graph) rather than a tree, and (2) it does not make the assumption, made by Knoblock, that the intermediate states lie on the optimal path to the goal.

There are a number of issues left for future research. First, one aspect of KDSA not explored by either the theoretical model or the experiments is how the size of the knowledge base will affect the depth of the beacon searches (d_p). Adding concepts to the KB randomly should cause more beacons to be added and thus should cause d_p to decrease, but more work is needed to model the level of decrease, and to investigate whether the benefit of beacon searches (Δd_p) is also affected. Second, we would like to have empirical tests of *all* of the theoretical results reported in Sect. 4. Currently, only the result in Fig. 3 has been verified experimentally. Third, while the analysis reported here provides evidence that KDSA will be a tractable mechanism for retrieving semantically distant analogues in very large KBs, it is important to continue testing this claim by scaling up the size of the actual knowledge bases to which KDSA is applied.

The theoretical model and experiments reported here are complementary methods of validating KDSA. The theoretical model shows that KDSA is likely to be tractable in large KBs, provided it can find beacon concepts in the KB that will lead it toward a final analogue. The program IDA demonstrates that these beacon concepts can be found in a real knowledge base for a real domain, and the experiments with IDA show that the beacon concepts can be utilized to efficiently guide a knowledge base search. Taken together, these two approaches provide evidence of KDSA's usefulness as an analogue retrieval mechanism for important problems.

Acknowledgements

This work was supported by a grant from NASA NAG2-581, and a contract from Texas Instruments 7554900. The author gratefully acknowledges Barbara Hayes-Roth for many useful discussions about this research, and the anonymous ICCBR reviewers for helpful suggestions about the paper.

References

1. A. Aamodt. Explanation-driven case-based reasoning. In S. Wess, K. Althoff, and M. Richter, editors, *Topics in Case-Based Reasoning*. Springer-Verlag, 1994.
2. J. Anderson. *The Architecture of Cognition*. Harvard University Press, 1983.
3. J. Anderson and R. Thompson. Use of analogy in a production system architecture. In S. Vosniadou and A. Ortony, editors, *Similarity and Analogical Reasoning*, pages 267–297. Cambridge University Press, 1989.
4. H. Bunke and B. Messmer. Similarity measures for structured representations. In S. Wess, K. Althoff, and M. Richter, editors, *Topics in Case-Based Reasoning*. Springer-Verlag, 1994.
5. P. Cunningham, B. Smyth, D. Finn, and E. Cahill. Retrieval issues in real-world CBR applications: How far can we go with discrimination-nets? In *IJCAI Workshop on Re-Use of Designs*, 1993.
6. C. Knoblock. *Automatically Generating Abstractions for Problem Solving*. PhD thesis, Carnegie Mellon University, 1991.
7. J. Kolodner. *Case-Based Reasoning*. Morgan-Kaufmann, 1993.
8. L. Rau. Knowledge organization and access in a conceptual information system. *Information Processing and Management*, 23:269–283, 1987.
9. P. Thagard, K. Holyoak, G. Nelson, and D. Gochfeld. Analog retrieval by constraint satisfaction. *Artificial Intelligence*, 46:259–310, 1990.
10. P. Winston. Learning and reasoning by analogy. *Communications of the ACM*, 23:689–703, 1980.
11. M. Wolverton. *Retrieving Semantically Distant Analogies*. PhD thesis, Stanford University, 1994.
12. M. Wolverton and B. Hayes-Roth. Retrieving semantically distant analogies with knowledge-directed spreading activation. In *AAAI-94*, 1994.
13. M. Wolverton and B. Hayes-Roth. Finding analogues for innovative design. In *Third Int'l Conference on Computational Models of Creative Design*, 1995.
14. R. Zito-Wolf and R. Alterman. A framework and an analysis of current proposals for the case-based organization and representation of procedural knowledge. In *AAAI-93*, 1993.

INRECA: A Seamlessly Integrated System Based on Inductive Inference and Case-Based Reasoning

E. Auriol[1], S. Wess[2], M. Manago[1], K.-D. Althoff[2], R. Traphöner[3]

[1] AcknoSoft, 58a, rue du Dessous-des-Berges, 75013 Paris, France
Phone: +33 1 44248800, Fax: +33 1 44248866, E-mail: {auriol, manago}@ipbc.fr

[2] University of Kaiserslautern, Dept. of Computer Science, PO Box 3049, 67653 Kaiserslautern, Germany. Phone: +49 631 205 3360, Fax: +49 631 205 3357, E-mail: {althoff,wess}@informatik.uni-kl.de

[3] tecInno GmbH, Sauerwiesen 2, 67661 Kaiserslautern, Germany
Phone: +49 6301 60660, Fax: +49 6301 60666

Abstract: This paper focuses on integrating inductive inference and case-based reasoning. We study integration along two dimensions: Integration of case-based methods with methods based on general domain knowledge, and integration of problem solving and incremental learning from experience. In the INRECA system, we perform case-based reasoning as well as TDIDT (Top-Down Induction of Decision Trees) classification by using the same data structure called the INRECA tree. We extract decision knowledge using a TDIDT algorithm to improve both the similarity assessment by determining optimal weights, and the speed of the overall system by inductive learning. The integrated system we implemented evolves smoothly along application development time from a pure case-based reasoning approach, where each particular case is a piece of knowledge, to a more inductive approach where some subsets of the cases are generalised into abstract knowledge. Our proposed approach is driven by the needs of a concrete pre-commercial system and real diagnostic applications. We evaluate the system on a database of insurance risk for cars and an application involving forestry management in Ireland.

1. Introduction

In the recent past, more and more research activities in AI have been re-directed towards application-oriented research and technology transfer. However, scaling-up from toy applications to complex real world tasks is not trivial. Further, single-paradigm systems seem to have reached their limit in several respects, and it is time to study more actively how to integrate multi-paradigm methods [Mikalski & Tecuci, 1994]. In this paper, we study integration along two dimensions: Integration of case-based reasoning (CBR) methods with methods based on general domain knowledge, namely rule-based methods [Golding & Rosenblum, 1991], and integration of problem solving and incremental learning from experience [Aamodt, 1994].

Examples of approaches in this direction are improving indexing in case-based reasoning by TDIDT [Kibler & Aha, 1987; Cardie, 1993; Ting, 1994], improving similarity assessment in case-based reasoning by learned rules [Sebag & Schoenauer, 1994], and combining nearest neighbour classification with symbolic learning [Zhang, 1990].

As basic features of the proposed architecture, we rely on two structures: decision trees [Quinlan, 1986] and k-d trees [Friedman, Bentley & Finkel, 1977; Moore, 1990].

The purpose of this paper is to present an implementation of an integrated structure called the INRECA tree, that permits both data structures to be used efficiently for diagnosis and classification tasks. The new structure fulfills the following objectives:

1. Extracting decision knowledge by induction;
2. Use this knowledge in the definition of the similarity measure;
3. Relating the current problem to the learned experience by case-based reasoning;
4. Maintaining classification accuracy of case-based reasoning when meeting unknown or noisy queries during consultation;
5. Maintaining the incremental behavior of case-based reasoning;
6. Gaining speed by using inductive learned and explicit knowledge;
7. Being flexible as in case-based reasoning;
8. Being straight forward as in decision trees.

Some of these objectives are explicitly geared towards the system end-user (e.g. flexibility and speed). For instance, a help-desk support technician needs sometimes to be guided by the system (induction), and at other times drives the search (CBR). On the other hand, some others are compelling for the system builder (i.e., definition of similarity assessment). Finally, some others are dedicated to system maintenance (i.e., incremental learning).

The integrated system, which we implemented within the INRECA[1] project, evolves smoothly along application development time, from a pure case-based reasoning approach, where each particular case is a piece of knowledge, to a more inductive approach where some subsets of the cases are generalised in abstract knowledge.

In the following section, we summarise basic features of k-d trees and decision trees and their associated building and search strategies. We present requirements on the integration of these mechanisms in the INRECA tree. In Section 3, we introduce improvements for the k-d tree approach that supports efficient processing of a system that seamlessly integrates inductive and case-based reasoning. We evaluate the integrated system on a database of insurance risk for cars and an application involving forestry management in Ireland. Finally, we discuss the main conclusions from the experiments and complete this with a short comment on open problems.

2. k-d Trees and Decision Trees

We describe the basic characteristics of these data structures and their associated building and search strategies to what extent it is necessary within the scope of this paper. We summarise their respective advantages and disadvantages and motivate their proposed integration in the INRECA system.

2.1 k-d Trees

The basic idea of k-d tree building [Friedman, Bentley & Finkel, 1977] is to structure the search space based on its observed density (respectively on its classification goal) and to use this pre-computed structure for efficient case retrieval (respectively for efficient diagnosis). It functions as a binary fixed indexing structure for case retrieval. Within the k-d tree an incremental best-match search is used to find the K most similar cases within a set of n cases with k specified indexing attributes.

Retrieval in a k-d tree is processed by the recursive application of two test procedures: Ball-Overlap-Bounds (BOB) and Ball-Within-Bounds (BWB) [Wess, Althoff & Derwand, 1994]. Both are relatively simple geometrical procedures. BWB is linear

---

[1] INRECA: INduction and REasoning from CAses, ESPRIT project P6322

with the number of indexing attributes and BOB is a binary test. While the search is going on, a priority list is defined that contains the ordered list of the current K most similar cases and their similarity to the query. The similarity *SIM* is computed as follow: for each attribute A_j, one computes a local (i.e., relative to this attribute) similarity sim_j between the values of the query and the target case. Then, all the local similarities are aggregated in a weighted sum. The priority list is modified when a new case comes in the "top K". The recursive procedure runs as follows:

```
currentNode = k-d-treeRoot; otherNodes = ∅   ; priorityList = ∅
k-d-treeSearch(Query, currentNode)
        previousNode = father(currentNode)
        IF currentNode = leafNode
        THEN
                computeSimilarity(query, currentNode)
                modify(priorityList, currentNode)
        ELSE
                nextNode = Value(Query, currentNode)
                otherNodes = childNode(currentNode) - nextNode
                k-d-treeSearch(Query, nextNode)
        END
        IF inspect(otherNodes) = TRUE THEN              *** BOB test ***
                FOR ALL node ∈ otherNodes DO
                        k-d-treeSearch(Query, node)
        IF priorityList ≠ full THEN                     *** BWB test ***
                k-d-treeSearch(Query, previousNode)
```

2.2 Decision Trees

TDIDT algorithms are nowadays popular. A decision tree is induced from a database of training cases, described by a set of attributes A_j, $j = 1, ..., p$. Each case belongs to a specific class M_l, $l = 1, ..., L$. The partitioning procedure attempts to find the most informative attribute in order to create the shortest tree possible. Traditionally, it uses a hill-climbing search strategy and a preference criterion often based on the information gain [Shannon & Weaver, 1947; Quinlan, 1986], like the C4.5 system [Quinlan, 1993][2]. At each node in the decision tree, the criterion is evaluated for all the attributes which are relevant and the one is picked which yields the highest increase of the information gain measure. The main steps of the TDIDT approach are:

```
IF currentNode = leafNode THEN
        label(currentNode, mostProbableClass)
ELSE
        develop(currentNode, relevantAttributes)
        select(bestAttribute, relevantAttributes)
        split(currentNode, bestAttribute)
```

2.3 Goals of the Integration

In their initial form, both k-d tree and TDIDT mechanisms are limited in several ways [Manago, Althoff et al., 1993]. We summarise the main points briefly:

- TDIDT: lack of flexibility and incrementality, sensitivity to errors and noise in the data during consultation[3];

---

[2] However, many other criteria have been proposed: Impurity reduction [Breiman et al., 1984], χ^2 statistic [Hart, 1984], G-statistic [Sokal & Rahlf, 1981] etc. For a comparison of selection criteria, see for instance [Mingers, 1989].

[3] Note that many TDIDT algorithms have been developed in order to encompass these problems (e.g., [Utgoff, 1988] for incrementality, [Quinlan, 1986] for tree pruning).

- *k*-d trees: lack of knowledge generalisation, problems with treatment of unknown and unordered symbolic data.

Table 1 aims at contrasting decision trees and *k*-d trees and at presenting the improvements gained with integration. The contrast calls especially for extending *k*-d trees with efficient classification abilities, also for symbolic attributes and unknown values in the query. Therefore, the extension of the usual *k*-d and decision trees attempts to encompass the objectives we presented in the introduction of this paper.

Table 1. Contrasting *k*-d trees and decision trees for diagnosis tasks

Aspects	Decision tree	*k*-d tree	INRECA tree
Similarity measure	not necessary	necessary, has to meet monotonicity requirements	multiple, class-specific similarity measures
Nearest neighbour classification using similarity measures	not possible (there are exceptions, e.g. ID5)	possible	possible
Result obtained	classification	*K* nearest neighbours	both
Backtracking in the tree	not necessary	necessary	possible
Cases during retrieval	not necessary	necessary	possible
Order of tests	fixed	query case has to be completely described w.r.t. indexing slots	arbitrary presentation of query
Unordered value ranges	possible	impossible	possible
Symbolic attributes	not necessary	necessary	possible
Unknown attribute values during tree building	costly copying of cases in all branches	not possible	extension of *k*-d trees to handle unknown values

3. The INRECA Tree

In this section, we present an extension of the *k*-d tree building and search methods, called the INRECA tree. We also describe how optimal weight vectors can be computed from such a structure by using intra- and inter-class similarity measures. The resulting system is completely integrated. The same tree can be used simultaneously as a *k*-d tree in the case-based reasoning process for case indexing and retrieval, or as a decision tree in the induction process for case generalisation. The interactions between both approaches are greatly enhanced. As we will illustrate, by this enhancement we obtain a more flexible and acceptable tool that is easier to use and to maintain.

3.1 Extending the *k*-d Tree Building and Retrieval Methods

This extension aims at creating a single INRECA tree that can be used indifferently as a *k*-d tree for retrieval and as a decision tree for knowledge and rules extraction. Like in TDIDT and in *k*-d trees, the branches of an INRECA tree represent constraints for certain attributes of the cases. Since we need to handle ordered and symbolic attributes as well as unknown attribute values, we introduce different kinds of branches. These branches are shown in Fig. 2.

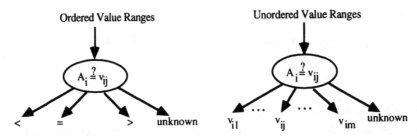

Fig. 2. Branches of the INRECA tree for ordered and unordered value ranges

As stated previously, the current k-d tree algorithms cannot handle unknown values and symbolic attributes. However, this arises often, whatever the attribute choice strategy. Therefore, the retrieval strategy in the k-d tree procedure has to be modified, such that it can deal with cases that contain symbolic or unknown attributes, as it can be done in TDIDT algorithms.

This modification is performed through an extension of the BOB and BWB Boolean tests presented in section 2.1, that work primarily on binary trees, towards more general multi-dimensional trees. Beside these two tests the basic retrieval procedure remains unchanged.

Extending the BOB Test

The BOB test is executed in order to recognise whether a node may contain some candidates that are more similar to the current query than those that have already been found. Therefore, the geometrical bounds of the node are used to define a test point that is most similar to the current query but still lies within the geometrical bounds of the current node. If this test point is in the ball it means that the ball overlaps with the node and then there may be a candidate to the priority list in this node.

The extension of the BOB test requires that the way how these test points are constructed also takes symbolic attributes and unknown values into account.

The definition of such a test point requires the assignment of a value to each attribute used in the case description. The value x_j for each attribute A_j must

a) lie within the geometrical bounds of the dimension defined by the attribute and the node to be investigated

b) be most similar (with respect to the local similarity for this attribute) to the value q_j of the attribute in the query.

For attributes A_j with ordered value ranges, we determine the bounds $[l_j ... u_j]$ defined by the attribute and the current node in the tree. The value x_j of the test point is as follows (1). In this definition, * denotes a new special value assumed in every value range. The similarity between * and every other value in the value range of attribute A_j is equal to 1.

$$x_j = \begin{cases} unknown \text{ if the node is in the unknown branch of } A_j \\ * \quad \text{ if the node is not in a branch of } A_j \\ q_j \quad if\ q_j \geq l_j\ and\ q_j \leq u_j \\ l_j \quad if\ q_j < l_j \\ u_j \quad if\ q_j > u_j \end{cases} \qquad (1)$$

For attributes with an unordered value range x_j is defined as follows (2):

$$x_j = \begin{cases} unknown \text{ if the node is in the unknown branch of } A_j \\ v_j \quad \text{if the node is in the } v_j \text{ branch of } A_j \\ * \quad \text{if the node is not in a branch of } A_j \end{cases} \qquad (2)$$

Extending the BWB Test

The extension of the BWB for correctly handling unknown values and unordered value ranges can be done similar to the extension of the BOB test. Let us recall that this test acts as a short-cut during the retrieval process by deciding at a given node of the tree whether all nearest cases have been found, or not. This results in a reduced number of examined cases. Unfortunately, this extension significantly increases the computational cost for executing this test. The gain obtained in the case of symbolic attributes is illusory, because the test has to verify each dimension of the attribute space, what can be very high for symbolic attribute. Instead of being in $O(k)$ where k is the number of indexing attributes in the tree, the complexity is in $O(k \times r)$ where r is the average number of values for the indexing attributes. However, the execution of this test can nevertheless pay-off, if the access to the cases is very expensive, for example if the cases are stored in some external storage.

3.2   Determination of Optimal Weight Vectors

A global similarity measure SIM between two cases a and b can be defined as a weighted sum of local similarity measures sim_j between the p attributes A_j that make up the cases (3). The weights w_{jl} evaluate the relative importance of the attribute A_j for each class M_l, $l = 1, ..., L$.

$$SIM(a,b) = \sum_{j=1}^{p} w_{jl} \times sim_j(A_j(a), A_j(b)) \qquad (3)$$

where $A_j(a)$ (resp. $A_j(b)$) stands for the value of case a (resp. b) for attribute A_j.

It is usual that the system user sets up these weights manually. They are normalised afterwards. This kind of approach presents the advantage to strongly implicate the user during the system building process. He generally enjoys this task. However, this kind of job is difficult and error-prone. After several steps (setting and normalisation), the resulting weights are no more easily understandable. Moreover, one usually evaluates only global weights for each attribute, without taking care about the class to which the cases belong. We propose that the system computes automatically the weights used in the similarity measures. For this purpose, we compute local intra- and inter-classes similarities. The class of each case is given by the set of constraints generated by the INRECA tree.

Determination of Weights through the INRECA Tree

The INRECA tree builds a partition of the set of cases in a set of classes. We know for each case its associated class. Let $M = \{M_1, ..., M_L\}$ be the set of classes. The INRECA tree may be viewed as a representation of a set of sufficient conditions (the *rules*) for a case to fall in some class M_l. Each condition refers to a single attribute A_j contained in the cases. On the basis of this knowledge acquired during tree building, we can compute the intra- and inter-class similarities for each attribute A_j as follow:

- The local intra-class distance measures to which extent a case a is near to the cases b that belong to its own class M_l with respect to attribute A_j are given by:

$$sim_{j,l}^{\cup} = \frac{1}{|M_l|^2} \sum_{a,b \in M_l} sim_j(A_j(a), A_j(b)) \qquad (4)$$

- The inter-class distance measures to which extent a case is far from the cases that belong to other classes with respect to attribute A_j are defined as follows:

$$sim_{j,l}^{\cap} = \frac{1}{|M_l||M - M_l|} \sum_{a \in M_l, b \in M - M_l} sim_j(A_j(a), A_j(b)) \qquad (5)$$

The goal of setting optimal weights is to minimise the intra-class distance and to maximise the inter-class distance between cases. For this purpose, the relative weight of each attribute A_j for each class M_l is defined by (6):

$$w_{jl} = \frac{\max\left\{0, sim_{j,l}^{\cup} - sim_{j,l}^{\cap}\right\}}{\sum_{l=1}^{L} \max\left\{0, sim_{j,l}^{\cup} - sim_{j,l}^{\cap}\right\}} \qquad (6)$$

The knowledge discovered in the INRECA tree about the class M_l of each case, is transferred to the similarity measure through the definition of the weights.

What did we Really Gained?

The introduced improvements allow the implementation of a CBR system and an inductive system within the same structure. The integrated system combines these approaches in a seamless way (Fig. 3) that is completely transparent for the user.

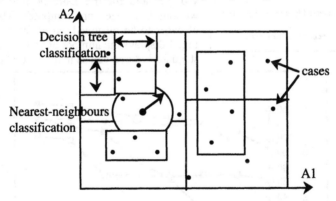

Fig. 3. Combining case-based and inductive classification

The INRECA tree encompasses all the requirements presented in Table 1. The objectives we wished to fulfill (Sect. 1) are completed:

- A single structure can be used either for CBR or for TDIDT retrieval. It can be straight forward and extract knowledge by induction, or flexible as in CBR;
- It enables incremental learning and adaptation of the similarity measure;
- This learning makes the retrieval quicker (see next section);
- It permits to evolve smoothly along application development time, from a pure case-based reasoning approach, to a more inductive approach;
- It offers a flexible tool configurable with respect to the end-user's needs.

4. Experiments

This section presents initial results on two databases. The database of insurance risk for cars[4] (called the CAR database) contains 205 cases described by 26 attributes. The goal is to determine a risk estimation factor (scaled from -3 to +3) for car insurance companies, based on several attributes such as manufacturing, price, technical data, etc. The second database (268 cases) comes from an application realised by IMS for Coïllte within the INRECA project involving the forestry management in Ireland (it is called the FORESTRY database). The underlying problem is to come up with a thinning strategy which maximises the overall value of the crop while minimising the risk of wind damage. There are 10 attributes. The choice of using nearest-neighbours or TDIDT classification for this problem is not fixed. It depends mainly on the forester and the location of the crop. Therefore, the integrated system offers the opportunity to be tuned with respect to the user's needs.

Let us recall that the objective of the k-d tree indexing mechanism is to avoid the computation of the similarity function between a new problem and all the cases of the case base. The goal of the experiment is the following: through the extension of the k-d tree into the INRECA tree and the computation of optimal weights, we intend to significantly decrease the number of "visited cases" (i.e., the number of cases on which the similarity is computed). Therefore, we have tested the average number of visited cases by cross-validation (80% of the database is used for training and the remaining 20% is used for test, repeated five times with different training and test sets) for the standard k-d tree and for the INRECA tree where the weights have been pre-computed. The number of cases to be retrieved varies from one to 30. Fig. 4 displays the number of visited cases in the standard k-d tree versus in the INRECA tree.

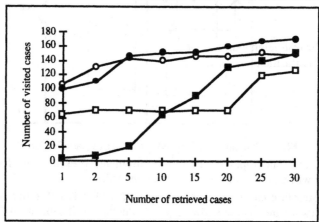

Fig. 4. Number of cases visited vs. cases retrieved (CAR and RORESTRY databases)

For the CAR database, we built the INRECA tree with an interquartile distance

---

4 It originates from the UCI Repository of Machine Learning Databases and Domain Theories: ftp ics.uci.edu, path pub/machine-learning-database/imports-85.

because there are many ordered attributes available. On the other hand, we built the tree with an entropy measure for the FORESTRY database because all the attributes but one are symbolic. The retrieval have always been performed without the BWB test because of the presence of many unordered attributes. The CAR database experiment can be interpreted in the following way. Due to the large number of attributes, it is necessary to browse many cases in the database even if we want to retrieve a small amount of cases only. The extraction of weights from the INRECA tree allows the similarity measure to be influenced by the acquired knowledge about the space structure. Therefore, the first retrieved cases reflect this structure, whereas the following ones do not. We have to note that the optimisation was achieved based on local criteria and, thus, turns to be adequate only for a limited number of nearest neighbours. However, it is rarely necessary to return more than ten cases to the user.

We obtain the same kind of results using the FORESTRY database. We can also notice that the introduction of automatically computed weights turns out to make the retrieval conducted on fewer cases and, as a consequence, quicker.

Note that since the k-d tree mechanism ensures to always retrieve the most similar cases, the accuracy of results is the same for both k-d and INRECA trees.

5. Conclusion

Our proposed approach corresponds to [Golding & Rosenblum, 1991] on a very abstract level. It includes also the aspect of improving case indexing with a TDIDT algorithm like [Cardie, 1993]. We extract decision knowledge by inductive learning to improve both the similarity assessment and the performance of the CBR system. Our main goal is to combine nearest neighbour classification with symbolic learning. Here the main motivation is similar to the underlying ideas proposed by [Wettschereck, 1994] and [Salzberg, 1991], though the means we selected to achieve it are very much different.

The experiments demonstrate that for both applications, the integrated system leads to a reduced number of visited cases and, thus, to an improved retrieval time. From these results, we can conclude that *the introduction of knowledge about classes has improved the similarity measure in the sense that it reflects the underlying space structure in a better way*. The system can learn incrementally from new cases.

On the other hand, the integration of k-d tree mechanism and TDIDT algorithms in a single INRECA tree makes the system much more *flexible* and enables the user to tune it to its own needs. The system can handle efficiently *unordered symbolic attributes* and *unknown values* in queries. It can produce *decision knowledge* by compiling cases or *interpret* the cases in a CBR manner.

6. Acknowledgement

Funding for INRECA has been provided by the Commission of the European Communities (ESPRIT contract P6322). The partners of INRECA are AcknoSoft (prime contractor, France), tecInno (Germany), Irish Multimedia Systems (Ireland), the University of Kaiserslautern (Germany). The authors are indebted to Guido Derwand who implemented the core parts of the integrated INRECA system. They also wish to thank the reviewers, whose the helpful comments contributed to make this paper much more readable and sound.

7. References

Aamodt, A. (1994). Explanation-Driven Case-Based Reasoning. *Richter, Wess et al.* , 274-288.

Breiman, L., Friedman, J., Olshen, R. & Stone, C. (1984). *Classification and Regression Trees.* Belmont, CA: Wadsworth.

Cardie, C. (1993). Using decision trees to improve case-based learning. *Proc. 10th Int. Conf. on Machine Learning*, 25-32.

Friedman, J. H., Bentley, J. L. & Finkel, R. A. (1977). An algorithm for finding best matches in logarithmic expected time. *ACM Trans. Math. Software 3*, 209-226.

Golding, A. R. & Rosenblum, P. S. (1991). Improving Rule-Based Systems Through Case-Based Reasoning. *Proc. AAAI Conference 1991.*

Hart, A. (1984). Experience in the use of an inductive system in knowledge engineering. M. Bramer (ed.), *Research and Development Systems*, Cambridge University Press, 117-126.

Kibler, D. & Aha, D. W. (1987). Learning representative exemplars of concepts: An initial case study. *Proc. of the Fourth International Workshop on Machine Learning*, pp. 24-30. Irvine, CA: Morgan Kaufmann.

Koopmans, L. H. (1987). *Introduction to Contemporary Statistical Methods.* Second Edition, Duxbury, Boston.

Manago, M., Althoff, K.-D., Auriol, E., Traphöner, R., Wess, S., Conruyt, N., Maurer, F. (1993). Induction and Reasoning from Cases. Richter, Wess et al. , 313-318.

Mikalski, R. & Tecuci, G. (Eds.) (1994). Machine Learning : A Multi-Strategy Approach (Volume IV). San Francisco, CA: Morgan Kaufman.

Mingers, J. (1989). An Empirical Comparison of Selection Measures for Decision-Tree Induction & An Empirical Comparison of Pruning Tree Methods for Decision-Tree Induction. *Machine Learning 3* (319-342); *4* (227-242).

Moore, A. W. (1990). Acquisition of dynamic control knowledge for a robotic manipulator. In: *Proc. of the Seventh International Conference on Machine Learning*, 242-252. Austin, TX: Morgan Kaufman.

Quinlan, R. (1986). Induction of Decision Trees. *Machine Learning 1*, 81-106.

Quinlan, R. (1993). *C4.5: Programs for machine learning.* San Mateo, CA: Morgan Kaufmann.

Richter, M. M., Wess, S., Althoff, K.-D. & Maurer, F. (eds.) (1993). *Proc. 1st European Workshop on Case-Based Reasoning (EWCBR-93).*

Salzberg, S. (1991). A Nearest Hyperrectangle Learning Method. *Machine Learning 6*, 277-309

Sebag, M. & Schoenauer, M. (1994). A Rule-Based Similarity Measure. *Richter, Wess et al.*, 119-131.

Shannon & Weaver (1947). *The Mathematical Theory of Computation.* University of Illinois Press, Urbana.

Sokal, R. R. & Rahlf, F. J. (1981). *Biometry.* W. H. Freeman and Co., San Francisco.

Ting, K. M. (1994). The problem of small disjuncts: Its remedy in decision trees. *Proc. of the Tenth Canadian Conference on Artificial Intelligence*, 91-97.

Utgoff, P. (1988). ID5: An incremental ID3. *Fifth International Conference on Machine Learning*, Morgan Kaufmann, Los Altos.

Wess, S., Althoff, K.-D. & Derwand, G. (1994). Using *k*-d Trees to Improve the Retrieval Step in Case-Based Reasoning. Wess, Althoff & Richter (Eds.), *Topics in Case-Based Reasoning,* Springer-Verlag, 167-181.

Wettschereck, D. (1994). A Hybrid Nearest-Neighbor and Nearest-Hyperrectangle Algorithm. Bergadano & De Raedt (Eds.), ECML-94, Springer Verlag, 323-335.

Zhang, J. (1990). A method that combines inductive learning with exemplar-based learning. *Proc. for Tools for Artificial Intelligence*, 31-37. Herndon, VA: IEEE Computer Society Press.

DOM-ArC: An Active Decision Support System for Quality Assessment of Cases*

Shirin Bakhtari[1] and Wolfgang Oertel[2]

[1] BSR Consulting GmbH, Wirtstrasse 38, D-81539 München, Germany
[2] Technische Universität Dresden, Institut Künstliche Intelligenz,
D-01062 Dresden, Germany

Abstract. There is a general acceptance that a case-based assistance system that can meet the requirements of real-world complex applications should maintain a core of domain specific knowledge in combination with its case store. The presented DOM-ArC incorporates a domain ontology and is situated within a case-based design support system. The domain ontology incorporates not only deep domain knowledge, but also the decision making knowledge that ensures the quality and reliability of the domain cases. The DOM-ArC undertakes the role of an active assistant that supports the case-based reasoner with the following services. It reviews and analyses a case and makes suggestions about which case to retain, how to overcome deficiencies in a proposed solution, which solution to reject, and how to construct a case from scratch.

1 Introduction

There is a consensus among researchers for what should constitute a knowledge-intensive case-based assistance system which can meet the requirements of real-world complex applications. Any case-based reasoner in a real-world application should maintain a core of domain specific knowledge in combination with its case store. Some of the developed case-based support systems specify – at least to some extend – specific domain knowledge and give different roles of this knowledge in order to support the case-based problem solving process [10] [2]. In planning applications for example, CHEF favours the combination of a case-based reasoner with a causal model that is used to record explanations of failures. In diagnosis applications, CASEY incorporates a causal model in order to support reasoning from first principles and the CREEK system combines its case-based reasoner with a deep knowledge model, which accompanies the case-based reasoner and may also be used as a last resort for problem solving from scratch.

---

* This research was supported by the Federal Ministry of Education, Science, Research and Technology (BMBF) within the joint project FABEL under contract no. 01IW104. Project partners in FABEL are German National Research Center for Computer Science (GMD), Sankt Augustin, BSR Consulting GmbH, München, Technical University of Dresden, HTWK Leipzig, University of Freiburg, and University of Karlsruhe.

DOM-ArC represents a sophisticated and elaborated *domain ontology*. It undertakes the role of an active assistant and supports the case-based reasoner with deep semantic and decision making knowledge. It provides the deep knowledge for a proposed case or a solution being obtained by a case-based reasoner and makes suggestions for which case to retain, how to overcome deficiencies in a proposed solution, which solution to reject, and how to construct a case from scratch due to the underlying domain ontology. The DOM-ArC provides the following multiple purposes:

- DOM-A assesses the reliability and quality of cases,
- DOM-r assists the rectification of cases and is viewed as a first and decisive step towards case adaptation support, and
- DOM-C supports problem solving from first principles.

In order to make clear which support services are already implemented and accessible, we sign them by writing capital letters, such as **A** for quality assessment and **C** which is the abbreviation for construction. The issue which is at the moment not fully implemented is made clear by the small letter r as an initial letter for rectification.

The DOM-ArC is situated within the open architecture [13] of the case-based design support system of the FABEL project [7]. The application domain imposed by FABEL is designing of the technical installation for highly complex buildings, e.g. office buildings. Our current focus is set on designing the heating, ventilating and air conditioning systems (HVAC). Figure 1 gives a very abstract view of some of the developed tools within the FABEL project[3]. It supports each single loop of the design process by using previous designs (cases) through the case-based reasoner and maintains the DOM-ArC component for the mentioned analytical and synthetical issues.

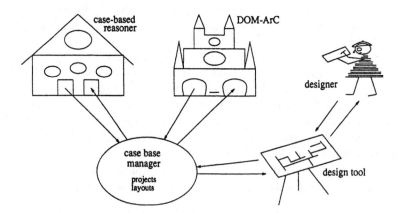

Fig. 1. The DOM-ArC system in the case-based design support environment

---

[3] DOM in the german language means cathedral. The given translation may help for a better understanding of the figures in this paper.

2 Some Characteristics of the Design Application

Considering a real-world complex domain, such as architectural and engineering design, the first step is to spell out what are the specific requirements and characteristics of that particular domain and to make clear what are the consequences for the formal representation of the design application [3]. In this section we give some significant characteristics of our considered domain. The implications and impacts of these domain specifics for the realization of the DOM-ArC system are described in the section 3.

I. An appropriate design assistance system must be accessible through a platform for specification of cases (design layouts), namely a CAD system. The realm of knowledge in the current CAD systems is limited to the representation of objects and arrangements of these objects syntactically [6]. They provide a platform for compositions of syntax primitives of the design vocabulary, e.g. lines, points, etc.

Hence, a significant departure from the current syntax oriented approaches within the design support environment is to maintain a rich core of deep design knowledge in order to be able to append semantic knowledge to the syntax primitives, e.g. a line could be the visualization primitive for a wall, a pipeline, etc.

II. The design process is characterized as continuous loops in a chain of synthetic and analytic activities.

Therefore, The DOM-ArC system has to be adapted within this process of designing an artefact. In order to obtain a well-formed and workable final state of an artefact, each single design case has to be designed in accordance with a set of design decisions and engineering judgements [4].

III. One major problem with architectural and engineering design is that the requisite knowledge is generally accumulated experimentally.

The important implication is that we have to deal with incomplete knowledge and take precautions for a stepwise extension as well as goal oriented modification of the stored knowledge without incurring the whole cost of re-representation and reorganization of the whole system. Therefore, to put it concisely, the DOM-ArC has a throughout object-oriented knowledge and system organization realization.

And last but not least, another characteristic of the complex real-world applications, such as design and planning, is that the activities are almost carried out in a multiple discipline collaborative framework using a common and shared knowledge platform, though with different foci of interest on the knowledge [3]. Within a collaborative framework the domain knowledge is referred to as an *ontology*[4]. The DOM-ArC considers a design ontology which is to be shared among different designers within the context of designing the HVAC systems.

---

[4] There are research and development investigations in this field, notably, the ARPA funded KNOWLEDGE SHARING AND REUSE EFFORT at Stanford [11] and the YMIR ontology [1] that is proposed by the group at Twente University for design applications.

3 DOM-ArC: A Conceptual View

The identification and formulation of the domain ontology is for our purpose not only a tool for analysing and computationally representing the deep design knowledge which can be shared among the designers with different foci of interest. Moreover, it provides the fundamental basis for the decision making whether a proposed layout (a case) fulfils the criteria that have been formulated as design decisions and engineering rules while designing a particular artefact. Accordingly, the key issue in modelling the design ontology is to make a symbiosis out of these two kinds of knowledge and provide support services that can meet the needs within the continuous loop of designing an artefact.

In order to meet the requirement I in the previous section, the DOM-ArC system incorporates and maintains a rich core of deep design knowledge. The first step towards the realization of the DOM system is the formulation of identification rules that enable the access to the semantic of the syntax primitives and their arrangement in a proposed case.

The represented deep knowledge in the DOM-ArC [5] establishes the meaning and permissible use of the design objects and the topological relation between these objects. It is built up as a network over a set of generic semantic structures that we call *concepts*. The relations between the concepts are identified by a set of identification rules and are specified as associations. The most important associations are specialization and partialization (partonomy). Due to the subsystem for which the design concepts are used, e.g. supply-air subsystem or heating subsystem, we have also formalized some subsystem characteristic features which are also appended to the concepts.

The semantic knowledge is accessible through the provided functionality that we call *Concept and Topological Information* – see section 3.1.

Getting adapted within the continuous process of synthetic and analytic activities has been addressed in the previous section as the second requirement. Hence, the qualitative leap forward that can make a meaningful contribution to the current design practice is to consider the deep knowledge and represent also decision making knowledge to ensure the quality and reliability of cases at multiple stages of case elaboration.

The knowledge for decision making support in DOM-ArC is formalized on the basis of a spatial ordering and coordination design methodology called ARMILLA [8] and the criterion of success is that of being conform with the underlying methodology of designing an artefact. For instance, we take the following quality assessment rules into account:

- Coherence assessment that examines all involved geometrical and topological arrangements in a proposed layout for their coherent connections. In general, the examination can be viewed as a check for a closed loop or chain of well arranged duct-systems that connect all well situated in- and outlets together in order to satisfy a certain functionality, where the functionality is given through the subsystem for which the layout has been designed.

- Spatial ordering and organization maxims that check the position of the geometrical design entities and their topological relations for their conformance relative to the underlying methodology or specific agreements for a particular project at hand.
- Coordination assessment that reviews a layout including more than one subsystem and draws the users attention to collisions. The coordination maxims give regulations and priorities for the spatial organization of different subsystems within the layer structure of the technical service space.

Over the period of our ontological engineering, we found out that the knowledge for decision making support has much in common with the knowledge for case adaptation. We also got an insight into the fact that constructing new cases from scratch relies also to a large extent on the same knowledge. Thus we decided to extend the support services on the basis of the domain ontology modelling for multiple purposes. Beside quality assessment we also supply case construction and case rectification as a first step towards case adaptation.

The case construction services are applicable for generating a solution from scratch as well as for the completion of a partially specified case. The construction can proceed in several steps and may serve as inspiration or as a coach for the designer while designing a specific layout for a certain subsystem. It indicates synthesis alternatives in order to give the user the opportunity to get informed about possible constructions that are conform with the underlying ontology. The DOM-ArC service support incorporates the following assistance services for designing the HVAC subsystems:

- the completion of a partially specified case,
- the indication of possible alternatives, and
- assistance for case construction from scratch.

Following the ultimate goal of supporting the adaptation of a retrieved case to the case at hand, the rectification support services are viewed as the first necessary step within a case adaptation framework. It is supposed to serve the following assistance calls with regard to the underlying model of design ontology: How to rectify the shortcomings and errors of omissions, how to adjust the geometrical dimensions in order to get the design entities well situated, and how to use the scope of validity in order to get some modifications on the case done.

A conceptual view of the DOM-ArC is given in figure 2 and a scenario concerning the support service for quality assessment of a proposed case is given in the next section.

Figure 2 illustrates the involved system components: an *interface gate* that serves the interaction between the DOM-ArC and an external drawing system or a case base manager, a *design board* that is the internal work bench, the *ontology* which builds the heart of the system. The call for assistance is managed by the component *assistance functions*.

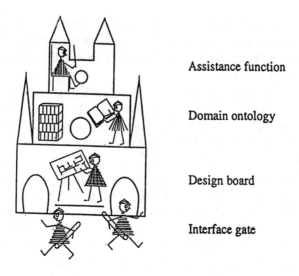

Assistance function

Domain ontology

Design board

Interface gate

Fig. 2. The DOM-ArC concept

3.1 A Scenario

The DOM-ArC system is accessible as soon as a case (a design layout) has been specified – partially or completely – through a design platform or through a call for assistance by the case-based reasoner. With the articulation of a requirement the cue is given to the *executive manager* sitting in the top storey of the DOM-ArC system, shown in figure 2. The executive manager expects as necessary inputs: an assistance call, a layout (case), the subsystem(s) for which the layout has been designed, and the design grid. Optional inputs are: a specific project in which the designed layouts has to be embedded, a particular structure of the technical service space. In the following we give two examples with different calls for assistance.

Consider a case as shown in figure 3[5], which gives the top view of a conceptual design of a return-air subsystem layout [9]. The assistance call is formulated as *Concept and Topological Information* in order to make the meaning of the syntactic primitives comprehensible. Due to this requirement the DOM-ArC executive manager undertakes the role of a *case critic* and causes a process of analytic examination. On the interface platform all syntactic design entities involved in the proposed case will be specified in terms of an internal representation due to each subsystem. This representation of the case incorporates a set of design entities representation. Each entity is represented in terms of its *geometrical data*, *descriptive data*, and *presentation data*. The next stage is characterized as a *design board*. If a specific project is given (as optional input) the design board is specified for that particular project in which all layouts have to be embedded. Otherwise, we activate a default initialization. On the design board, the design entities go through a qualification and aptitude test. The knowledge needed at

---

[5] Please note that the meaning of the entities is determined by the DOM-ArC and not given. We have outlined them to make the figure readable.

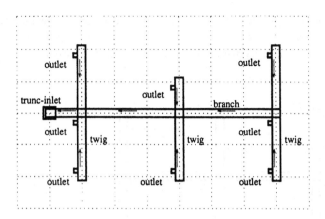

Fig. 3. A return-air subsystem case with the DOM-ArC determined meaning of the syntactically specified entities

this stage is formalized as syntax examination rules and consistency check.

The domain ontology provides a semantic view on the syntactically qualified design entities and identifies these as instances of generic semantic structures that we call *concepts*, e.g. outlet, main-connecting-duct, etc. Since each layout is designed syntactically, we have specified a set of includes concept identification and construction rules. The identification rules classify the syntactic design entities into classes of semantic structures. The concepts are – as mentioned above – allocated in a concept network where their subsystem characteristic features are also accessible. The relations between entities are identified in terms of their corresponding *topological relations*, e.g. contact, overlap, etc. Further, the design entities which have to be viewed as a whole will get aggregated and made explicit as instances of the *aggregate concepts*. The case shown in the figure 3 has the following representation[6]:

(entities
((1 800 400 2800 400 0 5000 0.01 ra c b 3 rectangle green nil nil)
(2 900 7200 2900 200 5000 200 0 0.1 ra c b 4 rectangle green nil nil) ...))
(relations ((modul 100)(planning-area (0 9000 0 6000 0 6000))))
(contacts ((1 2) (2 3) (2 4) (2 5)...))
(concepts ((1 trunc-inlet) (2 branch) ...(13 outlet) (g001 duct-system)))
(aggregates
((g001 800 7300 900 4200 0 5200 0 0.01 ra c b nil rectangle green nil ...)))

Having the deep knowledge determined for a proposed case, we are now able to establish useful information about the meaning and permissible use of the involved concepts and topological arrangements in the proposed case. We make all these information transparent for the user and thus serve the purpose for the call *Concepts and Topological Information*.

---

[6] The abbreviation ra stands for return-air, c for construction and b stands for the entity form *bounding box*. For the complete set of program packages see [5].

The next example shows how to meet the requirement of evaluation – that is to determine whether the obtained solution is assumable and workable due to quality assessment rules. Consider the case as shown in figure 4.

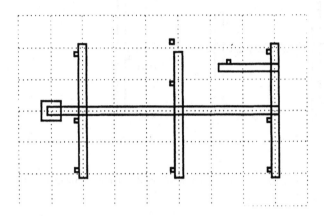

Fig. 4. A spatial and organizational well arranged, but not coherent return-air case

The quality assessment proceeds in terms of *Coherence Assessment* and *Spatial Ordering Organizational Maxims*. Some of the rules for the coherence examination of the return-air case, shown in figure 4, are the following:

- All involved ducts in the considered case have to be connected together in order to let the return air from all get into the trunk-inlet → O.K.
- All in- and outlets must be connected to ducts → Violation, there exists outlet which is not connected.
- The branch must occupy the whole space of the trunk-inlet completely (as shown in the fig. 3) → Violation, there is space left within the trunk-inlet.

The results of the examination of the spatial ordering and organizational maxims attest whether the proposed layout is conform with specific agreements. For instance, the maxims for the service space divisions indicate which layers of the technical service space are to be used for which kind of ducts laying in which directions, the maxims for the spatial ordering of outlets define which configurations of outlets are demanded, and the coordination maxims give regulations and priorities for the spatial organization of different subsystems within the layer structure of the technical service space. Examples of this examination are:

- All outlets have to be situated in the lowest or highest layer of the technical service space division within a certain distance and orderly due to a certain topological configuration → O.K.
- The branch is to be placed – per default – in middle layer of the installation service space → O.K.
- The laying direction of the ducts in each layer should be orthogonal to the ducts of its neighbor layers → O.K.

4 Implementation Framework

The DOM-ArC application system is the result of a cascade of system development, as shown in the figure 5. We started with the generic knowledge-based development system, FAENSY [12]. The next system was the DOM-ArC development system which is especially designed for development issues in the course of ontology formalization. It is implemented in Allegro Common Lisp under UNIX with a user interface based on TCL/TK. These main parts of the system are real-

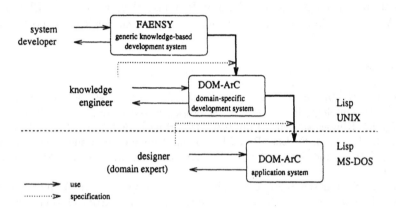

Fig. 5. The cascade of the system development

ized as classes of an object-oriented system. The system architecture is analogous to the conceptual description given in section 3:

- interface gate → transfer base,
- design board → shorttime data base,
- domain ontology → knowledge base, and
- assistance function → behavior base.

The DOM-ArC application system is our current state of the implementation. Our further work follows the same implementation framework: development on UNIX platform, evaluation by domain experts, and then transferring the formalized knowledge into the application system.

5 Summary and Outlook

We have shown – conceptually, implementationally and practically – that it is not only desirable, but – for dealing with design applications – it is demanded to extend a case-based reasoner with techniques of a powerful domain ontology modelling. One major advantage of the DOM-ArC is that it permits a significantly better understanding of the application and the evaluation of both: the solutions that are obtained and suggested by applying a case-based reasoner and cases that are specified by a designer.

The objectives of our further work are the following: Elaboration of the rectification part towards the ability of support services for case adaptation. Further, we use the potential of quality assessment results as basis for the realization of a reuse oriented structure for the case base organization.

Acknowledgement: We are indebted to Brigitte Bartsch-Spörl. Her valuable contributions permitted us to improve the DOM-ArC conceptualization and functional specification considerably. It is also thanks to Ulrike Eltz that the DOM-ArC development system have been implemented within a short time.

References

1. Alberts, L.K., Dikker, F.: Integrating Standards and Synthesis Knowledge Using the YMIR Ontology. In: Gero, J. S., Sudweeks, F. (eds): Artificial Intelligence in Design 94. Kluwer Academic Publishers, Dordrecht (1994) 517–534.
2. Aamodt, A., Plaza, E.: Case-Based Reasoning: Foundational Issues, Methodological Variations, and System Approaches. AI Communication, Vol. 7, Nr. 1 (1994) 39–59.
3. Bakhtari, S., Bartsch-Spörl, B.: Bridging the Gap between AI Technology and Design Requirements. In: Gero, J. S., Sudweeks, F. (eds): Artificial Intelligence in Design 94. Kluwer Academic Publishers, Dordrecht (1994) 753–768.
4. Bakhtari, S., Oertel, W.: Quality Assessment of Design Cases within the DOM Environment. In: Proceedings of the German Workshop on Case-Based Reasoning. LSA-95-02, University of Kaiserslauten, Germany (1995) 106–113.
5. Bakhtari, S., Bartsch-Spörl, B., Oertel, W., Eltz, U.: DOM: Domain Ontology Modelling for Architectural and Engineering Design. Fabel-Report Nr. 33, GMD, Sankt Augustin (1995).
6. Beheshti, M.R., Zreik, K. (eds): Advanced Technologies: Architecture, Planning, Civil Engineering. Elsevier (1993).
7. Fabel-Consortium: A Survey of FABEL. Fabel-Report Nr. 2, Sankt Augustin, GMD (1993).
8. Haller, F.: ARMILLA - ein Installationsmodell. Institut für Baugestaltung, Baukonstruktion und Entwerfen, Universität Karlsruhe (1985).
9. Hovestadt, L.: A4 Digital Building: Extensive Computer Support for the Design, Construction, and Management of Buildings. In: U. Flemming and S. van Wyk (eds): Proceedings of the Fifth International Conference on Computer-Aided Architectural Design Futures. North-Holland, Amsterdam (1993) 405–422.
10. Kolodner, J.: Case-Based Reasoning. Morgan Kaufmann (1993).
11. Neches, R., Fikes, R., Finin, T., Gruber, T., Patil, R., Senator, T., Swartout, W.: Enabling Technology for Knowledge Sharing. AI Magazin (1991).
12. Oertel, W.: FAENSY: Fabel Development System. FABEL Report Nr. 27, GMD, Sankt Augustin (1994).
13. Walther, J., Graether, W., Oertel, W., Schmidt-Belz, B., Voss, A.: An Open Architecture for Multiple Case Retrieval Methods. In: Keane, M., Haton, J.P., Manago, M. (eds): Preprints of the Second European Workshop on Case-Based Reasoning. AcknoSoft Press, Paris, France (1994) 373–380.

A Case-Based Reasoner Adaptive to Different Cognitive Tasks

Isabelle Bichindaritz

Université René Descartes, LIAP-5, UFR de Math-Info
45 rue des Saints-Pères, 75270 Paris Cedex 6, France
Email : bici@math-info.univ-paris5.fr

Abstract. Case-based reasoning systems are generally devoted to the realization of a single cognitive task. The need for such systems to perform various cognitive tasks questions how to organize their memory to permit them to be task-adaptive. The case-based reasoning system adaptive to cognitive tasks presented here is capable to adapt to analysis tasks as well as synthesis tasks. Its adaptability comes from its memory composition, both cases and concepts, and from its hierarchical memory organization, based on multiple points of view, some of them associated to the various cognitive tasks it performs. For analytic tasks, the most specific cases are preferably used for the reasoning process. For synthesis tasks, the most specific concepts, learnt by conceptual clustering, are used. An example of this system abilities, in the domain of eating disorders in psychiatry, is briefly presented.

1 Introduction

Case-based reasoning is classically presented as an artificial intelligence methodology to process empirical knowledge [1]. In order to achieve this goal, it studies how to design and implement memories dedicated to the realization of a precise cognitive task.

A *cognitive task* [17] can be characterized by an initial state space, containing the initial state, a final state space, containing the final state, and a path between these two states. When the final space is well-defined from the beginning, a cognitive task can be called an *analysis task* [7]. On the contrary, when the final space is unknown at the beginning, it must be constructed during the reasoning process, and the cognitive task is called a *synthesis task*. The general principle of case-based reasoning is to reduce a given cognitive task, whether analytic or synthetic, to the simpler analytic task of choosing the most useful case in the case library for realizing the given cognitive task. Nevertheless, some case-based reasoning systems also use synthetic sub-tasks, and particularly synthetic learning strategies [10], to perform some steps of their case-based reasoning. For instance, the problems related to the construction of elaborated cases and to their organization in MOPs [18] or clusters often involve the use of a synthetic learning strategy, which is a kind of synthetic task. The set of problems related to the process of learning the organizational units of the memory, which can be assimilated to concepts, meets that related to incremental concept learning in artificial intelligence. These problems have actually been in common from a longer time, since concepts have been used in case-based reasoning from the start to optimize the reasoning process. This article proposes to study how a case-based reasoning system can be made adaptive to the cognitive task it performs, when this task can take several forms, and moreover can vary between analysis and synthesis. In case-based reasoning, the memory is the key to adaptability. Its composition and organization do reflect all the reasoning abilities.

The system presented here is capable to realize both analysis and synthesis tasks. With that purpose, its memory possesses both cases and concepts, and is organized around several points of view, among which those associated to the cognitive tasks. The organization around several points of view permits the system to adapt to the different cognitive tasks. But the adaptation to both synthesis and analysis tasks comes from the composition of the memory ; the cases serve as the basis of reasoning for analysis tasks, and the concepts learnt serve as the basis of reasoning for synthesis tasks, thus allowing the system to adapt to these kinds of tasks as well as to analytic ones. The incremental concept learning, dependent upon the task performed, has been improved, especially in order to remedy the problem of the dependence upon the order of presentation of the instances, which is a crucial problem for conceptual clustering [8].

In this paper, the second part presents the adaptability problem in case-based reasoning. The third part details the system in order to show how a case-based reasoner can be made task-adaptive. Some result examples are set out in the fourth part. It is followed by the conclusion.

Throughout this paper, the word task refers to a cognitive task (such as diagnosis, or planning). For the learning tasks referred to in the machine learning literature, the expression learning strategy is used instead. In this system, the *learning strategy-adaptivity* is answerable for the *cognitive task-adaptivity*.

2 Adaptability in Case-based Reasoning

2.1 Classical Adaptability

Classically, several approaches to adaptability are combined in case-based reasoning. Their goals are first to increase the system skills in known situations, and secondly to broaden the system scope to new situations. The first goal is achieved by more specific knowledge, the second one by more abstract or general knowledge. To reach these goals, learning in case-based reasoning assumes several principal forms :

- **cases addition** : this is the earliest kind of learning in case-based reasoning; the issue here is to find a balance between mere accumulation, which serves a goal of specificity, the selection of the cases added, which controls the previous one, and the elaboration of cases from abstract schemas [16], which meets a goal of generality ;

- **indexes choice** : several approaches can be used, such as a pure inductive method, an explanation-based indexing or a knowledge-based indexing. It is the relative importance of background knowledge that guides towards one of these ;
- **memory organization** : the choice is between structured or unstructured memories. These systems evolution favors hierarchically structured memories, either in shared-features networks (such as in IPP [13]), or in discrimination networks (such as in CYRUS [11]). These organization variants are similar, and can be turned into one another. They rely upon the construction of clusters of similar cases in the memory, indexed under a common structure, generalized from them (a MOP [18]). To remedy the problem of incomplete new cases descriptions, they also propose redundant networks, such that cases are indexed under several clusters. These clusters, or MOPs, are kinds of concepts, and the algorithms used in case-based reasoning to deal with them are close to incremental concept learning [9], or conceptual clustering, algorithms in artificial intelligence. The advantage of these hierarchically structured memories is that they ease the search for the most similar cases, when the size of the memory increases. Instead of traversing all the cases in the memory, only the most general, limited in number, structures (the MOPs), are traversed in a first step. Then, progressively, more specific structures are traversed, until the most specific structure matching the new case is found, conversely with the set of cases indexed under it. If the general structures ease the extraction and the selection of cases, the utmost specificity of the cases selected facilitates their use. Moreover, this type of memory faces the future. Indeed learning occurs whenever a new case is processed, and following its results. Thus the memory keeps track of each of its experiences, whether success or failure, in a declarative way ; it is then as ready as possible to take advantage from future experiences. The drawbacks of these memories are first the place needed to store the network of these general structures, secondly the amount of learning inferences necessary to keep this network to date, lastly the lack of guarantee to lead to the most similar case [12].

2.2 Improving Case-based Reasoning through Incremental Concept Learning

The incremental concept learning practiced in several case-based reasoning systems deserves a thorough investigation. In fact, the concepts learnt during the case-based reasoning process may play several roles :

- **to facilitate the extraction** when the case-base grows ; as pointed before, the search through a hierarchy is more efficient than an exhaustive search through the whole case-base ;
- **to facilitate the selection** of the most useful cases for the reasoning : these are indexed under the concepts retrieved ; the comparison of these cases is reduced to their differences, and is thus more simple ;

- **to guide the use** of these cases : concepts provide general knowledge able to guide the use of the cases, for instance the adaptation ;
- **to increase the reasoning validity** : when similar cases are clustered together in the memory, the structure imposed by a common concept is an additional guarantee of the reasoning validity ;
- **to facilitate learning**, and thus the improvement through experience : learning is first localized in the extracted concepts, and in the cases depending from them ; a more global restructuring is achieved only if local restructuring is judged insufficient.

It appears that the construction of concepts, if it involves more learning inferences at each new case processing, facilitates, and increases the quality of the reasoning for subsequent cases. This advantage may be summarized by this property of dynamic memories, as quoted earlier : they face the future. Another advantage is that concepts, which are learnt structures, remain in memory, and can be used later throughout the reasoning ; not only to improve case-based reasoning in its field of application, but also to broaden this field. As a matter of fact, if the general methodology of case-based reasoning can be characterized as a heuristic classification, by performing an analytic or a synthetic task by an analytic strategy (that of choosing a case among all those of the memory), the concepts learnt while reasoning may serve as a basis for a synthetic strategy [4] to perform a task. The concepts learnt are thus similar to cases created by the system, as in some other case-based reasoning systems, such as CABOT [6].

3 A Task-adaptive Case-based Reasoning System

3.1 General Architecture of the System

The general architecture of the system presented here (see figure 1) is a current case-based reasoning system architecture. It has been improved in two ways in order to adapt to different cognitive tasks. In the first place, a specialized part of its memory contains models representing points of view. Each of these points of view is associated with a single cognitive task. In the second place, it is able to reason from concepts as well as from cases. The performance of an analytic task turns it towards the search for the most specific cases. But the performance of a synthetic task turns it on the contrary towards the search for the most specific concepts, and for the cases depending on those.

3.2 Knowledge Representation

The memory of the system can be divided into two parts : an experimental memory, and a theoretical memory. The experimental memory of the system is composed of cases, from a particular application domain, and of concepts learnt from the cases by incremental concept learning. Thus both the cases and the concepts are the entities composing the experimental memory. Each entity in memory is represented by a conjunction of description elements El_i where each

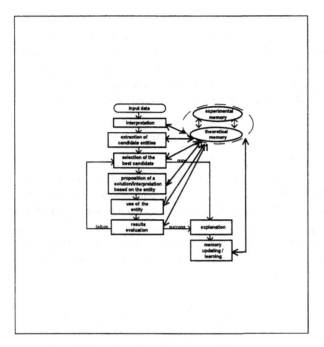

Fig. 1. Functional architecture of the system

El_i is a $< e_i, arg_i >$ pair ; the e_i are either attributes (in which case the arg_i are values), or relations (in which case the arg_i are entities in memory). So an entity E is expressed in this way :

$$E = \bigwedge_i < e_i, arg_i > \tag{1}$$

3.3 Memory Organization

For the adaptability problem presented here, only the experimental memory, and some specialized parts of the theoretical memory, called the points of view, are presented. The entities in the experimental memory (defined in 1) are organized in hierarchies which are dependent upon points of view in the theoretical memory of the system. Each cognitive task realized by the system is associated with a particular point of view. There are other types of points of view, all corresponding to coherent sub-domains of the application domain. Lastly, a neutral point of view is also defined, meaning that it is independent from the cognitive task realized. The concepts hierarchies depending on this point of view are constructed by a totally empirical conceptual clustering. On the contrary, the concepts hierarchies depending on the points of view associated to the cognitive tasks are ordered according to this task. More precisely, a point of view is a filter for the description elements El_i associated with each entity in memory. It can be expressed in the form of a conjunction of $< El_i, n_{i,pert} >$ pairs, where $n_{i,pert}$ is a pertinence weighted variable associated with the description element El_i. This pertinence weight is all the more increased as this element is important according to this point of view. The El_i element may be either an $< Att_i, val_i >$ pair, or a $< Rel_i, arg_i >$ pair, or simply an attribute Att_i or a relation Rel_i.

Consequently a point of view is expressed in this form :

$$P = \bigwedge_i < El_i, n_{i,pert} > \tag{2}$$

Each point of view element El_i is then associated with a set of entities Ent_j in memory, all sharing this description element. Moreover, a predictivity weighted variable $n_{j,pred}$ is here also associated with each entity in memory. This predictivity weight is the more increased as the corresponding element permitted to favorably select a case, and the more decreased as this selection leaded to a failure (credit and blame assignment). So each element El_i drives the search towards a set of entities in memory :

$$El_i \longrightarrow \bigwedge_j < Ent_j, n_{j,pred} > \tag{3}$$

Then, each entity in memory is a conjunction of $< e_k, arg_k >$ pairs (see 1). In addition, a concept associates to each description element e_k two discrimination weighted variables, a positive one $n_{k,disc+}$, and a negative one $n_{k,disc-}$. These variables are updated by learning : The positive discrimination variable is all the more increased as the description element has been matched positively during the search thru the memory, and all the more decreased as this element has been unmatched. These discrimination variables are used in the same way as the counters associated to each feature in the GBM system [14]. The concepts hierarchies are shared-features networks.

3.4 Extraction of the Entities

The extraction of the entities potentially interesting for the reasoning is realized following the several indexing levels from the point of view. The extracted entities do correspond to the Ent_j previously presented, and more precisely :

$$\{Ent_k\} = \bigcap_j \bigcap_i \{Ent_{j,i}\} \tag{4}$$

3.5 Selection of the Entities

The step of the selection of the entities on which reasoning will be based is essential, because it is here that the notion of similarity between the entities in memory is applied. Let Ent_e be a new case presented to the system. Two similarity notions are defined, one according to proximity, and the other one according to substitutability. The proximity similarity is calculated by the following scoring function :

$$sim(Ent_e, Ent_j) = \frac{\sum_{k=1}^{n} \alpha \times sim(El_{i,k}, El_{l,k}) + \sum_{k=1}^{n} n_{k_i,pred} \times n_{i,pert} \times sim(El_{i,k}, El_{l,k})}{\alpha \times n + \sum_{k=1}^{n} n_{k_i,pred} \times n_{i,pert}}$$

(5)

According to this measure, the set of entities extracted is ordered by decreasing order of similarity, in a set that is the set CA of the potential candidates for the reasoning. Nevertheless, these entities belong to different types : some are cases, others are concepts. The concepts held in the set $\{Ent_k\}$ are the heads of hierarchies in memory. The substitutability similarity is defined by a traversal algorithm though the hierarchies of concepts. For each concept C_k in the set Ent_k, a set of cases similar to the input case Ent_e is formed after the results from the traversal algorithm $SEARCH(Ent_e, C_k)$. Returning from this traversal, the set of the most specific concepts in which Ent_e is substitutable is returned, and the cases the most similar to Ent_e are the cases directly indexed under these concepts. The algorithm $SEARCH(Ent_e, C_k)$ is that of GBM [14].

3.6 Use of the Selected Entity

The entity(ies) selected is(are) then used for the reasoning process. For an analytic task, the cases, or a part of their representation, are adapted. For a synthetic task, the concepts, or a part of their representation, most of the time serve as a basis for constructing an argumentation. Yet other types of reasoning are possible.

3.7 A Priori Evaluation

An a priori evaluation of the validity of the inferences realized is possible, taking into account the adequacy between the most similar cases according to proximity, and according to substitutability. The more these sets of cases coincide with one another, the more valid are the inferences made.

3.8 Learning

Learning consists in the first place to take into account the results from the fulfillment of the processing proposed for the new case, and secondly to modify the hierarchy of concepts according to it.

Learning of Predictivity Variables. The predictivity variables (see 3) are dependent on the point of view, and thus on the cognitive task realized by the system. They are modified according to the results from the experimentation of the processing proposed (a posteriori evaluation). It is essentially a credit and blame assignment. If the processing is successful, the predictivity variables are incremented for the description elements in common between the selected case and the new case. If the processing fails, the predictivity variables are decremented for the description elements in common between the selected case and the new case.

Concept Learning. Before inserting a new case under the extracted concept, the system uses an improvement of GBM algorithm to remedy the problem of the order of presentation of the instances. If case-based reasoning benefits from a co-operation with incremental concept learning, at this point in the reasoning, the incremental concept learning takes advantage of a co-operation with case-based reasoning. This concept learning is more detailed in [5].

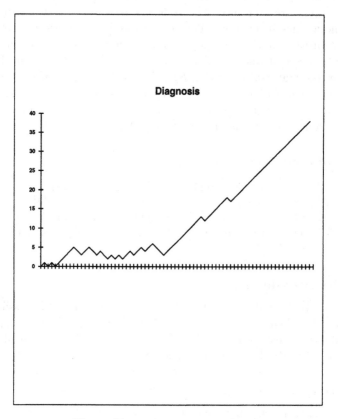

Fig. 2. Diagnosis accuracy evolution.

4 Application

4.1 Domain

The application domain is eating disorders in psychiatry. A restricted validation of the system, realized on the alimentary questionnaires of the patients, is presented here. These questionnaires, filled by the patients themselves, contain three types of information, about 232 foods :

- **the appreciation** of the food, having three possible values : "I like it", "I am indifferent to it" and "It disgusts me" ;
- **the avoidance** of the food, having two possible values : "I avoid it" and "I don't avoid it";
- **the reason of the avoidance** of the food, for each avoided food, with 22 possible values, such as "Sugar", "Fat" or "Taste" for instance.

The cognitive tasks realized by the system are diagnosis and treatment (analysis tasks), and research assistance (a synthesis task). They are detailed in [3].

4.2 Results

The results presented here are about one analysis task, diagnosis, and the synthesis task. For diagnosis, figure 2 presents the results for the classification obtained. The diagnostic category can take several values, the most important being Restrictive Anorexia, Bulimic Anorexia, and Control. Each point on the X-axis corresponds to a case ; each ascending line between two X-axis points represents a diagnosis success, and each descending line to a diagnosis failure. The results for the diagnosis are thus excellent after about 30 cases.

For clinical research assistance, an example of a concept learnt by the system is given in [2] for the neutral point of view, where learning is totally empirical. In this example, the case-based reasoning is an interpretation : the system gives an explanation for the concept learnt, on one hand from the theoretical knowledge contained in the memory about foods composition, and on the other hand by comparing this concept with those learnt from a control, that is to say non pathological, case-base.

5 Conclusion

Adaptability can be achieved in various ways in case-based reasoning. They all share the focus on the system memory, whether its composition, or its organization, or the processes involved with it. In the system presented here, the adaptivity to the different cognitive tasks comes from the organization of the memory around several points of view, each of them associated with a single cognitive task. The organization of the memory in hierarchies dependent on the points of view constrains strongly the case-based reasoning, and meets the set of problems of incremental concept learning. So the quality of this concept learning, in each point of view, permits not only to improve the reasoning thru experience, but to broaden the scope of case-based reasoning to the realization of true synthesis tasks. For these synthesis tasks, the concepts learnt by conceptual clustering, which is a synthetic learning strategy, form the basis for the reasoning, whereas for analysis tasks, the cases memorized are the basis for the reasoning. So the learning strategy permits to anticipate the processing of the cognitive tasks.

References

1. Aamodt A., Plaza E.: Case-based Reasoning : Foundational issues, methodological variations, and system approaches. AI Communications, 7(1) (1994)
2. Bichindaritz, I.: A case-based reasoning system using a control case-base. In : Proceedings ECAI-94, T. Cohn (Edt.) (1994) 38-42
3. Bichindaritz, I.: A case-based assistant for clinical psychiatry expertise. In : Proceedings 18th Symposium on Computer Applications in Medical Care, AMIA, Washington DC (1994) 673-677
4. Bichindaritz, I.: Apprentissage de concepts dans une mémoire dynamique : raisonnement à partir de cas adaptable à la tâche cognitive. PhD thesis of University René Descartes, Paris (1994)
5. Bichindaritz, I.: Case-Based Reasoning and Conceptual Clustering : for a Cooperative Approach. In : Proceedings of 1st UK CBR Workshop, I. Watson and F. Marir (Edts.) (to appear)
6. Callan J., Fawcett T., Rissland E.: CABOT : An Adaptive Approach to Case-Based Search. In : Proceedings of AAAI-92, Cambridge, MA (1992) 803-808
7. Clancey W.: Heuristic classification. Artificial Intelligence, volume 27 (1985) 289-350
8. Cornuéjols A.: Getting Order Independance in Incremental Learning. In: Proceedings of the European Working Session on Learning (1993) 196-212
9. Gennari J., Langley P., Fisher D.: Models of Incremental Concept Formation. Artificial Intelligence, 40 (1989) 11-61
10. Kodratoff Y., Michalski R. (Edts.): Machine Learning : An Artificial Intelligence Approach. Volume 3. Morgan Kaufmann Publishers, Inc., San Mateo, CA (1990)
11. Kolodner J.: Maintaining Organization in a Dynamic Long-Term Memory. Cognitive Science, 7 (1983) 243-280
12. Kolodner J.: Case-Based Reasoning. Morgan Kaufmann Publishers, Inc., San Mateo, CA (1993)
13. Lebowitz M.: Generalization From Natural Language Text. Cognitive Science, 7 (1983) 1-40
14. Lebowitz M.: Concept Learning in a Rich Input Domain : Generalization- Based Memory. In : Machine Learning : An Artificial Intelligence Approach, Vol 2. Michalski R., Carbonell J., Mitchell T. (Edts.), Morgan Kaufmann, Los Altos, CA (1986)
15. Lebowitz M.: Deferred Commitment in UNIMEM : Waiting to learn. In : Proceedings 5th Machine Learning Conference, Ann Arbor, Michigan (1988) 80-86
16. Ram A.: Indexing, Elaboration and Refinement : Incremental Learning of Explanatory Cases. In : Case-Based Learning, Kolodner J. (Edt.), Kluwer Academic Publishers, Boston (1993) 7-54
17. Rich E.: Artificial Intelligence. In : Encyclopedia of Artificial Intelligence, Shapiro S. (Edt.), Wiley Interscience (1987) 9-16
18. Schank R.: Dynamic memory. A theory of reminding and learning in computers and people. Camdridge University Press, Cambridge (1982)

On the use of CBR in optimisation problems such as the TSP

Pádraig Cunningham *, Barry Smyth **, Neil Hurley **

**Department of Computer Science, Trinity College Dublin, Ireland

**Hitachi Dublin Laboratory, Trinity College Dublin, Ireland

Abstract. The particular strength of CBR is normally considered to be its use in weak theory domains where solution quality is compiled into cases and is reusable. In this paper we explore an alternative use of CBR in optimisation problems where cases represent highly optimised structures in a huge highly constrained solution space. Our analysis focuses on the Travelling Salesman Problem where difficulty arises from the computational complexity of the problem rather than any difficulty associated with the domain theory. We find that CBR is good for producing medium quality solutions in very quick time. We have difficulty getting CBR to produce high quality solutions because solution quality seems to be lost in the adaptation process. We also argue that experiments with CBR on transparent problems such as the TSP tell us a lot about aspects of CBR such as; the quality of CBR solutions, the coverage that cases in the case-base offer and the utility of extending a case-base.

1 Introduction

Normally in CBR cases represent high quality solutions in weak theory domains. CBR is useful in situations where analytical models of interactions in the problem are difficult to determine and cases represent compiled quality solutions that are adaptable. It is a basic tenet of CBR that this solution quality should survive the adaptation process.* This paper examines solution reuse in a very different context; we explore case reuse in optimisation problems where cases can represent highly optimised structures in a large highly constrained search space.

There has already been some CBR research on scheduling, a particularly important category of optimisation problem. Two distinct approaches to case-based scheduling can be identified from the literature. The first one is used in Koton's SMARTplan (1989). Cases are used to propose preliminary schedules which are then adapted (refined and repaired) to satisfy the target schedule requirements. The second approach does not uses cases to propose schedules, but instead to adapt schedules proposed by other methods (for example, Sycara & Miyashita, 1994). In other words cases can encode actual schedules (the first approach) or they can encode repair procedures (the second approach). In this research we are interested in the first approach where the cases represent actual optimised structures in the problem domain.

So far we have looked at graph traversal problems (shortest path) and Travelling Salesman Problems (TSP). These are not weak theory domains because these

---

* Typical examples of this are; CAPLAN/CBC as described in (Muñoz, Paulokat & Wess; 1994) or Déjà Vu (Smyth & Cunningham, 1992)

problems are easy to model and the way in which solution components contribute to good quality solutions is easily understood. The problems are difficult because they involve a search through a huge highly constrained solution space. The fact that in optimisation problems solution components may be reusable in other situations suggest that CBR may be applicable. The transparency of these problems compared to problems in weak theory domains means that an analysis of the application of CBR in these areas can tell us a lot about CBR itself. In particular, it can tell us something about the quality of CBR solutions, the coverage that cases in the case-base offer and the utility of extending a case-base.

In this paper we focus on the use of CBR on Travelling Salesman Problems. Our findings have been mixed. Our CBR solution has been excellent from the point of view of speed but the solution quality has not been great. The CBR system produces good but not excellent solutions very quickly. In the next section we present a description of our CBR solution for the TSP. The cases are produced using Simulated Annealing (SA) and the performance of CBR system is compared with SA. The SA algorithm we use is described in an Appendix at the end of the paper. In section 3 we present a statistical analysis of case coverage. The performance of the CBR system is analysed in detail in section 4. The paper concludes with a summary of our findings and an indication of some future directions for research.

2 A Model for CBR in TSP

The basic idea behind a CBR approach to a problem like TSP is to shift problem complexity from the time domain into the space domain; that is, by storing cases we expect to find significant improvements in problem solving time. There is the worry however that the combinatorics of TSP will force the need for prohibitively large case-bases, in order to achieve significant performance improvements, thereby rendering a CBR solution infeasible in all but the simplest of TSP domains. We will defer discussion on the size problem to section 3 and describe our model of case reuse here.

The TSP problem involves sequencing a set of objects in order to minimise a cost function. There are many manifestations of this problem; for instance the problem of scheduling N jobs on a single machine where job set-up time is sequence dependent is a TSP (Cunningham & Browne, 1986). This is an example of a non Euclidean TSP in that solutions cannot be graphed in 2-dimensional space. This scheduling problem is also asymmetric in that the 'distance' from A to B is probably not equal to the 'distance' from B to A. The context of this scheduling problem motivates a case based solution. Typically schedules will be produced on a weekly or monthly basis and the set of jobs to be scheduled may be similar to a set scheduled in the past. The CBR solution described here is valid for non-Euclidean asymmetric TSPs even though the examples presented in the paper are shown as graphs.

In Figure 1 we show a 'world' of 100 cities, an optimised tour of 40 cities and a target problem of 40 cities. There is an overlap of 19 cities between the base and the target. In T-CBR the size and distribution of this overlap is the measure of similarity used in case retrieval. The first step in the adaptation process is to produce a skeleton tour from the overlap of the base and target; this is shown in the Figure. The first CBR solution is produced by adding the remaining cities on the target to this tour.

The algorithm for this is as follows:-

```
function Add-cities(tour, rem-cities)
{
    if rem-cities {
            best-city ← Select-best-city(tour, rem-cities)
            rem-cities ← Remove-city(best-city, rem-cities)
            tour ← Insert-city(tour, best-city)
            Add-cities(tour, rem-cities)
    }
}
```

The `Select-best-city` function takes each remaining city in turn and finds the point on the tour where it can be inserted with the minimum cost. The best city is the one that can be inserted in the tour with least cost. This first CBR solution is shown in Figure 2.

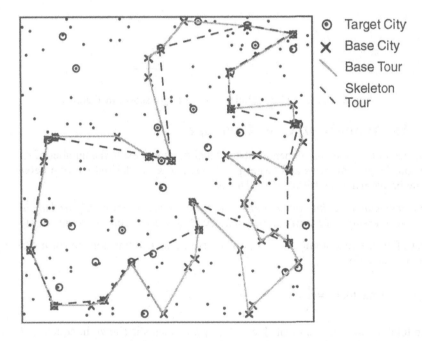

Fig. 1. A 'world' of 100 cities, a target problem of 40 cities and a base with 19 cities in common with the target.

This T-CBR solution is 365 units in length. The SA algorithm produced a solution of 338 units. This T-CBR solution is 8% longer than the SA solution. This adaptation mechanism is inspired by the geometric techniques for solving TSPs used by Norback and Love (1976). However it will work for non geometric or non symmetric problems. T-CBR goes on to improve this initial solution by examining each pair of cities in turn and testing to see if reversing the section of path between these two points produces an improved solution. We call this gradient descent 'Freezing' by analogy with what happens in Simulated Annealing.

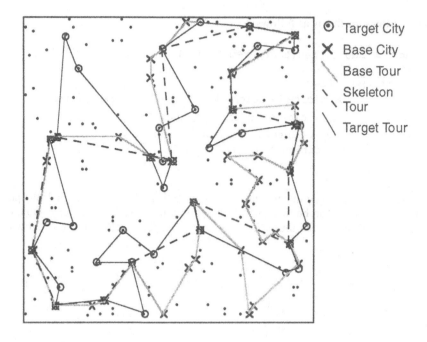

Fig. 2. The first CBR solution for the target shown in Figure 1.

3 An Analysis of Case Coverage

The size of the case-base depends on a number of quantities: n, the number of cities; r the tour lengths of cases and target problems; and k the desired overlap between a target problem and a retrieved case. That is:-

For a domain of n cities and a tour size of r, how many cases are required to ensure the presence of at least one case that shares k or more cities with the target?

First of all the total number of possible tours of size r in this domain (of n cities) is given by equation 1.

$$(1) \qquad \text{Total tours} = \binom{n}{r}$$

The total number of tours that share exactly k elements is shown in equation 2. The first factor is the total number of ways of choosing k cities from tours of r cities, and, given that k cities have now been fixed, the second factor is the total possible ways of filling the remaining r-k tour positions.

$$(2) \qquad \text{Total tours sharing } k \text{ cities} = \binom{r}{k} \cdot \binom{n-k}{r-k}$$

The total number of tours that share k or more cities is thus given by equation 3.

(3) Total tours sharing k or more cities $= \sum_{i=k}^{r} \binom{r}{i} \bullet \binom{n-i}{r-i}$

For a particular target specification of r cities, the probability of picking a random tour that shares at least k cities with this target is shown in equation 4; this is termed the probability of success and is denoted by S.

(4) $S = \dfrac{\sum_{i=k}^{r} \binom{r}{i} \bullet \binom{n-i}{r-i}}{\binom{n}{r}}$

Now in a CBR scenario, a case-base of C random cases means that we have essentially C attempts to find a successful tour, a tour that overlaps by at least k cities with the target. We would like the probability of failure (in other words the probability of there not being a suitable case) to be less than some fraction ε. So if $(1-S)^C$ is the probability of a finding no such case over C trials[*] then the relationship between ε and S is the simple one shown in equation 5.

(5) $(1 - S)^C < \varepsilon$

So from this we can form the function in equation 6 that computes the case-base size necessary to ensure that a suitable case is present for every target problem, all but $\varepsilon \bullet 100\%$ of the time.

(6) $C = \dfrac{\log(\varepsilon)}{\log(1 - S)}$

Figure 3 (A) & (B) illustrate how this function behaves for various values of n, r, and k. In each graph, the error value, ε, is kept static at 0.05, and n is varied from 50 to 500 in increments of 50, a separate curve is drawn for each n value and marked with that value. Both graphs plot the case-based size on the y axis, which is logarithmically scaled.

Figure 3(A) plots case-base size against the tour length (that is the case and target sizes). The desired overlap between target and case, k, is assumed to be 30% of the tour length. As expected there are large variations in the size of the case-base as n and r increase. It is interesting that for this 30% overlap restriction, the size of case-base needed for a given n peaks when r is 12.5% of n and trails off rapidly as r increases towards n. For example, for n = 500, the case-base size offering 30% overlap, peaks at $r = 40$, where over 10^5 cases are needed to provide the desired problem coverage. However, when the tour size is 100, less than 600 cases are needed.

---

[*] (1- S) is the probability of not selecting a successful tour in one attempt so $(1-S)^C$ is the probability of failure after C consecutive attempts.

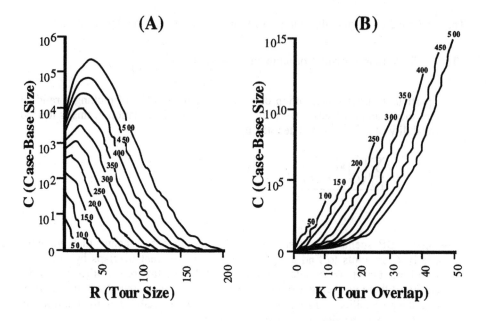

Fig. 3. Variations in case-base size.

Figure 3(B) plots the case-base size against varying overlap. For each curve r is fixed at 20% of n and the overlap, k, is varied from between 0 and $r/2$. So for example, the curve corresponding to $n = 500$ corresponds to a system where the tour length (that is the sizes of the cases and the target problems) is 100, and a varying overlap of between 0 and 50 cities. Again, as expected the case-base size rises exponentially with k. In a system where n is 500, r is 100, and k is 50 (that is 50% of the tour length), a case-base of over 1014 cases is required. However, as was mentioned above, if an overlap of 30 cities is acceptable for this system then less that 600 cases are needed.

A pessimistic interpretation of these results might suggest that CBR and TSP do not mix well, owing to the enormous case-bases required to provide adequate coverage and significant performance improvements. However this is not necessarily true in general, and there exist a great many TSP problems which *are* amenable to a case-base solution, at least in the sense that the case-base is of an acceptable size. In particular, this is true if the route size, r, is greater than roughly 20% of n and k is less that about 40% of r.

4 Evaluation

In order to evaluate the T-CBR process an artificial world of 500 cities was created and a case-base with 600 tours of 100 cities each was constructed. Good solutions for these tours were produced using the SA algorithm described in the Appendix. The case-base size was chosen to offer good target-base overlap. In fact, on average, about 10 cases are found that overlap the target by 29 or more cities.

The evaluation that we describe here has two parts. In the first part the potential of T-CBR to produce very quick medium quality solutions is considered. In this evaluation it is compared with SA and a Myopic algorithm that selects a starting city at random and chooses the nearest remaining city at each step. This is the standard quick solution to the TSP. This evaluation is described in section 4.1. We then attempted to use T-CBR to produce good quality solutions by seeding a Low Temperature version of the SA algorithm with solution produced from the case-base. This is described in section 4.2.

4.1 Producing quick & nasty solutions

In this situation we are evaluating five alternatives;

- the full Simulated Annealing
- the initial T-CBR solution
- the initial Myopic solution
- the T-CBR with Freezing
- the Myopic with Freezing

One hundred target tours were generated at random and solutions were produced using each of these algorithms. The average solution times and tour lengths are shown in Figure 4. The SA solution was used as a base-line for comparing the alternatives. The CBR+Freezing produces solutions that are within 6% of the SA solutions but in one tenth of the time. The Myopic+Freezing is extremely fast but the solutions are over 11% longer than the baseline. So CBR scores well as a means of producing medium quality solutions quickly.

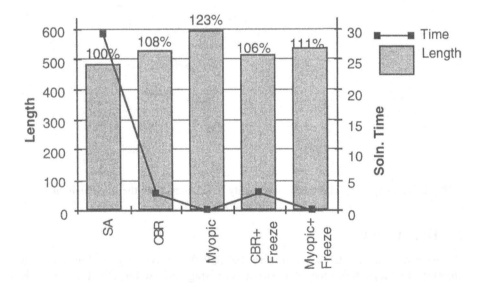

Fig. 4. Costs and lengths associated with different algorithms

4.2 Producing good quality solutions

The obvious question arising from this evaluation is whether T-CBR can be improved to produce high quality solutions. The strategy we came up with was to use the initial

CBR solution to seed a Low Temperature version of the Simulated Annealing algorithm (LTSA). After experiments with different temperatures we settled on a starting temperature of 1.0 for the LTSA. Temperatures much below this were akin to Freezing the solution while values greater than 1.0 allowed the structure of the good solution produced by T-CBR to deteriorate.

The experiment reported here describes tests over a range of target tour lengths from 40 to 160, with 20 tests being done at each length. This also illustrates the flexibility of T-CBR where base cases can be adapted to targets of different lengths. The main results of this experiment are shown in Figure 5. T-CBR+LTSA performs quite well with solutions found on average 2.5 times faster than SA. These solutions are now within 1-3% of the SA solutions. This would be great news for CBR except that we discovered that Myopic+LTSA (Low temperature SA seeded with a Myopic solution) produced solutions of similar quality. Myopic+LTSA is faster than T-CBR+LTSA and does not need a case base. This suggests that the main contribution to the good solution is the LTSA and not the CBR.

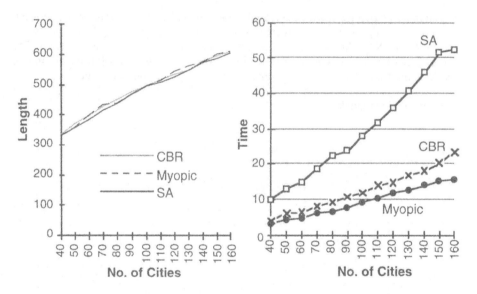

Fig. 5. A comparison of the cost and quality of solutions from the three high quality techniques.

5 Discussion

We have described a CBR solution to the TSP that provides good but not great solutions in very quick time. This is not surprising because the effect of the CBR solution is to shift the problem complexity from the time domain into the space domain. Indeed we have pointed out that this CBR solution is not practicable for many TSP problems because the required case-bases can be prohibitively large.

The more interesting issue raised in this paper is the fact that our CBR technique does not manage to produce solutions of high quality. Some of the solution quality is lost in the adaptation process. We have described a technique combining case retrieval and

Low Temperature Simulated Annealing that does produce very good solutions but we have argued that this is more due to the power of the SA than the contribution of the retrieved case.

It seems that the experience of research on Genetic Algorithms (GA) is informative in this regard. What is happening in T-CBR is that the retrieved case represents a highly optimised structure that is disrupted or broken in the adaptation process. GA research emphasises the importance of building blocks in the GA process. These building blocks are manipulated blindly in the process of reproduction and crossover to produce compositions of building blocks that are highly optimal. It is recognised that it is important for individual building blocks not to be broken in the crossover process (Goldberg, 1989). In our adaptation process the solutions are manipulated naïvely and building blocks representing optimal structure are broken. However, this is probably inevitable where there is so little intersection between the base and target problems. The base case provides a skeletal solution for the target problem but the detailed optimal structure from the base case is not transferred into the target.

This analysis suggests that a change in approach to the reuse of base cases might be fruitful. Instead of considering the base case as the source of a skeleton on which a target tour can be built several base cases could be used to provide tour segments to build into a good quality target solution. This alternative approach seems promising but there are new problems associated with combining tour fragments taken from different cases.

Conclusions

CBR can be used to produce medium quality solutions to optimisation problems. In the approach described here the base case provides a skeletal solution on which a solution for the target problem can be built. Efforts to use CBR to produce high quality solutions for optimisation problems need to focus on ensuring that solution building blocks survive the optimisation process. This might be achieved by using several cases to contribute to the target solution.

We have argued that the naïve manipulation of the solutions in the adaptation process results in the target solutions being of lower quality than the solution in the base case. This is evident in T-CBR because of the transparency of the problem domain. It is interesting to speculate on how prevalent this is in other CBR applications in domains that are not so transparent.

References

Cunningham P., Browne J., (1986) A LISP-based heuristic scheduler for automatic insertion in electronics assembly, *International Journal of Production Research*, Vol.24, No.6, pp1395-1408.

Goldberg D.E., (1989) *Genetic Algorithms in Search Optimization & Machine Learning*, Addison Wesley, Reading Massachusetts.

Kirkpatrick S., Gelatt C.D., Vecchi M.P., (1983) Optimization by Simulated Annealing, *Science*, Vol. 220, No. 4597, pp671-680.

Koton, P. (1989) SMARTplan: A Case-Based Resource Allocation and Scheduling System. *Proceedings of the Case-Based Reasoning Workshop*, pp 285-289, Florida, USA.

Muñoz H., Paulokat J.,. Wess S., (1994) Controlling Nonlinear Hierarchical Planning by Case Replay, in working papers of the *Second European Workshop on Case-based Reasoning*, pp195-203, Chantilly, France.

Norback J., Love R., (1977) Geometric Approaches to Solving the Travelling Salesman Problem, *Management Science*, July 1977, pp1208-1223.

Smyth B., Cunningham P., (1992) Déjà Vu: A Hierarchical Case-Based Reasoning System for Software Design, in Proceedings of *European Conference on Artificial Intelligence*, ed. Bernd Neumann, John Wiley, pp587-589.

Sycara, K. & Miyashita, K. (1994) Case-Based Acquisition of User Preferences for Solution Improvement in Ill-Structured Domains. *Proceedings of the 12th National Conference on Artificial Intelligence*, pp. 44-49. Seattle, USA.

Appendix A: The Simulated Annealing Algorithm for the TSP

The Simulated Annealing Algorithm is a modification of a basic gradient descent search based on some ideas from statistical mechanics (Kirkpatrick, Vecchi & Gelatt, 1983). A notion of temperature is introduced into the process and the system is gradually cooled to *freeze* at a near optimal solution. The key modification to standard gradient descent is the possibility that some dis-improvements in solution are accepted. The probability of this is greater at higher temperatures (see Step 3 below). This allows the gross features of the solution to be determined at high temperatures while details are worked out at low temperatures. The details of our implementation are as follows:-

1. Set $temp \leftarrow \dfrac{\sqrt{NCITY} \bullet longest - dist}{10}$
$$nsucc \leftarrow 10 \bullet NCITY$$
$$ntries \leftarrow 100 \bullet NCITY$$

   Generate a pseudorandom feasible solution T.

2. Generate a new feasible solution T' by reversing a section of T.
   $nt \leftarrow nt + 1$.

3. $\Delta E \leftarrow E_{final} - E_{initial}$ (where E is the cost of the solution)
   If $\Delta E \leq 0$ accept the move;

   If $\Delta E > 0$ accept the move with prob. $P(\Delta E) = e^{-\Delta E/T}$
   $$ns \leftarrow ns + 1.$$

4. Repeat from 2 while $nt < ntries$ and $ns < nsucc$

5. When nt reaches $ntries$ or ns reaches $nsucc$ drop temperature
   (i.e. $temp \leftarrow temp \bullet 0.9$), set ns & nt to 0 and start a new loop from 2.

   Terminate on the first pass that produces no successes.

Case-based Diagnosis of Multiple Faults

Ralph Deters

Universität der Bundeswehr München
Institut für Technische Informatik
85577 Neubiberg, F.R.Germany
E-mail: deters@informatik.unibw-muenchen.de

Abstract:
In order to maintain complex technical systems e.g. a telecommunication network, a rapid and precise recognition of faults and critical situations is required. But the large number of different components, the high degree of interdependencies among the components and the permanent changes in these systems make the diagnosis of faults and critical situations difficult.
Case-based Reasoning (CBR) seems particularly well suited for such a diagnosis. The ability to reuse old experiences by adapting them to current needs offers a possibility to handle the large number of diagnoses as well as the changes in the systems. However, the large number of components results in the problem of diagnosing multiple independent faults which leads to serious difficulties in retrieval and adaptation.
This paper focuses on the specific problems of diagnosing multiple independent faults. An incremental retrieval and adaptation approach based on an hypothesis and test strategy is introduced which is able to cope with data of multiple overlapping problems. At the end of this paper is given a report about the experiences in using the described algorithm for handling multiple faults in telecommunication networks.

Keywords: multiple independent faults, incremental case retrieval

1. Introduction

A major problem in maintaining large distributed technical systems such as telecommunication networks, power plants or assembly lines concerns the fast recognition of abnormal system states (e.g. faults, critical situations). In order to recognise abnormal system states the stream of messages produced by the components of the system are observed. Every message contains two types of information - the affected component and its report. The flood of messages and the large number of different components (e.g. components from different vendors), their high degree of interdependence and the permanent changes in these systems make the diagnosis an extremely complicated task for human operators. Rapid and precise diagnosing of the current system state is therefore a central problem of maintaining a large distributed technical system.

Case-based diagnosing seems to offer a possibility to support the operator, especially if the domain is ill structured and the number of possible diagnosis is extremely high. The case-based approach seems to require less and often easier to acquire knowledge than the classical approaches like simulation [Rie93] and pure model-based diagnosis [Rei87] [Kle93]. In addition, the ability to adapt old solutions to current problems offers a promising possibility to cope with the permanent changes (modifications/extensions) of these systems. In contrast to other learning approaches such as neural networks the results of case-based diagnosis are more understandable (explainable). A case-based reasoner is always able to deliver at least the used case(s) as an elementary explanation. This ability to explain the result is extremely important since an operator must trust the output in order to plan the required actions. With the development of the field of CBR [Rie91] [Kol93] a variety of diagnostic approaches have been implemented e.g. Protos, Casey, Swale which cover the full range from classification to explanation tasks. Unfortunately, until now developed case-based diagnostic approaches are limited to the detection of single faults. This is a serious shortcoming, since in a large distributed system multiple independent faults can happen at the same time. Therefore a diagnosis tool has to be able to cope with the problem of multiple faults [Ngu89].

The aim of this paper is to focus on the specific problems of case-based diagnosis in domains with multiple overlapping faults and to discuss a retrieval approach which uses an hypothesis and test strategy. The described approach for an incremental and opportunistic retrieval stems out of our research concerning the problems of analysing large message streams (each file containing several thousand messages) of telecommunication protocols [Det94]. At the end of the paper a report about the experiences of the described retrieval algorithm is given.

2. Case-Based Diagnoses of Faults

In case-based diagnosis the goal is to recognise faults by using diagnostic cases containing the experience of previous fault detection. A diagnostic case is at least a pair consisting of a set of symptoms and a diagnosis. Depending on the amount of possible diagnosis the process of diagnosing can be modelled either as a classification or explanation task.

As already mentioned, a large number of case-based diagnosis and explanation approaches have been developed. Unfortunately these systems are not able to detect multiple independent faults. In order to explain the specific difficulties of multiple fault detection an example from the field of telecommunication network faults is given.

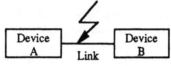

Fig. 1 - Link-Failure

Figure 1 shows a typical network fault called link failure. The link between two devices has become faulty. The result of such a fault is the emission of four messages. First devices A and B report that they can't communicate anymore. In addition, device A reports that the link A-B is faulty. Since every device has only a local view device B reports the same about "its" link B-A.

The detection of such a single fault is not difficult for a case-based diagnosis tool since this is a single fault detection problem. The observed messages (symptoms) can be used to form a search vector which is then used for case-retrieval (one-shot retrieval). But if several of these faults appear (multiple independent faults), which is not unusual in a large network, it is unclear which message belongs to which problem. This "problem of origin" makes applying a one-shot retrieval impossible, since using messages from different problems would be misleading.

Incremental retrieval approaches which "compose their target specification during the CBR process" [Cun94] seem better suited for multiple fault diagnosis than one-shot approaches. But current incremental retrieval approaches are also limited to single faults detection, because they can't compose for the *multiple* faults *multiple* target specification. In the following, an incremental CBR approach is described which is able to diagnose multiple independent faults by using a hypotheses and test strategy.

3. The Hypothesis Concept

The basic problem of multiple independent faults is that it is not possible to decide in advance if one or several faults have happened. This means that it is unclear if the observed symptoms belong to one or several independent faults. In order to solve this problem it is necessary to use an hypothesis and test strategy. Figure 2 shows the pseudo code of a retrieval approach using hypothesis and test. The algorithm starts with a list of observed messages (message-list), an empty list of unexplainable messages (noise-list), an empty list of hypotheses (hypothesis-list) and an empty list of retrieved cases (result-list). In the first step, one of the observed messages is taken out of the message-list and matched against all existing hypotheses. If the message is matched successfully with an hypothesis, it is added to the hypothesis. The adding of a message to an hypothesis is called instantiation. If an hypothesis is fully instantiated, that is all expected messages were observed, the hypothesis is called a retrieved case. The hypothesis can then be moved from the list of hypotheses to the list of found cases. If the message doesn't match any hypothesis all cases in the case-memory are matched against the message. All cases that the message has matched successfully are copied into the hypothesis-list. If no case was selected, the message is classified as not explainable and is added into the noise-list.

```
01. while (messages-list not empty)
02.      { take message from message-list
03.      set flag to false
04.      for (all hypotheses in the hypotheses-list)
05.           { select a hypothesis
06.           check hypothesis
07.           if ((hypothesis not valid) OR
08.                (message-list empty))
09.                { delete hypothesis
10.                if (first message nowhere else)
11.                {move first message to noise-list}
12.                add unused messages to message-list
13.                }
14.           if ((message not tried before) AND
15.                (message matches hypothesis))
16.                { add message to hypothesis
17.                adaptation of hypothesis
18.                }
19.           set flag to true
20.           if (hypothesis is no longer valid)
21.                { remove message again
22.                set flag to false
```

```
23.                            }
24.                 if (hypothesis full)
25.                     { copy hypothesis to result-list}
26.                 }
27.         if (flag equal false)
28.             {for (all existing cases)
29.                     {if(message matches case)
30.                         { set flag to true;
31.                         copy case into hypotheses-list
32.                         add message to hypothesis
33.                         adaptation of hypothesis  .
34.                 }      }       }
35.         if (flag equal false)
36.                 { add message to noise-list }
37.         }
```

Fig. 2 - The basic retrieval algorithm

3.1 An Example

The following example shows how the described algorithm works. A flat rather than an indexed case-memory is used, containing the following three cases. In order to simplify the example the justifications of the cases are not mentioned. The cases are:

Case 1 := (Problem Definition := {(device_a, can't communicate), (device_b, can't communicate), (link_ab, faulty), (link_ba, faulty)}, Diagnosis := Link-Failure)
Case 2. := (Problem Definition := {device_z-can't communicate, device_z, can't communicate}, Diagnosis := Internal Device Error)
Case 3. := (Problem Definition := {device_g-call establishment error, device_f-call establishment error}, Diagnosis := Call Establishment Error)

In addition it is assumed that all devices are different instances from the same class and that all reports are from different classes. A distance measure based on the class relations is used to define the similarity (see section 4).

The task is to analyse the following message stream:
{ 1. (device_e, can't communicate), 2. (device_z, call establishment error),
3. (device_a, can't recover), 4. (device_f, can't communicate), 5. (link_ef, faulty),
6. (link_fe, faulty), 7. (device_x, call establishment error) }
(Please note that a message is a pair consisting of component and report)
First comes Message 1. No hypotheses exist - so message 1 is used to search in the case-memory. The Cases {1, 2} are found applicable because only a simple reinstantiation is needed for adaptation. The cases {1, 2} are copied as hypotheses {H1, H2} into the hypotheses-list and instantiated with the message 1.
Message 2 is taken and is matched against the two existing hypotheses. The message doesn't match any existing hypotheses - a search in the case-memory is required. The case 3 is applicable and copied as hypotheses H3 into the hypotheses-list. H3 is instantiated with the message 2.

Message 3 is taken and matched against the three existing hypotheses. It matches only H1 since the same component is mentioned. It is added to H1.

Message 4 is taken and matched against the hypotheses. It matches H1 since only a simple reinstantiation is required. It is added to H1.

Message 5 is selected and matched against all hypotheses. It matches only H1 and is added to H1.

Message 6 is taken and matched against all hypotheses It matches only H1 and is added. H1 has now a complete consistent set of messages (1,4,5,6). This instantiation of the hypotheses H1 is moved with its messages into the result-list. As a result of the move H1 contains now only the message 3.

Message 7 is taken and matched against all hypotheses. It matches only H3 to which it is added. The hypotheses H3 is now complete and can be copied into the result-list. Since no message is associated any longer with this hypothesis it is removed.

No messages are left and the last hypotheses remaining are removed. Since the message contained in hypothesis H2 is already linked to a diagnosis it is deleted. The last message left is 3. Since no hypotheses are left the case-memory is searched. The case 1 is selected and copied as hypothesis H4 into the hypothesis-list. But since no messages are left this hypothesis is also removed again. Finally the message 3 is moved into the noise-list and the algorithm terminates.

3.2 Characteristics of the Algorithm

The above described algorithm performs a kind of hypothesise and test strategy for retrieving cases. The main characteristics of the described algorithm are:

• **Handling of multiple problems**

The described approach is able to handle *multiple* problems by creating *multiple* hypotheses. This is an important difference in comparison with other case-based reasoning approaches. *Typically CBR applications are not able to treat multiple independent problems.* This is a serious limitation for CBR as a cognitive approach (humans are able to handle multiple problems) and for CBR as a problem solving paradigm (model-based diagnosis approaches are able to handle multiple independent faults).

• **Incremental and Opportunistic**

The approach is incremental since the cases are retrieved step by step and opportunistic because the order of messages influences the generation of hypotheses. *This is again an interesting feature since humans show the same behaviour. Depending on the order of data humans develop different hypotheses.*

The development of different hypotheses leads to the problem of deleting unpromising candidates. If an hypothesis turns out to be wrong all messages which are contained in this hypothesis have to be freed again which means that they are added again into the message-list. Only the message which was used to generate the hypothesis is not added again to the message-list. This one is moved to the noise-list in order to avoid a cycle.

• **Adaptation is performed during retrieval**

The other important aspect of this approach is that the adaptation is performed during the retrieval. The retrieval component not only delivers similar cases it *creates adapted* cases. This is performed by creating copies of the cases called hypotheses and manipulating them. This manipulation is performed first by instantiating them with similar messages and then computing the effects of the instantiation. A result of an instantiation with a similar message is either local (no effect on other messages, trivial situation), or global as an increase/decrease of constraints concerning other messages.

4. The Matching and Adaptation Problem

The goal of the retrieval component is to find similar cases that are believed to be useful in solving the current problem. This is performed by searching for cases that contain a problem definition which is similar to the current problem (another approach could be to focus on the used explanations). This means that the retrieval component searches for a case that has similar messages in its problem definition. The problem definition of the cases contains two types of information. First a list of expected messages and second a list of constraints between the messages. In order to decide if a message can be matched with a case or hypothesis, the retrieval component checks if the message is similar to the expected one and then checks to see if no constraints are violated.

The similarity of a message is viewed as the combination of the similarity of the report and the similarity of the component. Both similarities are defined by use of a distance measure based on two abstraction graphs. One abstraction graph contains all the information about the abstraction relations of the reports and the other about the abstraction relations of the components. The overall similarity of a message is defined boolean. If both sub similarities are in a case specific tolerance range, it is accepted. After the similarity of the message is checked the constraints are checked. The goal is to detect if the message leads to conflicts with other messages.

Every addition of a message to a hypothesis invokes the adaptation which is performed step by step (incrementally) while retrieving the cases. This leads to the problem of making adaptation decisions without having all the information needed. An adaptation is required whenever a message is added to an hypothesis. Several possible effects of an adaptation are possible. The first possibility is that the result of the adaptation only effects the parts which should be instantiated with the message which means that all other parts of the problem definition are not affected. But the adaptation can also lead to modifications of the problem definition which can result in a limitation or extension of the matching possibilities. A limitation can result in either introducing new constraints as necessary pre-conditions or by simple constraint propagation. If, for example, the hypothesis "link-failure" is instantiated with the messages concerning a fault of a link_ab, a message about a link_ef leads to an inconsistency. If link_ab is reported faulty, only messages from the link_ba and the devices a and b are possible. But since several overlapping link faults could have happened, this leads to the problem of handling consistent variants (instantiation combinations) of a hypothesis. But besides the addition of constraints, it is also possible that the adaptation removes constraints. This leads to the effect that by adding a certain message, until then not matching, messages could be added.

5. Hypothesis Variants

The described algorithm tries to match the message with all known hypotheses. In order to cope with the problems of *different* ways to instantiate hypotheses with the set of messages it is necessary to handle *different* variants of a hypothesis.

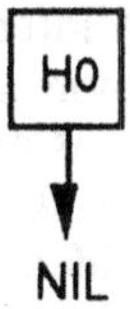

Fig. 3 -Hypotheses-List with only one Hypothesis

If for a given message no hypothesis is found to which it could be added, the case-memory is searched. If now a case is found, a copy of the case is moved as the hypothesis H0 into the hypotheses-list (fig.3).

To this hypothesis the message is added. If now the hypotheses could be instantiated in different ways it is necessary to create for every possibility an additional sub hypothesis called a variant. In the following it is assumed that two possibilities of adding the message exists. This leads to the creation of two new variants (V1,V2) which are both linked to the initial hypothesis H0. The variants V1 and V2 are the two possible variants of how to add the message M1 to the hypothesis H0 (fig.4).

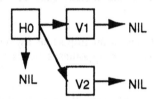

Fig. 4- Two Variants of the Hypothesis H0

If now another message is matched against the hypothesis H0 it is first checked to see if it fits all constraints of H0. If this is the case the children of H0 (V1,V2) are tested. Instead of again checking all constraints of V1 and V2 only constraints that differ from H0 are tested. If the message M1 meets all constraints of a variant it is added. If some constraints are violated the hypothesis is tested if this indicates a unacceptable dissimilarity. Depending on its similarity or dissimilarity it is added or not.

As already mentioned, every addition of a messages invokes the adaptation process. If, as a result of the adaptation, the scope of possible instantiation for another position in the hypothesis is limited (either by adding new constraints or by simple constraint propagation), a new variant has to be created. If for example the message M1 would lead to a reduced scope of another message in V1 it is necessary to create a new variant (V3) (fig. 5).

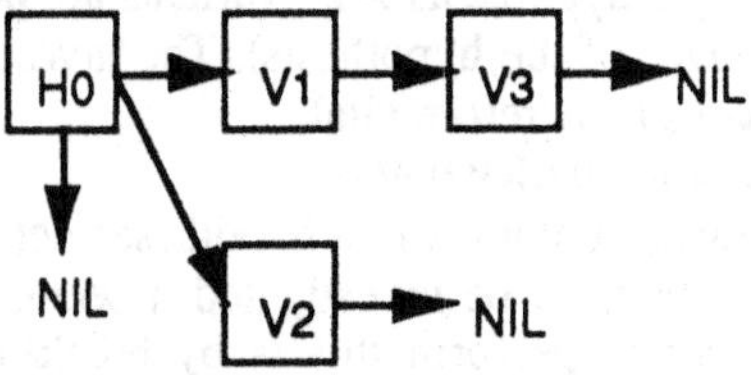

Fig. 5 - A new sub variant of V1

If a message should be matched against an hypothesis it is necessary to check also all variants. It is first tested to see if it is possible to match the root hypothesis (H0). Only if this is possible are the variants investigated by treating them again as root hypotheses. In this way only the children of successfully matched parents are investigated since children are always more specific.

Note that the creation of a new variant is only done if the instantiation of a variant with a message limits the scope of other messages. Instantiations that don't reduce the scope of other messages are simply added to the variant. If the position is already occupied by another message (as a result of a earlier instantiation) the message is still added as a different possibility. If the adding of a message (Mx) in a variant (Vx) would lead to a removing of a constraint, a new variant is created (Vy). Then the new variant (Vy), which is more general, is added as a child to the parent node of (Vx). If the constraint has been defined in the initial hypothesis (H0) then a new initial hypothesis instantiated with the message Mx is created.

6. Optimisation Strategies

The described hypothesise and test algorithm leads to serious performance problems if the growth of the hypotheses and their variants is not limited. In the following discussion possible limitation techniques are introduced.

Handling the Hypotheses

The handling of the hypotheses is an important aspect. The goal is to keep this number small since any increase of hypotheses leads to a significant performance reduction.

• **Limiting the creation**

The first and simplest approach is to limit the amount of hypotheses by introducing a maximum number of hypotheses. If this number is reached no further hypotheses are created. This number can be either a static value given by the user or a value calculated by the current performance which means that if the performance allows further hypotheses they are excepted but if it drops under a critical value no more hypotheses are accepted.

• **Evaluation**

Instead of simply stopping the creation of an hypothesis because the maximum number is reached, it is also possible to develop an evaluation function for hypotheses. Only the n (n defined as the maximum number of hypotheses) best hypotheses are then investigated.

Handling the Variants of a Hypothesis

The incremental expansion of all possible variants can lead to serious performance problems because for a single hypothesis $> 2^n$ variants are possible (n represents the number of expected messages of the hypothesis). The investigation of techniques to identify unpromising variants is therefore vital.

• **Breaking the cases into smaller pieces**

Since the number of messages contained in a hypotheses defines how many different variants of this hypothesis have to be investigated it seems reasonable to keep the hypotheses small. One way to perform this is by breaking the cases into small substructures. This can be done by use of the microcases [Zit93] or by multidimensional structuring [Det95]. In the current implementation of a case-based tool for analysing message streams the multidimensional approach was used. The substructures contain typically between 4 and 10 different messages.

• **Evaluating Variants**

An evaluation of the variants is also possible. The idea is to evaluate every variant and only expand the most promising ones. The difficulty in such an incremental expansion is the development of useful heuristics. It has therefore not yet been tested.

6. Empirical Results

The described algorithm has been implemented in C++ (GNU 2.4) on a Sun-Workstation under XVIEW. It was tested by use of various types of simulated net faults given by domain experts. The first question was if the used retrieval approach leads to performance problems if single faults have to be detected. A sequence of not overlapping single faults were given to the system and it turned out that the time needed for detecting all faults depends on the number of faults given. This was exactly what was expected since the detection of 5 faults takes typically 5 times as much time (when no learning is performed).

The next question concerned how the number of created hypotheses influences the performance. The number of hypotheses correspond to the number of overlapping problems. Allowing up to 6 hypotheses (fig. 6, curve A) the systems performance in processing a single message remained stable (30 seconds as max. tolerable time). Note that focusing on multiple faults leads a reduction in processing a single message but helps in early detection of serious faults since a breath search is performed. The result was obtained by use of an average message stream (given by the expert) containing the messages produced during a 48 hour period for a simple network containing 600 components. Artificial worst case scenarios showed that for complex hypotheses containing 15 - 30 messages only 3 hypotheses are tolerable(fig.6, curve B).

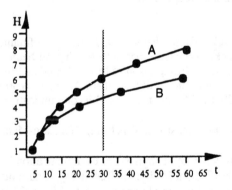

Fig. 6 - Hypotheses versus performance

The result of these empirical tests is that the described algorithm is in principle able to handle the problem of diagnosing multiple faults. However, it is necessary to limit the amount of parallel investigated hypotheses in order to guarantee a certain performance. This limiting of hypotheses can be performed either by the already described strategies or *by interaction of a user.* If the user is allowed to manipulate the hypothesis-list by deleting or modifying hypotheses it is possible to use experiences/knowledge in order to optimise retrieval and adaptation. In the current implementation a user has the possibility to delete or to create hypotheses. This enables to delete unpromising hypotheses as well as forcing the system to investigate new hypotheses (manipulation of hypotheses was not possible). The usefulness of allowing the manipulation of existing hypotheses is still an unanswered question and a field of further research. Until now no adequate approach for visualising the instantiations and variants have been found.

7. Conclusion

This paper reports on case-based diagnosis of multiple independent faults. The specific problems concerning the processing of mixed data from several, not necessarily dependent, problems are discussed. An incremental and opportunistic retrieval and adaptation approach is introduced which is able to overcome the "one-problem" limitation of classical retrieval approaches by use of a hypothesis and test strategy. Instead of using the observed problem data for a "one shot" retrieval an incremental approach is used by formulating and testing hypotheses. An interesting side-effect of the hypothesis approach is that interactive retrieval and adaptation is possible. The main contribution of this paper is the description of the algorithm for incremental and opportunistic retrieval. The algorithm which is implemented in C++ and is currently used in a message stream analysing tool is evaluated according to its specific strength and weaknesses.

Future work in the project will focus on the further enabling more interaction between the user of the case-based diagnosis tool. The current developed approach of enabling a user to manipulate the list of hypotheses and variants seems a good approach but further empirical tests are still needed.

Acknowledgements:
This works has been carried out in a Research project between the SIEMENS AG and the Universität der Bundeswehr München.

References
[Kol93] J. Kolodner: Case-Based Reasoning, Morgan Kaufmann, 1993
[Rie89] C. K. Riesbeck: Inside Case-based Reasoning, Erlbaum, 1989
[Cun94] P. Cunningham: A Comparison of Model-Based and Incremental Case-Based Approaches to Electronic Fault Diagnosis, AAAI'94 Workshop on CBR, 1994
[Det94] R. Deters: CBR for Maintenance of Telecommunication Networks, EWCBR-94, 1994
[Det95] R. Deters: Multidimensional Structuring of a Case-Memory, CBR-Workshop at XPS-95, 1995
[Rie93] M. Riese: Model-Based Diagnosis of Communication Protocols, Doctoral Thesis No. 1173, Swiss Federal Institute of Technology Lausanne, 1993
[Kle93] J. de Kleer: Characterising Diagnoses, AAAI-90, MIT-Press 1990
[Ngu89] T. A. Nguyen: Diagnosing Multiple Faults in Digital Systems, The Fifth Conference on Artificial Intelligence Applications
[Rei87] R. Reiter: A theory of diagnosis from first principles", Artificial Intelligence 32, 1987
[Zit93] R. Zito-Wolf: A Framework and a Analysis of Current Proposals for the Case-Based Organisation and Representation of Procedural Knowledge, Eleventh National Conference on Artificial Intelligence

On the Automatic Generation of Case Libraries by Chunking Chess Games

Stephen Flinter and Mark T. Keane

Trinity College Dublin

Abstract. As a research topic computer game playing has contributed problems to AI that manifest exponential growth in the problem space. For the most part, in games such as chess and checkers these problems have been surmounted with enormous computing power on brute-force search methods using massive databases. It remains to be seen whether such techniques will extend to other games such as go and shogi. One suggestion is that these games and even chess might benefit from a knowledge-based treatment but such approaches have met with limited success. The problem, as ever from such approaches, is the characterisation of the knowledge to be used by the system. This paper deals with the TAL system, which employs case-based reasoning techniques for chess playing. In the paper, rather than focus on playing, we concentrate on the *automatic* generation of suitable case knowledge using a chunking technique on a corpus of grandmaster games.

1 Introduction

Many games like chess and checkers have been mastered by computational techniques that use extensive search with massive computing power. The failure of such techniques to deal with other games, like go and shogi, is perhaps an indication that this approach does not constitute a general solution to such problems. One alternative is to use knowledge-based techniques, like case-based reasoning, to reduce the search overhead and speed-up solution generation. After all, human chess players play quite well, with relatively little search, through the use of extensive past experience. Several knowledge-based solutions have been attempted but with limited success (e.g. [2] [10]). As always, the fundamental problem with knowledge-based approaches is the isolation of the relevant knowledge in a suitable form for use.

Case-based reasoning (CBR) seems to be a plausible technique to apply to such games. However, again, with it we face the problem of defining a suitable case library to support the technique. In this paper, we consider a chess playing system, called TAL, that uses CBR. To date, the central problem we have focused on in TAL is the development of a case library. There are two problems to be faced in doing this. First, one has to develop a good case representation. It is not obvious what form chess cases should take: for example, whether they should contain parts of a game or a full game, whether they should represent all the details of a game at the level of actual moves from play or whether some abstracted representation should be developed. In TAL, cases are represented as abstractions of actual board situations.

Second, one needs to automate the method of building cases. For an adequate level of expertise, a considerable case library is likely to be needed. Given this factor, and the availability of extensive databases of chess games, it makes sense to have a method that will generate a case library *automatically* from records of previous games. In TAL, we use a *chunking* method to do just this. The reader should note that the notion of chunking to which we refer is inspired by de Groot's ([6]) and Chase and Simon's ([3]) ideas and is quite different to the chunking method used by Laird, Newell and Rosenbloom in SOAR ([9]).

1.1 Architecture

The TAL system consists of two major components: the Library sub-system and the Game-Playing sub-system. The Library component is responsible for converting the set of example games into populated knowledge bases, as described in Section 4. The Game Playing component is responsible for applying this knowledge to novel game positions to produce candidate moves and to perform some look-ahead.

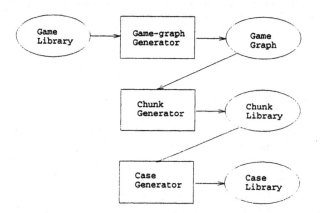

Fig. 1. TAL Library Sub-system

The Library component is shown in Figure 1. It has three main sub-components to generate the three knowledge-bases (game graph, chunk library and case library) used by TAL: the game-graph generator, the chunk generator, and the case generator. The *Game-graph Generator* takes a set of chess games and creates a game-graph based on those games. The *Chunk Generator* produces set of *candidate chunks* from the game-graph. The *Case Generator* takes the set of base chunks and recombines them into set of cases.

The Game-playing component is shown in Figure 2. It uses the knowledge-bases created by the Libraries Component to analyse a given current chess position, and to select a move to play from that position. Several interesting issues

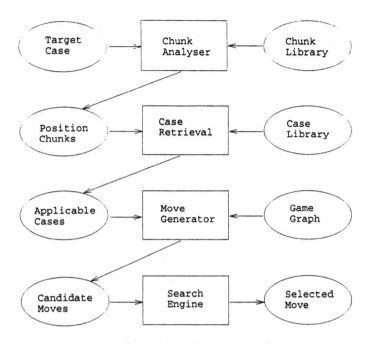

Fig. 2. TAL Game-Playing Component

arise in the design of this component, for instance, the generalisation and re-specialisation of candidate moves. However, this paper will not be concerned with the game-playing aspect of TAL, rather it focuses on the Library component and the generation of case knowledge.

1.2 Outline of Paper

In the following sections, the workings of TAL's Library component are sketched in detail. However, before doing this we consider some of the background to the ideas used in this component, in the form of psychological evidence on the use of chunks by chess players. While our idea of chunking is quite different to that used in the psychological work, and we do not make any claims for the psychological plausibility of TAL, we have been inspired by this research.

2 Psychological Evidence

According to psychological evidence, human chess players of all strengths perform what Newell and Simon called *chunking* ([6] [11] [7]). A *chunk* here is some portion of a board position represented by a meaningful grouping of pieces. Each complex board position can be broken down into a small number of chunks, each of which will contain a number of pieces. Consider the chess position shown in Figure 3. This figure is taken from [7], which itself is taken from [6]. The sets of ringed pieces represent the chunks which de Groot suggests his chess master subject used to represent the position.

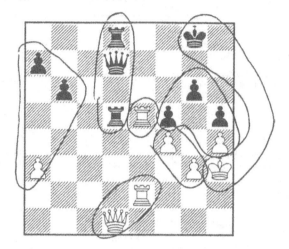

Fig. 3. Reference chunk position

As a chess player's expertise increases chunks change in two ways. First, the *size* of the chunks increase — that is, the chunks a master uses to represent a position will have more pieces than those of an intermediate level player, which in turn will have more than a rank beginner. Secondly, the *number* of chunks possessed by the player also increases with playing strength. So, not only will a master represent chess positions using richer and more complex chunks, but will also use more of them. It has been estimated that an intermediate club player will have about 1,000 chunks, while a master will have of the order of 100,000 ([6]).

TAL does not try to model this human chess playing skill — this has already been attempted a number of times, with varying success ([13] [3]) — but it does *borrow* ideas from this research. Specifically, the idea of breaking a complex situation, such as a chess position, into a number of smaller, more manageable pieces is a very useful technique for case-based reasoning; especially, if the cases can be generated automatically, using heuristic methods applied to a large data set. This process of automatically generating the required knowledge-bases is analogous to the learning which takes place as a human player gains experience.

3 Theory of Chunking Applied to TAL

As it appears in TAL, the *chunking hypothesis* could be stated as the belief that complex situations or episodes, such as chess positions, can be better understood in terms of a number of simpler component structures. Specifically, given a set of representative chunks (representative of the entire set of chess games, that is), one can break a previously unseen chess position into a set of such chunks. The composition, arrangement and relationships of the set of component chunks can then be used to retrieve similar previously seen positions (reminding). The hypothesis goes on further to postulate that a move made in a similar position to the one under examination is worthy of consideration as a move for the current position, once it has undergone the appropriate transformation or adaptation, which will express it in terms of the current position. Such a move is called a *candidate move*.

It is not necessary that every candidate move be relevant to the current position — in fact, it is important that *not* every move be relevant: otherwise, we return to the problem of exponential growth in our search which we are trying to avoid with this method. Once this set of candidate moves has been generated, it is then possible to search the game-tree, like any ordinary chess program, but using the candidate moves to guide the search. In this manner, the hope is to reduce the average number of moves to be searched at a given chess position from 35 down to about three or four. However, there are certain problems which must be resolved in implementing this chunking hypothesis. We should have:

- a, preferably, automatic method for refining the initial set of example games to a set of base chunks (achieved by our *chunking heuristic*).
- a means of filtering out unwanted and useless chunks from the set of candidate chunks, leaving only useful and meaningful base chunks.
- a way of creating a set of base cases from the set of base chunks, where these cases represent situations in which one or more chunks are present. Here a base case, will be a position expressed in terms of chunks from the chunk library rather than in terms of atomic pieces.
- a method for characterising novel, unseen positions into a collection of chunks from our chunk library.
- a retrieval method to find a set of relevant similar positions from the game graph to this characterisation of a target position
- a set of methods for generalising and re-specialising moves made from similar positions, to put them in terms of the new position. In the instances, where this is impossible, the candidate move is simply discarded. Once we have a set of candidate moves, we can then begin to search from them, and repeat the above process for as long as necessary.

4   The Inner Workings of TAL's Library Component

In the next three sections we will explain in more detail the nature and composition of each of TAL's knowledge bases.

4.1   Game-graph Generator and Game Graphs

The *Game-graph Generator* takes a set of chess games, in Portable Game Notation (PGN — a standard notation for chess games), and creates a game-graph based on those games. The game graph is a cyclic-directed graph which stores raw chess games. Each node in the graph represents a single, unique chess position and is stored in Forsythe-Edwards Notation (FEN — another standard notation, this time for chess *positions*). Each arc from one node to another represents a legal move made from one chess position to another. The graph is directed because the effects of a move are not (always) reversible, and cyclic because positions can repeat. The graph is tree-like in that it has a single root which is the initial chess position. Finally, both the nodes and the arcs have *counter tags*, which specify the number of times a given node or arc appears across the set of games submitted to the graph.

A complete chess game is represented as a path or *thread* through the graph, linking the positions occurring in the game by the moves made from position to position. Each unique position can be represented by one and only one node. If two or more games share the same position (which is inevitable), they must share the same node. The graph can have only one root — the initial chess position — and will have one or more leaves; with each leaf representing the termination of a game, corresponding to a win, draw or loss for white (or black).

4.2 Generating Chunks for the Chunk Library

The chunk library is a repository of base chunks. Each chunk is composed of a *salient piece* and one or more other pieces. The salient piece of a chunk is the most important piece: the one from which other pieces hang. For example, recall the position shown in Figure 3. If we consider a white pawn chunk, with the three pawns on f4, h4, and g3 (note that, this does not correspond exactly to the master's chunks shown in the diagram, and is used simply for the sake of argument). Together, these pawns make up a cohesive chess unit. The salient piece in this chunk is the pawn on g3, as it is the piece which relates all three — without this pawn the other two would just be single, separate, unrelated units.

The purpose of the Chunk Generator is to traverse the game-graph produced by the Game-graph Generator and to produce a set of *candidate chunks*. A candidate chunk is defined to be a chunk created according to some chunking heuristic, which will be either discarded or added to the chunk library according to some *chunk selection criterion*. So, there are two issues which the Chunk Generator must tackle: firstly, how should the chunks themselves be composed; and secondly, once they are composed, how can the most relevant and useful ones be selected, for inclusion in the chunk library.

In TAL candidate chunks are generated according to the principle of *direct interaction*. Two pieces are said to directly interact in situations where one defends the other (in the case where both pieces are of the same colour), or where one attacks the other (in the case where the pieces are a different colour). Specifically, each candidate chunk consists of a salient piece, and the enumeration of all direct interactions with that piece. The algorithm for the generation of the set of candidate chunks follows.

For each piece in the position:
let the piece be the salient piece;

if the piece is black, normalise the position to white;
determine all the direct interaction between the salient piece and the remainder
of the pieces in the position;
enumerate each possible permutation of salient piece and directly interacting
piece(s), and store as a candidate chunk.

The second issue facing the Chunk Generator is that of selecting a set of base chunks based on the set of candidate chunks. This task must yield a small set of chunks (relative to the set of candidate chunks) which are representative of the total set of chunks required to express each position. Obviously, there will be a large amount of duplication across the set of candidate chunks, and it is this factor which is used as the chunk selection criterion. Specifically, the frequency of each chunk is determined (by frequency here we mean the number of times it occurs across the entire game set), and a selection made on the basis of this frequency. Refer to Section 5 for more details on the results to date.

4.3 Case Library

Just as the chunk library is a repository of chunks, so the case library is a repository of cases. In the TAL system, a case is a representation of a board position in terms of a number of base chunks found in the chunk library. Specifically, a case consists of the set of base chunks which appear in the examined position. Thus, when a novel position is encountered, it is decomposed into its constituent chunks. Its similarity to other positions can then be measured by a distance metric between the current position and the other positions encoded in the case library.

5 Results

At the moment, the implementation of TAL's Library Component is complete, and work on the Game-Playing component is under-way. We have conducted experiments using a set of 350 games from the late grandmaster and ex-world-champion, Mikhail Tal. This game set yields a total of 43,592 unique candidate chunks. An analysis of this data reveals an L-shaped distribution. Those chunks which have a low frequency tend to have a very large count. For example, there are 16,352 different chunks with a frequency of 1; that is, from the set of 43,592 chunks from, approximately 38% of those appear only once. Conversely, those chunks which have a very high frequency have very low counts — typically only one or two.

Since we are looking for a representative set of chunks from the entire set of possible chunks, those points lying on the extremities of the distribution are uninteresting. Those with a low frequency and high count are not useful because they occur too infrequently to be of assistance in retrieving relevant positions. That is, the cost of storing them exceeds the benefit gained from greater coverage. Equally, those chunks with a high frequency and low count are not useful because they are not discriminating enough. Storing them would direct the system to retrieve too many cases to handle. For the current system, we use a chunk library approximately 10% the size of the complete set of possible chunks. From the candidate chunk set, we have pruned those chunks with a frequency 10 or less, and a frequency 500 or more. This selection criterion leaves a chunk library with a population of 4,533 base chunks. A graph of the distribution of the remaining chunks can be seen in Figure 4.

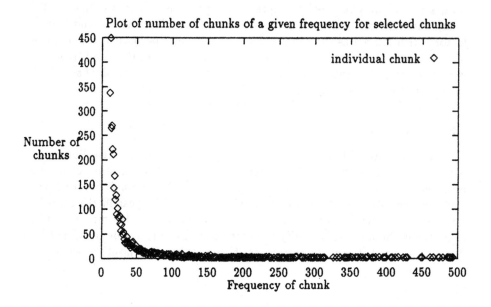

Fig. 4. Plot of selected chunks

When we chunk the reference position found in Figure 3 using TAL we get the *automatically generated* chunks shown in Figure 5. As can be seen, there is some similarity between the two sets of chunks, without them being identical. This is not a critical factor: we are not trying to reproduce the same chunks of a human master player, but simply using these chunks as aids to retrieval.

6 Future Work

The work described in this paper mainly revolves around the generation of the knowledge bases. In the next set of experiments we will focus on case retrieval, and in particular, on generalisation and re-specialisation of retrieved candidate moves. The primary issue here is to correctly map the move made from the retrieved case into an appropriate move for the target case, and to recognise the situations where no such meaningful maps exists.

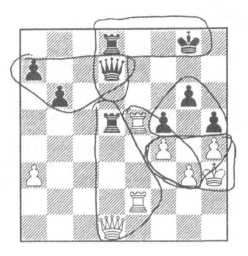

Fig. 5. Base chunks chosen by TAL

In this paper we have described TAL's current chunking heuristic and chunk selection criterion. These are the two most important factors in determining the quality of the system's chunk library, and hence ultimately its case library. In future experiments, we intend to investigate different chunking heuristics and selection criteria.

In the long term, while much of TAL is closely tied to the game of chess, we believe that the approach of automatically chunking complex situations and building cases out of such chunks is generally applicable and useful. One of the biggest problems with current CBR technology is the dependence on hand-crafted case libraries. While TAL does not completely solve this problem — we still had to encode the chunk representation and chunking and selection criteria — it does go a long way towards alleviating the time-consuming and pain-staking task of building the individual base cases.

7   Related Work

There is a large project underway in the Institute of Learning Sciences at North-western University named CASTLE. This project takes a Model-Based Reasoning (MBR) approach to computer chess ([4] [5] [1]). The ILS approach is a very knowledge intensive one, and involves planning, learning and high-level reasoning. Kerner has recently published work on a CBR approach to chess ([8]). However, his work focuses on developing a case-base *evaluation function* for a standard searching chess system, and so differs significantly from TAL. Pell's work on METAGAME ([12]) deals primarily with forcing programs to learn, and in particular, to create their own evaluation function.

8 Summary and Conclusions

In this paper, we have described the TAL CBR system, and in particular, its Library Component. We have demonstrated a method for automatically generating a case library from expert data. The hypothesis advanced by this work that positions composed of similar base chunks will tend to have a similar chess 'meaning', and that reasoning performed on one can usefully be applied to the other has so far been supported. Further work is necessary to refine the generation of base chunks and cases, but experiments indicate that this approach is a useful and fruitful one. Further, we propose that the approach to such problems, that of "chunking" complex situations, is one which could be generally applicable to case-based reasoning.

References

1. Lawrence Birnbaum, Gregg Collins, Michael Freed, and Bruce Krulwich. Model-based diagnosis of planning failures. In *Proceedings of the Eighth National Conference on Artificial Intelligence*, pages 318–323. American Association of Artificial Intelligence, AAAI Press/MIT Press, 1990.
2. M. M. Botvinnik. Three positions. *International Computer Chess Association Journal*, 16(2):71–75, June 1993.
3. William G. Chase and Herbert A. Simon. Perception in chess. *Cognitive Psychology*, 4:55–81, 1973.
4. Gregg Collins, Lawrence Birnbaum, Bruce Krulwich, and Michael Freed. A model-based approach to learning from planning failures. In *Notes of the 1991 AAAI Workshop on Model-Based Reasoning*. AAAI, 1991.
5. Gregg Collins, Lawrence Birnbaum, Bruce Krulwich, and Michael Freed. Model-based integration of planning and learning. *SIGART Bulletin*, 2(4):56–60, 1991.
6. A. D. de Groot. *Thought and Choice in Chess*. The Hague: Mouton, 1965.
7. Dennis H. Holding. *The Psychology of Chess Skill*. Lawrence Earlbaum Associates, 1985.
8. Yaakov Kerner. Case-based evaluation in computer chess. In *Proceedings of the European Workshop of Case-Based Reasoning*. Springer-Verlag, 1994.
9. John Laird, Allen Newell, and Paul Rosenbloom. *The SOAR Papers*. MIT Press, 1993.
10. Robert Levinson and John Amenta. Morph, an experience-based adaptive chess system. *International Computer Chess Association Journal*, 16(1):51–53, March 1993.
11. Alan Newell and Herbert Simon. *Human Problem Solving*. Prentice Hall, 1972.
12. Barney Pell. METAGAME: A new challenge for games and learning. In Jaap van den Herik and Victor Allis, editors, *Heuristic Programming in Artificial Intelligence 3*, Ellis Horwood Series in Artificial Intelligence, pages 237–251. Ellis Horwood Limited, 1992.
13. Herbert A. Simon and Michael Barenfeld. Information-processing analysis of perceptual processes in problem solving. *Psychological Review*, 76(5):473–483, 1969.

Learning to Refine Indexing by Introspective Reasoning[*]

Susan Fox and David B. Leake

Computer Science Department
Indiana University
Bloomington, IN 47405, USA

Abstract. A significant problem for case-based reasoning (CBR) systems is determining the features to use in judging case similarity for retrieval. We describe research that addresses the feature selection problem by using introspective reasoning to learn new features for indexing. Our method augments the CBR system with an introspective reasoning component which monitors system performance to detect poor retrievals, identifies features which would lead retrieval of more adaptable cases, and refines the indexing criteria to include the needed features to avoid future failures. We explore the benefit of introspective reasoning by performing empirical tests on the implemented system. These tests examine the effect of introspective index refinement, and the effects of problem order on case and index learning, and show that introspective learning of new index features improves performance across the different problem orders.

1   Introduction

Selecting the best set of features to use in indexing a case-based reasoning (CBR) system's memory may be difficult; determining which features are most appropriate may require experience [15]. An appealing alternative is to permit the system itself to learn what features are relevant in response to its experiences. Our research uses introspective reasoning to permit a CBR system to detect indexing problems and to alter its indexing criteria to correct the problems by learning to consider new features. Our method applies introspective reasoning to learn features implicit in the original problem description but not used explicitly in the CBR system's initial indexing scheme, in order to direct retrieval towards cases that can easily be adapted.

Our testbed computer system, ROBBIE[2], is a case-based route planner. Its CBR component learns by adding successful plans to its memory, as in other case-based route planners such as ROUTER [13]. However, our research focus is not the route planning task itself. Instead, the focus is on how introspective reasoning can be used by the CBR system to refine its indexing criteria. ROBBIE combines a case-based planner with an introspective component. The introspective component contains a declarative model of the *ideal* reasoning behavior of the system. The model provides expectations about the

---

[*] This work was supported in part by the National Science Foundation under Grant No. IRI-9409348.

[2] Re-Organization of Behavior By Introspective Evaluation

ideal case-based planning performance; these expectations are compared to the actual reasoning performance to discover discrepancies. A discrepancy indicates a reasoning failure; the failure is corrected by explaining why it occurred and revising the reasoning process to avoid future failures. Using introspective learning to improve the case-based reasoning process itself was first suggested by Birnbaum et al. [6].

Introspective improvement of reasoning processes is a relatively new approach, and there have been few evaluations of its effect on the performance of a system using it. We designed empirical tests to examine the effect of introspective learning on ROBBIE's performance, and to examine the effect of problem order on both case learning and index learning. Our results show that introspective reasoning for learning indexing criteria improves performance *and* efficiency across different problem orders.

We will first present the ROBBIE system and discuss its mechanisms for case-based and introspective learning, providing an example of its learning to illustrate the process. We will then describe our experiments and what we can conclude from them.

2   The ROBBIE System

The ROBBIE system demonstrates the application of an introspective self-model to the task of refining the indices used to retrieve cases from memory. The system has two main parts: a planner which develops plans through case-based reasoning [2, 14, 15] and applies them through execution in a simulated world, and an introspective model-based reasoner which detects, explains, and repairs reasoning failures caused by poor indexing criteria.

The performance task of ROBBIE is to navigate around a simulated set of city streets as a pedestrian. ROBBIE is situated in a "map" of streets and learns new routes to navigate around that map. ROBBIE is given a goal location and must create a plan for getting from its current location to the goal. Plan creation involves retrieving and adapting an old case. Because adaptation is not always guaranteed to be correct, ROBBIE executes the newly created plan using reactive planning [8] to fill in missing details and recover from failures. Execution evaluates the quality of the CBR-created plan, and permits ROBBIE to arrive at a solution despite flaws in the plan. This provides a form of execution-time case adaptation: the reactive planner can alter the plan given it by removing useless steps and adding new steps as necessary. In addition, the reactive planner handles facets of the simulated world that cannot be predicted by the CBR system, such as traffic lights and blocked streets. The plans resulting from execution are stored in memory for future use. The plans in memory are indexed by their starting and ending locations, plus features discovered through introspective learning. Plan retrieval in ROBBIE is a two-stage process: first ROBBIE gathers a pool of generally similar candidate cases, then it selects the best candidate from that pool.

ROBBIE's high-level task is to improve its reasoning process (in particular, its feature selection process) when it detects failures in its reasoning. As the planner reasons about *its* task, the introspective component monitors its reasoning process by comparing it to a declarative model describing the planner's ideal reasoning processes [6, 9, 12]. Reasoning failures occur when the model's expectations about the reasoning process are not fulfilled by the actual reasoning. Expectations are encoded as "assertions;" facts that would be ideally true of particular points in the case-based reasoning process. For example, one assertion states that *the index for retrieval will be most similar to the index of the best case in memory for adapting to the current problem.* This assertion reflects the desire to retrieve easily adaptable cases.

Some assertions describe the ideal behavior of specific implementation details for ROBBIE. Others describe ideal aspects at an abstract level, in terms of control and information flow through the CBR process. The assertion in the previous paragraph is an example of an abstract assertion. A specific one would describe, for instance, how similarity judgements are made and the ideal result. The assertions are clustered together by the part of the reasoning process to which they refer, and by how abstract or specific they are. Each assertion also contains links to other causally related assertions inside *or outside* its cluster. Fox and Leake [11] contains a detailed description of the model and its representation.

Failure detection for the introspective reasoner involves noticing discrepancies between assertions and actual behavior. At each point in the reasoning process, the introspective reasoner compares the actual reasoning to the ideal. When they fail to match, a reasoning failure has occurred (See [9] for a more extensive discussion of ROBBIE's failure detection). Detecting failures due to faulty indexing criteria requires monitoring the entire reasoning process: the failure may not be discovered until after the inappropriately retrieved case has been adapted and executed. The problem is compounded by the desire to recognize not only poor retrievals which lead to a failed solution, but poor retrievals that, despite leading to a successful solution, waste effort in adaptation or execution.

ROBBIE's introspective reasoner uses hindsight to detect when a successful solution was based on the wrong case (indicating wasted effort in adaptation and execution). After a successful plan has been generated, it is used as a standard for determining which case *should* have been retrieved. The final solution is compared to the plans in memory to determine whether the plan that was retrieved was really the most similar plan in memory. The goal to retrieve the most similar plan is captured in the model by the expectation that the final solution should be most similar to the *solution* of the retrieved case.

If the wrong plan has been retrieved, causing the adapted plan to contain wasted steps, execution of a plan will eliminate wasted steps, leading to a streamlined final solution. In storing a new solution, ROBBIE looks for the case in memory with the closest solution, according to the similarity of their plan steps (which may be quite different than when retrieved). If the final solution is now similar to another case, then a retrieval failure is indicated.

Once a reasoning failure is detected the model is used to create an explanation of the failure in terms of other failed assertions, and to suggest a repair. An explanation is formed by searching the model for other causally-related assertion failures. Other assertion failures might have been previously undetected, but may be suspected in the context of the detected failure. The introspective reasoner is guided in its search for an explanation by the links between assertions that are causally related.

Attributing a detected failure to faulty indexing criteria depends on the discovery of some relevant feature of the new solution and its closest matching case in memory whose explicit inclusion in the indexing criteria would have permitted a correct retrieval (i.e., retrieval of the case closer to ROBBIE's final solution). An assertion about the index formation process, when re-examined in light of a failure, is evaluated by looking for missing features which fit the above requirement. In searching for shared features, ROBBIE currently uses a set of abstract feature types, such as "starts-at X" and "moves-in-direction Y," which it attempts to instantiate for the current cases. ROBBIE looks for instantiations of feature types that apply to both the solution and the best-match case that was not retrieved, and that are not currently used in indexing. The feature types are ranked by a pre-defined importance hierarchy; if more than one instantiated type applies to the two cases, the more important one is selected to add to the indexing criteria.

Figure 1 illustrates an implemented example of ROBBIE's introspective index refinement. In this situation, ROBBIE has in memory plan A, which describes how to get from L1 to L2, and plan B, which describes how to get from L2 to L3. The current task is to get from L4 to L2. ROBBIE's initial indexing uses the geographic closeness of starting and ending locations; by this measure, plan A appears to be the closest because it shares the same ending location (ROBBIE's retrieval criteria do not include reversals of known routes, so plan B does not look similar at all). Plan A is selected and adapted to create plan C (dashed line in Fig. 1). During this process, the introspective reasoner compares the system's reasoning process to its ideal model, but cannot detect a problem.

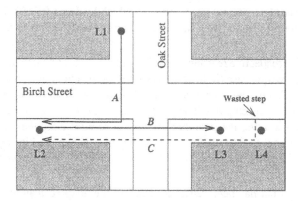

Fig. 1. example of ROBBIE's introspective learning

However, adaptation of plan C during execution eliminates the wasted step; moving south across the sidewalk makes no progress towards the goal. The final solution is a plan which moves straight west. When the resulting plan is stored in memory, the introspective reasoner detects a reasoning failure: the final solution is more similar to plan B than to plan A, the retrieved plan.

In explaining this failure, the introspective reasoner must search for other causally-related assertion failures. Some such assertions relate to the indexing criteria used. One assertion related to the original failure is that *the index for retrieval will include all the features needed to retrieve the closest case*. This assertion is assumed true unless another failure has been detected: if nothing appears wrong, we may assume that the current indices are sufficient. In the context of an existing failure, this assertion is examined by considering the features of the final solution and best matching case to determine if a feature exists which would enable avoiding the faulty retrieval. In this case a feature is found: that B and C both involve moving straight along an east/west street. This assertion suggests a repair to the indexing criteria: adding the feature "moves straight east/west" to the features used in indexing cases, and re-indexing the cases in memory to include the new feature.

3 Empirical Evaluation

There has been growing interest in evaluation of case-based reasoning systems to identify to what extent they succeed and what components of their processing are responsible for their success [1]. However, little work has been done to quantify the benefits of introspective reasoning for improving reasoning methods, and the relationship between case presentation order and learning is largely unaddressed.

We performed experiments to evaluate the effect of introspective learning of new index features on the overall performance of ROBBIE. We chose a range of situations in which to test ROBBIE's performance which would also demonstrate the effect of the problem order on the system's learning. Such tests should show that introspective re-indexing improves performance across the range of situations, that problem order had a distinct and dramatic effect on overall performance, and that introspective re-indexing causes improved performance even as quality of problem order declines.

It is acknowledged that problem order can strongly affect learning in general, and learning of CBR systems in particular (e.g. [4, 18]). A sequence of goals which gradually increases in complexity and distance from the original cases in memory, and which covers the range of possible situations, should maximize the effectiveness of the case-based reasoner's learning.

Guided by the principles outlined in the previous paragraph, we created by hand a "well-ordered" sequence which included 40 randomly generated goal locations on a set of streets, each appearing exactly once. In these tests, ROBBIE began at the first location, then moved from one to the next in sequence. From this ordered sequence of locations we derived five groups containing five sequences in each. For four of the groups, we permuted the original sequence by randomly swapping a percentage of its locations with other locations in the sequence. The groups had 25%, 50%, 75%, and 100% of their elements swapped. The final group contained random arrangements of the 40 goal locations. We did not attempt to create a deliberately bad sequence, although that would be an interesting extension of this experiment.

To examine the effect of introspective re-indexing, we compared the performance of ROBBIE on runs using just case learning with runs using case and introspective learning. We measured the number of successfully completed plans at the end of a test run and compared the results across runs and sequences. We also measured the percentage of cases in memory considered for each retrieval. Learning new index features increases the focus of retrieval; the decrease in percentage of cases considered over time forms a measure of retrieval efficiency. Because ROBBIE chooses randomly between two alternatives that are considered equally good, we ran each sequence twenty times under the same initial conditions to factor out the effect of individual random decisions.[3]

The initial case memory for these tests was very small to examine the effects of learning under difficult, knowledge-poor conditions. The initial cases in memory were clustered in one section of the set of streets, to examine how a learner with limited initial information could expand its knowledge to encompass its domain. The model used during testing contained a restricted set of assertions to streamline the diagnosis process.

We predict the rate of success should be highest for the initial "well-ordered" sequence, and the rate (with and without introspective re-indexing) should decline as sequences become more random. For each sequence, runs with introspective re-indexing should be more successful than those without. We do not expect introspective re-indexing to overcome the negative effect of poor problem order Learning new indexing features depends on the right features being available in cases in memory. The most difficult scenario for introspective re-indexing occurs when the initial memory size is small and the problem order produces poor performance: the smaller the case memory, the fewer the opportunities to learn useful new features for indexing.

We expect introspective re-indexing to improve retrieval efficiency by causing fewer cases to be considered in retrieval, as newly learned features allow finer-grained distinctions between cases. However, there is a possible danger in this restriction: when the system fails repeatedly and memory remains small over time, re-indexing could cause over-restriction of retrieval, leading to failures when applicable cases are ignored. Consequently, another question we studied was whether index learning decreases the planner's success rate by over-restricting the retrieval process.

4   Results

Success rate was measured by counting the number of successful plans created for each run of a sequence. Figure 2 illustrates the overall success rate of each group of sequences used. The success rate was averaged across each of the 20 runs of a sequence, then the results for each sequence in a group were averaged again. The trend as sequences became less ordered is as expected: performance drops as problems become less easy to match against known cases. The combination of case learning and introspective re-indexing of memory led to better performance than case learning alone for every group.

Figure 3 shows the success rate for each sequence individually. The tendency for performance to degrade with less ordered sequences can still be seen, and for all but one sequence the addition of introspective learning proved beneficial (we discuss the anomalous case below). The wide range of behaviors within each group warrants further explanation in the future: we describe a possible correlation with retrieval efficiency in the next section.

We measured the change in retrieval efficiency by considering the percentage of stored plans ROBBIE considered similar for each retrieval during a test run. We graphed the course of the run on the x-axis by counting each retrieval in sequence as a point in time. We considered "successive averages" of the percentage considered on the y-axis: each

---

[3] ROBBIE was presented with a total of 41,600 goals: 26 sequences, each 40 goals long, and 20 runs with introspection, 20 without.

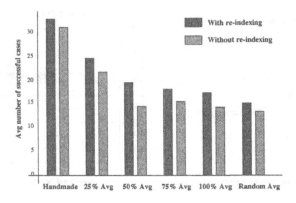

Fig. 2. Average success rate declines as order becomes more random; introspective reasoning slows the decline

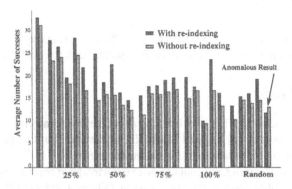

Fig. 3. Average success rate for each sequence; one anomaly demonstrates over-constraint of retrieval

value was the average of the percentages from the beginning of the sequence to that point. By putting runs of a sequence together on one set of axes, we see trends in the retrieval performance. For a more detailed discussion of these results see [10].

Figure 4 shows typical results for a sequence: the averages considered with re-indexing decrease over time to a much lower level than those without: 30-45% instead of 60-70%. A similar pattern appeared for every sequence except the anomalous one. In some cases the decrease with re-indexing was much more dramatic. The size and consistency of the drop were greater for sequences with high success rates, and for sequences with large differences between success rates with and without re-indexing.

The anomalous sequence led to poor performance under any measure. There was no apparent difference between the retrieval efficiency with re-indexing or without it, suggesting that the new features learned introspectively did not apply to later situations and so could not provide any benefit. The new features did not group together useful cases, but could occasionally cause an additional failure by restricting retrieval so that a useful case might not be considered at all. This limiting effect on re-indexing would be magnified by the small size of the case base, which in this case remained small throughout

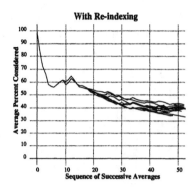
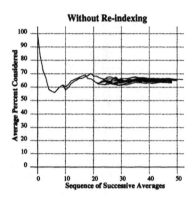

Fig. 4. Successive average of retrieval: with re-indexing, efficiency improves by considering fewer cases on average (50% permuted sequence)

the run as few goals were successfully achieved. Characterizing sequences like this one further and determining their frequency is an important task for the future.

5 Related Work

Other work has combined CBR with learning about the reasoning process itself. A proposal by Birnbaum et al. [6] inspired ROBBIE's framework, but that proposal was not implemented and did not use a hierarchical model. Meta-AQUA [7] performs failure-driven introspective learning, but contains no explicit model of correct behavior. Instead, it uses a set of template descriptions for reasoning failures which provide diagnosis and repair information. Autognostic [20] applies an existing framework for device modeling (SBF) to introspective modeling of the route planner ROUTER; their approach focuses on explanation of failures without strongly addressing failure detection. IULIAN [17] also performs introspective learning, but instead of using an explicit introspective model, it stores plans for repairing its reasoning which are recalled when failures occur. Arcos and Plaza [3] create a unified architecture for describing case-based and meta-level problem solving tasks by describing each process by decomposition into tasks and sub-tasks. IDEAL [5] investigates index learning, but uses a model of its domain, not the reasoning task, as well as cases from its domain, in order to learn new indices.

The focus of our research, by comparison, is the development of a framework for modeling reasoning processes which can address both detection and repair of reasoning failures. We believe the framework, using a model of ideal reasoning behavior to detect and explain failures, has wide applicability, but so far it has been applied only to the task of learning indexing criteria for retrieving plans in ROBBIE.

6 Conclusions

Using a model of reasoning behavior to detect and repair reasoning flaws permits a system to learn from experience how to reason best in its environment. We have applied this idea to the learning of indexing criteria for case retrieval. We propose a framework which combines case-based learning with an introspective reasoning component. The introspective reasoner uses a model of expected ideal reasoning performance to detect discrepancies in actual performance, and to diagnose and repair such expectation failures. ROBBIE implements this framework for a case-based planner that learns new plans as it creates them and introspectively learns which features are required for retrieving easily adaptable cases from memory. Because the quality of a retrieval scheme depends on retrieving cases that are easy to adapt, it is desirable to achieve more direct connections between similarity criteria and case adaptation ability in CBR systems (e.g., [16, 19]); our research is one way to make indexing criteria better reflect adaptability. In addition, introspective reasoning for self-improvement is a general approach that could be extended to other portions of the CBR process: altering adaptation, evaluation, and case storage (See [9] for a more general discussion).

Little empirical evaluation has been done to measure the effects of introspective reasoning on the behavior of systems which use it. We designed a set of empirical tests of ROBBIE to examine the effect of introspective learning of new index features by comparing its performance with and without index refinement. In addition, we examined the effect of problem order on the performance of case and index learning. It is well known that the order in which problems are presented to a learning system can have a large effect on the quality of the learning that the system performs. Case-based learning systems appear particularly susceptible to this effect.

We found that, even under knowledge-poor initial conditions, introspective learning of new index features improved the success rate of the system over case learning alone, while at the same time improving the efficiency of the retrieval process by focusing retrieval on the best cases. Problem order had a large effect on the learning of the system, but regardless of problem order the inclusion of introspective re-indexing outperform case learning alone. One anomalous case demonstrated that under difficult conditions re-indexing may cause over-constraint of the retrieval process, causing it to ignore applicable cases. That over-constraint, made worse by poor case learning performance, led to better performance without re-indexing than with it.

By gradually increasing the complexity of situations a case-based system faces, we can guide its learning to be more productive. The addition of introspective learning of index features also improves performance and eases the burden on the system designer to pick the right initial features. Further exploration of what "well-ordered" means for case-based systems is required, but extending ROBBIE to introspectively alter other portions of the CBR process is the next step.

References

1. D. Aha, editor. *Proceedings of the AAAI-94 Workshop on Case-Based Reasoning*, Seattle, WA, July 1994.
2. R. Alterman. An adaptive planner. In *Proceedings of the Fifth National Conference on Artificial Intelligence*, pages 65–69, Philadelphia, PA, August 1986. AAAI.
3. J. Arcos and E. Plaza. A reflective architecture for integrated memory-based learning and reasoning. In S. Wess, K.D. Altoff, and M. Richter, editors, *Topics in Case-Based Reasoning*. Springer-Verlag, Kaiserslautern, Germany, 1993.

4. W.M. Bain. *Case-based Reasoning: A Computer Model of Subjective Assessment*. PhD thesis, Yale University, 1986. Computer Science Department Technical Report 470.

5. S. Bhatta and A. Goel. Model-based learning of structural indices to design cases. In *Proceedings of the IJCAI-93 Workshop on Reuse of Design*, Chambery, France, September 1993. IJCAI.

6. L. Birnbaum, G. Collins, M. Brand, M. Freed, B. Krulwich, and L. Pryor. A model-based approach to the construction of adaptive case-based planning systems. In R. Bareiss, editor, *Proceedings of the Case-Based Reasoning Workshop*, pages 215–224, San Mateo, 1991. DARPA, Morgan Kaufmann, Inc.

7. M. Cox and A. Ram. Managing learning goals in strategy-selection problems. In *Proceedings of the Second European Workshop on Case-Based Reasoning*, pages 85–93, Chantilly, France, 1994.

8. R. J. Firby. *Adaptive Execution in Complex Dynamic Worlds*. PhD thesis, Yale University, Computer Science Department, 1989. Technical Report 672.

9. S. Fox and D. Leake. Using introspective reasoning to guide index refinement in case-based reasoning. In *Proceedings of the Sixteenth Annual Conference of the Cognitive Science Society*, pages 324–329, Atlanta, GA, 1994. Lawrence Erlbaum Associates.

10. S. Fox and D. Leake. An introspective reasoning method for index refinement. In *Proceedings of 14th international Joint Conference on Artificial Intelligence*. IJCAI, 1995.

11. S. Fox and D. Leake. Modeling case-based planning for repairing reasoning failures. In *Proceedings of the 1995 AAAI Spring Symposium on Representing Mental States and Mechanisms*, Stanford, CA, March 1995. AAAI. (ftp.cs.indiana.edu:/pub/leake/p-95-02.ps.Z).

12. M. Freed and G. Collins. Adapting routines to improve task coordination. In *Proceedings of the 1994 Conference on AI Planning Systems*, pages 255–259, 1994.

13. A. Goel, K. Ali, and Andrés Gómez de Silva Garza. Computational tradeoffs in experience-based reasoning. In *Proceedings of the AAAI-94 workshop on Case-Based Reasoning*, pages 55–61, Seattle, WA, 1994.

14. C. Hammond. *Case-Based Planning: Viewing Planning as a Memory Task*. Academic Press, San Diego, 1989.

15. J. Kolodner. *Case-Based Reasoning*. Morgan Kaufman, San Mateo, CA, 1993.

16. D. Leake. Constructive similarity assessment: Using stored cases to define new situations. In *Proceedings of the Fourteenth Annual Conference of the Cognitive Science Society*, pages 313–318, Bloomington, IN, 1992. Cognitive Science Society.

17. R. Oehlmann, P. Edwards, and D. Sleeman. Changing the viewpoint: Re-indexing by introspective questioning. In *Proceedings of the Sixteenth Annual Conference of the Cognitive Science Society*, pages 675–680. Lawrence Erlbaum Associates, 1994.

18. M. Redmond. *Learning by Observing and Understanding Expert Problem Solving*. PhD thesis, College of Computing, Georgia Institute of Technology, 1992. Technical report GIT-CC-92/43.

19. B. Smyth and M. Keane. Retrieving adaptable cases: The role of adaptation knowledge in case retrieval. In S. Wess, K. Althoff, and M Richter, editors, *Topics in Case-Based Reasoning*, pages 209–220, Berlin, 1994. Springer Verlag.

20. E. Stroulia and A. Goel. Task structures: What to learn? In M. desJardins and A. Ram, editors, *Proceedings of the 1994 AAAI Spring Symposium on Goal-driven Learning*, pages 112–121. AAAI Press, 1994.

Problem Solving with "The Incredible Machine"[*]
An Experiment in Case-Based Reasoning

Mehmet H. Göker, M.Sc.Eng., M.Sc.   Prof. Dr.-Ing. Herbert Birkhofer

Technische Hochschule Darmstadt
Maschinenelemente und Konstruktionslehre
Magdalenenstr. 4, D-64289 Darmstadt, Germany
{goker, birkhofer}@muk.maschinenbau.th-darmstadt.de

1 Motivation and Goals

In order to analyze the development, influence and application of experience during problem solving and to draw conclusions for the development of Case-Based Reasoning systems [Ko93, RiSch89] we observed and videotaped test persons while they were solving simple design problems with the computer program "The Incredible Machine"[*]. The video and audio recordings were protocolled and analyzed.

2 The Experiment

2.1 The Computer Program "The Incredible Machine"

The computer program "The Incredible Machine" (TIM) simulates a design environment in which simple machines can be built by using the 45 provided elements. A selection of these elements is shown in Table 1.

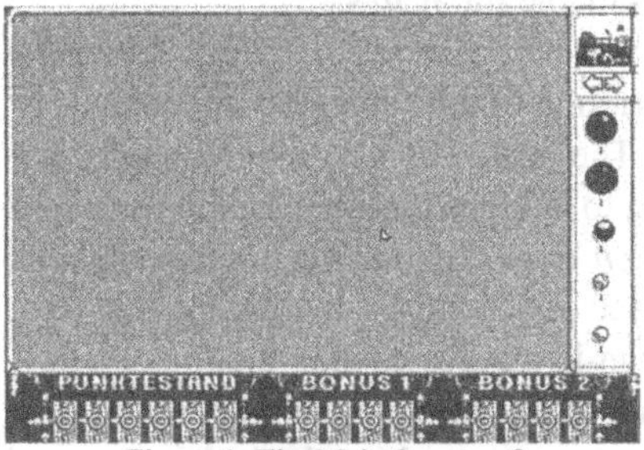

Figure 1: The Main Screen of "The Incredible Machine"

Figure 1 shows the main screen of the program. The machine is built and started in the main window. The parts can be selected from the list on the right hand side of the screen which can be scrolled using the arrows. By clicking on the field in the upper right hand corner of the screen, the environment (gravity, air pressure) is activated and the machine started. The point and bonus display at the bottom of the screen was of no interest to us and deactivated.

2.2 The Setup of the Experiment

During the experiments the test persons were asked to build machines to solve the given assignments. To reduce the pressure they were told, that their machines will not be evaluated in any way and that their time is not limited.

First the test persons had to read the introduction to the experiment and the computer program and were allowed to test the handling of the program. Then they had to solve four obligatory assignments in fixed order and to describe the elements they used in a description booklet. After the first four assignments, they were asked to select two more assignments out of the eight we provided, give the reason why they selected these particular assignments, and solve them. After all assignments were solved, the test persons had to write down the lessons they learned as if they wanted to give hints to a friend, taking this test the next day. Some of the test persons were also asked to solve the first assignment once more.

---

[*] "The Incredible Machine " is a registered trademark of Sierra On-Line Inc., Coarsegold, CA.

We observed 19 test persons (14 male / 5 female) while they solved our assignments. All of them were not familiar with the program beforehand.

Bowlingball	Basketball	Baseball	Rope	Conveyor belt	Belt
Wall	Board	Pipe	Boxing-glove	Pokey the Cat	Trampoline
Ape on a bike	Rocket	Colt	Cannon	Bucket	Cage
Balloon	Pulley	Switch / Outlet	Generator	Electromotor	Ventilator

Table 1: Some of the Elemets available in "The Incredible Machine"

2.3 Data Acquisition and Structuring

The test persons were asked to "think aloud" while they solved the assignments. Their comments and the computer screen were recorded with a video camera. At the end of each experiment the video and audio recordings, the computer files of the solved assignments and the description booklet were available for analysis.

The video and audio recordings were transcribed into a *protocol*, a *task list* and a *solution tree*. The *protocol* is a plain text transcription of the comments and actions of the test persons and the test administrator. The *task list* gives a chronological enumeration of the goals, the actions performed to achieve these goals, the results of these actions, and the new subgoals. The *solution trees* are graphical representations of the problem decomposition and solution space generated by the test person (e.g. Figure 2). The goals of the test person are shown in cursive capital, the hypothetical solutions in normal letters. Variants that have not achieved the posed goal are broken off with a horizontal line. The solution trees do not give a chronological account of the development of the solution but allow to analyze the reuse of elements.

3 Sample Analysis

In order to illustrate our experiments we will describe and analyze part of the experiment conducted with test person 13 (Tp13). A complete analysis of the experiment with Tp13 can be found in [GöBi95].

In the first assignment (Figure 2) the test person is asked to build a machine to propel the ball that rests on the wooden platform on the left hand side into the box to the right.

The test person divides the assignment "Ball in Box" into the sub-goals: "Propel Ball" and "Support Ball". She tries to achieve the sub-goal "Propel Ball" with the variants "Cable pull", "Ball in canon", Boxing glove", "Conveyor belt" and "Ramp and Ball". The combination "Ramp and Ball" is successful and fulfills the sub-goal. "Support Ball" is achieved by means of several trampolines. The meanwhile useless board is left over at the bottom of the screen.

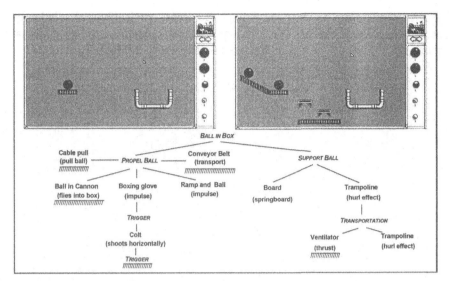

Figure 2 : Tp13, Assignment 1, Solution, Solution tree

The "Boxing glove", which was tried as a solution for "Propel Ball", has to be triggered to function. Such prerequisites cause the combination of elements to groups that work as an assembly. The test persons indexed these assemblies through the function which was originally needed (e.g. "Propel Ball") and retrieved and used

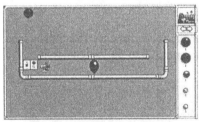

them in whole whenever this function was required. Each assembly extended the spectrum of available elements of TIM by one more, previously lacking, element.

In assignment 2 the test person had to "Free the Balloon". She solved the assignment by means of a ventilator which was powered by a switch/outlet, triggered by a basketball (Figure 3).

Figure 3: Assignment 2, Solution of Tp13

In assignment 3 the test person had to get the basketball which lies on the conveyor belt, around the wall, and into the box. Figure 4 shows the solution of Tp13. Please note the power source for the electromotor and the trampolines that come from assignment 2 and 1 respectively.

In Figure 5 the assignment 4 ("transport the basketball underneath the cage into the wooden box") is shown along with the solution and solution tree of Tp13. We can see that the test

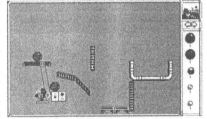

Figure 4: Assignment 3, Solution of Tp13

person split the assignment into the sub-goals "Free Ball" and "Ball to the left". "Ball to he left" was a situation with which the test person had experience and for which she employed the known solution directly. The sub-goal "Free Ball" on the other hand posed a problem to which a solution was found only after various objects and arrangements were tested. Assignments to which the test persons knew solutions, had experience with, can be identified through the deeper, straightforward solution trees of the sub-goals. A shallow tree with many spreading branches, on the other hand, shows that the test person was trying various alternatives and was inexperienced.

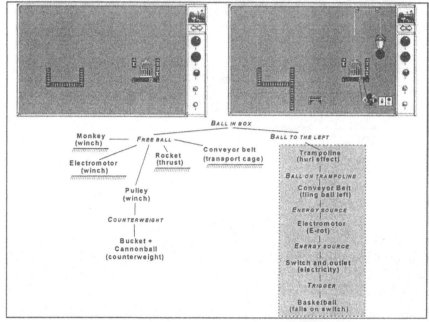

Figure 5: Tp13, Assignment 4, Solution, Solution tree

Figure 6 shows the first assignment the test person chose herself. The ball on the conveyor belt in the upper right corner has to be moved into the containment in the upper left corner.

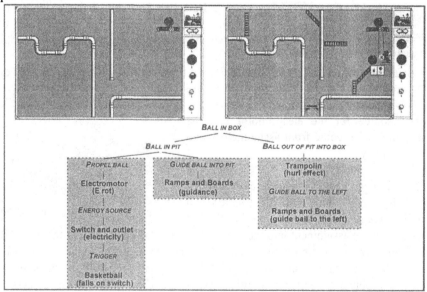

Figure 6 : Tp13, Assignment 5 (first selected assignment), Solution, Solution tree

Tp13 solved the assignment completely by applying prior experience. The "Electromotor/Switch/Basketball" combination from assignment 2 was used to propel the ball, the Trampoline from assignment 1 was used to fling and lift the ball, and several ramps and boards were used to guide the ball into the direction wanted.

Actually assignment 5 could only be solved by using a trampoline. As expected, only test persons that had experience with the trampoline in TIM and knew its peculiar property to generate energy selected this assignment.

Similar to assignment 5, Tp13 solved the second selected assignment also solely by means of experience.

4 Development and Utilization of Experience

4.1 Object Utilization

The test persons comprehended the assignments based on their experience. If they had experience with a similar assignment, they solved it directly and perceived it as a task. If no experience was available the assignment posed a problem and deductive or trial-and-error approaches were applied. Towards the end of the test, especially during the two assignments the test persons chose themselves, the assignments were solved by merely using the objects or assemblies learned during the course of the experiment.

Figure 7 shows the average percentage of new and previously known parts among the parts the test persons used to solve the assignments A1 to A4 and the two selected assignments SA1 and SA2.

Figure 7 : Development of the usage of known parts

One should note, that at the end of the experiment the test persons had in average used only 15 out of the 45 available parts (i.e. %33). Thus the reservoir of available new parts was by no means exhausted. The jump in the decrease in new parts from assignment 4 to the two selected assignments shows, that the test persons preferred assignments to which they could think of a solution in terms of their experience.

However, the unreflected application of experience to solve the assignments did not necessarily result in the most efficient and effective solution.

4.2 Object Identification

To achieve the goal "Free Ball" in assignment 4 (Figure 5 on previous page) test person 13 tried the "Monkey", the "Electromotor", a "Pulley", a "Rocket" and a "Conveyor Belt". While the "Monkey", the "Electromotor" and the "Pulley" are used to provide a similar function (i.e. "to pull") the "Rocket" and the "Conveyor Belt" provide different functions (i.e. they "push" or "move away"'). The test person tried objects with *different functions* to achieve *one purpose*.

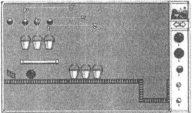

Figure 8:Tp6, Solution to Assignment 6
(Selected Assignment 2)

One function of an object was also used to achieve *different purposes*. In selected assignment 2 ("Get the basketball around the buckets into the box", Figure 8), test person 6 used the property of the bowling ball to fall (i.e. the function to store and release potential energy) to increase the weight of the buckets for a pulley and to create an impulse to propel the basketball.

By means of the description booklet, the solution trees and the protocols we saw, that the test persons assigned several functions to each object. The identification and selection of an object was done by comparing the function the object can fulfill with the desired purpose and evaluating the applicability of the object.

4.3 Development and Utilization of Methods

In the course of the experiment, the experience of the test persons did not only increase with respect to the objects they used, but also concerning the methods they applied to perform the actions necessary to achieve their goals. The basic actions we observed are described below.

4.3.1 Assessing the Assignment

The first action that the test persons performed was to assess and understand the assignment. The test persons achieved this by repeating, reformulating or summarizing the situation. Thereby the assignment was

- changed from a problem to a task by putting it into relation with previous experience and reformulating it "in their own words"

  "The ball has to be transported into the box. That means I have to build something around the wall so that the ball gets into the box." (Tp15/A3)

- divided into sub-goals

  "In principle all I need is something that joins the support of the ball with the box and something that hits against it."(Tp10/A1)

- solved on an abstract level.

  "The ball has to get over the wall first. Behind the wall it is easy, I will just take a ramp and let it roll down." (Tp8/A3)

4.3.2 Retrieving suitable solutions

In order to solve the assignments, the test persons had to retrieve, i.e. search and select appropriate solutions.

The test persons used mental objects on various levels of concretization as templates for search. The following forms could be observed :

A) Searching with no solution in mind: This, most abstract form of search can be considered a sort of brainstorming. The test persons saw the problem and started flipping through the list of parts to find something suitable by inspiration.

   "Now let's see what else we have, what else one can do." (Tp8/A1)

B) Searching with a concept of abstract objects in mind: In this form the test persons had a kind of functional description of the object(s) they needed in mind and searched the part list using this description.

   "Now I need something which moves it (the ball) upwards." (Tp11/A4)

C) Searching with a concept of known objects in mind: In this situation the test persons had a model of the machine, built out of objects they are familiar from their everyday experience, in mind, and tried to find something similar in the list.

   "I am going to build a conveyor belt, convince the ball somehow to

```
fall on it and transport it there afterwards. Let me see what parts
I will find.."(Tp6 / A1)
```

D) Searching with a concept made of TIM Objects: In this most concrete form, the test persons knew what they wanted in terms of TIM objects and looked for these objects in the list.

```
"Here I will first put a seesaw and afterwards some of those wooden
ramps. The boxing glove in the back. If that does not work the
ventilator." (Tp12/A6 - second selected assignment).
```

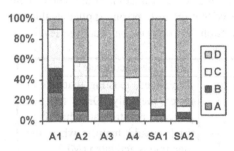

Figure 9: Development of search types

Figure 9 shows the development of the mental objects used for search for all test persons in the course of the experiment. It can be seen that Form D, being the most concrete form, constantly increases. The small amount of D type search in assignment 1 is due to the fact that some of the test persons tried out the program before they started with the first assignment.

Although search starts with a more or less abstract concept in mind, it always ends with looking up the part in the parts list. After a part is found in this list, the selection process, where the basic suitability of the object is determined, takes place. The result of the selection is a part that is moved into the main screen to be used in the machine. Following forms of selection could be observed:

I) Select after considering for some time: An object is found, but not selected immediately. The test person evaluates the object, seems to consider its suitability. Most of the time the cursor rests on the found object.

II) Select spontaneously: An object is selected without any time delay as soon as it appears on the list. It seems as if it does not matter if exactly this object is retrieved, any object of the class would do.

III) Select directly : An object - and only this object - is being sought after and selected in the list.

O) No selection : It also happens, that test persons look at a part for some time and then change their minds.

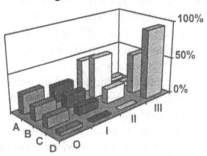

Figure 10: Combinations of search and selection types

Figure 10 shows for all test persons, over all assignments, the type of selection method applied with respect to the mental object type used for searching. Obviously, the more concrete the object the test person had in mind during the search phase is, the more concrete the selection type. The selection types II (select spontaneously any fitting object) and III (select exactly one) seem to be complementary to each other. The maximum of the type II selection occurs when the test persons look for a solution with a concept made of abstract objects (B). Any object that satisfies the functional description can - and apparently is- selected.

The selection of type III, on the other hand, has its maximum value when exact definitions of the searched objects are given. The more abstract search types (A,B) yield more abstract types of selection results (O, I).

4.3.3 Evaluation

One of the fundamental steps in problem solving is the evaluation of the objects with respect to the expectations. We could observe that the test persons applied evaluation methods on various levels of concretization to objects on various levels of concretization (Table 2).

Evaluation	Mental Object (abstract)	Real Object (concrete)
Mental evaluation (abstract)	A hypothetical object is tested by thinking how it would behave (MM). `"Lets' take a rocket ... but that's going to destroy the ball!" (Tp5/A9)`	A realized, existing machine is tested mentally. Often the test persons pointed at what they think would happen when the machine is activated (MR). `The Tp wants to start the machine, then stops and raises the right hand wall of the box with another piece of wood "...just in case..." (Tp16/A1).`
Real evaluation (test, concrete)	Parts of a machine which is planned, are being tested to see how they would behave if the machine was built (RM). `"Maybe a trampoline .. let's see, where does the ball roll to ?" (Tp6/A3).`	A realized machine is evaluated by starting it on the screen, thus performing a real test (RR). `Tp has fixed a balloon to the bucket and starts the machine - but nothing happens. "How many balloons does it take to make it work?" (Tp8/A6).`

Table 2: Evaluating solutions on various levels of concretization by combining objects and methods

Figure 11 shows the development of the evaluation types the test persons applied during the experiment. Evaluation of type RM could only be observed (or identified) once. It is possible that this type is included in the RR type evaluation count. The evaluation of type RR is the most concrete and efficient evaluation method and is increasingly used by the test persons.

The results of the evaluation were not only influenced by rational arguments but also by subjective impressions such as knowledge regarding the object, sympathy, previous successes, complexity and the availability of "chic" alternatives.

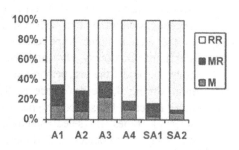

Figure 11: Development of evaluation types

4.3.4 Adaptation

Adaptation is the process of changing the solution after it has been evaluated. Two main types of adaptation were observed: mending, in which the quality of the existing solution is increased, and repair, in which the goal is to make the object fulfill its function (again). The function structure of the machine stays the same during mending, but is changed during repair.

Table 3 summarizes the actions that the test persons performed to adapt their "machines"

Adaptation	Mend	Adjust	
		Duplicate effect	
		Replace	
	Repair	Add	
		Remove	Leave Out
			Delete

Table 3: Adaptation Types

In the course of the experiment, with increasing experience, the test persons tended to mend more than to repair. They could foresee how the objects will perform and only had to make small adjustments to their machines. Only in assignments that posed problems they had to apply several repair steps, i.e. try out alternatives. This can also be deduced from the development of the solution trees.

4.3.5 Acquiring Information

During the experiment the test persons used various methods to obtain information (Table 4).

Inform	how	ask	expectant
			without expectations
		test	look at
			start
	what	identification	
		handling	
		triggering	
		function	
		arrangement	
	when	during search	
		before selection	
		after selection	

Table 4: Types of Information Acquisition

Simply asking the test administrator is the information acquisition type observed most. The test persons either asked if their expectation was correct or what the function of an object was. With growing experience the need for information decreased and the test persons preferred to test their hypotheses instead of asking the test administrator.

5 Summary and Conclusion

By means of the experiments described above we analyzed the development, utilization and influence of experience during problem solving.

We could see that while assignments to which the test person had no experience, were conceived as problems, assignments to which experience was available were conceived as tasks. The test persons understood an assignment through the experience they had with similar situations.

The solution trees that an experienced person generated were more straightforward and deep whereas an inexperienced person had to try out various alternatives and thereby created a shallow solution tree with many branches. Towards the end of the experiment the test persons solved the assignments by almost purely using their experience. This did not always result in the most optimal solution, sometimes the obvious was overlooked.

The test persons indexed the assemblies they built through the function these could fulfill and treated them as new, previously lacking, parts. They memorized all functions they knew a part or assembly could fulfill and applied the object whenever a purpose that could be achieved by means of its function(s) was needed.

In order to solve problems the test persons combined methods in various degrees of concretization with objects (mental models) on different levels of concretization. With growing experience both the mental models of the machine and the methods applied became more concrete. The effects of this concretization could be observed during assignment assessment, solution retrieval, evaluation, adaptation and information acquisition.

We believe that by taking these aspects into account the efficiency and effectivity of case-based reasoning systems can be increased. Although the basic actions we observed correspond to the steps proposed in standard case-based reasoning literature there is still a lot we can learn from the way "we" solve problems.

6 Literature

GöBi95   M.Göker, H.Birkhofer, "Problemlösen mit 'The Incredible Machine', Ein Experiment zum Falbasierten Schließen", in Proceedings, Case-Based Reasoning Workshop at the 3rd. German Expert Systems Conference, Kaiserslautern 28.2-1.3.1995, B.Bartsch-Spörl, D. Janetzko, S.Wess eds., Lernende Systeme und Anwendungen, Fachbereich Informatik, Universität Kaiserslautern LSA-95-02.

Ko93   J.Kolodner, „Case Based Reasoning", Morgan Kaufmann Publishers Inc, San Mateo, 1993

RiSch89   C.Riesbeck, R.Schank, "Inside Case-based Reasoning", Lawrence Erlbaum Associates, Publishers, Hillsdale 1989

Integrating Case Based Reasoning and Tabu Search for Solving Optimisation Problems

Stephan Grolimund   Jean-Gabriel Ganascia

Université Pierre et Marie Curie - Paris VI
LAFORIA - IBP - CNRS
4, place Jussieu, BP 169
F-75252 Paris Cedex 5, France
E-mail: {grolimund, ganascia}@laforia.ibp.fr

Abstract

Tabu search is an established heuristic optimisation technique for problems where exact algorithms are not available. It belongs to the same family as simulated annealing or genetic algorithms. It extends the basic iterative improvement scheme by adding control learning. A technique of this kind, intensification, captures experience established on a frequency-based analysis of past search. Experience is reused while the same optimisation process is going on in order to guide search to better solutions.

In this paper, we introduce a case-based reasoning approach for control learning in tabu search. Search experience concerns operator selection and is represented by cases. The aim of case reuse is to improve conflict resolution. While the proposed method is domain independent, we present its application to the NP-hard uncapacitated facility location problem. Experimental results show that adding our approach to a basic tabu search optimisation significantly improves solution quality on the evaluated benchmark problems. It reduces the gap to the optimal solution by a factor of nearly 2.

1. Introduction

There are important NP-hard optimisation problems which cannot be solved efficiently by exact optimisation from mathematical programming [15]. A local search iterative improvement technique, *tabu search* [7, 8] has regularly shown to be apt in producing high-quality solutions in such domains. Its success is based on the ability to learn about optimising a particular problem instance while optimisation is in progress, and to reuse this experience to control future search. This learning process, called intensification, is strongly domain dependent and essentially of statistical or frequency-based nature [23].

Case-based reasoning research recognised the importance of solving optimisation problems early, and various approaches have been investigated. For example EASe [20], demonstrated in the domain of logic synthesis, learns on simple problem instances how it can improve them, and reuses these acquired cases while optimising more complex ones. The system CABINS [21], designed for the repair problem in job shop scheduling, maintains the case library as an extensional definition of the optimisation criteria, providing the criteria for selecting repair actions.

This paper introduces a domain-independent case-based learning technique that is directly designed for experience learning at the intensification level inside tabu search.

As function-replacing hybrid system, it combines the strength of the renowned, general optimisation technique with CBR's capabilities of capturing experience in domains where only weak knowledge is available. The paper is structured as follows: Section 2 presents the test domain that will serve as example, uncapacitated facility location, Section 3 outlines the tabu search concepts necessary for understanding our method, Section 4 introduces the learning technique, and Section 5 presents a preliminary experimental evaluation.

2. Facility Location Problems

Facility location problems [17] deal with the optimal placing of an unknown number of facilities (e.g. plants or warehouses), within a finite set of possible locations, in order to minimise the cost of delivering demand to a given set of clients (Fig. 1). More precisely, for m possible facility locations, the binary variables y_i design the opening of a facility at location i by $y_i = 1$. For n clients with demand D_j, the real variables x_{ij} hold the flow from facility i to client j. Each opened facility i charges a fixed cost F_i. Further, unitary costs c_{ij} are charged for each flow x_{ij}. They are typically related to the distance between facility and client. The optimisation goal, expressed by the objective function $f(\cdot)$, is to find the facility configuration that minimises the total cost. The most simple and most studied variant of facility location is the Uncapacitated Facility Location Problem (UFLP), where the facilities' capacities are unlimited. It has important practical applications in transportation and other industry sectors [17]. Using the given notation, its mathematical programming formulation is :

(UFLP)   minimise: $\displaystyle f = \sum_{i=1}^{m}\sum_{j=1}^{n} c_{ij} x_{ij} + \sum_{i=1}^{m} F_i y_i$

subject to:

$$\sum_{i=1}^{m} x_{ij} = D_j, \qquad j = 1,\dots,n$$

$$\sum_{j=1}^{n} x_{ij} \le Q_{\max} \cdot y_i, \qquad i = 1,\dots,m; \qquad with: Q_{\max} \ge \sum_{j=1}^{n} D_j$$

$$x_{ij} \in \Re^{+}, \qquad i = 1,\dots,m; j = 1,\dots,n$$

$$y_i \in (0,1), \qquad i = 1,\dots,m$$

UFLP is NP-hard. Even though, its mathematical properties provide a means to find global optimal solutions efficiently, even for large problem instances[1] [3]. As soon as additional constraints are introduced, exact optimisation techniques are not available anymore and heuristic optimisation like tabu search has to be used. UFLP is interesting for an experimental evaluation because of benchmark problem instances. Results of heuristic approaches can thus be compared to the global optimal solutions.

---

[1] We distinguish *problem* from *problem instance*, a usual separation in operations research. The problem is "uncapacitated facility location", and a problem instance may be defined by giving let's say 21 clients and a set of 50 possible warehouse locations.

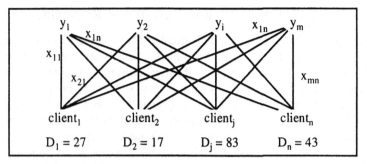

Fig. 1. General m × n facility location

3. Tabu Search

Local search (or hill-climbing) heuristics explore a search space by stepwise moving from one solution state S to another one, applying operators o, in order to improve the objective function $f(S)$ iteratively. Three variants of this classic deepest descent search scheme produce high quality solutions (optimal or near optimal ones) in a variety of different domains [19]: simulated annealing, genetic algorithms and tabu search. *Tabu search* [7, 8] is a general, domain-independent meta-heuristic that tackles search control. Its application to facility location problems has produced high-quality solutions [6, 12].

Operator selection is guided by an operator evaluation function $p(o)$ which reflects the change of $f(\cdot)$ before and after applying the operator, i.e. $p(o) = f(S) - f(o(S))$. Tabu search adds a three-level control structure to this general operator selection criteria. The base level of control consists of a *tabu list L* and copes with local minima where greedy local search often gets trapped in. During search, each visited solution S is put in L, which is managed by a first-in first-out strategy. As long as $S \in L$, operators that would lead back to S are declared *tabu* and, for this reason, are forbidden to apply. The idea is to force the search to move away from S and, in case S is a local minimum, to push it as far away for that it will not get attracted by S again. Tabu lists may either be of fixed size (length 7 seems to be well adapted to various problems) or, often a better alternative, of variable size [1].

Tabu search's two upper levels of control, *intensification* and *diversification*, build the so-called mid-term and long-term memories of the search process. They are meant to improve the future search, benefiting from learning by experience. This experience comes from search on the same problem instance. Intensification aims to focus the search on promising areas of the search space, while diversification tries to direct the search to yet unexplored regions. The interpretations of "promising" and "unexplored" are not rigorously defined and are problem dependent. Frequency-based criteria are used often in this case [23]. For example in facility location, typical intensification consists of fixing the number of opened facilities for some iterations, forcing the exploration of different similar configurations, while diversification may be achieved by compelling the opening (or closing) of a facility that did not change status for a given number of iterations [6].

4. Combining Tabu Search and Case-Based Reasoning

We claim that case-based reasoning is particularly well suited for control learning in tabu search, especially for intensification. First, intensification is a form of learning based on experience [7, 8]. Second, only shallow knowledge, resumed by "promising", is available to qualify experience. Consider any solution S. For S being of "high quality", $f(S)$ has to be close to $f(S^*)$, S^* the optimal solution. Of course, neither S^* nor $f(S^*)$ are known during optimisation. In practice, "high quality" and "promising" may not refer to S^*, but only to the best solution(s) found during past search. Case-based reasoning is well adapted to problems where experience extensively represents domain knowledge and where only a weak domain theory is available [13].

Control learning for planning has been investigated in machine learning as well as in case-based reasoning [11, 16, 22]. Optimisation differs from planning in nature: First, planning focuses on *how* to achieve solutions, while in local search optimisation, where solutions are usually constructed easily, the task is to find *good* ones [10, 23]. As consequence, memorising operator chainings, i.e. receipts for constructing solutions, is not necessary the best choice. We abandon it completely, focusing learning on single operators [18]. Second, there is no evidence that *good* solutions for one problem instance share any characteristics with *good* solutions for another problem instance [23]. We thus do not transfer acquired experience from one problem instance to another one, a practice that is of major concern in plan learning but completely uncommon in tabu search.

The remaining part of this paper introduces ALOIS ("Analogical Learning for Optimisation to Improve operator Selection"). Its local search technique is detailed below. A straightforward case-based learning technique is integrated: cases in ALOIS capture experimental, approximate qualifications, called *reward*, of operator firing outcomes. The hypothesis for case reuse is that, in a similar state, firing the operator again will result in similar qualifications. Cases are relevant to the operator schema they have been created from, and are composed of a description of the state the operator was fired in, together with the reward attributed to this firing. Case retrieval occurs for each operator becoming applicable again. The state's description is used to identify the most similar case between the relevant available cases, and the retrieved case's reward modifies the operators firing priority.

4.1 The Optimisation Algorithm

An optimisation problem is defined by a domain theory, a problem instance data-Instance and a stop condition stopCondition (Table 1). As in tabu search, an optimisation starts for each problem instance with an empty case library in an initial feasible solution. New solutions are generated iteratively, as long as the stop condition is not satisfied. Typically stop conditions are combinations of: CPU time, iterations or number of iterations without improving the best solution. For each operator, applied to achieve the new solution Next, a case is inserted in the case library.

A feasible state is build by iteratively applying operators to the Current state (Table 2). The Agenda contains the set of applicable operators without those that fall

	function Optimise(domain, dataInstance, stopCondition) : the best solution
1	initialise the engine with domain and dataInstance
2	Current := generate initial solution state
3	Best := Current
4	Caselibrary := **empty**
5	**while** stopCondition not satisfied
6	Next := Next_Solution(Current, Caselibrary)
7	O := the set of applied operators to achieve Next
8	**if** Next is better than Best **then** Best := Next
9	**for** each operator o_i in O **do**
10	$case_i$:= Generate_case(o_i, Current, Next, Best)
11	Insert($case_i$, Caselibrary)
12	Current := Next
13	**return** Best

Table 1. Main loop of optimisation in ALOIS

	function Next_Solution(Current, Caselibrary) : the feasible solution
1	O := **empty**
2	**repeat**
3	Agenda := set of non-tabu, applicable operators in Current
4	**for** each operator o_i in Agenda **do**
5	p_0 := priority of applying p(o_i)
6	p_1 := Retrieve_Reuse(Caselibrary, o_i, p_0)
7	set p_1 as new priority of o_i
8	reorder Agenda
9	o := select the operator with highest priority in Agenda
10	append o to O
11	Current := o fired in Current
12	**until** Current is feasible
13	**return** Current

Table 2. Solution generation, reusing experience in ALOIS

under the tabu conditions imposed by the tabu list. For conflict resolution, the agenda is sorted according to the operator evaluation function *p(o)*, which may be modified during conflict resolution according to relevant experience retrieved from case memory. To guarantee that a feasible state is constructed without any special planning effort (like backtracking), a hand-coded control structure must be provided by the user [9].

UFLP is modelled using three operator schemata: closeWarehouse closes one (open) facility and adds it to the tabu list, separateOneClient severs one client from the facility that had just been closed, and affectOneClient allocates one client with unsatisfied demand to a facility, opening it if necessary. The hand-coded control strategy imposes that, first, a facility is closed, second, all its clients are separated, and third, each of these clients is allocated to any facility except the one that just has been closed. As long as a facility is member of the tabu list, it is not possible to close it again, while opening it remains allowed. In the initial solution, each client is allocated to its closest facility.

4.2 Case Representation and Assessment

Cases are represented in a first order language to facilitate domain modelling. Similarity computation between cases requires therefore partial matching. Constructing the source-target mappings, a subgraph isomorphism problem, is NP-complete [4]. As consequence, worst case matching complexity grows exponentially with the number of descriptors. In case the number of descriptors is proportional to the problem instance size, which may be the case for UFLP as well as for single machine scheduling [10], source-target matching can become as complex as the optimisation problem itself. This is clearly undesirable. Case assessment has therefore to reduce the matching complexity.

For this means, one classic approach is predicate typing [14]. Combinatorial optimisation problems have in general both, symbolic and numeric characteristics. Predicate typing in KBG [5] copes with such numeric features in first order inductive learning. In this representation, literals have the form (predicateName [attribute]*), starting with the predicate name and followed by a variable number of attributes. Attributes have to belong to one of the two classes: object or value, and have to be typed. We consider the object attributes to represent the entities of the domain, while value attributes characterise both, these entities and the relations between them. For example in UFLP, facilities are object attributes of type Warehouse, and costs are value attributes of type Cost. A typical literal in this domain might be (clientArc warehouse19 client23 27 450), stating that warehouse19 delivers 27 units for a cost of 450 to client23.

However, predicate typing alone may not reduce matching complexity in case there is only one object type, as may happen in simple optimisation domains like single machine scheduling [10]. Another common technique for the complexity reduction of source-target matching, by reducing the length of the retained state description, is footprinting [22]. As in ALOIS a case focuses on only one single operator, footprinting only produces the operator's instanciated precondition. This is a somewhat restrictive description of the situation the operator was applied in. A case should ideally apprehend a description, as complete as possible, of the local configuration of its related solution state. For this task, we define the *instanciation context* as the set of literals, being present in the state the operator applied, describing the domain's entities which were concerned by the operator firing (Table 3).

Fig. 2 gives the operator schema closeWarehouse from UFLP. The left shows the (simplified) definition of closeWarehouse with its evaluation function, the precondition and the action part. The right shows closeWare-house(warehouse17), an instanciation of closeWarehouse where warehouse17 has the clients client11, client13 and clients45 allocated. Its instanciated precondition contains the entities warehouse17, client11, cli-

---

function Instanciation_context(operator) : the instanciation context
1   precond := the set of facts that are instanciated preconditions of operator in State
2   objects := extract the object attributes of precond
3   **return** I_context := the subset of facts of State where objects occur

---

Table 3. Instanciation context construction

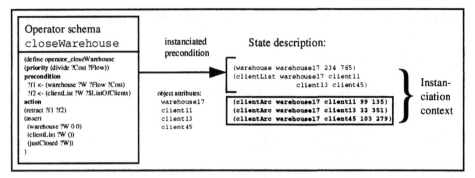

Fig. 2. Instanciation context for an application of `closeWarehouse`

ent13, and clients45. The middle box contains all facts where these object attributes occur and which lay outside the instanciated precondition. They compose, together with the instanciated preconditions, the instanciation context.

The second component of a case, going with the instanciation context, is the reward attributed to the operator firing. An operator's reward depends on the quality of the solution that has been constructed by the transformation the operator was involved in. For this first evaluation of ALOIS, we opt for a simple qualitative and heuristic reward attribution, assigning a fixed, positive amount, or *bonus*, to an operator that contributed to an improvement of solution quality. Otherwise a fixed, negative reward, or *malus*, is assigned. It is constructed once a new feasible solution is obtained, as $f(\cdot)$ may be defined for solutions only. Table 4 summarises case generation.

4.3 Case Reuse

For this experimental evaluation, aimed at clarifying the general interest of the proposed technique, the case library is only rudimentary organised. Cases are added into the base structure, a sequential list, by simply appending them at the end (Table 1). No evaluation concerning the cases originality or pertinence is performed. Case retrieval is as simple as insertion, the target is compared, using partial matching, to each case in the library in order to find the closest one (Table 5).

Source-target matching is done on a literal by literal base, with a one-to-one match between attributes of the same type, using a greedy partial matching heuristic. Literals are mapped in the order they appear in the instanciated precondition, respectively in the order they were added to the instanciation context. Similarity evaluation uses hit counts for mapped entities, and ratios in [0...1] for mappings between the two numeric attributes. The final evaluation of a partial mapping is normalised into [0...1]. The detailed algorithm for matching and similarity evaluation is

function Generate_case(operator, Current, Next, Best) : the case
1   **if** Current is better than Next **then** reward := bonus
2   **else** reward = malus
3   l_context := Instanciation_context(operator)
4   **return** case := {I_context, reward}

Table 4. Case generation and reward attribution

---

function Retrieve_Reuse(Caselibrary, operator, oldPriority) : the new priority

1	I_context := Instanciation_context(operator)
2	BestCase := **empty**
3	BestSim := 0
4	**for** each $case_i$ in Caselibrary **do**
5	sim := match I_context with $case_i$
6	**if** sim > BestSim **then**
7	BestSim := sim
8	BestCase := $case_i$
9	reward := the reward of BestCase
10	α := 1 + BestSim
11	**if** reward is bonus **then** p := α * oldPriority
12	**else** p := oldPriority / α
13	**return** p

Table 5. Case retrieval and priority adaptation

---

described in previous work [10].

Case reuse adapts an operator's priority according to the reward stored in the retrieved case. The bonus-malus reward attribution scheme leads to priority raising in case of bonus reward, and priority diminishing in case of malus (Table 5.11). Priority adaptation is weighted by the similarity value between the case and the operator.

5. Experimental results

The goal of the experimentation is to verify whether or not adding ALOIS to a tabu search optimiser improves the quality of the best solution found[2]. UFLP is chosen, because benchmark problem instances with known optimal solutions are available from the OR-library [2], making it possible to verify how close the different heuristics approach the global optimum. A cross validation scheme, separating training and test, is not appropriate here, because similar to tabu search alone, each new optimisation restarts from scratch with an empty case library. In other words, ALOIS is not designed to learn from one optimisation on how to conduct the next one, but for improving an optimisation while it is going on. The system is implemented in C++ and experimentation is conducted on a Sun Sparc workstation using an industrial forward chaining inference engine with Rete-like pattern matching.

The UFLP domain is modelled as introduced in Section 4. Two different tabu list implementations are tested, one with a tabu list of fixed size 7 (T-fix), the other with a list of variable size in the range of 6...10 (T-var), with transition probabilities of 20% for increasing or decreasing the list size after each main iteration. ALOIS has been added to both of these basic tabu methods. Eight medium size problem instances from the OR-library have been optimised (minimised), each one having 50 clients to be affected. Four instances (cap71 - cap74) have 16 possible facility location, the other four (cap101 - cap104) have 25. Optimisation stopped after visiting 30 solutions

---

[2] Due to the rudimentary case library design, we cannot yet appropriately evaluate the CPU time impact of our approach.

without finding a new best solution. In practice, no run required more than 150 iterations (i.e. generated solutions).

Results are shown in Table 6. The best solutions produced by each of the 4 methods are given after normalising them such that, for the global optimal solution S^* of each problem instance, $f(S^*) = 1$. The smaller the objective function of the best solution is, the better. The 'improvement' column gives the absolute solution improvement, i.e. the total cost reduction, due to ALOIS. These results show that integrating ALOIS improves solution quality on all but 2 problem instances. On problem instances where tabu search alone does not produce excellent results (e.g. on cap101), adding ALOIS is particularly beneficial. The average gap to the optimal solution is decreased, for T-fix, from 26% to 16%, and, for T-var, from 25% to 13%. Noteworthy, ALOIS improves solution quality on *both* tabu search designs in about the same extent, dividing the gap to optimum by nearly 2.

6. Conclusion

This paper introduces a case-based learning technique, ALOIS, to store and reuse operator selection experience encountered while a tabu search optimisation is in progress. Evaluation of the approach is conducted on the uncapacitated facility location problem. It shows that adding ALOIS to the tabu search framework is promising, as solution quality in the test domain is significantly improved for two different tabu search techniques. Further evaluations on other problem domains as well as on other tabu search implementations need to be done to comfort the general interest of the approach.

In order to gain a deeper understanding of the way by which adding a case-based reasoning technique to tabu search improves performance, the actually rudimentary case base organisation has to evolve, introducing an analysis of new cases for novelty, pertinence, relevance and contradictions compared to the one in the case library. Feedback from case reuse should allow the identification of high value cases. We are confident that a sophisticated case library organisation will further improve performance of the approach. Actual work addresses these topics.

problem instance	best solution T-fix	T-fix + ALOIS	improvement $f(S^*) = 100\%$	problem instance	best solution T-var	T-var + ALOIS	improvement $f(S^*) = 100\%$
cap71	1.08	1.07	**0.4%**	cap71	1.05	1.04	**1.1%**
cap72	1.10	1.06	**4.0%**	cap72	1.05	1.06	-0.9%
cap73	1.10	1.06	**3.7%**	cap73	1.07	1.07	**0.7%**
cap74	1.14	1.15	-0.7%	cap74	1.14	1.07	**7.1%**
cap101	1.41	1.05	**34.7%**	cap101	1.41	1.10	**28.3%**
cap102	1.44	1.26	**14.6%**	cap102	1.27	1.14	**11.6%**
cap103	1.51	1.36	**10.5%**	cap103	1.45	1.37	**5.4%**
cap104	1.57	1.24	**27.0%**	cap104	1.54	1.24	**24.8%**

Table 6. Solution quality improvement for UFLP due to ALOIS

Acknowledgement

We wish to thank Alain David and Geber Ramalho for fruitful discussions on this work.

References

[1] Battiti R., Tecchiolli G., The Reactive Tabu Search, *ORSA Journal on Computing* 6, 1994, p. 126-40

[2] Beasley J.E., OR-Library: Distributing Test Problems by Electronic Mail, *Journal of the Operations Research Society* 41, 1990, p. 1069-72

[3] Beasley J.E., Lagrangien heuristics for location problems, *European Journal of Operational Research* 65, 1993, p. 383-99

[4] Bunke H., Messmer B., Similarity Measures for Structured Representations, *First European Workshop on Case-Based Reasoning*, 1993

[5] Bisson G., Learning in FOL with a Similarity Measure, *AAAI*, 1992, p. 82-7

[6] Crainic T., Gendreau M., Soriano P., Toulouse M., A tabu search procedure for multicommodity location/allocation with balancing requirements, *Annals of Operations Research* 42 (1-4), 1993, p. 359-83

[7] Glover F., Tabu Search - Part 1, *ORSA J. on Computing 1* (3), 1989, p. 190-206

[8] Glover F., Tabu Search - Part 2, *ORSA J. on Computing 2* (1), 1990, p. 4-32

[9] Grolimund S., Ganascia J.G., *A Case-Based Reasoning Approach to Knowledge Transfer in Tabu Search*, Tech. Rep. 94/06, University Paris 6, Laforia - IBP, France, 1994

[10] Grolimund S, Ganascia J.G., *Case Based Reasoning and Tabu Search for the Single Machine Scheduling Problem: First Results*, Tech. Rep., University Paris 6, Laforia - IBP, 1995

[11] Hammond K., CHEF: A model of case-based planning, *AAAI*, 1986

[12] Hansen P., Pedrosa E., Ribeiro C., Location and sizing of offshore platforms for oil exploration, *European Journal of Operational Research* 58, 1992, p. 202-14

[13] Kolodner J., *Case-Based Reasoning*, Morgan Kaufmann, 1993

[14] Michalski R.S., A Theory and Methodology of Inductive Learning, in: *Machine Learning: An Artificial Intelligence Approach*, Tioga, Palo Alto, 1983

[15] Minoux M., *Mathematical Programming*, Morgan Kaufmann, 1989

[16] Minton S., *Learning Search Control Knowledge: An Explanation-Based Approach*, Kluwer Academic Press, Boston, 1989

[17] Mirchandani P., Francis R. (eds.), *Discrete Location Theory*, Wiley, 1990

[18] Mitchell T., Learning and problem solving, *IJCAI*, 1983, p. 1140-51

[19] Reeves C., *Modern Heuristic Techniques for Combinatorial Problems*, Blackwell, 1993

[20] Ruby D., Kibler D., Learning Episodes for Optimization, *ICML*, 1992, p. 279-84

[21] Sycara K., Miyashita K., Case-based acquisition of User Preferences for Solution Improvement in Ill-Structured Domains, *AAAI*, 1994, p. 44-9

[22] Veloso M., *Learning by analogical reasoning in general problem solving*, Ph.D. thesis, Carnegie Mellon University, Pittsburgh, 1992

[23] Woodruff D., *Proposal for Chunking and Tabu Search*, Tech. Rep., University of California Davis, Dec. 1994

Systems, Tasks and Adaptation Knowledge: Revealing Some Revealing Dependencies

Kathleen Hanney, Mark Keane[1], Barry Smyth[2] and Padraig Cunningham[1]

[1] Department of Computer Science, University of Dublin, Trinity College, Dublin 2, Ireland

[2] Hitachi Dublin Laboratory, University of Dublin, Trinity College, Dublin 2, Ireland

Abstract. This paper shows that the use of adaptation knowledge in CBR systems is heavily dependent on certain task and system constraints. Furthermore, the type of adaptation knowledge used in systems performing specific tasks is quite regular and predictable. These conclusions are reached by reviewing forty-two CBR systems and classifying them according to three taxonomies: an adaptation-relevant taxonomy of CBR systems, a taxonomy of tasks and a taxonomy of adaptation knowledge. We then show how different systems cluster with respect to interactions between these three taxonomies. The CBR system designer may find the partition of CBR systems and the division of adaptation knowledge suggested by this paper useful. Moreover, this paper may help focus the initial stages of systems development by suggesting (on the basis of existing work) what types of adaptation knowledge should be supported by a new system. In addition, the paper provides a framework for the preliminary evaluation and comparison of systems.

1 Introduction

The growth of CBR has led to a great diversity in the field. CBR systems perform diverse tasks in a multiplicity of domains. Some of these systems perform all the prototypical CBR processes (e.g., retrieval, reuse, adaptation, learning), although many employ only some subset of these processes. Other surveys of CBR have been carried out [1, 52] but our review is different in that it focusses on the diversity in the use of the adaptation process. Our aim is to learn from current practice, to review CBR systems to determine when, in practice, adaptation tends to be used; the sort of tasks requiring adaptation and the form adaptation takes in different tasks. Hence, we propose a taxonomy of adaptation knowledge (see section 3). However, we need two other taxonomies to fulfil our aim; a taxonomy of CBR systems (of relevance to adaptation) and a taxonomy of task types (see section 2). Such an analysis is useful for several reasons. First, it could help focus the initial stages of systems development by providing useful divisions of both tasks and adaptation knowledge and by suggesting the types of adaptation knowledge required by a new system. Second, it can provide a framework for the evaluation and comparison of different systems. Finally, it also tells us in a succinct way what is going on in the field. To date, our review has considered 53 CBR systems in detail, using available published sources and student dissertations (11 of these 53 systems were excluded because they were not reported in sufficient detail for our analysis).

2 Taxonomies of CBR Systems and Tasks

Adaptation is treated very differently in many CBR systems. First, many systems use no adaptation at all. Second, distinctions are often made between different types of adaptation, like derivational and transformational adaptation. Derivational adaptation involves a replay of the steps taken to find the old solution (using subgoal and justification structures) making any necessary adjustments to these steps, while transformational adaptation is more concerned with repairing discrepancies between a current problem and a previous case [10, 11]. Third, the location of adaptation knowledge varies. Some systems store adaptation knowledge in the case (e.g., ACBARR [34]), though most systems use an external knowledge source consisting of domain-specific adaptation procedures. Fourth, most systems use domain-specific adaptation procedures while others also employ more domain-independent adaptation strategies (e.g., plan step reordering in CHEF [21]). We have reduced this diversity to just four dimensions which we use to classify CBR systems with respect to adaptation:

- Presence or Absence of Adaptation - an obvious divide is between systems that have some form of automated adaptation and those that do not. We define adaptation as the modification of case solutions. This definition excludes systems that combine unmodified cases or case parts because they do not change past cases or their parts.
- Single or Multiple Cases - solutions may be based on single or multiple cases. The solution of a single-case system is the solution (either modified or intact) of a single past case (even if successive cases are considered before a solution is reached). Also included in this category are those systems which use multiple cases to reinforce the solution given by the best-match case. For example, some memory-based systems take the most common solution of the list of best-matching cases to avoid relying on a single close match. Multiple case systems may base their solutions on more than one case. In AIRQUAP [27], for example, the solution to the target problem is the mean value of the solutions to the most similar past cases. The case-based design system, CADRE [16], composes a design from several cases or case parts.
- Complexity of Case-solutions - system solutions may be atomic-valued solutions that are primitive and non-decomposable, compound solutions that are decomposable by processes other than adaptation (e.g., where only part of a previous solution is retrieved to solve a problem subgoal) or compound-manipulable solutions that have parts that can be modified by adaptation (see [14]). Solutions in AIRQUAP, for instance, are atomic numeric. CELIA [35] has compound solutions since they are composed of unmodified case snippets. PRODIGY [50] has compound-manipulable solutions since individual plan steps can be modified.

- Interactions within Case-solutions - systems differ according to whether parts of the solution are independent or interacting (e.g., where the adaptation of one part of a solution requires further modification of other solution parts). As an example, consider JULIA [23], which detects and fixes bad interactions between parts of meal designs.

Figure 1 combines these four dimensions into a hierarchy under which the reviewed systems are classified. At the leaves of this tree the first number indicates the number of the category and the number of systems found in this category is shown in brackets. It is immediately clear that systems cluster into particular categories, even though all the categories are, in principle, viable system-types. There are several possible reasons for the distribution found. First, there is clearly a reporting bias in the literature. Many of the simpler systems (e.g., 1, 5 and 7) are less likely to be reported in the research literature. Setting aside this reporting bias, it is also clear that some systems do not make practical sense. For instance, we found no instances of systems using adaptation with compound solutions that are not manipulated by adaptation knowledge (see 2 and 8); clearly, if compound solutions are available and adaptation is being used then it makes practical sense to decompose the problem and manipulate the parts of these solutions using adaptation knowledge (see 3, 4, 9 and 10). In addition, no reviewed system uses multiple cases without adaptation to reach an atomic solution. Obvious exceptions are those memory-based learning systems that use clustering algorithms [40]. These systems use multiple cases without adaptation to reach an atomic solution. Of the 42 systems reviewed the majority reasoned from multiple cases (33 or 79%). The clustering in the multiple-case categories (9 and 12) indicates an important focus for CBR systems. These categories are sophisticated reasoners that merge solutions from different problem-solving contexts and handle complex interactions between solution goals. What is clear from this initial

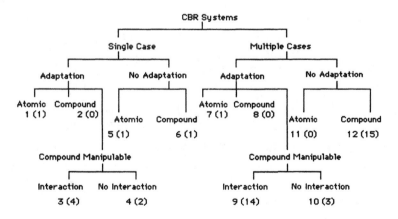

Fig. 1. Classifying Systems on Four Dimensions Relevant to Adaptation (N = 42)

classification is that the main systems in the literature are largely concerned with dealing with multiple cases, and that there is a roughly even split between those that use adaptation to do this and those that do not. To get a better understanding of how some systems deal with multiple cases without adaptation (and also to look at the spread in other systems), we categorised these systems in terms of the task they achieve. There should be some obvious task characteristics that permit us to distinguish between those that do and those that do not require adaptation.

2.1 Analysing System-Types by Task

Task classifications are not straight-forward as there is no canonical set used by system builders. One researcher's design system may be a simple classification system to another researcher. We tried to achieve some standardisation by adopting Clancey's [12] taxonomy of tasks for expert systems. Only three of Clancey's task types are needed to categorise CBR systems: identify (basically recognition or classification), predict, and design (subsuming configuration and planning). CBR systems either do identification alone (PROTOS [5], µI-CBR [15], ARCHIE-2 [17], ORCA [6], ASK-SYSTEMS [18], CASCADE [41], CELIA [35]) or identification and prediction (AIRQUAP [27], JUDGE [4], REBECAS [38]) or identification and design (PRIAR [24], CADSYN [29], CASEY [26], JULIA [23], CHEF [21], CYCLOPS [31], ROENTGEN [7], MEDIATOR [42], KRITIK [19], PRODIGY [50], COBRA [44], CASPIAN [32], CADRE [16], PLEXUS [2], DEJA VU [45], PANDA [37], DDIS [51], BOLERO [28], TOLTEC [49], ROUTER2 [20], BOGART [30], APU [8], PERSUADER [47], HYPO [3], CLAVIER [22], MBR-talk [46], CABARET [43], CAB Assembler [33], GREBE [9], CADET [48], SWALE [39]). One system uses cases for identification and control (ACBARR [34]).

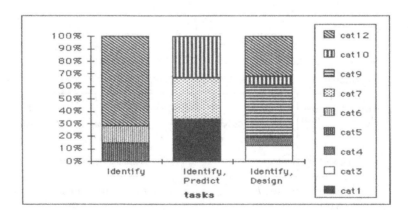

Fig. 2. Percentage of System-types used to achieve different Tasks

Figure 2 gives us some insight into the clustering found in our system taxonomy. It shows strong dependencies between system-types and types of tasks. First, identification tasks are the preserve of adaptation-free systems (5, 6 and 12), whereas prediction and design tasks for the most part require adaptation (e.g., 1, 3, 4, 9 and 10). Second, prediction can be achieved using solutions that are either atomic or the simpler form of compound-manipulable solution (1, 7 and 10). Third, design tasks largely require adaptation on compound-manipulable solutions (3, 4, 9 and 10), except when the systems are design assistants (i.e., category 12 systems like ARCHIE-2). The distribution of systems performing different tasks suggests that certain system-types are optimal for different tasks (clearly the complexity and completeness of domain knowledge is also an important, but more difficult to characterise, consideration).

3 When Types of Adaptation Knowledge are Used

Our initial taxonomies show that CBR systems using adaptation are predominantly used when prediction and design are required. In this section, we consider the nature of the adaptation knowledge used by these systems to determine whether there are any regularities in the use of adaptation knowledge across different system-categories and tasks. Several alternative taxonomies of adaptation knowledge have been proposed [13, 23, 25, 36], but none of them meet our specific needs. Kolodner's taxonomy of adaptation methods includes substitution (used when a substitute already exists) and transformation (used to change a solution or solution element by inserting or deleting a subpart). Various substitution methods are distinguished according to the method used to find a substitute. Transformational methods can be either model-guided or heuristically driven. It is our view that we need a taxonomy at a level of analysis that is general enough to show the commonalty between disparate systems but specific enough to tell us something about adaptation. We identify four main types of adaptation knowledge on the basis of the roles they play in the adaptation process: target-elaboration operators, role-substitution operators, subgoaling operators and goal-interaction operators:

- Target Elaboration Operators elaborate the target problem description to facilitate adaptation, resulting in a better specified target. Elaboration can either add new information to or re-describe (or re-categorise) some part of the target. These operators are clearly indispensable when aspects of the target are uncertain or under-specified. In CYCLOPS [31], for instance, similar cases can signal problems or opportunities within a new design resulting in the introduction of new criteria.
- Role Substitution Operators effect substitutions at various levels of granularity. These operators can be simple or complex. In simple role-substitution, a local substitution of parts of a solution (actions, values or roles) is made without reference to dependencies between these parts and other parts of the solution. For example, PERSUADER [47] adapts numerical parameters using special-purpose critics. Complex role substitution can change several

parts of a solution at once, where such substitutions are sensitive to causal or other dependencies between solution parts. In CHEF [21], for example, the substitution of a new ingredient in a plan may require the insertion of special preparation steps. In CASEY [26], the remove and add evidence modifications not only remove or add features but also update causal links.

- Subgoaling operators handle the decomposition of the adaptation task into smaller, simpler tasks. If a solution requires several distinct adaptations, then a subgoaling operator might sequence these adaptations [50]. DEJA VU [45] delegates its adaptation tasks to adaptation specialists. Each specialist makes a local modification to a retrieved case.
- Goal interaction operators - handle interactions between solution parts and handle both the detection and repair of bad interactions that occur. In DEJA VU, general adaptation strategies are used to handle bad interactions resulting from the local changes made by adaptation specialists.

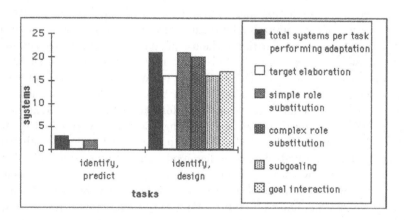

Fig. 3. The Number of Systems using different Types of Adaptation Knowledge

To look at "task by adaptation-knowledge" dependencies we plotted the number of prediction and design systems that use different types of adaptation knowledge (see figure 3). Several notable regularities arise. The adaptation requirements for prediction are quite simple; they merely involve target elaboration and simple role substitution. However, in design systems the whole range of adaptation knowledge tends to be employed; design systems use each type of adaptation knowledge at least 75% of the time. This figure shows that the main focus for adaptation knowledge is in design tasks and that relatively simple adaptation knowledge can be used in prediction (although assistants can circumvent this generalisation). It goes without saying that no types of adaptation knowledge are required for identification (see figure 2). A more fine-grained analysis is possible if we look at the "system-category by adaptation-knowledge" dependencies. In figure 4, we have a rough ordering of adaptation systems in terms of their complexity: 1 and 7 are the simplest with atomic solutions, 4 and 3 are more complex in that they have compound manipulable solutions (and use single cases), and 9 and 10 are the most complex as they have compound manipulable solutions and use multiple cases. The figure shows that the requirements for different types of adaptation knowledge increase as systems increase in complexity: Simpler systems can get by with target elaboration and role substitution, but more complex systems require diverse adaptation knowledge. It is also notable that almost every system with compound, interacting solutions (3 and 9) requires the full range of adaptation knowledge (irrespective of whether single or multiple cases are being used).

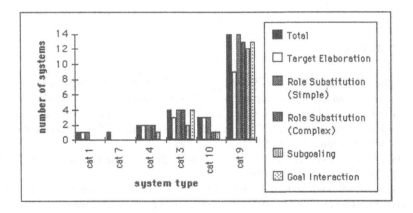

Fig. 4. The types of Adaptation Knowledge used in System Categories

4 Conclusions

In this paper we have produced three distinct taxonomies to plot when adaptation is currently used in CBR systems. In general, the space of systems explored by researchers is a good indicator of practical constraints on system construction. Accepting the restricted nature of our sample, it is clear that there are strong dependencies between the use of adaptation knowledge, the task to be achieved and the nature of the case solution. Several conclusions are possible:

- identification tasks can be achieved without adaptation
- prediction tasks require more adaptation but minimal amounts are required
- design tasks have the heaviest adaptation requirements in the amount and diversity of this knowledge (except when overridden by the use of a case-based assistant approach)

- systems using solutions with compound-interacting parts need all forms of adaptation knowledge (irrespective of whether solutions are based on single or multiple cases)

Other more detailed conclusions may arise as more and more systems are included in our on-going review. Many might think that these conclusions are obvious. To the extent that they conform to an expert's intuitions about the field, they will be successful if they are obvious. In spite of this, we think that finding a justified empirical basis for such intuitions is a useful task, as it places them on a firmer footing. Furthermore, the results of our analysis reveal interesting guidelines for system builders about when and what sort of adaptation knowledge is required. To date, such guidelines have merely existed as hearsay in the research community. This review shows that they have a firm basis in practice.

References

1. Aamodt A., Plaza E.: Case-Based Reasoning: Foundational Issues, Methodological Variations, and Systems Approaches. AI Communications. **7(1)** (1994) 39–59
2. Alterman R.: Adaptive Planning. Cognitive Science **12** (1988) 393–422
3. Ashley K.: Reasoning with Cases and Hypotheticals in HYPO. International Journal Man-Machine Studies **34** (1991) 753–796
4. Bain W.: JUDGE.: In Riesbeck C., Schank R. (Ed.) Inside Case-Based Reasoning. *Northvale, NJ : Erlbaum* (1989)
5. Bareiss E.: Exemplar-Based Knowledge Acquisition: A Unified Approach to Concept Representation, Classification, and Learning. *Boston: Academic Press* (1989)
6. Bareiss E., Slator B.: The Evolution of a Case-based Computational Approach to Knowledge Representation, Classification, and Learning. In Nakumura G., Medin D., Taraban R. (Ed.) Categorisation by Humans and Machines. *New York: Academic Press* (1993)
7. Berger J.: Roentgen: Radiation Theraphy and Case-Based Reasoning. In Proceedings of the 10th Conference on Artificial Intelligence for Applications. *IEEE Computer Society Press* (1994)
8. Bhansali S., Harandi M.: Syntesis of UNIX Programs Using Derivational Analogy, Machine Learning **10** (1993) 7–55.
9. Branting L.: Exploiting the Complementarity of Rules and Precedents with Reciprocity and Fairness. In Bareiss E. (Ed.) Proceedings: Case-Based Reasoning Workshop (1991) 39–50.
10. Carbonell J.: Learning by Analogy: Formulating and Generalizing Plans from Past Experience. In Michalski R., Carbonell J., Mitchell T. (Ed.) Machine Learning: An Artificial Intelligence Approach Vol. 1. *Morgan Kaufmann* (1983)
11. Carbonell J.: Derivational Analogy: A Theory of Reconstructive Problem Solving and Expertise Acquisition. In Michalski R., Carbonell J. Mitchell T. (Ed.) Machine Learning: An Artificial Intelligence Approach Vol. 2. *Morgan Kaufmann* (1986)
12. Clancey W.: Heuristic Classification., Artificial Intelligence **27(3)** (1985) 289–350.
13. Collins G.: Plan Creation. In Riesbeck C., Schank R. (Ed.) Inside Case-based Reasoning. *Northvale, NJ : Erlbaum* (1989)

14. Cunningham P., Smyth B., Veale T.: On the Limitations of Memory Based Reasoning In Keane M.T., Haton J-P., Manago M. (Ed.) Proceedings Second European Workshop on Case-Based Reasoning. (1994) 59–65

15. Cunningham P., Smyth B., Bonzano A. : An Incremental Case Retrieval Mechanism for Diagnosis. Technical Report TCD-CS-95-01. Department of Computer, Science Trinity College Dublin (1995)

16. Dave B., Schmitt G., Shen-Guan S., Bendel L., Faltings B., Smith I., Hua K., Bailey S., Ducret J-M, Jent K.: Case-Based Spatial Design Reasoning. In Keane M.T., Haton J- P., Manago M. (Ed.) Proceedings of the Second European Workshop on Case-Based Reasoning (1994) 115–123

17. Domeshek E., Kolodner J.: Using the Points of Large Cases AI EDAM 7(2) (1993) 87–96

18. Ferguson W., Bareiss R., Birbaum L., Osgood R.: ASK Systems: An Approach to the Realization of Story-Based Teachers. The Journal of the Learning Sciences 2(1) (1992) 95–134

19. Goel A. Integration of Case-Based Reasoning and Model-Based Reasoning for Adaptive Design Problem Solving. PhD Dissertation, Department of Computer and Information Science, The Ohio State University (1989)

20. Goel A., Callantine T.:An Experience-Based Approach to Navigational Route Planning. In Proceedings of the 1992 IEEE/RSJ International Conference on Intelligent Robots and Systems (1992) 705–710.

21. Hammond K.:Case-Based Planning: Viewing Planning as a Memory Task. *Boston: Academic Press* (1989)

22. Hinkle D., Toomey C.: Clavier: Applying Case-Based Reasoning to Composite Part Fabrication. In Proceedings of the Sixth Innovative Applications of Artificial Intelligence Conference (1994) 55–61

23. Hinrichs T.: Problem Solving in Open Worlds: A case study in design. *Northvale, NJ:Erlbaum* (1992)

24. Kambhampati S. Hendler J.: Validation-structure-based Theory of Plan Modification and Reuse. Artificial Intelligence 55 (1992) 193–258

25. Kolodner J.: Case-based Reasoning *Morgan Kaufmann* (1993)

26. Koton P.: Using Experience in Learning and Problem Solving. PhD Dissertation Department of Computer Science, MIT. (1989)

27. Lekkas G., Avouris N.: Case-Based Reasoning in Environmental Monitoring. Applied Artificial intelligence 8 (1994) 359–376.

28. Lopez B., Plaza E.: Case-based Planning for Medical Diagnosis. In Komorowski J., Ras Z.W. (Ed.) Methodologies for Intelligent Systems. Lecture notes in artificial intelligence 689 (1993)

29. Maher M., Zhang D.: CADSYN: A Case-Based Design Process Model. AI-EDAM 7 (2) (1993) 97–110

30. Mostow J.: Design by Derivational Analogy. Artificial Intelligence 40 (1989) 119–184

31. Navinchandra D.: Exploration and Innovation in Design, Towards a Computational Model.*New York Springer-Verlag* (1991)

32. Price C., Pegler I.S., Bell F.: Case- Based Reasoning in the Melting Pot. International Journal of Applied Expert Systems 1(2) (1993) 120–133.

33. Pu P., Reschberger M. Assembly Sequence Planning using Case-Based Reasoning Techniques. In Gero J. (Ed.) Artificial Intelligence in Design *Boston: Kluwer Academic Publishers* (1991)

34. Ram A., Arkin R., Moorman K., Clark R.: Case-based Reactive Navigation: A case-based Method for On-line Selection and Adaptation of Reactive Control Parameters in Autonomous Robotic Systems, Technical Report GIT-CC-92/57, School of Information and Computer Science, Georgia Institute of Technology (1992)

35. Redmond M.: Learning by Observing and Understanding Expert Problem Solving. PhD Dissertation, School of Information and Computer Science, Georgia Institute of Technology (1992)

36. Riesbeck C., Schank R.: Inside Case-based Reasoning *Lawrence Erlbaum Associates* (1992)

37. Roderman S., Tsatsoulis C.: PANDA: A Case-Based System to Aid Novice Designers. AI EDAM **7(2)** (1993) 125–133.

38. Rougegrez-Loriette S.: Prédiction de Processus à partir de Comportements observés: Le système REBECAS. Thèse du Doctorat de l'Université Paris 6 (1994)

39. Schank R., Kass A., Riesbeck C.: Inside Case-based Explanation. Lawrence *Erlbaum Associates, Hillsdale, New Jersey* (1994)

40. Schaal S., Atkeson C.: Robot Juggling: Implementation of Memory-Based Learning. IEEE Control Systems **14(1)** 57–71

41. Simoudis E.: Using Case-Based Reasoning for Customer Technical Support. IEEE Expert **7(5)** (1992) 7–13

42. Simpson R.: A Computer Model of Case-Based Reasoning in Problem Solving: An Investigation in the Domain of Dispute Mediation, Technical Report GIT-ICS-85/18, School of Information and Computer Science, Georgia Institute of Technology (1985)

43. Skalak D., Rissland E.: Arguments and Cases: An Inevitable Intertwining. Artificial Intelligence and Law **1** (1992) 3-44

44. Slattery S.: Case-based Reasoning. The derivational analogy approach. B.A. Project, Computer Science Department. Trinity College Dublin (1993)

45. Smyth B., Cunningham P.: Deja Vu: A Hierarchical Case-Based Reasoning System for Software Design. In Proceedings of the 10th European Conference on Artificial Intelligence. Vienna, Austria (1992)

46. Stanfill C., Waltz D.: Toward Memory-Based Reasoning. Communications of the ACM **29(2)** (1986) 1213–1228

47. Sycara E. P.: Resolving Adversarial Conflicts: An Approach to Integrating Case-Based and Analytic Methods. PhD Dissertation,.School of Information and Computer Science, Georgia Institute of Technology (1987)

48. Sycara E. P., Navinchandra D.: Influences: A Thematic Abstraction for Creative Use of Multiple Cases. In Bareiss E.R. (Ed.) Proceedings: Case-Based Reasoning Workshop (1991)

49. Tsatsoulis C., Kashyap R.: Case- Based Reasoning and Learning in Manufacturing with the TOLTEC Planner. IEEE Transactions on Systems, Man and Cybernetics **23(4)** (1993) 1010–1022

50. Veloso M.: Learning by Analogical Reasoning in General Problem Solving, PhD Thesis. School of Computer Science. Carnegie Mellon University, Pittsburgh, PA. (1992)

51. Wang J., Howard H.: A design-dependent approach to Integrated Structural Design. In Gero J. (Ed) Artificial Intelligence in Design. *Boston: Kluwer Academic Publishers* (1991)

52. Watson I., Marir F.: Case-based Reasoning: A Review. The Knowledge Engineering Review **9(4)** (1994): 1–39

Some Limitations of Feature-Based Recognition in Case-Based Design

Thomas R. Hinrichs

The Institute for the Learning Sciences
Northwestern University
Evanston, IL 60201

Abstract. A crucial part of Case-Based Reasoning is retrieving cases that are similar or otherwise relevant to the problem at hand. Traditionally, this has been formulated as a problem of indexing and accessing cases based on sets of predictive features. More generally, however, we can think of retrieval as a problem of recognition. In this light, several limitations of the feature-based approach become apparent. What constitutes a feature? What makes a feature predictive? And how is retrieval possible when the structure of an input is predictive, but its components are not?

This paper presents an analysis of some of the limitations of feature-based recognition and describes a process that integrates structural recognition with retrieval. This structural recognition algorithm is designed to augment the retrieval capabilities of case-based reasoners by facilitating the recognition of functional design clichés, natural laws, and sub problems for which individual features may not be predictive.

1 Introduction

Recognition is an important component of problem solving. Engineers and programmers recognize design clichés, scientists recognize natural laws at work in different situations, and people generally recognize problems they've solved before. In AI, one of the central tenets of case-based reasoning (CBR) is that problems can be solved by retrieving and adapting solutions to similar problems (Kolodner, 1993). To do this, problem solvers typically access and evaluate previous cases by recognizing their common features. Such an approach is called feature-based recognition. It seems plausible that reducing a problem to constituent features would sometimes be insufficient or inappropriate. In fact, the limitations of feature-based recognition was one of the cornerstones of Minsky and Papert's book Perceptrons (1969). Why, then, are most problem-solving accounts of retrieval based solely on feature-based recognition? This paper presents a problem for which this fails, proposes an alternative model that more closely integrates problem solving with perception, and outlines an algorithm to achieve this.

One reason that feature-based recognition is so ubiquitous is the assumption that recognition should be cheap. After all, human beings easily recognize faces and situations on the order of milliseconds. But the deceptive ease with which we recognize the familiar may lead us astray by suggesting computational models that emphasize reduction to simple primitives that are "immediate" or "free". Moreover, by reducing to primitive features, it is easy to see how to amortize the cost of recognition by indexing concepts and cases at storage time, rather than performing complex computations at retrieval/recognition time. This apparent computational efficiency can be an illusion, however, because it does not account for the cost of perceiving features, and in some ways it trades off competence for performance.

Some recent work in case-based reasoning has involved effectively extracting features from geometrical structure (Berger, 1993), and from traces of continuous parameters over time (Ram and Santamaria, 1993). In this paper, we concentrate instead on recognition and retrieval based on the topological structure of engineered designs.

2 An Example From Engineering

Recently, I was attempting to apply the case-based design system JULIA (Hinrichs, 1992) to some problems of engineering design. An issue that quickly became apparent was how to index and retrieve concepts as simple as a voltage divider. A voltage divider is not so much a component as a configuration of components: two resistors in series with a voltage source divide the voltage in proportion to the resistance of one of the resistors divided by the sum of their resistances (Fig. 1).

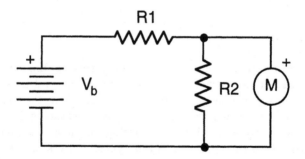

Fig. 1. Voltage Divider

Clearly this is not a problem for computational design in general. CAD systems perform such calculations all the time. In fact, the voltage divider example has been used previously to illustrate constraint propagation in ThingLab (Borning, 1981). In ThingLab, however, the voltage divider constraint must be added manually by the user in order to solve for the voltage across the meter M. Ideally, a computational model of design should not only perform such inference, but also be able to quickly recognize such configurations.

A case-based design system, for example, should be able to retrieve a similar circuit for which the voltage across M has been solved, and to transfer the reasoning or constraints that determined the value. However, because JULIA relies on feature-based recognition, it cannot do this. JULIA's memory is arranged as a multiple-discrimination network that discriminates based on deviations from and specializations of normative features. Consequently, it could retrieve circuits containing resistors and batteries, or even resistors with a specific value, but it could not retrieve only those circuits with two resistors in series. Unless, that is, the concept "two resistors in series" were explicitly represented in the input, or arbitrary procedures were permitted as discrimination tests. What makes this problem hard is that the primitive components of the circuit, its features, are for the most part the same; by themselves they are not predictive. What is predictive is relationships that are implicit in the input representation.

This is not merely a problem with discrimination networks and knowledge-poor matching. The same limitation is true of other retrieval feature-based recognition algorithms. For example, PROTOS (Bareiss, 1989) does not rely on discrimination to retrieve exemplars, but instead uses a two-phase retrieval algorithm in which the reminding strengths of the input features are combined to activate hypothesis categories, and exemplars of those categories are then matched against the input case using knowledge about the relationships between features. In addition, PROTOS permits categories to be features of other categories thereby representing complex features. Given the right category and the right relational vocabulary, PROTOS could distinguish between a circuit with resistors in series and one with resistors in parallel. Nevertheless, it could never be reminded of a category based solely on relationships in its input, even if those relationships were explicitly represented. This is a fundamental problem of feature-based recognition.

In effect, feature-based recognition reduces the input to a set of features, thereby losing all information about their configuration and cardinality. For some problems, this suffices to enable an efficient first pass retrieval, followed by a matching phase that ranks retrieved items or verifies a hypothesis category. From a pattern-recognition perspective, this is essentially pattern classification followed by template matching.

For many problems, however, this begs the question of exactly what should constitute a feature. If symbols in the input do not represent predictive features, then at what granularity and specificity are features to be found? For example, is a 5Ω resistor a different feature from a 500Ω resistor? Is a transistor a feature, or should it be translated into a 'small signal' model composed of passive elements such as resistors? One could appeal to basic level effects and argue that component types are natural categories (hence their designation by different schematic symbols.) But one could also argue that the voltage divider example shows that features can be at a larger granularity, and the existence of alternative representations of transistors suggests that, ultimately, there may not be a fixed set of primitives.

2.1   Feature Extraction

One standard solution to these problems is to employ pattern recognition processes as a front end in order to make explicit the relationships that are otherwise implicit in the input. These extrinsic relationships are then treated as features by the problem solving component. This process, called pattern classification, is illustrated in Fig. 2. Pattern classification takes as input a pattern that may be a perspective view or may be partially occluded, and transforms the pattern through a process of normalization. It then extracts symbolic features that can be used by the decision procedure to classify the input.

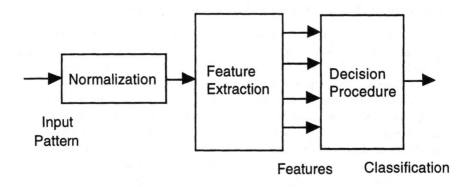

Fig. 2. The Feature Extraction process

Feature extraction has been used by many AI programs to recognize domain-specific configurations, such as chess positions (Simon and Gilmartin 1973). While it makes sense to exploit domain expectations in perception, this approach is limited because it effectively hard-wires the domain-specific part of the program; the sort of knowledge that is least likely to be innate in any cognitive model of intelligence.

Moreover, for recognizing relational structure, feature extraction can be like the tail wagging the dog. Not only is it a domain-specific black box, but there is typically no feedback from the decision procedure to the feature-extraction process. Feature extraction provides no general account of how to focus attention and it ignores cardinality and configuration information, so there must be a small number of relevant configurational categories. Most importantly, because features are extracted via arbitrary code, they are not systematically composed of simpler features that can be derived or learned from the input. The vocabulary of features is either fixed or determined by the task and the local features of the input. While top-down processing is important because it provides expectations in the form of a pragmatic (task-driven) context, it must be applied in a global-to-local fashion in order to provide a structural context as well.

2.2 The Problem With Parsing

An alternative to pattern classification is to re-represent the input to extract its relational structure. Syntactic pattern recognition extracts structural information through syntactic analysis (Fu, 1980). It translates local relationships into features using a pattern description language consisting of pattern primitives, composition operators, and a grammar. The generality of this approach depends on the existence of a natural or universal set of primitives, composition operators, and a common grammar.

One candidate for a common grammar that is increasingly used in engineering design representations is the bond-graph grammar (Paynter, 1961). Bond graphs are a mathematical notation used to model a very wide range of dynamic systems in terms of a small set of abstract primitive elements. Although they are almost universally applicable for modeling the flow of energy in dynamic systems, bond graphs are generally not applicable for modeling software systems or physical configurations. Choosing or learning an appropriate domain-specific grammar could be an arbitrarily difficult task.

Furthermore, parsing by itself can only extract the structure of formal languages. Informal languages, such as natural language, require some kind of semantic analysis as well. The basic problem with parsing is that it is fundamentally a bottom-up process. Contextual information might determine an initial pattern-description language, but after that there is no feedback from higher-level processes.

3 Toward Design Perception

To overcome the limitations of feature-based recognition in case-based design requires a greater integration of problem solving and perception. A theory of design perception should combine a model of memory retrieval with a model of attention. This changes the emphasis of case-based reasoning from retrieval to recognition, and changes the emphasis of perception from classifying an input to re-representing it. Design perception differs from visual perception in terms of its input or base-representation (which could be a topological space rather than a measure space) and in terms of the ambiguities it must address (Design perception need not address perspective transformations, occlusion, or noise.) The principle characteristics of a model of design perception would be:

1. *Recognition is based primarily on relationships.* Rather than recognizing concepts from sets of features, it must be possible to recognize configurations based solely on relationships that may be implicit in the base representation.
2. *Processing is primarily global-to-local.* Rather than building up an interpretation by composing primitive features, decompose the input representation and try to recognize concepts or features at progressively finer granularity.
3. *Higher-level processes feed back to decomposition strategies.* Flexible design perception can be neither purely top-down nor purely bottom-up, but must

entail feedback from higher-level recognition processes and from problem-solving processes in order to provide structural and pragmatic context to focus attention.

4. *Primitives are decomposition strategies.* Instead of relying on features of the world to serve as primitive building blocks, invariants would be strategies for decomposing patterns. This is in opposition to, for example, the idea of recognition by components (Biederman, 1987).

5. *Abstract relationships are recognized first.* At any given granularity, recognize relationships in the form of the base representation first. Domain-specific features are range-restrictions on these relationships.

6. *Decomposition knowledge is encoded as constraints or preferences, rather than as plans.* Decomposition knowledge must serve multiple uses. It should support both local-to-global and global-to-local recognition processes, and for problem solving, it should support both synthesis and problem reduction.

If recognition is to be based first on relational structure, this raises the problem of inductive bias. Since there are virtually infinitely many relationships implicit in an input, which should be attended to? Part of the answer is that expectations from pragmatic and structural context must provide preferences between decompositions. However, to rely solely on context is to invite infinite regress. Another part of the answer may be to focus attention using gestalt laws of perceptual grouping such as grouping similar elements, grouping highly interconnected clusters and contiguous elements (Rock and Palmer, 1990).

Although originally postulated to account for visual perception, these laws also provide guidance in recognizing abstract relationships in a topological representation. While topological representations have no analog for proximity relationships, there could be other decomposition strategies, such as identifying parallel and serial connections of two-terminal devices, disconnecting graphs at cut nodes that form points of cleavage, and separating circuits or loops. In effect, this would promote configurational information from the role of disambiguation to a more predictive role.

To see how this could work, let's revisit the voltage divider example. Given a structural description of the circuit, the first step would be to group similar elements R1 and R2. The next step would be to identify their relationships as a serial connection of two-terminal devices. If the components were complex sub-circuits, then this abstract relationship could provide a structural context to further constrain their interpretation. In this case, however, the components are simple resistors and their serial connection is enough to retrieve the concept 'voltage divider' from which the constraint equation can be transferred to solve the original problem. In this way, recognition can be seen as a process of searching through the space of decompositions for representations that further constrain the recognition process.

4 An Experimental Implementation

To make this process more concrete, we have implemented an experimental algorithm for structure-based recognition. This algorithm takes as input a topological structure of components rather than a set of features. It re-represents that input structure in a higher-level vocabulary that may be more useful for reasoning or for retrieving specific cases. The algorithm has three main components: 1) A feature-driven recognition component that uses features of the input to predict a domain and possible context, 2) A decomposition process that takes a domain and an input graph and breaks the input into subgraphs, and 3) A graph re-writing component that matches subgraphs against predicted conceptual features and replaces low-level features with higher-level features. The algorithm iteratively re-represents the input until no further refinement can be made.

This process is supported by a conceptual representation with a number of unusual characteristics. First, domains are represented explicitly as categories that determine equivalence classes. Because there is no uniform vocabulary of primitive features with which an input must be specified, the level of abstraction at which features are considered to be 'the same' is determined by the domain's equivalence classes. For example, in conceptually breaking apart a circuit design, sometimes you want to group all impedances together, and sometimes you need to distinguish resistors, capacitors, and inductors. In matching and decomposing the input, we progressively abstract the domain.

Next, topological structure is itself represented as a domain. While designs are often implicitly represented as graphs of components, structural recognition makes it necessary to manipulate a representation with respect to progressively more abstract domains, up to and including the purely structural.

In addition, for any domain, there are two privileged equivalence classes: the 'null device' and the 'infinite device'. In an electrical circuit, for example, we typically consider wire to be a null device (except for transmission line effects, etc.) In the high frequency domain, capacitors may also belong to the null device class, while inductors become infinite devices. The null device permits us to treat all of its terminals as a single node, while an infinite device can simply be removed from the representation (in the context of a particular domain).

Figure 3 shows some example representations for the electrical circuit domain. Here, compound devices are represented as graphs of features (i.e., components) and the relationships between their terminals. Features associate a name with a type constraint to support matching. Relationships also support matching by denoting connections between terminals. These connections need not be direct; they may pass through an arbitrary number of null devices (e.g., wires.) Concepts also indicate their domain, parent type, and any remindings for which the concept is predictive. A reminding is another concept in the same domain for which the first concept may be a component feature.

An input to the program is a graph consisting of a set of features (instances of devices) and terminals. All relationships are implicitly represented by terminals shared between features. This input representation is generated automatically by a simple drafting program.

```
(defdomain electric-Circuit          (defconcept resistor
 :type graph                          :domain electric-circuit
 :equivalence-classes                 :type two-terminal-device)
    ((null-device wire)
     (resistor)                      (defconcept voltage-Divider
     (voltage-Source)))               :domain electric-circuit
                                      :type series
(defconcept two-terminal-device       :terminals (r1.1 r1.2 r2.2)
 :domain graph                        :features ((r1 resistor)
 :terminals (t1 t2)                              (r2 resistor)))
 :remindings (series parallel))
                                     (defconcept CommonEmitter
(defconcept series                    :domain active-circuit
 :domain graph                        :type transistor-amp-config
 :type three-terminal-device          :terminals (Q1.1 Q1.2 Q1.3)
 :terminals (d1.1 d1.2 d2.2)          :features ((Q1 transistor)
 :features                                       (Rc resistor)
    ((d1 two-terminal-device)                    (BN1 Bias-Net))
     (d2 two-terminal-device))        :relationships
 :relationships                          ((connected Q1.2 BN1.2)
    ((connected d1.2 d2.1)))             (connected VD1.1 Rc.1)
                                         (connected Rc.2 Q1.1)
                                         (connected Q1.3 BN1.3)))
```

Fig. 3. The Circuit Domain

The RECOGNIZE procedure works by first determining if any feature in the input graph predicts (via remindings) a configuration or concept that can be directly matched. If not, it decomposes the input to subgraphs and progressively abstracts the domain and features until a feature is predictive of some configuration or concept. It then re-represents the input in terms of the new concept and repeats the process until no further refinement is possible.

The DECOMPOSE procedure first determines the domain of the input based on its features. It then combines all terminals connected via components in the null device equivalence class for the current domain and eliminates 'infinite devices'. Next, it groups together features based on similarity (defined by equivalence classes), and lastly, it decomposes those groups based on contiguity (i.e., connectivity).

The RE-REPRESENT procedure takes a subgraph and re-writes it in terms of features that are relevant to the domain. It works bottom-up by predicting the context of the subgraph, matching to find a classification and bindings, discriminating to specialize the classification, and finally re-writing the subgraph of the input in terms of the new feature. Verifying a reminding and discriminating to a specialization employ a subgraph matching algorithm that uses constraint propagation and marker passing to minimize the amount of non-deterministic graph matching performed.

To illustrate the algorithm, consider again the problem of recognizing a voltage divider in a common-emitter transistor amplifier (Fig. 4):

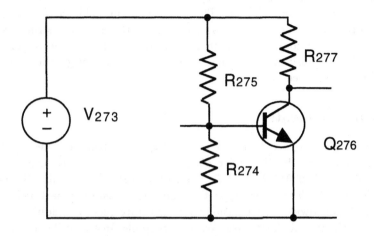

Fig. 4. A common emitter amplifier

With this input, the features do not immediately predict a configuration, so the procedure decomposes the circuit to the subgraphs ((Q276) (V273) (R274 R277 R275)). Q276 predicts transistor amplifier configuration, but by itself the transistor does not match anything. V274 is a two-terminal device so it predicts the concepts series and parallel configurations, but it too fails to match in isolation. The resistors predict series and parallel configurations and it succeeds in matching R275 to feature d1 of series and propagates the mapping d2 = R274 to complete the match. It then discriminates from series to voltage-divider and re-writes the circuit with R274 and R275 replaced by the new voltage divider. With this new feature, the process iterates and identifies the parallel combination of the voltage source and voltage divider as a bias network in the context of a transistor circuit. Given these higher-level features, it should be easier to retrieve cases from a long-term memory.

5 Conclusions

To retrieve cases based on structural properties requires treating retrieval as a recognition process. Classical pattern recognition methods fail us in two ways: Feature extraction is a top-down process that relies on a domain-dependent set of features and procedures for extracting them. Syntactic pattern recognition is a bottom-up parsing process that requires a pre-specified grammar and vocabulary of primitive tokens. We claim that an input can be decomposed and re-constituted in a more general way by reifying the domain-dependent expectations as explicit equivalence classes, by decomposing and identifying features with respect to an explicit domain and by allowing the recognition process to feed back upon failure so that it can progressively abstract the *domain* rather than directly abstract the features of the input. For pathological cases where only the configuration is predictive, the domain can be abstracted to the level of simple graph decompositions. This process is more akin to gestalt grouping than to the extraction of a fixed set of features. By using this structural recognition process in conjunction with the featural recognition processes of other case-retrieval algorithms, we can extend the range of design clichés and cases that can be retrieved.

Acknowledgments

This work was supported in part by the Defense Advanced Research Projects Agency, monitored by the Office of Naval Research under contracts N-00014-91-J-4092 and N-00014-91-J-4117. The Institute for the Learning Sciences was established in 1989 with the support of Andersen Consulting, part of The Arthur Andersen Worldwide Organization. The Institute receives additional support from Ameritech and North West Water Group plc, Institute Partners.

References

Bareiss, R.: Exemplar-based Knowledge Acquisition: A Unified Approach to Concept Representation, Classification, and Learning. San Diego: Academic Press (1989)

Berger, J.: Knowledge Acquisition and Design Support in a Medical Domain. In Case-Based Reasoning: Papers from the 1993 Workshop. Technical Report WS-93-01. Menlo Park, CA: AAAI Press (1993) 141–146

Biederman, I.: Recognition-by-Components: A Theory of Human Image Understanding. Psychological Review 94 (1987) 115–147

Borning, A.: The Programming Language Aspects of ThingLab, A Constraint-Oriented Simulation Laboratory. ACM Transactions on Programming Languages and Systems 3 (1981) 353–387

Fu, K.S.: Syntactic (Linguistic) Pattern Recognition. In K.S. Fu (Ed.), Digital Pattern Recognition, New York: Springer-Verlag (1980) 95–134

Hinrichs, T.R.: Problem Solving in Open Worlds: A case study in design. Hillsdale, NJ: Lawrence Erlbaum Associates (1992)

Kolodner, J.L.: Case-Based Reasoning. San Mateo, CA: Morgan Kaufman (1993)

Minsky, M., Papert. S.: Perceptrons. Cambridge, MA: MIT Press (1969)

Paynter, H.M.: Analysis and Design of Engineering Systems. Cambridge, MA: MIT Press (1961)

Ram, A. And Santamaria, J.M.: Continuous Case-Based Reasoning. In Case-Based Reasoning: Papers from the 1993 Workshop. Technical Report WS-93-01. Menlo Park, CA: AAAI Press (1993) 141–146

Rock, I. and Palmer, S.: The Legacy of Gestalt Psychology. Scientific American, December (1990) 84–90

Simon, H.A. and Gilmartin, K.: A simulation of memory for chess positions. Cognitive Psychology 5 (1973) 29–46

A Case Based Method for Solving Relatively Stable Dynamic Constraint Satisfaction Problems

Y. Huang and R. Miles

Faculty of Computer Studies and Mathematics
University of West England
Bristol BS16 1QY, United Kingdom
Email: huang@btc.uwe.ac.uk rgm@btc.uwe.ac.uk

Abstract This paper discusses some key issues in using case based methods to solve large constraint satisfaction problems. The problem addressed here is characterised by the large cardinality of the constraint tables. The aim is to reduce the amount of consistency checking carried out by database queries. We have addressed issues concerning the similarity measurement, adaptation/repair control in terms of conflict ordering strategies, the quality of the case base and issues concerning backtracking strategies. The results presented in this paper indicate an approach for improving case based methods in solving large constraint satisfaction problems.

1. Introduction

A general constraint satisfaction problem (CSP) involves a set of variables and a set of constraints. The goal is to assign each of these variables a value from its domain, subject to the constraints. Constraints can be represented by a set of tables, where each table contains the valid value combinations associated with the columns, the variables. A solution to the CSP is a full value assignment to the variables and the projection of the solution upon the columns of each of the constraint table is a member of that table. In many cases, constraints are not static in the sense that they may change from time to time. These CSPs are referred to as dynamic CSPs. Constraints which stay unchanged are static constraints, and those that change are dynamic. If only a small proportion of the constraints are expected to change and the number of valid value combinations which may change is also small, the CSPs may be referred to as relatively stable dynamic CSPs.

Constructive methods [Minton et al. 92, Dechter 90] for CSP solving use an approach in which a partial assignment to the solution is incrementally extended. These methods reason from scratch every time a new problem is presented. This is a drawback if these methods are used for solving relatively stable dynamic CSPs. It would be much more computationally economical to reason from a previous solution.

In contrast to the constructive CSP approach, [Minton et al. 92] discussed a repair based approach in solving CSP. The method is to generate, by a random mechanism, a set of complete yet inconsistent initial value assignments and then to start the repair process. The repairing method is based on the minimum conflicts heuristics. It is reported that the repair based method can outperform constructive methods in some problems, namely the n-queens problem and the Hubble Space Telescope scheduling problem. However, the issue of how the initial assignment should be made is not addressed by the repair based methods. For static CSPs, choosing a good initial assignment is equivalent to the original problem, but for dynamic CSPs, choosing a good initial assignment can be crucial to the efficiency of the repair algorithm.

Case based reasoning (CBR) "solves new problems by adapting solutions that were used to solve old problems" [Riesbeck & Schank 89]. An exemplar, which is a previous case that is included in the case base for later use, embodies domain knowledge which does not need to be justified by a reasoning process. In the context of CSP, the domain knowledge is the set of static constraints. When an exemplar is used, there is no need to worry about the static constraints unless some of the values in the case have been changed. The case base contains a set of representative value assignments, all of which satisfy the static constraints, but may violate the dynamic constraints. Given a set of dynamic constraints, solutions may be achieved more efficiently by repairing exemplars in the case base.

Integration CBR and constraint based reasoning (CBR-CSP) has been explored by CBR researchers. Hybrid CBR systems have been reviewed in [Hunt & Miles 94]. JULIA [Hinrichs 92] is a case based meal planning system which uses a constraint propagator to identify and subsequently resolve constraint violations. The constraint mechanisms keep track of the relationships between different component parts of the meal because they interact strongly with each other. In the CADSYN system [Maher & Zhang 93], design constraints are used to transform a previous design to fit the new requirements after conflicts are detected. In CADRE [Hua et al. 94], architectural and structural constraints are used to reduce the adaptation space. These systems either only deal with a relatively small number of constraints, or the extension of the constraints (the size of the constraint table) is also small. The performance issue is not addresses in these systems.

This paper investigates the problem of having the valid value combinations represented in large relational database tables. Checking consistency is carried out by undertaking a database query. To enhance performance, we wish to reduce the number of database queries. Conflict resolution becomes difficult because when a query returns a null response, we are not aware which variable assignment is inconsistent with the constraints. This can lead to the reissuing of unnecessary queries.

The work presented in this paper differs in a number of ways from other CBR/CSP systems

- Most CBR-CSP systems do not particularly address problems where the extensions of the constraints are large and are stored in databases, although the number of constraints involved may be potentially large. In our system, the complexity comes not only from the complicated inter-connections of the different constraints, but also, more importantly, from the large number of valid value combinations for each of the constraints.
- In problems dealt with in Minton's system, consistency checking of two value assignments is relatively easy. Also Minton's system uses a randomly generated value assignment, instead of a past successful case, as the start point of the repairing process. This is quite different from a case based method, which uses knowledge stored in the form of specific cases.
- In our experimental system, we make a distinction between checking constraints by way of database queries and by way of evaluating a formula. It is the database queries that cause the greatest concern. The aim is to reduce this kind of constraint check, even at the expense of increasing the number of other kinds of checking.

This paper presents some experiments on using the case based method to solve large relatively stable dynamic CSPs. In section 2, some key issues are addressed for using the case based method. Section 3 describes the backtracking method used in the repairing process. The overall view of the experimental system is given in section 4. Some experimental results are outlined in section 5. Section 6 concludes this paper.

2. Case Based Method

Restricting conflict propagation is the most important issue in the repair based and case based approaches. Because of the inter-connections between variables, a single change of value of one variable may trigger a lot of changes on other variables. Three issues are addressed in this paper to tackle this problem:

- Closeness between cases: measure of closeness determines which exemplar is going to be used in the adaptation process. This is the core issue of the indexing problem of CBR systems

[Kolodner 93]. In general CBR systems, a relevant exemplar needs to be retrieved to solve a new problem. For the CSP problem, we want to retrieve an exemplar which will greatly reduce the repairing complexity.

- Adaptation control in terms of conflicts ordering: once a exemplar is chosen, there will normally be a set of value assignments which are in conflict with the dynamic constraints. The system will have to resolve them, which may create more conflicts. The order by which conflicts are resolved can greatly affect the overall performance. This is the mirror image of the variable selection problem in the constructive methods of CSP solving [Tsang 93].

- Quality of the case base: even when we have a good closeness measure function, we still need a set of good exemplars. The construction of the set of exemplars, the case base, is an important issue in case based systems.

Another critical issue for reducing the computational complexity of the case based method is the backtracking strategy. Like the conventional constructive method, the repairing process implemented as reinstantiation can reach a point where no further reinstantiation is possible, in which case backtracking is necessary. Section 3 will describe a backtrack method in conjunction with the repairing process.

2.1 Closeness Measure and Conflict Propagation

Generally speaking, using a case similar to a current problem is better than using a less similar one. However, the most similar case is not necessarily the best exemplar with which to start the resolution. An exemplar is required, which causes the least conflict when its values are changed to those in the dynamic constraints. The most similar exemplar is not necessarily the one with least conflicts. The initial size of the conflict variable set does not determine the size of the derived conflict variable set. In order to retrieve the least conflicting exemplar, the attributes are weighted according to the constraint network topological information, which refers to the inter-connections between different variables in the constraint net, and conflict propagation potential of the attributes, which is calculated according to the information provided by the database tables representing constraints. The distance function is defined as,

$$Distance(Case_1, Case_2) = \Sigma \, W_{Att_i,Net} \, \Delta(Att_i(Case_1), Att_i(Case_2)) \qquad (formula\ 1)$$
$$where \quad W_{Att_i,Net} = \Sigma_j CP(Att_i, Att_j)(1 + W_{Att_j,Net-\{Att_k,k<j\}})$$
$$W_{Att_i,\{\{Att_i\}, \{\}\}} = 0$$
$$\Delta(a, b) = 1, \text{ if } a \neq b \text{ and } \Delta(a, b) = 0 \text{ otherwise}$$

Net is the constraint network consisting of a set of nodes and arcs, and *Net~{Att_k}* is a network derived from the *Net* by taking out the node *Att_k* and the arcs linked to it. *When all W_i are forced to be a constant, the distance is just a resemblance measure which tells how many different attribute values the two cases have. CP is the conflict propagation potential which is defined below. Figure 1 illustrates how weights are calculated.

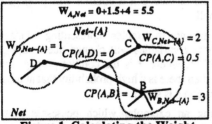
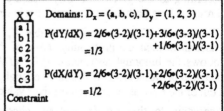

Figure 1. Calculating the Weight	Figure 2. Conflict Propagation Potential

The conflict propagation potential measures how likely a related variable Y will change its value to fit the constraints should the value of a variable X change. The information is contained in database tables involving X and Y. The conflict propagation potential of variable X is defined as the conditional probability

$$CP(X,Y) = P(dY/dX) = \Sigma_i w_i \ (n - k_i) \ / \ (n - 1) \qquad \text{(formula 2)}$$

where dX and dY mean that there have been changes to the values of variable X and Y respectively, n is the domain size of X, k_i is the size of ith group if we partition the table by the Y values and the weight w_i is, in normal cases, the frequency of the ith Y value, i.e. $k_i/\Sigma(k_i)$. The larger the value of the conflict propagation potential, the more important the variable is in calculating similarity. Figure 2 gives a simple example calculating the conflict propagation potentials.

It should be noticed that although computing a complete set of CP for each attribute can be expensive, it only needs to be calculated once since the constraint table is relatively stable. Alternatively, the influence information can be approximated by using the key reference information provided by the database schema or a E-R data model. Generally, there are four types of relationship between two attributes, i.e. one:one, one:many, many:one and many:many. Table 1 explains how the influence probabilities are approximated

Relationship (X:Y)	1:1	1:m	m:1	m:m
CP Approximation	1	1	0	0

Table 1: Conflict Propagation Potential Approximation

We will now use binary constraints to illustrate that if the exemplars are chosen carefully, the probability of conflict propagation along a long path (a domino effect) will be low, and the probability of only a small number of variables that will change due to the conflict propagating through direct connects in the constraint net (a fan-out effect) is high.

Let $X = \{X_i\}$ be the set of variables, and $T = \{C_i\}$ be the set of binary constraints. X_{i1}, X_{i2} are the two columns of C_i. The probability that changing X_{i2} will cause a change in X_{i1} is $P(dX_{i1}/ dX_{i2})$.

The domino effect: For any three variables, X_n, X_m, X_l through which a connection route is passing, if $d(X_n)$ causes $d(X_m)$, and $d(X_m)$ causes $d(X_l)$, then the probability that $d(X_n)$ causes $d(X_l)$ is $P(dX_m/dX_n) \cdot P(dX_l/dX_m)$, which is smaller than either of the component probabilities. If there are multiple intermediate variables X_{mi} $(i=1,s)$ between X_n, X_l, then

$$P(dX_l/dX_n) = 1 - \Pi_{i=1,s} \ (1 - P(dX_{mi}/dX_n) \ P(dX_l/dX_{mi})) \qquad \text{(formula 3)}$$
$$< 1 - [1 - max(P(dX_{mi}/dX_n)) \ max(P(dX_l/dX_{mi}))]^s,$$

which indicates that if s is small and the conflict propagation potential $max(P(dX_{mi}/dX_n))$ is small, then $P(dX_l/dX_n)$ will also be small. This shows that if an exemplar is chosen according to the given similarity measure, the chance that a conflict will propagate through a long path in the constraint net is small.

The fan-out effect: Assuming variable X_m appears in t tables representing t binary constraints, then the probability that s of these t variables will change due to $d(X_m)$ follows the binomial distribution $\binom{t}{s}P^s \ (1-P)^{t-s}$, where P is the conflict propagation potential of variable X_m. If P is small enough, then there is a high probability that at most s out of the t variables will change their values and s is small.

According to this simple analysis, choosing an exemplar which possesses close similarity on the variables with high conflict propagation potentials will reduce the repairing complexity.

2.2 Ordering of the Conflicts to be Resolved

The order by which conflicts are resolved can affect the efficiency. Heuristics described in [Minton et al. 92] only work for problems where conflicts between variables can be directly detected, such as the n-queen problem. For CSPs with constraints stored in database tables, a conflict may not be detected before database queries are issued

The following heuristics are used in the experimental system

- Choose the conflicts which do not involve queries to the data base table before choosing those that do. This is to reflect our overall goal of reducing the number of queries to the data base. Should there be any unresolvable conflicts, we will be able to detect them before we make any database query.

- Choose the conflicting variable with the maximum weight. These variables are most likely to propagate conflicts to other part of the network and therefore most likely to fail. This type of conflict should be resolved early in the process.

- When two variables have the same weight, we choose the one that corresponds to a small database table. The reason behind is that we want to commit heavy database queries as late as possible.

As a simple example, Figure 3 shows a problem with three variables, P, Q and R. A constraint C with two columns, P and Q, is represented as C(P, Q) in the figure. Given the exemplar and dynamic constraints, the conflict list has been evaluated. The variables P and R have changed values from p, r to p', r' respectively. The resolving process must confirm that:

c1: (p', q) is an valid value combination by sending a query to table C(P,Q), i.e. select P from C(P,Q) where P= p' and Q = q. If the query does not return a row, the condition Q = q in the query has to be dropped in order to bring back alternative values for the variable Q,

c2: (q, r') is valid by querying table C(Q, R).

Since both changing P and R involve database query and $W_R > W_P$, row (q, r') is less likely to be confirmed, so the correct order should be to confirm c2 and then to confirm c1. This will require three queries, while the reverse order will need five queries to reach the solution if we do not have a mechanism which can recognize a previous failed query.

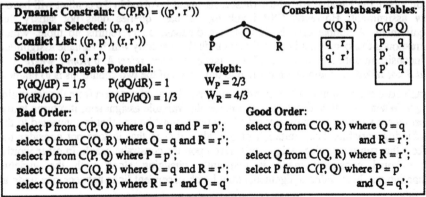

Figure 3. Ordering the Conflicts

2.3 Quality of the Case Base

The quality of the exemplar is important in reducing complexity. Limiting the potential of conflict value assignments incurred when part of the exemplar changes is important for choosing cases to be stored as exemplars. The topological information of the constraint net and the conflict propagation potential of each variable can also be used to judge how significantly different two cases are. Based upon the distance measure defined in section 2.1, a new case will be stored as an exemplar if it is significantly different from those in the case base on some critical features.

The quality of a case base can be defined as

$$\text{Quality(Casebase)} = \frac{1}{n} \Sigma \left(M(C_k, \text{Casebase}) \right) \qquad \text{(formula 4)}$$

where $M (C_k, \text{Casebase}) = \text{Min}(\text{Distance}(C_k, \text{Exemplar} \in \text{Casebase}))$ and $C_k \in R$, R is a randomly generated set of n new cases in the domain. The distance is defined by formula 1. The lower boundary of Quality is 0 an upper boundary is $nW_{Atti.Net}$. The smaller the value, the better the case base.

A distance threshold can be defined and the distances between exemplars in the case base should be greater than the threshold to avoid redundancy. A new case should be stored in the exemplar base if the minimum distance between the case and the exemplars in the case base is greater than the threshold to increase the quality of the case base. It is desirable that the exemplars cover some specific hyperplanes or subspaces characterized by important features.

3. Backtrack Strategies

Chronological backtracking, as a simple way of resolving conflicts and finding alternative solutions, has a number of disadvantages. Basically, the point being backtracked to is normally not the point that can resolve the conflict, therefore previous conflicts cannot be avoided by the chronological backtracking, and lots of computation may be wasted. In addition, useful value associations achieved by previous database queries and propagations are not reused after backtracking.

Dependency-directed backtracking [Stallman & Sussman 77] and backjumping [Dechter 90, Gashnig 79] are proposed to overcome these disadvantages. However, these methods also have their limitations when applied to CSP when the consistency check is in the form of a database query.

Dependency directed backtracking and backjumping methods require that the source of conflict be explicitly known to the algorithms. The search can then be backtracked to the point where the variable with the earliest assignment involved in the conflict will have a new assignment. However, CSP involving database queries does not satisfy this requirement. A simple case is that when a database query returns no tuple, which corresponds to a conflict, it is very difficult to find out exactly which variable assignment is inconsistent with the constraints. For instance, if query: *select A, B from T where A>a and B<b;* failed, it would be impossible to tell which of the two conditions is to blame.

Graph-base backjumping algorithms extract dependency information from the constraint graph. When a conflict is detected at a particular variable assignment, it returns to the most recent variable instantiation and this variable must be one that is connected to the conflicting variable. The limitation of this algorithm is that it does not consider the effects that run time value assignments have upon the constraint graph. In other words, the original constraint graph is constantly changing along with the variable instantiations. New value assignments may block dependent links between one node to another.

The backtracking control mechanism described in this section tries to enhance the above intelligent backtrack methods by using dynamic relevancy information contained in the constraint nets to rearrange the backtracking path. The idea is to avoid backtracking to a point which will not assist in the resolution of the original conflict and also to avoid unnecessary database queries.

The approach is to divide the set of constraints, and hence the set of queries, into independent blocks. Normally, two queries are related to each other because there are constraints relating to attributes contained in both queries. When issuing one, the query result will affect the other query. However, this interaction between queries can happen only when the related attributes are not instantiated.

In Figure 4, nodes represent variables, arcs represent constraints, and variables in a block relating to a single query are on the same horizontal level. Filled nodes represent instantiated variables and empty nodes represent non-instantiated ones. We can see that if two portions of the network are connected to each other only through instantiated variables, then no new value assignments within a portion will affect the other. The constant nature of the instantiated variables blocks the possible propagation between these two parts of the network. These two parts will be referred to as independent blocks. At the start of the instantiation process, very few independent blocks may exist, however, as query issuing and propagation proceeds, more independent blocks can be established.

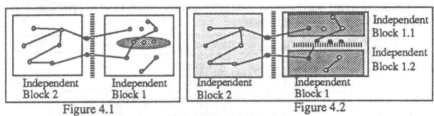

Figure 4.1   Figure 4.2

Figure 4. Independent Constraint Blocks

Within each independent block, queries are ordered according to some criteria. Once a query is issued and new value assignments are carried out, more independent blocks, which are sub-parts of the original independent block, may appear. Using Figure 4.1 as an example; suppose a query is issued which returns values for the three nodes as indicated, two more independent blocks have now been generated. This is shown in Figure 4.2; blocks 1.1 and 1.2 are children of the block 1.

A relevancy directed backjumping method is used in our experimental system. It requires that backtracking only be carried out within an independent block. For instance, if a conflict is found in the Independent-Block-1, we will not backtrack any value assignments appearing in the Independent-Block-2. If no further backtracking can be carried out within an independent block, the instantiation process will backtrack to its parent block. In other words, should there be an unresolvable conflict in either of the independent blocks, we will backtrack to the point where the boundary of independent blocks is generated. In the case described in Figure 4.2, if there is no consistent value assignment in the independent block 1.1, then we backtrack to the query associated with the interface variables as indicated.

The stack used to keep the instantiations resulting from queries and propagations is different from a conventional stack. It has a tree structure, reflecting the tree structure of the independent blocks. Figure 5 shows the corresponding stack organization for the example in Figure 4.2.

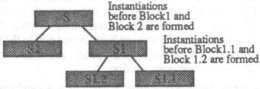

Figure 5. Stack Structure for Relevancy Directed Backtracking

In this way, not only the order of the instantiation, but also the relationship between the variables involved in the previous instantiations, are recorded. This stack structure allows the independence between the query ordering process and the backtracking process. It enables the system to reuse useful query results. Considering the example of the query ordering mechanism choosing to instantiate a variable *v1* in Block1, which helps to create Block1.1 and Block 1.2, and then to instantiate a variable *v2* in Block2. If it fails in trying to instantiate all variables in Block1.1, the backtracking mechanism will select an alternative value for *v1*. The relevancy directed backtracking method will still keep the state of S2 unchanged, while in an ordinary stack, the instantiation of *v2* would have been abandoned.

4. Experiments

Based upon the ideas presented in the previous sections, an experimental system has been built and a real world holiday packaging domain is used as an test problem. Figure 6 shows the architecture of the system.

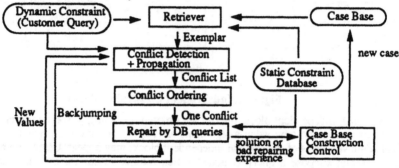

Figure 6. Case-based Approach to CSPs

Constructing a holiday tour package is a problem involving a large number of constraints stored in databases. A holiday can be seen as a structured object consisting of many components, e.g. accommodation, transportation, activities etc. There are four principal sources of constraints: firstly a set of static constraints specified in a logical model representing relationships amongst holiday components, secondly customer requirements, thirdly packaging constraints imposed by the holiday operator specifying the valid combination of holiday stocks, and finally the availability of the holiday stocks which are also constraining the set of possible holidays. Consistency checking is carried out in the form of database queries. Finding a solution can involve a large number of database queries resulting in a heavy load on the database server. If there are many concurrent customer requests being processed, the problem gets worse. Our key problem is to reduce the number of database queries needed for each customer query, thereby reducing the time to find a solution, i.e. a holiday that satisfies all of the constraints.

Results have been obtained using data supplied by a large holiday tour operator. This data contains a large number of constraints which are stored in databases and are of substantial size (there are 44 constraint tables, and some tables have over 1.2 million rows). Comparisons have been undertaken by comparing different characteristics of the case based methods. Two types of tests have been carried out. In the first type, the aim is to reduce the number of queries to obtain a solution and in the second to reduce the amount of searching when there is no solution.

The experimental results obtained compare different methods and strategies addressed in the previous sections. These results are based upon the recorded database queries corresponding to approximately two thousand customer queries. Figures in the tables are ratios between the number of data base queries issued using the contrasting methods.

The first experiment considered the effect of using conflict ordering on the number of database queries issued. In Table 2, c.o. and n.c.o. stand for conflict ordering and no conflict ordering. BJ and BT stand for relevancy directed backjumping and normal backtracking respectively. The Q_{xx} stands for the number of database queries made using method characterised by "xx". The results show that the number of queries is reduced by a factor of up to twenty if conflict ordering is used rather than having a random choice of conflict resolution.

Conflict ordering vs. No ordering (similarity measures (formula 1) are used)

Test type Methods	solution found	reported no solution	Additional condition
BJ	12.98	18.31	Using resemblance based simi-
BT	4.71	1.17	larity measure
BJ	15.03	21.38	Using similarity measure based
BT	4.09	1.18	on formula 1

Table 2: Average ratio: $Q_{n.c.o.}/Q_{c.o.}$

The second experiment contrasts the similarity measure based on formula 1 and the pure resemblance based measure where the weight is assigned to a constant 1. Table 3 shows that the number of queries is reduced by at least 50% when using a similarity comparison function which uses network topological information and conflict propagation measures rather than using a simple resemblance function.

Similarity based on formula 1 vs. Resemblance based similarity (BJ is used)

Test type Methods	solution found	reported no solution
c.o.	3.01	2.07
n.c.o.	2.67	2.14

Table 3: Average ratio $Q_{resemblance}/Q_{formula1}$

The third experiment was undertaken to show the effect of having case bases of different quality. For the holiday packaging example, we have $0 < $ Quality(Casebase) $ < 29$. In the experiment, we take two case bases CB1 and CB2 with Quality(CB1) = 9 and Quality(CB2) = 11.19. The results in table 4 show that the number of queries is reduced by 49% to 77% by having a better case base.

Using CB1 vs. CB2 (BJ and formula 1 based similarity measures are used)

Test type Methods	solution found	reported no solution
c.o.	1.98	4.43
n.c.o.	2.92	2.22

Table 4: Average ratio: Q_{CB2}/Q_{CB1}

Finally, search based on backjumping and backtracking are contrasted, table 5 shows that using the backjumping strategy, the number of queries is reduced by 70% up to 99% when the conflict ordering mechanism is enforced

Relevancy Directed Backjumping vs. Backtracking

Test type Methods	solution found	reported no solution
c.o.	3.64	93.26
n.c.o.	1.32	5.09

Table 5: Average ratio: $Q_{backtracking}/Q_{backjumping}$

5. Conclusion

A case based approach of solving large constraint satisfaction problems is presented in this paper. The application domain that we are considering is characterised by the large cardinality of the constraint tables which are relatively stable and our aim is to reduce the amount of consistency checking in terms of database queries. This paper has addressed issues concerning the similarity measurement, the quality of the case base, the conflict ordering problem and issues concerning backtracking strategies. Within the quality of the case base and when judging similarity between two cases, we include consideration of the ease of adaptation and repair. Assigning proper weights to attributes according to the constraint network topology and conflict propagation potential, enables the CBR system not only to select a reasonably good exemplar to start repairing, but also to order the conflicts to improve the repairing performance and to control the incremental construction of the case base. The experimental results show that the case based approach, taking into account the above issues, can offer improved performance through a significant reduction in the number of database queries.

The approach presented here can generally be applied to CSPs where a previous solution fits most of the present constraints. Most real world problem are relatively stable, consequences the CSPs involved are relatively stable. The method discussed in this paper is a general CSP solving method. However, for domains which involve drastic constraint changes and which do not have good exemplars, the method will not work well

References

Dechter R. (1990). Enhancement Schemes for Constraint Processing: Backjumping, Learning and Cutset Decomposition. *AI 41*, 273-312.

Freuder E. C. (1982). A sufficient condition of backtrack-free search, *J. ACM 29 (1) 24 - 32*.

Gaschnig J. (1979). Performance measurement and analysis of certain search algorithms, Tech. Rept. CMU-CS-79-124, Carnegie-mellon University, Pittsburgh, PA.

Haralick R. M.and Elliott G. L. (1980). Increasing tree search efficiency for constraint satisfaction problems, *AI 14, 263 - 313*.

Hinrichs T. R. (1992). *Problem solving in open worlds: A case study in design.* Northvale, NJ:Erlbaum.

Hua K., Smith I., Faltings B. (1994) Integrated Case-Based Building Design. *EWCBR 93, 246-51*.

Hunt J. and Miles R. (1994). Hybrid Case-Based Reasoning. *Knowledge Engineering Review, 9*.

Kolodner J. (1993). *Case Based Reasoning.* Morgan Kaufmann Publishers.

Maher M. L. and Zhang D. M. (1993). CADSYN: A Case-Based Design Process Model. *AI EDAM. 7(2), 97-110*, Academic Press.

Minton S., Johnston M. D., Philips A. B. and Laird P. (1992). Minimizing conflicts: a heuristic repair method for constraint satisfaction and scheduling problems. *AI 58, 161-205*.

Riesbeck C. K. & Schank R. C. (1989). *Inside Case-Based Reasoning.* Northvale, NJ:Erlbaum.

Stallman R. M. and Sussman G. J. (1977). Forward reasoning and dependency-directed backtracking in a system for computer-aided circuit analysis. *AI 9, 135-196*.

Tsang E. (1993). *Foundations of Constraint Satisfaction.* Academic Press.

Learning Strategies for Explanation Patterns: Basic Game Patterns with Application to Chess

Yaakov Kerner

Department of Mathematics and Computer Science
Bar-Ilan University
52900 Ramat-Gan Israel
kerner@bimacs.cs.biu.ac.il

Abstract. In this paper we describe game-independent strategies, capable of learning explanation patterns (XPs) for evaluation of any basic game pattern. A basic game pattern is defined as a minimal configuration of a small number of pieces and squares which describes only one salient game feature. Each basic pattern can be evaluated by a suitable XP. We have developed five game-independent strategies (replacement, specialization, generalization, deletion, and insertion) capable of learning XPs or parts of them. Learned XPs can direct players' attention to important analysis that might have been overlooked otherwise. These XPs can improve their understanding, evaluating and planning abilities. At present, the application is only in the domain of chess. The proposed strategies have been further developed into 21 specific chess strategies, which are incorporated in an intelligent educational chess system that is under development.

1 Introduction

Case-based reasoning (CBR) means adapting solutions of known cases to solve unknown cases. A potential domain is two-player board game playing (or in short, game playing) since human players use extensive knowledge in their playing. However, little research has been done on CBR in game playing in general and in evaluation of game positions in particular. Case-based playing programs have been constructed for the game of eight-puzzle by Bradtke & Lehnert (1988) and for the game of othello by Callan et al. (1991). A case-based program for evaluation of chess positions is described in Kerner (1994).

Most game playing programs do not make the evaluation process explicit. That is, there is a deficiency of evaluative comments concerning given positions. Current systems do not supply any detailed evaluative comments about the internal content of the given positions. An exception is the case-based system described in Kerner (1994), which evaluates chess positions.

In this paper we propose game-independent strategies capable of learning new explanation patterns (XPs) for evaluation of any basic game pattern. A basic game pattern is defined as a certain minimal configuration of a small number of pieces and squares which describes only one salient game feature. At present, the application is only in the domain of chess, which is known as an excellent test-bed for development of ML algorithms. Lessons learned in this research can be useful in other domains. Therefore, the learning strategies have been further developed into 21 specific chess strategies which are part of an intelligent educational chess system that is under development. At present, our model does not use search trees. Therefore, it is not useful to strong players. However, the proposed XPs should be helpful to weak and intermediate players wishing to improve their play in general and their understanding, evaluating and planning abilities in particular.

This paper is organized as follows: Section 2 addresses basic game patterns. Section 3 deals with evaluation of game positions. Section 4 presents XPs as suitable data structures for explanation and evaluation of basic game patterns. Section 5 describes learning strategies of XPs in previous case-based systems. Section 6 shows the strategies for the learning of XPs. Section 7 details an illustrative example. Section 8 summarizes the research and proposes future directions. In the Appendix we give a glossary of the main chess concepts mentioned in the paper.

2 Basic Game Patterns

It is known that human players use extensive knowledge in playing board games. A psychological study by de Groot (1965) shows that chess players base their evaluations of chess positions on patterns (typical positions) gained through experience. The player's patterns guide him either in deciding which move to play or rather which strategy to choose in a given position. Simon (1974) estimates that a master has a repertoire of about between 25,000 and 100,000 patterns.

In order to evaluate any game position, we have designed a game-independent evaluation tree that includes common positional features concerning evaluation of game positions. A tree containing a few hundred features concerning evaluation of chess patterns has been constructed with help of strong chess masters (see Kerner, 1994). Figure 1 presents the three highest levels of this tree that fit all board games.

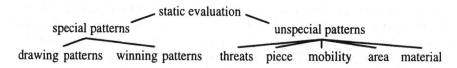

Fig. 1. The evaluation tree

Each feature at each level (except for the last level) is further divided into sub-features. Each leaf (a node at the last level) in this tree represents a unique basic pattern (examples in Kerner, 1994). Each basic pattern has two suitable explanation patterns (one for White and one for Black) that contain several important comments concerning the discussed pattern.

This tree is used primarily for two main tasks: (1) traversing the tree to find all basic patterns included in the position and (2) determining pattern similarity in the adaptation process proposed in Kerner (1994). The structure of the tree is analogical to the E-MOP, the memory structure introduced by Kolodner (1981). Our concepts resemble Kolodner's generalized information items and our basic patterns can be viewed as her "events."

3 Evaluation of Game Positions

Chess experts have established a set of evaluative terms for evaluation of chess positions. These general measures can be used for all two-person board positions. Table 1 presents a few qualitative measures and their meanings.

Table 1. A few evaluative terms and their meanings.

Evaluative terms	Meaning	Evaluative terms	Meaning
+−	White is winning	≈	approximately equal
±	White is better	∓	Black is slightly better
⩲	White is slightly better	∓	Black is better
=	equal	−+	Black is winning

Little research has been done concerning the task of giving more detailed evaluative comments for game positions. Most game-playing programs do not make the evaluation process explicit. They usually give as an evaluation only one evaluative term. More detailed explanations are given by the systems composed by Michie (1981), Berliner & Ackley (1982), Epstein (1989) and Pell (1994). However, they do not supply any detailed evaluative comments about the internal content of the given positions. An exception is the case-based system described in Kerner (1994) that gives detailed explanation concerning chess positions. In this paper we propose an extension that deals with evaluation of any two-player game position.

4 XPs as Explanations Structures for Two-Player Game Positions

In order to explain and evaluate basic game positions we have used XPs. Kass (1990, p. 9) regards XPs as "*variablized explanations that are stored in memory, and can be instantiated to explain new cases*". The XP-structure we use is similar to a certain type of an *intent explanation* proposed by Schank (1986). It contains the following slots: (1) a fact to be explained, (2) a belief about the fact, (3) a purpose implied by the fact, (4) a plan to achieve purpose, and (5) an action to take.

This XP structure has been applied to criminal sentencing (Schild & Kerner, 1993) and chess (Kerner, 1994). More general types of XPs have been applied in various story-understanding systems (e.g., Schank et al., 1994; Cox & Ram, 1994).

In game playing, the XP explains and evaluates a certain basic pattern of a game position from either White or Black viewpoint. Since we are concerned with the evaluation of a given position, we use an evaluation slot instead of an action slot. This slot contains one evaluative term (see Table 1).

Each basic pattern in the evaluation tree has two *general XPs* (one for White and one for Black). Five examples of chess XPs are presented in Fig. 6. For convenience we use some abbreviations: W for White, B for Black, and "e" for the endgame stage. Without loss of generality, our examples will be evaluated from White viewpoint, assuming that it is White turn to move.

The XP-structure seems to be a convenient data-structure for describing and explaining a specific basic pattern of a given position. However, each game position usually includes more than one basic pattern. Therefore, we have constructed a more complex structure called Multiple eXplanation Pattern (MXP) to explain an entire game position (Kerner, 1994). The learning of MXPs is described in general in Kerner (1994). In this paper we detail the learning of XPs.

5 Learning of XPs in Previous Case-Based Systems

The learning of XPs enable improving the correctness, quality and efficiency of an explanation system. Such a system becomes more adequate by deriving better and more creative explanations than those supplied with fewer explanations. In the domain of case-based learning of XPs we find two prominent systems: SWALE (Kass et al., 1986; Kass, 1990) and AQUA (Ram, 1993). These systems are based on Schank's theory of XPs (Schank, 1986). SWALE and AQUA construct new creative explanation patterns by adapting existing explanation patterns. However, these systems are different in their basic assumption and learning methods.

On the one hand, Kass's theory assumes that we work in a well-known domain and that past cases are well understood and can be used for future CBR. SWALE constructs new XPs by slightly altering existing XPs. It uses three kinds of strategies: generalize, replace and specify. On the other hand, Ram's theory assumes that we work in a novel domain. Past cases are unavailable or incorrect or incompletely understood or wrongly indexed in the case library. Ram proposes an incremental learning theory based on the revision of previously existing case knowledge. AQUA constructs new XPs by answering questions that underlay the creation, verification and learning of explanation.

The evaluation of game positions in general and of chess positions in particular, has been a well-investigated domain for a long time. Game-playing masters and books can serve as useful case libraries. Therefore, we adopt Kass's theory as a basis for our learning theory.

6 Learning Strategies in our Model

We have developed an extended theory of learning strategies for evaluation of game positions. It contains five kinds of game-independent strategies capable of learning XPs or parts of them as follows: replacement, specialization, generalization, deletion, and insertion. The first three strategies resemble Kass and Ram's strategies. The last two strategies are new.

6.1 Learning Strategies for Replacing Slot Fillers of XPs

These strategies are responsible for substitution of slot fillers. Each strategy substitutes only one slot filler in a given XP. Such a substitution causes a small change to an XP. The motivation is to fix the retrieved XP in order to better explain the given pattern. In principle, these strategies can operate on every slot filler included in the XP-structure. In our chess application, the belief and evaluation slot fillers cannot be changed since they are dependent on the fact slot filler.

6.1.1 Replacing a Slot Filler using the Appropriate Slot Hierarchy:
These strategies replace a certain slot filler using the specific slot's hierarchy. In chess we have only three specific strategies. Strategies 1-3 replace the fact, purpose, and plan slot fillers using the fact hierarchy (the evaluation tree), the purpose hierarchy (upper part of **Fig. 2**), and the plan hierarchy (lower part of **Fig. 2**), respectively. The belief and evaluation slot fillers cannot be replaced independently because of the reasons mentioned previously.

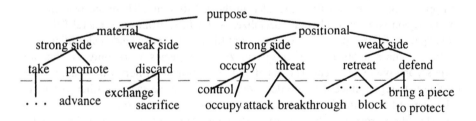

Fig. 2. A partial description of the purpose and plan hierarchies

6.1.2 Replacing a Slot Filler using the Stereotypical-Agent Links:
These strategies replace a certain slot filler using the game-independent agent link that replace either one certain type of a game-piece by another type of a game-piece or a White piece by the same Black piece. In our chess application we have two strategies, strategies 4 and 5 that replace the fact and plan slot fillers, respectively, using the chess stereotypical-agent links, which are described in **Fig. 3**. In addition to the belief and evaluation slot fillers, we also cannot change the purpose slot filler, since it does not contain any piece but rather describes a general purpose.

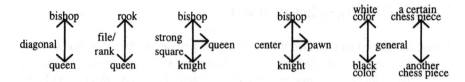

Fig. 3. The stereotypical-agent links

6.1.3 Replacing a Slot Filler using the Stereotypical-Area Links:

These strategies replace a certain slot filler using the game-independent area link that replace one certain type of a game-area by another type of a game-area that can play the same function. In our chess application we have only two strategies for the same reasons mentioned above. Strategies 6 and 7 replace the fact and plan slot fillers, respectively, using the stereotypical-area links that are described in **Fig. 4**.

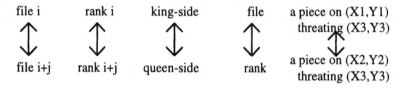

Fig. 4. The stereotypical-area links

6.2 Learning Strategies for Specializing Slot Fillers of XPs

These strategies specialize a certain slot filler of an XP. In principle, these strategies can operate on every slot filler included in the XP-structure. There are two kinds of specialization strategies: (1) that specializes a slot filler from one general filler to a more specific filler and (2) that joins two slot fillers into one extended slot filler.

In our chess application, both specialization strategies work only on the fact, purpose, and plan slot fillers. The belief and evaluation slot fillers are not appropriate for these strategies since they are dependent entirely on the fact slot filler. Strategies 8-10, derived from the first specialization strategy, specialize the fact, purpose and plan slot fillers, respectively, using the stereotypical-specification links described in **Fig. 5**. Strategies 11-13, derived from the second specialization strategy, specialize the fact, purpose and plan slot fillers, respectively, using two slot fillers into one extended slot filler.

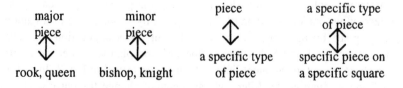

Fig. 5. The stereotypical-specification links

6.3 Learning Strategies for Generalizing XPs

These strategies generalize a certain slot filler of XP. In principle, they can operate on every slot filler included in the XP-structure. These strategies are opposite to the specialization strategies mentioned above. That is, there are two kinds of generalization strategies: (1) that generalizes a slot filler from one specific filler to a more general filler and (2) that deletes one problematic slot filler from two slot fillers. By a problematic value we mean a filler that is not valid for the discussed position.

In our application, both strategies work on the fact, purpose, and plan slot fillers. The belief and evaluation slot fillers are not appropriate for these strategies since they are dependent entirely on the fact slot filler. Strategies 14-16, derived from the first generalization strategy, generalize the fact, purpose and plan slot fillers, respectively, using the stereotypical-specification links described in **Fig. 5**. Strategies 17-19, derived from the second generalization strategy, generalize the fact, purpose, and plan slot fillers, respectively, by deleting one of two or more slot fillers.

6.4 Deletion and Insertion Strategies of XPs

The deletion strategy deletes a problematic XP and its related data from its data-base. The activation of this strategy is dependent upon the expert. In addition, the system can ask the expert for deletion of XPs that are used rather seldom. In contrast there is an insertion strategy enabling an insertion of a new XP and its related data to either DB1 or DB2. For instance, it can be performed in case the system has not satisfied the expert. In our application, these strategies are strategies 20 and 21.

7 Example

In this example, we illustrate an evaluation of a certain basic chess pattern "a backward pawn (a7) for Black on the closed a-file in the endgame stage" (call it *bp*) that is included in **Position 1**. Out task is to learn XPs that explain bp from White viewpoint. DB1 is a data-base of *general XPs* (XPs for the basic patterns) and *DB2* is a data-base of positions that include representative basic patterns and their XPs. All XPs involved in the evaluation of bp are presented in **Fig. 6**. A few important concepts mentioned in these XPs are defined in a chess glossary in the Appendix.

Here, the learning is as follows: XP-1 is retrieved from DB1 since its fact slot filler is bp. Applying a specialization strategy on it, we get XP-2, which is found as valid for **Position 1**. Thus, XP-2 is proposed as an explanation for bp. **Position 2** and its XP (XP-3) are retrieved from DB2 since the fact slot filler of XP-3 is considered as a near neighbor to bp in the evaluation tree. XP-4 is created from XP-3 after replacing its fact slot filler with bp. XP-4 is found valid for **Position 1** and it is also proposed as an explanation for bp. XP-5's slot fillers are the same as those of XP-2 and XP-4 except for the plan slot filler. By using a specialization strategy on these plan slot fillers we get a new elaborated plan slot filler.

By utilizing simple limited searching, we ensure that the new plan can be theoretically made on Position 1. We find a way to switch the White c5-rook to the a-file (a5) and to switch the White c2-rook to the 7th rank (c7). Due to the approval of XP-5 by our chess expert, Position 1, its bp and its XP (XP-5) are stored in DB2.

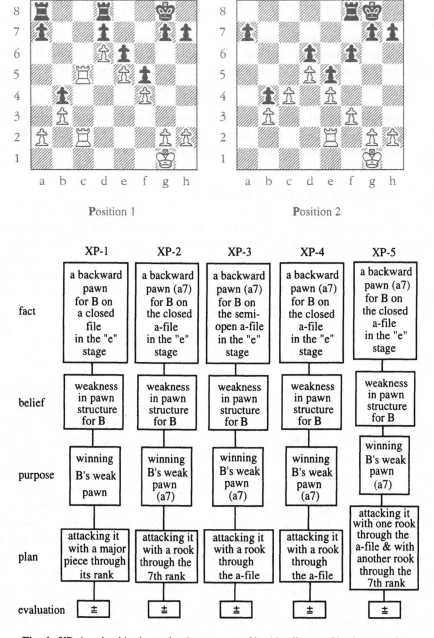

Fig. 6. XPs involved in the evaluation process of bp (the discussed basic pattern)

8 Summary and Future Work

We have developed an initial framework of learning strategies of explanation patterns for evaluation of basic game patterns. Our application, is to the best of our knowledge, the first application of case-based learning of XPs for game positions. These learning strategies seem to enable our system to supply better and more creative explanations for game positions than other existing computer game-playing systems. Experiments in the near future are planned to evaluate and improve the performance of our explanation system over learning new XPs.

In chess, profound understanding has been shown to be inefficient without playing and deep searching. Therefore, to strengthen our model there is a need to implement playing modules with searching capability. In addition to this, there is a need to implement specific learning strategies for other games. Case-based planning is another important issue we have to deal with more deeply using game tree search. The learning of multiple explanation patterns (MXPs) for evaluation of any game position remains for future work.

Acknowledgments

Thanks to Sean Engelson, Avraham Norin, Shlomit Zeiger, and anonymous referees for valuable comments and suggestions.

References

Berliner, H. J. & Ackley, D. H. (1982). The QBKG System: Generating Explanations from a Non-Discrete Knowledge Representation. In *Proceedings of the National Conference on Artificial Intelligence* (pp. 213-216). AAAI Press.

Bradtke, S. & Lehnert, W. G. (1988). Some Experiments With Case-Based Search. In *Proceedings of the Seventh National Conference on Artificial Intelligence* (pp. 133-138). San Mateo: Morgan Kaufmann.

Callan, J. P., Fawcett, T. E. & Rissland, E. L. (1991). Adaptive Case-Based Reasoning. In *Proceedings of a Workshop on CBR* (pp. 179-190). San Mateo: Morgan Kaufman.

Cox, M. T. & Ram, A. (1994). Interacting Learning-Goals: Treating Learning as a Planning Task. To appear in Keane, M.; Haton J. P.; and Manago M. (Eds.), *Topics in Case-Based Reasoning - EWCBR'94*, Lecture Notes in Artificial Intelligence. Berlin: Springer-Verlag.

de Groot, A. D. (1965). *Thought and Choice*. Mouton, The Hague.

Epstein, S. (1989). The Intelligent Novice - Learning to Play Better. In D. N. L. Levy & D. F. Beal (Eds.), *Heuristic Programming in Artificial Intelligence - The First Computer Olympiad*. Ellis Horwood.

Kass, A. M., Leake, D. & Owens, C. (1986). *SWALE: A Program that Explains*. In Schank, R.C. (Ed.) (1986). *Explanation Patterns: Understanding Mechanically and Creatively*. Hillsdale, NJ: Lawrence Erlbaum Associates, pp. 232-254.

Kass, A. M. (1990). *Developing Creative Hypotheses by Adapting Explanations.* Technical Report #6, p. 9. Institute for the Learning Sciences, Northwestern University, U.S.A.

Kerner, Y. (1994). Case-Based Evaluation in Computer Chess. In *Proceedings of the Second European Workshop on Case-Based Reasoning* (pp. 95-103). Paris: AcknoSoft Press. Extended paper to appear in Keane, M.; Haton J. P.; and Manago M. (Eds.), *Topics in Case-Based Reasoning - EWCBR'94*, Lecture Notes in Artificial Intelligence. Berlin: Springer-Verlag, 1995.

Kolodner, J. L. (1981). Organization and Retrieval in a Conceptual Memory for Events or Con54, Where are You? In *Proceedings of the Seventh International Joint Conference on Artificial Intelligence* (pp. 227-233). Los Altos: William Kaufmann.

Michie, D. (1981). A Theory of Evaluative Comments in Chess with a Note on Minimaxing. *The Computer Journal, Vol. 24, No. 3,* 278-286.

Pell, B. (1994). A Strategic Metagame Player for General Chess-Like Game. In *Proceedings of the Twelfth National Conference on Artificial Intelligence* (pp. 1378-1385). Seattle: AAAI Press/The MIT Press.

Ram, A. (1993). Indexing, Elaboration and Refinement: Incremental of Explanatory Cases. *Machine Learning 10 (3),* 201-248.

Schank, R.C. (Ed.) (1986). *Explanation Patterns: Understanding Mechanically and Creatively.* Hillsdale, NJ: Lawrence Erlbaum Associates.

Schank, R.C., Kass A. & Riesbeck C. K. (Eds.) (1994). *Inside Case-Based Explanation.* Hillsdale, NJ: Lawrence Erlbaum Associates.

Schild, U. J. & Kerner, Y. (1993). Multiple Explanation Patterns. In *Proceedings of the First European Workshop on Case-Based Reasoning,* Vol. II (pp. 379-384). Kaiserslautern: Germany. Extended paper in Wess, S.; Althoff, K-D.; and Richter, M. M. (Eds.), *Topics in Case-Based Reasoning - EWCBR'93*, Lecture Notes in Artificial Intelligence 837 (pp. 353-364). Berlin: Springer-Verlag, 1994.

Shannon, C. E. (1950). Programming a Computer for Playing Chess. *Philosophical Magazine, Vol. 41(7),* 256-277.

Simon, H. A. (1974). How Big is a Chunk? *Science No. 183,* 482-488.

Appendix

Chess Glossary

Backward pawn: A pawn that has been left behind by neighboring pawns of its own color and can no longer be supported by them.

Closed file: A file with pawns of both colors.

Endgame: The last and deciding stage of the chess game. In this stage the position becomes simplified and usually contains a relatively small number of pieces.

Major piece: A rook or a queen.

Minor piece: A bishop or a knight.

Open file: A file without pawns.

Semi-closed file: A file with pawn/s of only one's own color.

Semi-open file: A file with pawn/s of only the opponent's color.

A Memory-Based Hierarchical Planner

Deepak Khemani   P.V.S.R.Bhanu Prasad

Department of Computer Science and Engineering
Indian Institute of Technology, Madras
Madras - 600036
India
khemani@iitm.ernet.in   bhanu@iitm.ernet.in

Abstract. This paper describes a memory-based planning system. The memory constitutes a collection of generalized plans, which we call *skeletons*. Each skeleton embodies a style, and organizes planning knowledge in a packaging hierarchy. Traversal of this hierarchy results in hierarchical plan development, and the process is guided by a secondary memory which organizes the properties of ingredients into an inheritance hierarchy. A simple indexing hierarchy allows access to each skeleton, which is quite distinct and captures a whole class of plans in that style. Stepwise refinement of the plan is accompanied by modifications which add ingredient specific steps on the way. A system has been implemented in the culinary domain.

1 Introduction

A plan is a specific sequence of actions whose execution results in the achievement of some desired goal. The process of finding this sequence is the task of planning. Classical planning techniques [12, 16, 18] strive to do this by projecting into the future; essentially a trial and error process to explore various sequences with the aim of picking the winner. Memory (or knowledge) based techniques [4, 5, 6, 7, 9, 10] on the other hand, look into the past to reconstruct those sequences which worked before. The role of knowledge in the process has increased manifold; beginning with heuristic functions to guide search, present day systems, for example CHEF[4], rely entirely on knowledge, eschewing search.

Much of the progress in memory-based reasoning in fact came about due to work in (natural language) understanding. The key idea behind the development of knowledge structures [2, 13, 17] was that internal conceptual structures help in linking up the incoming sequences into meaningful patterns. And now in planning we endeavor to deploy the same knowledge structures to generate meaningful sequences of actions.

The main difficulty that any search based technique faces is the combinatorial explosion of possibilities. This happens specially if one tries constructing plans by trying out combinations of primitive actions, as was done in STRIPS[3]. One way to beat the combinatorial explosion, as humans tend to do, is to successively break up the goal into smaller sub-goals. This process of successive refinement indeed reveals a hierarchical structure in plans. Systems like NOAH[12], NON-LIN[17], and O-PLAN[1] aim at exploiting this by hierarchically refining goals in a space of partial plans. There are still choices to be made however, and if one is to avoid expensive backtracking then one must have adequate knowledge in the memory to facilitate the right choices. In this paper we present a hierarchical planner which essentially is memory-based. The task of plan generation will become more simpler if some of the intermediate states are generated from memory instead of a trial and error process. We explore the design of such a planner. This system is an attempt in bridging the gap between the classical and case-based approaches by keeping up the flavors of both the approaches. The system has been implemented in the domain of cooking vegetables in the South-Indian style. The motivation for taking up the culinary domain stems mainly from its wide access and its similarity to more complex domains, such as circuit construction [4]. The cooking domain is well represented in case-based reasoning community [4, 7].

Meanwhile the work in understanding [2, 10] postulated that knowledge in the memory is organized in various systems of hierarchies. The abstraction hierarchy links generalization to their specializations, with inheritance mechanisms to retrieve common features. The packaging hierarchies allow smaller units to be assembled into meaningful structures, and provide the basic structure needed for hierarchical decomposition. Indexing mechanisms aim at quick and relevant retrieval, and mostly employ discrimination networks to organize the knowledge into memory. In this paper we focus mainly on the packaging hierarchy; that which organizes our planning knowledge. The hierarchical plan expansion then follows directly from the organization. The packaging hierarchy of actions is aided by an inheritance hierarchy of properties of objects, in our case vegetables. Thus while the expansion of a higher level node using the packaging links unfolds a plan, the ingredient specific choices are dictated by the properties of the objects stored in an inheritance hierarchy. The two systems work in tandem to produce the plan.

Case-based reasoning is an enterprise [10] which attempts to store and reuse cases, which are specific sequence of units (events/operators). Cases are packaged chunks of specific experience, and case-based reasoners basically address the problem of capitalizing on past experience. We believe that, specially in structured domains, such experience as acquired by cases should get assimilated into more general memory structures. This is in accordance with Schank's notion [14] of how people may be acquiring scripts. This paper is (yet another) exploration of how such knowledge could be structured in the memory. We believe that insights obtained by such experiments will go a long way in designing systems that really learn from experience, extracting *lessons* [8] instead of just hoping to reuse that particular case. In some sense, such a learning system will understand the successful cases and internalize them. Cases will still exists as exemplars and existential evidence, and also as exceptions, surrounding the abstracted structures.

Before we go on to describing our system, one observation about our focus on the packaging hierarchy. This has been dictated by our planning viewpoint, since we believe that the planning knowledge itself should be organized in a packaging hierarchy. But a learning system may well emphasize others. For example in the domain of cooking, acquiring a new method of, say, chopping onions can only be done usefully with the aid of a finely tuned indexing and abstraction hierarchy. We now look at the operationalization of planning knowledge in our system for cooking South-Indian vegetables.

2 Memory Organization

The basic assumption is that there exist distinct and identifiable styles of cooking, each one being accessed via the root node of a packaging hierarchy. The root node itself is reached by a simple indexing mechanism. Unfolding the packaging hierarchy results in a hierarchical plan expansion, and is guided by knowledge of ingredients used to tailor the actions for the given ingredients. Plan generation, therefore, essentially uses two separate memories: The memory of properties and the memory of skeletons.

2.1 The Memory of Properties

The memory of properties is the system's knowledge of the ingredients, in our case, the vegetables. An ingredient is represented by the steps it introduces into the recipe when used. The memory of properties is organized using an abstraction hierarchy as shown in Figure 1. At the top of the hierarchy are more generalized properties. The names of the vegetables occupy the bottom most positions in the hierarchy. An ingredient inherits properties from all its ancestors. Associated with each property is a modification which adds relevant steps during plan expansion. For example, cluster-beans would be cut into small pieces because they are elongated having a large size. At the same time they will be boiled because they are legumes needing pre-boiling. Thus in this model, a vegetable is represented as a specific collection of properties needed for tuning the recipes.

2.2 The Memory of Skeletons

The memory of skeletons is the important part of the system's knowledge. It recognizes the existence of different styles like *frying, baking* etc which have some characteristic action patterns. For example, the recipe for fried *baingan* (brinjal) is very different from *baingan bharta*, but quite close to fried potato. For each style we build a skeleton. Such skeletons could be used to define regional and personal styles too. For example the well known *Chettinad* style of South-Indian cooking uniformly uses hot spices, while similar recipes in the North may be relatively bland. Each skeleton thus embodies a generic recipe.

This memory organizes both the operators and the modification knowledge and captures the various generic recipes. This memory consists of a set of skeletons of plan operators. Each corresponding to a class of plans. The skeleton

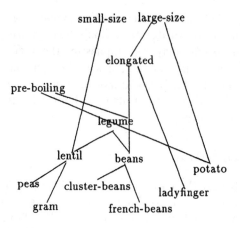

Figure 1: A part of the memory of properties.

itself is made up of the hierarchically organized primitive operators. These operators will be present in any plan of that class. Basically a skeleton consists of a highest level plan operator (like *roast, curry-form*), which is broken down into the sequence of plan operators that is pointed to by the packaging link of that operator. Again each of these operators in this sequence may be broken down as above until all the operators are of executable level (e-level) operators. Let us call this sequence of operators as the next-level plan of that operator. The packaging link of an operator points to the sequence of plan operators that will be present (in the same order, but not necessarily consecutive) in all the expansions of that operator.

The modification knowledge in our system is distributed over plan operators. This knowledge is in the form of a set of if-then-else rules. Each property of the ingredient may cause addition of new steps during expansion at that level. For example, a modification rule associated with *prepare-pieces* is: If the vegetable has *tough-skin* then remove the skin before chopping.

The modification rules are indexed by the properties of the ingredients. A modification rule is inherited by all the elements that are the specializations of the indexed node in the abstraction memory. Modification rules only add new operators. Since the new operators may be added at any level, an operator introduced at a higher level will be also expanded, and may itself be subject to further modifications. Figure 2 corresponds to the generated hierarchical plan up to the second last level for the fry of potatos. The underlined steps are specific to the ingredients. The arcs are used to connect the operators and their corresponding modified next-level plans.

In addition the modification knowledge of ground level operators assigns values to the variables. For example, time of cooking, and size of chopped pieces.

The root node of a skeleton represents its "recipe style". Since each skeleton corresponds to a class of plans, the number of skeletons is much smaller than

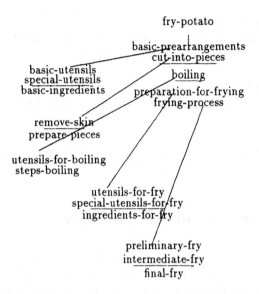

Figure 2: The plan for frying potatos.

the number of specific recipes. We thus expect a simple indexing mechanism to work, specially since each skeleton going to be quite distinct. Once a required skeleton is retrieved, a plan is created by stepwise expansion and modification.

3   The Planning Algorithm

A plan is created in a hierarchical fashion using the appropriate skeleton. Initially the root node is selected and the next-level plan is generated using its packaging link. The modification rules of the root node are applied (if necessary) on this next-level plan. A similar process is carried out with each of the operators in this plan. This is repeated until the ground level plan is generated. The algorithm is described below.

(1). /* INITIALIZATION */
For each level i in the hierarchy, create a list plan-list-i to store the operator identifiers at that level. Initialize each list to NULL.

(2). /* SKELETON SELECTION */
Select the operator representing the root node of the required plan skeleton. Add it to plan-list-0. Set $i \leftarrow 0$.

(3). /* EXPANSION */
For each element in plan-list-i generate the next-level plan elements and add them to plan-list-(i+1).

(4). /* MODIFICATION */

Apply each applicable modification rule associated with *i* level operators. Insert the *(i+1)* level elements in the indicated position.

(5). /* DESCENT */

Set *i* ← *i*+1. If all the operators are not e-level, go to (3). Else output the e-level plan.

An e-level plan generated by the system is given in the Appendix.

4 Comparison and Concluding Remarks

The hierarchical plan expansion in our system is similar to the one in AB-STRIPS[11]. An important difference between the utilization of skeletons in our system and generating plans from scratch in classical systems like NONLIN[16] is that in skeletons there already exists a partial plan. Because of this, generating a plan using skeletons is less expensive than solving from scratch. Unlike NON-LIN, our system has no backtracking facilities for undoing bad plan construction decisions. It is assumed that the system will have enough knowledge to make all choices. It may be observed that, in some sense, the major choices have already been made as soon as a skeleton is chosen, and only ingredient specific tuning remains.

Though both operate in the culinary domain, our system is very different from CHEF[4]. CHEF essentially stores and retrieves entire plans indexing them on styles, ingredients, and possible failures. A retrieved case is modified for current use. In our case the planning steps are distributed in the hierarchy and a recipe gets assembled relatively speaking from scratch. The packaging hierarchy attempts to capture the principles behind the recipes, which are then influenced by ingredient specific modification rules. Indexing is done only on styles.

Some case-based systems such as JULIA[7], MEDIATOR[15], and CELIA[9] organized the cases in terms of sub-goals. These systems store all the subplans corresponding to all the created cases. There is also some similarity between our approach and the one reported in PRIAR[5]: In PRIAR, the *partially reduced HTN*, that is created from a past suitable plan is used as the base for creating the final plan. Our system use a skeleton for this purpose. In addition, PRIAR has the capability of backtracking. Our system on the other hand employs a secondary memory of properties to guide the expansion along desired paths.

Some problems which case-based reasoning in general is likely to face is the difficulty of *pre-indexing* [6] and the effect on efficiency of indiscriminate storage of created plans. We hope to address both the issues by laying more stress on structures storing generalized knowledge. However in doing so, we reintroduce the problem of *selective learning*. For a memory-based system to be more realistic, it needs to learn new modification rules. We intend to incorporate a selective learning mechanism which will learn new modification rules for new ingredients at a suitable level, rather than storing all the created plans.

5   References

[1] K. Currie, A. Tate: O-Plan-Control in the Open Planner Architecture. In *BCS Expert Systems Conference*. Cambridge: Cambridge University Press, 1985.

[2] M. Dyer: *In-depth Understanding*. Cambridge MA: MIT Press, 1983.

[3] R.E. Fikes, N.J. Nilsson: Strips: A New Approach to the Application of Theorem Proving to Problem Solving. *Artificial Intelligence*, Vol. 2, pp. 189-208, 1971.

[4] K.J. Hammond: *Case-Based Planning: Viewing planning as a memory task*. Academic Press, Inc, New York, 1989.

[5] S. Kambhampati, A Theory of Plan Modification. In *Proceedings of AAAI*, 1990.

[6] B.P. Kettler, J.A. Hendler, W.A. Andersen, M.P. Evett: Massively Parallel Support for Case-Based Planning. In *IEEE EXPERT*, February, 1994.

[7] J. Kolodner: Capitalizing on Failure Through Case-Based Inference. In *Proceedings of the Ninth Annual Conference of the Cognitive Science Society*, Lawrence Erlbaum Associates, Publishers, New Jersy, 1987.

[8] J. Kolodner: *Case-Based Reasoning*. Morgan Kaufmann, San Mateo, CA, 1993.

[9] M. Redmond: Distributed Cases for Case-Based Reasoning; Facilitating Use of Multiple Cases. In *Proceedings of AAAI*, 1990.

[10] C.K. Riesbeck, R.C. Schank: *Inside Case-Based Reasoning*, Lawrence Erlbaum Associates, Publishers, New Jersy, 1989.

[11] E.D. Sacerdoti: Planning in a Hierarchy of Abstraction Spaces, *Artificial Intelligence*, 5(2), pp. 115-135, 1974.

[12] E.D. Sacerdoti: *A Structure for Plans and Behavior*. Amsterdam: Elsevier-North Holland, 1977.

[13] R.C. Schank, R.P. Abelson: *Scripts, Plans, Goals, and Understanding*. Lawrence Erlbaum Associates, Publishers, New Jersy, 1977.

[14] R.C. Schank: *Dynamic Memory: A Theory of Learning in Computers and People*. Cambridge University pres, 1982.

[15] R.L.Jr. Simpson: *A Computer Model of Case-Based Reasoning in Problem Solving*. Ph.D. thesis, Georgia Institute of Technology, Atlanta, GA, USA, 1985.

[16] A. Tate: *Project Planning Using a Hierarchic Non-linear Planner*, Research Report No. 25, Department of Artificial Intelligence, University of Edinburgh, U.K., 1975.

[17] R. Wilensky: *Planning and Understanding: A Computational Approach to Human Reasoning*. Addision-Wesley Publishing Company, Reading, Massachusetts, 1983.

[18] D.E. Wilkins: *Practical Planning-Extending the Classical AI Planning Paradigm*. Morgan Kaufmann Publishers, San Mateo, California, 1988.

Appendix

This program is for frying a vegetable.

The following is the list of vegetables that are considered in this program.

(beans french-beans potato ladyfinger brinjal cucumber peas gram snake-gourd bottle-gourd angular-gourd tomato)

Vegetable name ?

Potato

Would you like potato fried with onion. Y/N

Y

The final plan is:

Take a large vessel (approximately 1500cc.).

Take a peeler.

Take a table-knife.

Take 1kg. potatos.

Remove the covering skin of potatos with the peeler.

Chop the potatos into small pieces (approximately 1/2-inch) with the table-knife.

Put the pieces in the vessel.

Take a stove.

Take a pressure cooker of 2 liters capacity.

Take about 300ml. fresh water.

Put the potato pieces in the cooker.

Add water to the cooker.

Close the lid.

Keep the cooker on, and light the stove.

Wait for the whistle.

Reduce the flame to the lowest intensity and wait for 5 minutes.

Switch off the stove.

Replace the cooker onto the platform.

After some time open the cooker and remove the potato pieces.

Take a large frying dish (approximately 1500cc.).

Take a cutting board.

Take 100 ml. oil.

Take 1 table spoon salt.

Take 1/4 table spoon cumin.

Take 1/4 table spoon mustard seeds.

Take 15-20 curry-leaves.

Take one full garlic.

Take 1 table spoon black-gram.

Take 6-7 green-chillies.

Take a small piece of green-ginger.

Take a small piece of cinnamon.

Take 4-5 cloves.

Take 2-3 medium size onions.

Take a mixer.

Chop the onions on the cutting board.

Peel the garlic.

Make a paste of the green-chillies, green-ginger, garlic, cinnamon, cloves in the mixer.

Take 4-5 coriander stalks.

Switch on the stove.

Put the frying dish on the stove.

Add the oil to the dish.

Wait until the oil becomes hot.

Add the black-gram to the dish.

Wait until the color becomes light-brown.

Add the cumin, mustard, curry-leaves to the dish.

Wait for few seconds.

Drop the chopped onions into the dish.

Stir the onions until they turn brown.

Drop the potato pieces into the frying dish.

Add the salt to the dish and stir.

Add the paste of green-chillies, green-ginger, garlic, cinnamon, cloves to the dish and mix the pieces.

Continue the frying process until pieces are not-sticking to each other.

Chop the coriander leaves and add them to the dish.

Cook for a minute and switch off the stove.

Case-Based Reasoning for Cash Flow Forecasting using Fuzzy Retrieval

Rosina Weber Lee[1*], Ricardo Miranda Barcia[2] and Suresh K. Khator[1]

[1]University of South Florida, Tampa, Fl, USA

[2]Federal University of Santa Catarina, Industrial Engineering, Florianópolis, SC, BRAZIL.

Abstract. Case-Based Reasoning (CBR) simulates the human way of solving problems as it solves a new problem using a successful past experience applied to a similar problem. In this paper we describe a CBR system that develops forecasts for cash flow accounts. Forecasting cash flows to a certain degree of accuracy is an important aspect of a Working Capital Decision Support System. Working Capital (WC) management decisions reflect a choice among different options on how to arrange the cash flow. The decision establishes an actual event in the cash flow which means that one needs to envision the consequences of such a decision. Hence, forecasting cash flows accurately can minimize losses caused by usually unpredictable events. Cash flows are usually forecasted by a combination of different techniques enhanced by human experts' feelings about the future, which are grounded in past experience. This makes the use of the CBR paradigm the proper choice. Advantages of a CBR system over other Artificial Intelligence techniques are associated to knowledge acquisition, knowledge representation, reuse, updating, and justification. An important step in developing a CBR system is the retrieval of similar cases. The proposed system makes use of fuzzy integrals to calculate the synthetic evaluations of similarities between cases instead of the usual weighted mean.

1. Introduction

Case-Based Reasoning systems use successful past experiences to solve similar problems simulating human approach. Although CBR systems differ from one another, the basic procedure starts with a retrieval method that searches for cases similar to an input problem. This method must retrieve the case most similar to the given problem indicating the best match. An adaptation phase checks whether the solution of the best match can be readily used to solve the input problem. When the problem is solved, the adapted solution can be added to the memory of cases.

The nature of the cases and their retrieval methods may vary. Section 4 describes Fuzzy Set Theory and how its mechanisms are used to improve the evaluation of similarities on retrieval. The proposed system uses a fuzzy retrieval and it aims to forecast accounts in cash flows.

The Case-Based Reasoner is implemented under an Intelligent Hybrid System (IHS) in a unit called Case-Based Forecasting Unit (CBFU). Before detailing the unit,

---

* The research reported in this paper was supported in part by CNPq, Brazil.

let us briefly describe its environment (Weber-Lee et al. 1995). The IHS consists of units performing different functions. The IHS system is predominantly object-oriented although some units are still in prototype phase and their modeling into the object-oriented paradigm is being studied. Some of the units of the Intelligent Hybrid System are: *Firm*, the unit that embodies every function of the company; *Case-Based Forecasting Unit*, (the CBFU is discussed below separately); *Database*, it keeps the operations and feeds CBFU with all actual values; *Interface*, to input operations and the interface of decision support; *Expert System*, the unit that manages the IHS's interface and asks cash flow forecasts for CBFU. The Expert System[1] (ES), designed for IHS, manages the interface with the user and its knowledge representation is also object-oriented.

The CBFU is a CBR application that forecasts cash flows in the IHS that is the Working Capital Decision Support System. This paper proposes a fuzzy retrieval to improve the CBR application. Next section presents the importance of cash flow forecasting and how it is linked to the WC management. Then, the following section shows the advantages of the use of CBR as the forecasting technique. Section 4 describes the CBFU unit and its components. Lastly, section 5 presents the fuzzy retrieval, how it is implemented and the meaning of some of the Fuzzy Set Theory concepts applied.

2. Problem Description

Financial Management embodies a great number of issues that have to be resolved in order to maintain business activity. Monitoring the performance of an ongoing business embodies some important tasks such as funds financing, a budget and the distribution of the funds (Van Horne, Dipchand and Hanrahan 1985). Daily liquidity must be ensured to avoid unexpected costs. This is implemented by monitoring the funds that remain in current assets and liabilities. This monitoring is managing working capital. Working Capital management decisions reflect a choice among different options on how to arrange the cash flow. The decision establishes an actual event in the cash flow which means that one needs to envision the consequences of such a decision. Some decisions may cause losses or insolvency while others simply help make more money. Forecasting accurate cash flows can avoid losses caused by usually unpredictable events. Better management is attained when one estimates the consequences of an action more precisely.

Different techniques have been proposed to forecast cash flows (Wilson 1990; Lo 1993, Whalen and Schott 1985), although there are researchers that do not believe this task is possible (Singer 1994). Some of the techniques available are: regression analysis, historical trend smoothing, causal models, time series models, what-if models, goal seeking models, Monte Carlo models, constrained forecasting, etc. Cortes-Rello and Golshani (1990) presented a technique based on the Dempster-Shafer method. Neural Networks have also been used, (see for instance, Caporaletti et al. 1994 and Chiu and Scott 1994). Finally, several researches have described the use of expert systems, alone or combined with other techniques, in forecasting (Lo 1993, Whalen

[1] See Expert Systems: Principles and Programming, (Giarratano, 1994).

1985, Newquist 1990 and Shahabuddin 1990). Consequently, cash flow forecasting will always be an important subject due to the difference that it can make in financial performance of any business.

The use of human experts plays an important role in cash flow forecasting (D'Attilio, 1992, Randolph 1988, Jain and Chen 1992); mainly in terms of enhancing mathematical models and aggregating human feelings about the future. Human feelings about the future are grounded in past experience. The task of forecasting cash flows when performed by a human being works adequately under similar and sequential contexts. The expert aggregates information as a possible recession and becomes subjectively pessimistic. After a while, the expert cannot remember if the pessimistic approach used, for instance, 5 years ago, actually turned out to be effective, and if so, how effective. The CBR approach overcomes this shortcoming.

Time series methods have been of great help in different types of applications. The philosophy under time series methods is to model the actual numbers in functions and the forecast will be a point of a modeled function. This means that for this forecast to work, whatever it is that you are forecasting needs to have a consistent performance. Although, that is not always true in real life.

The uncertainty implied in real life is not an easy thing to be modeled. Both CBR and Neural Networks based systems have an implicit way of dealing with real life uncertainty. Neural Networks' strong limitation is being too implicit; they neither have a justification device nor can their solutions be adapted.

Another alternative to CBR is the Expert System (rule-based). Actually, expert systems work better in choosing a forecast technique than being used as one; (Lo 1993 and Whalen 1985) due to problems in knowledge acquisition and representation. Even if you could elicit all the knowledge necessary, the representation of this knowledge would generate too many rules and modeling all its interactions would be infeasible (Stottler 1994).

Using CBR as a forecast technique is simple. Suppose you have a series of observed data that occurred in the past, and you realize this same series is happening again, or a very similar one, you simply use the actual observation that followed your past series in order to forecast the new one.

3. Why Case-Based Reasoning?

Several drawbacks from alternatives to CBR have been discussed in previous section. Although CBR paradigm has its own limitations, it also has many advantages, which are discussed below.

Scientific research on CBR addresses issues in memory, planning and problem solving (Slade 1991) and describes CBR as paralleling the way humans solve problems. That is exactly what case-based reasoning systems do—whether implemented for diagnosis, machine learning or forecasting. A consequence of paralleling human beings is that CBR systems are able to give human justifications taken from the past experiences. These experiences can also warn about possible problems based on what has happened in the past. These justifications are reasonable and consistent to the problem.

With regard to expert knowledge, CBR systems are able to deal with incomplete and imprecise data and provide advantages on eliciting, representing, reusing and updating. Eliciting human expertise is a necessity difficult to achieve. CBR systems bypass such need as cases are automatically input by its features. Knowledge is updated as the system is used by aggregating each new problem into the system library of cases after an adaptation phase. As a consequence of this updating, CBR systems with use can evolve into more robust and efficient systems.

According to Stottler (1994), there is still another advantage related a consciousness that CBR systems have about their limitations. If no proper case can be retrieved, the system will not generate a solution, and thereby avoid problems that may be caused by systems under different paradigms.

Kolodner (1993) notes some other extremely important advantages. One is that CBR systems return solutions quickly unlike other methods that have to derive solutions from scratch. Another, is that solutions proposed do not need to be fully understood by the system. One does not have to input cases representing complete knowledge of a subject to enable the reasoner to provide a good solution. Also, CBR systems are able to evaluate solutions when no algorithmic method is available.

In the forecasting application, there is a strong motive to choose CBR paradigm and it is because it fits perfectly. Forecasting is not only by definition but by all its means, a task that uses experience to be solved. Most forecasting techniques are based on time series in an effort to model the past to infer the future. However, the conditions of that future may have changed. Sometimes the connection between past and future is not easily recognizable and only another similar event can represent such knowledge. That is exactly what the proposed system does.

4. Case-Based Forecasting Unit

The development steps in building a CBR system are described within the five main CBR problem areas: knowledge representation, retrieval methods, revise methods, retain methods and reuse methods. According to Aamodt and Plaza (1994), *"A set of coherent solutions to these problems constitutes a CBR method."*

4.1 Knowledge Representation

In a case-based system knowledge is represented through a case memory—the set of cases that embodies the proposed application. The representation problem is about deciding what to store in a case. So, the construction of this memory starts with the definition of the features of the cases.

The cases of the present application are all cash flow accounts. Descriptive features include account name and other relevant information that provide a proper retrieval. Some descriptive features are shown in Table 1. One type is the density feature, where the densities of each month reflect the seasonality factors.

Cases are hierarchically organized in an attempt to model all units under the same paradigm as the IHS, the object-oriented paradigm. Adapting case representation to the paradigm keeps some of the features of Schank's MOPs (Memory Organization Packages, Riesbeck and Schank 1989). MOP-based memory techniques use AI notions as abstraction and inheritance shared by the object-oriented paradigm.

Table 1. Descriptive features.

AccountName	cash sales	adm. expenses	suppliers
Year	1993	1993	1994
JanDensity	1.12	2.2	1.22
FebDensity	1	1.8	0.73
MarDensity	1.26	1	1.25
AprDensity	1.71	1.3	1.32
MayDensity	2.12	1.3	1
JunDensity	1.44	1	1.09
JulDensity	1.29	1	1.42
AugDensity	1.89	1.8	1.43
SepDensity	1.21	1.9	1.45
OctDensity	1.59	2.0	1.45
NovDensity	2.22	2.1	1.48
DecDensity	2.48	2.2	1.04

The two main bottlenecks on implementing MOPs under the object-oriented paradigm were avoided here due to the learning approach used as well as the extremely simple case library involved that did not demand the use of many different links.

The object-oriented analysis consists of one main *subject*[2]: cash flow accounts. The subject is presented in a classification structure consisting of two main abstract classes: income and expenses. All features are represented as attributes that assign values to the objects. According to Schank's terminology, every account is an instance and the classes that indicate the nature of the account are abstractions. There are no events or objects.

The most important descriptive feature of the example cases is the type of the account; as one wouldn't forecast salaries based on investment information. Although, it is possible to forecast one account using a different account. This is only possible when both accounts are related to Sales (in cash flow forecasting) at the same degree and the degree is high. Fixed costs such as rental or an interest payment may have the same degree of relation to Sales and this degree is very low for both. Hence, these type of accounts cannot be used in forecasting cash flows. Sales are a good point of reference because it controls the business activity.

Features become important as you use them in retrieving similar cases. Retrieval methods represent ways of accomplishing this task.

4.2 Retrieval Methods

Retrieval is implemented here in one set of tasks that receives the input problem and returns the best match.

The retrieval starts with a search that goes directly at the level of the hierarchic structure where the input problem account is. A matching function returns results showing how library cases are similar to the input case in terms of its seasonalities. A

---

[2] For definition of subject concept as well as other definitions within object-oriented paradigm refer to (Coad and Yourdon, 1990, Demster and Ireland, 1991, and Montenegro and Pacheco, 1994).

measure of seasonal similarity is obtained in order to ensure that there are cases sufficiently similar to the input case. This similarity is observed according to the case's past behavior, described through its density features, which are seasonality factors. This measure is a score that ranges in the interval [0,1]. A very low score reveals a change in the account behavior and it may result in not retrieving any case.

When an account has changed its performance to an extent that past cases of the same account do not reflect a similar behavior then it is time to consider something else. Experts seek for another account that could provide a fair forecast, otherwise the system is unable to retrieve any case. In the search function presented here, the second search for cases is verifying the feature ProportionToSales. This feature reflects the ratio of an account to Sales. This information itself does not add much although it can help a lot if used in combination with another feature: the degree of association of every account to Sales. This is an expert knowledge that asserts the associations as illustrated in Table 2. No matter how high the ratio is, the important point is the degree of association because it expresses how the behavior of an account depends upon sales volume.

If the input problem account belongs to a class labeled by a *Medium* or *High* degree of association to sales, the system performs a second search through the whole library seeking for accounts with the same fuzzy label. Otherwise, search ends and the function reaches a conclusion using a synthetic evaluation. The implementation of these two phases aims to reduce the time of the search as the second phase is not necessarily applied.

The results of the search throughout memory consist of another group of prospective cases. Cases sharing same account and fuzzy labels are then gathered and undergo a synthetic evaluation. The results of the synthetic evaluation are sorted and the best match is chosen. Section 5 presents how this synthetic evaluation is used in the fuzzy retrieval as well as some basic concepts of Fuzzy Set Theory, fuzzy measures and fuzzy integrals.

Table 2. Examples of accounts and their associations with sales volume.

Account	Degree of association	Fuzzy label	ProportionToSales
adm. expenses	0.02	*Low*	0.19
marketing costs	0.78	*High*	0.12
nonoperating income	0.00	*Low*	0.42
sales income	1.00	*High*	1.00

4.3 Reuse Methods

Using the best match returned by the retrieval function requires an adaptation phase while facing the differences from the input problem. In the CBFU, if the best match selected has a degree of association to Sales labeled *Low*, it will have the same AccountName of the input problem and the solution features used include the actual amounts inccurred and the densities. In the cases that the best match has a different AccountName, the solution features include ProportionToSales.

4.4 Revise Methods

Revise phase is when the solution is evaluated. According to (Aamodt and Plaza 1994), it is an opportunity to learn from failures. The revise phase is implemented in present example in conjunction with updating as long as the actual forecasts are known by the system when they occur.

4.5 Retain Methods

The learning capability of CBR system is presented here through an automatic updating implemented by a function that links the Database to the CBFU. This device updates the cases by informing actual values.

5. Fuzzy Retrieval

This paper proposes the use of a fuzzy retrieval. This means we use Fuzzy Set Theory[3] concepts in the retrieval function. As explained in Retrieval Methods the function retrieves a number of prospective cases that have to be evaluated in order to select the best match. This evaluation is a numerical function that assigns numbers for all the cases evaluated. Synthetic evaluations can be calculated through different formulas. CBR literature offers some algorithms like the nearest neighbor and the use of the weighted mean. We propose the use of the Fuzzy Measure Theory to perform this synthetic evaluation. Fuzzy integrals are used in Fuzzy Measure Theory. This is a generalization of the Classical Measure Theory that replaces the additivity axiom with weaker axioms of monotonicity and continuity.

Facing the multicriteria problem of the retrieval function, the synthetic evaluation obtained through the weighted mean fails due to its additivity nature. The classical weighted mean is based on the assumption that the effects of quality factors are additive: although, in real life they are interactive. The use of a synthetic evaluation, calculated through fuzzy integrals, is better because the results obtained have considered all the factors, and nothing has been overlooked. This process also considers the interactiveness of all the factors.

Let us see an example to demonstrate how the fuzzy approach excels the weighted mean. Suppose the input case is a cash sales account. Two different searches are performed: one among class cash sales and another through the whole hierarchy seeking for cases with fuzzy labels *High* and *Medium*. We evaluate the set of prospective cases using the weighted mean and the fuzzy measure approach.

For both evaluations we consider that from an object that we need to evaluate let $X=\{x_1, x_2,..., x_n\}$ be the finite set of quality factors of this object and X is called a factor space. Let $f(x_1), f(x_2),..., f(x_n)$ be the scores. Let function f be a measurable function defined on $(X, \zeta(X))$, such that $f(x_i) \in [0,1]$ for each $x_i \in X$.

In the example, let us use three quality factors: seasonal similarity, denoted by S, with possible values (scores) $x_i \in [0,1]$; account name, N, $x = 1$ when input and the case being examined accounts are the same and $x = 0$ when the accounts are not the same; and association to sales, A, $x = 1$ to same or $x = 0$ to other.

The examples for $f(x_i)$ scores are: $f(S)=0.612$, coming from a formula that evaluates the variability among the seasonal factors; $f(N)=1.0$, because the account name is the same; and $f(A)=0.0$, because the association to sales is not the same.

---

[3] About Fuzzy Set Theory refer to (Kaufmann, 1975, Zadeh, 1975, and Wang, 1992). For an application in CBR see (Baldwin, 1993).

Now let us assume that each subset E of the factor space X is associated by a real number, μ (E) between 0 and 1 that indicates the importance of E. The measure for the quality factors (weights) are elicited from experts and they are: $\mu(\{S\})=0.4$, $\mu(\{N\})=0.8$, and $\mu(\{A\})=0.6$. The weighted mean formula equals to an evaluation of .58.

Within the fuzzy measure approach, we consider that the empty set $\varnothing$ has the minimum importance 0 and the whole factor space X has the maximum importance 1. The set function μ must satisfy: (1) $\mu(\varnothing) = 0$ and $\mu(X) = 1$; and (2) If $E \subset F \subset X$, then $\mu(E) \leq \mu(F)$. μ is a fuzzy measure called an importance measure on X. E represents the use of fuzzy integral ($\int f d\mu$) of the scores $f(x_i)$ with respect to the importance measure μ to obtain a synthetic evaluation of the quality of the given object: $E = \int f d\mu$. The set function μ is the importance measure: $\mu(\{S\})=0.4$, $\mu(\{N\})=0.8$, and $\mu(\{A\})=0.6$, $\mu(\{X\})=1$, $\mu(\{S,A\})=0.8$, $\mu(\{S,N\})=0.9$, $\mu(\{N,A\})=0.0$ - also assigned by experts - and $\mu(\varnothing)=0.0$. The non additivity of this importance measure can be characterized by: $\mu(\{S,N\}) \neq \mu(\{S\}) + \mu(\{N\})$. The scores are as above: $f(S)=0.612$, $f(N)=1.0$, $f(A)=0.0$. The synthetic evaluation E follows:

$$E = \int f d\mu = \bigvee_{i=1}^{n} \left[f(x_i) \wedge \mu(F_i) \right] \qquad , F_i = \{x_i, x_{i+1}, \ldots, x_n\}$$

$$= [0 \wedge \mu(F_{0.0})] \vee [0.612 \wedge \mu(F_{0.612})] \vee [1 \wedge \mu(F_{1.0})]$$

$$= [0 \wedge \mu(X)] \vee [0.612 \wedge \mu(S,N)] \vee [1 \wedge \mu(N)]$$

$$= [0 \wedge \mu(X)] \vee [0.612 \wedge 0.9] \vee [1 \wedge 0.8]$$

$$= [0 \wedge 1] \vee [0.612] \vee [0.8]$$

$$= 0.8.$$

The result from the fuzzy integral came to a much larger number than the one resulted from the weighted mean. The feature's interactiveness brings the result much closer to a real life value.

Note that importance measures attributed to quality factors are still being tested to confirm their efficiency. This example is prototypical, synthetic operations in final implementation consider other quality factors as similarity features.

6. Conclusions

Forecasting with a CBR system represents a new approach to deal with forecasts as it does not try to predict assuming a continuity of behavior, but simply the possible repetition of patterns. The use of the fuzzy integral to obtain synthetic evaluations must be chosen over the weighted mean because it considers the interactiveness of the features that represent similarity. This results in a proper modeling of the human approach and above all this approach measures scores appropriately. Weighted mean has been widely used in the literature although it is not able to emulate human reasoning. Hence, when modeling fuzzy reasonings and trying to aggregate knowledge like humans do, the synthetic evaluation calculated through fuzzy integrals seems to be the best choice.

7. References

Aamodt, A. & Plaza, E. (1994). Case-Based Reasoning: Foundational Issues, Methodological Variations, and System Approaches. *Artificial Intelligence Communications, 7* (1), 39-59.

Baldwin, J.F. (1993). Evidential support logic, FRIL and case based reasoning. *International Journal of Intelligent Systems, 8* (9), 939-960.

Barnett, F. W. (1988). Four Steps to Forecast Total Market Demand. *Harvard Business Review, 66* (4), 28(6).

Caporaletti, L. E., Dorsey, R. E., Johnson, John D. & Powell, William A. (1994) Decision support system for in-sample simultaneous equation systems forecasting using artificial neural systems. *Decision Support Systems, 11* (5), 481-495

Catsimpoolas, N. & Marti, J. (1992).Scripting highly autonomous simulation behavior using case-based reasoning. *Proceedings of the 25th Annual Simulation Symposium*, Orlando, Fl, USA.

Caughlin, G. W. (1988). The cash management discipline. *CMA - the Management Accounting Magazine; March, 62* (2), 49(2).

Chiu, C. & Scott, R. (1994). Intelligent forecasting support system in auditing. Expert system and neural network approach. *Proceedings of the Hawaii International Conference on System Sciences, 3*, 272-280.

Coad, P. & Yourdon, E. (1990). *Object-oriented Analysis.* Prentice-Hall, Inc. New Jersey.

Cortes-Rello, E. & Golshani, F. (1990). Uncertain reasoning using the Dempster-Shafer method. An application in forecasting and marketing management. *Expert Systems, 7* (1), 9-18.

D'Attilio, D. F. (1992). Net working capital forecasting at DuPont. *Journal of Business Forecasting, 11* (1), 11(5).

Dempster, M. A. H. & Ireland, A. M. (1991). Object-oriented model integration in a financial decision support system. *Decision Support Systems, 7* (4), 329-340.

Fliedner, E. B. & Mabert, V. A. Constrained Forecasting: Some Implementation Guidelines. *Decision Sciences, 23*, 1143-1151.

Gage, T. J. (1988). Forecasts get clearer when current data, not history, is used. *Corporate Cashflow Magazine, 9* (11), 7(2).

Giarratano, J. & Riley, G. (1994). *Expert Systems: Principles and Programming.* 2nd ed. PWS Publishing Company, Boston.

Herbig, P. A., Milewicz,J. & Golden, J. (1993). The Do's and Don'ts of Sales Forecasting. *Industrial Marketing Management, 22*, 49-57.

Jain, Ch. L. & Chen, T. P. (1992). The role of judgment in business forecasting. *Industrial Management, 34* (6), 1(3).

Kaufmann A. (1975). *Introduction to the Theory of Fuzzy Subsets*, vol.1, Academic Press, New York.

Kolodner J. (1993). *Case-Based Reasoning.* Morgan Kaufmann, Los Altos, CA,.

Lo, T. (1994). An Expert System for choosing demand forecasting techniques. *International Journal of Production Economics, 33*, 5-15.

Loscalzo, W. (1982). *Cash Flow Forecasting.* McGraw-Hill Book Company.

Mcintyre, S. H., Achabal, D. D. & Miller, C. M. (1993). Applying Case-Based Reasoning to Forecasting Retail Sales. *Journal of Retailing, 69* (4), 372-398.

Montenegro, F. & Pacheco, R. (1994). *Orientação a Objetos em C++*. Editora Campus, Brasil.

Nakatani, Y., Tsukiyama, M. & Fukuda, T. (1991). Case organization in a case-based engineering design support system. *Proceedings of the IEEE International Conference on Systems, Man and Cybernetics, 3*, 1789-1794.

Newquist III, H. P. (1990). A maturing AI is finding its way in the world. *Computerworld, 24* (8), 23(1).

Randolph, A. (1988). Cash flow estimation practices of large firms. *Financial Management, 17* (2), 71(9).

Riesbeck, C.K.& Schank, R.C. (1989). *Inside Case-Based Reasoning*. Erlbaum, Hillsdale, NJ.

Shahabuddin, S. (1990). Expert systems and forecasting. *International Journal of Systems Science, 21* (10), 1997-2004

Shen, Z.L., Lui, H.C. & Ding, L.Y. (1994). Approximate Case-Based Reasoning on Neural Networks. *International Journal of Approximate Reasoning, 10* (1), 75-98.

Singer, A.E. (1994). DCF without forecasts. *Omega, 22* (3), 221(15).

Slade, S. (1991). Case-based reasoning: a research paradigm. *AI Magazine, 12*, 42-55.

Stottler, R. H.(1994). CBR for Cost and Sales Prediction. *AI Expert, (Aug.)*, 25-33.

Sugeno, M. (1977) *Fuzzy Measures and Fuzzy Integrals - A Survey*. In Fuzzy Automata and Decision Processes, Gupta Madan M., Saridis, George N. & Gaines, Brian R. (editors) ,North-Holland, New York.

Van Horne, J. C., Dipchand, C. R. & Hanrahan, J.R. (1985). *Fundamentals of Financial Management*. Prentice-Hall Canada Inc., Scarborough, Ontario,1985.

Wang, Z. & Klir, G. (1992). *Fuzzy Measure Theory*. Plenum Press, New York.

Weber-Lee, R., Viali, L., Pacheco, R., Martins, A. , Khator, S. & Barcia, R. (1995). Object Oriented Analysis and Programming for a Working Capital Management System. *Proceedings of the CIFEr, Conference on Computational Intelligence for Financial Engineering*, New York City, April 9-11.

Whalen, T. & Schott, B. (1985). Goal-Directed Approximate Reasoning in a Fuzzy Production System. *Approximate Reasoning in Expert Systems*. M.M.Gupta, A.Kandel, W.Bandler, J.B.Kiszka(editors) Elsevier Science Publishers B.V.(North-Holland).

Wilson, A. (1990). Effective cash and profit forecasting. *The Accountant's Magazine, 94* (1009), 45(3).

Womack, D. E. (1994). The numbers game: software that analyzes your cash flow. *Black Enterprise, 25* (2), 36(1).

Zadeh, L.A. (1975). The Concept of a Linguistic Variable and its Application to Approximate Reasoning-I. *Information Sciences, 8*, 199-249.

A Connectionist Indexing Approach for CBR Systems*

Maria Malek

TIMC-LIFIA
bat. Lifia, 46 ave Félix Viallet,
38031 Grenoble, France
Email: Maria.Malek@imag.fr

Abstract. An important factor that plays a major role in determining the performances of a CBR system is the complexity and the accuracy of the case retrieval phase. Both flat memory and inductive approaches suffer from serious drawbacks. In the first approach, the search time becomes considerable when dealing with large scale memory base, while in the second one the modifications of the case memory becomes very complex because of its sophisticated architecture.

In this paper, we show how we can construct a simple efficient indexing system structure. We construct a case hierarchy with two levels of memory: the lower level contains cases organised into groups of similar cases, while the upper level contains prototypes, each of which represents one group of cases. The construction of prototypes is made by using an incremental prototype-based network. This upper level parallel memory is used as an indexing system during the retrieval phase.

Key Words: Indexing, Incremental, Neural Network, Prototype.

1 Introduction

Case-Based Reasoning (CBR) means reasoning from prior examples that were stored in what we call a case base. This base of experience forms the memory or the library of the CBR system. The case-based reasoner is composed of two components: a case retriever and a case adapter. Given a new input problem, the case retriever identifies the most appropriate cases (in some similarity sense) in the case base and presents them to the case adapter. The case adapter then examines the retrieved cases and tries to solve the new problem by adapting these cases [1] [5] [14].

It is obvious that more the retrieval phase is efficient more the overall performances of the CBR system is increased. Hence, a particular attention must be paid to the design and the implementation of this phase. Indexing and memory organisation are the main issues for efficient retrieval of cases. In literature, two widely approaches for memory organisation are distinguished: flat memory systems and shared-features networks (hierarchical organisation of cases)[7].

In a flat memory system, cases are stored sequentially in a simple list or a file. They are retrieved by applying a matching function sequentially to each case in the file. The advantage of this approach is that the whole case library is searched, so accuracy is a function of quality of matching function, and adding new cases is cheap (incrementality). However this mechanism becomes very expensive when the case base becomes rather big.

Shared-feature networks provide a means of clustering cases so that cases that share many features are grouped together. Each internal node of a shared-feature network holds features shared by the cases below it. Leaves hold cases themselves. Building such a hierarchy is time consuming, but it can be used very efficiently during the inference process. Now, adding cases is a complex operation and it is hard to keep the network optimal as cases are added. The study of some inductive approaches like ID3/C4 [12] have shown that the costs of altering large case bases are very high and lead sometimes to a re-compilation of the complete case base after each alteration [4] [9]. This shows that using inductive approaches makes retrieval more efficient but

---

* This research is supported by the MIX ESPRIT Project-9119

it considerably complicates the learning phase because of the complex architecture of the used structure[17].

In this paper, we propose a simple and efficient indexing system. We construct a case hierarchy of two levels of memory. The lower level contains cases organised into groups of similar cases. The upper level contains *prototypes*, each of which represents a group of cases. The construction of prototypes is made by using an incremental prototype-based neural network. This upper level prototype memory is used as an indexing system during the retrieval phase.

In Sect.2 we describe incremental prototype-based networks. In Sect.3 we describe our prototype-based indexing system and we present a comparative study with other inductive approaches. In Sect.4, we give a short description of two models which uses neural networks to implement CBR modules. Finally some conclusion is given in Sect. 5.

2 Prototype-Based Incremental Neural Networks

Learning a given class of objects by accumulating representative exemplars of the class and slightly modifying existing ones is the approach used by prototype-based incremental networks. Each hidden network unit represents a *prototype*. These prototype units are grouped into their corresponding classes, each class identified by a category label. The first implemented model using this method was described in [13] commercially known as the Nestor Learning System (NLS). An incremental prototype-based neural network which is based on a " Grow and Learn" (Gal) algorithm is also described in [2].

In this section, we describe the incremental prototype-based neural network model (ARN2) proposed in [3]. Figure 1 shows the architecture of the model. The network is composed of three layers:

1. The input layer that contains one unit for each attribute
2. The output layer that contains one unit for each class
3. The hidden layer that contains one unit for each prototype and whose value is represented by the reference vector w_i^t

This model operates either in *supervised learning mode* or in *recognition mode*. The input vector at cycle t is denoted by X^t and is associated with a category label C_x^t. Comparison between the current input and the different prototypes is achieved by means of a similarity measure m_i^t which computes, using some pre-defined measure $M(X^t, w_i^t)$, the similarity between the input vector and the individual reference vectors.

An influence region of a reference vector w_i^t having n components is defined as the locus of points in the space that register a measure of similarity equal or greater than a given threshold Θ. Figure 2 shows two influence regions in a two-dimensional space (using an Euclidean similarity

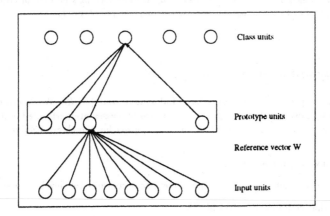

Fig. 1. General architecture of a prototype-based network

measure). In *learning mode*, the network learns to associate a training pattern to its correct category. Let U^t be the set of prototype units having the current input X^t within their influence regions:

1. If U^t is empty, then a new prototype is created (we call this *assimilation*)
2. Otherwise, a winner-take-all competition strategy selects the winning prototype U_s which registers the highest measure of similarity
   (a) If the wining prototype belongs to the same category of X^t then the network fine-tunes itself to render the winning prototype even more similar to the training input (we call this *accommodation*). This is achieved by applying the Grossberg learning law.
   (b) Otherwise, the influence region of the activated unit is decreased in order to exclude this wrong classified example (we call this *differentiation*). The example is then represented again to the network.

However, experience shows that the learning procedure may cause the creation of a considerable number of prototype units near the boundaries of classes in the input space [6]. This situation can be avoided by adding a new criterion to the differentiation process. This has been achieved by introducing an uncertain region between two classes in which *differentiation* is not allowed [6]. This region presents vectors that cause nearly the same activation to both prototypes. As a result, the network is unable to learn new cases that falls into this region (we call these cases: *boundary cases*) (Fig. 2). In the next section, we show how we can implement our CBR indexing system using this incremental neural network.

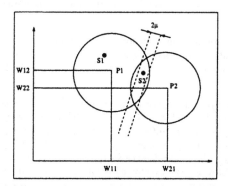

Fig. 2. Suppose that P1 and P2 are two prototypes which are associated to different classes. S1 is a situation vector which activates P1. S2 is a situation vector which falls into an uncertain region and the network is unable to give a decision because two different prototypes are activated.

3   Prototype-Based Indexing System

In this section we propose a Prototype-Based Indexing System (*PBIS*). We describe in the next, the memory organisation, how learning and retrieval processes are performed and we compare this system to two widely used inductive indexing approaches which are C4.5 and ID5R.

3.1   Memory Organisation

The idea is to construct a simple indexing system that contains two levels of memory [8]:

1. Memory that contains *prototypical cases*
2. Memory that contains *instances* or real cases

The *prototype* memory is used during retrieval phase as an indexing system in order to decrease retrieval time.

The first memory level is the hidden layer of the incremental prototype-based network described in previous section. The second memory level is a simple flat memory in which cases are organised into zones of similar cases. These two levels are linked together: at each prototype unit, is associated a memory zone which contains all instances belonging to this prototype. In addition, a memory zone is reserved for *boundary* cases which falls into an uncertain region as well as for cases that are not classified elsewhere. These cases form a group of *atypical* cases (or unusual cases). Figure 3 illustrates the architecture of the memory.

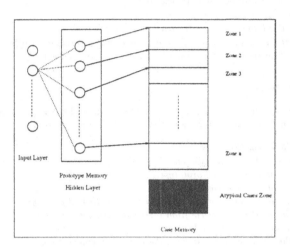

Fig. 3. The case memory is composed of two levels: Prototype memory and instance memory which are linked together.

3.2   Learning Process

Initially, the network contains no prototypes and the first memory level contains one zone: the *atypical zone*. Let's suppose that we want to construct our prototype memory given a training set S. Instances of S are initially placed into the atypical Zone. *No Boundary* instances are learned to the network, *boundary* instances are kept into the atypical zone. In fact the network can forget many previous learned instances during the *accommodation* or the *differentiation* process. These lost cases are then retrieved from their memory zone and are replaced into the atypical zone. The Learning Procedure is re-executed again until stabilisation of the atypical zone. (see Algorithm 1 and Algorithm 2):

Algorithm .1 *Learning Procedure*
 Repeat (n_{max} times) or (until stabilisation of the atypical zone)
     For each instance i belonging to the atypical zone do
         (Example Learning i) / see Algorithm 2 */*
     For each instance i in the second-level memory
         / memory of instances */*
         If i does not belong to the associated prototype then
             / This is a lost case */*
             Remove this instance from this zone
             Add it to the atypical zone

For each instances i, the following supervised learning procedure is applicated:

Algorithm .2 *Example Learning i*
> *If no prototype units is activated then*
>> *Create a new prototype unit (assimilation)*
>> *Associate at this prototype a new memory zone*
>> *Add this case to this memory zone*
> *Else If i falls into an uncertain region then*
>> *Keep i into the atypical memory zone*
> *Else If i belongs to the activated prototype then*
>> *fine-tune this prototype (accommodation)*
>> *add i to the associated memory zone*
> *Else /* i does not belong to the activated prototype */*
>> *Decrease the influence region of the activated unit to exclude i (differentiation)*
>> *(Example Learning i) /* Re-learn the example to the network */*

3.3 Retrieval Process

Once the system is learned, it can operate in retrieval mode. Let's suppose that a new case is presented to the network, the following retrieval procedure is executed:

Algorithm .3 *Retrieval Procedure*
> *If only one class unit is activated then*
>> *Retrieve the most activated prototype.*
> *Else many class units are activated*
>> *Determine the memory zones associated to the activated prototype*
>> *Retrieve the most similar case from these memory zones*
> *Else /* no prototype is activated */*
>> *Retrieve the most similar case from the atypical memory zone*

We mention here that at any moment, the system can switch from the *retrieval mode* to the *learning one* in order to learn new cases and then returns back to the *retrieval mode*.

3.4 Comparison with Two Inductive Indexing Approaches: C4.5 and ID5R

Inductive approaches to indexing in a CBR systems are suitable where case outcomes are well-defined and when there are enough examples. They aim to construct inductively a model by generalizing from specific examples. These methods have two advantages [5]:

1. They can automatically analyze the cases to determine the best features for distinguishing them
2. The cases are organized for retrieval into a hierarchical structure that increases the retrieval time by only the log of the number of cases

C4.5 [12] is an inductive method that generates a decision tree classifier from an initial set of cases. It is a descendent of the ID3 algorithm [11]. Each leaf in the tree indicates a class (or a prototype). A decision node specifies some test to be carried on a single attribute value.

A decision tree can be used to classify a case by starting at the root of the tree and moving through it until a leaf is encountered. The class of the leaf is predicted to be that recorded at the leaf.

To construct a decision tree, Quinlan [12] has pointed out that selecting an attribute with a lowest E-score is equivalent to selecting an attribute with a highest information gain. The E function is an information theoretical metric based on entropy, the attribute with the lowest E-score is assumed to give a good partition of instances into subproblems for classification and so is placed at the root of the tree. C4.5 is not incremental; this means that one needs to build a new decision tree to learn an additional case.

ID5R is an incremental method to build a decision tree [17]. The idea is to maintain sufficient information to compute the E-score for an attribute at a node, making it possible to change the test attribute at a node to one with the lowest E-score. The algorithm allows at each moment to restructure the whole tree and to expand it if possible.

In order to compare our indexing system to C4.5 and ID5R methods we have chosen the MONK's problems that were used to compare different learning algorithm performances [16].

The MONK's problems rely on an artificial robot domain, in which robots are described by six different attributes:

1. x_1: head_shape $\in$ {round, square, octagon}
2. x_2: body_shape $\in$ {round, square, octagon}
3. x_3: is_smiling $\in$ yes, no
4. x_4: holding $\in$ {sword, balloon, flag}
5. x_5: jacket_color $\in$ {red, yellow, green, blue}
6. x_6: has_tie $\in$ {yes, no}

The learning task is a binary classification task. Each problem is given by a logical description of a class. Robots belong either to this class or not. Instead of providing a complete class description to the learning problem, only a subset of all 432 possible robots with its classification is given. The learning task is then to generalize over these examples.

The MONK's Problems are:

1. Problem M1: (head_shape = body_shape) or (jacket_color = red)
   From 432 possible examples, 124 were randomly selected for the training set. There is no noise
2. Problem M2: exactly two of the six attributes have their *first* value. From 432 possible examples, 169 were randomly selected. There is no noise
3. Problem M3: (jacket_color is green and holding a sword) or (jacket_color is not blue and body_shape is not octagon)
   From 432 examples, 122 were selected randomly. Among them there is 5% of noise

Experimental Results Table 1 presents results of comparison of C4.5, ID5R and our proposed Prototype-Based Indexing System (PBIS), for the M1 problem. Table 2 presents results for the M2 problem and table 3 presents results for the M3 problem. We compare in the next the complexity of the generated structures (Leaves number and Prototypes number) and the classification and generalisation accuracies of the three approaches.

Table 1. M1 Problem, NbN is the number of nodes in the tree, NbP is the number of leaves in the tree or the number of prototype units in the network, TrS is the classification accuracy on the training set, TeS is the generalisation accuracy on the test set

Method	NbN	NbP	TrS	TeS
C4.5	15	28	90.3%	76.6%
ID5R	34	52	100%	79%
PBIS	-	33	98.4%	84%

Table 2. M2 Problem

Method	NbN	NbP	TrS	TeS
C4.5	27	46	85.5%	65.3%
ID5R	64	99	100%	69.23%
PBIS	-	78	97.63%	75.93%

We notice that ID5R registers a classification and generalisation accuracies which are higher than those registered by C4.5. The decision tree generated by ID5R (34 nodes, 52 Leaves, for M1 problem) is more complicated than the one generated by C4.5 (15 nodes, 28 Leaves, for M1 Problem). This means that using ID5R as an indexing system increases the accuracy of the retrieval phase but also increases the retrieval time because of the complex structure of the generated tree.

PBIS generates a neural network with an acceptable number of prototypes which is smaller than the ID5R one (33 for M1, 78 for M2 and 27 for M3 problems). The fact of using a *parallel* network with such a number of prototypes decreases considerably the retrieval time.

Table 3. M3 Problem

Method	NbN	NbP	TrS	TeS
C4.5	8	17	96.7%	92.6%
ID5R	14	28	100%	95.28%
PBIS	-	27	100%	87.5%

PBIS registers a classification accuracy which is near to 100% because it is able to learn most kinds of cases (*no boundary, boundary, lost*) (see previous section). The generalisation accuracies registered by PBIS are better than the ones registered by ID5R,for M1 and M2 problem.

ID5R and PBIS are both incremental. Adding a new case in ID5R is a complicated operation because it leads to a whole restructuration of the generated tree [17], whereas in PBIS, this is achieved by simply adding the treated case to the suitable memory zone and by modifying only one unit in the neural network (assimilation, accommodation or differentiation of a prototype).

4   Related Works

A natural relationship seems to exist between CBR and NN models where similar problems of associative retrieval, dynamic memory, and adaptation arise. Some neural network architectures for CBR systems have been proposed. In [15], a neural network model for case-filtering is proposed, a feed forward network is designed such that the inputs are factors from instances in a library of cases and factors from a new observed situation. The filter is designed to select relevant cases from the library. In [10] Authors propose another approach where case-based reasoning can be implemented on a connectionist network architecture. The method is based on implementing Pearl's probability propagation as a 3-layer hierarchical network. This architecture provides a possible solution to the case indexing problem based on a parallel architecture.

5   Conclusion

In this paper we show how we use a connectionist clustering method for creating prototypes from an initial training set. This prototype memory which consists of the hidden layer of the described neural network is used during retrieval phase. This model is implemented and is now under evaluation. Experience has shown that PBIS registers generalisation accuracies which are better than the C4.5 and ID5R ones, for the two first MONKs problems. In addition, the retrieval time is decreased because of using a parallel memory that contains a few number of prototypes.

In fact, using a simple memory hierarchy (two levels of memory) in stead of a shared-neural networks [7] simplifies learning new cases (incrementality); this is achieved by modifying one neural unit (prototype) and it is much simpler than the method used in ID5R for example.

We plan to study soon the effect of choosing a similarity measure on the retrieval accuracy. The currently-used similarity measure is the Euclidean one.

We have to mention here that prototype-based networks are suited for classification where little information on the input space is available.

We are evaluating now our system performance on a real set of medical diagnosis cases within the activities of the European project MIX.

Acknowledgement: *I would like to thank B. Amy for useful discussions and suggestions .*

References

1. A. Aamodt and E. Plaza. Case-based reasoning: Foundational issues, methodological variations, and system approaches. *AICOM*, 7(1), March 1994.
2. E. Alpaydin. Gal : Networks that grow when they learn and shrink when they forget. Technical Report TR 91-032, International Computer Science Institute, May 1991.
3. A. Azcarraza and A. Giacometti. A prototype-based incremental network model for classification task. In *Fourth International Conference on Neural Networks and Their Applications*, Nimes, France, 1991.
4. S.K. Bamberger and K. Goos. Integration of case-based reasoning and inductive learning methods. In *First European Workshop on CBR*, November 1993.
5. R. Barletta. An introduction to case-based reasoning. *AI Expert*, August 1991.
6. A. Giacometti. *Modèles Hybrides de l'Expertise*. PhD thesis, Telecom- Paris, 1992.
7. J. Kolodner. *Case-Based Reasoning*. Morgan Kaufmann Publishers, Inc, 1993.
8. M. Malek and V. Rialle. A case-based reasoning system applied to neuropathy diagnosis. In *Second European Workshop, EWCBR-94*, Lecture Notes in Computer Science. Springer-Verlag, November 1994.
9. M. Manago, K. Althoff, E. Auriol, R. Traphoner, S. Wess, N. Conruyt, and F. Maurer. Induction and reasoning from cases. In *First European Workshop on CBR*, November 1993.
10. P. Myllymaki and H.Tirri. Massively parallel case-based reasoning with probabilistic similarity metrics. In *First European Workshop on CBR*, November 1993.
11. J.R. Quinlan. Induction of decision trees. *Machine Learning*, (1):81– 106, 1986.
12. J.R. Quinlan. *C4.5*. Morgan Kaufmann Publishers, 1992.
13. D.L. Reilly, L.N. Cooper, and C. Elbaum. A neural model for category learning. *Biological Cybernetics*, (45):35–41, 1982.
14. C.K. Riesbeck and R.C. Schank. *Inside Case-Based Reasoning*. Lawrence Erlbaum Associates, publishers, 1989.
15. P. Thrift. A neural network model for case-based reasoning. In *Proceedings of the DARPA Case-Based Reasoning Workshop*, May 1989.
16. S.B. Thrun, J. Bala, E. Bloedorn, I. Bratko, B. Cestnik, J. Cheng, K. De Jong, S Dzroski, S.E. Fahlman, D. Fisher, R. Hamann, K. Kaufman, S. Keller, I. Kononenko, J. Kreuziger, R.S. Michalski, T. Mitchell, P. Pachowicz, Y. Reich H. Vafaie, W. Van de Welde, W. Wenzel, J. Wnek, and J. Zhang. The monk's problems a performance comparison of different learning algorihms. Technical Report CMU-CS-91-197, Carnegie Mellon University, December 1991.
17. P.E. Utgoff. Incremental induction of decision trees. *Machine Learning*, (4):161–186, 1989.

Using a Neural Network to Learn General Knowledge in a Case-Based System

Eliseo Reategui[1], John A. Campbell[1] and Shirley Borghetti[2]

[1] Department of Computer Science, University College London
Gower St, London WC1E 6BT, UK
(e-mail: e.reategui, jac@cs.ucl.ac.uk)
[2] Department of Transplants, The Heart Institute of São Paulo
Av. Dr. Eneas Carvalho de Aguiar 44
05403-000 São Paulo, SP - Brazil
(e-mail: dcl_edimar@pinatubo.incor.usp.br)

Abstract. This paper presents a new approach for learning general knowledge in a diagnostic case-based system through the use of a neural network. We take advantage of the self-adapting nature of the neural network to discover the most relevant features and combination of features for each diagnosis considered. The knowledge acquired by the network is interpreted and mapped into symbolic *diagnosis descriptors*, which are kept and used by the case-based system to guide its reasoning process, to retrieve cases from a case library and to build explanations. The neural network used in the learning process was the Combinatorial Neural Model, a network that has been combined with other symbolic approaches previously. The paper presents the method used to interpret the knowledge learned in the neural network, as well as the guidelines followed by the reasoning process of the CBR system. An initial experiment in clinical psychology is also reported, where the case-based model introduced here was used to learn and represent the psychological profile of patients in evaluation for heart transplant.

1 Introduction

Case-Based Reasoning (CBR) emphasises the use of particular experiences in reasoning. However, general knowledge often plays an equally important role in such systems. For example, a number of early CBR systems such as CYRUS [5] or CASEY [6] have compiled experiences in generalized episodes. These generalizations have been used to organize the case library and index the cases by exploiting the differences among them.

In the CBR model presented here, general knowledge acquired by a neural network is interpreted and stored in memory structures called *diagnosis descriptors*. Each descriptor is responsible for representing and highlighting the most important features for the identification of the diagnosis, and for associating the diagnosis with previous relevant experiences.

Other efforts in the combination of symbolic and connectionist representations can be seen in [3], where the author examines the limitations of each approach and the advantages of hybrid architectures, or in [4], where connectionist and symbolic processes have been combined in the design of a hybrid marker-passing model.

The neural network chosen for learning the general knowledge was the Combinatorial Neural Model (CNM) [10]. Our choice of neural network had much to do with our previous experience with this same network, as well as with the fact that it had been successfully combined with symbolic approaches previously, to solve problems in different application domains such as renal diseases [11], cardiology [7] and banking [16].

The paper is organized as follows: section 2 introduces the CNM, the operation of the network and its learning mechanism. Section 3 presents the structure of the *diagnosis descriptors* and details of how the knowledge stored in the neural network is interpreted and mapped into them. Section 4 introduces the reasoning process, which uses the *diagnosis descriptors* and previous cases to solve new problems. In the final sections we describes an experiment in clinical psychology and some initial results, discuss this work in relation to similar projects, and consider both lessons from our experience and possible future developments.

2 The Combinatorial Neural Model

The knowledge acquisition methodology of knowledge graphs inspired the development of the Combinatorial Neural Model. A knowledge graph is described as a minimal directed AND/OR acyclic graph representing the knowledge of an expert for a specific diagnostic hypothesis [8]. The structure of the CNM is therefore very similar to that of the graphs. The CNM has a feedforward topology with three layers. The input layer is formed by fuzzy-number cells. These fuzzy numbers (values in the interval [0,1]) represent the degree of confidence the user has in the information that is observed and inserted into the neural network. Cells in different layers are linked by connections with an associated weight which represents the influence of lower-layer cells on the output of upper-layer cells.

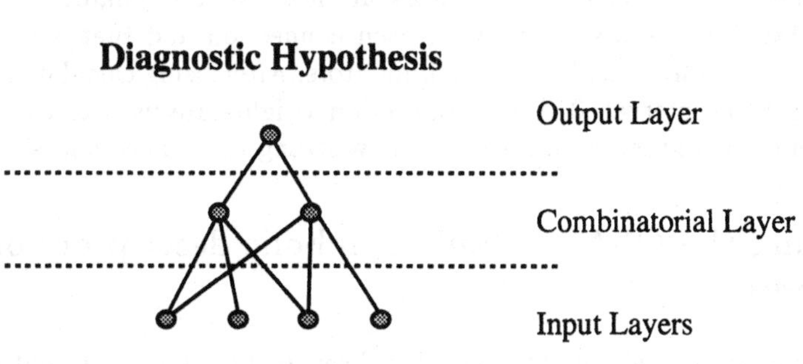

Diagnostic Hypothesis

Output Layer

Combinatorial Layer

Input Layers

Fig. 1. Basic structure of the Combinatorial Neural Model

Figure 1 depicts the basic structure of the CNM. Different types of information are contained in each layer of the neural network:

- output layer: contains nodes that represent the different diagnostic hypotheses;
- input layer: contains nodes that represent evidence such as symptoms, test results or any other information that supports the diagnostic hypothesis.
- intermediate layer: specifies different combinations of evidence that can lead to a particular diagnostic hypothesis.

The connections of the input layer can be either excitatory or inhibitory. An excitatory connection propagates the arriving signal using its weight as an attenuating factor. An inhibitory connection performs fuzzy negation on the arriving signal X, transforming it to 1-X. The combinatorial layers are formed by hidden fuzzy AND-cells. They associate different input cells in intermediate chunks of knowledge which are relevant in the classification process. The output layer is formed by fuzzy OR-cells. They implement a competitive mechanism between the different pathways that reach the diagnostic hypothesis.

2.1 The neural network learning mechanism

The neural network learning process is based on two main functions:

- determining the combinations of features that are influential for each diagnosis;
- adjusting weights of the connections that link the nodes of the input, the combinatorial and the output layers.

The CNM uses a punishment and reward learning algorithm to modify connection weights and force the network to converge to a desired behaviour intrinsically represented in a set of examples. This algorithm uses a simple version of the backpropagation mechanism [18]; it rewards the pathways that lead to correct results, and punishes the pathways that lead to incorrect results. Punishment and reward accumulators are stored for each connection of the network. The operant components of the network are not the accumulators though, but the weights that are associated with each connection and that are computed with the use of values held in the accumulators. After being calculated and normalized for the interval [0,1], the connection weights are used to calculate the output of each connection and to show how strong the connection is.

3 Using the CNM to build symbolic descriptors of diagnoses

One of our main goals in this work has been to transform the mathematical knowledge stored in the neural network as accumulators and weights into more intelligible symbolic knowledge. The main task was therefore to extract from the neural network symbolic descriptors for each diagnosis considered, in doing something similar to what is stated in some previous work [17] on combining the CNM with a frame system.

Three attributes were created to describe generalized knowledge about a diagnosis. The features referenced by these attributes are characterized by their frequency and specificity in relation to the diagnosis. Features that are specific are important for their discriminatory properties, being normally observed only in one diagnosis and not in others. Features that are frequent, on the other hand, are important for confirming a certain diagnostic hypothesis. The following attributes store the generalized knowledge of a *diagnosis descriptor*:

- **Triggers:** nodes of the neural network containing features and combinations of features that are highly significant, being very specific and frequent to the diagnosis. These are the nodes that, after the learning phase, have the punishment accumulator equal to 0 and the connection weight equal to 1.
- **Primary features:** nodes of the network containing features and combinations of features that are either very specific or very frequent to the diagnosis. These features usually provide a high degree of confidence when pointing out a diagnostic hypothesis. They were selected by taking the nodes of the network with high weight.
- **Supporting features:** nodes containing features and combinations of features that are not very frequent or specific, but that can reinforce the diagnostic conclusion. The weights of these nodes are lower than the weights observed in *primary features*.

Two additional attributes were used to identify cases of the case library that are likely to be relevant in the diagnostic process, but that would not normally be considered if only the generalized knowledge of the *diagnosis descriptors* were used.

- **Positive remindings:** the purpose of this attribute is to index the cases of the case library that are less typical and that can be useful in the analysis of new cases that do not conform with the norm. The positive remindings are selected by taking the nodes of the neural network containing features that are highly specific but not particularly frequent in such diagnoses. These are the nodes that have the punishment accumulator equal to 0 and a low reward accumulator.
- **Negative remindings:** the purpose of this attribute is to index previous cases containing features that would normally imply a diagnosis different from the one by which the case was classified. These nodes have the connection weight equal to 1 and the punishment accumulator different from 0. The cases used to punish these nodes during the training phase are indexed by this type of reminding.

It is important to point out here that, by eliciting the information above, we convert the "opaque" knowledge stored in the network into meaningful attributes. Furthermore, some attributes are formed with a type of knowledge that would not be taken into account in the neural network. For example, the nodes of the neural network referenced in the *negative remindings* would normally indicate a certain diagnosis with a high degree of confidence, without taking into account that in some previous circumstances, the same set of features contained in the node have been observed in cases diagnosed differently. The *negative remindings* are used by the symbolic system in such a way that these cases are always considered for further evaluation before a final solution is passed to the user.

In order to control the volume of redundant data in the case library, only a small set of cases is stored. These cases are classified as prototypical or atypical. Prototypical cases represent normative experiences, being selected from the whole set of existing cases as the ones that show the highest degree of similarity with the generalized knowledge of *diagnosis descriptors*. Although these cases contain the same kind of knowledge represented in the *diagnosis descriptors*, it was important to have them stored in the library to enable the system to present a similar previous experience that could help the user to understand the given results.

Atypical cases, on the other hand, are the cases that do not conform with the norm. They show rarer or exceptional features and contain knowledge that is not normally captured by systems that learn through generalization. The criterion for determining which cases are atypical is simple: all the existing cases that are indexed by both the *positive* and *negative remindings* of the *diagnosis descriptors* are selected as atypical.

4 The reasoning process

As mentioned earlier in this paper, CBR emphasises the use of particular experiences in reasoning, in contrast with adopting the more traditional artificial intelligence approach of using only generalized knowledge, such as production rules. However, CBR systems usually also maintain some form of generalized knowledge, in an attempt to hold a broader view of how to solve the problems that they address (e.g. at least for indexing purposes).

Here, the general knowledge learned from the neural network is represented in *diagnosis descriptors* and used to draw hypotheses for possible solutions, to index the cases in the library and to explain the reasoning performed by the system. The cases in the library are used to support a particular hypothesis (or to choose among suggested hypotheses) and to illustrate to the user previous experiences that resemble the current one, highlighting their similarities and implying that the solutions outlined for those cases should also apply for the new one.

When presented with a new case, the first step in the reasoning process is to match the given case with the *triggers* and *primary features* of the *diagnosis descriptors*. For simple cases, the system can usually find a single diagnostic hypothesis and exploit the *supporting features* just to reinforce the hypothesis. For more complicated cases, the system would follow the same step described above, but it would generate more than one hypothesis. In this event, the following procedure would be started:

- The cases indexed by the *positive remindings* of the hypotheses raised are retrieved and matched against the problem case. The best matches among those are selected as holders of possible solutions.
- The cases indexed by the *negative remindings* of the hypotheses raised are retrieved for further comparison with the problem case. Retrieved cases that match closely the problem case are also selected as holders of possible solutions.
- All the prototypical cases for the hypothetical diagnoses are matched against the problem case. The best match among these and the reminded cases from the steps above is selected to provide the final solution.

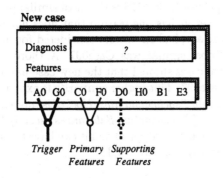

New case

Diagnosis   ?

Features

AO GO CO FO DO HO B1 E3

Trigger Primary Supporting
Features Features

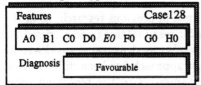

Retrieved prototypical case

Features	Case128

AO B1 CO DO *EO* FO GO HO

Diagnosis   Favourable

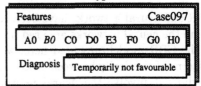

Retrieved more atypical case

Features	Case097

AO *BO* CO DO E3 FO GO HO

Diagnosis   Temporarily not favourable

AO - Psychological functioning: normal

BO - Use of psychoactive substances: no use

B1 - Use of psychoactive substances: social use

CO - Adherence to surgical treatment: good

DO - Motivation and knowledge about the
transplantation: good understanding

EO - Family dynamics: satisfactory

E3 - Family dynamics: unmanageable difficulties

FO - Psychosocial state: absence of symptoms

GO - Intellectual resorces: available

HO - Psychiatric antecedent in the
family: absent

Fig. 2. Some cases used in the construction of an explanation

After determining a final solution to the problem, the best-matching case is presented to the user and an explanation for the reasoning process is built, based on the importance of each attribute of the final *diagnosis descriptor* and on the similarities of the problem case with the best-matching case. Figure 2 shows an example of the reasoning carried out for a psychosocial evaluation case. Some features of the case presented as a problem are identified as *triggers*, *primary* and *supporting* features for the diagnosis *Favourable*. The prototypical *Favourable* case most similar to the new case is retrieved for further evaluation. A more atypical case is also retrieved, as not all the features of the new case could be explained by the *diagnosis descriptor* of *Favourable*. The new case is diagnosed *Temporarily not favourable* and the following explanation is produced:

> "The features A0 and G0 were identified as *Triggers* of the diagnosis *Favourable*. Thus, these features indicate the diagnosis *Favourable* with a high degree of confidence. The features C0 and F0 were identified as *Primary features* of *Favourable* cases, and as such they confirm this diagnosis with a high degree of confidence. The feature D0 supports the same diagnostic hypothesis. Case128 is the most similar prototypical case in the library. However, it has one feature that does not match the new case: E0. Other more atypical cases were considered for further analysis, among which the most similar was Case097. A thorough comparison among the three final cases showed that the new case has a higher degree of similarity with Case097. This higher similarity is explained by the fact that feature E3 - *Family Psychodynamics: blocked* is more important than the feature B1 - *Use of Psychoactive Substances: social*. Therefore, new case can also be catalogued as atypical and it can have the same diagnosis as Case097: Temporarily not favourable."

5 Discussion

CBR and neural networks have been combined in previous research, as in [1, 13] where the neural networks are used mainly for case matching and retrieval tasks. In the CBR model presented here, we have also used neural networks to learn patterns of similarity between cases, but our approach has been different in that we did not involve the neural networks themselves in the reasoning process. Instead, we tried to define symbolic interpretations for the knowledge stored in the neural networks, and use these interpretations, combined with specific cases, to support the reasoning.

The mapping of the knowledge stored in the neural network into *diagnosis descriptors* is similar to our previous work [17]. Here, however, we have discussed *diagnosis descriptors* more extensively and we have proposed a new method for eliciting symbolic knowledge of the neural network. Furthermore, by incorporating prototypical cases in the model, as well as *positive* and *negative remindings* in the *diagnosis descriptors*, we have defined a way to connect the diagnoses to real cases in the library.

In [16] we have introduced another approach for combining neural networks with CBR in a system for classifying credit card transactions. In that scheme the two reasoning mechanisms work in an independent fashion, the answers provided by each of the individual mechanisms being merged by a mediator. The approach described in the present paper is very different in that the neural network is not used to provide answers for a posed problem. It is used to learn and form the normative knowledge kept in the *diagnosis descriptors*. These descriptors are the actual components of the architecture that are used in the reasoning process.

The advantages of the architecture presented here over pure neural networks are very similar to those of symbolic systems over connectionist systems. For instance, the knowledge of the *diagnosis descriptors* is easy to understand. Hence, the *descriptors* can be consulted easily and used to build explanations for the reasoning process, unlike the knowledge of the neural networks.

We have started to use this model in the development of a system for the psychological evaluation of candidates for heart transplants. The psychological features of heart transplant patients have been studied since 1969 [9]. The initial studies showed the importance of a patient's psychological profile for a satisfactory outcome after the transplant [2]. At present, psychological evaluation is a routine procedure before heart transplants, used in 5 out of 6 of the transplantation centres worldwide. Between 1988 and 1994, 463 psychological evaluations were performed and catalogued in a case library at the Heart Institute of São Paulo University Medical School. Each case was described in terms of the following attributes: *psychological functioning, use of psychoactive substances, family dynamics, intellectual resources, adherence, motivation and knowledge about the transplant, psychological state* and *psychiatric antecedents in the family* [14].

We have started the development of a system for psychological evaluation using part of the cases set contained in this library. Regarding the performance of the system, we have not yet been able to collect statistical evidence showing conclusively that the CBR system is more accurate than a system using only the CNM, or vice versa. However, as the CBR system is based on the use of the general knowledge elicited from the neural network combined with a case-based matching algorithm, sometimes the two systems do present different answers. We are continuing to collect information about performance on new examples.

Another difference in the behaviour of the two systems is in the way they deal with features that are exceptional, e.g. the ones referenced by *positive* and *negative remindings*. When presented with a case in which not all the features can be explained by some *diagnosis descriptor*, the CBR system attempts to bring into consideration the cases pointed out by the *positive* and *negative remindings*. The goal here would be to determine whether these cases would not be more likely to have the correct answer than the prototypical cases of the hypotheses formed. The neural network, however, would behave differently ignoring nodes that were not activated with the highest output (which is usual for nodes with more atypical combinations of features).

Regarding the organization of the system's memory, it can often be observed that in CBR systems both normative experiences and distinctive ones are represented as cases. In Protos [15], a well-known system for the diagnosis of hearing disorders, normative experiences are stored in prototype cases. The same can be seen in more recent examples, such as in [12], where the memory of the system is split into two levels, one containing atypical cases and the other containing prototype cases. In the architecture presented in this paper, normative experiences are not represented in the same form of cases, but in the form of *diagnosis descriptors*. The reason for this is that by generalizing cases in *diagnosis descriptors* and by categorising their attributes into *triggers, primary features*, etc, we can guide the reasoning process of the system and build explanations.

6 Conclusion

We have presented here a new approach for learning general knowledge in a case-based system through the use of a neural network. After being trained with a set of real cases, the neural network is able to discriminate between relevant and irrelevant features for each of the diagnoses considered by the system. The network is not employed to solve new case-like problems, though. Instead, it is analysed, and the knowledge embodied in its connections is interpreted and stored in *diagnosis descriptors*. These descriptors are then used to guide the reasoning process in a case-based system.

We are currently using the case-based model described in this paper to develop a system that performs psychological evaluation of candidates for heart transplants. For this system, we have also collected knowledge graphs showing the relevance of possible combinations of features for each of the diagnoses considered. We have compared these knowledge graphs with the knowledge acquired and stored in the *diagnosis descriptors*. So far, we have been able to recognise that the kind of information stored in the *diagnosis descriptors* is often different from the knowledge represented in the experts' knowledge graphs. However, when used in practice, the knowledge graphs have a lower rate of correct classification than the method described here, although it is important that the two representations (the one given by the expert and the one given by the computer) match. This is particularly demanded because it is one of our goals that the knowledge stored in the *diagnosis descriptors* be not only comprehensible but also useful for building appropriate explanations.

The case-based model presented here is also being expanded for use in the development of other systems in different application domains: in particular, one in geology and one in banking. In the geological application, the main goal of the system is to classify sandstone deposits in accordance with previous cases of rock classification collected by a geologist. In the banking application, the system has to determine whether a client has the profile of a good or bad payer, in accordance with previous cases in credit scoring.

References

1. L. Becker and K. Jazayeri. A connectionist approach to case-based reasoning. In K. J. Hammond, editor, *Proceedings of the Case-Based Reasoning Workshop*, pages 213–217, Pensacola Beach, Florida, 1989. Morgan Kaufmann.

2. S. A. Borghetti-Maio. Quality of life after cardiomyoplasty. *Journal of heart and lung transplantation*, 13(6), 1994.

3. J. Dinsmore. Thunder in the gap. In J. Dinsmore, editor, *The connectionist and the symbolic paradigm: closing the gap*. Lawrence Erlbaum Associates, Hillsdale, NJ, 1992.

4. J. A. Hendler. Marker-passing over microfeatures: towards a hybrid symbolic/connectionist model. *Cognitive Science*, 13:79–106, 1989.

5. J. Kolodner. Maintaining organization in a dynamic long-term memory. *Cognitive Science*, 7:243–280, 1983.

6. P. Koton. Reasoning about evidence in causal explanations. In *Proceedings of the AAAI*, pages 256–261, St. Paul, Minnesota, August 1988. Cambridge, MA: AAAI Press.

7. B. F. Leão and E. B. Reategui. A hybrid connectionist expert system to solve classificational problems. In *Proceedings of Computers in Cardiology*, London, UK, 1993.

8. B. F. Leão and A. F. Rocha. Proposed methodology for knowledge acquisition: a study on congenital heart disease diagnosis. *Methods of Information in Medicine*, 29:30–40, 1990.

9. D. T. Lunde. Psychiatric complications of heart transplant. *American Journal of Psychiatry*, 126(3):117–129, 1969.

10. R. J. Machado and A. F. Rocha. The combinatorial neural network: a connectionist model for knowledge based systems. In B. Bouchon-Meunier, R. R. Yager, and L. A. Zadeh, editors, *Uncertainty in knowledge bases*. Springer Verlag, 1990.

11. R. J. Machado and A. F. Rocha. A hybrid architecture for fuzzy connectionist expert systems. In A. Kandel and G. Langholz, editors, *Hybrid architectures for intelligent systems*, pages 135–152. CRC Press, Boca Raton, 1992.

12. M. Malek and V. Rialle. A case-based reasoning system applied to neuropathy diagnosis. In M. Keane, J. P. Haton, and M. Manago, editors, *Proceedings of the European Workshop on Case-Based Reasoning*, Chantilly, France, 1994.

13. P. Myllymaki and H. Tirri. Massively parallel case-based reasoning with probabilistic similarity metrics. In K-D. Althoff, K. Richter, and S. Wess, editors, *Proceedings of the First European Workshop on Case-Based Reasoning*, pages 48–53, Kaiserslautern, November 1993.

14. M. E. Olbrich and J. L. Levenson. Psychosocial evaluation of heart transplant candidates: an international survey of process, criteria and outcomes. *Journal of heart and lung transplantation*, 10(6):948–955, 1991.

15. B. W. Porter, R. Bareiss, and R. C. Holte. Concept learning and heuristic classification in weak theory domains. *Artificial Intelligence*, 45(1-2):229–263, September 1990.

16. E. B. Reategui and J. Campbell. A classification system for credit card transactions. In M. Keane, J. P. Haton, and M. Manago, editors, *Proceedings of the European Workshop on Case-Based Reasoning*, Chantilly, France, 1994.

17. E. B. Reategui and B. F. Leão. Integrating neural networks with the formalism of frames. In S. Grossberg, editor, *Proceedings of the World Congress on Neural Networks*, Portland, Oregon, 1993. Lawrence Erlbaum Associates.

18. D. E Rumelhart, G. E. Hinton, and J. L. McClelland. Learning internal representations by error propagation. In D. E Rumelhart, J. L. McClelland, and The PDP Research Group, editors, *Parallel Distributed Processing: explorations in the microstructures of cognition*, volume 1. MIT Press, Cambridge, MA, 1986.

"Fish and Sink"
An Anytime-Algorithm to Retrieve Adequate Cases

Jörg Walter Schaaf

GMD – Artificial Intelligence Research Division
e-mail:Joerg.Schaaf@gmd.de
Sankt Augustin, Germany

Abstract. The main idea of the presented approach is based on the observation that identical data can be interpreted and used differently in different situations and by different persons. Data is considered individually and according to the actual situation. This phenomena can be interpreted as regarding different aspects. Here, the notion of aspects is applied to cases in the area of Cased Based Reasoning. This requires special representation of cases, special structure of case bases and a new algorithm to work on the defined structure. In this paper we will focus on description and discussion of an anytime algorithm that searches for cases regarding the relevant aspects.

1 Motivation

The present approach was developed to solve a problem that is common in CBR projects. According to the idea of CBR, a case similar to the users query should be able to support the user. This raises the question of detecting similarity of cases. Many approaches have been developed to meet this requirement e.g., in the FABEL project in the area of architectural design [12]. While evaluating these algorithms, we found that given a query, different "similar" cases were delivered. We then tried to answer the question, whether some of them were simply *incorrect*, or whether different results were based on different views of cases. Now the question is, which aspects should be taken into account to determine similarity? [7] To me this question can not be answered in general. Each algorithm can have its advantages under certain circumstances. Depending on the actual task[1].

This paper presents a concept that makes it possible to combine similarity concepts according to the actual needs. It describes a "shell" named AsPECT, which contains a data structure to store cases in various aspects, organize them in special case bases and suggest a global search algorithm to work on that structure. The presented paper focuses on the search algorithm that will be called the "Fish and Sink" algorithm (FaS) from now on. As far as I know, "Fish and Sink" is the only anytime algorithm that is able to handle *changing views* on

---

[1] In the following, the term "actual" means "at the moment the retrieval is activated".

cases and that delivers a demanded number of best cases of a case base before having examined all.

By December 1995 the CBR system of FABEL prototype will be equipped with the ASPECT shell, that will support the finding of useful cases in the area of architectural design.

2 An Approach to Integrate Similarity Concepts

Many of todays similarity concepts contain at least three main parts. The first part deals with representation of original data of a case. This representation can be very simple, like counting elements of a case (e.g., ASM in [12])), but others can be knowledge intensive and very time consuming (e.g., finding the case silhouette [1] or detection of Gestalten in [9]). Often, the generated representations were used to index cases for the support of further retrieval. A significant and independent representation of a case shall be called an *aspect*[2] in further description.

The second main part of similarity concepts is a function which states similarity for two given cases in the previously created representation. To simplify further description, it will help to replace the notion of similarity[3] from now on by the notion of distance. The range of values for distance functions should be restricted to $[0, 1]$ here. So, whenever we speak about a distance, we mean a normed distance. The used distance functions are often explicitly given by the integrated algorithms but must sometimes be deduced from the specific case organization (see associative memory in [6] and search tree of the ODM-algorithm in [1]).

The third part of similarity concepts often consists of a specific retrieval method based on its own case representation and distance function. Whenever a similarity detecting algorithm consists of at least a representation method and a distance function (as described above), ASPECT is able to integrate it with others and offer a general retrieval method called *Fish and Sink*. ASPECT is able to combine all different case representations (aspects) to various degrees, taking into account different *views*[4] on cases, while retrieving them from the case base. The varying importance of aspects depends on the actual task the user is going to perform. The case base of ASPECT consists of cases connected with weighted edges. Cases are objects containing original representation and some derived aspects. Edges relate same aspects of different cases and quantify their distance regarding the related aspect. Distances of stored cases are precalculated by aspect specific distance functions and stored in the data structure to keep access time down .

ASPECT should be used if a case base is worth being examined for several different types of queries, to fulfill different tasks or to satisfy users of different

---

[2] Here, we do not want to discuss what we think the differences are between aspects and for example, attributes or features. It is described in [10]

[3] Comp. e.g., [13]

[4] The notion of "views" is based on that used in database systems.

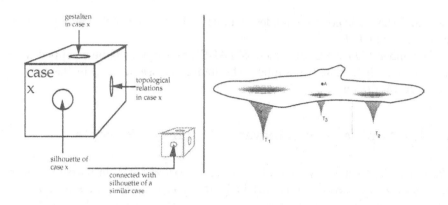

Fig. 1. A case object, and the metaphor of "Fish and Sink"

professions. If a case base is only used to answer very specialized questions regarding no more than one special case representation, other approaches may be more effective. For our domain in FABEL, it makes sense to use same cases to support different tasks in different work flows.

We now have to answer the question of how cases that fit the query in actually relevant aspects can be retrieved. Retrieval for similar cases should avoid testing every single case of the case base. To still obtain cases of high quality, comparison of one case with the query should deliver more than a single evaluation. As a common approach, one can examine one node in a search tree and cut off branches that do not contain adequate solutions. (See e.g., kd-trees of [14], "granulation trees" of [1] etc.) These approaches do not work if users want to define their own views (see Definition 5) on cases. Case organizations can not be static and must depend on the users actual tasks and interests.

Therefore, the dilemma is that without a structure on a case base, an efficient search is impossible, but unfortunately the information necessary to structure the case base (actual weights of aspects) is not available until the time of which the query is given. So we had to develop an algorithm that is able to spontaneously structure the case base and search through it, while the user is waiting for results.

The main idea is not to predefine relations between entire cases, but to relate their smallest ingenious interpretations – their aspects – and to combine them spontaneously according to the actual task. The view specific structure on the case base now is a result of elementary operations on aspect specific preorganized bases.

3 The Search Algorithm "Fish and Sink"

In the following sections, I will present an anytime algorithm whose task is to search for cases regarding each aspect according to the actually defined importance. Let cases be decomposed in aspects and be related by edges connecting them. Furthermore, let us suppose that the importance of all aspects are fixed manually or by an analysis tool. The algorithms aim is to test the probably useful cases before it tests those cases for which negative hints were found. The neighborhood of a case to a useless case should be seen as such a negative hint. This statement is based on the belief that for realistic case bases, the following is true:

Presumption 1 *If a retrieved case is not able to support the user in a given situation, then any similar case would not support him either.*

Consider the following metaphor (see Figure 1 on the right hand). Imagine all cases being distributed on a plain. You will find that they are without neighbors or within small or large groups. Imagine also, query (A) as a point in that plain. *Fishing* means taking a close look at one particular test case (T), selected by catching a point in the plain. First, suppose a test case is selected randomly[5]. After having tested the test case, imagine *sinking* it according to its distance to the query. Test cases with a small distance to the query will remain closer to the surface, whereas those with greater distances will be sunk deeper. If a test case has neighbors in the area, these neighbors will be influenced by the depth to which the test case is sunk. The closer the neighborhood is, the greater the influence will be. With each test of a case a crater appears around the location it was sunk. Cases that are part of a crater can not be test cases in the first pass anymore, but can be sunk further by influence of a test case in their neighborhood that is being sunk deeper. The closer a case is to the surface, the greater its distance is to every case that was sunk up to that time and the more rises the probability that this case will be tested early in the second pass.

3.1 Formal Description of "Fish and Sink"

To simplify further description I would like to state the following definitions: Let F_x, F_y be cases of the case base. In the given definitions we do not distinguish between queries and cases.

Definition 1 distance. A distance (normed to the interval [0,1]) defined on a set of objects Ω is a real function $\delta : \Omega \times \Omega \rightarrow [0,1]$ with $\delta(x,y) > 0$ and $\delta(x,x) = 0$ *We do not demand symmetry for the defined distance function here. Let Ω be the set of all stored cases.*

Definition 2 aspect. An aspect of a case is a function $\alpha_i: \Omega_0 \rightarrow \Omega_i$. Let Ω_0 be the set of all cases in their source representation. *The function α_i often has the nature of a transformation or a projection, but sometimes of a knowledge intensive interpretation.*

---

[5] In our implementation, we use the strategy to select the case with the most edges first.

Definition 3 aspect distance. We call a distance $\delta_i : \Omega_i \times \Omega_i \to [0,1]$ an aspect distance between F_x and F_y in the aspect α_i and simplify $\delta_i(\alpha_i(F_x), \alpha_i(F_y))$ to $\delta_i(F_x, F_y)$.

Definition 4 aspect neighbor. F_y is aspect neighbor of F_x in the aspect α_i, if an edge from F_x to F_y exits in the case base (for aspect α_i) .

Definition 5 view. A weight vector $\mathbf{W} = (w_1...w_n)$ with $\sum w_i = 1$ defines the "importance[6]", for each aspect α_i. Each given combination of weighted aspects, defined by the vector $\mathbf{W}$ is called a view on a case. α_i belongs to the actual view if $w_i > 0$.

Definition 6 view distance. The view distance of two cases is defined[7] as a function $SD_{Name} : \Omega \to [0,1]$. It is a combination of aspect distances weighted by the view $\mathbf{W}$. Examples:

$$SD_{med}(F_x, F_y, \mathbf{W}) := \sum_{i=1}^{n} w_i \delta_i(F_x, F_y) \qquad \text{weighted}$$

$$SD_{max}(F_x, F_y, \mathbf{W}) := Max\Big(w_i \delta_i(F_x, F_y)\Big) \qquad \text{conservative}$$

$$SD_{min}(F_x, F_y, \mathbf{W}) := Min\Big((1 - w_i)\delta_i(F_x, F_y)\Big) \qquad \text{innovative}$$

Definition 7 view neighbor. A case F_y is defined as a view neighbor of case F_x, if the view distance $SD_{actual}(F_x, F_y, \mathbf{W}) < 1$.

Definition 8 query and test case. Depending on the context, we define a query as only that part of it comparable with cases or the whole working situation context included.

Definition 9 Test- and base distance. The view distance between query A and a test case T is called the "test distance". The view distance between test case T and one of its view neighbors V_i is called "base distance[8]".

Fish and Sink The steps of the algorithm can be described as follows:

Given: A case base as described above, a query A, the distance functions δ_i, the actual view $\mathbf{W} = (w_1...w_n)$ and a definition of the preferred view distance $SD_{preferred}$. All cases are available in a data structure NT (not tested) of not yet tested cases.

Searched: Those cases of the case base with the minimal view distances to the query. The up to the moment of interruption calculated evaluation of (minimal) view distances should be available anytime.

---

[6] The importance of an aspect regarding the actual situation and task is now manually defined. This should be replaced by an automatic way soon.

[7] Definition of view distances and their influence to case selection is discussed in [10]. $SD(x,x) = 0$ is still current and SD is symmetric if all δ_i are symmetric.

[8] The notion "base distance" shall stress that this particular distance is stored in the case base.

Fish and Sink

WHILE NT (not tested) not empty AND not interrupted
    choose test case T from NT[9]
    move T to DT (directly tested)
    $depth_{DT}(T) := test\ distance$
    FOR ALL cases V (not directly tested view neighbors of T)
        If V not yet tested then move V to IDT
    $depth_{IDT}(V) := MAX\Big(test\ distance - base\ distance,\ depth_{IDT}(V)\Big)$

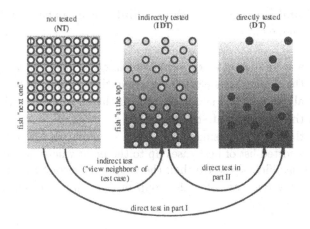

Fig. 2. "Fish and Sink"

In a first pass of FaS the data structure NT of not yet tested cases is examined. In aspects belonging to the actual view, cases are directly compared with the query *(directly tested)* beginning with the "first one" of a predefined order[10] (Figure 2). By direct test, the view distance between query and test case is now exactly known. The case base contains aspect distances between the test case and all its view neighbors. So, the view distances between the test case and all its view neighbors is easy to calculate. Let us suppose the worst case, that the entire stated distance between a test case and one of its view neighbors makes this neighbor come closer to the query. As a result, we get[11] the *expected minimum distance* between the query and each of the view neighbors of the test case. We also refer to the calculation of the expected minimum distance as the *indirect test* of a view neighbor of a test case. Each view neighbor of the test case is moved to the data structure IDT to a position corresponding to its expected minimum distance from the query. (This process corresponds to the *sinking* in

---

[10] A criteria to sort the cases in order to minimize run-time is suggested in [10]
[11] This is only true if the Triangle Inequality is supposed. See discussion in [10]

the metaphor.) Therefore, the data structure NT is decreased by the test case with each direct test and by the set of its view neighbors with indirect tests. The algorithm terminates its first pass if every case has been tested either directly or indirectly. The more view neighbors of a test case exist, the earlier it happens.

In a second pass Fish and Sink works on IDT to move some more cases to DT. This pass is similar to the previous pass but differs in the fishing strategy and in the way the result is interpreted. We fish cases from the top of IDT. These are cases for which the fewest negative hints were found until now. The depth of the top case in IDT is very important to us, as you can see in the next section where the finding of the n-best cases is discussed.

Termination and Results of "Fish and Sink" FaS can be activated expecting various results, e.g.:

- To obtain a sorted list of cases, recommending the most similar cases first.
- To obtain the n best cases (sorted regarding their similarity to the query)
- To obtain all cases with a similarity greater than a predefined threshold.
- To obtain the best cases after a predefined run-time.
- To obtain the most promising cases after a spontaneous user interruption.
- To obtain a sorted list of best cases up to the point where the quality of the next one is significantly worse than the previously recommended one.
- To obtain only one case of each group of cases where elements are very similar.

If the user wants a list of all cases sorted according to their similarity to the query, then FaS has no advantage over other algorithms. FaS must test each single case directly. FaS terminates after DT and IDT are completely empty with the above result.

FaS shows a completely different behaviour if the user wants to have the n cases that are most similar to the query. After DT is empty and all cases are located in IDT according to their actual expected minimal distance to the query or they are fixed in DT due to their exact distance, the n best cases can be determined if a certain condition is true. FaS has found the n best cases if there are n cases in DT with a position higher than the case on top of IDT. None of the cases in IDT can "rise" while changing to DT, because the depth in IDT represents the *minimal distance* to the query. The exact distance (depth in DT) can only be greater (deeper). The n-best cases are the n top cases of DT. You can see how FaS saves time by recognizing that FaS does not know the (n+1) best case at that moment.

If the user wants to have cases with a similarity to the query above a defined threshold, then FaS terminates with the same argument as above if there are no more cases in IDT which are "deeper"than the given threshold. Keep in mind, that every position in IDT and DT stands for an analog distance to the query. Cases on the top have a small distance, those deeper a greater one.

If FaS is interrupted by a user, the quality of results depends extremely on the run-time. If FaS is interrupted during part I, the only exact results are represented by the depths of cases in DT. The longer FaS runs, the more confident are the positions in IDT. If FaS is interrupted in part II, one can state the result of how many of the first best cases have been found so far, depending on the level of the top case in IDT. FaS shows the number of best cases found so far, permanently, after having switched to part II. Therfore, it is easy to determine the best time to interrupt FaS. If the user wants to make a decision dependent on a quality discontinuity, FaS shows the distribution of cases over the continuum of similarity so the user is able to decide or let an algorithm make the decision.

Complexity of "Fish and Sink" To estimate the complexity of FaS, one should look at three main operations after the user has pushed the retrieve button.

First, the query must be represented. Some of the algorithms representing aspects of cases use plenty of time. The complexity of a single representation (creating an aspect) can not be influenced by the ASPECT shell but the overall complexity can be reduced by selecting those aspects that are worth representing. ASPECT selects (or helps select) those that help discriminate helpful cases from useless cases.

After having represented the relevant aspects, FaS tries to find cases similar to the query by exploring the same aspects of those cases being stored in the case base. Therefore, FaS performs direct and indirect tests. The complexity of *direct tests* is given by the aspect specific distance functions and can not be influenced by ASPECT except in the same way the overall complexity of aspect representation is influenced. It is the complexity resulting calculating the actual view distance $SD_{actual}(A, T, \mathbf{W})$ between query (A) and test case (T).

To maximize the effect of one of those (probably expensive) direct tests, FaS tries to derive information about some other cases from it. This information results from frequent but cheap *indirect tests*. Complexity of one *indirect test* derives from the calculation of the view distance between the test case (T) and one case (V_i) of its view neighbors. Depending on the actual valid definition of view distance, the complexity of one indirect test is either a sum of aspect distances or the determination of their maximum or minimum. Access to aspect distances is implemented with a list operation, so that costs are minimal.

Reduction of the number of (expensive) direct tests through (cheap) indirect tests is not easy to predict, but one can state the following relations. The greater the number of aspect neighbors of each case, the greater is the average number of view neighbors of a randomly selected test case. The greater this number, the greater the number of cases being moved to IDT through one direct test. Because we know the minimal view distance of every case in IDT to the query, these cases are in a way "presorted". Quality of this assortment is permanently increased and influences positively the time it takes to satisfy the user, regardless of the desired result.

4 Summary, Comparison and Outlook

The presented approach differs from others mainly in the following points:

Changing views of cases The idea of making case bases useful for several different users for performing many different tasks, has not yet been explored consequently as far as I know. Using different and freely definable views on cases makes it possible to use episodical knowledge for tasks that one did not think about while the case base was created. This makes it possible to hitherto existing users to get more information from their cases and may make it possible for new user groups to participate. Some ideas regarding aspects can also be found in [3]. He uses decomposition of cases to aspects mainly to reduce storage capacity needs.

Spontaneous structuring of the case base To realize the idea of *changing views*, cases of the case bases can not be sorted statically to support the retrieval. To solve the retrieval problem without a static case organization, the FaS algorithm has been developed. FaS creates an easy to calculate local structure around a randomly selected case, using only the predefined structure between aspects and a given function to calculate view distances. A similar relationship between cases is used in [5]. He connects entire cases according to similarity to perform his "Hillclimbing on case neighborhoods". [8] describe a method to find cases without searching. At a first glance it looks similar to the procedure performed by FaS, but there are big and far-reaching differences. (See the following item and [10])

Using exclusion to retrieve Many approaches like [5] and [8] try to make statements about the *usefulness* of cases that are not directly tested. This has a lot of disadvantages. Retrieval methods based on this become e.g., sensitive if case neighbors are missing. FaS on the other hand, uses indirect tests only to make statements about the *uselessness* of cases. *Usefulness* is only stated by direct tests. If an aspect neighbor is missing, no fact stating the uselessness is generated, so the case will be tested early in the process. The only consequence of a missing aspect can therefore be, that the overall run time increases. In [4] and [8] cases can only be found confidently if every neighborhood is accurately existent. Missing neighbors can lead to neglecting the best cases. In FaS, a missing neighbor can not lead to a loss of quality if the user is willing to accept a slight delay. Nevertheless, he should initiate calculation of every known aspect similarity between each pair of his cases.

The presented approach is completely worked out, formally described in [10] and implemented as a prototype. Creation and maintenance of case bases belong as well to the implementation as a data structure to contain case aspects, a data structure to connect similar aspect occurences and the search algorithm "Fish and Sink". Up to now, we have integrated the aspect "case silhouette" [1] for a case base (in FABEL) in the domain of architectural design. Integration of the aspects "Gestalten" [9] and "topological structure" [2] is in progress. Run-time tests are still to be made.

Acknowledgments

First, I would like to thank my colleague Carl-Helmut Coulon who was ready at any state during the work to be my counterpart. Special thanks also to Angi Voß (GMD) and Merinda Johnson who helped with the editing of this paper. I would also like to thank the collegues in the FABEL-Project, and Ralf Steffens who implemented. Finally, I would like to thank Prof.Dr.M.M. Richter for his initial impulse and for several important hints.

References

1. Carl-Helmut Coulon and Ralf Steffens. Comparing fragments by their images. In Angi Voß, editor, *Similarity concepts and retrieval methods*, pages 36–44. GMD, Sankt Augustin, 1994.
2. Carl-Helmut Coulon. Automatic Indexing, Retrieval and Reuse of Topologies in Complex Designs. In *accepted at the ISCCSE-95*, 1995.
3. R. Deters. Multidimensional structuring of a case-memory. In Stefan Wess Brigitte Bartsch-Spörl, Dietmar Janetzko, editor, *Fallbasiertes Schließen - Grundlagen und Anwendungen*, pages 21–29, Universität Kaiserslautern, Germany, 1995. Zentrum für Lernende Systeme und Anwendungen, Fachbereich Informatik.
4. Klaus Goos. Preselection strategies for case based classification. In B. Nebel and L. Dreschler-Fischer, editors, *KI-94: Advances in Artificial Intelligence*, Lecture Notes in Artificial Intelligence 861, pages 28–38, Berlin, 1994. Springer-Verlag.
5. Klaus Goos. *Fallbasiertes Klassifizieren. Methoden, Integration und Evaluation.* PhD thesis, Bayerische Julius-Maximilians-Universität, Würzburg, 1995.
6. Wolfgang Gräther. Computing distances between attribute-value representations in an associative memory. In Angi Voß, editor, *Similarity concepts and retrieval methods*, pages 12–25. GMD, Sankt Augustin, 1994.
7. Janet L. Kolodner. *Case-Based Reasoning.* Morgan Kaufmann, San Mateo, 1993.
8. M. Lenz and H.D. Burkhard. Retrieval ohne suche. In Stefan Wess Brigitte Bartsch-Spörl, Dietmar Janetzko, editor, *Fallbasiertes Schließen - Grundlagen und Anwendungen*, pages 1–10, Universität Kaiserslautern, Germany, 1995. Zentrum für Lernende Systeme und Anwendungen, Fachbereich Informatik.
9. Jörg W. Schaaf. Gestalts in CAD-plans, Analysis of a Similarity Concept. In J. Gero and F. Sudweeks, editors, *AI in Design'94*, Kluwer Academic Publishers, pages 437–446, Dordrecht, 1994.
10. Jörg W. Schaaf. ASPECT: Über die Suche nach situationsgerechten Fällen im Case Based Reasoning. Fabel-Report 30, GMD, Sankt Augustin, December 1995.
11. Ralf Steffens. Kantenreduktion in aspect-fallbasen. Master's thesis, Universität Bonn, 1995. Diplomarbeit in der Entstehung.
12. Angi Voß. Similarity concepts and retrieval methods. FABEL-Report 13, GMD, Sankt Augustin, 1994.
13. Stefan Weß, Jürgen Paulokat, and Klaus-Dieter Althoff, editors. *Fallbasiertes Schließen - Ein Überblick -, Band I: Grundlagen.* Universität Kaiserslautern, 1992.
14. S. Wess, K.D. Althoff, and G.Derwand. Improving the retrieval step in case-based reasoning. In *Pre-Prints First European Workshop on Case-Based reasoning*, Universität Kaiserslautern, Germany, 1993. Zentrum für Lernende Systeme und Anwendungen, Fachbereich Informatik.

Knowledge Engineering for CBR systems from a Cognitive Science Perspective [1]

G. Strube, A. Enzinger, D. Janetzko & M. Knauff
Center for Cognitive Science, University of Freiburg
IIG, Friedrichstr. 50, D-79098 Freiburg, Germany
{strube | enzinger | dietmar | knauff}@cognition.iig.uni-freiburg.de

Abstract

Although CBR has been advertised as a technique to elude knowledge engineering (KE), we argue that knowledge-level modeling in KE is of eminent importance to the success of CBR systems, both for practical and theoretical reasons. Cases are knowledge structures linked to some underlying database (although not necessarily in a one-to-one fashion), and in order to define case structures and their relations to the database, domain knowledge is needed. In this paper, we focus on KE for CBR in the domain of architectural design, first looking at general analyses of work processes and information use, then discussing micro-analyses of task structure in order to define case size, finally proceeding to knowledge-level evaluation of the domain knowledge acquired and modeled so far.

Keywords: Knowledge Engineering, CBR Systems, Knowledge-Level Modeling, Architecture, Design, Task Analysis.

1 The Need for KE in CBR System Development

In the early years of expert systems, issues of knowledge acquisition, modeling, and maintenance quickly became identified as the major obstacle to rapid success. Many attempts to deal with KE tried to work around the problem by constructing tools to eliminate the knowledge engineer. Automated KE tools have been a limited success, however, and nowadays it is generally felt that KBS system development needs to be anchored in analyses of the workplace, the tasks to be supported, the interactions relevant for cooperation, and the kind of knowledge deployed in expert work (Strube, Janetzko & Knauff, in press). Especially in Europe, many researchers have realized that knowledge-level modeling in KE is of eminent importance to the success of KBS (e.g., the KADS and CommonKADS groups). To summarize, it took AI some time to recognize the importance of KE, and to integrate KBS development with the experience gained in the software engineering community.

---

[1]This research was supported by the Federal Ministry of Education, Science, Research and Technology (BMBF), within the joint project FABEL under contract 01-IW-104-D7. Project partners in FABEL are the German National Research Center for Computer Science (GMD), Sankt Augustin, BSR Consulting GmbH, München, the Technical University of Dresden, the HTWK Leipzig, the University of Freiburg, and the University of Karlsruhe.

Now CBR seems to re-enact for episodic knowledge (cases) what has happened before with respect to general knowledge. Some CBR practitioners attempt to skip KE altogether and, in fact, advertise CBR as a technique that relieves you of the problems of domain-specific knowledge. In doing so, they can rely on the opinion of distinguished researchers that were early promoters of CBR (see Riesbeck & Schank, 1989, p. 26).

Human expertise is neither identical to rules nor to cases, of course: It consists of both general and specific (often episodic) knowledge. For example, students in US business schools learn from cases, but they become also acquainted with the general principles applicable to these cases (or highlighted as an exception). Between rules and cases, we find generalized cases, or schemata. For this reason, cases and general knowledge cannot be kept apart completely. A second reason for KE in the context of CBR systems is a technical one: Cases are structures like frames, or feature-value lists - both call for clear distinctions (i.e., the attributes that constitute a case have to be clearly defined) - but in order to define attributes and case structures, domain knowledge is needed.

In our domain of application, the design of office buildings and the layout of pipes for air, water, etc., in those buildings, one of the fundamental problems that had to be solved was how to define a case. Should a case be a whole building? Or should smaller units be considered? Was CBR indeed the appropriate method of problem-solving in our domain? As it turned out in our case, we needed KE first to determine where and how CBR could be used in our application. KE is even needed for CBR applications that start out from a wealth of cases already accumulated, because those projects often involve heaps of data in dubious condition. The first author became acquainted as a reviewer with a CBR project that had to deal with several thousands of failure reports on complex equipment from different sites. Many of the data in the report forms were not relevant to diagnosis and troubleshooting, and important information was encoded in free-style handwriting – not only difficult to read, but also difficult to interpret. KE proved an essential step to success there. Similar experiences have been related from medical domains.

Practical and theoretical reasons both emphasize how important KE is in CBR. For practical success, you need to acquire domain knowledge in order to define cases or to understand existing ones. As for theory, research on expertise has shown that experts command and deploy both general and episodic knowledge (VanLehn, 1989): Domain knowledge is needed to determine which features are relevant (and hence, which cases are similar to a problem at hand). General knowledge is also needed to relate a problem to old cases, and to adapt old solutions to new requirements. *Central functions of KE for the development of CBR applications* are:

- determine when and how episodic knowledge is already used, when it could be helpful in the tasks that the system is expected to support, or even determine which tasks could be supported by CBR,
- determine typical problem-solving processes in the domain, and the corresponding format (size, attributes, etc.) that cases have or should have,

- determine which cases have already been collected (and in what shape these data are, how they should be reprocessed), or how cases should be collected, and how the integrity of the case-base should be maintained,
- acquire the general domain knowledge ('background knowledge') that is needed to model problem-solving in the domain, and describe the structure of cases,
- assess the changes the CBR systems introduces in the workplace, and evaluate the system (e.g., for further development).

2 CBR in Architectural Design - Whether, When, and How

CBR is meant to address various problem types like diagnosis, planning and design, monitoring etc. Although a lot of research on reuse of knowledge has been carried out, especially in software design (e.g., Burkhardt, & Détienne, 1995), only few studies have shown empirically whether, when, and how experts use case-knowledge (e.g., Visser, 1987). In our studies of 'real world'-domains, we try to find out how experts work, what knowledge and information they use, which plans, strategies, and working steps they take, and which quality of results and solutions they achieve. The study reported here is concerned with the design of industrial buildings.

2.1 Design of the Study. Two teams of architects were asked to design the ground plan of a conference building. The teams were investigated at their usual working places, at an architectural engineering office in Solothurn (Switzerland) and at the Institute for Industrial Building Production at the University of Karlsruhe (Germany). The Swiss group *(practitioner group)* consisted of two architects who had been designing many houses and buildings for decades and of one younger architect less experienced. The German group *(academic group)* were three architects with some practical but mostly theoretical experience in computer-aided building design. Both groups were presented with a 'room book' containing a detailed functional description of the building to be designed. Each group was given two days time to work out a solution. – Two knowledge engineers observed the design process according to a semi-structured schedule and took notes independently of each other. After each 'working step', the architects were interrupted and interviewed on the input used, their actions and outputs. In additional trials each team had to evaluate its own solution as well as the result from the other group. All interviews were tape recorded. For each team data from notes, tape-transcripts and sketches were collected in a protocol of the design process containing all available information. Using protocols were subjected to repeated cycles of qualitative content analysis. Along pre-prepared coding schemes, several raters iteratively coded, rated and interpreted the data. Apart from looking at the categories *action*, *output* and *working topics*, we paid particular attention to the *input* category, that is to all kinds of information and knowledge used during working steps.

2.2 Results

2.2.1 To what extent do experts use cases during problem solving? How important are they compared to schemata, scripts, and rules?

The practitioners proposed a solution after 139 working steps with 193 identified input units. The theoreticians worked with 227 steps and employed 334 identifiable input units. Table 1 shows absolute frequencies of the most relevant input categories. These data assign no prominent status to cases (including examples). Schemata and scripts are used almost twice as often. Overall, both groups seem to employ a well-balanced mixture of different kinds of input units. – A closer and qualitative look at the protocols shows, however, that the frequencies of knowledge units do not exactly reflect their valence or importance. The practitioners, for instance, took one project from their archive as a prototype with respect to quality, almost a schema with respect to mode of usage. This complex case was used extensively during the whole design process, both in an explicit and implicit way. ('Implicit' means that parts of the project were copied without identifiable consideration.) The academic group, in contrast, who naturally have no cases of their own available, consulted examples from several catalogs and plans, as well as the very rooms they were working in.

input category	Pract. Grp.	Acad. Grp.
examples	2	18
cases	16	0
schemata	20	14
scripts	20	16
rules	11	12
norms	10	20
principles	7	29
requirements	40	67
prior results	53	99

Table 1: Absolute frequencies of most relevant 'input' categories. *Examples* means solutions from other people, e.g., from design catalogs. *Cases* are solutions the architects worked out themselves at a former time. *Schemata* are generalized case structures, which represent abstract complex knowledge. *Scripts* are action schemata representing generalized knowledge about action sequences, planning and strategies. *Rules* are abstract, context-free prescriptions. *Norms* refers to laws, standards, or administrative prescriptions. By *principles* we mean personal values, standards, and esthetic principles. *Requirements* are the demands stated in the room book. *Prior results* are solutions from earlier working steps.

We may conclude that cases do not have the significance which CBR theory (e.g., Kolodner, 1993) suggests. Compared to other kinds of input they are used rather infrequently and mostly in connection with schemata and norms. However, even a single case may be used extensively, and guide much of the design process.

2.2.2 In which phases of the design process do experts use cases, and what are these cases used for? Generally speaking, a design process, just like every other problem solving process, consists of problem analysis, idea generation, evaluation and execution. These phases are modified in each application field by domain-specific characteristics.

We identified ten domain-specific steps in the design process for the practitioner group: analyzing the requirements and constraints, estimating sizes, exact calculation, checking alternatives, etc. They showed a peak of case usage during the first steps when they structured the problem, filled in lacking information on sizes, functions, and usage. They compared problem and prototype especially with respect to differences, then copied and sometimes adapted solutions for overall and partial problems. For checking the solutions, especially the adapted ones, they did not employ cases but norms, rules and standards of their own.

The academic group showed a different pattern of case usage over 13 domain-specific design steps. They too had a small peak in the first phase, but then a concentration in the second half of the design process. This reflects differences in the design process rather than in case usage, because they had more iterations and recursions in the whole design process. In the beginning they used examples to get a rough estimate of floor and room sizes. Then they freely designed the general building structure without explicit reference to cases or examples. Nevertheless their sketches show a combination of various experiences, and indeed a tendency to avoid existing solutions. When solving smaller problems, like toilets, or furniture, they copied examples from several sources, checking them with norms and rules.

Interestingly, both groups tended to copy cases or examples, at least for subproblems, but avoided to do a lot of adaptational work. The practitioners sometimes even changed the problem requirements (stated in the room book) to make them fit to an available solution, e.g., they canceled the bedrooms. This behavior seems to be concordant to results from cognitive research on transfer. Most people succeed in transferring solutions only if the requirements of source and target are identical or extremely similar.

2.2.3 What criteria are employed in finding good cases?
A 'good case' is relevant to the problem at hand. Its solution is correct and reliable with respect to norms, safety standards, etc. Both teams of architects looked for relevant cases and examples according to function and usage, and considering the context at different levels of abstraction. 'Function' means the kind of use of a building entity, like floor, toilets, etc. 'Usage' means the amount of people using a building entity. If they wanted to fix the size of a floor, of computer rooms or corridors, for example, they looked for a functional unit of the same category, like a school building, a working room for groups, or corridors in public buildings. This seems to be a weak and clumsy heuristic strategy, mostly ending up in a couple of alternatives. But cases or examples seem to be indexed by criteria of function and usage with a lot of context. In addition, the frequency of similar or different solutions might be a useful piece of information for making a choice. Concerning the reliability and correctness of cases and examples both teams only chose sources with well-known high standards. The practitioners chose one of their own prototypical projects. The academic group also used the plans and catalogs of the practitioners (due to availability), but additionally checked the examples with the help of norm-books.

In sum, the strategy of both teams was to look for identical function. The more abstract a functional feature, the more additional criteria like usage, size and structure were employed. – Due to data analyses still running and lack of space, we have presented only some of the results and first interpretations. More detailed descriptions and discussions of the study will be available in Enzinger (forthcoming). As a conclusion we would like to suggest that CBR projects should take the human tendencies in use of cases into account, and enrich case formats (or indexes) with information on function and usage at different abstraction levels, if possible.

3 Problem-Solving Steps: Determining the Format of Cases

Given a real world domain, especially when synthetic problems are concerned, cases are not simply given (e.g., in files etc.) but have to be identified and acquired. Until now, CBR has mainly been applied to analytic tasks. Here properties or symptoms and corresponding concepts or diagnoses are quite ready at hand. There is an ongoing debate how to determine, or 'cut' cases in synthesis tasks. Issues at stake are the method to cut cases and, as a consequence, the grainsize of cases. Note that there is no need to identify cases with units in the underlying database (in architecture, often CAD data): Although cases should be systematically related to the underlying data, there is considerable freedom how to define and implement the relations.

3.1 The Problem of Determining Cases in Design Problems

What is a case in building design? The literature on CBR does not provide an answer. Obviously, cases could be cut *ad lib* from an overall architectural plan – in a word, no particular method is applied. Case acquisition may, on the other side, be carried out by using a rationale that points out how to derive cases. Such a method is to use a task-structure (Drury, Paramore, van Cott, Grey & Corlett, 1987). The main reason for employing a well-founded method for cutting cases is not the size of cases as such, but the need to arrive at cases that are *usable* in CBR. Cases should reflect and support problem solving in a domain; they should allow to tackle specific problems that are known to reoccur in the application domain. Embarking on specific problems becomes extremely hard if the grainsize of the problem to be solved (e.g., the design of the supply air system for an aisle or a room) and the grainsize of the case (e.g., a complete building) do not match. A mismatch is likely to happen if no particular method is employed or oversized units in the domain are viewed as cases.

3.2 Deriving a Task Structure to Guide the Acquisition of Cases

A task-structure is both *knowledge* that can be directly used for system design and a *tool* that supports further knowledge acquisition, especially cases. Using empirical methods like observations, interviews, card sorting, or analysis of traces allows to derive a task structure. The methods used should be objective (independent of the knowledge engineer), reliable (yielding similar results when different experts are examined) and valid (providing results that truly reflect an expert's organization of knowledge). This is how the task structure depicted in Fig. 1 has been derived. Only when these criteria are met the knowledge that feeds into the system is sound, and the system as a whole has a chance to be accepted by the expert.

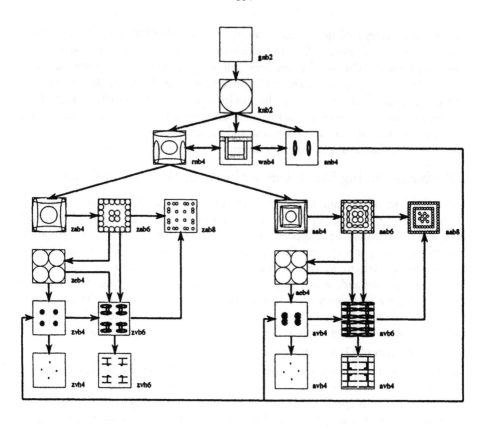

Figure 1. Task-decomposition schema used in planning and design of an air-conditioning system Tasks are described by expressions made up of three letters and a number. The first letter relates to the subsystem of the building (e.g., **a** = used air, **g** = building, **k** = climate, **r** = rooms, **w** = paths, **s** = shaft, **z** = supply air). The second letter denotes the general function of the area addressed by the task (e.g., **a** = linkage, **e** = development, **v** = connection). The third letter specifies the degree of resolution (e.g., **b** = area, **h** = bounding-box). The number relates to the part of the building that is envisaged (e.g., **2** = building, **4** = floor, **6** = room, **8** = areas within a room). For example, **knb2** is the task of designing the area of climate use that covers the whole building. The arrows indicate the standard sequence of tasks that are addressed. They do neither point out the necessary requirements that have to be fulfilled to tackle a particular task, nor do they exclude other sequences an architect may possibly choose when addressing these tasks. Simple arrows refer to a transition between two adjacent tasks with the former providing input to the latter. For example, the ground plan **gnb2** provides input for the task of designing the areas of a building that are intended to have a homogeneous climate **knb2**. The double arrows connect two adjacent tasks that interact strongly (loop), i.e., they provide input to each other, e.g., the layout of the rooms **rnb2** and the layout of the paths **wnb2** in a building have to be tuned to each other.

To establish a task-structure, (1) the overall domain task (e.g., planning and design of supply nets in a building) is factored into manageable subtasks to be accomplished. As a rule of thumb, the subtasks should have the same grainsize as the problems experts deal with. This can be done along the physical components involved in the overall domain task. The task-structure may reflect the structure of the physical components that occur in planning or design. Another way of factoring an overall task into subtasks is by focusing on reoccurring problems that are separated from other problems by having unique input and outputs.

(2) Input and output of each of the resulting subtasks is specified. In so doing, the flat list of subtasks is replaced by a structure made up of tasks and enabling relations. The task-structure is constructed in collaboration between domain experts and knowledge engineers using knowledge elicitation techniques that range from observation and interviews to highly structured methods.

(3) Dependencies, i.e., interactions between tasks are specified. There are dependencies between two or more tasks if one task cannot be achieved without considering the realization of one or more other tasks.

(4) The task-structure should be tested empirically, e.g., by predicting subsequent problem solving steps and comparing the prediction with experts' behavior (see also section 4). In cases of divergencies the task-structure has to be adjusted accordingly.

(5) Finally, cases are determined corresponding to the tasks to be tackled: A case is nothing but an instance of a reoccurring task. Cases should represent the problem solving goal, the initial state, and the solution. Thus, cases relate immediately subsequent states in problem solving for means of reasoning. Additionally, in domains like building design, not only knowledge about attributes of case objects is important but also their inherent relations. Knowledge representation schemata have to meet this fact. In the FABEL project, the task structure provided guidance not only for cutting cases, but also helped to design suggestions for what to do next to the user, and to determine exactly which design steps the system should support.

4 Knowledge-Level Debugging of Acquired Knowledge

The concept of the knowledge level (Newell, 1982) is very popular in KE. Therefore, it seems surprising that approaches to system evaluation have not attached much significance to the knowledge level so far. We propose an evaluation method that operates at the knowledge level. *Knowledge Level Debugging* (KLD) is a kind of high-level 'walk-through'. It integrates theories from cognitive psychology and KE and takes the cooperative character of expert system design and knowledge acquisition into account.

The main idea of KLD is to base the process of knowledge-base evaluation and debugging on knowledge-level models rather than on an implementation. (The success of operational knowledge-level specifications turned out to be very limited, at least in the FABEL project.) During knowledge acquisition, the knowledge engineer together with an expert builds a model of the expert's task-relevant knowledge. This model can be tested directly for correctness, completeness, and consistency. If the knowledge base seems to be sufficient for the task, the implementation can begin, while interim results of the debugging process provide a guideline and the framework for later phases of a cooperative knowledge acquisition process. Since KE does not strictly follow a sequence of knowledge acquisition–evaluation–implementation, but requires many cycles through the acquisition–evaluation loop, KLD has also the decisive economic advantage of spotting and repairing gross (and also a lot of subtle) errors before implementation and re-implementation, where corrections are much more costly.

To show how KLD works in practice, we describe a pair of methods developed by Dietmar Janetzko: *Forced-Choice Card Sorting* and *Replay of Cards*. The first method (not identical to the well-known hierarchical sorting of concepts) generates a problem solving trace obtained from observing an expert who solves a problem. The second method tests and extends the results obtained. This is achieved by having another subject solve a similar problem, using (replaying) the cards produced by forced-choice card sorting.

4.1 Forced-Choice Card Sorting. The leading principle is to make task-relevant knowledge explicit. A non-trivial problem has to be selected, which can be solved without regard for other problems. This is possible even in domains where cross-dependencies abound, because the necessary preconditions can be fixed experimentally, and co-dependencies may be neglected at that stage. Methods of task decomposition may be applied to isolate suitable problems (Janetzko, Börner, Jeschke, & Strube, 1994). A set of cards, which denote basic functional relations, has to be provided to express the knowledge that may be applied. This set is the result of theoretical considerations (cognitive theories of problem solving) and practical experience in KE. There are different types of cards that draw on central concepts: Primitive cards just express a single concept, relation, or rule; compound cards combine a number of other cards so that a knowledge base can be constructed incrementally. Linkage cards code the initial state, goal state, case, etc. The set of cards is intended to bridge the gap between a structured interview and a formal representation of knowledge.

The method proceeds as follows. The experts are given a preselected problem and are asked to solve it. In particular, they are given the set of problem solving cards that they can use to express their way of solving the problem. The cards presented in the beginning are generic in nature. When the experts employ a domain concept, they take an empty concept card, write the name of the concept on the card, and place the card in the temporal sequence of other cards. In this way, a problem solving trace is attained. The knowledge engineer has to watch that the trace actually covers all kinds of knowledge required for understanding the trace. The experts may use each type of card and may even introduce new types of cards if required.

Forced-choice card sorting intervenes in the way experts solve a problem. To lessen the experts' burden of documenting each problem solving step, two knowledge engineers are required to conduct forced-choice card sorting: One of them selects and writes cards, and the second one observes and interviews the expert.

4.2 Replay of Cards. The leading principle behind replay of cards is the reapplication of the problem solving trace to similar problems by a different intelligent agent. The method proceeds as follows: A problem solver, for example, a knowledge engineer, is presented with a problem and with the problem solving trace produced by an expert who solved a similar problem using the forced-choice card sorting technique. The expert is also present. The cards provide the only expert knowledge the non-expert problem solver can use. Usually, the non-expert runs into difficulties quickly when trying to solve the problem given. This situation is similar to forced-choice card sorting: The non-expert has to ask the expert for the additional knowledge he needs to overcome the impasse. This additional knowledge is also written on cards taken from the forced-choice card set. Additional cards are inserted into the trace. At times, a concept used by the expert as a primitive turns out to be a compound one that has to be resolved into a number of primitive cards. This process leads to a cooperative change of the original problem solving trace generated by the expert. By using replay of cards the non-expert slips into the role of the computer, which is given a knowledge-based program to tackle a problem. However, replay of cards is more economical than the test of a program on the symbol level, for example, in rapid prototyping. When errors are detected, they can be alleviated on the spot.

5 Discussion

Emphasis on the knowledge level has become the common denominator of the majority of approaches in the expert system community, particularly in the so-called 'modeling approach'. In order to make good use of the knowledge level approach, further structuring is required. There is, however, no general agreement to date concerning the structuring of knowledge on the knowledge level (Wielinga et al., 1993). Clancey's model of heuristic classification can be seen as the first elaborated approach to expert systems on the knowledge level (Clancey, 1985). In recent years the KADS and CommonKADS groups (Schreiber et al., 1993; Wielinga & Breuker, 1986; Wielinga et al., 1992), the generic tasks approach (Chandrasekaran, 1986) and the components-of-expertise theory (Steels, 1990) are the most representative approaches to knowledge-level modeling in the KE literature.

Our experience from project FABEL is that knowledge-level oriented KE is an essential foundation for CBR systems. Empirical analyses of expert work helped to determine the role of cases in the work of architects. Empirically based micro-analyses of the tasks into subtasks and their dependencies resulted in defining case size and case structure, and in fact provided a reference grid for the various methods devised and implemented for case-based support in the prototype. Since our KE activities aimed at knowledge modeling, we also evaluated and 'debugged' it at the knowledge level.

References

Chandrasekaran, B. (1986). Generic tasks in knowledge-based reasoning: High-level building blocks for expert system design. *IEEE Expert*, 1, 23-30.

Clancey, W. J. (1985). Heuristic classification. *Artificial Intelligence*, 27, 289-350.

Burkhardt, J.-M., & Détienne, F. (1995) An empirical study of software reuse by experts in object-oriented design. *Proceedings of Interact '95*. Lillehammer (Norway), 27-29 June.

Drury, C. G., Paramore, B., van Cott, H. P., Grey, S. M., & Corlett, E. N. (1987) Task analysis. In G. Salvendy (Ed.), *Handbook of Human Factors* (370-401).New York: Wiley.

Enzinger, A. (forthcoming). *Experts' working input.* Phil. Diss., University of Freiburg.

Janetzko, D., Börner, K., Jäschke, O. & Strube, G. (1994). Task-oriented Knowledge Acquisition and Reasoning for Design Support Systems. *Proceedings of the First European Conference on Cognitive Science in Industry, 28th - 30th September, 1994, Luxembourg,* 153-184.

Kolodner, J. (1993). *Case-based reasoning.* San Mateo, CA: Morgan Kaufmann.

Newell, A. (1982). The knowledge level. *Artificial Intelligence,* 18, 87-12.

Riesbeck, C. K., & Schank, R. C. (1989). *Inside case-based reasoning.* Hillsdale, NJ: Erlbaum.

Schreiber, G., Wielinga, B., & Breuker, J. (1993). *KADS. A principled approach to knowledge-based systems development.* London: Academic Press.

Steels, L. (1990, Summer). The components of expertise. *AI Magazine.* (also VUB AI Lab Memo 88-16).

Strube, G., Janetzko, D. & Knauff, M. (in press). Cooperative construction of expert knowledge. In P. B. Baltes & U. M. Staudinger (Eds.), *Interactive minds.* Cambridge: Cambridge University Press.

Van de Velde, W. (1993). Issues in knowledge-level modelling. In J. M. David, J. P. Krivine, & R. Simmons (Eds.), *Second Generation Expert Systems* (pp. 211-231). Berlin: Springer.

VanLehn, K. (1989). Problem solving and cognitive skill acquisition. In M. I. Posner (Ed.), *Foundations of cognitive science* (pp. 527-579). Cambridge, MA: MIT Press (Bradford)

Visser, W. (1987). Strategies in Programming programmable controllers: field study on a professional programmer. In G. Olson, S. Sheppard, & E. Soloway (Eds.), *Empirical Studies of Programmers. Second Workshop.* Norwood, NJ: Ablex.

Wielinga, B. J., & Breuker, J. A. (1986). Training of knowledge engineers using a structured methodology. In T. Bernold (Ed.), *Expert Systems and Knowledge Engineering* (pp. 133-139). Amsterdam: Elsevier (North-Holland).

Wielinga, B. J., Schreiber, A. T., Breuker, J. A. (1992). KADS: A modelling approach to knowledge engineering. *Knowledge Acquisition,* 4 (Special Issue "The KADS approach to knowledge engineering").

Wielinga, B., Van de Velde, W., Schreiber, G., & Akkermans, H. (1993). Towards a unification of knowledge modelling approaches. In J. M. David, J. P. Krivine, & R. Simmons (Eds.), *Second Generation Expert Systems* (pp. 299-335). Berlin: Springer.

Towards using a Single Uniform Metric in Instance-Based Learning

Kai Ming Ting

Basser Department of Computer Science
University of Sydney, NSW 2006, Australia

Abstract. In instance-based learning, two different metrics are usually used for continuous-valued attributes and nominal attributes. The problem of using different metrics in domains which have both types of attribute has been mitigated by methods such as attribute and instance weightings in instance-based learning.

This paper investigates a method that treats both types of attribute using a single uniform metric in instance-based learning. The method transforms continuous-valued attributes into nominal attributes through discretisation at the outset. We empirically examine the approach using both real-world and artificial datasets to characterise the benefits of discretisation and using a single uniform metric in instance-based learning. Results indicate that our approach can be beneficial to instance-based learning in domains which have noise or irrelevant attributes.

1 Introduction

Research in instance-based learning or IBL [1, 3, 12] has brought about different metrics for continuous-valued attributes and nominal attributes. By metric, we strictly refer here to a measure used to obtain the value-difference of an attribute. The problem of using two different metrics in domains which have both types of attribute has been mitigated by methods such as attribute and instance weightings. This problem can be very serious. For example in the hypothyroid domain, decision trees have an error rate of 0.8% and one of the IBL algorithms used in this paper has an error rate of 72.4%. When a uniform metric is used, the same IBL algorithm achieves an error rate of 1.7%. The huge difference in performance exemplify the problem. Intuitively, we prefer the use of a uniform metric rather than different metrics.

Here, we investigate an approach of using a single uniform metric in IBL by transforming continuous-valued attributes to nominal attributes through discretisation at the outset. One recent discretisation method [4] used under the framework of decision trees provides a useful starting point for the work reported in this paper. However, the motivation of using a discretisation method differs. In the framework of decision trees, the emphasis is in computational efficiency [2, 4, 11] that results in speeding up the evaluation process for continuous-valued attribute discretisation. Others have used discretisation in rules [5] and in naive Bayesian classifiers [6] because these systems only accept nominal attributes. The ability of treating continuous values directly without discretisation gives IBL an advantage over other systems mentioned above. Thus, it seems to be counter-intuitive to discretise continuous-valued attributes. On the contrary, our results show that discretisation during preprocessing can improve the performance of IBL algorithms in most of the real-world domains studied.

The objective of this paper is to investigate the effects on the performance of IBL of using a single uniform metric through discretisation. We intend to characterise the conditions under which the approach can be beneficial to IBL.

We begin the next section with a brief description of IBL and a recent improvement in the treatment of nominal attributes. Section 3 reports in brief a current method of discretisation of continuous-valued attributes, which we will employ in conjunction with IBL. Section 4 presents the empirical results and is followed by discussion and future work.

2   Instance-Based Learning

IBL distinguishes itself from other types of learning which induce theories in the form of decision trees, rules and neural networks. The basic IBL algorithm simply stores the training instances and classifies a new instance by predicting that it has the same class as its nearest stored instance (according to some distance measure, see [1, 3, 12]). For a continuous-valued attribute, the value-difference between two values is simply an arithmetic difference. In a nominal attribute domain, the "overlap" metric is usually used, counting the number of attributes that differ. In order to handle domains that have both types of attribute, the different metrics are simply combined in a similarity function (e.g., Euclidean distance in the IBn series algorithms in [1]) calculation.

A different metric for nominal attributes, called modified value-difference metric (MVDM) is proposed in the literature [3]. The value-difference between two possible values (v_1, v_2) of a nominal attribute is defined as follows [3]:

$$\delta(v_1, v_2) = \sum_{i=1}^{n} \left| \frac{C_{1,i}}{C_1} - \frac{C_{2,i}}{C_2} \right| \tag{1}$$

where $C_{1,i}$ is the number of times v_1 was associated with categories i, and C_1 is the total number of times value v_1 occurred.

In the experiments reported in Section 4.1 and Section 4.2, we use two IBL algorithms i.e., IB1 [1] and IB1-MVDM, a modified version of IB1 that incorporates MVDM rather than the overlap metric for nominal attributes. Collectively, they are referred as IBx hereafter and use only one nearest-neighbour. We also employ a sophisticated IBL algorithm, WV-VSM [12], which incorporates attribute and instance weightings in the same section. All three algorithms employ linear normalisation method [1] which normalises all continuous-valued attributes to the interval from 0 to 1. We describe a discretisation method used in decision trees in the next section.

3   Discretisation of Continuous-Valued Attributes

Fayyad and Irani [4] devised a method for multi-value splitting for continuous-valued attributes. The same criterion (i.e., information gain) as used in binary splitting (in the popular ID3 algorithm) is employed. Multi-value splitting is realised by recursively applying the same criterion to the subsets of the previous split until the stopping criterion based on the minimum description length principle, MDLP [8], is satisfied. This criterion [4] is re-stated as follows:

MDLP Criterion: The partition induced by a cut-point T of attribute A for a set S of N examples is accepted iff

$$Gain(A, T; S) > \frac{log_2(N-1)}{N} + \frac{\Delta(A, T; S)}{N} \qquad (2)$$

and it is rejected otherwise. Where

$$\Delta(A, T; S) = log_2(3^c - 2) - [cEnt(S) - c_1 Ent(S_1) - c_2 Ent(S_2)] \qquad (3)$$

Gain(A,T;S) is the information gain of a cut-point T. Ent(S) is the class entropy of a subset S, and c is the number of classes in subset S, and S_1 and S_2 are two disjoint subsets of S due to cut-point T.

We will employ this discretisation method in IBx and WV-VSM which converts all continuous-valued attributes into nominal attributes. An appeal of this approach is that it avoids any problems arising from the combination of two different metrics. Intuitively, using a single uniform metric is preferred over using different metrics because combining different metrics is analogous to summing two numbers of different units, which may bring about poor performance to the IBL algorithms that use them.

In the following experiments, we first use ten real-world datasets which have continuous-valued attributes to investigate the effect of this preprocessing on the performances of IBx and WV-VSM. In order to gain insight into the factors that affect IBx's performance, we then examine some artificial domains.

4   Experiments

The aim of the experiments is to test the following hypothesis:

Discretisation of continuous-valued attributes at the outset is an effective means to achieve the aim of using a single uniform metric and to improve IBL's performance in domains that have noise or irrelevant continuous-valued attributes.

Recent machine learning research [9] has shown that there is no such thing as a universally best learning algorithm. Thus, it is important to discern the conditions under which the bias i.e., the discretisation of continuous-valued attributes imposed on IBL algorithms, will improve their performances.

In Section 4.1, we first conduct the experiments in ten well-known domains which have continuous-valued attributes, obtained from the UCI repository of machine learning databases [7]. They are Wisconsin breast cancer (bcw), pima diabetes, waveform-40, Cleveland heart disease (heart), glass, hypothyroid (hypo), hepatitis, automobile (auto), echocardiogram (echo) and horse colic. The first five domains are domains with only continuous-valued attributes and the other five have both continuous-valued and nominal attributes. Though the primary concern is in the domains with mixed attribute types, the performance difference of using one type of uniform metric (i.e., continuous-valued) to another (i.e., nominal) also warrants investigation. In Section 4.2, we will examine two artificial datasets. We will also investigate the effect of the approach when these datasets have noise or irrelevant attributes.

In all experiments, discretisation of continuous-valued attributes during pre-processing is conducted using the training data first, and then the testing data is converted according to the cut-points obtained from the training data conversion. Algorithms run with data conversion are postfixed with "*".

4.1 Real-World Domains

The experiments first employ IB1 and IB1-MVDM, and are conducted in the ten UCI domains. In each domain, we randomly select 90% of the instances for training and using the remaining 10% for testing, and repeat over 50 trials. The average error rates for IB1, IB1*, IB1-MVDM and IB1-MVDM* are shown in Table 1. The best result among these four algorithms in each domain is in bold-face. The "$\oplus$" (or "$\ominus$") symbol in front of a figure indicates that the algorithm with discretisation performs significantly better (or worse) than that without (using two-tailed, t-test, p<0.05).

Table 1. Average Error Rates for IBx, IBx*, WV-VS and WV-VSM*

Domain	IB1	IB1*	IB1-MVDM	IB1-MVDM*	WV-VSM	WV-VSM*
bcw	4.5 ±0.3	$\oplus$ **3.3** ±0.2	4.6 ±0.3	4.6 ±0.3	3.7 ±0.4	4.1 ±0.4
diabetes	29.8 ±0.8	29.5 ±0.7	29.8 ±0.8	**28.8** ±0.6	24.6 ±0.6	24.1 ±0.6
wave	36.5 ±1.3	$\oplus$ 31.1 ±1.1	36.5 ±1.3	$\oplus$ **21.7** ±1.1	22.0 ±1.0	$\ominus$ 25.5 ±1.2
heart	24.7 ±1.0	$\oplus$ 21.1 ±1.0	24.7 ±1.0	$\oplus$ **19.4** ±0.9	19.9 ±1.1	$\oplus$ 17.7 ±0.9
glass	30.0 ±1.2	**27.3** ±1.1	30.0 ±1.2	27.7 ±1.2	23.7 ±1.3	23.2 ±1.3
hypo	2.7 ±0.1	$\oplus$ **1.4** ±0.1	72.4 ±0.3	$\oplus$ 1.7 ±0.1	2.2 ±0.1	$\oplus$ 1.5 ±0.1
hepatitis	19.3 ±1.3	19.0 ±1.2	**18.8** ±1.4	20.6 ±1.6	20.0 ±1.2	19.2 ±1.4
auto	24.2 ±1.3	$\oplus$ 18.8 ±1.1	23.0 ±1.3	$\oplus$ **14.8** ±1.0	27.9 ±1.6	$\oplus$ 15.8 ±1.1
echo	43.9 ±1.6	$\oplus$ **35.4** ±1.6	44.4 ±1.6	$\oplus$ 36.0 ±1.9	37.6 ±1.8	$\oplus$ 32.3 ±1.7
horse	24.1 ±1.0	$\oplus$ 22.1 ±1.0	**19.9** ±0.9	20.0 ±1.0	17.5 ±1.0	17.1 ±0.9

$\oplus$, $\ominus$: two-tailed, paired t-test with IBx or WV-VSM; p<0.05.

IB1* outperforms IB1 in all domains. IB1-MVDM* achieves better results than IB1-MVDM in seven domains and has equal performance in the bcw domain, and performs marginally worse in the hepatitis and horse colic domains. Both IB1* and IB1-MVDM* achieve the best results in four domains each. In the hepatitis and horse colic domains, IB1-MVDM has the best result. These results·clearly indicate that using the converted data is more desirable for IBx. IB1-MVDM* gains substantially in some domains, and there is a modest improvement for IB1*.

Table 1 also shows the results using a recent weighted vote variable-kernel similarity metric, WV-VSM [12] which uses a gradient descent method to learn the attribute weights and the votes of the k nearest neighbours are weighted inversely proportional to their distances. The same experimental method is used except we conduct leave-one-out for $k < 10$ in the training data and only the best k is employed for testing. WV-VSM* has better performance in three out of the five domains which contain solely continuous-valued attributes. Whereas in all domains with mixed attribute types, WV-VSM using a uniform metric is again shown to be better than WV-VSM using different metrics. In comparison to IBx, WV-VSM performs better than IBx in eight out of the ten domains, while employing discretisation can still improve its performance. These results reveal that the attribute weights together with weighted votes and the use of multiple nearest neighbours (k) are unable to counter the problem due to the use of different metrics.

The extremely poor performance of IB1-MVDM in the hypothyroid domain needs special attention. An analysis on the matrix for MVDM produced for the eighteen binary attributes indicates that all the value-differences are less than 0.01. When these value-differences are used in conjunction with the continuous-valued attributes in the distance calculation, they have virtually no impact. Thus, the eighteen binary attributes are deemed irrelevant in IB1-MVDM. Omitting the binary attributes has confirmed our analysis by showing similar results. Because of the discretisation, the value-differences for the (original) continuous-valued attributes have comparable "weight" to that of the binary attributes. As a result, all twenty five attributes play a part in classification. Further examination of the data reveals that it has large proportion of missing values and most of the values (91.8%) of the last attribute are missing. We conduct experiments by deleting the last attribute and using a different scheme which ignores the missing value attributes when computing the distance between instances. The results of these experiments are shown in Table 2 which shows that IB1-MVDM's poor performance in this domain are actually due to the use of different metrics, the missing value scheme used and the peculiar missing value situation.

Table 2. Average Error Rates in the hypothyroid domain

No. Attribute	MV Scheme[1]	IB1	IB1-MVDM	IB1*	IB1-MVDM*
All attr	Max Diff	2.7	72.4	1.4	1.7
Delete 18 binary attr	Max Diff	72.6	72.6	1.7	1.6
Delete last attr	Max Diff	2.7	6.9	1.4	1.6
All attr	Ignore	2.3	2.0	1.4	1.7

Since the waveform domain has 19 irrelevant attributes, its result shown in Table 1 seems to suggest that discretisation increases IBx's tolerance for irrelevant continuous-valued attributes. It is also reasonable to assume these UCI domains have noise (the waveform domain contains Gaussian noise). Discretisation of continuous-valued attributes could have the effect of noise reduction which leads to a better performance in almost all of the experimental domains. In domains which have both types of attribute, we hypothesise that combining different metrics has contributed to the loss of the accuracy. We use artificial datasets to test these hypotheses in the following section.

---

[1] Schemes used in treating missing values. Max Diff : value-differences equal to 1 for nominal attributes and for continuous-valued metric, replace the missing value with 1 or 0, whichever gives the larger value-difference or it is 1 if both testing and the stored instances have missing values for an attribute. Ignore : a scheme that ignores any missing value attributes when computing the distance between examples. We use the default setting i.e., Max Diff for all experiments unless otherwise specified.

4.2 Artificial Datasets

The purpose of using artificial datasets is to investigate under what conditions the discretisation of continuous-valued attributes will improve/degrade the performance of IBx. We construct artificial data which has special characteristics. The first data concerns ultra-violet (UV) radiation with one binary attribute indicating AM or PM and one continuous-valued attribute indicating the time from zero to twelve. This data has the characteristic where each value of the binary attribute is correlated to a specific range of the continuous-valued attribute. The target concept is:

If (AM and TIME ≥ 11.0) or (PM and TIME ≤ 3.5) then HIGH UV else LOW UV.

We designated the concept as UV1. The same experimental method is used except the same testing data of size 1000 is employed in all trials.

Single Uniform Metric versus Different Metrics. We first examine the performance difference due to the use of two different metrics and a single uniform metric in the UV1 dataset. We run IBx on the original data, the data discretised using the actual cut-points in the concept described and the data discretised using the method described in Section 3. Table 3 shows the experimental results. Note that IB1 and IB1-MVDM on the original data have the same performance. The results in the given cut-points indicate that *IBx using a single uniform metric performs better than IBx using two different metrics.* However, using the discretisation method to find the cut-points has *degraded* the performance of IBx. This shows that the discretisation method does not find the right cut-points. Also note that the discretisation method employed performs better as the data size increases.

Table 3. Average Error Rates for IBx and IBx* in the UV1 dataset

Data Size	IBx	Given Cutpts		Find Cutpts	
		IB1*	IB1-MVDM*	IB1*	IB1-MVDM*
100	1.3	⊕ 0.2	⊕ 0.6	⊖ 3.0	⊖ 3.8
150	0.9	⊕ 0.1	⊕ 0.1	⊖ 1.7	⊖ 2.3
200	0.8	⊕ 0.0	⊕ 0.0	0.9	⊖ 1.2

⊕,⊖ : significant in two-tailed, paired t-test with IBx

Attribute Noise. We use another dataset, denoted as X+Y>1 which has class boundary diagonal to the axes for further investigation. The concept description has two continuous-valued attributes[2]: *If (X+Y>1) then class 1, else class 0.*

Gaussian noise with mean zero and varying standard deviations (sd) is introduced to the continuous-valued attributes in this experiment and the noisy data is allowed to be out of the range. The results for the 150 training data items in the UV1 and X+Y>1 concepts are shown in Figures 1(a) and 1(b) respectively. Note that the graphs in Figure 1(b) for IB1* and IB1-MVDM* are almost overlap. In both the UV1 and X+Y>1 datasets, the discretisation has *degraded* the performance of IBx in the noise-free (when sd=0.0) or 'low noise' cases; whereas in the 'high noise' data, the discretisation has *improved* the performance of IBx. In the UV1 dataset, the performance differences are significant

---

[2] Two decimal points are used here. The range of X and Y is from 0.00 to 1.00.

except at sd=0.5,2.0 and 2.5 for IB1 and sd=1.0-2.5 for IB1-MVDM. In the X+Y>1 dataset, there are significant performance differences at all noise levels.

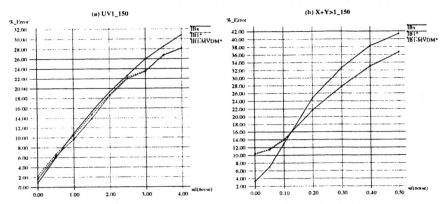

Fig. 1. The effect of noise on IBx and IBx*

The average number of cut-points produced are 4.1 for the noise-free data and 2.5 for the noisy data (at sd=3.0) in the UV1 datasets. Obviously, the discretisation method employed produces more cut-points than necessary. The example cut-points in the UV1 noisy dataset are: -0.3,4.6,13.4.

One explanation to the effect of discretisation is that the discretisation has made the attribute-values' granularity coarse. For noise-free and low noise data, fine attribute-value granularity would be the best choice. However, in the case of high noise data, coarse-grain attribute-value granularity can be a better choice as *this achieves an effect of noise reduction*. Nevertheless, correlation between values of different attributes in the UV1 dataset disorients the discretisation process. This accounts for the creation of a cut-point far away from the actual cut-points in both noise-free and noisy datasets. Note that the X+Y>1 concept has class boundary diagonal to the axes but by forcing axis-parallel splits through discretisation, it can still improve the performance of IBx at high noise levels. This is because noise has blurred the boundary. At high noise levels, the 'blurring' errors are higher than those caused by axis-parallel splits.

Table 4. Average number of predictions made using more than one instance

Dataset	IBx	IB1*	IB1-MVDM*
UV1_150	417.5	994.6	995.5
noise (sd=3.0)	258.8	997.2	997.2
X+Y>1_150	19.0	970.7	967.5
noise (sd=0.3)	6.0	980.9	979.8

Another issue we would like to explore is to examine the number of predictions made using more than one nearest neighbour. IBx employs a majority vote when two or more stored instances have the same minimum distance. Table 4 shows the average number of predictions, N, when they are made using more than one nearest instance for the two artificial datasets. Without discretisation, N in the noisy data is less than that of the noise-free data in both datasets. This coincides with the intuition that noise causes instances to be less similar to each other. But this does not necessarily translate into a lower error rate, as shown in the case of noise-free data in Figures 1a and 1b.

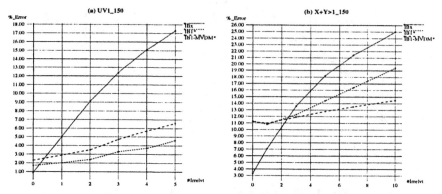

Fig. 2. The effect of irrelevant attributes on IBx and IBx*

Irrelevant Attributes. Using noise-free data, the effects of irrelevant continuous-valued attributes in the UV1 and X+Y>1 concepts are shown in Figures 2a and 2b respectively, where a fixed number of irrelevant continuous-valued attributes are added to the original concepts. Note that IB1 and IB1-MVDM perform similarly, and their performances quickly degrade as the number of irrelevant attribute increases. In both datasets, the performances of IB1* and IB1-MVDM* degrade more gracefully. The performance differences are significant in all cases. These results indicate that *discretisation increases IBx's tolerance for irrelevant continuous-valued attributes.* In all cases, the irrelevant continuous-valued attributes are converted into binary attributes which have skewed distributions (i.e., one value occurs more often than the other). This explains why IBx* performs better than IBx, especially IB1* which uses the overlap metric. The effect of irrelevant attribute on the performance of IB1 decreases as the skewness of the binary value distribution (of irrelevant attributes) increases.

We summarise the experimental results with the artificial datasets as follows:

i In the UV1 dataset, IBx using a single uniform metric (given the actual cut-points for the discretisation) performs better than IBx using different metrics.

ii In two datasets which are noise-free or *low noise*, the discretisation has been demonstrated to *degrade* the performance of IBx.

iii In the same two datasets which have *high noise*, the discretisation has *improved* the performance of IBx. This is achieved through noise reduction by discretisation. This effect also applies in one dataset which has a class boundary not parallel to the axes.

iv Discretisation has been shown to *increase IBx's tolerance for irrelevant continuous-valued attributes* in two datasets by producing binary attributes with skewed distributions.

v Correlation between values of different attributes in the UV1 dataset disorients the discretisation process.

5 Discussion

With discretisation of continuous-valued attributes, we have actually transferred the source of the errors from those due to using different metrics to discretisation errors (problems caused by incorrect and spurious cut-points). However, the errors induced by the discretisation mistakes are smaller in most of the UCI domains studied. The empirical results indicate that a naive approach in instance-based learning which uses two different metrics for continuous-valued and nominal attributes can lead to poor performance in domains with mixed attribute types (an example is the hypothyroid domain). Converting continuous-valued attributes to nominal attributes at the outset proves to be a simple yet effective approach. In this way, IBx uses only one metric rather than two different metrics for continuous-valued and nominal attributes. This provides a coherent approach to the treatment of these two types of attributes. Three methods commonly used in IBL such as instance weighting, attribute weighting and multiple nearest neighbours only mitigate the problem of using two different metrics.

Experiments with artificial data have provided some insight into the effects of the data character (i.e., data characteristics, noise and irrelevant attributes) on the performance of IBx*. Since most real-world cases possibly contain 'high noise' and irrelevant attributes, this explains the better performances of IBx* and WV-VSM* over IBx and WV-VSM in most of the ten UCI domains. This finding is also true even if the actual concepts have boundaries not parallel to the axes. Although discretisation could only approximate these types of boundary, it has been shown (in the X+Y>1 concept) that it is better to have coarse axis-parallel approximation in 'high noise' situations. This also explains why the nominal attribute treatment is preferable even in domains with only continuous-valued attributes. Though it is hard to define what is high (or low) noise in a domain, the experimental results seems to suggest that most of the real-world domains studied contain 'high noise'.

Since discretisation only provides decision boundaries parallel to the axes of the description space, it is anticipated that this approach would degrade IBx's performance when the target concept's boundaries are not axis-parallel (in noise-free cases). One weakness of the current discretisation method is that it would fail to find the exact cut-points in domains which has similar data characteristics as in the UV1 dataset, even in noise-free cases. Because the method determines the cut-points using the whole training set, correlation between values of different attributes in the data 'blurs' the actual cut-points and makes them hard to find using the information gain criterion.

We have also attempted other discretisation methods. Variations of the method motivated by unsupervised learning [11] and a simple method that discretises the continuous-valued attributes into equal-width intervals have been tried [10]. However, the discretisation method using the information gain and the MDLP criteria seems to work best with the IBL algorithms used here. Another approach of achieving the aim of using one single uniform metric in IBL is the exact opposite – converting nominal attributes to continuous-valued attributes. However, it is found to degrade the performance of IBx as well.

6 Conclusion

The main contributions of this paper are (i) unveiling the problem of using two different metrics in IBL and (ii) the proposed use of discretisation of continuous-valued attributes to counter the problem. This approach achieves the aim of using one single uniform metric in IBL and its advantage over using different metrics is supported by empirical results in domains with mixed attribute types. We also show that this approach can improve three IBL algorithms' performances in domains with only continuous-valued attributes. The investigation has characterised two situations i.e., domains which have noise or irrelevant attributes, where the discretisation can be beneficial to IBL. The investigation also reveals that the data character is influential in the discretisation process. The proposed approach, although it limits the representable concepts to hyper-rectangular regions that are orthogonal to the attribute axes, has been shown to improve the performances of IBx and WV-VSM in almost all of the UCI domains studied.

7 Acknowledgements

This research was partially supported by an ARC grant (to J.R. Quinlan) and by a research agreement with DEC. This author is partially supported by the EMSS. Numerous discussions with J.R. Quinlan, N. Indurkhya, M. Cameron-Jones and Z. Zheng, have been very helpful. Thanks to D.W. Aha for providing IB1 and D. Wettschereck for providing WV-VSM. Thanks to anonymous referees' comments

References

1. Aha, D.W., *A Study of Instance-Based Algorithms for Supervised Learning Tasks*, PhD Thesis (1990), Department of Information and Computer Science, University of California, Irvine, Technical Report 90-42.
2. Catlett, J. On Changing Continuous Attributes into Ordered Discrete Attributes. In *Proceedings of the European Working Session on Learning*. (1991).
3. S. Cost and S. Salzberg. A weighted nearest neighbor algorithm for learning with symbolic features. *Machine Learning*, 10:57–78 (1993).
4. U.M. Fayyad and K.B. Irani. Multi-interval discretization of continuous-valued attributes for classification learning. In *Proceedings of the Thirteenth International Joint Conference on Artificial Intelligence*, (1993) 1022–1027.
5. Kerber, R. ChiMerge: Discretization of Numeric Attributes, in *Proceedings of the Tenth National Conference on Artificial Intelligence*, (1992) 123-128.
6. Kononenko, I. Inductive and Bayesian Learning in Medical Diagnosis, *Applied Artificial Intelligence*, Vol.7, (1993) 317-337.
7. Murphy, P.M. and D.W. Aha, UCI Repository of Machine Learning Databases [machine-readable data repository]. Technical report (1991), Department of Information and Computer Science, University of California, Irvine, CA.
8. Rissanen, J. *Stochastic Complexity in Statistical Inquiry*, (1989) World Scientific.
9. Schaffer, C. A Conservation Law for Generalization Performance, in *Proceedings of 11th International Conference on Machine Learning*, (1994) 259-265.
10. Ting, K.M. *Discretization of Continuous-Valued Attributes and Instance-Based Learning*, TR.491, (1994) Basser Dept of Computer Science, University of Sydney.
11. Van de Merckt, T. Decision Trees in Numerical Attributes Spaces, in *Proceedings of 13th International Joint Conference on Artificial Intelligence*, (1993) 1016-1021.
12. Wettschereck, D. *A Study of Distance-Based Machine Learning Algorithms*, PhD Thesis, (1994), Department of Computer Science, Oregon State University.

Main Topic Index

Case and Knowledge Representation

KBS maintenance as learning two-tiered domain representation............................109
Gennady Agre

Separating the cases from the data: Towards more flexible case-based reasoning......157
Mike Brown, Ian Watson, Nick Filer

Cases as terms: A feature term approach to the structured representation of cases....265
Enric Plaza

Case Retrieval

Some limitations of feature-based recognition in case-based design......................471
Thomas R. Hinrichs

Case memory and retrieval based on the immune system................................205
John E. Hunt, Denise E. Cooke, Horst Holstein

Retrieving cases in structured domains by using goal dependencies....................241
Héctor Muñoz-Avila, Jochem Huellen

"Fish and sink": An anytime-algorithm to retrieve adequate cases........................538
Jörg Walter Schaaf

Experiments on adaptation-guided retrieval in case-based design........................313
Barry Smyth, Mark T. Keane

An investigation of marker-passing algorithms for analogue retrieval...................359
Michael Wolverton

Nearest Neighbour Methods

An average-case analysis of k-nearest neighbor classifier................................253
Seishi Okamoto, Ken Satoh

Weighting features...347
Dietrich Wettschereck, David W. Aha

Case Adaptation

Systems, tasks and adaptation knowledge: Revealing some revealing
dependencies..461
Kathleen Hanney, Mark T. Keane, Barry Smyth, Pádraig Cunningham

Case adaptation using an incomplete causal model...........................181
John D. Hastings, L. Karl Branting, Jeffrey A. Lockwood

Learning to improve case adaptation by introspective reasoning and CBR...........229
David B. Leake, Andrew Kinley, David Wilson

Adaptation using constraint satisfaction techniques..........................289
Lisa Purvis, Pearl Pu

Learning

Learning to refine indexing by introspective reasoning.....................431
Susan Fox, David B. Leake

Learning strategies for explanation patterns: Basic game patterns with
applications to chess...491
Yaakov Kerner

A connectionist indexing approach for CBR systems........................520
Maria Malek

Using a neural network to learn general knowledge in a case-based system...........528
Eliseo Reategui, John A. Campbell, Shirley Borghetti

Learning a local similarity metric for case-based reasoning.................301
Francesco Ricci, Paolo Avesani

Towards using a single uniform metric in instance-based learning.....................559
Kai Ming Ting

Cognitive Modeling

Reasoning with reasons in case-based comparisons...........................133
Kevin D. Ashley, Bruce M. McLaren

A case-based reasoner adaptive to different cognitive tasks..................391
Isabelle Bichindaritz

On the automatic generation of case libraries by chunking chess games...............421
Stephen Flinter, Mark T. Keane

Problem solving with "The incredible machine": An experiment in case-based
reasoning..441
Mehmet H. Göker, Herbert Birkhofer

Knowledge engineering for CBR systems from a cognitive science perspective......548
G. Strube, A. Enzinger, D. Janetzko, M. Knauff

Reuse of knowledge: Empirical studies... 335
Willemien Visser

Integrated Reasoning Methods

INRECA: A seamlessly integrated system based on inductive inference and
case-based reasoning..371
Eric Auriol, Stefan Wess, Michel Manago, Klaus-Dieter Althoff, Ralph Traphöner

Towards the integration of case-based, schema-based and model-based reasoning
for supporting complex design tasks...145
Brigitte Bartsch-Spörl

Integrating case-based reasoning and tabu search for solving optimisation
problems..451
Stephan Grolimund, Jean-Gabriel Ganascia

Using case data to improve on rule-based function approximation......................217
Nitin Indurkhya, Sholom M. Weiss

ADAPtER: An integrated diagnostic system combining case-based and abductive
reasoning..277
Luigi Portinale, Pietro Torasso

Integrating rules and cases for the classification task......................................325
Jerzy Surma, Koen Vanhoof

Application-Oriented Methods - Planning

Route planning by analogy..169
Karen Zita Haigh, Manuela Veloso

A memory-based hierarchical planner...501
Deepak Khemani, P.V.S.R. Bhanu Prasad

Application-Oriented Methods - Various

A case-based approach for developing writing tools aimed at non-native English users..121
Sandra M. Aluísio, Osvaldo N. Oliveira Jr.

On the use of CBR in optimisation problems such as the TSP...........................401
Pádraig Cunningham, Barry Smyth, Neil Hurley

A case based method for solving relatively stable dynamic constraint satisfaction problems..481
Y. Huang, R. Miles

Evaluating the application of CBR in mesh design for simulation problems.........193
Neil Hurley

Case-based reasoning for cash flow forecasting using fuzzy retrieval...................510
Rosina Weber Lee, Ricardo Miranda Barcia, Suresh K. Khator

Applications - Decision Making in General

Integration of case based retrieval with a relational database system in aircraft technical support...1
Jonathan R. C. Allen, David W. R. Patterson, Maurice D. Mulvenna, John G. Hughes

Cost estimation of software projects through case base reasoning........................11
Rossella Bisio, Fabio Malabocchia

Operator decision aiding by adaptation of supervision strategies..........................23
Béatrice Fuchs, Alain Mille, Benoît Chiron

Representing and indexing building refurbishment cases for multiple retrieval of adaptable pieces of cases..55
Farhi Marir, Ian Watson

Case-based reasoning for expertise relocation in support of rural health workers in developing countries...77
Elisha T. O. Opiyo

Applications - Diagnosis and Interpretation

Case-based diagnosis of multiple faults..411
Ralph Deters

MacRad: Radiology image resource with a case-based retrieval system..................43
Robert T. Macura, Katarzyna J. Macura

Large-scale fault diagnosis for on-board train systems..67
B. D. Netten, R. A. Vingerhoeds

Applications - Design

DOM-ArC: An active decision support system for quality assessment of cases.......381
Shirin Bakhtari, Wolfgang Oertel

PROFIL: A decision support tool for metallic sections design using a CBR
approach..33
Fréderic Geffraye, Jean Luc Wybo, Aline Russeil

Spatial composition using cases: IDIOM..88
Ian Smith, Claudio Lottaz, Boi Faltings

CBR and machine learning for combustion system design...............................98
Jutta Stehr

Author Index

Agre, G.   109
Aha, D. W.   347
Allen, J. R. C.   1
Althoff, K.-D.   371
Aluisio, S. M.   121
Ashley, K. D.   133
Auriol , E.   371
Avesani , P.   301
Bakhtari, S.   381
Barcia, R. M.   510
Bartsch-Spörl, B.   145
Bichindaritz, I.   391
Birkhofer, H.   441
Bisio, R.   11
Borghetti, S.   528
Branting, L. K.   181
Brown, M.   157
Campbell, J. A.   528
Chiron, B.   23
Cooke, D. E.   205
Cunningham, P.   401, 461
Deters, R.   411
Enzinger, A.   548
Faltings, B.   88
Filer, N.   157
Flinter, S.   421
Fox, S.   431
Fuchs, B.   23
Ganascia, J.-G.   451
Geffraye, F.   33
Göker, M. H.   441
Grolimund, S.   451
Haigh, K. Z.   169
Hanney, K.   461
Hastings, J. D.   181
Hinrichs. T. R.   471
Holstein, H.   205
Huang, Y.   481
Huellen, J.   241

Hughes, J. G.   1
Hunt, J. E.   205
Hurley , N.   193, 401
Indurkhya, N.   217
Janetzko, D.   548
Keane, M. T.   313, 421, 461
Kerner, Y.   491
Khator, S. K.   510
Khemani, D.   501
Kinley, A.   229
Knauff, K.   548
Leake, B. D.   229, 431
Lee, R. W.   510
Lockwood, J. A.   181
Lottaz, C.   88
Macura, K. J.   43
Macura, R. T.   43
Malabocchia, F.   11
Malek, M.   520
Manago, M.   371
Marir, F.   55
McLaren, B. M.   133
Miles, R.   481
Mille, A.   23
Mulvenna, M. D.   1
Muñoz-Avila, H.   241
Netten, B. D.   67
Oertel, W.   381
Okamoto, S.   253
Oliveira Jr., O. N.   121
Opiyo, E. T. O.   77
Patterson, D. W. R.   1
Plaza, E.   265
Portinale, L.   277
Prasad, P. V. S. R. B.   501
Pu, P.   289
Purvis, L.   289
Reategui, E.   528
Ricci, F.   301

Russeil, A. 33
Satoh, K. 253
Schaaf, J. W. 538
Smith, I. 88
Smyth, B. 313, 401, 461
Stehr, J. 98
Strube, G. 548
Surma, J. 325
Ting, K. M. 559
Torasso, P. 277
Traphöner, R. 371
Vanhoof, K. 325
Veloso, M. 169
Vingerhoeds, R. A. 67
Visser, W. 335
Watson, I. 55, 157
Weiss, S. M. 217
Wess, S. 371
Wettschereck, D. 347
Wilson, D. 229
Wolverton, M. 359
Wybo, J. L. 33

Springer-Verlag
and the Environment

We at Springer-Verlag firmly believe that an international science publisher has a special obligation to the environment, and our corporate policies consistently reflect this conviction.

We also expect our business partners – paper mills, printers, packaging manufacturers, etc. – to commit themselves to using environmentally friendly materials and production processes.

The paper in this book is made from low- or no-chlorine pulp and is acid free, in conformance with international standards for paper permanency.

Lecture Notes in Artificial Intelligence (LNAI)

Vol. 835: W. M. Tepfenhart, J. P. Dick, J. F. Sowa (Eds.), Conceptual Structures: Current Practices. Proceedings, 1994. VIII, 331 pages. 1994.

Vol. 837: S. Wess, K.-D. Althoff, M. M. Richter (Eds.), Topics in Case-Based Reasoning. Proceedings, 1993. IX, 471 pages. 1994.

Vol. 838: C. MacNish, D. Pearce, L. M. Pereira (Eds.), Logics in Artificial Intelligence. Proceedings, 1994. IX, 413 pages. 1994.

Vol. 847: A. Ralescu (Ed.) Fuzzy Logic in Artificial Intelligence. Proceedings, 1993. VII, 128 pages. 1994.

Vol: 861: B. Nebel, L. Dreschler-Fischer (Eds.), KI-94: Advances in Artificial Intelligence. Proceedings, 1994. IX, 401 pages. 1994.

Vol. 862: R. C. Carrasco, J. Oncina (Eds.), Grammatical Inference and Applications. Proceedings, 1994. VIII, 290 pages. 1994.

Vol 867: L. Steels, G. Schreiber, W. Van de Velde (Eds.), A Future for Knowledge Acquisition. Proceedings, 1994. XII, 414 pages. 1994.

Vol. 869: Z. W. Raś, M. Zemankova (Eds.), Methodologies for Intelligent Systems. Proceedings, 1994. X, 613 pages. 1994.

Vol. 872: S Arikawa, K. P. Jantke (Eds.), Algorithmic Learning Theory. Proceedings, 1994. XIV, 575 pages. 1994.

Vol. 878: T. Ishida, Parallel, Distributed and Multiagent Production Systems. XVII, 166 pages. 1994.

Vol. 886: M. M. Veloso, Planning and Learning by Analogical Reasoning. XIII, 181 pages. 1994.

Vol. 890: M. J. Wooldridge, N. R. Jennings (Eds.), Intelligent Agents. Proceedings, 1994. VIII, 407 pages. 1995.

Vol. 897: M. Fisher, R. Owens (Eds.), Executable Modal and Temporal Logics. Proceedings, 1993. VII, 180 pages. 1995.

Vol. 898: P. Steffens (Ed.), Machine Translation and the Lexicon. Proceedings, 1993. X, 251 pages. 1995.

Vol. 904: P. Vitányi (Ed.), Computational Learning Theory. EuroCOLT'95. Proceedings, 1995. XVII, 415 pages. 1995.

Vol. 912: N. Lavrăç S. Wrobel (Eds.), Machine Learning: ECML – 95. Proceedings, 1995. XI, 370 pages. 1995.

Vol. 918: P. Baumgartner, R. Hähnle, J. Posegga (Eds.), Theorem Proving with Analytic Tableaux and Related Methods. Proceedings, 1995. X, 352 pages. 1995.

Vol. 927: J. Dix, L. Moniz Pereira, T.C. Przymusinski (Eds.), Non-Monotonic Extensions of Logic Programming. Proceedings, 1994. IX, 229 pages. 1995.

Vol. 928: V.W. Marek, A. Nerode, M. Truszczynski (Eds.), Logic Programming and Nonmonotonic Reasoning. Proceedings, 1995. VIII, 417 pages. 1995.

Vol. 929: F. Morán, A. Moreno, J.J. Merelo, P.Chacón (Eds.), Advances in Artificial Life. Proceedings, 1995. XIII, 960 pages. 1995.

Vol. 934: P. Barahona, M. Stefanelli, J. Wyatt (Eds.), Artificial Intelligence in Medicine. Proceedings, 1995. XI, 449 pages. 1995.

Vol. 941: M. Cadoli, Tractable Reasoning in Artificial Intelligence. XVII, 247 pages. 1995.

Vol. 946: C. Froidevaux, J. Kohlas (Eds.), Symbolic Quantitative and Approaches to Reasoning under Uncertainty. Proceedings, 1995. X, 430 pages. 1995.

Vol. 954: G. Ellis, R. Levinson, W. Rich. J.F. Sowa (Eds.), Conceptual Structures: Applications, Implementation and Theory. Proceedings, 1995. IX, 353 pages. 1995.

Vol. 956: X. Yao (Ed.), Progress in Evolutionary Computation. Proceedings, 1993, 1994. VIII, 314 pages. 1995.

Vol. 957: C. Castelfranchi, J.-P. Müller (Eds.), From Reaction to Cognition. Proceedings, 1993. VI, 252 pages. 1995.

Vol. 961: K.P. Jantke. S. Lange (Eds.), Algorithmic Learning for Knowledge-Based Systems. X, 511 pages. 1995.

Vol. 981: I. Wachsmuth, C.-R. Rollinger, W. Brauer (Eds.), KI-95: Advances in Artificial Intelligence. Proceedings, 1995. XII, 269 pages. 1995.

Vol. 984: J.-M. Haton, M. Keane, M. Manago (Eds.), Advances in Case-Based Reasoning. Proceedings, 1994. VIII, 307 pages. 1995.

Vol. 990: C. Pinto-Ferreira, N.J. Mamede (Eds.), Progress in Artificial Intelligence. Proceedings, 1995. XIV, 487 pages. 1995.

Vol. 991: J. Wainer, A. Carvalho (Eds.), Advances in Artificial Intelligence. Proceedings, 1995. XII, 342 pages. 1995.

Vol. 992: M. Gori, G. Soda (Eds.), Topics in Artificial Intelligence. Proceedings, 1995. XII, 451 pages. 1995.

Vol. 997: K. P. Jantke, T. Shinohara, T. Zeugmann (Eds.), Algorithmic Learning Theory. Proceedings, 1995. XV, 319 pages. 1995.

Vol. 1009: M. Broy, S. Jähnichen (Eds.), KORSO: Methods, Languages, and Tools for the Construction of Correct Software. X, 449 pages. 1995.

Vol. 1010: M. Veloso, A. Aamodt (Eds.), Case-Based Reasoning Research and Development. Proceedings, 1995. X, 576 pages. 1995.

Vol. 1011: T. Furuhashi (Ed.), Advances in Fuzzy Logic, Neural Networks and Genetic Algorithms. Proceedings, 1994.

Lecture Notes in Computer Science

Vol. 967: J.P. Bowen, M.G. Hinchey (Eds.), ZUM '95: The Z Formal Specification Notation. Proceedings, 1995. XI, 571 pages. 1995.

Vol. 968: N. Dershowitz, N. Lindenstrauss (Eds.), Conditional and Typed Rewriting Systems. Proceedings, 1994. VIII, 375 pages. 1995.

Vol. 969: J. Wiedermann, P. Hájek (Eds.), Mathematical Foundations of Computer Science 1995. Proceedings, 1995. XIII, 588 pages. 1995.

Vol. 970: V. Hlaváč, R. Šára (Eds.), Computer Analysis of Images and Patterns. Proceedings, 1995. XVIII, 960 pages. 1995.

Vol. 971: E.T. Schubert, P.J. Windley, J. Alves-Foss (Eds.), Higher Order Logic Theorem Proving and Its Applications. Proceedings, 1995. VIII, 400 pages. 1995.

Vol. 972: J.-M. Hélary, M. Raynal (Eds.), Distributed Algorithms. Proceedings, 1995. XI, 333 pages. 1995.

Vol. 973: H.H. Adelsberger, J. Lažanský, V. Mařík (Eds.), Information Management in Computer Integrated Manufacturing. IX, 665 pages. 1995.

Vol. 974: C. Braccini, L. DeFloriani, G. Vernazza (Eds.), Image Analysis and Processing. Proceedings, 1995. XIX, 757 pages. 1995.

Vol. 975: W. Moore, W. Luk (Eds.), Field-Programmable Logic and Applications. Proceedings, 1995. XI, 448 pages. 1995.

Vol. 976: U. Montanari, F. Rossi (Eds.), Principles and Practice of Constraint Programming — CP '95. Proceedings, 1995. XIII, 651 pages. 1995.

Vol. 977: H. Beilner, F. Bause (Eds.), Quantitative Evaluation of Computing and Communication Systems. Proceedings, 1995. X, 415 pages. 1995.

Vol. 978: N. Revell, A M. Tjoa (Eds.), Database and Expert Systems Applications. Proceedings, 1995. XV, 654 pages. 1995.

Vol. 979: P. Spirakis (Ed.), Algorithms — ESA '95. Proceedings, 1995. XII, 598 pages. 1995.

Vol. 980: A. Ferreira, J. Rolim (Eds.), Parallel Algorithms for Irregularly Structured Problems. Proceedings, 1995. IX, 409 pages. 1995.

Vol. 981: I. Wachsmuth, C.-R. Rollinger, W. Brauer (Eds.), KI-95: Advances in Artificial Intelligence. Proceedings, 1995. XII, 269 pages. (Subseries LNAI).

Vol. 982: S. Doaitse Swierstra, M. Hermenegildo (Eds.), Programming Languages: Implementations, Logics and Programs. Proceedings, 1995. XI, 467 pages. 1995.

Vol. 983: A. Mycroft (Ed.), Static Analysis. Proceedings, 1995. VIII, 423 pages. 1995.

Vol. 984: J.-P. Haton, M. Keane, M. Manago (Eds.), Advances in Case-Based Reasoning. Proceedings, 1994. VIII, 307 pages. 1994. (Subseries LNAI).

Vol. 985: T. Sellis (Ed.), Rules in Database Systems. Proceedings, 1995. VIII, 373 pages. 1995.

Vol. 986: Henry G. Baker (Ed.), Memory Management. Proceedings, 1995. XII, 417 pages. 1995.

Vol. 987: P.E. Camurati, H. Eveking (Eds.), Correct Hardware Design and Verification Methods. Proceedings, 1995. VIII, 342 pages. 1995.

Vol. 988: A.U. Frank, W. Kuhn (Eds.), Spatial Information Theory. Proceedings, 1995. XIII, 571 pages. 1995.

Vol. 989: W. Schäfer, P. Botella (Eds.), Software Engineering — ESEC '95. Proceedings, 1995. XII, 519 pages. 1995.

Vol. 990: C. Pinto-Ferreira, N.J. Mamede (Eds.), Progress in Artificial Intelligence. Proceedings, 1995. XIV, 487 pages. 1995. (Subseries LNAI).

Vol. 991: J. Wainer, A. Carvalho (Eds.), Advances in Artificial Intelligence. Proceedings, 1995. XII, 342 pages. 1995. (Subseries LNAI).

Vol. 992: M. Gori, G. Soda (Eds.), Topics in Artificial Intelligence. Proceedings, 1995. XII, 451 pages. 1995. (Subseries LNAI).

Vol. 993: T.C. Fogarty (Ed.), Evolutionary Computing. Proceedings, 1995. VIII, 264 pages. 1995.

Vol. 994: M. Hebert, J. Ponce, T. Boult, A. Gross (Eds.), Object Representation in Computer Vision. Proceedings, 1994. VIII, 359 pages. 1995.

Vol. 995: S.M. Müller, W.J. Paul, The Complexity of Simple Computer Architectures. XII, 270 pages. 1995.

Vol. 996: P. Dybjer, B. Nordström, J. Smith (Eds.), Types for Proofs and Programs. Proceedings, 1994. X, 202 pages. 1995.

Vol. 997: K.P. Jantke, T. Shinohara, T. Zeugmann (Eds.), Algorithmic Learning Theory. Proceedings, 1995. XV, 319 pages. 1995. (Subseries LNAI).

Vol. 998: A. Clarke, M. Campolargo, N. Karatzas (Eds.), Bringing Telecommunication Services to the People – IS&N '95. Proceedings, 1995. XII, 510 pages. 1995.

Vol. 999: P. Antsaklis, W. Kohn, A. Nerode, S. Sastry (Eds.), Hybrid Systems II. VIII, 569 pages. 1995.

Vol. 1009: M. Broy, S. Jähnichen (Eds.), KORSO: Methods, Languages, and Tools for the Construction of Correct Software. X, 449 pages. 1995.

Vol. 1010: M. Veloso, A. Aamodt (Eds.), Case-Based Reasoning Research and Development. Proceedings, 1995. X, 576 pages. 1995. (Subseries LNAI).

Vol. 1011: T. Furuhashi (Ed.), Advances in Fuzzy Logic, Neural Networks and Genetic Algorithms. Proceedings, 1994. (Subseries LNAI).